iusticia nram ptiner eu p posse nro manutenebim̄.
⁊ psonas illi᷒ in maximo honore ⁊ reuerentia sicut
bre ᷒suetim̄: exactiori si fieri potri diligentia
uen̄abim̄. Hec ⁊ q̄ alia p̄fatis domib; expedire
credidim̄: nuncias nris magistro·] archidiacono
ticestrie·⁊ magistro·O· dico secreci᷒ intimauim̄· ut
uob ea fidelit exponant: ⁊ sup hiis nob ᷒silium utrm
reporrent. Epistola sci Gileberti ad canonicos·matrone·

G ileber᷒ de semptingha uiria dei hi q; est uirino q̄d
fiure dilectis filiis suis canoniceis ⁊ frib; de mal
tona·saℓ᷒·ppetuam in dn̄o cū di benedictione ⁊ sua.
dū licuit·dū dīs facultate sedm suā nram ih
ministrauit: solebam eṽndoq; sic filios meos kmo᷒
uos cōpali psentia uisitare·⁊ doctina q̄ potui·q̄
noui·ad amore diuinū inuitare·ac allicere. Vt
iam efficatia mea sollicitudine sequeret᷒·s; ih
uirib; corpis omnino destruro: ita ut me oporter
caruis uelamina exeundo hinc migrare ex hac
uita·ih longo tempe amara ⁊ tediosa. Et cū ā m
uos uoce uiua alloq̄ ñ poco: hac cedula arrenci᷒
q̄intū possum admone ñ desisto. quatinus p di
amore ⁊ salute aīa᷒ uiia᷒ diligenci᷒ q̄n hucusꝗ.

British Library, Cotton MS Cleopatra B. i, f. 100ᵛ (Lc): see pp. 162–4

THE BOOK OF
ST GILBERT

EDITED BY
RAYMONDE FOREVILLE
AND
GILLIAN KEIR

OXFORD MEDIEVAL TEXTS
CLARENDON PRESS · OXFORD
1987

Oxford University Press, Walton Street, Oxford OX2 6DP

Oxford New York Toronto
Delhi Bombay Calcutta Madras Karachi
Petaling Jaya Singapore Hong Kong Tokyo
Nairobi Dar es Salaam Cape Town
Melbourne Auckland
and associated companies in
Beirut Berlin Ibadan Nicosia

Oxford is a trade mark of Oxford University Press

Published in the United States
by Oxford University Press, New York

British Library Cataloguing in Publication Data
The Book of St. Gilbert. —(Oxford medieval texts)
1. Gilbert, of Sempringham, Saint
I. Foreville, Raymonde II. Keir, Gillian
III. Un Procès de canonisation a l'aube
du XIII siècle, 1201—1202
271'.12042 BX4700.G65
ISBN 0—19—822260—2

Library of Congress Cataloging-in-Publication Data
The Book of St Gilbert
(Oxford medieval texts)
Bibliography: p.
Includes indexes.
1. Gilbert, of Sempringham, Saint, 1083?—1189.
2. Christian saints—England—Biography—Early works
to 1800. 3. Gilbertines—History. I. Foreville,
Raymond. II. Keir, Gillian. III. Title. IV. Series.
BX4700.G65B66 1987 271'.49 [B] 86—28619
ISBN 0—19—822260—2

Set by Joshua Associates Limited, Oxford
Printed in Great Britain
at the University Press, Oxford
by David Stanford
Printer to the University

GENERAL EDITORS' NOTE

THIS book contains the first full edition of the *Life*, miracles and canonization dossier of St Gilbert of Sempringham—the *Book of St Gilbert*, compiled by a canon of Sempringham in the opening years of the thirteenth century as a monument to the founder and a *pièce justificative* of his canonization and translation, on the instruction and with the encouragement of Archbishop Hubert Walter.

An incomplete text of the *Life* was printed in the 1830 and 1846 editions of Dugdale's *Monasticon*, vi; and the rest of the *Book*, with full commentary, by Raymonde Foreville in a volume published in Paris in 1943, during the Second World War, and so always a rare book in this country. Some years ago Professor Christopher Cheney advised us that Professor Foreville had in mind a complete edition; and at our invitation and to our great pleasure she agreed to include it among the Oxford Medieval Texts. We were so fortunate as to enlist the collaboration of Gillian Keir as translator; and Mrs Keir has also helped materially in revising the notes. The introduction has been translated by Mrs Kathleen Dockrill (to whom we are greatly indebted) and C.N.L.B.: the first part has also been published as a Lincoln Minster Pamphlet by arrangement between the Oxford University Press and the Dean and Chapter (we are grateful to the Reverend Chancellor John Nurser and Miss Joan Williams, Cathedral Librarian, for their help in these plans). Ready access to the manuscripts has dictated that final checking of the text fell to the General Editors, all three of whom have taken a share; and M.W. has also checked the translation and C.N.L.B. revised the historical notes. In an edition projected in Paris and published in Oxford we naturally have a particular responsibility for its final condition; and we owe a special debt to Gillian Keir for her generous help. All concerned in this edition are much indebted to Vera Keep of Joshua Associates Ltd for skilled type-setting, and to the staff of the Press, and especially Ivon Asquith, Robert Faber, and Leofranc Holford-Strevens. We are also grateful to the Keeper of Manuscripts in the British Library, and to the Curators and Keeper of Manuscripts of the Bodleian for their kind

approval of our use of their manuscripts; to Sir Roger Mynors for some amendments he noted long ago; to Veronica Ortenberg for valuable help in obtaining microfilms; to Peter Keir for expert medical advice; to Mr M. Marschner for the Map on p. xxvii; to Brenda Bolton, Henry Chadwick, Giles Constable, Robert Markus, and Richard Sharpe for generous help; and to Dr M. R. Abbott, Dr J.-M. Bienvenu, and Dr S. Thompson for permission to refer to their unpublished theses.

In all essentials this book reflects the scholarship and aims of Professor Raymonde Foreville and it is our privilege thus to welcome this notable addition to our series by the doyenne of Gilbertine scholars.

C.N.L.B.
D.E.G.
M.W.

PREFACE

FROM the very first research I undertook in London shortly before the Second World War, I was able to appreciate the remarkable interest of British Library Cotton MS Cleopatra B. i for medieval canon law. It was this aspect of the book—its place in the history of the canonization of saints at the turn of the twelfth and thirteenth centuries—which held my attention and inspired the publication of the canonization process of St Gilbert of Sempringham in 1943, in the form of a *thèse secondaire* for the Sorbonne doctorate; a publication which remained imperfect, owing to the sad events which for a number of years prevented any further study of the manuscripts, and any renewed discussion with British scholars. For this reason I have been particularly grateful to Professor C. R. Cheney for his welcoming response to my wish for a new edition, and to Professor C. N. L. Brooke and his colleagues as General Editors of OMT, Dr Diana Greenway and Dr Michael Winterbottom.

I wish first of all to render homage to the late Gabriel Le Bras, who first taught me medieval canon law, and urged me to pursue this path, which the work of Stephan Kuttner had opened up. If I am able, some forty years later, to revise and polish my earliest work and bring it up to date, I owe it to the generous help which has been given me. I wish next to express my thanks to the President and Fellows of Clare Hall, Cambridge, for electing me to a Leverhulme Visiting Fellowship in 1979 which enabled me to spend the Lent Term, 1980, working in the Cambridge University Library, and to the Council of the British Academy for the award of a Visiting Professorship in 1983. In 1981 and 1984, during renewed visits to Clare Hall, I was able to complete my researches. In the course of them I have been indebted to my English friends and colleagues, above all to Marjorie Chibnall who introduced me to Clare Hall and much aided me in my visits there.

This edition could not have been realized without an English collaborator, and I next acknowledge Gillian Keir, whose special responsibility has been the elegant English translation of the Latin

texts, and who has helped in the annotation and in many other ways.

The General Editors have checked the text of the manuscripts and Michael Winterbottom in particular has revised the text and translation to bring them into conformity with the norms of OMT; Christopher Brooke has given ceaseless help and scholarly advice, and Mrs K. Dockrill and he have translated the introduction. Christopher Cheney read the French text of the Introduction, and advised me in particular on the pages relative to the crisis in the Order of Sempringham. Allen Brown permitted me to present them in a provisional form to the Sixth Battle Conference in 1983.

My thanks are also due to Anne Duggan for sending me, and giving permission to publish, in advance of her full edition of Thomas Becket's Correspondence, her critical text of the archbishop's letters to Gilbert of Sempringham; to Dom Jacques Dubois, OSB, of the Abbey of Sainte-Marie de la Source, Paris, and to Cecily Clark, for their contributions to Appendices 1 and 3. Arthur and Dorothy Owen have given precious aid from their close knowledge of the landscape and religious houses of Lincolnshire, and in the identification of place-names.

Nor can I pass over the kindness of the archivists and librarians who have permitted me to consult the manuscripts in their care and made available photographic reproductions for my use, and especially the staff of the Cambridge University Library, and the Keepers of Manuscripts in the British Library and the Bodleian Library at Oxford, by whose leave we use the manuscripts on which this edition is based.

I express my warm thanks to all those who have assisted me.

September 1985   R.F.

CONTENTS

ABBREVIATED REFERENCES

AASS	*Acta Sanctorum Bollandiana*, Antwerp, Brussels, etc., 1643– .
BJRL	*Bulletin of the John Rylands Library*.
BL	London, British Library.
Bodl.	Oxford, Bodleian Library.
CC	*Corpus Christianorum*.
Cheney and Cheney	*The Letters of Pope Innocent III (1198–1216) concerning England and Wales*, ed. C. R. and M. G. Cheney (Oxford, 1967).
Cheney, *Innocent III and England*	C. R. Cheney, *Pope Innocent III and England* (Päpste und Papsttum, ed. G. Denzler *et al.*, ix, Stuttgart, 1976).
Cheney, 'Papal Privileges'	C. R. Cheney, 'Papal Privileges for Gilbertine Houses', *Bulletin of the Institute of Historical Research*, xxi (1946), 39–58, cited from the revised edition in Cheney, *Medieval Texts and Studies* (Oxford, 1973), pp. 39–65.
Councils and Synods, i	*Councils and Synods with Other Documents Relating to the English Church*, i, ed. D. Whitelock, M. Brett, and C. N. L. Brooke (2 parts, Oxford, 1981).
DACL	*Dictionnaire d'archéologie chrétienne et de liturgie*, ed. A. Cabrol, H. Leclercq, *et al.* (15 vols., Paris, 1907–53).
Danelaw Charters	*Documents Illustrative of the Social and Economic History of the Danelaw from Various Collections*, ed. F. M. Stenton (British Academy, London, 1920).
DNB	*Dictionary of National Biography*, ed. L. Stephen and S. Lee (66 vols., London, 1885–1901; repr. 22 vols., Oxford, 1921–2).
EEA i–iii	*English Episcopal Acta*, i, Lincoln *1067–1185*, ed. D. M. Smith; ii–iii, Canterbury *1162–1205*, ed. C. R. Cheney, B. Jones and E. John (British Academy, London, 1980, 1986).
EHR	*English Historical Review*.
EYC	*Early Yorkshire Charters*, i–iii, ed. W. Farrer, Edinburgh, 1914–16; iv–xii, ed. C. T. Clay

(Yorkshire Archaeological Society Record Series, Extra Series, i–iii, v–x, 1935–65; Extra Series iii is Index to *EYC*, i–iii, ed. C. T. and E. M. Clay, 1942).

Fasti   John Le Neve, *Fasti Ecclesiae Anglicanae, 1066– 1300*, i–iii, ed. D. E. Greenway (London, 1968– 77).

Fontanini, *Codex*   G. Fontanini, *Codex Constitutionum quas summi pontifices ediderunt in solemni canonizatione sanctorum a Johanne XV ad Benedictum XIII* (Rome, 1729).

Foreville 1943   R. Foreville, *Un procès de canonisation à l'aube du XIIIe siècle (1201–1202), Le Livre de saint Gilbert de Sempringham* (Paris, 1943).

Foreville, 'Crise'   R. Foreville, 'La crise de l'Ordre de Sempringham au XIIe siècle. Nouvelle approche du dossier des frères lais', *Anglo-Norman Studies*, vi (Proceedings of the Battle Conference 1983), ed. R. A. Brown (Woodbridge, 1984), pp. 39–57.

Foreville, 'La diffusion du culte de Thomas Becket'   R. Foreville, 'La diffusion du culte de Thomas Becket dans la France de l'Ouest avant la fin du XIIe siècle', *Cahiers de civilisation médiévale*, xix (Poitiers, 1976), pp. 347–69 = Foreville, *Thomas Becket dans la tradition historique et hagiographique* (Variorum, London, 1981) ch. IX.

Foreville, *Latran*   R. Foreville, *Latran I, II, III et Latran IV* (Histoire des Conciles Œcuméniques VI, Paris, 1965).

Foreville, *L'Église et la royauté*   R. Foreville, *L'Église et la royauté en Angleterre sous Henri II Plantagenêt (1154–1189)* (Paris, 1943).

Foreville, 'Miracula'   R. Foreville, 'Les "Miracula S. Thomae Cantuariensis"', *Actes du 97e Congrès National des Sociétés Savantes, Nantes, 1972. Section de philologie et d'histoire jusqu'à 1610* (Paris, 1979), pp. 443–68 = Foreville, *Thomas Becket . . .* (Variorum, London, 1981) ch. VII.

Foreville, 'Naissance'   R. Foreville, 'Naissance d'un Ordre double: L'Ordre de Sempringham', *Les Réseaux monastiques et canoniaux*. Actes du Colloque international du C.E.R.C.O.M., sous la direction de Pierre Roger Gaussin (Saint-Étienne 16–18 septembre 1985). Paris, forthcoming.

Foreville, 'Saint Gilbert'   R. Foreville, 'Saint Gilbert de Sempringham', *Encyclopédie de la sainteté*, vi *(1054–1274)* sous la direction d'André Vauchez (Paris, 1986).

GFL — *The Letters and Charters of Gilbert Foliot, Abbot of Gloucester (1139—48), Bishop of Hereford (1148—63) and London (1163—87)*, ed. A. Morey and C. N. L. Brooke (Cambridge, 1967).

Gilbertine Charters — *Transcripts of charters relating to the Gilbertine Houses of Sixle, Ormsby, Catley, Bullington and Alvingham*, ed. F. M. Stenton (Lincoln Record Society, 18, 1922).

Gilbertine Rite — *The Gilbertine Rite*, ed. R. M. Woolley (2 vols., Henry Bradshaw Society, 59–60, 1921–2).

Giraldus, *Opera* — *Giraldi Cambrensis Opera*, ed. J. S. Brewer, J. F. Dimock, and G. F. Warner (8 vols., RS, 1861–91).

Graham, *S. Gilbert* — Rose Graham, *S. Gilbert of Sempringham and the Gilbertines. A History of the Only English Monastic Order* (London, 1901, repr. 1904).

Heads — *The Heads of Religious Houses, England and Wales, 940—1216*, ed. D. Knowles, C. N. L. Brooke, and V. C. M. London (Cambridge, 1972).

JBAA — *Journal of the British Archaeological Association*.

JL — P. Jaffé, *Regesta Pontificum Romanorum ad annum 1198*, ed. W. Wattenbach, S. Loewenfeld, F. Kaltenbrunner, and P. Ewald (2 vols., Leipzig, 1885–8).

John of Salisbury, *Letters* — *The Letters of John of Salisbury*, i (nos. 1–135), ed. W. J. Millor, H. E. Butler, and C. N. L. Brooke, NMT, 1955; ii (nos. 136–325), ed. W. J. Millor and C. N. L. Brooke (OMT, 1979).

Knowles and Hadcock — (M.) D. Knowles and R. N. Hadcock, *Medieval Religious Houses, England and Wales* (edn. of London, 1971).

Knowles, *Episcopal Colleagues* — (M.) D. Knowles, *The Episcopal Colleagues of Archbishop Thomas Becket* (Cambridge, 1951).

Knowles, 'The Revolt of the Lay Brothers' — M. D. Knowles, 'The Revolt of the Lay Brothers of Sempringham', *EHR* l (1935), 465–87.

Life — *The Life of St Gilbert*, below, pp. 2–133.

M1, M2 — The miracles of St Gilbert, formal and informal collections, below, pp. 264–303, 304–35.

MB — *Materials for the History of Thomas Becket, Archbishop of Canterbury*, ed. J. C. Robertson and J. B. Sheppard (7 vols., RS, 1875–85).

MLD — *Dictionary of Medieval Latin from British Sources*, 3 Fasc. so far (ed. R. E. Latham and D. R. Howlett, London, 1975–).

Monasticon	W. Dugdale, *Monasticon Anglicanum*, ed. J. Caley, H. Ellis, and B. Bandinel, 6 vols. in 8, London, 1817–30, repr. 1846. References to Gilbertine documents are to pp. i*–xcix* in vi. 2 (1830) and *in brackets* to pp. i*–lix* in vi. 2 (1846) between pp. 946 and 947; in the reprint the additional pages are in double columns, and so take fewer pages.
NMT	Nelson's Medieval Texts.
OMT	Oxford Medieval Texts.
Owen, *Church and Society*	D. M. Owen, *Church and Society in Medieval Lincolnshire* (History of Lincolnshire, ed. J. Thirsk, v, Lincoln, 1971).
Pipe Roll	*Pipe Rolls*, cited by the regnal year (ed. in Pipe Roll Society, London, 1884–).
PL	*Patrologiae cursus completus, series Latina*, ed. J. P. Migne (221 vols., Paris, 1844–64).
Potthast	*Regesta Pontificum Romanorum* A.D. *1198–1304*, ed. A. Potthast (2 vols., Berlin, 1874–5).
PUE	*Papsturkunden in England*, ed. W. Holtzmann (3 vols., Abhandlungen der Gesellschaft der Wissenschaften zu Göttingen, phil.-hist. Klasse, Berlin, Göttingen, i, n.s. XXV (1930–1), ii, 3rd ser. XIV–XV (1935–6), iii, 3rd ser. XXXIII (1952).
RS	Rolls Series, London, 1858–1911.
St Bernard, *Opera*	*Opera Sancti Bernardi*, ed. J. Leclercq, C. H. Talbot, and H. M. Rochais (8 vols., Rome, 1957–78).
Sempringham Charters	'Charters relating to the priory of Sempringham', ed. E. M. Poynton, *Genealogist*, n.s. xv (1898–9), 158–61, 221–7; xvi (1899–1900), 30–5, 76–83, 153–8, 223–8; xvii (1900–1), 29–35, 164–8, 232–9 (cited by vol. and page of *Genealogist*).
VCH	*Victoria History of the Counties of England*.
William of Newburgh	William of Newburgh, *Historia rerum Anglicarum*, ed. R. Howlett, in *Chronicles of the reigns of Stephen etc.* (RS, 1884–9), i–ii.

INTRODUCTION

I. ST GILBERT OF SEMPRINGHAM, THE FOUNDER[1]

Gilbert's family and youth

GILBERT, the founder of the religious Order which bears his name, was born before 1089 and, according to an unverifiable tradition, perhaps as early as 1083, into a family of the lesser nobility recently settled in Lincolnshire. It was established, so far as we know, in the wapentakes of Aveland and Wraggoe, around Sempringham and West Torrington. The knight Jocelin, his father, was of Norman origin; his mother, whose name has not been recorded, was of English stock.[2] The hypothesis that Jocelin received his estates from Gilbert de Gant, Domesday Lord of Folkingham, has long prevailed.[3] Numerous documents, published by antiquaries, but with limited circulation, throw some light on the family's status and allow us to trace Jocelin's descendants as far as the middle of the thirteenth century. Gilbert's father held meadows, woods, and arable lands on which lived sokemen and villeins, not from Gilbert de Gant, but from Alfred of Lincoln, at Alvingham (Louthesk), West Torrington, and Sempringham.[4] He belonged to the gentry and the family's status remained the same for generations. If the family won some renown, it was owing to the founder and Master of the Gilbertine Order.

[1] The biographical data are based on the *Life*, which gives no dates most of the way; but it evidently preserved a chronological sequence of events, as can often be checked by other documents.   [2] *Life*, c. 1.

[3] Graham, *S. Gilbert*, pp. 2–3. In *EYC* vi. 252–4 (1939) Sir Charles Clay gave the first accurate account of Gilbert's family, based on the Sempringham and Gilbertine Charters; for a brief résumé and revision, see M. Abbott, 'The Gant Family in England 1066–1191' (Cambridge Univ. Ph.D. Thesis, 1973), pp. 231–2.

[4] *Lincolnshire Domesday and the Lindsey Survey*, ed. C. W. Foster, T. Longley, and F. M. Stenton (Lincs. Rec. Soc., 1924), pp. 126, 130, nos. 20–2, 57. Sempringham was the most important of Jocelin's holdings, with 14 sokemen, 8 villeins, 2 borders, and a fourth of a church. On sokemen and villeins, see Stenton, ibid., p. xxvii, where he points out the decline in the status of *ceorls* (Domesday *villani*) in the generation or two after the Conquest.

The charters of Sempringham and those of other priories of the Order have preserved the names of his kinsmen, the benefactors of the foundations of Sempringham, Alvingham, Bullington, and Sixhills. In this way we know Gilbert's family: his father Jocelin; his brother Roger, the lay founder of Alvingham priory; his sister Agnes.[1] Roger, founder of the priory of Alvingham and benefactor of Sempringham, left no heir except his sister Agnes. Her husband can probably be identified as Hugh Mustel, and they had three sons, Roger, Hugh, and William. Roger Mustel, the eldest, was a benefactor of the priories of Bullington and Sixhills; and to Sixhills his uncle, the Master, admitted his two daughters; he had also a son, William, whose assent was specified in all his charters.[2] William Mustel confirmed his father's gifts in his turn, and among the witnesses to his charters were his own sons, Geoffrey and Thomas Mustel.[3] Geoffrey left one son, Thomas Mustel of Torrington, who confirmed various charters in favour of Sixhills and Bullington: labelled 'iunior' in a charter of Odo of Kilkenny about 1250, he appeared again in a charter of William of Kyme in 1256.[4]

[1] 'Rogerus filius Gocelini' (Sempringham Charters, xv. 158); 'de donatione Rogeri filii Gocelini' (Gilbertine Charters, p. 203); 'Agnes filia Jocelini', among the 'veteres feodati' of 1135 in the carta of Hugh of Bayeux of 1166 (Red Book of the Exchequer, ed. Hall, RS, 1896, i. 387). For Hugh Mustel, probably Agnes's husband, see Sempringham Charters, xv. 223.

[2] 'Rogerus Mustela de assensu Agnetis matris mee et Hugonis fratris mei' confirms the charter of his uncle: 'Rogerus filius Jocelini avunculus meus' (Sempringham Charters, xv. 227). At Michaelmas 1176, Roger Mustel was amerced 5 marks for a forest offence in Lincolnshire; and in 1178, he rendered account of 5 marks for securing his right against William Paynel (Pipe Roll 22 Henry II, p. 86; 24 Henry II, p. 8). 'Rogerus Mustelie et Willelmus filius eius et heres' occur in Gilbertine Charters, p. 17. 'Willelmo Mustele, Willelmo Mustele avunculo eius de Tirintonna' are among the witnesses in Sempringham Charters, xv. 160, of c. 1160. There is a confirmation by Roger Musteile to the nuns and brethren of Bullington of all the land given them by his men of Torrington (1165), and a grant to William Musteil his brother (late Henry II) in Danelaw Charters, p. 66, nos. 101, 102. For Gilbert's niece Matilda, see pp. 284–5.

[3] 'Willelmus filius Rogeri Musteile de Tiringtona' confirms to the nuns of Bullington and their brethren all his father's grants and charters in the parish of Bullington, witnessed by 'Galfrido Musteile, Thoma Musteile' (Gilbertine Charters, p. 95). Charters for Bullington priory were attested by Geoffrey Mustel and Thomas Mustel his brother (Danelaw Charters, pp. 68–72, nos. 104, 106, 108–9, 111). 'Emma quondam uxor Willelmi Mustela de Tirigtona . . . in libera uiduitate' confirmed all the grants of her husband to Bullington priory (c. 1200; Danelaw Charters, p. 70, no. 108). In the year 1212, the heirs of Roger (son of Jocelin) were still tenants of Hugh of Bayeux, who married Margaret heiress of Alan of Lincoln, and was then lord of the Mustel fee in (West) Torrington (The Book of Fees, PRO Texts and Calendars, 1920–31, i. 171).

[4] Thomas Mustel witnessed Danelaw Charters nos. 107 and 110; in the latter appears 'Thoma filio Galfridi Mustel' (Danelaw Charters, pp. 70–1; cf. Book of Fees, ii. 1053, 1062, s.a. 1242–3). Geoffrey's son must be this donor, who appears in a charter of Odo of

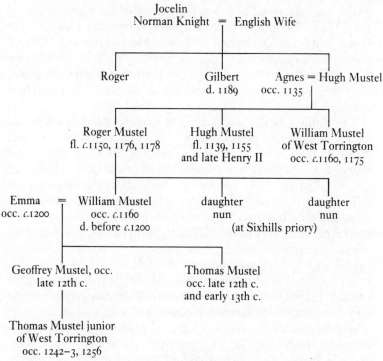

Fig. 1. Gilbert's family

Such was the family of Gilbert of Sempringham over six generations. Hitherto no trace of his ancestry has been found in Normandy before the Conquest.

From the second generation of the lords of Folkingham–Lincoln, they appear in the history of the Gilbertine Order as distinguished benefactors. Walter, son and heir of Gilbert de Gant, was the lay founder of Sempringham as donor of the land on which Gilbert was to establish his first priory: this was attested by his son, Gilbert II (†1156), in a charter of confirmation.[1] Countess Alice, daughter of Gilbert II, and his heiress, lady of the fief, widow of Simon of Senlis, was in *c.* 1184–5 to bequeath her body to God, St

Kilkenny as 'Thomas Mustell minor' (the younger: *Gilbertine Charters*, p. 9). Under the name of Thomas Mustell of Torrington, he witnessed charters for Sixhills (ibid., pp. 10, 27) and as Thomas Mustell for Bullington (ibid., p. 92), of 1256.

[1] *Sempringham Charters*, xv. 223. For the Gant family, see M. Abbott, 'The Gant Family . . .' (p. xv n. 3), ch. II.

Mary, and the nuns of Sempringham, with an ample group of properties: all the mills of Folkingham, pasture for a flock of 200 sheep, and holdings situated at Barton, Heckington, and Walcot.[1] Countess Alice was outlived a few years by Gilbert; so he knew four generations of the House of Gant–Folkingham–Lincoln, from the founder of the dynasty (†1095) during Gilbert's earliest years.

The future founder learned the rudiments of letters while still young, at a humble parish school or at Crowland abbey, the sole monastic foundation in the region prior to the Conquest. But it was in France that he was initiated in the *ars litteratoria*.[2] We can imagine that he made his way to Normandy, the home of his father's family; established perhaps between the mouths of the Orne and the Couesnon, if we bear in mind his kinsmen's ties with the Paynels and the house of Bayeux. Mont Saint-Michel and the school at Avranches had attracted young minds eager to complete their learning: Lanfranc and Anselm of Bec had for a time given lustre to the school at Avranches. At the end of the eleventh century, thanks to the impact of the ducal abbeys—Saint-Étienne and La Trinité—the school at Caen had taken over this role. Theobald of Étampes was called *doctor Cadumensis* before he transferred his teaching to the collegiate church of St George at Oxford and was known thereafter as *doctor Oxenefordiae*.[3] It was perhaps under the aegis of the doctors at Caen, like Master Arnold and Master Theobald of Étampes, that Gilbert acquired the title of master under which he is known to posterity.

On his return to his own country, he undertook the instruction in Sempringham of children, boys and girls of the district, teaching them Latin grammar and vocabulary by the classic method of the psalms, inculcating in them moral principles and imposing upon them an almost monastic discipline.[4] This leads us to the view that there was a dearth of schools in the area. After this Jocelin, exercising his right of patronage over the churches of his domains, presented his son to the rectories of Sempringham and West Torrington. Gilbert consented to this for the sole purpose of preserving his father's rights of patronage, which were the object of

---

[1] *Sempringham Charters*, xv. 161. [2] *Life*, c. 2.

[3] Foreville, 'L'École de Caen au xiᵉ siècle . . .', *Études médiévales offertes à . . . Augustin Fliche* (Montpellier, 1952), pp. 81–100; R. Foreville and J. Leclercq in *Studia Anselmiana*, xli (1957; = *Analecta Monastica*, iv), 10–14.

[4] *Life*, c. 3.

dispute. He had received only the simple tonsure, or was at most in minor orders; he nevertheless embarked on a common life with the chaplain of Sempringham. The biographer who, throughout the *Vita*, seems to have shown a healthy respect for chronology, specifies that he passed to orders during his stay at the episcopal court. He had entered the house of the bishop of Lincoln, Robert Bloet (†1123), and then remained for several years with his successor, Alexander (1123–1148). The latter admitted him to major orders, and despite his reservations—for he considered himself unworthy— ordained him priest. Gilbert did not, however, forget his pastoral duties while in the bishop's service: allocating for his own subsistence the revenues from the church of Sempringham, he assigned those from the church of Torrington to the poor and continued to visit and instruct the parishioners despite his distance from them.[1]

First steps

The bishop offered him the dignity and the benefits of one of the archdeaconries of the vast diocese of Lincoln: he refused the office, which was full of peril for the life of the spirit. It was no doubt at this time that he left the episcopal court in order to fulfil his own pastoral vocation. But he was always to find support and protection with Alexander and his successor Robert de Chesney (1148–66). Resolving to devote his ministry to the service of the poor so that they might lead an honourable life in the fear and love of God, and with no men responding to the call, he gathered together seven young women, whom he thereafter guided towards the religious life. For them he built an enclosure on the model of anchorites' cells along the northern side of the parish church of St Andrew. For them he laid down a discipline of life enjoining them to practise chastity, humility, obedience, and charity. And because they were cloistered, and thus unable to go out to attend to the necessities of life, he obtained for them the services of some girls living in the world, who could communicate with them through a window which the rest of the time remained carefully closed.[2]

Gilbert was at that time in communication with the first Cistercians to become established in the north-east of England. Rievaulx, founded in 1132—some months before Fountains—and contemporary with the humble beginnings of the Gilbertine

[1] *Life*, cc. 5–7.   [2] *Life*, cc. 8–9.

Order, had as its first abbot William, a monk of Clairvaux.[1] On his advice—for he reckoned it unfitting that girls involved in secular life, who were likely to introduce the gossip of the outside world into the cloister, should be in the service of the nuns—Gilbert proposed to these simple souls that they also follow the religious life, 'contempt for the world, and the abandonment of all property; restraint upon the will and mortification of the flesh; continual work and infrequent rest; many vigils and little sleep', fasting and prayer for the love of God and the salvation of their souls, and also for security in this life. He imposed on them one year of probation.

These serving girls formed the first community of lay sisters of the Gilbertine Order.[2] However, 'because women's efforts achieve little without help from men', Gilbert was led to found the third branch of the Order, that of the lay brethren.[3] Every institution, whether secular or religious, was at that time based upon the possession and exploitation of the land. To the first very modest endowments, those indeed of the founder, came to be added those of his kinsmen, of Gilbert de Gant, of Bishop Alexander, and others stemming from the generosity of local squires; later, those of King Henry II. In order to put this land to effective use, Gilbert brought together farm hands—day-labourers, defecting serfs—and in the first place those who were working on his own lands, as well as unfortunate souls whom he had taken in and brought up from infancy, for poverty was endemic to the region. Acceptance of the religious status—after probation—ensured their daily bread and their social and cultural promotion, without for all that radically transforming the labour to which they were accustomed. In this new foundation, Cistercian influence was of primary importance. It appears in the constitutions which he drew up, prescribing rules for the monastic discipline and the labour of the brethren. It is so deliberate that it is manifest even in the outward appearances: 'I have taken mercenaries from around me,' he said, 'and I have given them religious habits, such as the Cistercian brothers wear.'[4]

The Order and its Master

Around the initial house founded in 1131 or shortly before, and then about 1139 raised to the status of the priory of St Mary on

---

[1] St William, abbot of Rievaulx, 1132–45 (*Heads*, p. 140). [2] *Life*, c. 10.
[3] *Life*, c. 11. [4] *Life*, c. 11; 'Institutiones', *Monasticon*, vi. 2, p. xxx* (xix*).

adjoining lands given by Gilbert de Gant, there had developed subsidiary branches to serve the 'handmaidens of Christ'. The great number of vocations was matched by the generosity of donors, both stimulated during Stephen's reign by the reputation for saintliness which already surrounded the founder, and by the renewal of religious life in the simplicity and austerity of a particularly strict rule. The foundation of new Gilbertine houses in Lincolnshire posed the problem of their direction; Gilbert, who had not belonged to any order of monks or canons, believed himself unworthy to govern them. Linked by friendship to the Cistercians, who from that time onwards were established to the north and south of the Humber, and whose rigour and originality he admired, he therefore thought them to be more suited than all others to preside over his work. Like the abbots of Savigny and Obazine, he wished to bind his foundations to the great Cistercian family. To this end, he went to the general chapter of the Order in Cîteaux in 1147. Eugenius III, himself a Cistercian monk, and the chapter declined, alleging that it was not lawful to govern monks of another religious order, still less nuns. The pope conferred upon the founder the care of his foundations and, if we are to believe his biographer, he would have elevated him to the archiepiscopal see of York if the fame of his merits had reached him sooner.[1] Gilbert went on to Clairvaux where he remained for some time.

On his return to England, having accepted the papal decision as a judgement from God, but not by himself feeling equal to the responsibility for several houses, Gilbert resolved to create the fourth branch of the Order, that of canons regular, for the spiritual direction of the monasteries.[2] Knowing that canon law forbade monks or clerks to live in the same quarters with women, but wishing nevertheless to ensure the stability of foundations primarily intended for nuns, he resolved the problem by instituting double monasteries within which, by a series of ingenious architectural arrangements and stringent regulations banning any exchanges between men and women, male communities and female communities were to live in partnership although strictly separated. It

---

[1] *Life*, cc. 13–14. After the deposition of William FitzHerbert and a disputed election, the see of York was confirmed by Pope Eugenius III to the Cistercian monk and abbot of Fountains, Henry Murdac, who was consecrated by the pope himself on 7 Dec. 1147 (D. Knowles, 'The Case of St William of York' in *Historian and Character and Other Essays* (Cambridge, 1963), pp. 76–97, esp. p. 90).

[2] *Life*, c. 15.

was surely at Sempringham that the Gilbertine plan was first evolved. It comprised a common church with an aisle to which the nuns and lay sisters had access, and another aisle adjacent, accessible to the canons and lay brethren, each coming from their respective enclosures, but separated by a wall running down the centre of the church from west to east in such a way as to prevent either group from seeing anything of the other. Between the two enclosures, a narrow window, hermetically sealed on each side, provided for the necessary exchanges.[1]

The biographer insists on the union of heart and mind animating the two groups, even though the founder laid down a double monastic discipline: on the nuns, as well as on the lay brethren and sisters, he imposed the Rule of St Benedict according to the Cistercian tradition; on the clerks he imposed the so-called Rule of St Augustine; to all he proposed the example of Christ and the saints and the teaching of the Gospels and the Apostles. And because he considered it right to adapt constitutions to times, places, and people, Gilbert selected from amongst the statutes and practices of various churches and monasteries that which appeared to him most fitted to human needs, right down to points of detail. He brought these together in a kind of anthology or florilegium, the text of which was approved by a privilege of Eugenius III, then confirmed by Adrian IV, Alexander III, and other popes.[2] If we refer to those traces of the founder's writings which have come down to us, we shall observe that he had himself set up the division of labour and responsibility among the various branches of the Order; but we shall also observe that he borrowed from the Cistercians the institution of which they were, if not the first inventors, at least the promoters *par excellence*, the annual general chapter of the Order.[3]

Gilbert is presented to us as the good shepherd. He practised the virtues of humility, mercy, sincerity, and above all chastity and poverty, not setting himself apart in anything from those over whom he presided, unless by his mortifications in food and clothing, even refusing fish in Lent and the use of a fur-lined cloak in winter. He exercised the power of punishment with discretion

---

[1] Graham, 'Excavations', pp. 79–83; below, p. lxxxiii n. 2; H. Braun and R. Graham in *JBAA*, 3rd ser., v (1940), 79–83.

[2] *Life*, c. 17; *PUE*, i, no. 154, esp. pp. 426–7, 25 June 1178 (from the Malton cartulary, BL Cotton Claud. D. xi, f. 9).

[3] 'Institutiones', *Monasticon*, vi. 2, pp. xxix*–xxx* (xix*–xx*).

but also with an inexorable severity until the sinner had sincerely repented and done penance, in order to eradicate all transgression and to inspire the fear of sin. He had the gift of tears, but he was jovial and showed great urbanity in his conversation.[1] Although the founder and Master of the Order, he himself acted in all observances as one of its members, without for all that wearing the canons' habit and without having made his profession to a Rule. Fearing that after his death a stranger to the Order would be imposed upon them, his disciples persuaded him first to take the habit, then to choose his successor. It was at Bullington priory, probably in the 1170s, that he made his profession in the Order of Sempringham, in the presence of Roger, one of the first canons, the prior of Malton. Thereafter the latter was associated with the administration of the Order, Gilbert taking his advice and seeking his approbation. The Master had become very advanced in years.[2]

Crisis in the Order

This decision was made after two ordeals. The first was in connection with the exile of Thomas Becket. Compelled to flee in secret from the Council of Northampton (October 1164), the archbishop had taken refuge in the houses of the Order, escorted by a Gilbertine brother.[3] Gilbert was accused of having forwarded sums of money to the exile, thereby disobeying the king's orders. He was obliged to visit London and appear before the royal judges. Refusing to take an oath upon the Scriptures or upon relics—in spite of being threatened with the exile of the officials and bursars of all his monasteries—he was cleared when the king, who was sojourning on the Continent, ordered the cessation of all proceedings against him (probably in the spring of 1165).[4]

[1] *Life*, cc. 21–2.

[2] *Life*, c. 23. Gilbert must be in his 90s. He laid down his responsibilities as head of the Order between 1176 and 1178. See Cheney, 'Papal privileges', pp. 46–52, where the author discusses the titles given to the heads of the Gilbertine Order in the 12th c.: Master, prior, *summus prior*—correcting several entries in *Heads*: in particular, the mention (*Heads*, p. 203) of a Gilbert prior of Malton must be cancelled.

[3] Herbert of Bosham, *MB*, iii. 323–5.

[4] *Monasticon*, vi. 2, p. lxix* (xlii*); Foreville, *L'Église et la royauté*, pp. 209–10, 210 nn. 2, 3. William FitzStephen describes the enquiry about bishops and abbots suspected of giving the exiled Becket financial support, and notes that they left Henry bishop of Winchester in peace; he also noted that when the king returned to London, he stopped the proceedings (*MB*, iii. 106–7).

The second ordeal, much more serious, occurred about the same period. It touched the Order at its heart, since its own constitutions were at stake. It concerned a revolt of lay brethren, starting in houses in Lincolnshire; they cast the worst aspersions on the canons, claiming that the double monasteries lent themselves to scandal, and asserting that they had been compelled to make a new profession.[1] The affair went all the way to Rome and the Master was required to make reply in court before judges delegate.[2] Gilbert had to comply with papal injunctions stipulating that the separation of the male and female communities be rendered even more strict. Nevertheless, he refused to modify the constitutions of the Order. He consented to receive the repentant lay brethren to the kiss of peace. However, a handful who were irreconcilable, led by Ogger, none the less pursued their revolt. At this time, indeed, towards the end of the twelfth century, other religious Orders—Cîteaux, Prémontré, and Grandmont—experienced similar stirrings amongst their lay brethren.[3]

Last years, death, and canonization of Gilbert

An ordeal of a personal nature overtook Gilbert in his extreme old age: he lost his sight. He now travelled only by litter, from this time on unable to ride a horse. Devoting himself more to contemplation, he left to Roger, prior of Malton, the care of his houses, but he himself still received the written professions of the members of the Order.[4] By the saintliness of his life and the extent of his work he had won for himself not only renown, but the veneration of the

---

[1] *Life*, c. 25; see below, pp. lv–lvi.

[2] This inquiry took place during the vacancy of the see of Lincoln after the death of Robert de Chesney, if not during his last illness. He probably died on 27 Dec. 1166 (*Fasti*, iii. 2). For the Lincolnshire houses, the pope commissioned William bishop of Norwich and Henry bishop of Winchester. For Watton priory, he commissioned the archbishop of York, Roger of Pont-l'Évêque, and Hugh du Puiset, bishop of Durham.

[3] The condition of the Gilbertine lay brother did not differ from the Cistercian, who was deprived of any intellectual education, entirely subject to his abbot and to the needs of the community, engaged in vigils, fasting, hard labour, humility, and austerity; knowing that even his labours were of no merit the lay brother, if he did not accept his status, ventured to seek money, or to enter into open revolt (C. Van Dijk, 'L'instruction et la culture des frères convers dans les premiers siècles de l'Ordre de Cîteaux', *Coll. Ordinis Cisterciensis ref.* xxiv (1962), 243–58, esp. pp. 254–6). For Grandmont, see J. Becquet, 'La première crise de l'Ordre de Grandmont', *Bull. Soc. arch. hist. Limousin*, lxxxvii (1960), 283–324.

[4] See above, p. xxiiin.; *Life*, cc. 26–7.

leading figures of the kingdom. The king himself honoured him, even visiting him in person with his barons and asking for his blessing. On learning of the founder's death, he was to exclaim 'Truly I realize now that he has departed this life, for these misfortunes have befallen me just because he no longer lives.' At that time Henry II was waging war on the Continent against Philip Augustus, the king of France, who was supporting Prince Richard in his claims to Aquitaine.[1]

Weighed down by his years and by his infirmities and with ordeals heaped upon him, Gilbert had laid aside the administration of the Order before 1178, perhaps at the time of the Pierleone legation (1175–6). He none the less remained the central figure of the whole Order. The austerity of his life, the fruitfulness and the firmness of his rule, his unshakeable will to maintain the Order along its original lines, his constancy in adversity, and already, if we are to believe the biographer, miraculous signs occurring upon his intercession—all these contributed to an aura of sanctity in his extreme old age. It was then that he agreed, with the consent of the chapter of the Order and with the arbitration of the bishop of Lincoln, St Hugh, to moderate the severity of the statute governing food and clothing for the lay brethren (after 21 September 1186, the date of Hugh's consecration).

Gilbert, now over a hundred years old, scarcely any longer took nourishment. It was to extreme debility that he succumbed. He was on the island of Cadney, where lay of the priory of Newstead-on-Ancholme. For fear he might depart this life in this place and his mortal remains might elude his spiritual sons, his companions and chaplains conveyed him secretly, with all speed and by an indirect route, to Sempringham, the first and chief house of the Order. Priors and officials of the monasteries flocked to receive his final blessing and catch his last words—which were to preserve the peace, unity, and strictness of the Order. Roger received the final confirmation of his ministry: 'Tibi amodo incumbit . . .'—'Upon you the responsibility rests . . .'—the last words barely audible on the lips of the dying man. It was the hour when the monastic community was intoning Lauds, on 4 February 1189. His body, duly bathed[2] and clothed in priestly vestments, was

---

[1] *Life*, c. 29. King Henry II was in his last days. His forces were routed in Touraine and elsewhere: he died on 6 July after the conclusion of a truce at Chinon two days before.

[2] For the use of the water in which Gilbert was bathed see the miracles, M1, nos. 5, 10, 14, 18, 28, etc.

buried on Tuesday, 7 February, in the priory church of Sempringham between the altar of St Mary and the altar of St Andrew. His tomb was embedded in the wall between the choirs in such a way that it was accessible, from both sides of the wall, to each of the communities, nuns and sisters on the one hand and canons and brethren on the other.[1]

Gilbert's funeral was the occasion of a great gathering of people: religious of various orders, knights, and humble folk of the region. Soon there were signs appearing—visions reported by some, cures received by others on the Master's intercession—giving credence to his reputation for sanctity.[2] The founder of the Order of Sempringham was solemnly canonized at Anagni on 11 January 1202 by Pope Innocent III, who promulgated his decree by a bull of 30 January.[3]

II. THE GILBERTINE FOUNDATIONS

The Gilbertine countryside in the twelfth century: the geographical and social background

The Gilbertine houses originated and multiplied primarily in the county of Lincoln, especially in the Lincolnshire Fens. Domesday Book and the Lindsey Survey have allowed modern geographers and social historians to chart the demographic structure and way of life of the population at the time of the Norman Conquest. The situation remained very similar in the twelfth century, the great social changes not really appearing until the eighteenth century, the era of industrialization and the beginning of scientific agriculture. The basic features of physical geography—the hills, the distribution of soils, the changing pattern of flowing waters, the vast marshlands—all had a direct bearing on the economy of the country and the lives of its inhabitants.

If we consider the situation of Sempringham, the origin and centre of Gilbertine expansion in the twelfth century, we cannot

---

[1] *Life*, cc. 52, 55. The separation between men and women is perfectly clear when looking at the witnesses of miracles: they did not visit the tomb of Gilbert if they were not of the same sex as the disabled, but could only certify the condition of the cured before and after the miracle (see e.g. M1, nos. 9, 24, 30). Braun and Graham, art. cit. (p. xxii n. 1), 80–3 and pl. XI, described the new church (14th c.) in which the shrine of Gilbert was left in its original situation—embedded in the wall between nuns' and canons' choirs.

[2] Below, pp. c–cvii, 92–117, 264–335.   [3] Below, pp. xcvi–ci, 168–259.

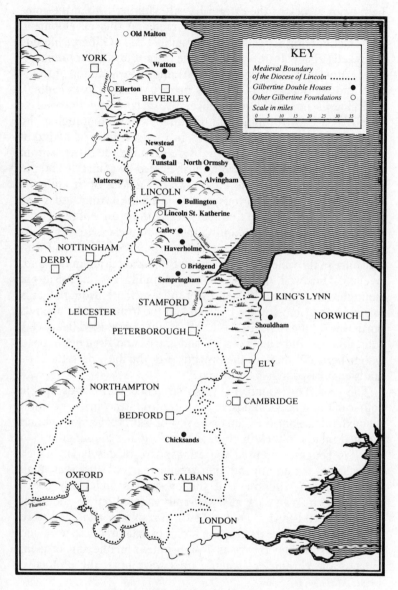

KEY

Medieval Boundary
of the Diocese of Lincoln ....
Gilbertine Double Houses ●
Other Gilbertine Foundations ○
Scale in miles
0 5 10 15 20 25 30 35

Old Malton ○

YORK □

Watton ●

Derwent

Ellerton ○

Don

Trent

BEVERLEY □

Newstead ○

Tunstall ●

North Ormsby ●

Mattersey ○

Sixhills ●   Alvingham ●

LINCOLN □

Bullington ●

Lincoln St. Katherine ○

Catley ●

Witham

Haverholme ●

NOTTINGHAM □

DERBY □

Bridgend ○

Sempringham ●

Welland

STAMFORD □

KING'S LYNN □

LEICESTER □

NORWICH □

PETERBOROUGH □

Shouldham ●

ELY □

Ouse

NORTHAMPTON □

CAMBRIDGE ○ □

BEDFORD □

Chicksands ●

OXFORD □

ST. ALBANS □

Thames

LONDON □

Sempringham and the Gilbertine Order.
Drawn by Max Marschner.

help being struck by the extraordinarily rapid growth of the communities and the strongly local character of this development. Eleven out of thirteen foundations established in Gilbert's lifetime belonged to Lincolnshire.[1] Within the county, except for the short-lived Tunstall in the wapentake of Manley (West Riding of Lindsey), and Newstead-on-Ancholme in Yarborough (North Riding), nine houses lay in the wapentakes of Aveland and Flaxwell in Kesteven, Wraggoe (in the South Riding), and Ludborough in the southern part of the North Riding, in Lindsey, forming a kind of arc around the Wash. Moreover, if we examine the districts from which the pilgrims came—both those healed by a miracle and the witnesses quoted by name in the two collections of St Gilbert's miracles—apart from various members of the Order and some persons of high rank, we find that the great majority of those who frequented Sempringham and Gilbert's tomb came from wapentakes which likewise described an arc around the Wash and with its centre in the valley of the Witham; Elloe and Kirton in Holland; Aveland, Flaxwell, Langoe, Threo, Winnibriggs in Kesteven; Bolingbroke, Gartree, Wraggoe in Lindsey (South Riding): that is to say, in the Lincolnshire Fens and on the fringes of the uplands bordering on the Fens. In these regions there prevailed heavy clay soils, alluvial lands: beds of sand and gravel, and stretches of peat; woods here and there in the uplands. For the most part, the lowlands comprised marsh and water.[2]

The great fens round the Wash stretched northwards up the course of the Witham almost to the latitude of Lincoln; in the south they extended along the Cam to the very outskirts of Cambridge and reached inland in the direction of Stamford and Huntingdon. No one has better recaptured the atmosphere of desolation which bathed the region during the greater part of the year than J. R. Green: 'A wilderness of shallow waters and reedy islets, wrapped in its own dark mist-veil and tenanted only by flocks of screaming wild-fowl.'[3] To the desolation of the landscape were sometimes added the destructive forces of a natural disaster. Such was the case in the 1170s—as a punishment for the sins of men, remarks the chronicler—when a tidal wave burst the protective

[1] See *VCH Lincs.*, ii. 179–99.

[2] H. C. Darby, *The Domesday Geography of Eastern England* (3rd edn. Cambridge, 1971), pp. 34–6; id., *The Medieval Fenland* (Cambridge, 1940), esp. fig. 2, p. 5.

[3] Green, *The Making of England* (London, 1881), p. 351, cited by Graham, *S. Gilbert*, pp. 1–2 (wrongly ascribed to p. 56).

dikes on the coast of Holland and invaded the lowlands with exceptional violence, devastating villages and drowning a great number of animals and men.[1]

Situated on the western fringe of the Fens, Sempringham therefore extended its influence over lands which were not very fertile. The people lived principally by wild-fowling and fishing, by the exploitation of the salt-marshes, some domestic crafts, and sheep-shearing based on the Cistercian and Gilbertine granges. The region was sparsely populated, the villages were scattered save on the edge of the Wolds, in contrast with the inland areas of Lincolnshire, as can be seen from the insignificant number of plough-teams recorded in Domesday Book.[2] Most of those from Sempringham who had been healed by a miracle were humble folk, the majority freemen, who travelled about on foot, or were conveyed in a hand-litter if their condition so required. Their family ties and bonds with neighbours, expressed in the procession of witnesses coming from the same village or the same hamlet, testify not only to family connections, but to a community life and solidarity in the exploitation of the soil.

The deeds of gift generally involved very small parcels of land resulting from the generosity of peasants: such was the case for the priories of Alvingham and Ormsby, the latter maintained by properties scattered across Lincolnshire and the southern plain of Yorkshire.[3] If, on the other hand, certain deeds of Sixhills derived from great feudal lords and involved important domains pledged for ready money to pay for a pilgrimage to Jerusalem, this was a general phenomenon in western Christendom at the time of the crusades. The properties thus granted certainly differed from one priory to another, but their description, as in the case of Alvingham, shows the diversity of the parcels of land, which were often tiny: tofts, salt marshes, sand pits, furlongs of arable land.[4] Sempringham, owing to the impact of Gilbert and his foundations, became the centre of an intense religious life spreading throughout

---

[1] William of Newburgh (RS, i. 204–5) records the cataclysm on 7 Jan. 1176(?), when Hugo Pierleone was acting as legate in England. The Waverley annalist dates it 12 Jan. 1178 (*Annales monastici*, ed. H. R. Luard (RS, 1864–99), ii. 241). We cannot exclude the possibility of two successive catastrophes.

[2] Cf. Darby, *The Domesday Geography of Eastern England*, esp. figs. 5, 7, 8, pp. 35–49 (place-names, plough-teams by settlements, plough-teams' densities).

[3] *Gilbertine Charters*, pp. xii–xiii.

[4] *Gilbertine Charters*, p. 106; cf. p. xvi; Owen, *Church and Society*, pp. 48–51.

the county and even beyond, over the immense diocese of Lincoln and the south of Yorkshire, but it also became one of the driving forces behind the development of the region and its economic transformation. Today not one house, not one stone, remains of either the village or the priory. It is a deserted village from which there emerges a single, solitary witness, the parish church of St Andrew, which raises its square tower above a broad expanse of meadows, fields, and heath.

The Gilbertine foundations in the time of Gilbert

Parallel with the increase in vocations, donations multiplied, to the extent that from the reign of Stephen the Gilbertine Order numbered many houses. The piety of the donors and the desire to bring renown to their families by the establishment of some religious foundation were at that time stimulated by the incentive to make amends, by a charitable deed, for the depredations in which both sides had indulged as a result of their involvement in the civil war. At that period reforming movements were in vogue among both monks and canons. Cistercians and Premonstratensians were substantially increasing the number of their establishments on the Continent and were spreading in England too. The Gilbertine inspiration was of the same stamp and had originated at home, in the county of Lincoln, which had not been spared by the struggle between the supporters of Stephen and Matilda. The reputation for saintliness which Gilbert was very soon to enjoy, the success of the first foundations, Sempringham and Haverholme, and the support of the bishop of Lincoln all worked in favour of the new Order. However, the founder's fame remained restricted to the area from which he came, Lincolnshire; it spread incidentally to a part of Yorkshire: to the East Riding and southern parts of the North and West Ridings. It was only after Gilbert's death—with the exception of Chicksands in Bedfordshire—that the Order of Sempringham was to penetrate into a few other counties, and even then it never reached the west of England.[1]

[1] The Gilbertine foundations are listed and briefly described in *Monasticon*, vi, 2. 947–82, whose accounts are revised and corrected in *VCH*, esp. *Lincs.* ii; see also Graham, *S. Gilbert*. Very useful, though not perfect, is Knowles and Hadcock, pp. 194–9. For Lincolnshire, the best summary is in Owen, *Church and Society*, app. III, pp. 146–53, which includes Holland Marsh, omitted in Knowles and Hadcock. See also R. Midmer, *English mediaeval monasteries (1066—1540)* (London, 1979: lists and maps).

The first tiny house of the Order, built round the parish church of St Andrew of Sempringham, was established on the advice and with the help of Alexander bishop of Lincoln, then transferred a certain distance and raised to the status of a priory dedicated to St Mary about 1139. At the same date, a second monastery was founded, at Haverholme on a site which the bishop had initially offered to the Cistercians of Fountains, who had begun the construction of monastic buildings before abandoning their plan. But the rapid rise of the Gilbertine Order dates from the last years of Stephen's reign, when peace was returning to the country. Robert de Chesney, the successor to Bishop Alexander (†1148), took up this role and, after the creation of the Gilbertine canons and the confirmation of the Order by Eugenius III, founded a priory in Lincoln intended for canons, to the exclusion of nuns: St Catherine Without the Walls, a very amply endowed house, with a hospital attached after an appeal had been made to the lay sisters to care for the sick.[1]

Eight other foundations sprang up between 1148 and 1154, at the prompting from that time onwards of secular lords, and of these five were in Lincolnshire. These were: Alvingham, founded by Roger, Gilbert's brother, whose work was completed by his nephew, Roger Mustel; Bullington, founded by Simon of Kyme, who was the son of William of Kyme, and whose wife Roesia was the daughter of Gilbert de Gant's steward; Catley, endowed with the whole island of the same name, in the marsh of Walcot, by Peter, son of Henry of Billinghay; North Ormsby, given the name of Nun Ormsby, founded by Gilbert of Ormsby with the consent of his lord, William of Aumale; and Sixhills, founded by a member of the Greslei family. The year 1150, that is to say about ten years after the founding of the first priory at Sempringham, marks the beginning of Gilbertine expansion beyond the county of Lincoln. Old Malton and Watton in Yorkshire owe their establishment to Eustace FitzJohn. Henry I had appointed him castellan of Bamburgh. Eustace had then joined his

---

[1] St Catherine's priory foundation charter is known from an *inspeximus* of 1327 of the confirmation of Henry II (*EEA, Lincoln*, i, no. 163). The accepted date of *c.* 1148 seems too early, since the branch of the Order consisting of houses of canons was planned after the Cistercian general chapter of Sept. 1147, and the priory was founded by Robert de Chesney, who was elected and consecrated in Dec. 1148 (*Fasti*, iii. 2)–unless he completed a scheme prepared by Bishop Alexander. Bishop Robert and Gilbert were involved in a charter of Hugh of Bayeux 'ecclesiae beatae Mariae de Torentona et canonicis inibi degentibus': Canon Venables, who discovered and published it, identified this with Torrington, and supposed a link with St Catherine's (*Archaeological Journal*, xxxiii (1876), 183–9, esp. 185); but in fact it related to the Augustinian house of Thornton.

forces to King David I of Scotland's, and these were finally defeated at the Battle of the Standard (1138), not without causing much destruction, laying waste the fields, burning churches and villages, and claiming a number of victims. Having, through the mediation of Thurstan, archbishop of York, recovered his estates, confiscated by Stephen, Eustace set up these two priories on the advice of Henry Murdac, the Cistercian successor to Thurstan. Finally, Chicksands (Bedfordshire) owes its foundation, also in 1150, to Roesia, the widow of Geoffrey de Mandeville, earl of Essex (who had died in 1144), the second wife of Pain de Beauchamp of Bedford.

After 1150, the Gilbertine foundations marked time. The reign of Henry II saw the setting up of only three new institutions. Even so, the priory of Tunstall (Lincolnshire), founded before 1164 on the island of the same name and endowed by Reginald de Crèvecœur, was only short-lived, its endowments having been joined to Bullington priory by his son before 1189. Newstead-on-Ancholme (Lincolnshire) had the king himself as founder: it received part of the island of Cadney, on which it was sited, as well as estates at Hardwick and elsewhere. The last foundation established in Gilbert's lifetime was effected by Roger, son of Ranulf of Mattersey, whose name it took: it was set up probably about 1185 on an island of the River Idle in Nottinghamshire, and was dedicated to St Helen.

The numbers of religious at the end of the twelfth century

Such were the Gilbertine houses at the founder's death. The *Life* and the letters postulating the canonization (1201) certify the existence in 1189 of nine nunneries, that is to say, according to the institutions established by Gilbert, nine double monasteries, and four priories of canons. These same documents put forward the number of 1,500 nuns and lay sisters, and 700 canons and lay brethren.[1] These figures have been challenged and it is difficult to accept them without submitting them to careful criticism. Every foundation for monks or canons was established with a fixed number of religious in view, related to the resources with which it was endowed. A calculation of the number of nuns and lay sisters on the one hand, and canons and lay brethren on the other, whose

[1] *Life*, c. 19; see also below, pp. 54–5, 128–9, 192–3, 250–1.

figure had been set by the founders, indicates that there were very approximately 930 female religious and 524 male religious, that is to say, nearly 1,500 all told.[1]

TABLE I. *Total strength of Gilbertine establishments, c. 1200*

	Nuns and lay sisters	Canons and lay brethren
Sempringham	120	60
Haverholme	100 (120)	50
Lincoln (St Catherine)	20	16
Alvingham	80	40
Bullington	100	50
Nun Ormsby	100	50
Catley	60	35
Sixhills	120	55
Chicksands	80 (120)	40 (55)
Malton	–	48 (35)
Watton	150 (140)	70
Newstead	–	? (13)
Hospital (Clattercote)	–	– (55)
Mattersey	–	10
TOTALS	930 (980)	524 (594)

These figures are probably an underestimate. It is possible that the numbers originally specified may in fact have been exceeded, considering the surge of donations and the prosperity due to the early development of the region.[2] The enrichment of the Order had not taken place without reservations on the part of the founder. It continued during the first half of the thirteenth century. Thus, Watton priory—the largest in the Order, designed for 150 women and

---

[1] The figures are those given in the Institutiones: *Monasticon*, vi. 2, pp. xcvii* (lix*); they are noted *in brackets* where they differ from other evidence. The figures in Knowles and Hadcock, pp. 491–3, seem to be an underestimate.

[2] The flow of gifts from *c.* 1150 is clearly illustrated in the *Sempringham* and *Gilbertine Charters*: see e.g. the elaborate confirmation of 1 Richard I attested by the queen mother Eleanor, archbishops, bishops, etc., in *Sempringham Charters*, xvi. 226–8.

70 men (its plan was revealed in full by the excavations carried out in 1893–8)—housed no less than 200 women in 1247.[1]

In 1301 the prior of Sempringham undertook the reconstruction of the church, which was threatened with collapse, on an ampler scale better adapted to the fashions of the time. It is known that in 1319 Walter Reynolds, archbishop of Canterbury, blessed on a single day 52 nuns of Sempringham, 25 of Haverholme, five of Catley, and 'une haute Cercheresse' (scrutatrix).[2] This prosperity faltered from the middle of the fourteenth century owing to the disasters of the age and to mounting debt, and it took more than a century to complete the new priory church at Sempringham. But it remains true that from the end of the twelfth century, the Order commanded substantial resources, thanks to the system of granges, used both by Cistercians and Gilbertines, and the building of dikes to direct the flow of water, from the enlargement of pasture-land, the rearing of sheep, and the sale of wool. The confiscation of all the wool-production of the Order of Sempringham, as of the Cistercian abbeys, for the ransom of Richard I, four years after Gilbert's death, bears witness to the growing wealth of the Gilbertines.[3] At this period William of Newburgh could write, echoing their common reputation, 'The sons and daughters of the venerable Gilbert are still as numerous and his seed proliferates in our land.'[4]

At the end of the twelfth century a whole world revolved around Sempringham and the other priories. Gilbert had not merely founded thirteen conventual churches. Hospices and hospitals for the poor, the sick, the handicapped, widows, and orphans were attached to some of the houses of canons.[5] Thus Malton took upon itself the responsibility for running three hospitals; Clattercote (Oxon.) in the time of Bishop Robert de Chesney (1148–66) was

[1] W. H. St John Hope in *Archaeological Journal*, lviii (1901), 1–34; Graham, *An Essay on English Monasteries* (Hist. Association Pamphlet, 1930), both with plans of Watton priory; see also D. Knowles and J. K. S. St Joseph, *Monastic Sites from the Air* (Cambridge, 1952), pp. 246–7.

[2] *Le Livere de Reis de Brittanie*, ed. J. Glover (RS, 1865), Sempringham Continuation, pp. 326–7, 336–7. On the new church, 'Our Lady of Sempringham', see Graham, 'Excavations', H. Braun and R. Graham, in *JBAA*, 3rd ser., v (1940), 85–94.

[3] *Chronica Rogeri de Hovedene*, ed. W. Stubbs (RS, 1868–71), iii. 210–11. For the wool-production in Lincolnshire monasteries, see Owen, *Church and Society*, p. 66 and map p. 67.

[4] William of Newburgh, i. 55 (after Gilbert's death and before the canonization: 1190×1200).

[5] *Life*, c. 19.

a leper-house for the care of Gilbertines stricken with leprosy and was to become a priory in the second half of the thirteenth century.

The Order likewise maintained modest establishments whose function was economic. Thomas Becket, fleeing in secret from the Council of Northampton, was welcomed into various Gilbertine houses and found refuge in a hermitage situated some forty miles from Lincoln, all but inaccessible, surrounded by water. It may perhaps have been Holland Marsh, which, about 1180, made its appearance as a chapelry dedicated to St Thomas the Martyr, for two canons, no doubt supplemented by an unspecified number of lay brethren. Its establishment is attested at that time by a grant to Sempringham by the knight Ralph of Wyberton, son of Stephen of Holland.[1] In the years following Gilbert's death, certainly before 1199, a comparable foundation made its appearance: a modest priory for two or three canons at the place named Bridge End, or Holland Bridge, established at the junction of the new dike and the causeway crossing the fens to Donington. The canons were obliged to maintain the causeway. One can scarcely imagine that they devoted themselves personally to such duties: it was the concern of the lay brethren, of whom, however, the charters make no mention—unless they employed hired labourers to carry out this work. No doubt Holland Marsh took charge of similar tasks in relation to water drainage, soil improvement, and the reclamation of the land. These few examples reveal to what extent the Gilbertines, spread across the lowlands of Lincolnshire, contributed to the transformation of a particularly desolate region. Without disregarding their charitable and social mission towards the people, we shall recall here the view expressed by Rose Graham: 'Nowhere has the country round a Gilbertine priory changed so completely. A good high-road, with fields on every side, has taken the place of the deep, dangerous fen with its thirty bridges.'[2] The process was well on the way at the end of the twelfth century.

[1] 'Cappella sancti Thome martiris infra marescum Hoylandie sita', *Sempringham charters*, xv. 76; Owen, *Church and Society*, app. III, p. 149. The editors of the *Monasticon*, *VCH Lincs*. ii, and Knowles and Hadcock were not aware of this small priory. Herbert of Bosham pointed out the first settlement as one of Becket's stops in his flight from Northampton, saying that he went from Grantham to Lincoln, and 'ad locum quendam solitarium in medio aquarum situm, qui dicitur Hermitorium et pertinet ad sanctam illam sanctimonialium congregationem de Simpligeham, per aquam venit [i.e. the Witham] millia circiter quadraginta' (*MB*, iii. 324).

[2] Graham, *S. Gilbert*, p. 147. See Owen, *Church and Society*, pp. 57–8.

Further growth of the Order

After Gilbert's death, the foundations recorded were on the whole modest, intended for canons together with a complement of lay brethren, with the exception of two nunneries, one established just before the end of the twelfth century, the other in the middle of the fourteenth. The second half of the thirteenth century saw only two new priories, and the fourteenth century two more. In nearly two centuries, the Order barely managed to double the number of its foundations. Leaving out of account Owton (or Overton) and Ravenstonedale, since the facts concerning their establishment remain problematic, let us say thirteen foundations, whereas the first thirteen came into existence in a half-century, from 1139 to 1189.[1] We need only briefly note their locality, date, and intended purpose.

Holland Marsh (Lincs.)	priory of St Thomas the Martyr, *c.* 1180.
Bridge End (Lincs.)	priory of St Saviour, before the end of the twelfth century (1189–99).
Shouldham (Norf.)	double priory of St Mary and the Holy Cross, founded by Geoffrey FitzPeter, earl of Essex and Chief Justiciar (1189–99).
Marlborough (Wilts.)	St Margaret, a royal foundation, presumed to be by Henry II, but first mentioned in 1199–1200.
York	St Andrew, by Hugh Murdac, for twelve canons, *c.* 1200.
Marmont or Mirmaud (Cambs.)	On the Isle of Ely, by Ralph de Hauville, *c.* 1203; confirmed by King John in 1204.
Ellerton (Yorks.)	on Spalding Moor, St Mary, by William FitzPeter, hospital for thirteen poor, before 1207.
Fordham (Cambs.)	St Mary Magdalene and St Peter, before 1227, the date of the confirmation by

[1] Owton (Durham) was confirmed by King John as a priory founded by Alan of Wilton. Probably a grange was settled on the spot (Knowles and Hadcock, p. 199). A similar state of things may be suggested of Ravenstonedale (Westmorland), where a small establishment might have been an economic centre for lands and pastures listed in John's charter to Watton priory (ibid.). For what follows, see D. M. Owen, *Church and Society*, pp. 147–9; Knowles and Hadcock, pp. 194–9; for Ellerton, *Heads*, p. 202.

	Henry III of the freedoms granted by John to the Order and its priories.
Clattercote (Oxon.)	former leper-hospital (before 1166). Became a priory during the episcopate of Richard de Gravesend, 1258–79.
Stamford (Lincs.)	St Mary, Sempringham Hall, for some students of the Order. After 1266; closed by 1334.
Cambridge	St Edmund, a Gilbertine college earlier than all the Cambridge colleges with the exception of Peterhouse, c. 1291.
Poulton (Gloucs.)	St Mary, chantry chapel, by Sir Thomas Seymour, lord of Poulton, for five chaplains, c. 1348, Gilbertine from 1350.
New Biggin (Herts.)	at Hitchin, St Saviour, a small double priory, founded by Sir Edward Kendale, 1361–2.

With the exception of Shouldham, which belonged to the first Gilbertine period, and the later, modest foundation of New Biggin, both conforming with the normal plan for a Gilbertine institution as conceived by the founder, these were essentially small priories of canons: chapelries, chantries, university halls, hospices, dependent on or attached to other houses. Nevertheless, in this second period, the Order expanded beyond the boundaries of the county of Lincoln. Little priories had sprung up in Hertfordshire, Oxfordshire, Cambridgeshire, Norfolk, and Wiltshire, and strengthened the position of the Order in Yorkshire. However, when we consider these new establishments, we must recognize that most still belonged to the vast diocese of Lincoln, which at that time covered Lincolnshire, Oxfordshire, Bedfordshire, and part of Hertfordshire. Cambridgeshire had only recently been detached from it at the time of the foundation of the see of Ely in 1109. Norfolk and Wiltshire (and, of course, Yorkshire) alone lay outside the traditional rule and management of the Lincoln diocese from the time of the Norman Conquest. And there is more to it than this. Each time the Gilbertine Order was called to spread to more distant regions, the result was failure or refusal.

Whereas the Cistercians were settled in Scotland in the twelfth

century, it was only in the thirteenth century that an appeal was made to the Gilbertines. As a result of negotiations, Walter Fitz-Alan announced to the Master of the Order, Robert, his intention to establish a cell 'apud Novum Castrum super Are', Dalmilling upon Ayr. Before 1228, a small group of Gilbertines from Sixhills priory, which was particularly well endowed, took possession of the site. Ten years later, in 1238, the two resident canons, upon the command of the priors of Old Malton and St Andrew's, York, proctors of the Order, gave the abbot of Paisley seisin of the lands, revenues, and properties, on payment of rent of assize based on the wealth of this Cluniac abbey, a rent which subsequently gave rise to interminable disputes and lawsuits.[1]

No less significant was the affair of St Sixtus in Rome. Innocent III had devised a plan to amalgamate several institutions of female religious and establish a common monastery in the church of St Sixtus, near the church dedicated to the saints Nereus and Achilleus. Informed of the constitutions and the merits of the Order of Sempringham by the contacts made in the Curia at the time of Gilbert's canonization, he appealed to the Gilbertines to take over the care of the church and the spiritual direction of the nuns.[2] The old and ruinous St Sixtus was only partially rebuilt at the pope's death in 1216. In August 1218, Honorius III reproached the Master of the Order for having left the church without qualified priests in charge and called on him to send four canons the following Christmas to set up at the pope's expense arrangements in accordance with their statutes.[3] The Gilbertines, pleading difficulties in carrying out the agreement, allowed more than a year to elapse before sending a new delegation to Rome. Finally, the pope released St Sixtus from all obedience to the Master and the Order and he established there the sons of St Dominic—later transferred to St Sabina.

[1] See G. W. S. Barrow, 'The Gilbertine House at Dalmilling', *Ayrshire Archaeological and Nat. Hist. Soc. Collections*, 2nd ser., iv (1955–7), 50–67, esp. 58; cf. J. Edwards in *Transactions of the Glasgow Arch. Soc.*, n.s., v (1908), 66–95; and for the history of the foundation, I. B. Cowan and D. E. Easson, *Medieval Religious Houses, Scotland*, 2nd edn. (London, 1976), pp. 105–6.

[2] M. Maccarrone in *Italia Sacra*, xvii (1972), 272–8; Cheney, *Innocent III and England*, p. 238; V. J. Koudelka in *Archivum Fratrum Praedicatorum*, xxxi (1961), 5–81, esp. 43–53; xxxv (1965), 5–20, esp. 11–13.

[3] *Monumenta diplomatica S. Dominici*, ed. V. J. Koudelka and R. J. Loenertz, *Monumenta Ordinis Fratrum Praedicatorum Historica*, xxv (1966), nos. 92, 108, from Honorius III, Reg. Vat. 10, ff. 2, 148; *Calendar of the Entries in the Papal Registers relating to Great Britain and Ireland*, i, ed. W. H. Bliss (London, 1893), pp. 57, 69; cited Cheney, *Innocent III and England*, p. 238.

The examples of Dalmilling and St Sixtus demonstrate to what extent, once the euphoria that accompanied the beginning of the Order was over, the creation of new priories entailed lengthy bargaining and a considerable lapse of time before a foundation, formally endowed and legally established, could become a concrete reality. To what degree did the Gilbertines at the beginning of the thirteenth century possess the resources in terms of men to face such problems? Were they not after all apprehensive about the difficulties of maintaining the strict rule and authority of Sempringham in institutions remote from the centre? At all events, having refused the opportunities for establishing communities which it was offered outside the kingdom, the Gilbertine Order lacked any bases capable of ensuring its survival, when the English monasteries were dissolved in the sixteenth century.

Extinction of the Order

When the hour of dissolution struck, the Gilbertine houses had for the most part fallen into a state of great poverty. In point of fact, they had not recovered well from the fifteenth-century crisis, following on the Black Death, which had swept down upon England as upon the Continent in 1348 and 1349, with renewed outbreaks until the end of the century. At least half of their members died from the epidemic and the numbers could not be replaced. Fatal for men, the epidemic was even more so for livestock. The scarcity and rising cost of paid labour brought about— as a result of the shortage of lay brethren—the abandonment of estates, a reduction in farming, and the leasing for rent of numerous parcels of land. The war with France in the course of the fourteenth and fifteenth centuries aggravated the situation by burdening the monasteries with heavy charges. With the decline in the number of men and the decrease in revenues, the standards of both intellectual and spiritual life deteriorated, though not to such a point that charges of a moral nature were levelled against the Order.

In c. 1535 only four Gilbertine houses commanded annual revenues exceeding £200. That is to say that almost all came under the provisions of the Act for the suppression of the lesser monasteries. The influence of the Master of the Order, Robert Holgate, with Thomas Cromwell, one of whose chaplains he was, gained

them some respite.[1] At Sempringham, the prior Roger and sixteen canons '... by unanimous ... consent, with deliberate purpose ... being especially moved by [their] minds and consciences, ... of [their] own will and desire, granted the Priory ... to [their] most illustrious prince and lord, Henry VIII, Supreme Head of the English Church' (30 September 1538).[2] Before the end of the year all the Gilbertine priories, with the exception of Watton and Old Malton, had been put in the hands of the commissioners. One year later Robert Holgate, Master of the Order probably by royal nomination from *c.* 1534, prior *in commendam* of Watton from *c.* 1536, personally initiated the surrender of these two houses: on 9 December 1539 he resigned Watton, with seven canons, two prioresses, and twelve enclosed nuns; on the 11th, in his presence, the prior and nine canons resigned Old Malton.[3] At the dissolution, the Order is reckoned to have totalled 143 canons, 139 nuns, and 15 lay sisters; no mention is made of the lay brethren.[4] Were any of them still left? Yet without them, how were the estates maintained which provided the livelihood of the communities?

III. THE CHARACTER OF THE ORDER OF SEMPRINGHAM

Cîteaux general chapter of 1147

We may at first be surprised at the fact that Gilbert's request to the general chapter of 1147 was not considered favourably like those of the abbots of Savigny and Obazine. Certainly, as has often been emphasized, the refusal with which he met stemmed from a policy already determined: the opposition of the Cistercian Order as such to any assumption of responsibility for communities of women and their incorporation into the Order. A closer analysis of the facts reveals other reasons for discrimination in the 1147 verdict. Stephen of Obazine had managed to win the support of the Cistercian pope Eugenius III, who particularly recommended him to the abbot of Cîteaux: Obazine entered the filiation of Cîteaux,

---

[1] Graham, *S. Gilbert*, ch. vii, pp. 162–208; J. A. Youings, *The Dissolution of the Monasteries* (London, 1971), p. 77.

[2] Graham, *S. Gilbert*, p. 192; T. Rymer, *Foedera*, xiv (edn. of London, 1712), 604–5, 618.

[3] Graham, *S. Gilbert*, p. 195.

[4] Ibid., p. 167; *VCH, Lincs.*, ii. 186.

bringing with it the priory of Coyroux, a priory of women.[1] The abbot of Savigny, Serlo, successor to Vitalis of Mortain, was in close contact with St Bernard: his Order, already famous, comprising monasteries spread across France, England, and Normandy, was incorporated whole—including the Abbaye Blanche—in the filiation of Clairvaux.[2]

Savigny and Obazine were bringing their respective male filiations, in which were already integrated, by established tradition—*de facto*, without economic and juridical autonomy—the female communities of the Abbaye Blanche and Coyroux. Gilbert, a humble priest of the diocese of Lincoln, probably supported by Bishop Alexander,[3] was offering two nunneries, Sempringham and Haverholme—the only houses properly attested at the time—served by lay brethren and lay sisters, in which the nuns did not yet have, properly speaking, either Rule or statutes, but lived in accordance with the Cistercian spirit in 'chastity, humility, obedience, charity'.[4] Serlo at Savigny, Stephen at Obazine remained at the head of their congregations: Gilbert, for his part, intended to place his foundations in the hands of the Cistercians and pursue his own vocation as a hermit and contemplative. Nevertheless, he went to stay at Clairvaux, under the patronage of St Bernard (1147–8).[5] Familiarizing himself with the Cistercian institutions, he studied possible adaptations of them, without for all that, as we shall see, brushing aside other influences to religious fervour.

[1] *Statuta capitulorum generalium Ordinis Cisterciensis*, i, ed. J.-M. Canivez (Louvain, 1933), p. 38. The Obazine congregation comprised at the time four abbeys and two priories at least: B. Barrière, *L'Abbaye cistercienne d'Obazine* (Tulle, 1977), pp. 73–4.

[2] *Statuta*, ed. Canivez, i. 37–8. On the origin of the Order of Savigny, the circumstances, conditions, and consequences of its incorporation in the Clairvaux filiation, see B. D. Hill, *English Cistercian Monasteries and their Patrons in the 12th Century* (Chicago and London, 1968), pp. 84–115. At the time, the Order comprised twelve houses in England, of which eight were founded from Savigny itself, three from Furness, and one from Calder.

[3] In Aug. 1147 Alexander, bishop of Lincoln, went to meet Pope Eugenius at Auxerre, but he was afflicted by the excessively hot weather, returned to England, and died soon after (Feb. 1148: Henry of Huntingdon, *Hist. Anglorum*, ed. T. Arnold (RS, 1879), p. 280; *Fasti*, iii. 1–2). The pope's journey brought him to Auxerre *c.* 14 July–*c.* 6 Sept. 1147; then he went on to Cîteaux for the general chapter of the Order (*c.* 14–17 Sept.).

[4] *Life*, c. 9.

[5] Did Gilbert stay one year at Clairvaux as suggested by Brian Golding, 'St Bernard and St Gilbert', in *The Influence of St Bernard*, ed. B. Ward (Oxford, 1976), pp. 41–52, at p. 47? Or did he make two separate visits, the first when coming back from Cîteaux, after the middle of Sept. 1147, the second in Oct./Nov. 1148? The *Life*, c. 14, is not clear on the point, but this last meeting with Malachy could not be earlier than Oct. 1148, when the latter came for the second time to Clairvaux, where he died on 3 Nov. in the same year.

The verdict of 1147 carried in it the seeds of the Gilbertine Order. Confronted with his own responsibilities, supported by the pope's decision, Gilbert found himself at the crossroads. Several paths opened before him. Which was he going to follow and for what reasons? In order to answer the question, we must examine the situation of women in the religious life and institutions of the period, as well as the nature of the patronage granted them—or refused them—by the male communities, monastic or canonical.

The double monasteries from their origin

The originality of the Gilbertine foundations from 1150 onwards lay in the organization of double monasteries at a time when such a religious structure had been practically condemned and abandoned, although revived in the houses of Fontevraud at the beginning of the century. A double monastery, according to Dom Ph. Schmitz, consists in the union of 'two communities, one of monks ..., the other of nuns, established in the same place, not necessarily within the same enclosure', in completely separate buildings, under a single authority, generally disposing of a common endowment and forming a legal unit.[1] In this sense, the communities of Sempringham and Haverholme cannot be termed double monasteries before the middle of the century.

The double monastery goes back to the foundations of St Pachomius in Egypt and St Basil in Asia Minor. It spread in the Byzantine world and flourished in the West in the sixth and seventh centuries: suffice it to mention, amongst many others, Faremoutiers and Jouarre in Gaul, Hartlepool and Whitby under the great abbess Hilda in the Anglo-Saxon world. The Anglo-Saxon missions introduced it into Germany in the circle of Winfrith (St Boniface).[2] The case of Spain is of special interest. Double monasteries grew up in the Visigothic kingdom, then in the Suevic kingdom, despite the prohibition of the council of Agde (506) and the opposition of St Isidore, under the influence of three factors: the *tuitio* (or patronage) of nunneries by monks; the appearance of

[1] Ph. Schmitz, *Histoire de l'Ordre de Saint-Benoît*, vii (Maredsous, 1956), pp. 45–6.
[2] H. Leclercq and J. Pargoire, 'Les monastères doubles chez les Byzantins', *Échos d'Orient*, ix (1906), 21–5, reprinted in *Dict. d'Archéologie chrétienne et de liturgie*, xi. 2 (Paris, 1934), cols. 2184–7; M. Bateson, 'Origin and Early History of Double Monasteries', *Transactions of the Royal Hist. Soc.*, n.s., xiii (1899), 137–98; J. Leclercq, 'Should Contemplative Nuns Govern Themselves?', *Cistercian studies* v (1970), 111–30.

family monasteries, which were often mixed, on the fringe of canonical discipline; and finally, the singular form of religious life established by St Fructuosus of Braga in the *Regula communis*, which gave rise to whole monastic cities under the jurisdiction of an abbot-bishop, notably at Dumio under St Martin of Braga.[1] The institution was strengthened in Galicia by a substantial Celtic immigration, which gave birth to the abbey-bishopric of Britonia in the Bierzo, between the Minho and the sea.[2] Double monasticism lasted in Spain until the eleventh century, notably amongst the Mozarabs, whereas it declined and died out as early as the ninth century throughout nearly all Christendom. The antiquity and geographic spread of the phenomenon reflects its spontaneous character.

In contrast, Gilbert's initiative, like that of Robert of Arbrissel at Fontevraud, was perfectly deliberate, but the two paths diverged.[3] Gilbert's was modest and pragmatic and fitted into a context quite different from the Northumbrian and Celtic traditions, which were, however, known to the founder through his contacts with the Celtic world. It was set within the framework of territorial jurisdiction, under the authority of the diocesan bishop, and from the beginning enjoyed the patronage of the bishop of Lincoln, Alexander, and his archdeacons. Gilbert was not guided by the Cluniac example of Marcigny, still less by that of Molesme, whose female priory was very early transferred to Jully, but by lessons drawn from experience closer at hand and more direct.[4]

[1] On the double monasteries in Spain, see the well-documented study of J. Orlandis Rovira, *Estudios sobre instituciones monásticas medievales* (Pamplona, 1971), pp. 19–202.

[2] The fact was pointed out by P. David when he published the *Parochiale*, an authentic witness of the Breton migration to the north coast of Spain (*Études historiques sur la Galice et le Portugal*, (Lisbon and Paris, 1947), pp. 57ff.). It was confirmed by E. A. Thompson, in *Christianity in Britain*, ed. M. W. Barley *et al.* (Leicester, 1968), pp. 201–5. See also Ch. J. Bishko, 'The Date and Nature of the Spanish *Consensoria monachorum*', *American Journal of Philology*, lxix (1948), 377–95.

[3] After several years of wandering, preaching both to men and women, Robert of Arbrissel established his followers at Fontevraud. It became the chief monastery of a new religious Order in which men and women lived in the same precincts but in separate houses. See J.-M. Bienvenu, *L'Étonnant Fondateur de Fontevraud* (Paris, 1981). In fact, neither Robert nor his foundations had direct influence on Gilbert (below, p. liii).

[4] St Hugh, abbot of Cluny, founded Marcigny as a double monastery *c.* 1055. The castle of Jully had been given to Molesmes by Miles count of Bar *c.* 1113; it became a priory, Jully-les-Nonnains, for the wives and relatives of the noblemen who retired to Molesmes and of those who followed Bernard at Clairvaux. But Jully had never been, strictly, a Cistercian house. See p. xliv.

The status of women in the new orders

In the early religious communities, both Columban's foundations and those following the Benedictine rule, abbesses as well as abbots had power of jurisdiction temporal as well as spiritual, sometimes in independence of the diocesan bishop, over a territory comprising villages and churches, clerics and laity. In the eleventh and twelfth centuries there was a deliberate return to the *Vita apostolica*, the ideal of poverty and the common life in imitation of the apostles, whether in founding institutions of monks or of canons. The religious status of women could not but be constrained by this movement, and it was further narrowed by other causes.

If the twelfth century was pre-eminently the century of the renewal of monastic life and the flowering of vocations, the new models were conceived to satisfy the aspirations of men, and they believed their ascetic ideal to be beyond the reach of women. To be sure, at the end of the eleventh century, Robert of Molesme had founded a double monastery; but the female community was transferred as early as 1113 to Jully, some 20 km distant from Molesme, and was not strictly speaking a Cistercian house. Stephen Harding founded the abbey of Tart about 1123; although privileged, it was not treated as a daughter of Cîteaux until the end of the century, and the abbey of Las Huelgas was not acknowledged to be part of the filiation of Tart until after it was ceded to the abbot of Cîteaux by the king of Castile, its founder.[1] It was only from 1213 that the general chapter of Cîteaux began to legislate for the nunneries incorporated by the favour of Cistercian abbots who protected them.[2] All the same, it was a case of prescribing strict enclosure for

[1] M. Fontette, *Les Religieuses à l'âge classique du droit canon* (Paris, 1967), pp. 28–30; cf. S. Thompson, 'The Problem of the Cistercian Nuns' in D. Baker (ed.), *Medieval Women* (Oxford, 1978), pp. 227–52, at p. 230. It was only at the end of the twelfth century that a letter of Guy, abbot of Cîteaux, admitted the close link: 'propria est filia domus Cisterciensis' (ibid.). Under strong royal pressure the Cistercian general chapter gave some measure of recognition to Las Huelgas in the late 1180s (Thompson, pp. 237–8; M. Connor, 'The First Cistercian Nuns and Renewal Today', *Cistercian Studies*, v (1970), 131–68, at p. 133).

[2] '... non ... admittantur ad ordinis unitatem, nisi penitus includendae' (1213, *Statuta ... Ordinis Cisterciensis*, i, ed. J.-M. Canivez (Louvain, 1933), p. 405). In 1228 Cistercian legislation was even more restrictive: 'In future, no nunnery shall be built under or associated with the name and jurisdiction of our Order. ... We do not accept the *cura animarum* [of nuns] nor the duty of ministering to and visiting them'; if an abbot, monk, or lay brother infringed this rule, he was to know that he would incur severe punishment (*Statuta*, ii (1934), 68).

them. Sister Michael Connor was able to write in this connection: 'If they were going to accept responsibility for these nuns, they were going to have peace while they were about it.'[1] In the thirteenth century, the houses governed by Cistercian statutes and uses were not for all that fully Cistercian, *pleno jure*.

In England at the beginning of the twelfth century, Gilbert of Sempringham faithfully expressed the spirit of his times. The years 1130 to 1150 saw the birth of a number of monasteries of women which professed, in different degrees, the Cistercian life, under the authority of a master or prior and under episcopal control. Most were in Lincolnshire and Yorkshire, regions to all intents and purposes devoid of monastic foundations *c.* 1100— 'monastic wildernesses' in the words of Janet E. Burton,[2] in comparison with the south-east, still more the west of England, where the ancient and prestigious Benedictine foundations flourished. If several of these houses received, from kings or bishops, privileges naming them 'Cistercian' in their district of origin, they were nevertheless not incorporated into the Order after the fashion of certain continental nunneries.[3] The Gilbertine priories enjoyed a structure which was lacking in female monasticism in general in the region, at that time in search of particularly austere ways of religious life. From then onwards until the end of the thirteenth century, vocations flowed towards an Order which, well before Cîteaux, recognized the female religious life; more than that, which, by reason of its origins and its organization, declared itself founded for women.

Other ideas then current were to inspire Gilbert. Various orders of Augustinian canons were at that time in process of expansion and organization, more particularly in the north of France, on the route for travellers from the British Isles disembarking at Wissant. In 1120–1 St Norbert had founded a monastery at Prémontré into which he welcomed men and women. They lived apart within the

---

[1] M. Connor, *Cistercian Studies*, v (1970), 149; cf. S. Thompson, art. cit.

[2] *The Yorkshire Nunneries in the Twelfth and Thirteenth Centuries* (Borthwick Papers 56, York, 1979), p. 5. The situation was the same in 12th-c. Lincolnshire.

[3] C. V. Graves, 'English Cistercian Nuns in Lincolnshire', *Speculum*, liv (1979), 492–9. Some two abbeys and 27 priories of nuns followed the Cistercian observance in England and Wales, most of them in Lincolnshire and Yorkshire; the oldest houses were Stixwould and Nun Cotham, founded *c.* 1135 and 1147–53 (Knowles and Hadcock, pp. 272–7); but for problems of labelling, see S. Thompson, art. cit., and ead., 'English Nunneries: a Study of the Post-Conquest Foundations *c.* 1095–*c.* 1250' (London Ph.D. thesis, 1984–5). Dr Thompson discusses double monasteries in chap. IV.

same enclosure; the women looked after household services—
sewing, weaving, laundry—and did not have access to the canons'
choir.[1] Nevertheless, between the setting up of the first two Gilbertine cells and Gilbert's journey to Cîteaux (1139–47), the Order
of White Canons had undergone an important change: Norbert
had left Prémontré, and the general chapter, in 1140 or 1141, had
decreed the separation of the double communities.[2] The sisters of
Prémontré were despatched to Fontenelle 4 km away, and similar
measures separated the nuns from the abbeys of Tongerloo, Tron-
chiennes, Cuissy, Belval, etc. Having become autonomous,
deprived of their original *raison d'être*, bereft of proper resources
and always dependent upon the houses of men, the sisters of the
Order, where their houses survived, changed into choir nuns
(*sorores cantantes*) under the title of canonesses. In England there
were some separated communities settled in Lincolnshire: about
1143 canons from Licques in the county of Guînes settled at Newhouse; later some canonesses at Irford and Brodholme, 'sufficiently remote and forbidding . . .' to commend 'itself to the canons
of Newhouse as the site for a house of canonesses . . .'.[3] Gilbert
could draw a lesson from the experience of failure in the Premonstratensian Order; but also from the parallel evolution of the
Arrouaisian foundations.

In the heart of the forest of Arrouaise, in the frontier zone
between Artois and Vermandois, Abbot Gervase, a native of the
Boulonnais, welcomed women as well as men and, as the numbers
grew large, organized new houses in the country around called
curtes. The house at Ruisseauville in the diocese of Thérouanne

---

[1] 'Hermanni monachi de miraculis sanctae Mariae Laudunensis', *AASS, June*, i
(1695), 865–6.
[2] Cf. H. Lamy, 'L'abbaye de Tongerloo depuis sa fondation jusqu'en 1263', *Recueil de
travaux publiés par les membres des conférences d'Histoire et de Philologie de l'Université de
Louvain*, xliv (1914), 92–103, esp. p. 97; S. Roisin, 'L'efflorescence cistercienne et le
courant féminin de piété au XIIIe siècle', *Revue d'Histoire ecclésiastique*, xxxix (1943), 342–
78, at p. 350; G. Hymans, *L'Abbaye de Saint-Feuillien de Roeulx en Hainaut* (Averbode,
1967), p. 67. The authors agree on the date, not 1137, but 1140/41, as shown in the
Fontenelle charter of the bishop of Laon (J. L. Le Paige, *Bibliotheca Praemonstratensis
Ordinis* (Paris, 1633), pp. 421–2). For a great number of female communities, the separation had been a sentence of death, as they were deprived of any endowment of their
own, in spite of renewed papal injunctions to the male communities, from Eugenius III
to Adrian IV.
[3] H. M. Colvin, *The White Canons in England* (Oxford, 1951), p. 331: see chap. vii,
passim, esp. pp. 328–31. The Newhouse charters (*c.* 1148–*c.* 1166) refer to the church of
St Michael Irford and the land of Broadholme (*EEA*, i, *Lincoln*, nos. 178–81).

sent a colony to Carlisle at the time of the first bishop, Adelold (1133–56/7), prior of St Oswald, Nostell (Yorks.), an older house of canons—if not before.[1] From 1133, the first Arrouaisian house was planted in Buckinghamshire at Missenden, soon followed by priories of women at Harrold (Beds., 1136–8), of men at Bourne (Lincs., 1138), and Dorchester (Oxon., c. 1140), all in the diocese of Lincoln: a noteworthy point, amongst others, was the house at Dorchester established in the seat of the former bishopric, transferred to Lincoln in the 1070s. If there is no direct evidence of Bishop Alexander's patronage, we cannot question his acquiescence and favour with regard to the houses of canons as to the Cistercians. As A. G. Dyson writes: 'At least it is clear that the diocese proved a congenial milieu for the new Order, whose interest in female religious may well have influenced the thinking both of the bishop and of Gilbert of Sempringham.'[2]

Other contacts could only strengthen Gilbert in his purpose. Such were the meeting, or meetings, with Malachy O'Morgair, former archbishop of Armagh and pioneer of ecclesiastical and monastic reform in Ireland. On his journey to Rome as early as c. 1140, via Carlisle, Grantham, Lincoln, Wissant, Thérouanne, and finally Clairvaux, Malachy had, stage by stage, established relations with the communities of canons of Arrouaisian observance.[3] No doubt he had also met Bishop Alexander and perhaps Gilbert too. Before this first journey to Rome, he had reformed a number of monasteries in Ireland where the Celtic tradition of double houses was maintained as also the Rule of St Columbanus. It seems established that on his return he favoured the Rule of St Augustine as well as that of St Benedict, at least where there

[1] L. Milis, L'Ordre de chanoines reguliers d'Arrouaise (2 vols., Bruges, 1969), i. 88–9, 114–18; ii. 324–8, 600–1. For Carlisle, the dates offered by modern authorities vary from c. 1102 to the 1130s: see esp. D. E. Greenway in Fasti, ii. 19, 21 and references; cf. Knowles and Hadcock, p. 152; H. S. Offler, Trans. Cumberland and Westmorland Antiquarian and Archaeol. Soc., N.S., lxv (1965), 176–81 (1102); J. C. Dickinson, ibid. lxix (1969), 102–4 (c. 1122).

[2] A. G. Dyson, 'The Monastic Patronage of Bishop Alexander of Lincoln', JEH, xxvi (1975), 1–24, at p. 11. The author points out very clearly the importance of the Arrouaisian foundations in the diocese and the influence of the bishop—and the possible existence of a double monastery of Arrouaisian observance at Harrold (pp. 10–13, 20).

[3] J. Wilson in Scottish Hist. Review, xviii (1921), 69–82; Milis, i. 324–7. On Malachy's journey and contacts, see also H. J. Lawlor in Proc. Royal Irish Academy, xxxv, ser. C (1918–20), 238–43, esp. 241; J. A. Watt, The Church and the Two Nations in Medieval Ireland (Cambridge, 1970), pp. 25–7 and references.

existed earlier houses of canons.[1] His second journey to Rome, in 1148, is better documented, thanks to the *Life of Malachy* of St Bernard. Gilbert's *Vita* attests the meeting of the founder of Sempringham with the reformer of the Irish church who died at Clairvaux on 3 November in the same year.[2]

Nuns and canons

Gilbertine tradition has it that in the course of his sojourn at Clairvaux, the Master of Sempringham received at the hands of Malachy a pastoral staff, and another at the hands of Bernard. For the hagiographer, these were *media*, instruments in the working of miracles.[3] In fact, this tradition conveys a symbol, the sign of a double consecration, in the Cistercian way on the one hand, and on the other in the more complex way of the Irish archbishop, who combined in his inspiration aspects of the canons' reform as well as of that of the monks. From that time on, Gilbert set the Rule attributed to St Augustine beside the Rule of St Benedict. What remains of the original Gilbertine constitutions drawn up by Gilbert includes, in the first person, the institution of canons: '. . . I have associated clerks [with my ministry] for the direction and protection of both [nuns and lay sisters, and lay brethren] . . . so that in vigils and fasts, they live under the Rule of St Augustine, separated from the nuns and having no access to them save to administer the last sacrament to the dying.'[4] A careful examination of the Gilbertine customs allows us to discern the impact of these two powerful influences. This is not the place to analyse them. The Cistercian model was emphasized in the *Life* and historians have continually invoked it, and rightly: its features are echoed in the similarity of the claustral offices, the lay brethren and the system of granges, and the general chapter. But parallel or similar institutions are found in orders of canons, for example at Prémontré.[5]

[1] See G. Carville, *The Occupation of Celtic Sites in Medieval Ireland by the Canons Regular of St Augustine and the Cistercians* (Cistercian Studies Ser. 56, Kalamazoo, 1982).

[2] Below, pp. 44–5; *Vita Malachiae* in St Bernard, *Opera*, iii. 370–8.

[3] *Life*, c. 14.   [4] *Monasticon*, vi. 2, p. xxx* (xix*).

[5] F. Giraudout and J. de la Croix Bouton, 'Bernard et les gilbertins', *Bernard de Clairvaux* (Paris, 1953), pp. 327–38. The new orders of canons—Prémontré, Arrouaise, Saint-Victor—like Cîteaux very early legislated for lay brethren, granges, and the annual general chapter: on Prémontré, G. Van der Broeke, *Analecta Praemonstratensia*, xv (1939), 121–8; M. Cocheril, *Studia Monastica*, i (1959), 423–36, esp. 433; P. Lefèvre, *Analecta*

There is no doubt that insufficient note has been taken of the fact that the Gilbertine Order originated at a time when the legislation of Cîteaux, like that of Prémontré, was still evolving. The *Carta Caritatis*, the 'Charter of Divine Love', in its second edition, ruled the Cistercian Order;[1] Hugh of Fosses, successor to Norbert, completed a first codification of the Premonstratensian constitutions, the *Institutiones Praemonstratenses* (*c.* 1125–35), which was typical of canons' regulations, even though the later *Ordo* generally attributed to him showed a clear orientation toward the monastic model made famous by the followers of St Bernard. About 1150, the *mandamenta* or instructions concerning the lay brethren and sisters disappeared from this code. Only those concerning lay brethren reappeared in the second half of the century.[2] Of the original Gilbertine constitutions drawn up by the founder, there remain only a few scanty traces: the surviving statutes are later than Gilbert's canonization. Consequently, we can only compare parallel practices. The sisters of Tongerloo, for example, appear to have been pious anchorites, like Gilbert's very first young women; but at Prémontré Norbert entrusted the hospice to them. At Tongerloo they were completely separated from the canons: in case of need they could communicate with the male community through a narrow window; yet never singly, one to one: the superiors on the one side and the other were required to have two witnesses in attendance. In the church the same separation

Praemonstratensia, xxx (1954), 12–19; P. Lefèvre and W. M. Grauven, *Les Statuts de Prémontré au milieu du XII^c siècle* (Albervode, 1978: Bibliotheca Analectorum Praemonstratensium 12); for Arrouaise, *Constitutiones canonicorum regularium Ordinis Arroasiensis*, ed. L. Milis and J. Becquet (Turnhout, 1970). Saint-Victor only penetrated the west of England: *c.* 1131 at Shobdon, eventually settling at Wigmore *c.* 1172; and in the 1140s at Bristol.

[1] On the legislation of Cîteaux, from the immense literature, we select: P. Guignard, *Les Monuments primitifs de la règle cistercienne* (Dijon, 1878); J. A. Lefèvre, *Collectanea Ord. Cisterciensium Reformatorum*, xvi (1954), 5–29, 77–104, 157–82, 241–66; D. Knowles, *Great Historical Enterprises* (London etc., 1963), pp. 197–222; J. de la Croix Bouton and J. B. Van Damme, *Les Plus Anciens Textes de Cîteaux* (Achel, 1974); B. Lucet, *La Codification cistercienne de 1202 et son évolution ultérieure* (Rome, 1964), id., *Les Codifications cisterciennes de 1237 et 1257* (Paris, 1977), with a survey of the early legislation, pp. 1–9.
[2] On the early legislation of Prémontré, see esp. C. Dereine, *Revue bénédictine*, lviii (1948), 84–92; P. F. Lefèvre, *Analecta Praemonstratensia*, ix (1913), 1–4, xxv (1949), 96–103; id., *L'Ordinaire de Prémontré* (Louvain, 1941); id., *La Liturgie de Prémontré* (Louvain, 1957). A common purpose and intent inspired both Cîteaux and Prémontré: the return to the purity of primitive rules. St Norbert, founder of Prémontré, did indeed seek a canonical discipline, but his Order was later influenced by large borrowings from monastic customs.

was maintained; the canons alone sang the psalms and intoned the Office.[1] Comparable arrangements existed from the establishment of the first double houses of the Gilbertine Order: the example of the new orders of canons cannot therefore be ruled out at its very beginning. Furthermore, if Gilbert opted for small groups of canons rather than communities of monks, it was because he was familiar with the canons' mode of life; but also because this formula was more flexible and lent itself more readily to a varied ministry, as had become plain in the course of the Premonstratensian expansion. It seems likely that Bishop Robert de Chesney gave this advice and supported this option at the time when he established St Catherine's priory at Lincoln.[2]

It remains clear that these diverse and undeniable influences cannot obscure the founder's care in adapting them and the genuine originality of the Gilbertine Order. His biographer gives a striking image of this when, taking up a biblical figure, he compares Gilbert to the famous charioteer Aminadab: 'The chariot', he writes, 'has two sides, one of men, the other of women; and four wheels, two of men, clerks and laymen, and two of women, educated and unlettered; the two animals drawing the chariot are the clerical and monastic disciplines. St Augustine directs the clerks and St Benedict guides the monks, while Father Gilbert drives the chariot high and low over places rough and smooth. The way along which they go is a narrow path, but the prize they seek is everlasting life.'[3]

The originality of the Gilbertine Order

The originality of the Order of Sempringham did not lie only in the combination of the two Rules. They were not, after all, without

[1] H. Lamy, art. cit. (p. xlvi, n. 2), pp. 92–5. Similar arrangements could be found at Coyroux: B. Barrière, L'Abbaye cistercienne d'Obazine (Tulle, 1977), pp. 100–3. The eclecticism of the Gilbertine Institutions has been noted by B. Golding, 'St Bernard and St Gilbert' (p. xli, n. 5), pp. 49–50. We do not, however, accept Golding's view that Grandmont or Fontevraud directly influenced Gilbert (see above, p. xxiv, and below, pp. lii–liv).

[2] See above, p. xxxi n. In the context of the religious renewal of the age, the amalgam between the Benedictine and Augustinian Rules is not surprising. On all this see now also S. K. Elkins, 'The Emergence of a Gilbertine Identity', in J. A. Nichols and L. T. Shank (eds.), Medieval Religious Women, i, Distant Echoes (Kalamazoo, 1984), pp. 169–82.

[3] C. 19.Cf. 'Nesciui: anima mea conturbauit me propter quadrigas Aminadab' (S. of S. 6: 11). See Appendix 1, pp. 336-7.

affinities; and Gilbert set before his disciples an ideal which all could seek: the example of Christ and the saints, preaching to them the gospel and the teaching of the apostles, that is to say the return to the life the apostles led, holding all things in common. He strove to inculcate in them a single spirit, adapting their common practices to the capacities of women on the one hand and of men on the other. Or rather, it was the institutional basis of the Gilbertine Order which made it into an Order *sui generis* from the middle of the twelfth century. We have here, in fact, double monasteries: they united two religious communities of choir nuns and canons in a juridical and economic unit, completely autonomous, differentiated from contemporary experiments emanating from the orders of canons or monks, which were doomed to failure and in decline at the very time when canonical rules were becoming more and more restrictive towards convents of women.

The Gilbertine foundations were designed from the outset to meet women's aspirations to the religious life, and were established in their favour. We need only consider the form of the donations. The charters are as explicit as we could wish: the very first concerning Sempringham are worded 'concessi' or 'confirmaui sanctimonialibus de Sempringham', 'I have granted' or 'I have confirmed to the nuns of Sempringham'; subsequently, whether for Sempringham, Haverholme, Alvingham, Bullington, Catley, Ormsby, or Sixhills, they specify: 'sanctimonialibus de . . . et fratribus earum clericis et laicis'—'to the nuns of . . . and their brethren, clerical and lay'.[1] The pope ratified this situation when in 1178 he confirmed the possessions and rights of the communities of Alvingham and Chicksands in the person of Roger, prior of the Order: 'Alexander . . . Rogero priori et monialibus Beate Marie de Alvingham [*al.* de Chikesande] et reliquis fratribus canonicis et sororibus . . .'—'Alexander . . . to Prior Roger and the nuns of St Mary of Alvingham [*al.* of Chicksand] and to the other brother-canons and sisters . . .'.[2] This affirmed both the pre-eminence of the nuns and the economic and legal unity of the double monasteries, thus ensuring the necessities of life for all their members, in contrast to earlier experiments involving monks

---

[1] e.g. *Sempringham Charters*, xvi. 77, nos. 38–9, etc.; *Gilbertine Charters*, pp. 91–3 and *passim*.

[2] Cheney, 'Papal privileges', pp. 57–62 (the Chicksands privilege has lost its date, but was probably contemporary with those for Alvingham and Malton, dated 1178: cf. ibid., pp. 39–40).

or canons. In the hour of crisis, when attacks were made upon the Order during the 1160s, this was a weighty argument, an anchorage, in favour of maintaining the double houses. Robert de Chesney, bishop of Lincoln, could still write to the pope: 'If the canons and (lay) brothers were really put a great distance from the nuns . . . , as some suggest, these houses could not maintain themselves.' And Henry II, urging the pope to confirm afresh the Order as originally established, made it clear that if the establishment should happen to be overturned, he and his barons would resume the possessions and domains they had granted to these houses for the pursuit of the religious life and the holy purpose which inspired them.[1]

One further essential point. The Order was governed by the Master or prior of the Order, and the canons exercised a certain authority in it. But if we consider its internal organization, the statutory role of its female members is confirmed. The canonical visitors of the houses comprised, on the one hand, a group of men, two canons and one lay brother, and on the other hand, a similar group made up of two nuns and one lay sister. The priors and cellarers from the houses of canons were invited to the annual general chapter of Sempringham, but so were two officials from each house of nuns, which at the time constituted a liberal attitude in comparison with the general chapter of Cîteaux.[2] The nuns also played a part in the election of the prior of the Order, the person who would take the founder's place after Gilbert's death. This election was carried out according to the canonical method of compromission (via compromissi), one of the forms already in use in ecclesiastical elections and which was to be ratified by the Fourth Lateran Council (c. 24) in 1215. The election was made by thirteen canons chosen by their peers: four of the first grade, nine of the second; but the nuns, like the canons not chosen among the thirteen, gave their assent to the form of the election, to the nomination of the thirteen, and finally, through obedience, to the canon elected.[3]

We are then entitled to assert that, for the period, Gilbert showed himself to have been shrewd and well informed and, to a certain extent, an innovator. There is no doubt that from the outset he conceived his foundations as for women and instituted a

---

[1] Letters 6, 12, pp. 150–1, 162–3.
[2] Institutions, Monasticon, vi. 2, pp. xcv*–xcvi* (lvii*).
[3] Ibid., pp. xxx*–xxxi* (xx*).

religious Order for women.[1] Nevertheless, an objection comes to mind. Was he not anticipated and perhaps inspired by the model of Fontevraud? If we have hitherto passed over the Order of Fontevraud in silence, it is not only because it was settled late in England, in the second half of the twelfth century; it is essentially because, though founded as a double community according to the views of its founder, Robert of Arbrissel, once it was settled at Fontevraud, it was changed into a mixed community merely. The growing pre-eminence of the aristocratic ladies of the cloister—the Prioress Hersende, then from 1115 the Abbess Petronilla de Chemillé, and their kinswomen—relegated the male members of the community, even if they were clerks, to the rank of nuns' servants, dependent upon the cellaress for their livelihood, with only the same standing as the lepers and the penitent women. The pattern became assimilated to the classical monastic mould on the model of Cluny. The privileges conferred by various bishops and a succession of popes, beginning with Paschal II in 1106 and 1112, recognized the Order of Fontevraud only as an institute of nuns.[2] In its recruitment as in its first benefactors, it contrasted with the Gilbertine Order: at Fontevraud an aristocratic power, at Sempringham a religious movement thrusting its roots into the strata of the common people and sustained by the gentry of the region. Robert of Arbrissel pursued his hermit's vocation and lacked the power or skill to resist the pressure of great ecclesiastical and secular lords like Geoffrey abbot of Vendôme and the families of Montsoreau and Chemillé. Gilbert held to his first ideal against every wind that blew, with the support of the bishop of Lincoln, first Alexander, then Robert de Chesney, and of the local abbots and lesser lords—and finally, of the whole episcopate of England and King Henry II in the crisis which afflicted the Order of Sempringham. Upon emerging from this crisis, contrary to the evolution of the Order of Fontevraud, the Gilbertine canons had secured, in addition to their pastoral ministry, total authority in the administration of property and in the government of the Order,

---

[1] William of Newburgh bestowed on him the palm among all those who undertook to establish and govern religious women (i. 55).

[2] J. M. Bienvenu, *Les Premiers Temps de Fontevraud (1101–1189). Naissance et évolution d'un Ordre religieux* (Thèse de Doctorat d'État, Paris IV; Sorbonne, 1980) is the most comprehensive study and the best documented on the Order of Fontevraud. See also J. Dalarun, 'La véritable fin de Robert d'Arbrissel . . .', in *Cahiers de civilisation médiévale*, xxvii (1984), 303–17.

and they had firmly established their pre-eminence over the nuns and the lay sisters as well as over the lay brethren.

IV. CRISIS IN THE ORDER

The episode of the nun of Watton

The crisis came when Gilbert had already reached his eighties: it clouded his old age, which was to last twenty years longer. The documents which bear witness to it essentially consisted of a score of letters, of which thirteen were inserted in the manuscripts; and in spite of the paucity of chronological data they allow us to determine the origin, the outbreak, and the settlement of the crisis. It seems to have begun with a moral scandal, the affair of the nun of Watton, who had been brought up in the house since the age of four: of this Aelred, abbot of Rievaulx, left a circumstantial account which turned on the miracle which rescued the nun and the punishment administered to the guilty brother, whose status— canon or lay brother—is not certain. When Gilbert learnt of their guilt he hastened to Watton and at his request Aelred intervened, doubtless in order to confirm the reconciliation of the communities of men and women severely disturbed by the violation of the most sacred laws at the heart of a double community's life.[1] The biographer makes perhaps a discreet allusion to it when he

[1] The story reported by Aelred of Rievaulx was first printed by R. Twysden, *Historiae Anglicanae Scriptores X* (London, 1652), cols. 415–22, and reprinted by Migne (PL 195, cols. 789–96); for comment see Sir Maurice Powicke in Walter Daniel, *Life of Ailred of Rievaulx* (NMT, 1950; OMT, 1978), pp. lxxxi–lxxxii; A. Squire, *Aelred of Rievaulx: a Study* (London, 1969), pp. 117–18, 139; and especially G. Constable, 'Aelred of Rievaulx and the nun of Watton . . .', in D. Baker (ed.), *Medieval Women*, pp. 205–26 (see p. 205 n. 1 for corrections to the text in Twysden). Professor Constable thinks that in the 12th-c. context the punishment of the man by castration was 'not exceptionally harsh' (p. 214), and the miraculous events related to the 'nun' might be accepted as a sign of Christ's mercy. Nevertheless, since the girl was at most about 15, the question must be asked: was she really a nun, or had just received a veil and not yet taken vows? The *Institutiones* reads: 'Nec fiat novicia nisi adulta quindecim annorum' (*Monasticon*, vi. 2, p. lxxxvi* (li*)). But her punishment was the one stipulated ibid., p. lxxi* (xliii*). Examples of the unfastening of chains or miraculous delivery of prisoners were fairly common from apostolic times (Acts 5: 19) and throughout the Middle Ages. Alcuin tells the story of a thegn caught in battle:

> Vinciri numquam potuit, nam cuncta resolui
> Vincula sponte sua mirando more solebant.

(*The Bishops, Kings and Saints of York*, ed. P. Godman, OMT, 1982, pp. 66–7, ll. 804–5.) In the 12th c. and later St Leonard de Noblat was widely known for delivering prisoners.

describes the Master's severity towards a nun burning with sinful passion under the inspiration of the devil.[1]

The revolt of the lay brethren

This episode seems to have been the prelude to the rebellion of the lay brethren which broke out *c.* 1164–5.[2] Alexander III and Thomas Becket, then in exile, were informed of it by a handful of brethren in breach of discipline. They appeared before the pope, who was then staying at Sens, and appealed against the Master and canons. We know the names of the three ringleaders: Ogger, Gerard, and Denis. Some of the rebels were serfs, brought up from childhood on the domain and freed by entering religion.[3] They had not scrupled to bring weighty charges against the Order: of relaxation of regular discipline among the other groups in the Order, of scandals in double houses, of the exaction of a new profession contrary to that which they had given to Sempringham. Alexander III issued a mandate to the archbishop of Canterbury to proceed if necessary to the reform of the Order. The archbishop, in exile, wrote to Gilbert, expressing his sorrow at learning that such scandals could arise at the heart of an Order which he cherished among all the others, and sending him at the same time the papal order to correct abuses and to institute reform, under penalty of having to appear before the archbishop, giving him as a term the Feast of Purification (2 February 1166), to reply to the faults of which the religious were accused and of disobedience to papal instructions.[4]

As Gilbert was to testify in the sequel, these letters never reached him, whether because the king had already erected an obstacle to communication between the exiled archbishop and his province, or because the bearer, Ogger himself, had hesitated to deliver them. A first arbitration, however, took place: in the presence of Robert de Chesney, bishop of Lincoln, Gilbert released those brethren who had taken an oath to preserve the

---

[1] *Life*, c. 21.

[2] In the *Life*, c. 25, the lay brethren's revolt immediately follows Gilbert's appearance before the royal justices in London, on the charge of helping the exiled Becket with money (c. 24), Henry II being at the time on the Continent (i.e. *c.* Feb.–May 1165: Eyton, pp. 77–9). For the chronology of the crisis see below, pp. 343–4.

[3] *Life*, c. 25, esp. pp. 78–83; letters 1, 7 on pp. 134–9, 150–3.

[4] Appendix 6, below, pp. 346–7.

Order—doubtless as a counter to the rebels.[1] As for Thomas Becket, he addressed a second letter to the Master, enjoining him to restore peace and unity to the heart of his institution. This instruction was based on the highest authority—in virtue of the office of papal legate, conferred by Alexander III in the spring of 1166—but it had no new citation attached to it, since the exiled archbishop was deprived of any means of effective action.[2] The lay brethren repeated their complaint to the Curia; and Alexander III, now back in the Lateran, determined to proceed by judicial enquiry, immediately naming judges delegate. Gilbert was summoned to appear before the bishops of Norwich and Winchester to answer for the houses of the see of Lincoln, and before the archbishop of York and the bishop of Durham for the double house of Watton.

The reports of the judges delegate for the diocese of Lincoln (1166) inform us fully of the charges made against the Order and the Master of Sempringham. In the absence of Henry of Winchester, who was ill, William of Norwich investigated the matter with the aid of various abbots and priors. The issues were: the question of a new profession contrary to that made at Sempringham, and of an oath of an unaccustomed kind; suppression of papal letters or refusal to receive them on the grounds that they were forged; and charges about the common life of canons and nuns. Gilbert denied exacting a new profession prejudicial to the first, save for the incident of the oath arranged in the presence of the bishop of Lincoln. He equally defended himself from any knowledge of the papal letters addressed to himself and the chapter of the Order, and from having excommunicated the bearer, a statement which was formally admitted by Ogger. The bishop of Norwich explained that the male and female communities had separate enclosures: none the less, in obedience to the papal mandate, and although it was to the prejudice of the Order, he made Gilbert promise to forbid access by canons or lay brethren to the nuns' choirs. Henceforth, two or three canons only were allowed to celebrate solemn mass, and the lay brethren were to attend matins not in the nuns' choir but in their own. As for the rebels, Gilbert had to bind himself to receive back to communion with the Order those who submitted in humility to him. Some, such as Denis and a certain W., refused to return and announced

---

[1] Letter 1, pp. 134–7.   [2] Appendix 6, below, pp. 347–8.

that they would join another Order. Ogger and the other brethren present tried to demand a change of statute giving in every priory an equal status to the four kinds of religious—canons, nuns, lay brethren, and lay sisters—under obedience to a single prior.[1] These proceedings concerned the double houses in the see of Lincoln, probably seven at that date: Sempringham, Haverholme, Alvingham, Bullington, Catley, Ormsby, and Chicksands.

In the see of York the instructions were carried out in two stages (c. 1166–7). The archbishop, Roger of Pont-l'Évèque, assisted by his suffragan Hugh du Puiset of Durham, testified to the existence in his diocese of only one double house, in which canons and nuns lived apart and in good repute, within a single ample *enceinte*; he explained that Gilbert had not imprisoned or excommunicated any of the brethren, or exacted an oath contrary to their former profession from any of them; and that he could not have claimed that the papal letters were forged since he had neither received nor seen them.[2] But an injunction had been given him to make effective the separation of canons and nuns in this priory of Watton.

The lay brethren of Watton were insufficiently informed about a case which probably did not concern them, and obtained a delay. The affair was resumed in the absence of the bishop of Durham, but with abbots and priors present. The archbishop described how the rebellious brethren were not able to prove their charges; and that furthermore those in his see, where nothing contrary to their profession had been introduced, were received to the kiss of peace by the Master. They requested, however, some relaxation in return for peace; but since there was no papal instruction on this point, their request was rejected. As for Ogger, he demanded that new rules in the life of the Order be laid down at his dictation.[3]

It seems that the rebels, disenchanted after some thirty or forty years of the regular life, had formed a kind of organized band of malefactors. Besides the calumnies which they heaped on the canons, they tried to lay hands on the goods of the Order, and even engaged in brigandage and murder; they also tried to reorder its organization so as to appropriate to themselves the temporal

---

[1] Letter 1, pp. 134–9.

[2] Letter 7, pp. 150–3. In 1167–8 Gilbert was pardoned a fine he had been charged 'pro concelamento' (of papal letters: *Red Book of the Exchequer*, ed. H. Hall (RS, 1896), iii. 821; cf. *Pipe Roll 13 Henry II*, pp. 42, 47–8; *14 Henry II*, pp. 70–4).

[3] Letter 7, pp. 150–3; *Life*, c. 25.

administration of the Gilbertine houses.[1] Their complaints had, however, a genuine foundation: they were subject to a rule which was harsher than those of the canons or the nuns; and these constraints had become unbearable at the point when the canons had taken over the effective administration of the houses of the Order, leaving the lay brethren the subordinate tasks. Such movements were far from being confined to the Order of Sempringham: they affected also Cistercian houses and those of the Premonstratensian, Arrouaisian, and Victorine canons; later they were to shake the Order of Grandmont.[2] The rebellion of the Gilbertine lay brethren could not but bring a grave crisis to the heart of the Order in the diocese of Lincoln. This crisis ensured for the founder a popular canonization during his lifetime.

In the event, the ecclesiastical judges did not fail to offer in their reports to the pope a plea in favour of Gilbert, bearing witness to his reputation for sanctity and the radiance spread by his work through English society. A number of bishops, abbots, and priors joined their petitions to the dossier taken to the Curia. By way of example there have survived the letters of the bishops of Lincoln and Winchester, and also King Henry II's: he urges the pope to listen to the prayers of the bishops and the religious, to give a mandate to the bishops of the sees involved to coerce the rebels, and to keep the nuns under the close vigilance of the Master and the canons.[3] We have no account of the proceedings in the Curia at Rome. One can, however, infer that, according to the rules of the Curia, the dossier would have been passed to an *auditor*, a cardinal or papal notary; that the witnesses on the two sides would have been cited and given their depositions at an *audientia contradictoria* before the pope; that a record would have been drawn up and a demand sent for further information, which implies a further process in the Curia before a definitive settlement was made. So much is implied by several letters of Alexander III in reply to the petitions: they show the case in suspense in 1169 and the call for a final process.

Two of these letters are privileges dated at Benevento, 30 July and 20 September 1169; and they form together a group which can

---

[1] Letter 3, pp. 142–5; see also pp. 78–81.

[2] J. Becquet, 'La première crise de l'Ordre de Grandmont', *Bulletin de la Société arch. et hist. du Limousin*, lxxxvii (1960), 283–324; cf. above, p. xxivn.

[3] Letters 6 (on author and date see p. lxxxviii), 4, 3, pp. 142–51.

be assigned to the summer of 1169. The pope addressed the archbishops, bishops, and archdeacons of the sees which contained
Gilbertine houses, and ordered them to defend the members of the
Order and to excommunicate on papal authority any fomenters of
trouble.[1] He wrote to the king to constrain and correct, without
bloodshed, the lay brethren who were unyielding rebels against the
Order, and who would not submit to ecclesiastical censures.[2] On
20 September he sent to Gilbert a privilege (*lettres de non-préjudice*)
confirming to him and to his lawfully appointed successors the
power to correct and reform abuses, with the advice of the priors;
and the previous mandates to religious of other orders to allay the
dissensions and scandals in the houses of the Gilbertine Order
were not to prejudice this privilege.[3] A fourth document, however,
needs to be taken into account.

The privilege of 30 July 1169 was set aside from the rest of the
dossier, both by Dom David Knowles and myself, as of purely
local concern.[4] The reconstruction and publication by C. R.
Cheney of the privileges of 25 June 1178 addressed to Roger prior
of Alvingham and Roger prior of Chicksands, linked to a privilege
of the same date addressed to Roger prior of Malton[5]—establishing
that they all refer to one man, Gilbert's successor and head of the
Order—lead to reconsideration of the privilege of 1169 addressed to
Gilbert prior of Malton. This text is the only evidence for a prior of
Malton of this name, inserted between Prior Robert and Prior
Roger, who was indeed prior of Malton before he succeeded the
founder as Master.[6] It is clear in fact that Prior Gilbert was the
Master himself. The Yorkshire priory has preserved a remarkable
range of his titles in its cartulary, whose significance is not dimin-
ished by the lack of similar addresses to other Gilbertine houses.[7]

---

[1] Letter 10, pp. 158–9, evidently about contemporary with no. 9, dated 20 Sept.
[2] Letter 11, pp. 158–61.   [3] Letter 9, pp. 156–9.   [4] *PUE*, i. 377–9, no. 112.
[5] Cheney, 'Papal Privileges', pp. 46–50, points out the interchangeability of the titles
given to Gilbert: *Magister*, *prior*, *superior prior*. The 12th-c. charters exhibit this
diversity; Gilbert said: 'G. . . . prior ordinis de Sempyngham' (*Gilbertine Charters*, p. 95)
and Roger Mustel confirmed his gifts 'in manu magistri Giliberti auunculi mei' (ibid.,
p. 29).
[6] *Heads*, p. 203.
[7] The Sempringham cartulary was 'burnt in a fire at Staples Inn, London' (quoted by
Poynton in *Sempringham Charters*, xv. 158). As Cheney remarks: 'Since the constitution
varied from house to house it was not easy to achieve precision in a privilege designed
for the Order'; and he also suggested that 'the proctors of the Gilbertines at Rome may
well have sought simultaneous confirmations of the properties and liberties of every
house in the Order' ('Papal Privileges', p. 42).

Now in the second letter of Henry II to the pope in the dossier,[1] the *epistola gratulatoria*, the king thanked Alexander III for having taken the brethren and the convents of the Order under his protection and for confirming it by a privilege, *autentico scripto*. In the Oxford manuscript, in place of 'fratribus et conuentibus', we read 'canonicis et monialibus et uniuersis conuentibus eius'. We should not infer from this that the affair was at an end. The privilege of 30 July in the version for Malton, in addition to papal protection and the confirmation of the *ordo canonicus* according to the Rule of St Augustine and the constitutions of the Order of Sempringham, confirms the priory's possessions, forbids acts of violence and theft and concludes with formal sentences. The question remains whether other houses of the Order were similarly provided with privileges analogous to that of 1169, and in what measure such grants also applied to the double houses, as the *Life* seems to bear witness.[2] However that may be, the crisis was not over nor the process concluded. The first and most original of the Order's customs remained in suspense, especially the statute governing the double priories.

The final settlement, 1176–8

The letter of Henry II, furthermore, also bears the character of petition, carrying with it a warning. 'So we earnestly beg you to ensure that the Order is rigorously obeyed in the form in which it was established by Master Gilbert and confirmed by yourself.' There follows the threat that its possessions and domains granted by himself and his barons will be forfeit if 'the Order's organization should be altered.' But 'if you will see that the Order, in its original form as approved and confirmed by you and your predecessors, is strictly and properly obeyed, then as far as our secular justice is concerned we shall support it to the height of our powers'.[3] This was a direct response to Alexander III's previous request.[4] Doubtless it would be reasonable to accept that the king's petition, taken

---

[1] Lay brethren's dossier, Letter 12. See textual discussion and p. lxxxvi.

[2] *Life*, c. 25, *ad fin.*, where after a summary of the papal privilege of 20 Sept. (Letter 9) and a general reference to other privileges, it is said: 'Alias etiam plurimas inmunitates et dignitates ad perpetuum firmamentum domnus papa Alexander sancto patri Gileberto successoribusque eius . . . dedit et concessit'.

[3] Letter 12, pp. 160–3.

[4] Letter 11, pp. 158–61: an exhortation to ensure the safety of the canons and nuns 'contra potentiam omnium laicorum'.

to the Curia by Jordan archdeacon of Chichester (Lewes) and O., was one of the items in a dossier also containing the petitions of the bishops, abbots, and priors, of which the letter from the prior of Bridlington seems to give us the gist.[1] He reproaches the pope for infringing the privileges of his predecessors: those of Eugenius III, who approved and guaranteed the constitutions which Gilbert had submitted to him in perpetuity as they applied to both sexes, of Adrian IV who confirmed them, and his own. It is impossible to assign a date to the new royal initiative: it was later than the summer of 1169 and must fall in the period 1169–76.

Nearly ten years passed away before the final settlement, a decade punctuated by crises at the heart of the kingdom. At the very end of 1169 Henry II had tightened the watch on the coast in the fear of receiving censures from pope and primate. In 1170 the coronation of the young king, followed by the murder of Thomas Becket, sharpened the tension between Henry II and Alexander III. These obstacles and setbacks were scarcely overcome before the end of 1174. True, the king had been released from the interdict laid on him and reconciled at Avranches (May–September 1172); but there had followed the appeal of the young King Henry to Rome, his revolt, hostilities in Normandy, and the Scots invasion. It was only in 1176 that the affair of Sempringham surfaced again in our documents, during the legation to England of the Cardinal of Sant'Angelo, Hugo Pierleone, who visited the mother house of the Order in January.[2] In his report to the pope, the legate bore witness in favour of Gilbert and the nuns, attested the ceaseless obduracy of the conspiracy by Ogger and the other irreconcilable brethren to breach and subvert the constitutions of the Order, and reported the sentence of excommunication which the Master had laid on them, in accordance with the papal privileges. He also passed on the petitions from Gilbert and the canons and nuns of various houses of the Order.[3]

[1] Letter 8, pp. 154–7.
[2] The legate remained in England from late Oct. 1175 until early July 1176. He met the king at Winchester on 31 Oct. At Christmas he was at York with the archbishops; in Jan.–Feb. he attended a royal council at Northampton (H. Tillmann, *Die päpstlichen Legaten in England* (Bonn, 1926), pp. 73–7; Eyton, pp. 196–205; *Councils and Synods*, i. ii. 996–8). He certainly visited the diocese of Lincoln in the beginning of 1176, and went to Sempringham; 'Sane cum per Lincolniensem episcopatum transirem, contigit me ad domum religiosarum monialium de Sempyngham ...' (below, Appendix 6, pp. 348–9). See Foreville, *L'Église et la royauté*, pp. 431–40; *Councils and Synods*, i. ii. 993–1010.   [3] Below pp. 348–9. On Ogger's pertinacity (*Life*, c. 25), see Appendix 2.

The documents published by Christopher Cheney, which can be securely dated to 25 June 1178, on the basis of those addressed to Alvingham, are solemn privileges securing papal protection. They concern the double priories of Alvingham and Chicksands, but every Gilbertine house must have had one. They confirmed not only the possessions of each foundation, threatened by the rebels; they specified the concessions made by Henry II and the young Henry. Finally, on the application of the parties and to settle the fundamental issue in the dispute, these privileges confirmed the constitutions of the Order established by Archbishops Theobald of Canterbury and Henry of York, and by Gilbert 'its first father'. It is noteworthy that the various branches of it were deliberately specified: 'the Order of nuns and lay sisters, of canons and lay brethren ...'.[1] Thus the institution of the double houses was validated and the fundamental unity of the Order confirmed.

The canonization

Gilbert was full of years and infirmities, now unable personally to visit his houses, burdened with trials for more than ten years, summoned before civil judges, suspected of supporting the exiled archbishop with money, then several times cited before ecclesiastical judges in the affair of the lay brethren, his reputation affected by calumny; and at last, before 1178, perhaps during the legation of Hugo Pierleone in 1175–6, he laid down the government of the Order. He remained just as much the figurehead, the symbol or image of the whole Order. The austerity of his life, the fruitfulness and rigour of his direction, his inexorable determination to maintain the Order in its original form, his constancy in adversity and already, if one may believe his biographer, some miracles performed at his intercession: all this surrounded his extreme old age with an aura of sanctity. Gilbert then agreed, with the consent of the chapter of the Order and on the intervention of the bishop of Lincoln, Hugh of Avalon, to temper the rigour of the constitutions of the lay brethren in regard to food and clothing (after 21 September 1186).[2] After his death, numerous miracles around his tomb, in the great priory church at Sempringham, gave credit to the popular

---

[1] Cheney, 'Papal privileges', pp. 57–62; *PUE*, i. 425–7, no. 154.

[2] *Life*, c. 30. Hugh of Avalon was consecrated to the see of Lincoln on 21 Sept. 1186 (*Fasti*, iii. 3).

acclamation of his sanctity, the *fama publica*.[1] The authorities of the Order set the affair in motion.

At the turn of the twelfth and thirteenth centuries a simple translation by the bishop was no longer regarded as satisfactory in England. The Gilbertine canons turned towards Rome, and with the support of the hierarchy and after an enquiry led by Archbishop Hubert Walter, they requested the founder's canonization.[2] Innocent III was in process of refining the procedure to the *ordo iudiciarius*, and prescribed a new, better-founded enquiry, and the dispatch to Rome of witnesses to Gilbert's life and miracles, who could testify in his presence under seal of oath to the truth of the facts reported.[3] It was in the wake of this process that the pope added Gilbert to the catalogue of confessor saints on 11 January 1202. By a bull of 30 January he announced the canonization and ordered the archbishop to proceed to the translation of Gilbert's mortal remains.[4] This took place on Sunday, 13 October 1202 amid a great throng of people.[5]

It is to the canonization process that we owe our knowledge of the founder and of almost sixty years in the life of the Order of Sempringham during the first century of its existence; and this in turn is due to the diligence of one of the canons, who was author of the *Life* and compiled the documents—the two collections of miracles and two series of letters. He gathered them into a collection, *The Book of St Gilbert*, which he presented to the archbishop of Canterbury,[6] between 13 October 1202, the date of the translation, and 13 July 1205, when Hubert died, and probably before the first solemn festival of the new saint on 4 February 1203.[7]

V. THE BOOK OF ST GILBERT

The manuscripts and transmission of the Book

The Book of St Gilbert has come down to us in two manuscripts certainly deriving from the Gilbertine Order, now in the British Library: Cotton Cleopatra B. i, of the early thirteenth century, and Harleian 468, of the mid- or late thirteenth century. A third MS,

---

[1] See the two collections of Miracles.   [2] Below, pp. xcviii, 170–1.
[3] See pp. xcviii–xcix, 234–7.   [4] See pp. 244–53.   [5] pp. 184–9.
[6] pp. 2–3.   [7] Below, p. lxxiii.

Oxford, Bodleian MS Digby 36, of the fifteenth century, is of a markedly different character. It is selective, it has finely illuminated initials, its careful script is adorned with rich floral decoration; and it has lacunae and additions. It is related to books of devotion.

Lc   *BL Cotton Cleopatra B. i* is a collection of pieces apparently put together in the Cotton Library; rebound in 1982–3 and comprising 183 ff. *The Book of St Gilbert* takes up ff. 33–168 (now 32–167),[1] and is followed (ff. 168–71ᵛ) by somewhat later copies of papal bulls of Alexander III, Clement III, Honorius III, and Gregory IX, concerning the Order of Sempringham, some of them mentioned in the *Vita*. The other items are:

(1) ff. 1–22 (now 2–23), 3 gatherings, 8 + 8 + 6. A *Historiola* of the Holy Land, from the death of Baldwin IV to the fall of Jerusalem (1184–7). Begins 'Quantis pressuris et calamitatibus oppressa'.

(2) ff. 24–31 (no f. 23 in old foliation) (now 24–31), 1 gathering of 8. A thirteenth-century copy of the Life of St Edmund of Abingdon by Eustace of Faversham (with a note on the vision of St Paul and St Anselm's letter on the Immaculate Conception), ed. C. H. Lawrence, *St Edmund of Abingdon* (Oxford, 1960), pp. 203–21; on this manuscript see pp. 32–3.

(3) ff. 33–171ᵛ (now 32–170), *The Book of St Gilbert*. 17 gatherings of 8, with 4 folios added, the 4th cancelled (i.e. 3, ff. 169–71).

(4) ff. 173–8 (now 171–6), 1 gathering of 6. Heroic verses in honour of King Henry V, garnished with attacks on the Lollards. Begins 'Ad saluatoris laudes titulos et honores'.

(5) ff. 179–82ᵛ (now 177–80ᵛ) a fragment of the *Liber Aureus* of St Bonaventure, on the Life of Jesus; f. 182ᵛ (180ᵛ), a prophecy from Valencia in Spain and the legend of the jar of oil given by the Blessed Virgin to St Thomas of Canterbury for anointing the English kings; f. 183 (181) a note on various problems relating to the moon's cycle; ff. 183ᵛ–186 (181ᵛ–184), a letter from Lucifer to the pope and prelates, composed in the time of Richard II. Ff. 179–86 form a single gathering of 8 leaves; f. 187 (no new number) is an old guard-leaf; on f. 186ᵛ is a quire number 'xij quat''.

At f. 33 the first line has been erased; but it may be restored from the guide-note in the margin as 'Incipit (?) prologus in uitam sancti

---

[1] Throughout this edition the old foliation of Lc has been used since this facilitates cross-reference to the edition of 1943, in which the old foliation was consistently noted in the margin.

Gileberti confe[ssoris]'; the explicit, on f. 168, which alone gives a title to the whole collection, originally read 'Explicit Liber beati Gileberti'. Thus the marginal guide; a later scribe wrote at the foot of the text 'Explicit Liber Vite beati Gileberti'. The leaves are approximately 140 × 185 mm; the written space approximately 85 × 135 mm, leaving margins of 10 mm above, 35 mm below, 40 mm outer margin—but very variable, since they were cut by the seventeenth-century binder. It is written in a single hand of the very early thirteenth century, who has also written *testis* or *testes* by the names of witnesses to the first collection of miracles but once only in the second (p. 320), in the margins between ff. 140ᵛ and 168. There are normally 22 lines to a page in black, with appropriate rubrics. Such are the external characteristics of the book.

The structure of the *Liber* is defined by the prologue, a dedicatory letter to Archbishop Hubert Walter, in which the author of the *Vita* and the compilation lists the stages in its composition: a short Life, written at the request of the prior of the Order, Roger, Gilbert's successor as the Order's head,[1] and of Canon Albinus, the Master's chaplain;[2] the miracles of which the author was witness in the church at Sempringham; an amplification of the short Life; the canonization process; the narrative of the translation; letters written in Gilbert's lifetime and after his death for causes involving him; brief extracts from the *Life* intended to be read at the solemn celebrations of his feast, but not the proper responses and antiphons that the author proposes to extract from Holy Scripture.

The Cotton MS presents the documents thus listed (apart from the short Life and the brief extracts) in the identical order.

ff. 33–6	Prologue: dedicatory letter to Hubert Walter.
ff. 36ᵛ–37	Capitula (contents of the *Vita*, cc. 1–56).
ff. 37ᵛ–74	The *Vita*, in its definitive form, concluding with:
ff. 74–83ᵛ	miracles performed by Gilbert in his lifetime;
ff. 83ᵛ–86	illness and death of Gilbert; and
ff. 86–9ᵛ	burial, and appointment of his first successor (c. 56). *Explicit Vita* ...
ff. 89ᵛ–101ᵛ	Letters of the bishops relating to the affair of the lay brethren.

---

[1] Roger, a native of Sempringham and one of the first canons of the Order, prior of Malton, coadjutor and later Gilbert's first successor as prior of the Order (*Life*, Prologue (pp. 8–9) and cc. 23, 56).

[2] See *Life*, cc. 31–2 and nn.

Thus the various strata in the compilation of the *Liber* are clearly presented to us.

The manuscript shows marks of long use, evidently by the religious of the Order and by Cotton's Librarians. There are numerous seventeenth-century notes, guides to the contents of the MS. Other marginal notes of the late thirteenth and fourteenth centuries, and a few of the fifteenth, are listed in Appendix 3, and show how it was used in the late Middle Ages. After the end of the book (ff. 168ᵛ–171ᵛ) a small hand of the mid-thirteenth century, which also appears in notes on pp. 156, 158 below, has added summaries of a series of papal bulls; Alexander III (*PUE*, i, no. 103); Clement III (*PUE*, i, no. 258, with variants of no. 310 of Celestine III interlined); a privilege of Alexander III not identified; Clement III (*PUE*, i, no. 256); an indulgence of Honorius III; five letters of Gregory IX; one of Clement III (*PUE*, i, no. 257); seven of Honorius III; and a fragment of Clement III, possibly also referring to *PUE*, i, no. 257.

Lh   *BL Harleian 468* contains only *The Book of St Gilbert*; it has been rebound in red leather and is distinctly smaller than Lc, with leaves of 120 × 155 mm and written space approximately 90 × 125 mm. It was written by various hands of the mid-thirteenth century or slightly later, in single columns varying from 21 to 27 lines. The MS is made up of 16 gatherings of 8 ff.; f. 128ᵛ has drafts for letters, etc., following the end of the text. A bifolium was wrapped round the last gathering, and is now represented by a stub between ff. 120 and 121, and by f. 129, on which are verses and notes, including, in a sixteenth-century hand, a prayer addressed to Gilbert:

> Geleberte singularis signa gerens gracie
> Discipline regula signifer exennie [?*for* eximie]
> Vita sacer potens signis meritis egregie
> Nobis reis et indignis locum posce uenie.

This is repeated on f. 129ᵛ almost illegibly; but this confirms the reading 'locum', which on the recto is unclear. Apart from these external forms, and the glosses and marginal notes, the Harleian MS reproduces exactly both the text and the arrangement of the Cotton MS to quite an exceptional degree: thus Lc contains a number of alternative readings between the lines, and there were evidently similar readings in Lh's source. The scribe of Lh started by repeating them, then wearied of it, and noted fewer and fewer original readings; he invariably reproduces either the first reading or both, never chooses a variant however obviously better. Most of the way he reproduces Lc's errors faithfully, though he occasionally corrects an obvious slip, and Lh is useful in the rare cases when Lc is illegible—as, for instance, with the opening rubric, erased in Lc. The tables of *capitula* on ff. 36ᵛ–37 in Lc and ff. 3ᵛ–4ʳ in Lh are particularly close, and minor errors of order made by the scribe of Lh are made slightly more intelligible by odd variations in capital letters in Lc. An omission of two lines at p. 30 lines 1–2 in Lh corresponds exactly to two lines in Lc. It is just possible that Lh was copied from a twin of Lc; much more probable that it was copied from Lc itself; and we have proceeded on this assumption. Lh was doubtless made in or for Gilbertine religious for the use of one of their houses. Some initials are discreetly decorated, but the marginal words *testis*, *testes*, were omitted. The rubrics, as on the model, have been only partly executed: for the most part the spaces set aside are left blank, while guide-words are written on the outside margin. In short, it is a book carefully planned, but never quite finished.

Oxford, Bodleian Digby 36 (15th cent.) is markedly different from Od both the other manuscripts. It is bound in worn, brown leather, with two metal clasps, 130 mm × 185 mm, some 30 mm thick; containing solely Gilbertine material, on vellum folios numbered 4–116ᵛ, measuring 120 × 180 mm. ff. 1–3 are paper and contain a table of contents, sixteenth or seventeenth century, in several hands. Prick-marks appear on the outer margins of ff. 4–27, and f. 27 and several others have suffered from damp. At the same time that the table of contents was made, a sixteenth- or seventeenth-century hand numbered in roman numerals the chapters of the *Vita*, and the numeration then, somewhat incoherently, carries on to number the items which follow: canonization, translation, miracles, and letters, down to no. CLXII for the last letter of the lay

brethren's dossier, and no. CLXIII at the head of the *Seruicium*, the solemn office for St Gilbert, at f. 110ᵛ. Od is very carefully written, on double columns of 26 lines to the page. Marginal notes are rare. On f. 13ᵛ (p. 28 below) we read: 'aduerte . . . beati Gileberti cum ei oblatus erat archidiaconatus ecclesie Lincolniensis', and near the end of the column, opposite 'animarum multi uero causa', 'causa'. On f. 16ᵛ is a gloss in the lower margin commenting on 'suis sumptibus nutritos' which reads 'Et quosdam a dominis suis transfugas quos nomine religionis emancipauit'. On f. 49 by 'uxor boni uiri de Hauuilla', 'Radulphi'. All three glosses are in a single sixteenth-century hand.

Characteristic of Od is the richness, not to say profusion, of its decoration. Illuminated initials open the rubric of every paragraph of the *Vita* and of every miracle and letter. Every major section has a large initial to its rubric, framed in pink or blue on a blue or pink ground with white fillets; and from the initials garlands of flowers spread out towards the top and the bottom of the leaves on the outer margin; they sometimes extend right across the upper and lower margins to the right of the text, even penetrating between the columns on occasion. The profusion of leaves and flowers and buds grows as the volume goes on, with green and gold for leaves and stems predominating, and red and pink tints for flowers and buds.

There are twelve of these profusely decorated initials, marking significant points in the structure of the book's contents, at the opening of the prologue, *Life*, miracles in his lifetime, canonization, visions and revelations before his canonization, translation, miracles after his death, and (f. 77ᵛ) the letters on the canonization. All these rubrics are reproduced in Appendix 7; the MS concludes with:

f. 110ᵛ: 'Seruicium in sollemnitatibus sancti Gilleberti confessoris . . .'

f. 115: 'Missa de eodem in diebus Deposicionis et Translacionis sancti G(illeberti)'.

The *Seruicium* and *Missa* were printed in *Gilbertine Rite*, i. 115–26.

Thus the opening of each major section is always sumptuously decorated. There is no similar treatment of an explicit, even at the end of the book; but blank spaces are left at the end of the relevant columns, sometimes extending over two columns, perhaps intended

for further illumination, so that the final effect is of a book finished but not perfected. At the very end, on f. 116ᵛ, a hand about 50 years later than that of the text has added along the side of the left-hand margin: 'Qui scripsit . . .'.

Thus there are very clear differences between the structure of the Book of St Gilbert as described in the prologue—and as it is laid out in Lc and Lh—and the organization of the material in Od. But the differences go further than this. In Od the text of the *Life* follows the normal order until c. 29, though divided into more numerous paragraphs; but from c. 30 on the miracles of Gilbert performed in his lifetime are copied in a different order, and there are various lacunae.[1] The collections of documents which follow the *Life* and the accounts of the canonization and translation in Lc are arranged in quite a different order in Od: the letters related to the canonization are put after the miracles, and the letters about the affair of the lay brethren are put at the end of Od instead of between the *Life* and the canonization dossier. Od indeed adds in conclusion the liturgical office and proper of the mass in the Gilbertine rite for the feasts of St Gilbert, which are not included in Lc and Lh. When they were copied these liturgical texts were integrated into the service-books of the Order; whereas in a book like Od intended for someone with a special devotion to St Gilbert it was natural to include a copy of the *seruicium*.

If we examine the contents of the dossiers, we find many lacunae in Od among the canonization letters, of which it has 23 out of 34; a lacuna and two additions among the letters on the lay brethren's revolt; 29 as against 56 (30 + 26) miracles, and no distinction between their sources, official or unofficial; the sworn witnesses are omitted, and most of the time the name and standing of the persons involved are also omitted. In Appendix 7 tables of concordance allow us to juxtapose the two forms of the Gilbertine tradition: that in Lc contemporary with the process of canonization, designed to record the *pièces justificatives*; Od late—two centuries after the events—and designed to edify, and in consequence not concerned to preserve the precise memory of men and women long dead. We should also note that so sumptuous a volume was hardly made for a conventual library: it can scarcely have belonged to any of the Gilbertine houses, unless one supposes that it was given or bequeathed to one. It was assuredly compiled from the

[1] See Appendix 7.

Gilbertine material, doubtless for a rich patron with a special devotion to St Gilbert. In the seventeenth century it was acquired, whether by purchase or inheritance, by the celebrated bibliophile Sir Kenelm Digby, whose arms are engraved in metal on the new binding of the period, and who himself wrote on the first folio of the original MS (now f. 4) in large capitals his motto 'Vindica te tibi Kenelme Digby'—'do justice to yourself, Kenelm Digby'.

An inspection of the comparative tables reveals the eclecticism of the compiler of Od. He has made a selection both among the miracles and among the letters relating to the canonization. Thus it is clear among the miracles that he avoids offering a second, still more a third, example of a similar cure from the same illness, or fever or blindness, for example. A similar selection dictated his choice of letters. Only four out of six episcopal petitions are included, those from the bishops of London, Ely, Norwich (but see p. 218 n.), and Bangor; Coventry and Rochester are excluded. Of petitions from abbots, the compiler has kept only that from the abbot of St Albans, discarding those from the abbots of Kirkstall, Kirkstead, Revesby, and Barlings, as well as the priors of Kirkham and Kyme. He has not seen fit to include the only petition from a layman, that from Geoffrey FitzPeter, earl of Essex. Last, and significantly, he has omitted the letter (no. 1) which Philip the papal notary addressed to the bishops, urging them to proceed to the investigation of the miracles 'so that to God's honour you can openly demonstrate the clear truth of these matters both to the lord Pope and to the sacred church of Rome'. It is evident that the patron of the Bodleian MS was not at all interested in having copies of the documents which authenticated the process, but only in the presentation of some examples. Similarly the omission of one of the letters attributed to Roger of Pont-l'Évêque, archbishop of York, in the letters on the lay brethren reflects the same deliberate purpose of excluding any duplication.

Can we, then, speak of two different contemporary traditions in the transmission of the Gilbertine documents, as Dom Knowles and Jane Cowan Fredeman proposed? This was based on the omissions in Od and on its additions, consisting only of two letters on the lay brethren, on certain details relating to the canonization letters, and on two miracles without named witnesses.[1] Assuredly,

---

[1] See pp. xix, lxxxv, 357–63; for a further detail, p. 324 n. *a*, *Matild'* for M. in Lc. For Knowles and Fredeman see Knowles, 'The Revolt of the Lay Brothers', p. 474; Jane Cowan Fredeman in *BJRL* lv (1972–3), 112–45.

all the letters came from the Order's records and there must have
been an element of choice. Those on the canonization were contemporary with the planning of the *Book*; those on the lay brethren
had been in existence for thirty or forty years when they were
incorporated in it. Thus we should speak of the Gilbertine tradition, not as representing two different traditions, but as transmitted in two forms, one contemporary with the canonization,
aimed to preserve the *pièces justificatives* of the two processes, the
other much later, aimed to preserve the cult of St Gilbert in a context of personal devotion and edification.

Summary: the method of this edition

This edition is based on Lc, of the early thirteenth century, which
is a faithful copy close to the original *Book*. Lh is a copy of Lc made
later in the thirteenth century, and we only cite its readings where
it has by conjecture improved on Lc. Od is a fifteenth-century
book for devotional use, and an abbreviated and adapted version of
the archive. Not infrequently it retains correct readings where Lc
is wrong. Of its other readings we give a selection, where it seems
to have something of interest to offer. No deductions as to its readings elsewhere should be drawn from our apparatus, except that
where a variant of Lc is given alone it is to be assumed that Od
gives the reading printed in the text. The apparatus states whether
Od contains each letter and miracle: for additional letters in Od,
see Appendix 6, nos. 3–4. Elsewhere we note ('*def.* Od') where
Od's evidence is not available.

An analysis of the dossier in the Book of St Gilbert

The prologue and composition

It is unusual for a hagiographer to reveal to his readers his method,
his sources, and his plan. The author of the *Book of St Gilbert* does
just this in his prologue, a letter of dedication to Hubert Walter,
archbishop of Canterbury, who had instructed him to the task. In
respect of the *Life*, we learn that there was first a short version,
probably written with a view to the request to the Roman authorities for the canonization of the founder of the Order of Sempringham. This *Vita breuior* was presented to the archbishop and

carried to Rome by the envoys of the mother house of the Order, two canons, Gamel and W.,[1] and it must have been completed at the latest at the end of 1200, before the first investigation of the miracles achieved by the intercession of Gilbert in his lifetime and after his death. Subsequently, the author was set to the task of expanding the *Life* by adding a recital of such facts as he knew from his own experience or could learn from eye-witnesses. Since he served in the conventual church at Sempringham itself, where the body of the saint lay, he was, he tells us, in course of time a witness of numerous miracles—'multa ibi insignia uidi, plura audiui'—accounts of which he added to the *Life*. The collection was submitted to men of great learning, especially William de Montibus, master in theology and chancellor of Lincoln Cathedral,[2] and corrected on their advice. Perhaps we should identify this second *Vita amplior et emendata* as the version taken to the Curia by the second embassy. Finally, after the canonization of Gilbert on 11 January 1202 and his translation on 13 October 1202, a full description of these events was added to the *Life*, and also the documents relating to the processes in which Gilbert was involved—the revolt of the lay brethren and his own canonization, and two collections of letters, and an official collection of miracles (M1), emerging from the second legal enquiry in accordance with Innocent III's instructions, which was presented to the Roman Curia. The author added a second group of miracles (M2) containing a substantial number of details not included in the first.

The compilation shows some marks of incomplete revision: some details are given twice, in both the *Life* and the Miracles: thus M1, c. 13, gives a briefer version of the story in the *Life*,

---

[1] 'G. et W. fideles et discretos canonicos ordinis de Sempingham' (below, Letter 6, pp. 214–15). Gamel is named in the 'Visiones et revelationes', below, pp. 182–3; canon W. must be the canon William, witness of two miracles (M1, nos. 1, 19).

[2] William de Montibus, chancellor of the church of Lincoln, appears in episcopal documents between 1194 and *c.* 1212; he died in 1213 (*Fasti*, iii. 16–17). In his *De rebus a se gestis*, Giraldus Cambrensis says that he came to Lincoln intending to learn theology under this celebrated doctor, called de Monte because he studied in Paris on the Montagne-Sainte-Geneviève (Giraldus, *Opera*, i. 93). It was not uncommon to send books and to submit works to William de Monte or Montibus: a letter Giraldus directed to him shows that, after receiving some works of his former disciple, *Topographia* and *Expugnatio Hibernica*, the chancellor expressed some criticism; Giraldus hoped that his *Gemma ecclesiastica* and *Vita S. Remigii Lincolniensis* would be better received (*Speculum Duorum*, ed. Y. Lefèvre, R. B. C. Huygens, B. Dawson, and M. Richter (Cardiff, 1974), pp. 168–75); on William see H. MacKinnon in *Essays in Medieval History Presented to Bertie Wilkinson*, ed. T. A. Sandquist and M. R. Powicke (Toronto, 1969), pp. 32–45.

cc. 31–2, of which Canon Albinus was the occasion, the witness, and the agent. Similarly, a vision of eternal reward promised to Gilbert is reported in the *Life* (c. 54) following the vision of the wife of Ralph de Hauvilla,[1] between Gilbert's death and burial (cc. 52, 55), and repeated word for word between canonization and translation under the rubric 'Visions and revelations of St Gilbert the confessor'. Finally, the vision of Robert, prior of Watton, copied after the episcopal documents contemporary with the translation, seems to be a later addition after the book had been completed. In Od it has been integrated into the text between canonization and translation with the other 'Visions and revelations'.

However this may be, it emerges from the Prologue that the compiler of the *Book* was also the author of the *Life* and the narratives which expand it or were added to it. But it is equally clear that the author and compiler was inspired by a real desire to provide an authentic memorial, and in particular that Archbishop Hubert Walter appears as the guarantor of the authenticity not only of the witnesses to the canonization process, but also of the *Book of St Gilbert* as a whole, which was executed at his request, in accordance with his instructions and under the control of the ecclesiastical authorities, in virtually the form in which it survives in Cotton Cleopatra B. i. The Prologue also gives us the clue to its date. In the list of the contents of the *Book*, the author specifies at the end the lessons of the solemn office of the new saint, which are not actually copied in Lc or Lh, but he leaves out of the volume presented to the archbishop the proper responses and antiphons that he intends, as he tells us, to extract later from the Old and New Testaments. Thus it was in all probability before the celebration of the first solemn feast of St Gilbert, but after the translation, that the *Book of St Gilbert* was presented by its author to Hubert Walter—that is, between 13 October 1202 and 4 February 1203.

We have traced the author and compiler in many parts of his work, but nowhere in it does he reveal his identity. Although he observes the convention of modesty adopted by every regular author of the age—claiming 'imperitia sermonis et uerecundia minoris etatis'—he emerges as a man both well qualified and involved. He was sacrist of the conventual church of St Mary,

---

[1] Ralph de Hauvilla married Matilda daughter of Richard of Dunwich. He founded Mirmaud priory, a cell for three Gilbertine canons (p. xxxvi). Probably his family came from Hauteville-sur-Mer in Cotentin (Manche, canton of Montmartin-sur-mer).

Sempringham, as he implies in the Prologue, and he plays the
role of witness to the cure of Simon, priest and canon of Haverholme, which took place about twelve years earlier, when Simon
was still a secular. 'Ralph, a canon of Sempringham and a priest,
said on oath that when he was sacrist of the church of Sempringham ...' (M1, c. 1). This was one of the first miracles performed near the tomb of Gilbert, a little after his death in 1189.
But was Ralph still exercising his ministry when the editing of
the *Book* was completed? Surely so, since he describes the cure of
a poor sick child on the very night of the translation
(12–13 October 1202): 'On the night of the translation I myself,
who have written this account, handled his body with my own
hands; I saw that his limbs were rigid like the branches of a tree,
and in my pity for him I took him away from the pathway where
he was lying into the church, so that he would not be trampled
underfoot by the crowd' (p. 329). Once again we must cite the
words 'Cogitans mecum', which open his account of the pro-
phetic words attributed to Gilbert on the end of all flesh (*Life*,
c. 42). Thus notable events later than the translation have been
inserted in the *Book*, some of them at least duly attested by credible witnesses, such as Ralph the sacrist, probable author of the
Book of St Gilbert.

But there is more to it than that. Here and there the author gives
his personal convictions: his assurance of the divine presence in
the history of mankind, his unyielding faith in the glory of the
world to come, and the ineffable joy evoked by the illumination of
the elect, in a paradise in which everyone has his precise place in
the hierarchy according to his merits. 'What greater joy is there
than that which is bestowed upon men at the same time as upon
angels? We are firm witnesses of it, and because of our joy we are
unable, and indeed ought not, to keep silence about what we know'
(c. 30). Thus he comments on the dream of the knight Adam de
Amundeville, who received assurance of the eternal glory promised to Gilbert in a vision of St Thomas.[1] The account of another

---

[1] The Amundeville family from Mondeville (Calvados), now a part of the town of
Caen, is known as hereditary tenant of the stewardship of the bishopric of Lincoln in
the 12th c. (*EEA*, i. *Lincoln*, Introduction, p. xlii). One Adam, son of Jordan, was a canon
after his father (*Fasti*, iii. 18–19).. Adam, *miles opulentus*, seems to be identified with
Adam, son of Jocelin de *Amundavilla* and of Beatrix, daughter of Ralph Paynel. Jocelin
had been steward of the bishopric, and two of his sons, Walter and William, occupied
successively the office. Adam was probably the younger son of Jocelin, who we know

vision, the dream of one of the members of the second embassy to the Curia, is in the same vein. During the description of this memorable journey, when some of the envoys were assailed by doubt on the issue of their mission, Gilbert 'appeared in a dream to one of them, called Ralph de Insula' (p. 183). It was the revelation of final success: 'the work is accomplished—it is accomplished—it is accomplished'. The author describes this with an excitement which strongly suggests he is passing on his own exultation. Can we doubt that he was one of the embassy? It seems impossible to avoid the conclusion that he was present, at once an actor and a careful observer, so precise, circumstantial, lit up with specific details, is his account of the events, especially when he reaches the public consistory at which the canonization of Gilbert was decreed and proclaimed. It appears, then, that Ralph the sacrist, author of the *Book of St Gilbert*, and Ralph de Insula, member of the mission to Rome, were one and the same person.

The Life and other narratives

These form a group, complex in their mode of composition and in their literary forms: they are no doubt hagiographical pieces, but closely related too to history and chronicle.

Gilbertine hagiography. The lives of the saints have formed a literary genre since the Merovingian age—since the period, indeed, when, after the end of the persecutions, confessors of the faith came to be venerated by the faithful. Expressive of the cults of saints, hagiography had the task of preserving the memory and example of the saints in the Christian community. In England these cults had been proliferating, so that in many a major church there was veneration of the holy patrons whose miracles were recounted in prose or verse.[1] In the course of the twelfth century, moreover, with the advent of formal papal canonization, the production of *Vitae sanctorum* had become *de rigueur*. Ralph the

had two other sons, Elias and Ralph. Adam held lands in Lincolnshire, in part from Gilbert of Gant, and had interests in Edenham and Scotterthorpe (C. T. Clay, 'The Family of Amundeville', *Lincs. Archit. and Archaeol. Soc. Reports and Papers*, iii, ii (1948), 131–2). I could not find information about a link between Adam and Becket's household.

[1] For examples of poems on Anglo-Saxon saints' lives and miracles, see *Frithegodi monachi Breviloquium vitae b. Wilfredi, et Wulfstani cantoris Narratio metrica de S. Swithuno*, ed. A. Campbell (Zürich, 1950). Anglo-Saxon saints' legends flourished in the 11th c.: see D. W. Rollason, *The Mildrith Legend. A Study in Early Medieval Hagiography in England* (Leicester, 1982); S. Ridyard, *The Royal Saints of Anglo-Saxon England* (Cambridge, 1987).

sacrist very likely knew the *Vita Wulfstani*, written by Coleman and translated into Latin by William of Malmesbury, and that of Edward the Confessor by Osbert of Clare.[1] Beyond doubt is the interest he had in St Thomas, the martyr of Canterbury, whose lives and collections of miracles formed the most recent and famous example of the genre.[2] Witness the parallel Ralph established between martyr and confessor in his Prologue and again in c. 2 of the Life: 'following the wonderful example of steadfastness shown by the martyr St Thomas of Canterbury, we may appreciate in the confessor blessed Gilbert of Sempringham the essential lessons about the care of souls' (Prol.); 'already a martyr, . . . he was found worthy to bear the vessels of the Lord until the hundredth year of his life' (c. 2)—and other references to St Thomas in the course of his work. Besides the 'Passiones', the *Lives* of St Thomas of Canterbury provided the most relevant example of a hagiographical mode grafted into the stem of recent, well-known historical events. The problem is to disentangle the elements proper to hagiography from the facts of history.[3] Needless to say, each life of a saint is a case by itself. In the *Life of St Gilbert* history which had been lived mingled with hagiographical commentary throughout the literary narrative.

A marked characteristic of hagiography, in conformity with the monastic tradition, is the use of Holy Scripture, including explicit quotations and the impregnation of the Latin with the style of the Vulgate and biblical images.[4] It is easy to detect in the *Life* the impact of the Bible.

From the Old Testament we find at least 123 citations from 111 passages, with the Psalms predominating (43 citations from 40 passages), followed by Genesis (15 from 13), the Song of Solomon,

[1] *The Vita Wulfstani of William of Malmesbury*, ed. R. R. Darlington (Camden 3rd ser., 40, London, 1928); 'La vie de s. Édouard le Confesseur par Osbert de Clare', ed. M. Bloch, *Analecta Bollandiana*, xli (1923), 5–131.

[2] *MB* i, ii (Miracles); ii–iv (Lives). For the authors, dates, and textual history, see: E. Walberg, *La Tradition hagiographique de saint Thomas Becket avant la fin du XIIe siècle* (Paris, 1929); Foreville, *L'Église et la royauté*, pp. xxvi–xxxi; Anne Duggan, *Thomas Becket, a Textual History of his Letters* (Oxford, 1980): 'The Twelfth-century Biographers', pp. 175–204, esp. 182–7 on William of Canterbury. On the miracles, Foreville, 'Miracula', pp. 443–68.

[3] B. de Gaiffier, 'Hagiographie et historiographie', *Recueil d'hagiographie* (Brussels, 1977: Subsidia hagiographica, 61), no. IV (repr. from *La storiografia altomedioevale, Settimane di studio del Centro italiano di studi sull'alto medioevo*, xvii, Spoleto, 1970).

[4] Examples of sanctity from the Bible, ibid., p. 155; Biblical influence, ibid., pp. 160–1.

Proverbs, Job, and, among the prophets, Isaiah. From the New Testament, there are 149 citations from 119 passages: Matthew leads with 55 from 41 passages, then Luke (26 from 19) and John (17 from 13); the Pauline epistles furnish 36 from 32: Romans 13 from 12; Acts 4 from 4; Revelation is cited three times from three passages.

Biblical comparisons flow naturally from the pen of a biographer nourished on the Scriptures: they furnish familiar images destined to characterize the behaviour and actions of Gilbert. To take a single example: the organization and novelty of the Order inspire him to biblical comparisons pushed at times to extremes. The founder gathered the children of God from the four cardinal points of the earth, between four walls built on humble foundations, having Christ Jesus as corner-stone.[1] It was like the vessel which Peter saw descending from heaven, full of animals of every species, which he transferred from the world to the bosom of the Church.[2] It was like the vast chariot of God which the Lord draws endlessly towards him, filled with the just by tens of thousands, of every kind, of both sexes, of every tongue, humble and serene in their hope, grace, and charity. It is the chariot of Aminadab; in it are those who have chosen to be Christ's poor.[3] Having evoked this Old Testament image as an enigmatic figure of the Order in the unity and diversity of its structure under Gilbert's direction, the author proceeds to insist on its apostolic charisma. Here the wolf, once hunting its prey in the world, and the gentle lamb full of kindness dwell together. Here the fox forgets its wiles and the crow abandons the search of carrion. A wonderful unity: a community of every good quality united in the hearts[4] and in the diversity of convents; a unique example which he has derived from no man, but from the Holy Spirit, for none before him had imagined such an Order—and no such Order existed before him (c. 19).

Some chapters of the *Life*, set between the account of the trials of the Master in his later years and of his death, are dedicated to the virtues he exhibited through his long life. These consisted not only in piety, humility, and obedience to God and the Rule even before he had himself clothed as a canon, like his disciples (cc. 21–3), but

[1] Matt. 21: 42; Eph. 2: 20; 1 Pet. 2: 6. *Life*, c. 19.

[2] Acts 10: 9–16; *Life*, c. 19.

[3] S. of S. 6: 11; *Life*, c. 19. See above, p. l; and on the enigmatic character of Aminadab, Appendix 1.

[4] 'Mirabilis hec unitas . . . et inaudita rerum omnium communio' (*Life*, c. 19); cf. Acts 4: 32.

also mercy, sincerity, and justice, and above all chastity in devotion to virginity, and the rejection of every compromise with the world (cc. 4, 54). This did not hinder him from heavy tasks—visiting the houses of the Order, answering the king's appeal, frequenting the households of bishops and great nobles, if needs must, this side and beyond the Channel.

It is needless to emphasize that the *Life* is a panegyric in which the author deploys more or less faithfully the catalogue of virtues appropriate to sanctity.[1] Doubtless it fitted numerous founders and pastors. None the less, we discern several special traits which give us a concrete image of Gilbert's personality. It was natural for certain of his characteristic sayings and actions to catch the attention of his disciples and the companions of his travels. These stories must have been familiar and passed from house to house with the *circatores* and *circatrices*, the visitors appointed to undertake the canonical visitations. They particularly recalled his behaviour in extreme old age: feeble and blind, he had preserved his acute hearing (*auditus penetrabilis*), his firm hand (*manus intremula*), his eloquent speech (*lingua diserta*), his tenacious memory (*herens memoria*) (c. 27). When he could no longer walk and had to be carried into the refectory, the brethren who suggested that they bring him his meals to his chamber received this reply: 'Gilbert will not provide his successors with the example of eating delicacies in his own room' (c. 28). In his youth, in the household of Alexander bishop of Lincoln, when he shared a room with a bishop who was staying in the house, the bishop had observed in jest that he had seen a dancer practising his art during the night, for Gilbert was awake and praying with many genuflexions and prostrations, and his movements cast shadows on the chamber wall (c. 5).

Every life of a saint must contain some exceptional deeds, making clear while the saint lived the impact of his nature, a *virtus* emanating from his personality; this was a convention of hagiography. But no less necessary was the presentation of 'signs' which together with his merits constituted the evidence of sanctity. The *Life of St Gilbert* was originally conceived as the centre-piece in the canonization process. Such evidences must have had a place in the *Vita breuior*: the effect of his words or the force of his prayers

---

[1] On catalogues of virtues and classical types of sanctity, see de Gaiffier, 'Hagiographie et historiographie', p. 158: cf. the use of superlatives in the *Vita*: 'uir sanctissimus et sapientissimus' (c. 24), 'uir pacientissimus' (c. 25).

appeared in his mastery over attacks of fever (cf. cc. 31–2), over the
wind when he crossed the Humber (c. 45), over fire in an outbreak
of fire at London (c. 46), or again in the manner of his brotherly
correction (c. 39). The spirit of prophecy of the immediate future
appeared in his prediction about the duration of civil war in the
reign of Stephen, or of the extinction of a generation of princes and
bishops at the end of the century (cc. 43, 42). Finally, his vision—
supernatural in a blind man—of the tears inspired by his preaching
in the nuns of Elstow, bore witness to his spiritual clairvoyance
(c. 44).[1] But here again Gilbert remains a man of flesh and blood
and feeling, and sometimes witty: and thus we see him in the story
of how, like Elisha with the Shunammite woman, he passed the
night on the couch offered him by a woman at Stamford and
predicted that she would bear a son, and 'being a cheerful and
generous person' when he heard news of the happy event, 'he sent
the boy a cow to supply him with food, acting just as if the boy had
been his own son'.[2] As for his posthumous miracles, we cannot tell
which were presented in or annexed to the *Vita breuior*, for the
surviving collections which have been transmitted in the *Book*
belong to the second phase of the canonization process.

Another notable species of phenomena common in medieval
hagiography appears in the 'visions and revelations' in the *Life of St
Gilbert*. These consist especially in premonitory dreams before
certain events or other visions. Every saint's life and many of other
famous men attempt to point out the prodigies announcing the
birth of an exceptional person.[3] The author of Gilbert's *Life* has
his share in this genre. But equally he does not hide the fact that
Gilbert as a boy, ill-favoured in physique, unattractive in manner,
was despised by his family circle (c. 1). Throughout, the *Life*
makes few concessions to hagiographical wonders. It is only at the
hour when the Master passed from this world to the next that
visions and revelations make their appearance. We have quoted
the announcement made to the knight Adam de Amundeville,

---

[1] Elstow (Beds.), a Benedictine abbey founded *c.* 1078 (Knowles and Hadcock, p. 258).

[2] C. 47: cf. 4 Kgs. (2 Kgs.) 4: 8–17.

[3] As examples: *The Life of Christina of Markyate, a Twelfth Century Recluse*, ed. and trans. C. H. Talbot (Oxford, 1959), pp. 34–5; the visions before Philip Augustus' birth: Rigord, *Oeuvres*, i, *Gesta Philippi Augusti*, ed. F. Delaborde (Paris, 1882), c. 1, pp. 7–9, and Giraldus, *De principis instructione*, ed. G. F. Warner, *Opera* (RS), viii. 291–2. See Foreville, 'L'image de Philippe Auguste dans les sources contemporaines', in *La France de Philippe Auguste* (Paris, 1982), 124–5.

formerly of the household of Thomas Becket, of the glory to come for Gilbert, made by the martyr himself.[1] On the night of Gilbert's death, however, several people had foreknowledge of it in their dreams. The Prioress Agnes of Nun Appleton in the diocese of York assisted in the solemn obsequies of a noble person and saw the Master of Sempringham, whom she knew personally while he was alive, rise from his coffin (c. 53).[2] Likewise the wife of Ralph de Hauvilla:[3] she saw in a dream a host of angels singing sweetly, leading more angels bearing three boys on their way to heaven, dressed in linen garments. The tallest of the three, 'bald-headed though he had the face of a boy', was no other than the Master of Sempringham (c. 54). We are here amid characteristic medieval imagery: numerous illuminations and Limoges caskets on their higher surface show the soul in the likeness of a child similarly carried by two angels to their eternal rest.[4] A little later a Gilbertine canon also had a revelation of a confrère recently dead, whom he asked about Gilbert's place in the hierarchy: 'He is not with us; he occupies a higher position ... amongst the choirs of virgins'—a just reward, comments the author, for one who in his lifetime gathered so great a throng of virgins (c. 54).

As his holy death brought visions, so Gilbert's canonization gave equal occasion for dreams inspiring the event. We have already quoted that of Ralph de Insula which gave comfort to the envoys of the Order on their journey to Rome.[5] But Pope Innocent himself, as he hesitated to pronounce on Gilbert's cause, was also favoured by a vision whose meaning a holy hermit, approached to this end, alone explained to him.[6] To decipher a dream was in the best tradition of sacred history: the hermit and the pope were in the succession to the prophet Daniel and Nebuchadnezzar, and in the earliest biblical period, to Joseph and the Egyptian Pharaoh.[7] Finally, a cousin of the pope, John Hodeline, as he lay on his couch had a dream of a chamber so spacious and brilliantly lit that he seemed to see within it the majesty of God enthroned. But when he

---

[1] Above, p. lxxiv, and n. 1.

[2] The priory of St Mary and St John the Evangelist, Nun Appleton (Yorks.), was founded by Alice of St Quentin, later wife of Eustace de Merc, c. 1150; it was of Cistercian use (*EYC*, xi, pp. 94–5; Knowles and Hadcock, pp. 272, 275).

[3] See above, p. lxxiii, and n. 1.

[4] Foreville, 'La diffusion du culte de Thomas Becket', esp. figs. 3 to 9.

[5] Above, p. lxxv.

[6] Below, pp. 174–7.

[7] Dan. 2: 24–45, 4: 16–27; Gen. 41: 1–36.

tried to enter, encouraged by an elderly man, 'God's majesty spoke to him: "You cannot enter here now; but Master Gilbert of Sempringham shall bring you in".'[1] Human history touches on eternity, the vision of God, face to face, the hope of the saints and of those who aspire to be saints. In the Christian tradition, since Gregory the Great, the phenomenon of the vision in a dream has played a didactic role: it has been the medium of teaching, both doctrinal and moral. It is also the witness of the mentality of an age and of its milieu.[2]

Gilbertine history and chronicle. The visions described in the *Life of St Gilbert* have been integrated into the historical narrative. It is a modest historical narrative, perhaps, of a religious order confined to the east of England; but it has an actuality and a precision—emphasized by the naming of the people who take part in it and of the places in which its events occur—accentuated by the same traits in the collection of miracles. Furthermore this history in miniature is set in its place amid great events, the history of the realm at certain times—of Henry I, King Stephen, of Henry II both as duke of Normandy and king. It spread beyond the confines of England across the western world to Cîteaux and St Bernard, to Rome and the papacy from Eugenius III to Innocent III. The author's talent as a historian is undeniable, and in full conformity with the grand style expected at this date. The preface or prologue in which fine language displays the author's contemplation of sanctity, St Gilbert's in comparison with the sanctity of Thomas, the martyr of Canterbury, a 'wonderful example' 'in our lifetime and in our country' ('diebus nostris et regione nostra'), developing an argument adorned with biblical and patristic citations, yet also informing the reader about the sources and the plan of the work: these are elements necessary, indeed fundamental, to the historical mode.[3]

Once he reaches the last chapters of the *Life*—and especially in the narratives of the canonization and translation attached to it—

[1] Below, pp. 184–5.

[2] The author of the *Vita* refers several times to Gregory the Great's *Dialogues*. For Gregory, visions were the sole way to catch a glimpse of the spiritual realities of the world to come. But he advises us to be cautious about illusions ((*Dial.*, iv. 49–51, ed. A. de Vogüé, 3 vols., Sources Chrétiennes, 251, 260, 265, Paris 1978–80, 168–77). See M. Aubrun, 'Caractères et portée religieuse et sociale des "visions" en Occident du vi[e] au xie siècle', *Cahiers de civilisation médiévale*, xxiii (1980), 109–30.

[3] Cf. B. Guenée, 'Histoire et chronique: nouvelles réflexions sur les genres historiques au Moyen âge', in *La chronique et l'histoire au Moyen âge* (Paris, 1984), pp. 8–9.

he becomes a chronicler in the accepted sense of the term: from the middle of the twelfth century the chronicle combined precision in dating, sometimes developed like the dating clauses of charters, with historical narrative.[1] The first chronological note appears in c. 52, describing the death of Gilbert: 'on that Saturday which was 4 February 1189'; and his obsequies followed on the fourth day after his death, in conformity with the constitutions of the Order, to allow time for the priors of several houses and other notables to reach Sempringham (c. 55).[2] Embarking on the canonization, Ralph stated his intention thus precisely: 'we shall briefly describe the course which events took'. The author traces the process from its beginning, more than eleven years after Gilbert's death, in the course of 1200; he notes the date of the first enquiry into the miracles, 9 January 1201, and the dates of the arrival of the second embassy at Rome, 31 December 1201, and at Anagni, where the pope was staying, 2 January 1202. Finally, Ralph deployed all his chronological learning to mark the solemn day of Gilbert's canonization; 'on 11 January, during the sixth age of the world, on the sixth day of Epiphany, on the sixth day of the week, at the sixth hour of the day, in the sixth year of the nineteen year cycle, the sixth letter of the Dominical alphabet (F), at Anagni by Pope Innocent III acting through the full Roman curia, while John, son of King Henry II, was ruling in England, Hubert presiding over the see of Canterbury and Our Lord Jesus Christ reigning everywhere, to whom is honour and glory world without end'. Although these formulae have been inflated, they are none the less clearly parallel with those in use at this time in charters and stone inscriptions authenticating consecrations of bishops, altars, and churches.[3]

The narrative of the canonization, furthermore, takes the form of a report detailing the legal context and the facts of the case, as well as the circumstances of time and place.[4] The Curia had been gathered in solemn session, sitting in public consistory—open for clergy and people to attend; the envoys of the Order, who came as postulants and witnesses, stood aside, while the pope gave a formal sermon on the merits and the miracles of St Gilbert, after which the witnesses

---

[1] Guenée, p. 10; M. Paulmier-Foucart et M. Schmidt-Chazan, 'La datation dans les chroniques universelles françaises du XIIe au XIVe siècle', in *Comptes-rendus de l'Académie des Inscriptions*, 1982, p. 819.

[2] Cf. *Monasticon*, vi. 2, pp. xxx*–xxxi* (xx*).

[3] See Foreville, 'La diffusion du culte de Thomas Becket', pp. 365–8 and fig. 19.

[4] See below, pp. 168–79.

were called and the arguments expounded. Last of all came the proclamation that the new saint had been inscribed in the catalogue of confessors, by the common assent of the whole assembly.

To the precision of the narrative of the solemn canonization corresponds an equally precise narrative of the translation.[1] Time and place were noted, and the gathering of the suffragans of Canterbury for the event. On the morning of 13 October 1202, following the opening of the tomb and recognition of the relics which had taken place the night before, the archbishop proceeded to the blessing and dedication of the relic chest. The author describes in order the procession, followed by a numerous crowd, preceding the reliquary; the relic-chest and the relics themselves carried by a group of nobles; the sermon preached by Hubert Walter, mass solemnly chanted; the holy relics wrapped in fine linen covered with precious silk, the gift of the archbishop; their laying of the relics in the chest, with a charter, containing a short narration of the life, miracles, canonization, and translation of the saint, adorned with the seals of the bishops present at the celebration. Ralph transcribed the charter in full, together with that attesting the indulgences granted to those who should visit the shrine. A fiery globe of light, a sweet savour, and other marvels have their place in the story; but so too does the hard work of the labourers: during the night preceding the translation, they had shifted the coffin, now empty, a certain distance, and raised on the spot a marble wall to form the base of the shrine on which the relic chest itself would be laid, on the site of the tomb itself: a vital indication for the archaeology as well as the liturgical arrangement of the conventual church of Sempringham.[2]

It remains to characterize the style of the author: his Latin is not classical indeed, though it follows some of the classical rules—the verb set at the end of the sentence, the short subordinate before the main clause. It is a compromise close to the language of speech, a flowing discourse giving a lively narrative, adorned with interjections, happily reverting to the interrogative form and to dialogue,

---

[1] See below, pp. 184–95.

[2] Gilbert's tomb, and after the translation on 13 Oct. 1202 his shrine, were incorporated in the wall separating the two churches, the nuns' and the canons'. They were situated in the eastern part of the building between the altars of St Mary and St Andrew. But in the late Middle Ages, Sempringham priory church was enlarged and the choir extended, so that the shrine, which stayed in the same spot, was more distant from the altars (H. Braun and R. Graham, *JBAA*, 3rd ser., v (1940), 73–101, esp. pp. 80–3).

or again to the demonstrative 'Hinc est quod'. In this way the attention of the reader is caught at a point where he will meet an eloquent passage. Thus Ralph gave way to the literary tradition of the lament, and cried: 'it was that sad day which took from us our father and pastor, our brother and friend . . . a man who begot us all, however many we were or had been, in the word of the gospel. . . . What then shall we do, Lord, now that you have been taken from our midst? To whom shall we go? Whom shall we follow? We are afraid that now you are struck down we shall be scattered, like sheep wandering without a shepherd.' Then he changes course. 'We should weep, not for you, but for ourselves and those who come after us. But . . . that moment saw our comfort begin and everlasting glory descend upon you. Therefore it is not fitting to grieve for you or for ourselves; rather let us rejoice with you, and let all rejoice with us' (c. 52). There follow the visions of eternity already cited (cc. 53–4) and, a special miracle, the unanimous election of Gilbert's successor, 'without any hindrance or gainsaying . . . for it was regarded almost as a certainty by some . . . that . . . a secession of his limbs from the house of Sempringham would take place. So they were all amazed and, marvelling at what they had done, they could after discussion find no other explanation but that one who had always devoted himself to the cause of peace during his lifetime successfully petitioned for perpetual peace amongst his followers as soon as he entered the presence of God' (c. 56). And there follows 'The end of the life of St Gilbert the Confessor'.

The search for literary effect is clear. He makes use of the *cursus*; and the rhetoric carries a dramatic, emotional note, such as one can discern in a contemporary author, Giraldus Cambrensis, also at times a hagiographer, who rewrote in the taste of his day the lives of several English and Welsh saints.[1] In this literary enterprise we may suppose that the *periti* mentioned in the Prologue, and particularly William de Montibus, had played a part.

The lay brethren's dossier

In the *Book of St Gilbert* the letters concerning the lay brethren's revolt were placed after the *Life*: in Od, in contrast, they were moved back after the canonization process, as a kind of appendix.

---

[1] On the literary and stylistic standards of the late 12th c., as illustrated by Giraldus' *Lives* of St David and St Ethelbert, king of the East Angles, see R. Bartlett, 'Rewriting Saints' Lives. The Case of Gerald of Wales', *Speculum*, lviii (1983), 598–613.

The dossier is in any case not complete: it represents a selection from the original archives of the Order, now lost. It is by other routes that a sizeable number of documents has come down to us. They have been almost entirely overlooked hitherto, but are indispensable to the serious study of this crisis in the Order of Sempringham, both in its length and in its true character.

The Gilbertine documents in Lc are thirteen in number: Table 2 shows them in parallel columns with those copied in Od and edited by Knowles.

TABLE 2. *The letters relating to the affair of the lay brethren*

Lc (and Lh), numbered as in this edn.		Od, numbered as in Knowles's edn. (no. of this edn. in parentheses)
1 The bishop of Norwich to the pope	I	(1) William, bishop of Norwich, to Pope Alexander III
2 The bishop of Norwich to the pope	II	(7) Roger, archbishop of York, to the pope
3 King Henry to the pope	III	(5) William of Norwich to St Gilbert
4 The bishop of Winchester to the pope	IV	(not in Lc) King Henry II to St Gilbert (see p. 348)
5 The bishop of Norwich to St Gilbert	V	(2) William of Norwich to the pope
6 Robert bishop of Lincoln to the pope	VI	(4) Henry, bishop of Winchester, to the pope
7 Roger (arch)bishop of York and Hugh bishop of Durham to the pope	VII	(from Lc 6) Roger, (arch)bishop of York, to the pope
8 The prior of Bridlington to the pope	VIII	(8) The prior of Bridlington to the pope
9 Pope Alexander to St Gilbert and his Order	IX	(not in Lc) The Cardinal-legate Hugo to the pope (see pp. 348–9)
10 The pope to the bishops	X	(3) The king to the pope
11 The pope to the king		(Knowles omitted the three papal letters 11–13, since they were in *PUE*, iii, nos. 103, 184–5).
12 The king to the pope	XI	(12) The king to the pope
13 St Gilbert to the canons of Malton	XII	(13) St Gilbert to the canons of Malton

No. 6 was omitted in Od but copied by Knowles from Lc; no. 13 (in the dossier in Lc) was incorporated in the *Life* in Od.

The basic material is thus the same in both manuscripts: three letters are different, twelve the same. Dom Knowles chose to follow Od, which he reckoned the more correct; and he did not take note of the fact that the lay brethren's dossier is an integral part of the *Book* as described in its preface, of which the archbishop was in some sense the guarantor. Od is notably different. True, the material relative to the lay brethren is less secure in the *Book* than the canonization dossier, which was incorporated at first hand in 1201–2, a collection of documents virtually contemporary with the *Book* itself. It was not the same for the letters about the lay brethren's revolt, already a generation old; doubtless they had formed part of an earlier collection of material. What has come down to us, in both Lc and Od, represents only a sample: a significant number of documents which must once have existed are not in either (see Appendix 4).

So far as the text is concerned the variants between the two forms of the tradition mostly comprise minor variants due largely to the two centuries which separate them in time. Where they differ significantly is in the text of the two letters of Henry II to the pope. The long passage at the end of letter 12 (p. 162 at n. b) has been moved to follow letter 3 in Od (Knowles, no. X; see p. 144 n. a). On the other hand, Od completes letter 12 thus truncated by adding two sentences copied in a different hand (so Knowles no. XI), unsatisfactory both in syntax and sense for their context, and apparently extracted from another document probably later in date, rather fitting in style the occasion of the canonization, and in the manner of King John (see p. 162 n. b). Letter 3 in Lc is a request from the king for the coercion of the rebels by ecclesiastical censures: its final sentence—'Quod [*sc.* totius ordinis excidium] ne ullo modo contingat, sanctitas uestra malignantibus medullitus resistat'—does not seem to anticipate any further points linked to it by 'Proinde', 'in consequence'. To Henry II's letter Alexander III replied positively: on the one hand, he instructed the bishops and archdeacons of the sees involved to pronounce sentence of excommunication on those who attacked members of the Order with violence (letter 10); on the other hand, he requested Henry II to exercise royal justice against rebellious and contumacious brethren whom the Church's censures had not brought to submission (letter 11). Finally, the pope addressed a reassuring letter to Gilbert confirming his right to correct abuses

in the Order (letter 9). These formed a bundle of measures of a conservative character in no way touching the root of the argument, the constitution of the Order.

Let us now examine the argument of letter 12. The king first expresses his thanks to the pope for the protection he has accorded the Gilbertine Order, in which some of the lay brethren of dissolute life are attempting to disturb the primitive constitution. In consequence, he prays the pope immediately to grant one or several privileges guaranteeing the constitution established by Master Gilbert which the pope himself had confirmed: 'Proinde obnixe rogamus quatinus ordinem prefatum faciatis inuiolabiliter obseruari, secundum quod a prefato magistro prestitus est et confirmatus a uobis.' If this were not done, the king and his barons would be ready to revoke the grants with which they had endowed the houses of the Order. In return, adds the king—and here he is answering Alexander III's letter—if you confirm the order in its original constitution, for our part we shall strive to preserve it, so far as pertains to our justice. The petition, with a serious proviso thus attached, was to be presented to the pope and followed to the Curia by two envoys, Master O. and J(ordan) archdeacon of Chichester.[1] Clearly what is in question here, as in the previous letter, is not just the repression of the rebels, but the economic and juridical integrity of the Gilbertine Order's endowments: that is to say the maintenance of the double houses to which the grants had been made—'sanctimonialibus de ... et fratribus earum clericis et laicis'—as well as the authority of the canons over the whole complex of communities.[2] Syntax and argument appear thus in perfect harmony; and Lc seems preferable to Od in its transmission of the documents concerning the affair of the lay brethren, though neither is perfect.

The original tradition is strongly confirmed by the passage in the *Life* which concludes the long chapter on the revolt of the lay brethren (c. 25). This chapter, which is both in Lc and Od, gives details of the letter 12 here in question. It takes note of the unanimity of the witnesses, of bishops and others, in Gilbert's

---

[1] Archdeacon of Lewes, but always named after the diocese, Jordan of Melbourne was in office *c.* 1154/64–1173/4 and later dean, *The Acta of the bishops of Chichester 1075–1207*, ed. H. Mayr-Harting (Canterbury and York Soc., 1964), pp. 211–13.

[2] *Sempringham Charters*, *passim*: e.g. xvi. 31–4. The formula is attested at least until the end of the 12th c., as in a deed of two portions of Stainton church, 'concessione uiri uenerabilis Hugonis Lincolniensis episcopi' (1186–1200), *Gilbertine Charters*, p. 107.

favour and of the tenor of the petitions to the effect that the Master should be confirmed in his original purpose, and goes on: 'The illustrious King Henry II himself also sent with royal messengers his own letter giving the same evidence and making the same requests. At the end of it he stated categorically that if the Order was altered through the machinations of these peasants and (as he put it) former serfs, he would take back in entirety the estates and possessions which, along with his magnates, he had granted to the house because of the devotion to the religious life shown by its inmates. But if the pope would ensure that this Order and the original form of its constitution were observed with proper strictness, then as far as secular justice was concerned he would maintain it to the height of his powers, and regard it with the greatest honour and reverence, as he had always done.'[1]

A final word on these documents: the heading to letter 6 in Lc, the letter from that MS transcribed by Dom Knowles, reads 'Epistola R. Eboracensis episcopi ad eundem pro eodem', and enshrines a double error. It was not addressed to St Gilbert as was the preceding letter, and it was not written by the archbishop of York. Doubtless the order of letters had been altered in a preceding text, or else one or more letters have been omitted. If we correct the addressee to Alexander III, the author is still wrongly named, as is clear if we compare the text with no. 7, which was indeed from the archbishop of York. He and the bishop of Durham, having made enquiry in the see of York, observe: 'For there is only one house in the diocese of York where canons and lay brethren dwell alongside nuns within the same enclosures', that is, the priory of Watton. But the so-called 'bishop of York' of no. 6 refers three times to the *houses* in his see; and he is certainly referring to double priories since he says distinctly that allegations have been made 'concerning those houses subject to the rule of Master Gilbert of Sempringham; namely, that canons, lay brethren, and nuns all dwell together. . . . If the canons and brethren were really put a great distance away from the nuns . . . those houses could not survive.'

The see of Lincoln alone contained several double houses; the letter must therefore come from Bishop Robert de Chesney, that is be earlier than 27 December 1166, the probable date of his death.[2]

---

[1] Below, pp. 82–5.

[2] *Fasti*, iii. 2—and almost certainly *c.* 25 Dec. 1166. There followed a lay vacancy in the see.

The involvement of the bishop of Lincoln is attested by the report of the bishop of Norwich (letter 1) of an arbitration between Gilbert and some of the lay brethren 'coram domino Lincolniensi episcopo'.

The related documents require no critical discussion, since their transmission is clear and they are published elsewhere. They comprise four series:

(1) Two letters of Thomas Becket to Gilbert. The first accompanied a papal mandate citing Gilbert to appear at the Feast of the Purification, 2 February [1166]. In the second Thomas writes as papal legate, so that it must be later than mid-May 1166. The text of the two letters and the legatine title have now been established by the new edition being prepared by Dr Anne Duggan: see Appendix 6, nos. 1–2.[1]

(2) The letters of Alexander III published by Walther Holtzmann in *Papsturkunden in England*, i (Berlin, 1931), nos. 103, 112, 154, 184–5 (from the Malton Cartulary, BL Cotton Claudius D. xi), of which nos. 103, 184–5 are in the Gilbertine dossier. They were omitted in Knowles's edition. They are dated at Benevento and assigned by Holtzmann to the years 1167–9.

(3) Two letters in Od alone (ff. 101ᵛ, 104ᵛ; Knowles, nos. IV, IX), the latter from the cardinal legate Hugo Pierleone, of early 1176: see Appendix 6, nos. 3–4.

(4) Two papal privileges concerning the double priories of Alvingham and Chicksands, published by Christopher Cheney. The first, dated from the Lateran 25 June 1178, was one of a string of privileges of like date in favour of the Order of Sempringham including those to Chicksands and Malton: *PUE*, i, no. 154.[2]

Thus new evidence enables us to grasp the length of the crisis— its opening *c.* 1164–5 and final settlement in 1178, after the legation of Hugo Pierleone in 1175–6—and also the stages of its development. Viewed as an affair of long duration, the chronology of the crisis appears markedly different from earlier discussions of it— including my own dates of 1165–70, those of Dom Knowles,

---

[1] I am greatly obliged to Dr Anne Duggan for the critical text of 'Quantum te' and 'Nos uobis': see Appendix 6. The protocol of Thomas Becket's second letter, including the legatine title, is attested only by MS Paris Bibl. Nat. Lat. 5372 (Roger of Crowland's *Quadrilogus II*). For the legation, see JL 11270–1 (24 Apr. 1166) = *MB*, v, nos. 172–3 (cf. *GFL*, p. 218n.).

[2] On the whole series, see Cheney, 'Papal privileges', pp. 39–65, esp. pp. 57–62, repr. with corrections from *Bulletin of the Institute of Historical Research*, xxi (1946), 39–58.

1167–9, and those suggested by Rose Graham, 1170–87.[1] The new dates fit well both the data of the *Life* and the slow progress of such cases in the Roman Curia. They allow for the likelihood of a suspension of negotiation in the unfavourable circumstances of the years 1170–4. Furthermore, they offer a better approach to the heart of the crisis—not only in the status of the lay brethren as serfs freed by their religious profession, but in the essentially unique structure of the Gilbert Order and its *raison d'être* amid the proliferation of foundations for monks and canons in the twelfth century.

The rebellion of the lay brethren of Sempringham and all it implied could well have found a place in the chronicles. But in fact the historians of the late twelfth century were prudent and laconic. The satirists, who were sparing neither of monks nor canons—still less of nuns—spared the Order of Sempringham. Nigel de Longchamps in his *Speculum Stultorum* gives it a passing notice, to which, however, the ass Burnellus adds the note of the spontaneous popular reaction: What goes on at Sempringham, I know not, but I distrust all these novelties.[2] Walter Map sets in the future his image of a combat between Venus and Minerva.[3] As for Giraldus Cambrensis, having castigated Irish monastic practice, taking shelter under the authority of St Jerome—'Nulla securitas est uicino serpente dormire . . .'—he turns to ecstasy over the almost miraculous achievement of Gilbert, whose wisdom has built multiple walls within his double houses.[4] It is true that he wrote shortly after the canonization pronounced at Rome, as he says, 'diebus nostris'. The last word lies with William of Newburgh: 'Grace was granted him [Gilbert] from on high in his ministry for women.'[5]

The canonization dossier

The canonization dossier of St Gilbert, as it has come down to us, consists of two series of documents: first, an important group of letters from the years 1200–2, which, if not exhaustive—of letters

---

[1] Knowles, 'Lay Brothers', pp. 468–9; Graham in *VCH Lincolnshire*, ii. 181.

[2] Nigel de Longchamps, *Speculum Stultorum*, ed. J. H. Mozley and R. R. Raymo (Berkeley etc., 1960), ll. 2451–2, cf. 2401–12 and nn.; also ed. T. Wright, *Anglo-Latin Satirical Poets . . .* (RS, 1872), i. 94–6.

[3] *De nugis curialium*, Dist. i, c. 27, ed. M. R. James, revised by C. N. L. Brooke and R. A. B. Mynors (OMT, 1984), pp. 114–17.

[4] *Opera*, iv. 184.

[5] *Historia rerum anglicarum*, ed. R. Howlett, *Chronicles of the reigns of Stephen etc.* (RS, 1884–9), i. 55.

from lay magnates, only one is included—is at least a very adequate sample; second, the record of the sworn inquest on the miracles, presided over by Archbishop Hubert Walter at Sempringham on 26 September 1201. To this document the compiler has added a second collection of miracles. The first collection was authenticated by the seal of the papal commissioners and so invested with an official character like the letters; the second carries interesting evidence none the less, including two accounts of miracles performed after the closing of the inquest and duly attested (M2, nos. 15, 23). First we must relate the dossier to normal canonization procedures in the twelfth century.

Anglo-Saxon England, the 'Isle of the Saints', knew a great number of popular cults based on venerable tombs; many a notable church, cathedral or abbey, honoured the remains of patron saints. Among the most notable were the martyrs Edmund of East Anglia (died 869) and Ælfheah, archbishop of Canterbury (1012), both murdered by the Vikings; and the confessors Cuthbert, bishop of Lindisfarne (687), Swithun (c. 862) and Æthelwold of Winchester (984), Dunstan archbishop of Canterbury (988) and several of his predecessors.[1] Æthelwold had built a new shrine at the Old Minster at Winchester for Swithun; Ælfheah, then bishop of Winchester, had translated Æthelwold; and the relics of Ælfheah himself were translated in 1023 from St Paul's in London to Canterbury Cathedral, on the orders of King Cnut.[2] Thus numerous popular cults had received diocesan approval, from the bishop or ordinary, by receiving translation at the bishop's hands, after the relics had been inspected and declared authentic. It was the custom in western Christendom at this time to recognize a 'canonization' of local effect, representing a single church, by the local diocesan; and thus it was the *bishop's* consent on which the Council of Westminster of 1102, presided over by Anselm, insisted.[3] This decree in effect ratified the traditional procedure,

[1] See D. H. Farmer, *Oxford Dictionary of Saints* (Oxford, 1978), s. nn., and refs.; for Swithun, especially *Winchester Studies*, iv (2 parts), ed. M. and B. Biddle and M. Lapidge (forthcoming), on the Old Minster and the cult; cf. also William of Malmesbury, *De gestis pontificum*, ed. N. E. S. A. Hamilton (RS, 1870), pp. 167, 170.

[2] *Anglo-Saxon Chronicle*, esp. D, s.a. 1023; cf. William of Malmesbury, p. 171; Gervase of Canterbury, ed. W. Stubbs (RS, 1879–80), ii. 56.

[3] *Councils and Synods*, i, ii, 678 (and nn. for parallels); Eadmer, *Hist. Novorum*, ed. M. Rule (RS, 1884), p. 143: 'Ne quis temeraria novitate corporibus mortuorum aut fontibus aut aliis rebus, *quod contigisse cognovimus, sine episcopali auctoritate* reverentiam sanctitatis exhibeat.'

but was clearly aimed at concrete examples and was a warning against unauthorized deviations, due solely to the faithful fostering extravagant cults which had not been authenticated.

On the Continent, in the first half of the twelfth century, episcopal prerogative found itself in competition with papal. The latter was in a continuous tradition going back to an ancient custom of canonization in general council. Urban II had refused to examine the case of Urloux, first abbot of Sainte-Croix de Quimperlé, declaring: 'No one can enter the canons of the saints unless eyewitnesses attest his miracles, and unless he receives confirmation by the assent of the full synod'—that is to say a general council summoned and presided over by the pope.[1] This is indicated by the sentence of Innocent II in the case of Godehard bishop of Hildesheim, postulated by his successor, Bernard, 'in plenaria synodo, quae Remis ... fuerat congregata, attestatione fratrum nostrorum episcoporum et abbatum ...'.[2] The same pope canonized Hugh, bishop of Grenoble, with the advice of some cardinals, bishops, and other dignitaries, then gathered about him (c. 1134–6);[3] and he referred to the Second Lateran Council of 1139 the case of Sturm, abbot of Fulda,[4] in conformity with the procedure already followed by Calixtus II in favour of Conrad, bishop of Constance, at the First Lateran Council of 1123.[5] The support of a synod of bishops, whether a general council or not, was thus required in an act as solemn as the canonization of a saint, without, however, obscuring the role of the pope. The general council was seen as the place specially privileged for postulating a process of canonization.

If we turn to England, it was in 1139 or just before—perhaps on account of the Second Lateran Council of that year—that a first attempt was mounted at Rome for the canonization of Edward the Confessor, whose cause was presented by Osbert of Clare, prior of Westminster abbey.[6] Twenty years later, the proposal was revived

---

[1] *Cartulaire de l'abbaye de Sainte-Croix de Quimperlé*, ed. L. Maître et P. de Berthou (Paris, 1896), p. 250; E. W. Kemp, *Canonization and Authority in the Western Church* (Oxford, 1948), p. 67.

[2] Fontanini, *Codex*, p. 11; Kemp, pp. 74–5.

[3] *PL* clxxix. 256; JL 7742.

[4] Innocent II, *Epistola* 392, *PL* clxxix. 450–1; JL 8007; French translation in Foreville, *Latran*, p. 187.

[5] Calixtus II, *Bullaire*, ed. U. Robert (Paris, 1891), ii, no. 358; JL 7028; French translation in Foreville, *Latran*, pp. 171–2.

[6] The fullest and most recent account of the canonization of Edward the Confessor is

in more favourable circumstances: the stabilization of the realm after the accession of the Angevin king, and the recognition of Pope Alexander III by the English Church in 1160.[1] The demand was renewed by the bishops and the king—and by Abbot Laurence and the monks of Westminster; and the canonization of Edward the Confessor was pronounced by the pope on 7 February 1161, after an examination of the catalogue of miracles—'libro miraculorum inspecto'—and the witness of the bishops.[2] Acting on his own authority with the counsel of the cardinals alone—'de communi ... fratrum nostrorum consilio'—Alexander none the less recalled the normal procedure: 'although it is not frequently the custom to assent to business so difficult and noble except in solemn councils'—'quamuis negotium tam arduum et sullime non frequenter soleat nisi in sollempnibus conciliis de more concedi'— following the model of Eugenius III in the bull of canonization for the Emperor Henry II. It was in the light of this that several canonization causes were introduced at the Council which Alexander III opened at Tours on 19 May 1163, among them the cause of Anselm of Canterbury, presented by Thomas Becket. The pope deferred examination of the canonization causes, and owing to adverse circumstances, that for Anselm was not pursued.[3]

In contrast, the canonization of Thomas Becket was declared scarcely more than two years after his death. The temptation was strong among the archbishop's disciples to call him 'Saint', convinced as they were that the justice of his case made him a martyr, but they were none the less convinced that they were

in F. Barlow, *Edward the Confessor* (London, 1970), chap. xii; cf. *The Letters of Osbert of Clare*, ed. E. W. Williamson (London, 1929), pp. 85–8; JL 8182.

[1] The circumstances of the recognition were recorded by Arnulf, bishop of Lisieux (*Letters*, ed. F. Barlow (London, 1939), nos. 27–9, pp. 36–50), John of Salisbury (*Letters*, i, nos. 124–5, 130, pp. 204–17, 226), and by Gilbert Foliot (*GFL*, no. 133, pp. 175–7); see Foreville, *L'Église et la royauté*, pp. 95–6 and 95 n. 1; M. G. Cheney, 'The Recognition of Pope Alexander III: Some Neglected Evidence', *EHR* lxxxiv (1969), 474–97; *Councils and Synods*, i. 2, 835–41.
[2] Barlow, *Edward the Confessor*, pp. 323–4; JL 10654; the whole dossier is critically edited by Barlow, pp. 309–24
[3] See Foreville, 'Regard neuf sur le culte de S. Anselme à Canterbury ...', *Les Mutations socio-culturelles au tournant des XIe–XIIe siècles, Études Anselmiennes IVe* (Colloques ... CNRS, Le Bec-Hellouin, 1982, publ. Paris, 1984), pp. 299–316; ead., 'Alexandre III et la canonisation des saints', in *Miscellanea Alexandri tertii* (Siena, forthcoming); and 'Canterbury et la canonisation des saints au XIIe siècle', in D. Greenway, C. Holdsworth, and J. Sayers (eds.), *Tradition and Change: Essays in honour of Marjorie Chibnall* (Cambridge, 1985), pp. 63–75.

obliged to apply to Rome.[1] The Roman church was never in doubt of the reality of the martyrdom in the archbishop's violent death, as the pope's letters in 1171 and 1172 attest; but the Roman church had not dispensed with the rule governing the examination of the merits and the miracles of a saint, nor that prescribing the approval of the cardinals. The letters announcing the canonization (March 1173) instruct the chapter of Canterbury Cathedral to proceed to the elevation of the martyr, the English bishops to celebrate solemnly the day of his death, and all the faithful to pray to him for the remission of their sins. Finally, all the hierarchy throughout Christendom—'tam in Anglia quam in Gallia, nec non et in aliis regionibus'—was instructed to solemnize every year the day of his death so that the faithful might pray for his intercession.[2] This is an injunction which makes the cult universal, which fitted the fame of St Thomas and his merits as a martyr, but derived from the universality of the Roman prerogative, solemnly affirmed in the bull addressed to the archbishops of Christendom.

The examination of other canonizations in this pontificate, and especially those of Cnut Lavard (1169) and Bernard of Clairvaux (1174), illustrate clearly the authority of the pope in this matter and also a more open consciousness of the relation of the kingdom of God to papal jurisdiction.[3] The letters of Alexander III furnish no fundamental text decreeing papal reserve, but it was none the less in force. From his accession a general consensus steered towards the see of Rome petitions in favour of numerous candidates to the title of sanctity. The authority of the bishop was not specifically rejected, but it was effectively checked by the attraction to Rome, a movement in which the English in course of time played a part one may reasonably judge preponderant.[4] Clement III and Celestine III indeed deemed it advisable to canonize Étienne de Muret or

---

[1] 'Martyres discernit causa, non poena' (St Augustine, *Sermones*, no. 275, *PL* xxxix. 1254); cf. John of Salisbury, *Letters*, ii, no. 305, pp. 726–7; Herbert of Bosham in *MB*, vii. 352, no. 779; C. Duggan, 'Bishop John and Archdeacon Richard of Poitiers ...', in *Thomas Becket*, ed. R. Foreville (Paris, 1975), pp. 71–83, at p. 78.

[2] One copy only of this important letter has been preserved (to the archbishop of Aversa) ordering the archbishop to transmit the document to the bishops of his province (*MB*, vii, 549–50, no. 786).

[3] Foreville, 'Alexandre III et la canonisation des saints', forthcoming.

[4] For the development of papal reservation see S. Kuttner, 'La réserve papale du droit de canonisation', *Revue historique de droit français et étranger*, 4th ser. xvii (1938), 172–228, repr. in Kuttner, *The History of Ideas and doctrines of Canon Law in the Middle Ages* (Variorum, 1980), no. VI, with *Retractationes*, pp. 7–11. For English involvement, see Foreville, 'Canterbury et la canonisation des saints', pp. 63–75.

Tiers, the founder of the Order of Grandmont, and Gerard, the founder of La Sauve Majeure, respectively, who had been added to the calendar by their successors.[1] Celestine III, furthermore, thought it necessary to confirm by papal authority the canonization of Rosendo, bishop of Dumio, which he had pronounced 'in minori gradu positi' when he was iegate in Spain, in order to give it the requisite strength and force, 'robur debitum . . . et vigorem'.[2] But it was Innocent III who finally asserted the papal reserve in cases of canonization, and gave better shape to the procedure and made it more effective.

In this process the year 1200 was the turning-point. The new pope, himself an eminent jurist as well as a theologian, had already to his credit two canonizations, of Homobonus, a simple burgher of Cremona (12 January 1199) and the Empress Kunigunde, wife of the Emperor Henry II (3 April 1200). These had given him the opportunity to define the Roman doctrine of canonization, making the authenticity of the merits and the miracles of the saint, and the papal reserve of the right of canonization in virtue of the *plenitudo potestatis* granted by Christ to Peter and his successors, the *sine qua non* of the process.[3] This reserve had already its echo in England in the postulation of the cause of Gilbert in the petition of the Master and chapter of Sempringham (letter no. 5): 'Because it is only lawful to call someone holy with the approval of the Holy See we beg your advice . . . ; we ask your approval, we beg for your mercy.' Canonization is a sentence declared by a supreme and universal judge, following a judgement of the most exalted kind. Such a judgement requires 'true and incontestable proof . . . [for] neither merits without miracles nor miracles without merits are properly enough to prove sanctity among men, since occasionally an angel of Satan transforms himself into an angel of light'.[4] The bull of canonization of St Kunigunde also defines the need to make appeal to witnesses on oath. Still, it was the canonization of Gilbert of Sempringham which was to be the occasion and the model for the renewal of the process: not novel in its basis but in its form, by uniting the rigorous juridical procedure and the extension to all such cases of the rules newly defined.

[1] Fontanini, *Codex*, pp. 26–7, 33–4.

[2] A. García y García, 'A propos de la canonisation des saints au xiiᵉ siècle', *Revue de Droit canonique*, xviii (1968), 3–15, at p. 9 (Letter to Martin archbishop of Braga, 9 October 1196).

[3] Fontanini, *Codex*, pp. 34–9.

[4] Below, p. 247.

Down to Innocent III, in fact, the evidence required on the life and miracles rested essentially on written testimony: the Life of the saint, furnished with miracles, and letters from dignitaries attesting the authenticity of his virtues and miracles. It was thus that Alexander III had proceeded in the case of Edward the Confessor; in that of Thomas Becket, he had required the attestation of numerous witnesses to the enquiry held by the legates in Normandy, Albert and Theoduinus, who, as the pope explained, had explored the truth and learned it 'uisu et auditu'. This evidence was received at the Curia in the form of depositions, according to tradition. In the case of Homobonus, however, canonized only fourteen months after his death, it was Innocent III himself who presided over the enquiry into his life and miracles and received the depositions of witnesses under oath—just as Calixtus II had earlier in the case of Hugh, abbot of Cluny, an analogous case owing to the pope's proximity in time and place.[1] The bull of canonization of Gilbert, dated 30 January 1202, extended this procedure to cover all cases of canonization: an enquiry into their lives and miracles, not only with supporting evidence, but with written depositions of witnesses supported by their oaths and the seals of papal delegates; the renewal of such depositions at the Curia in the presence of the pope; and a papal sentence after receiving the written and hearing the oral depositions (no. 27). The new procedure grew out of cases in which witnesses were near at hand and the events recent; it might have remained confined to such particular cases. But it was applied in the case of St Kunigunde, 160 years after her death, and defined in the bull of canonization of St Gilbert of Sempringham, a bull which we must reckon on a par with a definitive decree, setting aside the traditional procedure and introducing new canonical models. Analysis of the letters of the dossier will make clear the procedure followed.

The letters

The collection of letters is of exceptional interest: it is the most complete example to date of the unfolding of the procedure from the postulation to the canonization itself and the translation of the saint's body. These thirty-four documents were indeed an extract from a yet larger number, but they exemplify to perfection the various phases in Gilbert's process.

[1] At the time, Pope Calixtus was staying at Cluny (*AA SS*, Apr. iii (1675), 659).

The first phase was the postulation to the Roman Curia. The proceedings were opened by Master Philip, the papal notary, then on a mission to England.[1] He invited the prelates, who had been informed of what was afoot by the canons of Sempringham, to make an enquiry into the miracles, so that, once the facts had been established, the pope and the Roman church could pass judgement on them (no. 1). It was the archbishop of Canterbury, during a vacancy in the see of Lincoln, who set the machinery to work and organized the enquiry. To this end he set up a commission of inquiry entrusted to the abbots of Swineshead, Bourne, and Croxton (no. 2). The commissioners held their inquiry at Sempringham on 9 January 1201; they drew up a record of it, also attested by the abbot of Barlings and the priors of Kyme, Chicksands, and Catley, and addressed it to Hubert Walter (no. 3), but enclosed it in a letter to the pope, begging him to give ear to the writings of the brethren of the Order and their messages (no. 4). To this document was added the petition of Roger, Master of the Order of Sempringham (no. 5), and it was sent first by the archbishop to the bishops of the province of Canterbury so that they might add their petitions to the dossier (no. 8). There are included in it letters from the bishops of London, Coventry, Norwich, Rochester, Bangor, and Ely (nos. 9–14), and from thirteen abbots and six priors (nos. 3, 4, 15–17, 19–21; cf. pp. 170–1). The dossier only contains a portion of the petitions from bishops and religious houses, since the whole body of suffragans and major abbeys had been approached by the archbishop. Similarly, besides the petition of King John (no. 7), only one lay magnate figures in the list, the justiciar Geoffrey FitzPeter, earl of Essex, founder of the double priory of Shouldham (no. 22), his letter copied as an example. We observe that with the exception of the ancient and celebrated abbeys of Chertsey and St Albans, and the royal foundation of Waltham, the houses in the list all belonged to Lincolnshire or the adjacent counties in the diocese of Lincoln, or else to Yorkshire—that is to say within the sphere of influence of the Order of Sempringham as it was in 1200. Not less remarkable, in the list as it is preserved, is the spread of orders, Benedictine,

[1] Master Philip, subdeacon and notary of Pope Innocent III, was sent as nuncio to expedite the payment of the fortieth for the crusade. He arrived in England before 24 Apr. 1200, and left some time before Aug. 1200. See C. R. Cheney, 'Master Philip the Notary and the Fortieth of 1199', *EHR* lxiii (1948), 342–50; id., *Pope Innocent III and England* (Stuttgart, 1976), pp. 54–6, 243–6. For what follows see also *EEA*, iii, nos. 607–15.

Cistercian, Augustinian, Premonstratensian, Gilbertine, including
the double houses of Catley and Chicksands.[1] In the see of
Lincoln, vacant since the death of Hugh of Avalon on 16 November
1200, it fell to the dean, Roger of Rolleston, and the chapter of
Lincoln to present the petition from the diocese (no. 18). The
dossier of the postulation, the short *Life*, petitions, and the report
of the enquiry, including the evidence of miracles not included in
the *Book* (no. 3), was sent to Innocent III under the seal of the
archbishop of Canterbury, who attested the veracity of the
miracles (no. 6), by envoys of the Order, to wit two canons,
Gamelus and W., accredited by Roger, the Master, and the chapter
of Sempringham, and recommended by name by Hubert Walter
(nos. 5–6, *ad fin.*).

The dossier as it has come down to us is not a complete file of
the petitions, but it is at least a perfectly adequate sample. It is not
certain that the original *Book of St Gilbert* as it was presented to
Hubert Walter was an exhaustive collection: the prologue and
letter dedicatory to the archbishop leaves the possibility of doubt.
In any case the surviving documents form an exceptional archive
for the conduct of a canonization process at the opening of the
thirteenth century, in its preliminary phase. It started in England
with the approaches made by the Gilbertine Order and the archbishop of Canterbury: the affair then passed to Rome and the
canonization letters are equally revealing of the Roman procedure.
They show us a turning-point in the procedure for canonization, a
decisive stage set in motion from the beginning of Innocent III's
pontificate.

The second phase is marked by the check to the process in the
Roman Curia and the renewal of the procedure on new foundations. The Order's envoys were sent back furnished with instructions: Innocent III did not reject the case, but complained that the
procedure had been insufficient. He had received the attestations
of the English church, but he proposed to make a judgement based
not so much on these as on the witnesses themselves, on public

[1] Petitions recorded in the *Book* came from the Benedictine abbots of Bardney
(Lincs.), Chertsey (Surrey), St Albans (Herts.), and Selby (Yorks.), the Cistercian
abbots of Kirkstall (Yorks.), Kirkstead, Revesby, and Swineshead (Lincs.), and Wardon
(Beds.), the Augustinian abbots of Bourne (Lincs., Arrouaisian) and Waltham (Essex),
the Premonstratensian abbots of Barlings (Lincs.) and Croxton (Leics.), the Augustinian priors of Bridlington, Guisborough, and Kirkham (Yorks.), and Kyme (Lincs.),
and the Gilbertine priors of Catley (Lincs.) and Chicksands (Beds.).

opinion, and authenticated written evidence. He demanded a new inquiry, following three days of fasting and prayer in all the houses of the Order, and he laid down that the depositions of the witnesses to the miracles, instead of being passed on by the prelates instructed to this end, should be taken down directly from the same witnesses under oath, and that some of them should be summoned to the Curia. The process was then taken in hand by the pope, who set up a new commission of inquiry; and the identical letters sent to the archbishop of Canterbury and the papal commissioners—Eustace, bishop of Ely, Acharius, abbot of Peterborough, and the abbot of Wardon (no. 23)—are a crucial document revealing a turning-point in canonical procedure, which was fully absorbed into the *Ordo iudiciarius*. It is a document all the more significant because addressed to the English church, already experienced in such cases.

Three other letters relate to the execution of the papal mandate. The archbishop and the papal commissioners passed it on to Roger, the Master, and the chapter at Sempringham, instructing them to produce the witnesses for the new inquiry, fixed for 26 September 1201 (no. 24). After the inquiry, Roger and the chapter sent the pope a letter accrediting the witnesses sent to the Curia, five canons of the Order (no. 25), who were accompanied by six laymen (p. 172), most of them beneficiaries of miracles. On the pope's instructions they were to take with them the report of the new inquiry, in the course of which some religious, some seculars, clerks and laymen, men and women, had appeared as witnesses, and their depositions were copied down. The representatives were accredited to certify the fact in the presence of the pope: no. 26, from the archbishop of Canterbury, the bishop of Ely, and the abbot of Peterborough.[1] We owe to this new inquiry the authenticated dossier of the miracles of St Gilbert (M1).

The process was completed by the solemn canonization on 11 January 1202.[2] The bull of canonization of 30 January describes the first investigation of the evidence and the new procedure. The pope ordered the archbishop to proceed to the translation of the saint's body and to prescribe the celebration of his feast in the province of Canterbury; he attached the text of the prayers which

---

[1] At the time of the inquiry, the abbot of Wardon was absent, attending the general chapter at Cîteaux, in accordance with the statutes of his Order.

[2] pp. 178-9.

he himself had composed in the honour of the new saint (no. 27).[1] As in the first phase, the author of the *Book* has carefully copied the documents executing the mandate: the archbishop instructed the Master and the chapter of the Order to celebrate the feast of St Gilbert, and announced that he was prepared to perform the translation (no. 28); to the bishops of the province he announced the canonization 'de consilio fratrum cardinalium', that is in consistory, and instructs them to celebrate the feast (no. 29); the mandate was presented by the bishop to the clergy of his diocese, for example, by John, bishop of Norwich (no. 31); and by the dean and chapter of Lincoln, since the see was still vacant, to the archdeacons of the see of Lincoln (no. 30). At the request of the brethren of the Order of Sempringham, made on 13 September 1202, Hubert Walter invited the bishops to join him at Sempringham on 13 October for the solemnity of the translation (no. 32); and the archdeacons of the see of Lincoln invited all the faithful under their care to join in the translation of St Gilbert (no. 33). The last document (no. 34) was addressed by the archbishop to all the faithful. After a brief description of the canonization and translation, he promulgated an indulgence of forty days 'de iniuncta penitentia', on prescribed conditions, for whoever went to pray, after confession, at the tomb of St Gilbert, in letters dated on the day of the translation, 13 October 1202.[2] To complete the file of documents, the dossier of the canonization included two collections of miracles, the first comprising the report of the inquiry.

The miracles

The procedure introduced by Innocent III aimed to record only the miracles worthy of credence, duly attested by witnesses under oath. This was the object of the first collection (M1). The name, status, place of origin, and condition of each person cured before and after the cure, and its manner, were all noted down. Similar details were given for the witnesses, identified by the marginal note, *testis*. The first collection, authenticated at Sempringham and at the Roman Curia, is undoubtedly more reliable than the second (M2), but this contains, besides brief, though precise,

---

[1] Cf. p. 252 with *Gilbertine rite*, ii. 26–7 (cf. i. 123–6).

[2] Any bishop is empowered to grant an indulgence of forty days: the additional 160 days noted in the record of the translation included indulgences granted by four other bishops present at the translation.

descriptions, two particularly circumstantial narratives: the case of Ralph of Attenborough, described in the letter from the parishes of Chilwell, Attenborough, and Bramcote, with mention of witnesses, a miracle which occurred while the papal commissioners were still gathered but after the end of their inquiry, and was certainly invoked at the Curia, since Ralph was one of the witnesses called to give evidence before the pope (M2, no. 15); and the cure of William of Bourne, whose illness had been duly attested by Ralph the sacrist on the night of the translation itself (M2, no. 23). The attestation has a modern ring: the canons of Sempringham acted with prudent care, demanding evidence both of the illness and of the cure, and only accepted certain cases, and insisted on a delay to put the miracles to the proof of time (M2, nos. 15, 22–3).

Both collections present a diversity of cures, benefiting all the strata of Anglo-Norman society which gravitated round Sempringham priory at the end of the twelfth century. Among those who were cured we meet canons and nuns, lay brethren, clerks and laymen; men and women, peasants and knights. The first collection includes fourteen men—three canons and one lay brother of the Order, one priest and one chaplain, three noblemen, five peasants—and eighteen women, of whom five were nuns and the rest local peasant women. The second collection includes six men—one canon, one doctor, one warden of the Hospital of Castle Donington, the vicar of the subprior of Sixhills, one clerk, and one of uncertain status—and five peasant women, including one lay sister. We also meet a crowd of witnesses, clerks and layfolk of both sexes, all identified and people of the neighbourhood. Of all these, the cured and the witnesses, some came from Gilbertine priories, Sempringham, Haverholme, Malton, Sixhills, Chicksands, and Catley; but far more from places within a few miles of Sempringham in Nottinghamshire, Lincolnshire, and Norfolk— Moulton, Anwick, Willoughby, Houghton, Threckingham, Folkingham, Pointon, Marston, Pickworth, Horbling, Quadring, Newark, Braceby, Cressey, Leasingham, Attenborough, Chilwell, Bramcote, Walcot, Bourne, King's Lynn—of which some, like Sempringham itself, have virtually disappeared. Sometimes a single family included several cured or a single village was the scene of several miracles.

The details demanded by the papal inquiry—or the narrator's interest, evident in the second collection—have given us lively

narratives in which the symptoms of the disease are noted and circumstances of the cure, the behaviour of the patients and their
feelings and those of their families. We see them suffer, fervently
pray, weep for joy, help each other to carry a sick person to Sempringham, chase a mad woman with a whip. We follow the frantic
sons whose demented mother had escaped across the fens of
Holland (M2, no. 26); the proud mother who showed her baby who
had just recovered his sight in the villages around (M2, no. 22); the
mother leading her daughters to the priory to seek a cure for her
husband (M1, no. 18); the stepfather who forces his wife to abandon her sick son (M2, no. 23). We learn of the remedies administered to the sick: at the hospital at Castle Donington, where they
were treated with herbs and roots (M2, no. 2), or in the infirmaries
of the Order, where massages and ointments were used (M1, nos.
15, 17; M2, no. 23)—or again in their families, where the nursing
was purely empirical.

Numerous and diverse were the kinds of illness or infirmity, or
the accidents described in the two collections. The deaf, the blind,
the deformed, the lame, those sick of a fever, in turn enjoyed relief
or cure: such were the clerk whose right leg and foot had withered
and shrivelled (M1, no. 1); the young girl whose hand was 'bent
back in the opposite direction to her arm' (M2, no. 16); the knight
who suffered from a swollen belly for two and a half years and who,
when he sat down, could scarcely see his thighs (M1, no. 18); the
doctor who could not shake off a tertian fever (M2, no. 2); the nun
who suffered from leprosy to the roots of her hair (M1, no. 15); the
nun who had a fish-bone stuck in her throat and the nun who had
dislocated her foot (M1, nos. 16, 17); the man made dumb by an
abscess in his throat (M1, no. 8); and the woman violently mad so
that she spat out bread and began to gnaw a stone (M2, no. 26).
Most of the time the remedies tried had remained without effect
and medical skill had proved ineffective.[1] The dislocated foot,
massaged then put in a plaster, had become as black as the nun's
veil, and the doctor saw no alternative but to amputate it. Beside
the physical cures were those of the mind: the mad recovered their
wits and repented of the violence and lunatic acts committed while

---

[1] Surviving evidence for physicians of *c.* 1200 is scarce for Lincolnshire as compared
with Yorkshire or Cambridgeshire: before 1183 one Walter is recorded in Lincs.: C. H.
Talbot and E. A. Hammond, *The Medical Practitioners in Medieval England: a Biographical
Register* (London, 1965), p. 364.

they were mentally ill (M1, nos. 20, 21; M2, no. 26). The forces of nature obeyed the saint: fever fled at his command (M1, no. 13); the storm abated, the waves subsided and a favourable breeze, after Master Gilbert's scapular had been lifted up while the ship was in passage, filled its sails and ensured a good crossing of the Channel to the Constable John of Chester and the knights in his company (M1, no. 19).

From the descriptions of the symptoms we cannot always diagnose the illnesses with certainty. There are accidents described,

TABLE 3. *St Gilbert's healing miracles*[a]

Illness	*Life*	M1	M2
Blindness and eye problems		3	5
Childbirth, problems with	2	1	
Constipation	1		
'Contraction'[b]		3	4
Deafness		2	3
Dropsy		2	1
Dysentery		1	
Fever	3	(2)	7
Gout	1	?1[c]	
'Leprosy'[d]		1	
Madness		2	1
Paralysis		4	3
Quinsy		1	1
Ulcer (*fistula*)	1	1	1

[a] The terms used to describe the illnesses cured by St Gilbert do not make a firm diagnosis possible in every case. This list is based upon the practical observations made by those who recorded the cures and follows categories established in Foreville, 'Miracula'. In addition tentative diagnoses may be suggested of angina (M1, 10), dislocated ankle (M1, 17), Parkinson's disease (M2, 15), and torticollis (M2, 18). Compare with this table St Thomas's list of cures: Foreville, 'Miracula', pp. 461–2; and cf. R. C. Finucane, *Miracles and Pilgrims* (London, 1977), chap. 4; for the general context, B. Ward, *Miracles and the Medieval Mind* (London, 1982).

[b] See p. civ.

[c] M1, 4: 'gout' here probably means stomach ache.

[d] The term 'leprosy' (M1, 15) was used to describe a variety of skin complaints.

and infirmities of sight and hearing, of childbirth, leprosy, various swellings and ulcers, phlebotomy, dropsy, paralysis, and dysentery; but a number of uncertainties remain in conditions of arms and legs—rheumatism, withering, and shrivelling, whose recurrence could be comparable to that of a fever. One might be tempted to think that this part of Lincolnshire was particularly unhealthy, with its pools and fens which may well have bred fevers, with a soil permanently humid favouring gout, rheumatism, and contraction (see Table 3). The various *contracti* present diverse symptoms; but a diagnosis has been made of the disease called 'St Anthony's fire', which was 'an endemic disease whose spread is favoured by damp and by all the factors which tend to spoil corn, since its basic cause is malnutrition . . .—a chronic illness leading to the loss of the limb attacked more often than to the patient's death'. As for its symptoms, they take two forms: 'convulsive ergotism or St Andrew's disease which consists above all of a muscular contraction, and gangrenous ergotism or St Anthony's disease properly so called, marked by a dry gangrene on feet and hands, leaving behind it infirmities more or less serious and often incurable'.[1] The Miracles of St Gilbert offer relevant examples of both forms of ergotism, and the second and apparently the less widespread was clearly described in the miracle entitled 'A withered clerk' (M1, no. 1). It is clear that poor folk, peasants, villeins, and day-labourers, were particularly prone to ergotism.

The sick person who prayed for cure by the intercession of St Gilbert of Sempringham usually had himself measured, and a candle was made ,ᶠ the same height.[2] Then he was carried to

---

[1] J. Morawski, *La Légende de S. Antoine ermite* (Poznań, 1939), pp. 173–4. The author of the *Magna Vita sancti Hugonis*, Adam of Eynsham, gives a vivid picture of the effects of St Anthony's fire, before and after healing, from a visit with St Hugh to the shrine of St Anthony in France (ed. D. Douie and D. H. Farmer, NMT, ii (1962, repr. OMT, 1985), pp. 159–60).

[2] The making of candles in this way is well attested in some parts of Normandy, especially at Savigny (Manche) at the shrines of Vitalis, Geoffrey, Haimon, Peter, and William, the 'saints of Savigny', and also at the shrine of St Thomas of Biville (Manche); other examples can be found in Burgundy and the Île de France. From 1357 a candle symbolizing the circumference of the city of Paris was offered at the altar of St Mary in the cathedral of Notre-Dame (L. Delisle, 'Notice sur une forme de vœux usitée en Normandie au moyen âge', *Mémoires de la Soc. nat. académique de Cherbourg*, xix (1912), 111–20). A similar offering of a candle by the barons of the town of Dover occurred every three years before St Thomas's feast on 7 July (BL Add. MS 59616, f. 9, from 'Customary of the Shrine of St Thomas' by John Vyel and Edmund Kyngyston', guardians, 1428). It took three years to burn.

Sempringham with his candle, and requested admission to the church of St Mary. The sick person approached the tomb of the founder from the outside by the canons' enclosure if he was a man, or the nuns' enclosure for a woman; and passed one or several nights in prayer, sometimes stretched out on the tomb, and commonly slept a restful and restorative sleep, often visited by a dream: the good Master of the Order appeared to the suppliant with the appearance of a venerable old man, or a pilgrim on his road, staff in hand, or a priest dressed in alb or chasuble, with consecrated hosts in his hand, or his right hand raised in blessing. He urged the sick person to arise. Then the person awoke and felt as it were a great internal rupture of the infirm limbs, or spat out a quantity of liquid. Sometimes the person was cured in the twinkling of an eye; sometimes he became convalescent and his strength revived little by little. If the miracle was striking, as when an infirm limb was restored to health or a notorious sickness healed, the canons sounded the bell and intoned the *Te Deum*; in other cases they ordered an enquiry and demanded proof of the time of the cure.

Other cures followed contact with an object which had belonged to Gilbert: a belt, a cloak, a sandal, a coverlet, a towel, a staff. The sick member was wrapped in it or touched by it, while some drops of holy water, which had been used to wash his body and had been most carefully preserved in phials, were poured into the patient's mouth or spread over the affected part of the body. The effect was instant: the fever departed, the swelling abated, the limb recovered its shape and strength, the flesh recovered its normal, healthy look.[1] Neither the illnesses nor the mode of cure varied from one collection of miracles to the other: in the first as in the second we find the use of objects belonging to the saint, venerated as relics and endowed with a kind of curative power on his intercession, or the use of 'the water of St Gilbert', or again the practice of incubation, that is to say of passing the night near the saint's tomb. At Sempringham this last practice was common and the patient was generally accompanied by a candle of his own height, which was set to burn beside the sick person. Sometimes the patient stayed awake and prayed, sometimes the patient slept and dreamt, and on awaking found that cure or convalescence had set in.

Incubation, as it was practised at Sempringham, could at first sight recall a pagan practice at the sanctuaries of healing gods or

[1] M1, nos. 5, 8, 10, 12, 14, 16–18, 25, 27, 29; M2, nos. 2, 3, 5.

heroes like Serapis, Amphiaraus, and Asclepius, at Athens and Epidaurus above all. We know that offerings of sacrificial animals accompanied pagan incubation, that the patient sometimes fasted, that the arrangement of lights and the incantations prepared the patient to dream.[1] We do not find an identical *mise en scène* at Sempringham, and the canons did not assume the role of priests of Asclepius, whose injunctions made up for the god's negligence by prescribing instructions and applying remedies. The patients at Sempringham were for the most part simple uneducated folk, peasants and villeins of the neighbouring villages. They brought their offerings and came to the tomb for a vigil of prayer, an essentially Christian practice deriving from the vigils of the primitive Church. At Sempringham none the less incubation wore almost the character of an institution: it appears in the account of a great number of miracles, and it was an almost ritual observance inspired by the form of veneration practised from early Christian times at the *confessiones* of the martyrs. For where would the intercession of the saint be more effectively sought than at the very place where his mortal relics lay? But it also extended to the objects he had touched, dead or alive, tangible intermediaries of the graces he had obtained, while incubation never appeared, in spite of its frequency, as a *sine qua non* for a cure. A number of patients were cured in their beds and only visited the tomb on a pilgrimage to give thanks.[2] This practice was perhaps less common, but it occurred at the shrines of other saints, for example at Canterbury at the tomb of St Thomas.[3]

Nor was incubation, as in pagan antiquity, the necessary condition of a favourable dream: it was not uncommon for the saint to appear or to be heard in what one takes to be the sick man's chamber (M2, nos. 10, 20, 25), or in open country, and to a third person, if the patient was not in full possession of his or her reason (M2, no. 26). Its function then was to incite the sick person to visit his tomb, or his relations to lead him or her there. Thus dream or

---

[1] On the practice of incubation in ancient Greece and Rome there is no real consensus: see J. Gessler, 'Notes sur l'incubation et ses survivances', *Mélanges Th. Lefort: Le Museon*, lix (1946), 661–70 and D. Mallardo, 'L'incubazione nella cristianità medioevale napoletana', *Mélanges Paul Peeters*, i = *Analecta Bollandiana*, lxvii (1949), 465–98. A good summary may be found in the notice 'Incubation' by Dom H. Leclercq, *DACL*, vii. 1 (1926), 511–17.

[2] M1, nos. 8, 18; M2, nos. 1–3, 10, 25.

[3] William of Canterbury, *MB*, i. 175, and Benedict of Peterborough, *MB*, ii. 208.

vision were not necessarily linked to incubation. Further, Gilbert's appearances were accompanied by visions of other saints, St Andrew, St Clement (M2, no. 6), the Blessed Virgin above all, whose mediation seems often to have been linked with his intercession (M1, nos. 6, 15). The dreams were also related to his priestly function: he was preparing to celebrate the eucharist or distribute communion, in this way inciting the patient to lift up his prayers to Christ whose servant Gilbert was (M1, nos. 17, 2). Such were the chief features of Christian incubation as practised at Sempringham. If it had given way to abuse or superstition, one imagines that it would have incurred an episcopal sanction, of which we have no record. Furthermore, the papal commissioners described the practice without any criticism, and the pope himself neither forbade nor condemned it, although its almost ritual frequency appeared very clearly in the sworn enquiry into the miracles. Such were the various methods of cure worked by the intercession of St Gilbert of Sempringham. They were not exempt from features of Christian marvels—nor did the miracles described, especially in the first collection whose authenticity was better established, fail to satisfy the criterion of proof of his sanctity.

The canonization process of Gilbert of Sempringham proves itself a model of its kind on various grounds. It was a process in two stages, the first traditional, the second according to the new method recently introduced by Innocent III, which required not only attestations, but actual witnesses of the life and miracles, ready to give their evidence under oath in the pope's presence, as in every case referred to Rome. The papal commission of enquiry was similar to the papal delegation to judges delegate *de ueritate inquirenda* set up after the case had been referred. Henceforward, the canonization process was related to the *ordo iudiciarius* currently set on foot by Innocent III, whose stages were minutely described in Innocent's letters. Gilbert's cause was also a model in the number and authenticity of the documents which have survived, in the care taken by their compiler to have them transcribed immediately after the canonization and to obtain the endorsement of the archbishop of Canterbury to the *Book of St Gilbert*. A third ground for calling it a model lies in the fact that neither before nor in the years immediately following the canonization of Gilbert of Sempringham does a comparable work seem

to have been undertaken, or at least preserved. On 21 April 1203 Pope Innocent III canonized Wulfstan, formerly bishop of Worcester: the bull of canonization reproduced that for Gilbert. True, besides the bull of canonization, the surviving dossier includes only two books of miracles, each provided with a prologue, of which the first gives an account of the revised procedure. The much earlier *Life* by William of Malmesbury was closely based on the Old English Life by Coleman, Wulfstan's chaplain; and the modern editor of these documents, R. R. Darlington, has admirably demonstrated the irregular nature of their arrangement. In 1220 the canonization of another English bishop, Hugh, bishop of Lincoln, showed that the procedure followed in 1201–2 remained in force under Honorius III. But the dossier—eighteen letters, including a report on the miracles and a short abridgement of the *Life*—is not comparable to that for Gilbert.[1]

We cannot doubt that England contributed much to the movement, virtually spontaneous, which in the course of the twelfth century brought to Rome the causes for canonization of the saints, by affirming the centralized jurisdiction of the pope. In return, it was also the kingdom which benefited most fully from this movement. In the space of half a century, between 1161 and 1203, England had received the record of four papal canonizations: Edward the Confessor, Thomas Becket, Gilbert of Sempringham, and Wulfstan of Worcester. Continuing this course, during the thirteenth century four new English saints were to be added to the liturgical calendar: Hugh, bishop of Lincoln, in 1220; William, archbishop of York, in 1227; Edmund Rich, archbishop of Canterbury, in 1246; Richard, bishop of Chichester, in 1262. In short, by the outcome of papal canonizations—as, at an earlier date, by translation by the bishops—the land of the English earned its title of 'the isle of the saints'.

Previous editions of the documents in the Book of St Gilbert

Did the various houses of the Gilbertine Order each possess a complete copy of the *Book*, or perhaps of the *Life* in some shape,

---

[1] *The Vita Wulfstani of William of Malmesbury*, ed. R. R. Darlington (Camden 3rd Series, xl, 1928), Introd., esp. pp. v, vii–x, and on the miracles, pp. xlv–lii; (D.) H. Farmer, 'The Canonization of St Hugh of Lincoln', *Lincs. Architectural and Archaeological Soc. Reports and Papers*, vi. 2 (1956), 86–117.

brief or full? The existence of the copy in Lh leads us to think that some at least treasured a full copy already in the thirteenth century.[1] It is not surprising that in course of time the lay brethren's dossier became separated from it or set apart within it—it figures as an appendix in Od—or that some documents fell out or were added, since the original interest related to the *Book* as a record of the canonization process, a record inspired by Hubert Walter,[2] who was himself concerned to preserve documents in his archives, but also aimed to preserve the memory and spread the cult of the founder within the fold of the Gilbertine Order itself. It is not surprising, furthermore, that in course of time the interest shown in details of places and persons faded, since they were no longer considered as proofs of sanctity, but valued rather as examples of it.

No catalogue of a Gilbertine library seems to survive, and the literary production of the Gilbertines appears very scanty. A manuscript at Oxford, once in the possession of the canons of Sempringham, contains parts of the Latin treatise of Maurice of Kirkham against the Salomites, who believed Mary Salome to have been a man (*c.* 1170–5).[3] Some four chapters of the Anglo-Norman tale 'La Lumière as Lais', which is supposed to have been written by Master Peter of Peckham, a black canon of Newstead who ended his life as a Gilbertine at Shouldham, figured in a beautiful late thirteenth-century manuscript in the Shouldham library, at a time when the house flourished, and contained nuns from such celebrated families as the Beauchamps and the Mortimers.[4] But Latin culture was in decline in the houses of nuns, as the Master of the Order acknowledged; and this helped to inspire Capgrave's *The Life of St Gilbert*.[5] In any

---

[1] From the regulation about exchange of books between the communities of nuns and canons, we learn that there were two libraries in the double houses (*Institutiones*, c. 5: *Monasticon*, vi. 2, p. xxxii* (xxi*)).

[2] For Hubert Walter's archives, see C. R. Cheney, *English Bishops' Chanceries 1100–1250* (Manchester, 1950), pp. 130–2; for the academic element in his entourage, Cheney, *Hubert Walter* (London, 1967), pp. 164–8.

[3] Oxford, Lincoln College (deposited in Bodl.) 27. There is a dedicatory letter to Master Gilbert. The treatise exists more fully in another Bodleian MS, Hatton 92 (15th c.): it is a refutation of this minor but curious heresy, and contains evidence of some knowledge of Hebrew in Gilbertine circles (M. R. James, 'The Salomites', *Journal of Theological Studies*, xxxv (1934), 287–97).

[4] M. D. Legge, 'La lumière as Lais. A Postscript', *Modern Language Review*, xlvi (1951), 191–5.

[5] Below, p. cxi.

case the Order's constitutions were reluctant to allow the nuns to use Latin.[1]

Only three manuscripts of the *Book*—unless others are found—have survived the centuries; and this was obviously due in part to the decay of the Gilbertine houses, which had become notorious at the end of the Middle Ages.[2] A sharp decline in numbers and in income from land carried with it also a decadence in culture and learning. The spoliation of the houses at the dissolution and the suppression of the Order in 1539 led to the dispersion, if not immediately to the destruction, of books exalting St Gilbert, a saint canonized at Rome. The spread of printing had not advanced so far as to compensate. It was without doubt the interest of the bibliophiles, such as Sir Kenelm Digby, which rescued the Oxford manuscript. Copies of the *Book* as a whole had little chance to survive the Gilbertine Order, since there was no diffusion of it outside the Order or the kingdom.

It was not until the revival of interest in the Middle Ages, inspired by the romantic movement, that large extracts from the *Life*, taken from Lc, were printed in 1830 in the revised edition of the *Monasticon Anglicanum*, in the form of a supplement between pp. 845 and 846, as a kind of introduction to the text of the 'Institutiones beati Gilberti et successorum eius . . .': *Monasticon Anglicanum*, ed. J. Caley, H. Ellis, B. Bandinel, vi. ii (London, 1830, repr. 1970), pp. v*–xxix*; edn. of 1846, pp. v*–xix*.[3]

In 1935 Dom David Knowles published in 'The Revolt of the Lay Brothers of Sempringham', *EHR* l. 465–97, at pp. 475–87, an edition of the letters of the bishops based on Od, except for nos. VII and XII which were taken from Lc (see above, pp. lxix, lxxxv).

R. Foreville, *Un procès de canonisation à l'aube du XIIIe siècle (1201–1202), Le Livre de saint Gilbert de Sempringham*, Paris, 1943, was an edition of the Prologue, the canonization documents—letters, collections of miracles, and, in an appendix, some unpublished fragments from the *Life*, some 'Visions and Revelations', and the letters concerning the revolt of the lay brethren, from Lc.

Thus three partial editions published over the course of a

---

[1] 'Omnino prohibemus Latinam linguam inter omnes nisi conueniens occasio compellat. Quae autem fecerit, disciplinetur in capitulo, uel in pane et aqua poeniteat' ('Institutiones ad moniales ordinis pertinentes', c. 25, *Monasticon*, vi. 2, p. lxxxii* (xlix*)).

[2] See above, p. xxxix.

[3] The edition of 1846 printed the insertion in double columns and fewer pages.

century, each justified by its own particular purpose, together
added up to a complete edition. These texts inspired various
studies listed in the Select Bibliography. But the notice by T. A.
Archer on 'Gilbert of Sempringham' in the *DNB*, which was
among the most widely read, shows how inexact was the knowledge of the manuscripts in the late nineteenth century. It was
based on Od and the *Monasticon*: Lc was misunderstood until the
edition of 1943, owing to an *a priori* judgement which proved
mistaken—in Archer's words that Lc 'as printed in the *Monasticon*,
... seems to be an abbreviated, or perhaps an earlier, form of this
biography', i.e. as it appears in Od.[1] Archer had only a superficial
knowledge of Lc.

Two collections of *Lectiones legendae* were printed in the *Acta
Sanctorum Bollandiana*: 'Vita auctore coaeuo ex antiqua historia
sanctorum' (9 *lectiones*), *Febr.* i. 570–1; 'Alia Vita ex MS. Rubeæ-
Vallis et Capgrauio' (7 *lectiones*), *Febr.* i. 572–3.

The ignorance of Latin of the Gilbertine nuns in the fifteenth
century is attested by John Capgrave's enterprise, to wit the translation into Middle English of the *Life of St Gilbert* at the request of
the Master of the Order, Nicholas Reysby, whom the author
addressed in the Prologue: '... made for the sake of the cloistered
women of your Order who have little understanding of Latin, so
that in their spare moments they may study in this book the great
virtues of their Founder. For here they may see as in a mirror how
they too may transfigure their souls just as did that model whom
they are to contemplate.'[2]

John Capgrave, *Life of St Gilbert*, was edited by J. J. Munro in
John Capgrave's Lives of St Augustine and St Gilbert of Sempringham,
Early English Text Society, London, 1910, pp. 61–142, based on
the author's autograph, BL Add. MS 36704, from King's Lynn
(Norfolk), the birthplace of Capgrave (1383–1464), and from the
Augustinian house there, where Capgrave was a friar, and later
prior. The manuscript carries a colophon with the date 1451: 'Thus
endeth the life of St Gilbert, translated into our mother tongue the
year of the incarnation of Our Lord Mccccli.'[3]

The translation by Capgrave was almost contemporary with—or
made very soon after—the making of Od. In each case the purpose

[1] *DNB*, xxi. 315–17, at p. 317.
[2] Paraphrase from *Life of St Gilbert*, p. 61.
[3] Ibid., p. 142, spelling modernized.

was evidently didactic, both in the moral and the spiritual orders. The author does not explain on what text he worked, save that he used a single manuscript which the Master of the Order entrusted to him. This manuscript has been identified by the editor with Lc, since certain passages, from c. 14 on, where Capgrave announces a second part of his work, were translated literally from the same text as Lc.[1] In fact the work draws on two different versions of the *Life of St Gilbert*: (1) a short Life, cc. 1–13, pp. 62–80, more developed than the 'lectiones legendae', but close to this genre; (2) a translation from the *Life*, amplified in certain particular ways, with etymologies, *exempla*, and comments which Capgrave in his Prologue explains and justifies. 'This is the preamble or eke the prologue of St Gilbert's Life, which Life I have taken on hand *to translate out of Latin right as I find before me*, save some *additions* will I put thereto which *men of the Order have told me*, and eke *other things that shall fall to my mind in the writing which be pertinent to the matter*.'[2]

The identification of the manuscript entrusted to Capgrave has been challenged by Jane Cowan Fredeman.[3] She supposes the existence of another branch of the Gilbertine tradition, different from but contemporary with Lc, and develops an argument based on this 'unknown manuscript'. The case is discussed in Appendix 9. The present edition and its apparatus should clarify this subsidiary question, as well as others of more moment.

The Gilbertine tradition has not hitherto been the object of a full study owing to the partial nature of earlier editions: sound criticism required a full text based on a codicological study and an analysis of the contents of the surviving manuscripts. Yet the interest of a new edition is not confined to that. As has been shown, the *Book of St Gilbert*, in the form transmitted in Lc, is not only a history of the founder and the first century of the Gilbertine Order: it is a precious document because it is unique in its overall character at such an early date as the opening of the thirteenth century. It was this special interest which led me first to publish in 1943 the collection of documents in the canonization dossier of Gilbert, a dossier still little known in spite of that edition, as witness the note by J. Shlafke: 'Cum textum bullae s. Gileberti non inuenerim, de hoc processu non tracto', *De competentia in causis*

---

[1] *Life of St Gilbert*, pp. ix, 80 ff., 156–9.
[2] Ibid., p. 62, spelling modernized; italics mine.
[3] 'John Capgrave's Life of St Gilbert of Sempringham', *BJRL*, lv (1972–3), 112–45.

sanctorum decernendi a primis post Christum natum saeculis usque ad annum 1234 (Rome, 1961), p. 90.

The present edition has been entirely recast to take its place in the Oxford Medieval Texts, and aims to satisfy the needs of scholars and to make available to scholars and students of the Middle Ages a full knowledge of a remarkable document.

LIBER SANCTI GILEBERTI

SIGLA

Lc	British Library, Cotton Cleopatra B. i, original reading
Lc^1	Corrections by the scribe
Lc^2	Early corrections by a second hand
Lc^3	Much later corrections
Lc corr.	is used when the author of the correction is uncertain
Lh	British Library, Harley 468
Od	Oxford, Bodleian Library, Digby 36
s.l.	Above the line

INCIPIT PROLOGVS DE VITA SANCTI GILEBERTI CONFESSORIS[a]

REVERENTISSIMO domino et patri in Christo Huberto, Dei gratia Cantuariensi archiepiscopo, tocius Anglie primati,[1] unus ex minimis fratribus ordinis sancti Gileberti Sempinghamensis, sanctorum meritis et premiis coequari.

Diuine gratie largitati tanto nouit, pater uenerande, prudentia uestra nos debere esse gratiores, quo minus meritis uberiores contulit usus gratiarum. Sicut enim cum gratiarum actione crescunt munera gratie, ita se priuat acceptis quisquis non pari commetitur honore donorum dignitatem, secundum illud: 'Omni habenti dabitur et habundabit, ei autem qui non habet et quod uidetur habere auferetur ab eo.'[2] Ad nos communiter, iudex serenissime, hanc arbitror spectare rationem, quos extremos tempore, exteros loco, presentes scilicet carne, Anglicos natione, ad equalitatem antiquorum deduxit nouissimos, orientalis orbis glorie coequauit diuina bonitas ab orbe fere remotos. Hec est summi patris Dei gratia et uenerabilium patronorum nostrorum, sanctorum scilicet, insule nostre gloria, quorum alios in omni gradu et utroque sexu martirii decorauit corona, alios uero fidei ueritas et uite sinceritas confessorum Christi sacro numero copulauit. Inter quos, diebus nostris, in regione nostra, post beati Thome | Cantuariensis martiris admiranda constantie exempla, habemus in beato Gileberto Sempinghamensi confessore amplectenda[b] zeli animarum rudimenta. In illo discimus quanti sit meriti animam propriam pro ouibus suis dare,[3] in isto nouimus quanta sit merces animas proximorum lucrifacere. In illo perpendimus quod nemo in seculo recte conuersatus a Deo sit derelictus, in isto uidemus quam gratum sit Deo holocaustum quilibet a seculo exclusus. In eo tenemus certum penitentie remedium

f. 33ᵛ (margin)

---

[a] So Lh; Lc has no contemporary title; Hic incipit prologus de uita sancti Gilleberti confessoris Od   [b] amplectenda Lc¹Od; amplectanda Lc

---

[1] Archbishop Hubert Walter: see above, pp. lxv, lxxi; C. R. Cheney, *Hubert Walter* (London, 1967); *EEA* iii, *Canterbury 1193–1205*, ed. C. R. Cheney (London, 1986).
[2] Matt. 25: 29 (and cf. Luke 19: 26 etc.).   [3] Cf. John 10: 11.

HERE BEGINS THE PROLOGUE TO THE LIFE OF ST GILBERT THE CONFESSOR

To the most venerable lord and father in Christ Hubert, by the grace of God archbishop of Canterbury, primate of all England,[1] one of the least of the brothers of the order of St Gilbert of Sempringham, [praying that he] be equalled to the merits and rewards of the saints.

Venerable father, you know in your wisdom that we ought to be the more grateful to the largesse of divine grace, the less we have deserved the rich benefits of grace it has conferred. For just as the gifts of grace grow with the giving of thanks, so he robs himself of what he has received who does not measure the value of gifts with honour equal to them, according to the saying 'To everyone who has shall be given and he shall have abundance, but from him who has not shall be taken away even what he seems to have'.[2] I think, serene judge, that this formula applies to all of us, late in time and furthest in place, present in the flesh and English by race, whom God in His goodness has led, though most recent, into equality with the ancients, making men all but cut off from the world equal to the glory of the eastern world. This glory of our isle is the grace bestowed by God our supreme father and by our holy patrons the saints; some of these, drawn from all ranks of life and from both the sexes, He has adorned with a martyr's crown, whilst others their true faith and pure lives have joined to the sacred number of Christ's confessors. Among them in our lifetime and in our country, following the wonderful example of steadfastness shown by the martyr St Thomas of Canterbury, we may appreciate in the confessor blessed Gilbert of Sempringham the essential lessons about the care of souls. From the former we learn how meritorious it is to give up one's life for one's flock;[3] from the latter we discover the great reward enjoyed by the man who wins the souls of those about him. From the one we become aware that no-one who lives a good life in this world can be abandoned by God; from this other we see how pleasing to God is the sacrifice made by any man who withdraws from the world. In one we perceive the sure remedy of

et debitam finalibus operibus remunerationem, in isto amplec-
timur perpetue iustitie et finalis perseuerantie retributionem. In
utroque ergo probamus quia, siue uiuimus siue morimur, Domini
sumus.[1] Vnde nulli est mirandum si tanta circa nos acta Dei
beneficia recognoscamus, et pro eis saltem uerborum relatione et
uilium menbrarum commendatione grati curemus existere,
cum ex eorum taciturnitate discrimen immineat ingratitudinis, et
in eorum reuelatione laus Dei et sanctorum decus, necnon et
hominum procuretur profectus. Ad exemplar enim posterorum
formauit Deus uitam priorum, et ad institutionem futurorum
manifestari iubet facta preteritorum.

    Vt autem gratia loquar sanctorum, legimus quidem et cotidie
pronuntiamus multorum actus et nomina sanctorum, quorum
f. 34 quidam licet non tantum forte ut sanctus iste | profecerint in
domo Domini, quia tamen in initio fidei et primitiue ecclesie
laborauerunt plantatione, laudem eorum nuntiat ecclesia, et
nomina eorum uiuent in seculum seculi.[2] Nunc autem etsi fidei
robore opus est, sine qua impossibile est placere Deo, quanta
utilitas consistit in moribus et operibus, 'cum fides sine operibus
mortua sit'![3] Et quidem quanta fuit in illis diebus necessitas
exemplis et firmitate fidei quam multi morte sua testati sunt,
tantum in his diebus malis, in hoc seculo nequam, credimus
expedire ad salutem opera fidei operantis per dilectionem,
quando multi non uerbis sed moribus fidei contradicunt, et
confitentes Christum factis negant.[4] Hoc perpendens sagax et
sollers circa salutem animarum sancta Romana ecclesia, cum
prius esset celebre martirum nomen, adiecit et confessorum
Christi uenerationem, quatinus qui documenta fidei acceperant a
martiribus, uite exempla sumerent a confessoribus, et qui initium
uirtutum per primogenitam fidem sortiti sunt, per finalem cari-
tatem consequerentur meritorum consummationem, licet tam in
his quam in illis fides et opera simul effulserint. Non enim hec
dixerim in suggillationem sanctorum qui per fidem uenerunt ad
opera, et supra firmam petram fundati[5] fidelis uite munus
martirium acceperunt.

[1] Rom. 14: 8.
[2] Cf. Ps. 21: 27 (22: 26).
[3] Cf. Jas. 2: 20.
[4] Cf. Titus 1: 16.
[5] Cf. Matt. 7: 25.

penitence and the reward earned by a man's last acts; in the other we understand the recompense for being always just and for persevering to the end. Thus in both men we receive proof that we belong to the Lord whether we live or die.[1] No one should marvel, then, if we acknowledge the great works which God has performed about us and if we take care to remain grateful for them, at the very least putting them into words and committing them to humble parchment. To keep silent about them would be to invite the risk of ingratitude; to reveal them is to secure not only the praise of God and the honour of His saints but also the profit of mankind. For God has made the life of those who come before to be an example to those who come afterwards, and He commands proclamation of the deeds of past generations for the instruction of those yet to come.

I hope I may speak with the favour of the saints. We read, and indeed recite daily, the deeds and names of many saints. Although some did not achieve as much in the house of the Lord as this saint of ours, nevertheless the Church proclaims their praise and their names will live throughout eternity:[2] for they laboured at the very beginning of our faith, at the first founding of the Church. But now, although we need a firm faith—without which it is impossible to please God—especial value is attached to a man's conduct and to his actions, 'since faith without works is dead'.[3] Indeed just as at that time there was urgent need of good examples and strong faith, to which many testified by their death, so in these evil days of our wicked age, when many men contradict their faith not in what they say but in the way they lead their lives and by their actions deny the Christ whom they confess,[4] we believe that it is the works of a faith acting through love which brings us to salvation. The holy Church of Rome realizes this and takes wise and prudent measures for the salvation of souls; for although the title of martyr was famous in early days, this Church added the veneration of Christ's confessors, so that those who had learnt from the martyrs the articles of faith might be shown by the confessors how to live, and those who gained an entry into virtue aided by the early stirring of faith within them might at the end obtain perfect merit through love. However, in both martyrs and confessors faith and works were equally conspicuous. For I do not say this to insult the saints who came through faith to works and, resting upon a firm rock,[5] received martyrdom as the reward of a faithful life.

f. 34ᵛ Hic autem uir Domini, etsi | martyris nomen et gradum proprii sanguinis effusione in ecclesia militante non meruerit, confessorum tamen Domini uestigiis adherens, a numero sanctorum in ecclesia triumphante non creditur exclusus: quippe qui fidei specular et exemplar iustitie tanquam lucerna luxit in hoc loco caliginoso, donec illuscescat dies futuri seculi;[1] cuius quasi in aurore crepusculo, ita in huius noctis extremis temporibus, teste beato Gregorio, 'tam multa de sanctis clarescunt ut apertis reuelationibus atque ostensionibus uenturum seculum inferre se nobis atque aperire uideatur'.[2] Quo enim, ut ait idem doctor, mundi finis urget, eo necesse est ut uiui lapides in edificium celestis Ierusalem colligantur.[3] Cum tamen lateant et pateant hodieque multi qui etiam in seculari conuersatione Deo placiti inuenti sunt, et relicti sunt infiniti qui non curuauerunt genua ante Baal,[4] non asserimus singulis sollemnem deberi in ecclesia honorem, cum sufficere uideantur ad fidem et bonos mores astruendos tot exempla precedentium; sed, ut ait Leo papa, 'propriam sibi uenerationis obsequio uendicant dignitatem qui ecclesiam Dei et documentis pre ceteris erexerunt et patrociniis adiuuerunt'.[5] Quis, queso, post

f. 35 antiquos patres ecclesiam Dei ita in hoc tempore nutantem | tam sane predicando tantum erexit, cum in forma serui euangelici exiit in uicos et plateas ciuitatis, et quoscumque inuenit compulit intrare in domum Domini?[6] Quis eam tot patrociniis adiuuit, cum quicquid de patrimonio suo habere potuit, primo largitus, tot eam diuitiis ex suis iustis acquestibus accumulauit, tot ei propugnatores prestituit? Vnde, etsi signa que fecit non fecisset, facientibus tamen plerisqueᵃ impar non fuisset, 'uiteᵇ namque', ut ait sanctus Gregorius, 'uera estimatio in uirtute est operum, non in ostensione signorum'.[7] Verum, licet 'segnius irritent animum demissa per aurem, quam que sunt oculis subiecta fidelibus',[8] mira tamen et miserabili cecitate quidam obuoluti sunt: cum dictis et gestis ueterum sanctorum, que uel quos nunquam uiderunt, tantam ut

---

ᵃ plurimis que Lc (but see Greg. Dial. i. 12)   ᵇ uite Lc³Od, Greg.; unde Lc

---

[1] Cf. 2 Pet. 1: 19.
[2] Gregory, Dial. iv. 43 (ed. de Vogüé, iii. 154–5), put in the mouth of Petrus.
[3] Cf. Rev. 21: 2, 10–11.
[4] Cf. Rom. 11: 4.
[5] Pseudo-Leo I, Sermo xiii. 1, PL lix. 501 (also attributed to Augustine, Maximus, and Leander of Seville; cf. B. de Gaiffier in Analecta Bollandiana, lxvii (1949), 280–6; Clavis Patrum Latinorum, ed. E. Dekkers and A. Gaar² (Bruges, 1961), no. 1185; we owe these references to Professor Henry Chadwick).   [6] Cf. Luke 14: 21.

This man of God did not earn the title and rank of martyr by shedding his own blood in the Church Militant; but because he followed closely the footsteps of those who confessed Our Lord we do not believe he is excluded from the number of saints in the Church Triumphant; as a model of faith and pattern of justice he shone like a lamp of righteousness in this dark place until the day dawns of the age to come;[1] as in the half-light of dawn, so in the last hours of this night 'so much is revealed about the saints', according to St Gregory's testimony, 'that by clear signs and revelations the approaching age is seen to open and come upon us';[2] and because the end of the world is hard upon us, as the same doctor says, living stones must be gathered to build the heavenly Jerusalem.[3] But although many appear and disappear today who have been found pleasing to God even in their conduct in the world, and there are countless left who have not bowed the knee before Baal,[4] we do not urge that solemn reverence should be paid in the Church to each one of these, because there are so many earlier examples which are clearly sufficient to support the faith and right living; but in Pope Leo's words, 'those who more than any others have raised God's church with their instruction and assisted it with their patronage deserve the dignity offered to them in the service of veneration'.[5] Who, I ask you, since the fathers of antiquity has with his sound preaching so raised the church of God as it wavers at this time, when like the servant in the gospel he went out into the highways and byways of the city and compelled whomsoever he found to enter the house of the Lord?[6] Who assisted the Church with such generosity, when he first bestowed upon it all that he could secure from his own patrimony; who lavished upon it all he had from his lawful gains; who established so many to defend it? Thus even if he had not performed the miracles which he did, he would have been a match for most who accomplished them, for as St Gregory says 'a true assessment can be made from the character of a man's deeds, not from the manifestation of signs'.[7] But although 'what comes in through the ear is less effective in stirring the mind than what is put before our faithful eyes',[8] some men are wrapped in an amazing and pitiable form of blindness. While quite properly they accept and venerate the things which saints of past ages said and did—which they never witnessed any more than they saw the saints themselves—yet although they saw for themselves the most holy

[7] Gregory, *Dial.* I: 12, ed. cit. ii. 116–17. [8] Horace, *Ars Poetica*, 180–1.

decet habeant fidem et deferant honorem, huius sancti quem in
carne uiderunt uitam sanctissimam conspexerunt, facta mirifica
contuentur, tot et tantorum testium uoces audiunt, summi pontificis et sancte Romane ecclesie auctoritatem susceperunt, operibus
derogant, laudatoribus contradicunt, uenerationi resistunt. Vnde
hoc nisi quia excecauit eos malitia eorum, 'habundat iniquitas et
refrigescit caritas?'[1] Reliquerunt 'prophetam sine honore in patria
f. 35ᵛ   sua',[2] cum multi extranei et ignoti, fama eius | excitati, tam magni-
fice eum predicant, tam frequenter adeunt, tam deuote honorant.

Ego igitur hec attendens, licet aliquamdiu prohibuisset imperitia sermonis et uerecundia minoris etatis, ad nutum tamen uenerabilis patris nostri Rogeri, et ex hortatu karissimi fratris nostri
Albini canonici,[3] silentibus doctioribus, manum apposui ad scrib-
endum, et que ipse noueram, uel que a plenius noscentibus
didiceram, scribere cepi, et textum uite ipsius, quem primo excellentie uestre quasi breuiatumᵃ porrexeram, qualibuscumque
uerbis exaraui. Sane processu temporis, cum in ecclesia Sem-
pinghamensi ubi sanctus requiescit ministrarem, multa ibi insignia
uidi, plura audiui, que pro mei negotiatione talenti antescriptis
adieci,[4] uestreque deuotioni quam erga ipsum sanctum satis inten-
sam probaueram, prout a uiro in theologia eruditissimo magistro
Willelmo, Lincolniensi ecclesie cancellario,[5] et multis aliis peritis
emendata sunt et commendata, sicut iussistis, transmitto. In
quibus tota conuersatio eius a puero et monasteriorum fundatio, et
in uita sua gesta miracula, obitusque finis,ᵇ prout hic enumerantur,
f. 36 | describuntur. Deinde ordo canonizationis eius apud Romanam
curiam facte et translationis a uobis sollemnissime ut nostis celebrate, cum epistolis tam in uita quam post mortem eius causa
ipsiusᶜ directis, et cum miraculis post eius obitum patratis adiciun-
tur. Lectiones etiam ex hac legenda summatim excerptasᵈ et in
sollemnitatibus eius legendas huic opusculo inserui. Responsoria
uero et antiphonas de eo canendas ex canonica scriptura utriusque
Testamenti passim prout ei sententie que de aliquo alio nondum

---

ᵃ breuiarium Od (rightly?)   ᵇ One expects eius or suus (Winterbottom)
ᶜ causa ipsius Lc³Od; causasius Lc   ᵈ exceptas Lc

---

[1] Cf. Matt. 24: 12.   [2] Cf. Matt. 15: 37.
[3] For Roger, Master of the Order from 1178; formally so 1189–1204, see above, p. xxv
and below, esp. pp. 280–1 (dates in Heads, p. 204, corrected by C. R. Cheney, Medieval
Texts and Studies (Oxford, 1973), pp. 45–8). For Albinus, see pp. 316–17.
[4] Cf. Matt. 25: 14–30.
[5] Master William de Montibus, from before 1194 to 1213 (Fasti, iii. 16–17; H. Mac-

life of this saint of ours, whom they observed in the flesh, although they see his wonderful deeds and hear evidence from many important witnesses, although they have received the authoritative judgement of the pope and the holy church of Rome, still they detract from what he did, contradict those who praise him, and oppose his veneration. It can only be that their malice has blinded them, 'iniquity abounds and love grows cold'.[1] They have left 'the prophet without honour in his own country'[2] at a time when many foreigners and strangers, stirred by his fame, are lavishing such praise upon him, coming so frequently to this place and honouring him so devoutly.

With this in mind, although my inexperience in literary matters and the modesty of youth held me back for some while, I have nevertheless applied my hand to the task of writing at the request of our venerable father Roger and at the persuasion of our dear brother canon Albinus,[3] since those who are more learned remain silent. I began to copy down what I myself knew or had learnt from those better acquainted with the facts, and I have written as best I can the text of this man's life, which I first offered to your excellency in a rather abbreviated form. For as time went by, while I was serving in the church of Sempringham, where the saint lies, I saw many remarkable things and heard of even more, which, to make proper use of my talent,[4] I have added to what I wrote before. Since I have discovered that in your piety you are zealous for our saint, according to your instructions I am sending you this, corrected and commended by the very learned theologian Master William, chancellor of Lincoln,[5] and by many other experts. Here are described all his way of life from childhood days, the foundation of religious houses, the miracles performed during his lifetime, and his eventual death, in that order. Then follows the procedure at the Roman curia for his canonization and his translation, which you recall you celebrated with solemn pomp, together with letters sent in his cause both during his lifetime and after he died, and a description of miracles performed after his death. I have also put in this little work lessons extracted and summarized from this account which are to be read upon his feast-day. My purpose has been, with God's help, to extract for future use from various parts of the canonical writing of both Testaments responses and

Kinnon in *Essays in Medieval History presented to Bertie Wilkinson*, ed. T. A. Sandquist and M. R. Powicke (Toronto, 1969), pp. 32–45.

cantantur congruerint, Deo dante, in posterum excerpere proposui. Quibus igitur minus uidetur a recto quod hic dicitur, si qua desunt suppleant, quibus amplius superflua tollant, quibus male precor ut corrigant, quibus bene non michi sed Deo[a] mecum gratias agant.

EXPLICIT PROLOGVS. INCIPIVNT CAPITVLA

[*ff. 36ᵛ—37ʳ contain a table of contents of the Vita: see pp. lxv, lxvii.*]

f. 37   INCIPIT VITA SANCTI GILEBERTI CONFESSORIS

f. 37ᵛ Oriens splendor iustitie, qui illuminat omnem hominem uenientem in hunc mundum[1] et ad agnitionem sui nominis uult uenire, orbis occidui partes occiduas nouis lucis sue[b] radiis tempore occiduo illustrauit. Cuius iubare celitus inmisso, uelut infusum sydus ethereum fulsit sub noctis nostre tenebris uir uite admirabilis nomine Gilebertus, qui electus Dei famulus in Anglie partibus, loco qui dicitur Sempingham, spectabili, quod solet et debet esse incitamentum uirtutum, prosapia genitus, prerogatiua morum genus uicit et seculum. Pater eius Iocelinus nomine, miles strenuus et uir bonus et opulentus, Neustrigena natione, plures habens possessiones in partibus prouintie Lincolnie; mater uero ortu Anglica, a parentibus fidelibus[c] inferioris tamen conditionis originem trahens. In medio populi sui habitantes[2] totam suam progeniem tanti filii illustrarunt generatione, cuius future magnitudinis gloria tali, ut fertur, reuelata est matri eius inditio.[d] Nam priusquam infans nasceretur, uisum est ei in somnis quod quasi descendentem a supernis lunam suscepisset in synum: hoc nimirum presignante, ut post claruit uisione, prolem illam tanquam lucernam mundi a f. 38 Deo paratam | assiduis in posterum profecturam incrementis. Scintilula etenim prius latens in cinere super candelabrum posita magnum luminare emicuit ad lucendum omnibus qui in domo Dei sunt.[3] Nec inmerito lune comparauit eum Spiritus Domini, quia

---

[a] deo *Lc³Od; om. Lc*   [b] sue *Lc³Od;* sui *Lc*   [c] *ins.* non *Lc³*   [d] inditio *LcOd;* uel presagio *s.l. Lc¹*

[1] Cf. Mal. 4: 2; John 1: 9.
[2] Cf. 4 Kgs. (2 Kgs.) 4: 13.
[3] Cf. Matt. 5: 15.

antiphons to be sung concerning him, ensuring that the sentences were appropriate for him and are not yet sung for any other person. Those who consider that what I have said here does less than justice to the subject I ask to supply whatever is necessary; those who consider it too long, I ask to remove unnecessary additions; those who consider it badly written, I beg to correct it; those who consider it well written I pray to offer thanks not to me but, with me, to God.

HERE ENDS THE PROLOGUE. THE CHAPTERS BEGIN

[1] HERE BEGINS THE LIFE OF ST GILBERT THE CONFESSOR

The glory of righteousness arises and lights every man who comes into this world[1] and wishes him to come to knowledge of His name; at its setting it has cast rays of new brilliance upon the western lands of the western world. When its radiance had been cast into our midst from on high, there shone in the darkness of our night like a heavenly star brought among us a man of exemplary life called Gilbert. Chosen to be God's servant in the land of England, he was born in a place called Sempringham of a distinguished family (something that usually and properly acts as an encouragement to virtue); but by the special nature of his life this man overcame both the world and his worldly origin. His father was called Jocelin; he was a worthy knight as well as a virtuous and wealthy man: a Norman, who owned many properties scattered throughout Lincolnshire. But his mother was English by birth, of parents who were faithful folk but came from an inferior rank. As they dwelt amongst their people[2] they brought fame to the whole of their line by begetting a wonderful son. According to tradition, the glory of his future greatness was revealed to his mother by a sign. Before the child was born she dreamt that the moon seemed to come down from the heavens and she received it in her womb; without doubt this vision foretold what later became clear, that the child would thereafter steadily increase and become great like a light for the world established by God. For the spark which first lies amongst the ashes, when placed upon a candlestick, shines with great brilliance to give light to all who are in God's house.[3] With justice did the Lord's spirit compare this man to the moon. As

menbrum ecclesie que est luna perfecta in eternum in principio sui quasi modice forme apparuit, sed inter mundanas uarietates mutuato a sole Christo lumine, post alterna detrimenta eternis[a] proficiens augmentis, tandem decidit in synum matris diuine pietatis ac deinde susceptus est in secreta requie Ierusalem superne matris. Nempe in primeuo sui tempore, sicut etate, ita notitia et uirtute modicus, adeo erat abiectus in domo patris, ut nobis narrare consueuerat, quod nec famuli domus dignarentur cum eo cybum sumere. Porro corporali scemate incompositus et incultus, nulla que adhuc emineret redemit uitium exterioris deformitatis animi uirtute. Erat tamen intrinsecus latens, in bono scilicet eximie nature, quicquid postmodum, adueniente gratia, esse poterat uel fuit in maiori etate, tanquam lampas contempta apud cogitationem[b] diuitum parata in tempus statutum.[1] Sic Dominus superne gratie, non humane efficatie, suarum uolens attribui dona uirtutum, 'pauperem facit et ditat, humiliat et sub-

f. 38ᵛ leuat, suscitans | de puluere egenum et de stercore erigens pauperem ut sedeat cum principibus et solium glorie teneat'.[2] Sic educit nubes ab extremo terre, qui uocat ea que non sunt tanquam ea que sunt, infirma mundi eligens ut fortia queque confundat.[3]

2. De adolescentia eius

Igitur non sine dispositione diuina, cuius melior est misericordia super uitas, in etate paruula traditus est litteris eo quod, ut credi fas est, in hoc uiuendi genere ampliora bona ex hoc uase electionis et armario Spiritus Sancti fuerant proferenda.[4] In primis tamen segniter usus et exiliter institutus est rudimentis puerilis doctrine, quoniam cum deterreret teneros annos labor discendi, qui grauius solet affligere pueros, modicum adhibuit ei cura parentum iuuamen ad disciplinam donec uehementer correptus a suis super inertia sua, pudore nescio an timore, patriam suam deserens in Galliarum se transposuit regiones; ubi dum esset in se reuersus, cepit euacuare que erant paruuli,[5] et pristinam exuens socordiam institit sollicite arti litteratorie non tamen multa suffultus amicorum stipe.

---

[a] eternis *LcOd;* uel felicibus *s.l. Lc*[1]   [b] cogitaciones *Od (as Job 12: 5)*

[1] Cf. Job 12: 5.   [2] 1 Kgs. (1 Sam.) 2: 7–8.
[3] Cf. Ps. 134 (135): 7; Rom. 4: 17; 1 Cor. 1: 27.
[4] Cf. Ps. 62: 4 (63: 3); Acts 9: 15.   [5] Cf. 1 Cor. 13: 11.

a member of the church which is the perfect moon to all eternity, he appeared at his beginning in somewhat humble guise; but borrowing light from Christ our sun, amid the changes of this world, after alternate wanings grew bigger in things eternal until at last he sank into the womb of our mother holy piety and was then received into the secret rest of Jerusalem our heavenly mother. To tell the truth, at his earliest period he was as modestly endowed with distinction and virtue as with age, and occupied such a lowly position in his father's house that, as he used to tell us, even the household servants refused to eat with him. In addition his bodily form was misshapen and disfigured, and no greatness of soul had yet emerged to redeem the misfortune of his external deformity. But there lay hiding within, in the goodness of his excellent nature, whatever he was able to be or was afterwards when grace was bestowed upon him as he grew older, like a lamp despised in the thoughts of the wealthy but prepared against a certain hour.[1] Thus, since the Lord wishes the gifts of His virtue to be attributed not to human abilities but to His heavenly grace, 'He impoverishes and enriches, humbles and raises up, lifting the poor man from the dust and the beggar from the dunghill that he may sit among princes and occupy the throne of glory.'[2] Thus He who summons what does not exist in the same way as that which does draws the clouds from the end of the earth, choosing the weak vessels of the world to confound those that are stronger.[3]

2. *His youth*

And so by Divine Providence, whose pity is better than life, he was destined for study whilst still very young; for, as we are right to believe, in this type of career larger benefits were to be brought forth from this chosen vessel and receptacle of the Holy Spirit.[4] However, at first he made slow progress and was inadequately instructed in the rudiments of elementary education; although the difficulty in learning, which often hampers boys seriously, deterred one of his tender years, his parents' attention served only as a modest encouragement to this discipline until he was sternly rebuked by those about him for his laziness and, either through shame or fear, he fled from his own country and crossed to France. Whilst there he came to his senses, put away childish things,[5] and throwing off his former indifference applied himself earnestly to literary skills, supported by meagre gifts from his friends.

Adolescens autem bone spei in scola uirtutum[1] didicit maturius morum disciplinam, et cuius postea erat magister cepit mox tocius f. 39 honestatis fieri discipulus. | Institutus est itaque tam diu liberalibus et spiritualibus studiis donec magistri nomen mereretur et gradum. Sane quoniam mores ornant scientiam et sine uirtute uidua est omnis sapientia, studuit liberali[a] scientie maritare disciplinam probatissime uite; inmunis siquidem ab his quas ministrat mundus uitiorum illecebris, iam tunc quendam religionis, ad quam aspirauit, respirauit odorem. Illa nempe etate, qua iuxta quod[b] corpus corruptibile aggrauat animam,[2] estus feruentior libidinum grauius depascit corda mortalium, in qua etiam pugna plerumque succumbunt seniores et docti, ille uas suum ita Domino sanctificabat[3] ut magisterio spiritus intus cohibente nec ingenite cederet carnalitati nec exteriores expleret uoluptates. Nam nec illum tetigisse mulierem ab ineunte etate usque ad finem uite quisquam unquam audiuit: iam tunc martyr effectus, holocaustum se Domino exhibebat, unde factum est ut quia se mundum seruauit, ferre uasa Domini usque ad centesimum uite annum mereretur,[4] et quia grauius adolescentie certamen superauerat ad forcius infirmioris sexus regimen haut inmerito postmodum assumptus est.

3. *Qualiter rexit scolas*

Reuersus denique a Galliis ad natale solum, de talento scientie f. 39ᵛ quod | copiosius acceperat negociari cepit et tradidit illud pueris et puellis prouincialibus, ex quibus reportauit postea maximum lucrum ad mensam Domini sui.[5] Hii sunt enim primitiui illi in quibus fundatus est ordo de Sempingham, quos adhuc seculares,[c] et ipse habitu secularis, non modo scolaribus[d] rudimentis sed et moralibus et monasticis instituit disciplinis, ita quod pueros a iocandi et uagandi libertate cohercitos cogeret secundum statuta monasteriorum silere in ecclesia, cubitare simul quasi in dormitorio, non nisi locis statutis loqui et legere, et alia

---

ᵃ litterali *Od*   ᵇ quod *om. Lc; placed by Od after* corruptibile   ᶜ secularis *Lc*
ᵈ scolaribus *Lc;* secularibus *Lc*³*Od*

[1] No specific source identified.
[2] Cf. Wisd. 9: 15.
[3] Cf. 1 Thess. 4: 4.
[4] Cf. Isa. 52: 11; and see pp. 124–5, etc.
[5] Cf. Matt. 25: 14–20.

As a youth of promise, he soon came to learn disciplined behaviour in the school of virtues,[1] and soon began to be a pupil in
complete integrity, of which he was later a master. Thus for a long
period he received instruction in liberal and spiritual studies until
he achieved the name and rank of master. And because knowledge
is embellished by proper conduct and all wisdom is empty without
virtue, he endeavoured to unite to knowledge of the arts the rigour
of a most upright life; for, being free from the snares and vices
offered by the world, even at that time he gave off a whiff of the religious life to which he aspired. He was, indeed, at the age when,
because the body, which perishes, oppresses the soul,[2] the growing
heat of sensual desire consumes mortal hearts to their increasing
danger. But while many older and well-educated persons succumb
in the struggle, this man sanctified his vessel unto the Lord[3] so
completely that the spirit exercised mastery and control within
him and he neither yielded to the desires implanted in his flesh nor
tasted the delights proffered by the world outside. For no one has
ever heard that he touched a woman, from his youth to the end of
his life; already a martyr, he offered himself as a sacrifice unto the
Lord. And so it happened that because he kept himself clean, he
was found worthy to bear the vessels of the Lord until the
hundredth year of his life;[4] and because he had overcome the
serious conflict of youth he was later deservedly raised to the firm
direction of the weaker sex.

3. *How he governed his school*

Having at last returned from France to the country where he was
born, he began to do business with the talent of knowledge which
he had received in such abundance; he distributed it amongst the
boys and girls of the countryside, who afterwards supplied him
with the large profit which in turn he brought back to his Lord's
table.[5] These are the pioneers on whom the Order of Sempringham was founded; whilst himself clothed in secular dress, he
taught them as seculars not merely the rudiments of learning but
also moral and monastic discipline. Thus he forbade the boys to
jest and wander about at will, and following the rules of religious
communities he compelled them to keep silence in church, to
sleep together as if they were in a dormitory, to talk and read only
in places where this was allowed, and to practise other things

honeste uite experiri insignia. Hoc enim erat ei a puerilibus annis summum studium, hic labor continuus, hec indefessa sollicitudo, quod in uirtutibus estimatur optimum, animas scilicet lucrifacere Deo et quibuscumque poterat uerbo et opere proficere et exemplo. Ipse uero inmaculatum se custodiens ab hoc seculo,[1] semper honestis et spiritualibus negociis se tenuit occupatum.

Habitu tantum et fronte populo conueniens, intus habuit omnia dissimilia: preciosis et nitidis secundum natalium suorum dignitatem utens indumentis, ducens cultum in contemptum, usum pocius et formam eorum quantum potuit ad humilitatis modum conuertit. Iusticie et ueritatis amator, castitatis et | sobrietatis ceterarumque uirtutum sedulus cultor, enituit: propter que uenerabilis et laudabilis omnibus factus, omnium sibi fauorem comparauit et gratiam. Sed et pater ipsius super probitate filii admodum gauisus, paterno cepit iuuenem confouere affectu et de propriis diuitiis ministrauit ei necessariorum sufficientiam. Demum ad uacantes ecclesias parrochiales de Sempingham et de Tiringtona, in suo dominio fundatas,[2] ex more patrie personam illum episcopo loci presentauit, licet, ut aiunt, renitentem, sed ut tueretur iura patris in eisdem ecclesiis uix consentientem: ad quas legitime admissus est et canonice institutus. Post multos autem et molestos causarum conflictus, quas ei intenderant aduersarii nitentes tollere patri patronatum et sibi personatum, tandem pacifice possidens ecclesiasticum beneficium, satis suum exsoluit pro officio debitum, tam mistice quam materiali congruum exhibens ecclesie ministerium.

4. *Qualiter rexit ecclesias*

Mansionem habens in atrio ecclesie beati Andree de Sempingham,[3] solus cum capellano uite probate, Galfrido nomine, et ipse uitam satis duxit laudabilem. Prius enim apud quendam patremfamilias simul hospitati sunt in uilla. Sed cum super forma filie hospitis, que eis sedulo ministrauit, occulta utrique surreperet contagio, uisum est | Gileberto in somnis quod manum suam in synum predicte puelle iniecisset, nec inde eam extrahere posset; quod somnium uehementer expauescens uir castissimus, ne forte, ut est humana fragilitas, futurum fornicationis crimen portenderet,

---

[1] Cf. Jas. 1: 27.   [2] See p. xviii.   [3] See p. xix.

characteristic of a good life. From his childhood his chief study, his unceasing labour, and his unwearying concern was—what is reckoned the highest of virtues to gain souls for God and to help whomsoever he could by word, by deed, and by example. And so, keeping himself unspotted from this world,[1] he busied himself always with holy and spiritual matters.

He conformed to other people only in dress and appearance, for inside everything was different from them. Thus while he wore the costly and elegant clothes befitting the dignity of his birth, he thought fashionable garments contemptible, and as far as he could he altered their use and shape to a modest style. He became famous for his love of justice and truth and for his persistent fostering of chastity, sobriety, and the other virtues; hence everyone thought him worthy of reverence and praise, and he won for himself the grace and favour of all. His father, too, rejoiced wholeheartedly in his son's upright character, began to cherish the young man with fatherly affection, and provided him with a competency from his own wealth. Finally he presented him, following the custom of the country, to the local bishop, as rector of the vacant parish churches of Sempringham and Torrington, which were built upon his demesne.[2] It is said that his son opposed him in this but reluctantly agreed in order to ensure that his father's rights in these churches were preserved. He was lawfully admitted to the churches and instituted in accordance with canon law. When, after many troublesome lawsuits which his enemies brought against him in the hope of depriving his father of his right of patronage and himself of his rectories, he at last occupied his ecclesiastical benefice in peace, he fully discharged his obligations, giving proper service to the church both in its spiritual and its material sphere.

4. *How he looked after his churches*

He occupied a dwelling in the churchyard of St Andrew's at Sempringham,[3] and with a chaplain of proven virtue called Geoffrey he too led a solitary and commendable existence. Earlier they had both lodged with a family in the town. But a hidden infection stole upon them both from the beauty of the daughter of the household, who looked after them attentively; for Gilbert dreamt that he put his hand into this girl's bosom and was unable to draw it out. The most chaste of men was terrified that, human frailty being what it is, his dream foretold a sin of fornication,

confestim suam sacerdoti exposuit cum somnio temptationem. Cui ille itidem eadem se fatigari molestia confessus est, unde consilium apostoli sequentes[1] uelocius se ab illo hospitio remouerunt et in cymiterio ecclesie domum sibi edificauerunt, in qua, postposita frequentia uici, semper circa ecclesiam pariter commorati sunt. Veruntamen hec somnii uisio non futuri peccati sed gloriosi meriti fuit prefiguratio; hec enim uirgo postmodum una erat de septem illis primitiuis in quibus idem pater inchoauit tocius ordinis sui congregationes. In cuius synum quasi in secretum et requiem ecclesie, cuius fuit fundamentum, manum inmisit pastor et amicus diligentissimus, nec auelli poterat quia ad edificandum ei bone conscientie et perpetue pacis archanum totam operationem suam et uirtutem ministrauit, nec ab eius sollicitudine uiuus erui poterat

f. 41 nec a protectione defunctus. | Igitur in ecclesia sacris meditationibus assiduus familie dominice tritici mensuram, tanquam fidelis dispensator et prudens,[2] instanter erogauit. Et auditores suos ita instructos reddidit ut magna ex parte regulam monastice uite seruarent etiam seculares. Enimuero a comessationibus et impudicitiis, a spectaculis et potationibus publicis abstracti, opera misericordie exercere et ecclesiasticos census rite persoluere didicerunt.[3] Nam quocumque[a] basilicam intrassent, discerni poterant a ceteris parochianis[b] de Sempingham per orationum deuotionem et inclinationum humiliationem, quas eos docuerat prelatus eorum Gilebertus.

Quoniam autem uulneribus saucii nunc uinum nunc oleum infundere debet Samaritanus, qui interpretatur custos, studuit pro loco et tempore medicus iste animarum utroque uti genere medicamenti.[4] Quam seuerus enim extiterit in corripiendo rebelles, sicut iustis, mitibus et subditis mansuetum se exhibuit in exhortando, docet unum ex factis eius, quod non pro miraculo sed pro recti operis ponimus exemplo. Quidam ex parochianis suis fraudem fecerat de decimis frugum suarum in collectione earum, et quas in partes ecclesie debuerat sequestrasse, cum reliquo blado domum

f. 41ᵛ allatas | reposuit in horreo suo, propriis usibus profuturas. Quod ut nouit rector ecclesie, concito compulit rusticum illum totum

---

[a] Probably quandocumque *(Winterbottom)* or quotienscumque *(Holford-Strevens)*
[b] parochianis *Brooke;* parochiani *LcOd*

[1] Possibly 'fugite fornicationem', 1 Cor. 6: 18?
[2] Cf. Luke 12: 42.   [3] Cf. Rom. 13: 13.
[4] Cf. Luke 10: 34.

and so he immediately described his temptation and dream to the
priest. In his turn this man confessed to him that he was being
affected by the same trouble. Accordingly, following the apostle's
advice,[1] they speedily left those lodgings and built a house for
themselves in the churchyard. Here, remote from the village
crowds, they dwelt with one another, always staying close to the
church. But what he saw in his dream heralded not future sin but
glorious merit, for this girl was later one of the seven original
persons with whom the father founded the communities of his
whole Order. Her bosom into which our pastor and assiduous
friend put his hand was like the mysterious peace of the church, of
which he was a foundation. And his hand could not be torn away
because he directed all his endeavours and his strength towards
constructing for the church a secret refuge of true innocence and
everlasting peace, and could no more be prevented from looking
after it whilst alive than from protecting it after his death. Thus he
was constant in holy meditations within the church and yet
promptly issued the measure of corn to the Lord's household like a
loyal and prudent steward.[2] He imparted such instruction to those
who heard him that to a large extent even seculars observed the
rule of monastic life. For when he had drawn them away from
rioting and from wantonness, from evil displays and from public
drinking-bouts, they learnt to perform works of mercy and scrupulously to pay church dues.[3] Whenever(?) they entered church they
could be distinguished from the other parishioners of Sempringham by their devoutness at prayer and humble bows, taught
them by Gilbert, their religious superior.

Just as the Samaritan, whom we interpret to mean a protector,
must pour wine on one occasion and oil on another upon the
wounds of an injured man, so this doctor of souls endeavoured to
employ both types of treatment as time and place required.[4] We
cite one of the things he did, not as a miracle but as an example of a
proper course of action, for it illustrates how strict he was in
chastening those who rebelled, just as he showed himself mild in
encouragement to the righteous, gentle, and submissive. One of
his parishioners cheated him of his tithes of produce as they were
being collected, and the amount which he should have put aside
for the Church he carried home with the rest of the corn and put
in his barn for his own use. When the rector of the church discovered this he immediately forced the peasant to throw all of his

bladum suum ex grangia eicere et per singulos manipulos coram se numerare. Quorum totam decimam partem, que sibi et ecclesie uidebatur competere, in unum aceruum congestam*a* in media platea uici, accenso rogo, fecit consumi, in detestationem utique tanti criminis et ad terrorem aliorum, arbitrans indignum cedere in usus hominum quod Deo et sancte ecclesie furtiue fuerat sublatum. Erat enim uir magnanimus et rerum dispendia paruipendens dummodo equitatis ordo et iura ecclesiastica seruarentur illesa.*b*

5. Qualiter conuersatus est in curia Alexandri episcopi

Interim accessit ad obsequium diocesani sui pontificis, Roberti uidelicet cognomento Bloet, Lincolniensis episcopi, in cuius domo primo clericus ministrauit; deinde, post decessum ipsius, in curia Alexandri successoris eius sine querela conuersatus est.[1] Bonum enim iudicauit sub episcopali regimine degere et episcopum se semper intendentem intendere quam, more acephalorum, huc illucque dissoluta libertate discurrere. Sed licet curie

f. 42 implicaretur inquietudine, nunquam tamen | pretermisit officium pastoralis cure. Quin pocius sui[2] primo et precipue agens sollicitudinem, quicquid de debitis redditibus uel annuis pensis aliisue iustis acquestibus habere poterat, totum, preter stipendia uite, que tamen ex ecclesia de Sempingham consecutus est (nam de illa de Tiringtona nichil in suos usus conuertit), in sumptus pauperum seruauit et dedit. Cumque proprio abesset hospicio circa episcopum commoratus, Deum in eo suscepit et retinuit hospitem in orphanis et uiduis,[3] senibus, egris et debilibus, quos propriis agriculturis et ecclesiarum obuentionibus aluit et uestiuit.

Quanta autem ferueret in eo erga Deum dilectio, qui precepta caritatis ita seruauit ad proximos, testatur crebra orationum instantia et frequens in precibus mentis deuotio. Nam quamuis uita et moribus oraret omni hora, quandocumque potuit secreto furabatur orandi horas. Hoc autem fecit non motis tantum ut plerique labiis, nec corde in diuersa disperso, sed mente cum

---

a congestam Winterbottom; congestum LcOd   *b* illesa om. Lc

[1] See p. xix. Alexander succeeded Robert Bloet in 1123 (Fasti, iii. 1–2).
[2] The construction is not entirely clear, but sui seems to be for eius.
[3] Cf. Matthew 25: 35 (as cited in Reg. S. Benedicti, c. 53. 1); Jas. 1: 27. For 'Deum . . . hospitem . . .' cf. Thesaurus Linguae Latinae s.v. hospes, col. 3027, l. 13.

corn out of the store and measure it out before him handful by handful. A whole tenth of this, which clearly belonged to himself and his church, he caused to be heaped in one pile in the middle of the village street, set alight, and burnt, to show his utter hatred of such a crime and to inspire fear within others. For he considered it improper that what had been stolen in secret from God and His holy Church should go to men's use. He was a high-minded man who set little store by loss, so long as natural justice and ecclesiastical law were preserved intact.

5. *How he conducted himself in the household of Bishop Alexander*

After a while he entered the service of his diocesan, Robert surnamed Bloet, bishop of Lincoln, in whose household he first served as a clerk. Later, after Bishop Robert died, he lived blamelessly in the court of his successor, Alexander.[1] For he considered it wise to live under the rule of the bishop and to attend to one who always attended to him, rather than running hither and thither with unbridled licence like men who acknowledge no authority. But although he was involved in the turmoil of the household he never neglected the obligation of his pastoral office. Far from it. Rather it was his[2] primary and particular concern, so that he kept and gave to relieve the poor all that he could draw on from the rents owed to him, from yearly payments, and other lawful sources of income, apart from the payment of his living expenses, which he obtained, however, from the church of Sempringham, spending none of the revenue from the church of Torrington upon himself. When he was away from his own dwelling in attendance upon the bishop, he received and retained God as a guest in his house, in the shape of orphans and widows,[3] the elderly, the sick, and the feeble, whom he fed and clothed from his own farms and from the income of his churches.

His frequent resort to prayer and the concentration which he always showed in his devotions illustrate the great love for God which burnt in this man, who observed so scrupulously the commands of charity towards his neighbours. For although his life and behaviour was a prayer offered at all hours, he stole opportunities for secret prayer whenever he could. And this he performed not like most people just with movements of the lips, nor with his mind set on other matters; by raising his thoughts as well

manibus et oculis in superna erecta, tunsione pectoris et genuflexione, interioris hominis desiderium indicauit. Ad quod probandum aliqua ponantur exempli gratia. Inuitauit aliquotiens unum de con-
f. 42ᵛ decurionibus suis clericum ad orationem: | qui cum starent pariter ante gradus altaris decantantes psalmos Dauid, ubicunque occurrit nomen Domini uel Dei uel si quid tale in psalmo, ad prolationem dictionis humi stratus genuflexit Gilebertus. Ad cuius exemplum cum idem faceret clericus, id tam diu egit donec adeo fessus factus est ut iuraret se numquam amplius cum eo oraturum. Alio tempore cum quidam episcopus, a domino suo susceptus hospitio, in camera episcopi ubi Gilebertus de more dormiebat iaceret uigilans, uidit idem episcopus, in pariete opposito ad lumen lucerne, effigiem hominis per totam noctem nunc ascendentem nunc descendentem in umbra, et ignorans quid esset, putans autem fantasma esse, in magnum incidit mentis stuporem. Inuestigans tamen diligentius quid hoc esset, inuenit uirum Dei ante suum grabatum stantem et orantem, et manus sursum genua deorsum crebro ponentem deprehendit. Quod mane facto referens episcopus arguit iocose hospitem suum quia saltatorem haberet in thalamo, qui eum nocte preterita ita terruerat. Hec ideo ponimus in exemplum quia, sicut quandoque suis protestatus est, magis dum esset in curia quam postea ieiuniis, |
f. 43 uigiliis et orationibus ceterisque spiritualibus exerciciis corpus suum edomabat. Vt enim sui referunt domestici, arguit quandoque se ipsum quia magis ante conuersionem quam post conuersionem corpus suum afflixerat, cum tamen post susceptum sancte religionis habitum satis sue uideretur carni aduersari. Si quid tamen talium minus peregisset quando positus custos in uineis uineam suam non itaᵃ custodiuit,[1] hoc non torpori et negligentie sed necessarie et caritatiue rei familiaris occupationi est imputandum, cum et beato Martino ⟨non⟩ᵇ minorem post episcopatum quam ante episcopatum fuisse uirtutem legatur.

6. *Quod primo clericus*[2] *ordinatus est*

Quoniam igitur in sortem Domini uocatus est et dispensator domus Dei constitutus, consensit ecclesiasticorum ordinum insignibus signari, ubi singulis officiis, quantum humana permittit fragilitas,

---

ᵃ *ins.* districte *Od, perhaps rightly (cf. pp. 30 and 40 below)*   ᵇ *non* Brooke: *see n. 1.*

[1] Cf. S. of S. 1: 5; for what follows, Sulpicius Severus, *Vita S. Martini*, ed. J. Fontaine, i (Sources Chrétiennes, Paris, 1967), p. 282: '*Nec* minorem . . . uirtutem edidit'.
[2] i.e. not as a regular canon.

as his hands and eyes to heaven, by beating his breast, by kneeling, he revealed the longings of the inner man. Examples may be quoted to prove this. Several times he invited one of his fellow clerks to pray with him. They stood together before the altar-steps chanting the psalms of David; and whenever they came to the name of the Lord or of God or some similar reference in the psalm, upon mention of the word Gilbert knelt and prostrated himself upon the ground. Following his example, the clerk made the same obeisance; Gilbert did this for a long while until the clerk grew so weary that he swore he would never pray with Gilbert again. Another time, another bishop accepted hospitality from his master. As he lay awake in the room belonging to the bishop where Gilbert usually slept, he saw on the wall facing the light from the lamp the shape of a man in shadow alternately rising and falling all night long. Not knowing what it was but thinking it an apparition, he was struck with amazement and horror. However, when he investigated this phenomenon more carefully, he discovered our man of God standing praying in front of his couch, and he observed him frequently raising his hands and kneeling down. When morning came the bishop related what had happened, and laughingly accused his host of keeping a dancer in his chamber, who had given him such a fright during the previous night. We cite these cases to exemplify what Gilbert once said to his followers: that he used to subdue his body more strenuously with fasting, vigils, prayers, and other spiritual exercises while he was in the bishop's court than later on. As those of his household tell, on occasion he accused himself of having scourged his body more before his entry into the religious life than afterwards, although after he took the habit of holy religion he seems to have been by no means negligent in warring against the flesh. But if he engaged in fewer of these practices when, after being made keeper of the vineyards, he did not guard his vine as before,[1] we must attribute this not to laziness or negligence but to a necessary and charitable preoccupation with household affairs; in the same way we read that no less virtue resided in St Martin after he became a bishop than before.

6. *How first he entered ecclesiastical orders as a clerk* [2]

When he was summoned to share Our Lord's calling and was appointed a steward of God's house, he agreed to be marked with the signs of ecclesiastical orders. As far as human frailty allows he

se coequauit et, crescente dignitate graduum, creuit et sanctitas uite. Dignum sibi inuenit, immo preparauit Spiritus Sanctus in eo habitaculum, ut manifestum esset ipsum cum caractere rem percepisse sacramenti. Illi enim, ut testatur auctoritas,[1] in

f. 43ᵛ quorum mentibus diffusa est septiformis | gratia Spiritus Sancti, cum ad ecclesiasticos ordines accedunt, in ipsa spiritualis gradus promotione ampliorem gratiam percipere creduntur. Hunc itaque Dei ministrum ex digno digniorem et ex sancto effecit[a] sacrum collatum sanctiorem. Vestis illi non lasciua sed moderata et clericalis, cibus sobrius et potus parcus, corona patens et tonsura conueniens, modestia in uerbis, grauitas in incessu, ut iam tunc non clericus secularis sed canonicus regularis putari potuisset.

7. *Quod presbiter inuitus factus est*

Talem ergo tantumque uirum cum fama admirata aduerteret, quod cognouerat de eo circumquaque diffudit et aput aures omnium sanctum et sapientem predicauit. Ipsi quoque presuli, cuius uenerat uitam imitari, factus est norma et exemplar iustitie, et ex discipulo factus[b] magister in uia morum pontem fecit pontifici. Quocirca attendens pontifex eius prudentiam simul et iustitiam, dignum duxit et necessarium claues ei committere ligandi et soluendi,[2] eo quod per sanctitatem posset et per discretionem nosset iudicium ecclesie rationabiliter excercere; uoluitque illum tam suorum quam tocius populi delic-

f. 44 torum iudicem ac conscium constituere. Quod factum est: | cui tamen rei uehementer obnitebatur uir sanctus, tanto sacramento se reputans indignum et in accepto gradu stare nimis arduum arbitrans fore. Considerauit enim misterii magnitudinem, ministerii[c] dignitatem, humane actionis inperfectionem, percepti muneris reddendam rationem, et quam periculosum sit constitui mediatorem qui opus habet intercessore. Considerauit sacramentorum altitudinem, quam qui nanciscitur uel utitur indigne se facit inferiorem. Ab altiori semper nociuior est ruina,

---

[a] efficit *Lc*　　　[b] *ins.* est *Lc*　　　[c] misterii *Lc*

---

[1] Cf. Isa. 11: 2–3.
[2] Cf. Matt. 16: 19.

was equal to each office in turn, and as the dignity of the orders increased so did the sanctity of his life. The Holy Spirit found, indeed prepared for Itself, a worthy habitation in him, so that all might see that this man had received the substance of the sacrament along with its indelible seal. For we have it on authority[1] that, when those in whose minds is shed the sevenfold blessing of the Holy Spirit approach ecclesiastical orders, they are understood to receive greater outpourings of grace as they proceed through the spiritual grades. And so the sacrament conferred made of this worthy servant of God an even worthier one and of this holy man one yet holier. His dress was not luxurious but moderate and suitable for a clerk; he ate temperately and drank sparingly; he kept the crown of his head bare and was properly tonsured; he displayed modesty in speech and dignity in his gait; so that even at that time he could have been taken not for a secular clerk but a regular canon.

7. How he was made a priest against his will

As admiring fame took notice of his qualities and his greatness, it spread abroad in every place what it had learned about him and in the hearing of all pronounced him holy and wise. For the bishop, too, whose life he had come to emulate, he became the pattern and exemplar of righteousness, so that from being a disciple he became a master and on the road of good conduct he made a bridge for his pontiff's benefit. Therefore, having regard to both his wisdom and his integrity the bishop thought it proper and necessary to make over to Gilbert the keys of binding and of loosing,[2] for he had the ability derived from his holiness and the knowledge bestowed by his prudence to exercise judgement over the church in a responsible fashion. He also wished to appoint Gilbert to discover and judge both his own sins and those of all his people. And so it happened: but the holy man forcefully objected to this course of action, for he considered himself unworthy of such a great sacrament, and thought that it would be extremely difficult to live up to his order once he had accepted it. He meditated upon the greatness of the mystery and the dignity of the ministry, the imperfections of human deeds, the reckoning to be made for the gift received; he realized how dangerous it is for someone to be appointed a mediator who himself needs someone to intercede for him. He bore in mind the high office of the sacraments: anyone who obtains or uses it improperly makes himself inferior. The higher one's position the worse one's downfall,

et quod delictum uidetur in gradu infimo, crimen iudicatur in summo. Aggrauat enim culpam gradus eminentior, et prerogatiua ordinis presumptorem deicit eleuatum; copiosiorique debito obligatur copiosius mutuans, et cum fenore exigit quod commodat Dominus.[1]

Attamen uidens preses ecclesie utilitatem et persone gratiam, pie nolenti piam intulit uiolentiam, et iuxta exemplum beatorum Valerii et Epiphanii, licet inuitum, presbiterum ordinauit.[2] Honus autem impositum, quia sic oportuit, pie tulit, quia reuerentia que honorem fugiendum dictauit, eadem persuasit esse amplectendum pro obedientia. Sic suam agnouit infirmitatem, sed prepositi preposuit | uoluntatem, qui subditorum sepe solet melius nosse qualitatem. Sic et in hoc quod uoluit[a] et in hoc quod noluit[a] utrobique meruit, quia nolle eius pretendit reuerentiam, uelle autem pretulit obedientiam. Sic centurio, Domini presentia se estimans indignum, laudatur et Zacheus, eundem hospitio suscipiens, benedicitur; Petrus autem, dum se peccatorem fatetur miraculum expauescens piscium, Christum repellit et uituperatur; Iudas uero, quia irreuerenter sumere non timuit, condemnatur.[3]

8. *Quantum spreuit diuitias seculi*

Factus ergo presbiter pristinis spiritalibus excercitiis adiecit instantiam, maturior in moribus, crebrior in doctrina, efficatior in exemplis, ut tam nominis quam officii sui non uoce sed uita loqueretur interpretationem: ut qui non nosset auditu posset uisu uerum Domini cognoscere sacerdotem. Ita transcensis septem gradibus altaris, septem donis diuini doni donatum demonstrauit caritas nunquam ociosa. Quoniam igitur inchoatio bonorum est contemptus malorum,[4] et uitiorum abiectio uirtutum solet esse excercitatio, prius studuit se inmaculatum ab hoc seculo custodire, ut quicquid post ageret religionem mundam et immaculatam Deo deferret. | Spreuit se suaque cum mundo, ut abiectis impedimentis

f. 44ᵛ (margin note beside "posuit")

f. 45 (margin note beside "deferret")

---

[a] *Od reverses the words, perhaps rightly (note the order of* nolle . . . uelle)

[1] Cf. Matt. 25: 14–28.
[2] St Valerius was the bishop of Hippo who compelled St Augustine to take priestly orders, and St Epiphanius did likewise with St Jerome's brother (Posidonius, *Vita Aug.* 4; Augustine, *Sermo* 335. 1. 2, *PL* xxxix. 1569–70; St Jerome, *Lettres*, ed. J. Labourt, ii (Paris, 1951), no. 51). We owe the substance of this note to Professor R. A. Markus.
[3] Cf. Luke 7: 6–7; 19: 1–10; 5: 8; Matt. 27: 3–5, 26: 69–75, etc.; John 14: 26.
[4] Not identified.

and what seems a fault in the lowest rank is judged a crime in the highest. A greater status carries with it increased blame and the exercise of higher orders casts down the man who presumes on his elevation; the more freely a man borrows, the greater the debt by which he is bound, and the Lord demands what he lends with interest.[1]

Yet when the bishop observed how valuable he would be to the church and what grace resided in his person, he brought pious force to bear against his pious reluctance, and he ordained Gilbert priest after the example of St Valerius and St Epiphanius although it was against his wishes.[2] When the burden had been laid upon him he bore it dutifully as was right and proper; because the same reverence which led him to shun the honour persuaded him to embrace it out of obedience. Thus he acknowledged his weakness but set above this the will of his superior, for a superior often knows the worth of his subjects better than they. Thus both in what he wished and in what he did not wish he was equally meritorious, because his unwillingness showed his reverence, his willingness his obedience. Thus the centurion who holds himself unworthy of Our Lord's presence is praised, and Zacchaeus who receives Him into his house is blessed; but Peter, in confessing himself a sinner when he trembles at the miracle of the fish, rejects Christ and incurs censure; and Judas, because he was not afraid to take (the sop) irreverently, is condemned.[3]

8. *How he spurned worldly wealth*

After he was made a priest he gave himself more urgently to the spiritual exercises which he had engaged in before; he became more mature in conduct, more constant in teaching, more effective in setting an example, so that he expounded the meaning both of his title and his office not just by what he said but by the way he lived: thus whoever did not know by listening could recognize with his own eyes a true priest of God. When he had climbed the seven steps to the altar, his untiring exercise of charity showed that he had been endowed with the sevenfold gift of God. Because the beginning of virtue is the despising of evil,[4] and to shun vice is normally to perform good works, he tried first to keep himself unstained by the world so that whatever he did later might offer to God pure and spotless worship. He spurned himself and what belonged to him, together with this world, in order that, having

expeditus posset sequi crucifixum. Spreuit dico, quoniam etsi mundialibus usus est propter uite necessitatem, postposuit omnem superfluitatem et herentem habendi cupiditatem. Accepit uiaticum tanquam peregrinus in uia, nec subsidium uie computauit premium patrie.[1] Quantum satis esse iudicauit satisfecit nature, ut quod ipse reliquerat alteri posset esse supplementum indigentie.

Hinc est quod cum quidam archidiaconatus ecclesie Lincolniensis opibus et honoribus prepollens ei fuisset oblatus, noluit recipere, dicens non se nosse aliam promtiorem et paratiorem uiam esse ad interitum.[2] Viam dixit non causam sed occasionem, quoniam non cogit administratio peccare, sed difficile est absque peccato huiusmodi administrare. Bonum est ministerium ecclesie et utile bene ministranti, sed pauci sunt qui causas agunt causa animarum, multi uero causa pecuniarum. Timuit ergo ne augmentum culparum foret incrementum diuitiarum, et si plus sumeret de fonte pecunie non posset quandoque saciari ex situla[a] auaritie. Maluitque paucas animas quibus preerat bene procurare quam f. 45[v] multis commissis | non posse quod debuit impendere. Sane quia iustitie pars[b] est mala uitare, profectus autem bona perpetrare, et non sufficit aliena non rapere uel appetere nisi studeamus nostra largiri, studuit sollicite uerus sacerdos ligna cotidie subicere sacro igni qui ardebat in tabernaculo pectoris sui, in quo et se ipsum cremauit Domino holocaustum.[3] Ad hoc autem non ceca presumptione nec inconsideratis motibus utebatur, sed quia meritorum summam uoluit apprehendere, quis modus melior, que uia uerior esset ad perfectionem diligenter inuestigauit, et eam arripuit. Primum ergo operationis fundamentum huius iecit in alto humilitatis, que est proprie excellentie contemptus, cuius locus in summo celorum est. Omnium itaque terrenorum, que[c] falso

---

[a] situla *LcOd;* uel calice *s.l. Lc*[1]   [b] *Perhaps* prima pars *(Winterbottom)*
[c] que *Lc*[2]*Od;* qui *Lc*

---

[1] i.e. all for his personal use; but the meaning of 'patrie' is far from clear. A possible rendering is '. . . and did not count his support for the road as his prize' or 'as an augmentation of his patrimony'.

[2] Cf. John of Salisbury, *Letters*, ii, no. 140. It is odd that the *Vita* seems to make Gilbert a priest at the time when he was invited to become archdeacon, since archdeacons were normally deacons at this date; but this passage may not be in chronological order (see C. N. L. Brooke in D. Greenway, C. Holdsworth, and J. Sayers, *Tradition and Change: Essays in Honour of M. Chibnall* (Cambridge, 1985), pp. 1–19 at pp. 3–4). The archdeaconry was presumably that of Lincoln itself, perhaps offered to Gilbert when William of Bayeux succeeded, before *c.* 1132 (see *Fasti*, iii. 24–5): there was not a possible vacancy at Huntingdon or Oxford, nor a likely one at Northampton, but there

cast away all hindrances, he might be free to follow the crucified Christ. I say 'spurned' because, although he made use of worldly things where they were necessary to life, he put behind him every excess and persistent desire for possessions. He took his travelling-allowance like a pilgrim on his journey, and did not count the reward he had at home as meant for his support on the road.[1] What he judged sufficient satisfied his nature, so that what he had left might supply another's need.

It was for this reason that when he was offered a certain arch-deaconry belonging to the church of Lincoln which surpassed others in wealth and distinction, he refused to accept it, saying that he knew of no more apt or handy path to ruin.[2] By 'path' he meant occasion rather than cause: it is not that taking up a responsibility makes sin inescapable, but that it is difficult to perform this kind of responsibility without sinning. Service to the Church is useful and beneficial to the man who performs it well, but there are few who plead to save men's souls and many who do so to make money. He feared that the access of wealth would increase his share of blame, and that if he drew more from the well of riches the time would come when he would not be satisfied out of the bucket of avarice. Moreover, he preferred to take good care of the few souls under his authority rather than fail to do what he should for great numbers entrusted to his charge. To shun what is evil is a (? the first) part of righteousness, but to do good is a mark of progress, and it is not enough to avoid seizing or coveting things which belong to others if we do not study how to spend generously what is our own. For this reason our true priest strove manfully every day to cast wood upon the holy fire burning in the tabernacle of his breast, where he burnt himself as an offering unto the Lord.[3] He was motivated in this not by blind presumptuousness or by any unconsidered impulses; because he wished to attain the highest merit he patiently investigated which was the better method, which the truer path to perfection, and then pursued it. The first foundation of this endeavour he laid in profound humility: this signifies contempt of one's own good qualities, and it occupies a place in the highest heaven. Thus, along with pride at his inner goodness, he excised the substance of all those earthly possessions which are wrongly

are other possibilities among the archdeaconries of the diocese of Lincoln—and according to Henry of Huntingdon, a man named Gilbert actually held the arch-deaconry of Buckingham in the early 12th c. (see *Fasti*, iii. 39).   [3] Cf. Gen. 22: 13.

excellentes et uere deiectos faciunt, amputauit materiam cum interiorum bonorum extollentia, uocem Domini audiens: 'si uis perfectus esse, uade et uende omnia que habes, et da pauperibus, et ueni sequere me.'[1] Dispersit ergo, dedit pauperibus non respectu uanitatis sed intentione caritatis, unde et iustitia eius manet in seculum seculi.[2] Cumque propria decreuisset communicare pauperibus, tales elegit pauperes quorum paupertas f. 46 timore Dei pariter et amore esset ho|nestata,[a] ut seminans in benedictionibus de benedictionibus et meteret.[3]

9. De exordio ordinis de Sempingham et inclusione monialium

Erant tempore illo, regnante in Anglia Henrico primo, ut idem ait in libro quem de constructione scripsit monasteriorum,[4] puelle quedam seculares in uilla de Sempingham, quarum mentes semen uerbi Dei, quod ipse eis sepius ministrauerat, susceperant et iam albe ad messem et rore et calore germinabant.[5] Hee sexum cum seculo uincere cupientes celesti sponso sine impedimento optabant adherere. Quod uidens sanctus Gilebertus, Dei caritate plenus, cum pretaxatas ecclesias de Sempingham et de Tiringtona diuino cultui mancipare et sua egenis largiri disposuisset, cum non inueniret uiros qui tam districte uellent pro Deo uiuere, in usus talium sua omnia conferre dignum duxit que uere pauperes spiritu et sibi et ceteris possent celorum regnum uendicare.[6] Fecit ergo sibi amicos de mammona iniquitatis qui eum in eterna reciperent tabernacula.[7] Non tamen mares primo sibi fecit amicos, sed mulieres ad congaudendum de dragma inuenta conuocauit amicas,[8] que multos ei postea in sua castitate genuerunt amicos. Infirmioribus autem libentius benefaciendum et compatientis f. 46ᵛ nature | ratio dictat et consilium admonet diuinum, et merces uberior inde speratur. Virginum uero fructus est centesimus, ideo propter earum statum conseruandum sua relinquens centuplum recepit et uitam eternam possidet.[9] Preterea recto ordine dandi sua iustis contulit secundum illud: 'Da bonis et ne receperis

---

[a] honesta *Lc*

---

[1] Matt. 19: 21.   [2] Cf. Ps. 111 (112): 9; 110 (111): 3.
[3] Cf. 2 Cor. 9: 6.   [4] See pp. 78–81.
[5] Cf. Matt. 13: 3–23, etc.; John 4: 35.   [6] Cf. Matt. 5: 3.
[7] Cf. Luke 16: 9.   [8] Cf. Luke 15: 9.
[9] Cf. Matt. 19: 16, 29.

held to distinguish men when in truth they degrade them, and he heard the Lord's voice: 'If you wish to be perfect, go and sell all that you have, give to the poor, and come and follow me.'[1] So he distributed and gave to the poor, not out of conceit but prompted by charity, and for that reason his righteousness shall endure unto eternity.[2] Having determined to share his own goods with the poor, he chose only those whose poverty was made honourable by their fear and love of God, that as he sowed in blessings he might reap of them too.[3]

9. *The origin of the Order of Sempringham and the enclosing of nuns*

At that time, when Henry I reigned in England, as Gilbert says in the book which he wrote about the building of his monasteries,[4] there were in the village of Sempringham some girls living a secular life; their minds had received the seed of God's word, which he had constantly supplied to them, and, with the help of moisture and warmth, they grew until white already to harvest.[5] Wishing to overcome the temptations of their sex and of the world, these girls longed to cling without hindrance to a heavenly bridegroom. Holy Gilbert, filled with God's charity, had arranged to devote to His service the churches of Sempringham and [West] Torrington mentioned above, and to distribute his own possessions to the needy. When he found no men willing to lead such strict lives for God's sake, Gilbert thought it right to make over everything he owned to the use of such girls as, being truly poor in spirit, could obtain the kingdom of heaven for themselves and for others.[6] Thus he made for himself friends of the mammon of unrighteousness that they might receive him into everlasting habitations.[7] However, he did not at first make friends for himself of men, but, to rejoice with him over the coin which had been found, he called together women as his friends,[8] who in their chastity later too brought him forth many men to share in this friendship. The natural law of pity instructs us, and divine counsel urges us, to do good without stinting to weaker folk, and for this a richer reward is to be expected. Because the fruit of virgins is one hundredfold, when he abandoned his own possessions in order to preserve their virgin status he received a hundredfold and possesses eternal life.[9] Moreover, following the correct way of giving, he bestowed his goods upon the righteous, in accordance with the saying: 'Give to the good and do not harbour

peccatores.'[1] Septem itaque ex hiis uirgines ad celeste desiderium accensas septiformi spiritui templa dicauit, ut fieret uirginitas earum meritoria si fuisset uirtutibus adornata. Quid enim prodest lampas ab oleo uacua?[2] Quid caro integra mente corrupta, corpus mundum et cor maculatum? Sic essent uirtuosi infideles quorum tota uita peccatum est. Vt autem fierent sancte mente et corpore instrumenta sanctitatis eis preparauit et proposuit quibus suam ipsarum operarentur salutem; et quia nemo militans Deo implicat se negotiis secularibus, ut ei placeat cui se probauit, et uirginitas tenera facile solet temptari ab astutia serpentis si passim pateat ⟨in⟩[a] omnibus quod patet in Dina, seclusit eas a strepitu mundi et ab aspectu hominum ut regis ingresse cubiculum solius sponsi solitarie uacarent amplexibus.[3] Cumque non sufficiat ad salutem

f. 47 abstinere a malis nisi bonorum operum sequatur | effectus, legem sanctimonie eis dictauit et docuit qua celesti sponso placerent et facte dilecte castis eius amplexibus semper inhererent. Dedit ergo eis precepta uite et discipline, et castitatem et humilitatem, obedientiam et caritatem, ceterasque uite uias seruare suasit et iussit: que omnia gratanter susceperunt et deuote impleuerunt.

Fulsit enim in earum mente species preciose margarite pro qua et se et sua dederunt et eam comparauerunt.[4] Ad hec licet in carne essent sed preter carnem uiuerent, tamen quia in carne erant et extra carnem uiuere non poterant, omnia que carnalis indigentie conditio exigit in uictu et uestitu et edificiis ceterisque uite necessariis secundum modum et mensuram discrete dispositionis eis ministrauit ad usum. Hoc modo constructis rite domibus religioni competentibus et claustro circumquaque clauso,[5] inclusit ancillas Christi solitarie uicturas sub pariete ecclesie beati Andree apostoli, in uico de Sempingham, ad aquilonalem partem, habito auxilio et consilio uenerabilis Alexandri antistitis, fenestra tantum patente per quam necessaria intromitterentur.[6] Voluit in mundo sitas extra mundum ponere et

---

[a] Supplied by Winterbottom

---

[1] Ecclus. 12: 5.
[2] Cf. Matt. 25: 3 ff.
[3] Cf. 2 Tim. 2: 4; Gen. 34; S. of S., *passim*.
[4] Cf. Matt. 13: 46.
[5] *Claustrum* meant both the monastic enclosure (as in St Benedict's Rule) and the cloister walk or garth—cf. *clôture* and *cloître* in French, *Kloster* and *Kreuzgang* in German, a distinction not made in Latin or English.
[6] See p. xix.

sinners.'[1] From their number he consecrated seven virgins aflame with desire for heaven as temples to the sevenfold spirit, so that if adorned by virtue their virginity might win merit. For what use is a lamp which is empty of oil?[2] And what advantage is it if the flesh is wholesome but the mind corrupt, or the body pure and the heart tainted? On this basis the heathen would be virtuous when their whole life is a sin. That the girls might become holy in mind and body he prepared for them and put forward the means of sanctity with which they might secure their own salvation. In order to please Him in whose service he has enlisted, he who fights on God's side never involves himself in secular business; and, if what is clear in Dinah's case applies to all women everywhere, tender virginity is frequently and easily tempted by the serpent's cunning; therefore he shut them away from the world's clamour and the sight of men, so that having entered the king's chamber they might be free in solitude for the embrace of the bridegroom alone.[3] And since to obtain salvation it is not enough to desist from evil unless this is followed by the performance of good works, he dictated for them and taught them the law of holiness, by which they might please their heavenly bridegroom and, when they had become beloved, always remain in his chaste embrace. He gave them instructions concerning their life and discipline, urging and ordering them to preserve chastity, humility, obedience, charity, and the other rules of life, all of which they willingly accepted and devoutly kept.

In the minds of these women there gleamed the image of a valuable pearl, which they bought, giving themselves and their possessions for it.[4] Further, although they lived in the flesh, their life transcended it; but because they did live in the flesh and could not exist outside it, he made available for their use all that the condition of fleshly need requires in the form of food, clothing, shelter, and the other necessities of life according to the degree judged right by his prudence. In this way dwellings suitable for the religious life were duly built, together with an enclosure sealed on every side.[5] Then, with the aid and counsel of the venerable bishop Alexander, he enclosed the handmaidens of Christ to live a solitary life under the wall on the northern side of the church of St Andrew the Apostle in the village of Sempringham.[6] Only a window was preserved which could be opened so that necessaries could be passed in through it. They lived in the world but he sought to set

f. 47ᵛ a terra sua et cognatione et paterna domo | relegare,[1] quatinus ad modum ecclesie, immo ecclesia facte, populi sui et paterne domus oblite, id est ab omni curiositate, concupiscentia et ambitione egresse, summo regi facerent sue speciei concupiscentiam. Voluit, inquam, per hanc corporum incarcerationem animarum ad Deum ostendere, immo facere, relegationem, eo quod frequentia mundi multum soleat plurimumque separare a familiaritate Dei.[2] Et quia quoquam eis egredi non licebat etiam pro administrandis uel adquirendis sibi necessariis, deputauit obsequio earum puellas aliquas pauperculas in habitu seculari seruientes, que per fenestram illam que danda erant uel accipienda prout oporteret trahicerent. Illud enim tantum foramen reliquerat apertum tempore tantum congruo aperiendum, quod etiam perpetuo obserasset si homines sine rebus humanis uiuere potuissent. Nam hostium erat sed nunquam nisi ad eius nutum reseratum, non per quod ille egrederentur, sed quo ille ad eas cum opus esset ingrederetur: cuius hostii ipsemet erat clauiger et hostiarius. Quocunque enim pergeret uel ubicunque maneret, clauem illius hostii, ceu pudoris earum signaculum, fortis zelotes secum ferebat.[3]

10. *Vocatio sororum laicarum*

f. 48 Porro paci et quieti earum prouidens ne quid extrinsecus | perturbationis accideret, didicit a uiris religiosis et prudentibus non esse tutum iuuenculas seculares circumquaque uagantes ministrare religiosis, ne, quia corrumpunt mores bonos colloquia mala,[4] aliquid nuntiarent uel agerent rerum secularium quod animos offenderet monialium. Vnde factum est, persuasu et consilio ipsorum, ut habitum cum uita religionis peterent predicte famule sibi dari, quo possent in paupere uita sed honesta Christi famulabus famulari. Ecce granum frumenti cadens in terram in aliam spicam pullulauit.[5] Quod uidens beatus Gilebertus corde letatus est ob fidei deuotionem, sed inexpertis et presertim simplicibus et ydiotis, que plerumque promittunt que non intelligunt et plura quam possunt,

---

[1] Cf. Gen. 12: 1.
[2] Cf. Rom. 8: 39.
[3] Cf. Ex. 20: 5.
[4] Cf. 1 Cor. 15: 33.
[5] Cf. Matt. 13: 8.

them apart from it, to exile them from their land, their kin, and their father's house;[1] so that they should be like a church, or rather be made a church themselves, and oblivious of their families and homes—in other words leaving behind all curiosity, concupiscence, and ambition—might cause the highest King to feel desire of their beauty. I repeat he sought by imprisoning their bodies in this way to display, or rather bring about, the exiling of their souls to God, because the world's throng often makes a great barrier—very great indeed—separating us from a sense of God's presence.[2] And as the women were not allowed to go out anywhere, even to perform or obtain necessities, he appointed to their service some poor girls, who served them dressed in secular attire; they were to transfer whatever had to be given or received through the window in a proper fashion. He had left this single opening to be used only at a suitable time; in fact he would have fastened it permanently if humans could have lived without human things. There was a door, but it was never unlocked except by his command, and it was not for the women to go out through but for him to go in to them when necessary. He himself was the keeper of this door and its key. For wherever he went and wherever he stayed, like an ardent and jealous lover he carried with him the key to that door as the seal of their purity.[3]

10. *The calling of lay sisters*

Further, he took care that no trouble from outside should break in upon the peace and quiet of these women, because he learnt from wise religious that it is not safe for young girls in secular life who wander about everywhere to serve those in religious orders. Since evil conversation destroys good behaviour,[4] he was anxious that they should not report or perform any worldly deed which might offend the nuns' minds. And so, on the persuasion and advice of such men, it came about that these serving women asked, along with the life of religion, for a habit to be granted them in which they could minister to the handmaidens of Christ, leading a poor but honourable existence. See how the grain of corn produced another shoot as it fell to the earth.[5] When blessed Gilbert saw this, his heart was filled with joy because of their zeal for the faith. But he was unwilling hastily or lightly to impose the heavy yoke of a vow upon untried souls and especially upon simple and ignorant women, who commonly promise what they do not understand and more than they can perform.

36 LIBER SANCTI GILEBERTI

noluit eis cito uel leuiter graue iugum uoti imponere, ne forte postmodum penitudine ducte abicerent illud ad maiorem sui ruinam et
sancte religionis subuersionem. Probandi sunt enim spiritus
neophitorum ne se transfiguret Sathanas in angelum lucis,[1] ne
pellem ouinam lupus, pennas accipitris strucio, menbraque leonis
induat asellus agrestis. Vt ergo intelligerent quod agerent et etatem
habentes pro se responderent, predixit eis et prestruxit omnem
monastice discipline asperitatem, uiuendique modum quam
f. 48ᵛ nouerant unquam | uel uiderant uspiam arctiorem. Predicauit eis
mundi contemptum et omnis proprietatis abiectionem, sue uolun-
tatis restrictionem et carnis mortificationem, laborem continuum
et quietem raram, uigilias multas et somnum tenuem,ᵃ ieiunia
prolixa et cibaria uilia, uestem asperam et cultum nullum, claustri
carcerem ne malaᵇ agerent et silentii uicem ne eadem dicerent,
orationis et meditationis frequentiam ne illicita cogitarent. Que
omnia sibi placere pro Deo asserebant, et duritiam pro mollitie,
laborem pro quiete, molestias pro dulcedine computabant, dummodo possent consequi quod optarunt.ᶜ Compulit eas tamen
paupertatis necessitas et labor mendicitatis ardua uelle subire,
dummodo de perpetuo uite stipendio fierent secure. Illexit interim
Dei amor et animarum salus quo possent per temporalem laborem
eternam mereri quietem. Sicque ex necessitate facta est uirtus, et
licet finis cepte intentionis minus forte in quibusdam esset a
perfecto, non impediuit tamen sed adquisiuit consummationem
operationis bone. Set nec sic uoluit uir prouidus eas adhuc astrin-
gere uoto, propter ritum probationis, uerum anni transeuntis
f. 49 indixit illis expectationem, ut etiam ex dilatione | cresceret desi-
derium.

11. *Conuersio fratrum laicorum*ᵈ

Sane quoniam sine solatio uirili parumᵉ proficit sollicitudo
feminea, assumpsit mares et eos exterioribus et grauioribus
illarum prefecit operibus quos habuit domus sue et agriculture
famulos: quosdam autem ab infantia suis sumptibus nutritos et

---

ᵃ tenuem *Lc²Od;* tetuem *Lc*   ᵇ mala *LcOd;* uel praua *s.l. Lc¹*   ᶜ optarent
Od; perhaps optarant *(Winterbottom)*   ᵈ fratrum laicorum *Lc index, Od;* laicorum
fratrum *Lc (but cf. heading of ch. 10)*   ᵉ parum *Lc;* uel modicum *s.l. Lc¹*; modicum
Od

---

[1] Cf. 2 Cor. 11: 14.

For he was afraid that later perhaps, overcome by regret, they would renounce their vow, bringing greater ruin upon themselves and destroying the holy life of religion. Truly the souls of novices must be tested lest Satan transform himself into an angel of light[1] and the wolf put on sheep's clothing, the sparrow the feathers of a hawk, and the wild ass the limbs of a lion. So that they might understand what they were doing and reply for themselves as mature adults, he spoke to them in advance and laid before them all the rigour of monastic discipline and a way of life which was stricter than any that they had ever experienced or anywhere witnessed. He preached to them contempt for the world and the abandonment of all property; restraint upon the will and mortification of the flesh; continual work and infrequent rest; many vigils and little sleep; extended fasting and bad food; rough clothing with no adornment; confinement within the cloister to ensure that they did no evil and periods of silence lest they speak it; constant prayer and meditation to prevent them from thinking what was forbidden. The women claimed that for God's sake all these things pleased them and they reckoned austerity to be comfort, work rest, and tribulations a delight so long as they could attain what they had chosen. It is true that the want they suffered in their poverty and the labour of begging forced these women to undertake difficulties willingly so long as they were assured of a permanent livelihood. However, the love of God and their souls' salvation led them on to endure hardship for a time that they might earn everlasting rest. Thus virtue was made out of necessity and, although in some of them the object of their original resolution was perhaps less than ideal, this did not prevent but secured for them the accomplishment of good works. But even so, being a prudent man, Gilbert did not wish to bind them as yet with a vow, in order that they might undergo the usual probation; instead he told them to wait for a year to pass, that their desire might actually increase with the delay.

11. *The conversion of lay brethren*

Now because women's efforts achieve little without help from men, he took on men, and put those he kept as servants about his house and on his land in charge of the nuns' external and more arduous tasks; some of them he had raised from childhood at his own expense,

quosdam a dominis suis transfugas, quos nomen religionis emancipauit, quosdam uero pauperimos et mendicantes. Erat enim
seruus euangelicus qui ad preceptum Domini exiit in uicos et pla-
teas ciuitatis et quoscumque inuenit pauperes et debiles, cecos et
claudos compulit intrare ut impleretur domus Domini.[1] Qui et
ipsi, tum ex inopia humane tum ex ardore celestis uite, idem quod
conuerse laice appetierunt et petierunt: circa quos eodem modo
quo circa illas operatus est, et tandem tam hiis quam illis quendam
signatiuum humilitatis et renuntiationis mundi tradidit habitum.
Indixitque illis grauia multa et pauca leuia que supra memoraui-
mus, preter ea que sunt anime propria, ut est humilitas, obedientia
et pacientia et huiusmodi, quorum est actus difficilis sed merces
f. 49ᵛ multa, que omnia libentissime concesserunt et seruare | sub uoto
spoponderunt. Ecce talentum duplicatum quod quasi simplum
accepit in feminis et quasi duplum ex feminis simul et maribus
adquisiuit.[2] Ecce 'iunctura feminum sponse quasi monilia que
fabricata sunt manu artificis'.[3]

12. *Propagatio monasteriorum*

Iam tempus aduenit ut egrederetur dilectus cum dilecta in agrum
mundi, ut commorarentur in uillis et ciuitatibus populorum.[4] Iam
dies instabat quo uinea, cuius plantauit Dominus radices, impleret
terram, expanderet palmites suos usque ad mare, et usque ad flumen
propagines eius.[5] Processu ergo temporis, uolente Domino dilatare
semen quod ipse seminauerat in illis primis huius uite parentibus,
multi diuites et nobiles Anglie, comites et barones, uidentes et
approbantes opus quod inchoauit Dominus et que sequerentur
bona preuidentes, fundos et predia possessionesque plurimas
sancto patri optulerunt, et monasteria multa per multas prouincias
sub eius regimine edificare ceperunt, inchoante ipso episcopo
Lincolniensi Alexandro et consummante illustri rege Anglorum
Henrico secundo.[6] Que omnia uir Domini cum timore et tremore et
f. 50 quadam coactione accepit, plurima autem refutans | et omnino con-
temnens, eo quod honestam paupertatem semper diligeret et in

---

[1] Cf. Luke 14: 21–2. [2] Cf. Matt. 25: 14–28.
[3] S. of S. 7: 1. [4] Cf. S. of S. 7: 11.
[5] Cf. Ps. 79: 8–9, 12 (80: 8–9, 11).
[6] See pp. xxx–xxxii. The foundations were begun both in the time of Bishop Alexander and under his patronage.

others were fugitives from their masters freed in the name of religion, and others again were destitute beggars. For he was the true
servant of the Gospels who, following his Lord's command, went
out into the streets and open spaces of the city and forced all those
that he found poor, weak, blind, and lame, to enter, that the Lord's
house might be filled.[1] Because all these men, spurred both by the
poverty of their human life and by their longing for the life of
heaven, wanted exactly what the lay sisters desired and requested,
he took the same course of action in their case as in the women's,
and finally bestowed the habit upon both in token of humility and
renunciation of the world. He imposed on them many heavy tasks
and a few light ones, which we have recorded above, as well as
spiritual qualities like humility, obedience, and patience and the
like, which are difficult to perform but are greatly rewarded; all
these they accepted most willingly and promised under oath to
observe. See how the talent was doubled, as if he received it single
in the women and obtained it double from the women and men
together![2] See how 'the joints of the thighs of the bride were linked
together like a necklace made by a craftsman's hand'.[3]

12. *The multiplication of convents*

Now the time came for the lover to go out with his beloved into the
field which was the world, to dwell in the villages and cities of the
people.[4] Now the day was at hand when the vine, whose roots the
Lord had planted, should fill the land, stretching its shoots
towards the sea and its branches towards the river.[5] As time went
on the Lord wished to scatter more widely the seed which He
Himself had sown in those first progenitors of this life; thus many
wealthy and nobly born Englishmen, earls as well as barons, when
they observed and approved the work which the Lord had begun,
and foresaw what good things would follow, offered lands and
estates and a great number of possessions to the holy father, and
under his guidance proceeded to build many convents in many
different regions. This process was begun in person by Alexander,
bishop of Lincoln, and was completed by Henry II, the illustrious
king of the English.[6] The man of God received all such possessions
with fear and trembling, and under a certain amount of coercion;
he also refused and utterly rejected a great deal, because he always
loved honourable poverty and was frightened that to have large

numerositate*ª* subditorum neuum timeret elationis secundum illud: 'In multitudine populi gloria regis.'¹ Nam primitus primis illis septem inclusis, plures illis uiuentibus superapponere non arbitrabatur. Sed cum uideret opus Dei in multiplicitate monasteriorum multiplicari, noluit Dei uoluntati obuiare, deuotionem largitorum prepedire, sustentationem seruorum Dei negligere: sciens hanc esse Dei uirtutem, non suam, profunditati consiliorum Dei omnia committens, qui bonorum et malorum bene semper ad suum libitum utitur ministerio.

13. *Quod adiit dominum ᵇ papam Eugenium*

Videns ergo filios Dei cotidie succrescentes et de die in diem proficientes donec magni fierent ualde,² putauit se, ut est bonarum mentium, ad tantam sullimitatem indignum quia sensit infirmum, cogitauitque hoc honus simul et honorem a propriis humeris exuere et alicuius uel aliquorum quos adhuc inueniret aptiores et ualidiores committere potestati, tanquam alter Moyses diceret Domino: 'Obsecro, Domine, mitte quem missurus es et quem dabis, Domine, ut presit huic multitudini maxime f. 50ᵛ quam incepisti facere in gentem magnam.³ | Tu nosti quod ex quo locutus es ad seruum tuum ut preessem populo huic, factus sum inferioris uite, utpote homo secularis horum respectu, quos deberem meritis sicut et gradu precedere. Scio enim graue iuditium his qui presunt, et timeo ne, si non fuero grege melior, fiam ante te ex priore posterior.' Tunc adiit capitulum Cisterciense, ubi forte tunc aderat bone memorie papa Eugenius, ut curam domorum suarum manciparet custodie monachorum Cistercie.⁴ Hos enim ceteris habuit, ex frequenti hospicii susceptione, familiariores, quos et iudicauit aliis religiosiores, quia erant recentiores et regule arctioris: unde etᶜ tutius credidit illos suo operi preficere, eo quod rigor ordinis et nouitas eorum conuersionis conuersationem illam quam ille excogitauerat districtius faceret custodiri.

ª numerositatem *Lc*   ᵇ dominum *omitted in Lc index, marked for deletion in Od*
ᶜ et *Lc¹Od; om. Lc (perhaps rightly)*

---

¹ Proverbs 14: 28 ('dignitas regis', Vulg.).
² Cf. Gen. 26: 13.
³ Cf. Ex. 4: 13; Gen. 12: 2.
⁴ 1147. See pp. xl–xlii.

numbers under his authority would prove a mark of pride, according to the saying: 'A king's glory lies in the multitude of his people.'[1] In the beginning when he enclosed those first seven women he did not expect to add more to them during their lifetime. But when he saw how God's work increased with the growing number of convents, he was reluctant to oppose God's will, obstruct the devotion of generous donors, or neglect the support of God's servants. For he recognized that this achievement was God's, not his own, and he committed everything to the deep wisdom of God's counsels, since He always turns the service of the virtuous and the wicked to good advantage in accordance with His will.

13. *How he visited Lord Pope Eugenius*

And so daily he saw the sons of God grow up, gaining strength from day to day until they became very great.[2] As is typical of right-thinking men he considered himself unworthy of such great authority because he was conscious of his own weakness; he planned to divest his shoulders of what was at the same time an obligation and an honour, and to entrust it to the abilities of one or more of those whom he should yet find to be stronger and more capable. It was as if another Moses should say to the Lord: 'I beg Thee, Lord, send the man Thou wilt send and him whom Thou wilt provide, Lord, to rule this great multitude which Thou hast begun to turn into a mighty nation.[3] Thou hast known that from the moment Thou toldest Thy servant that I should lead this people, I have led a lower life, as a worldly man, compared with these people, whom I should surpass in merit as in rank. I realize the heavy judgement which rests upon men who exercise authority, and I fear that if I am not better than my flock from being first before Thee I shall be last.' Then he went to the Chapter of Cîteaux, where Pope Eugenius of happy memory chanced to be present at that time, for Gilbert intended to entrust the responsibility for his religious houses to the care of Cistercian monks.[4] Because he had often received hospitality from them, he was more at home with these men than with others. He also considered them more perfect in the religious life since they had entered it more recently and their rule was stricter; and for this reason he believed it the safer to put them in charge of his work, in that the discipline of the Order and the recent date of their entry into the religious life would ensure that the pattern of life which he himself had devised was more strictly observed.

Dominus autem papa et abbates Cistercie dixerunt sui ordinis monachos aliorum religioni, et presertim monialium, non licere preesse: et sic quod optauit non optinuit, sed ad imperium apostolici et consilium sanctorum iussus est quod inchoauerat prosequi in gratia Christi. Noluit Dominus congregationem de Sempingham proprio priuare[a] pastore qui melior erat ei futurus f. 51 quam decem alii, cuius etiam meritum | disposuit perducere ad centesimum fructum in collectione, qui adhuc restabat alterius conditionis hominum.[1] Soror nempe nostra, congregatio scilicet ista, adhuc paruula est, et ubera non habet prepositorum et predicatorum qui eam lacte nutriant, solido cibo sustentent, interius disponant, exterius protegant, undique et ubique confirment.

14. *Quod commissum est ei a domino papa regimen ordinis sui*

Data est igitur et iniuncta beato Gileberto a sancto papa Eugenio collecti gregis custodia, quia non inueniebatur nec inueniri poterat melior conseruator quam is qui fuerat conquisitor, nec fortior esse poterat boni status zelator quam qui primus et summus fuerat ad statuendum laborator. Veruntamen uir sanctus ad tanti pondus regiminis uergentis etatis causabatur inportunitatem; ad honorem indignitatem, ad magisterium imperitiam, ad prelationem suam pretendit humilitatem. Timuit namque suam quibus preferendus erat inparitatem, timuit placide mentis sue soliditatem dissipandam, timuit dilecti sui secreti et assidue contemplationis dulcedinem debellaturam occupationem. Que f. 51ᵛ omnia deuote humilitatis apologe|tica intellexit, ut erat uir prudens domnus apostolicus, et eo procliuius et securius pastoris ei deputauit offitium quo nullum uidit illi inesse prelationis appetitum. Propositum enim eius erat semper humilibus adherere,[b] et Domini fuit uoluntas illum se semper humiliantem amplius exaltare.

Cognoscens autem beatus Gilebertus diuinum circa se exactum iuditium, non est ausus diu superne reniti dispositioni que

---

[a] priuari *Od*   [b] humilibus adherere *LcOd;* uel humilia appetere *s.l. Lc*[1]

---

[1] Cf. Matt. 13: 8.

However, the lord Pope and the Cistercian abbots said that monks of their own Order were not permitted authority over the religious life of others, least of all that of nuns; and so he did not achieve what he desired but, by the Pope's command and the advice of the holy brethren, he was ordered to continue what he had begun in the grace of Christ. The Lord would not deprive the community of Sempringham of their own pastor, who was to prove better for them than ten other men. He purposed to guide Gilbert's merit till it brought forth its fruit a hundredfold in the harvest, though he at this time remained in the second [non-religious] state of men.[1] Indeed our sister, this same congregation, remains very small and does not possess resources in the form of prelates or preachers to feed her with milk, or strengthen her with solid food, to organize matters within, protect her from without, and support her in all things everywhere.

14. *How the lord pope committed to him the control of his Order*

Thus holy Pope Eugenius bestowed and enjoined upon St Gilbert the duty of guarding the flock which he had gathered together; a better person to look after them than he who originally gained them had not and could not have been found, nor was it possible for any-one to be more fervently concerned for their good standing than the man who laboured first and foremost to establish them. However, the saint used the demands of his declining years as an excuse from so heavy a responsibility; he pleaded his unworthiness for honour, his inexperience of teaching, his humility in the prospect of high office. He was afraid he would not equal those he would have under his charge; he feared that the calm assurance of his thoughts would be scattered, and that preoccupation with business must defeat the sweetness derived from the inner life so dear to him and from his continual meditation. Because the lord Pope was a wise man, he realized that all these arguments were the excuses of devout humility, and so, observing that the saint harboured no desire for ecclesiastical rank, he conferred pastoral office upon him all the more promptly and confidently. It was Gilbert's intention always to cleave to what was humble, and it was the Lord's will to raise him, in his constant self-abasement, still higher.

When the blessed Gilbert learnt the divine judgement delivered in his case, he did not dare to oppose for long the heavenly plan

illum ad hoc opus asciuerat, sed ne ceteris quibus pollebat se priuaret uirtutibus, si pertinaciter obsisteret, amplexatus est deuote obedientiam Dei eiusque uicarii pape,[1] ampliorem inde sperans mercedem quia nullam ex hoc habuit delectationem, suique solius postposuit utilitatem ut multorum adipisceretur salutem. Contemplationis studiis iamdudum eruditus, pie actionis nunc consensit inseruire operibus, ut utriusque uite meteret fructus. Porro licite poterat earum rerum fieri dispensator quarum pristinus fuerat possessor, quoniam pauperibus ea conferens et ipse pauper effectus, ut minister sibi credita, non ut dominus propria gubernauit. Propter hec et huiusmodi sanctitatis signa, et multorum consona testimonia, doluisse fertur papa Eugenius quoniam uirum | antea non nouisset, eo quod uoluisset, ut dixit, illum sullimasse in archiepiscopum Eboracensem, cuius sedes tunc uacabat, si fama meritorum eius illi prius innotuisset.[2a]

f. 52

Beatis quoque Malachie Hyberniensi archiepiscopo et Bernardo Clareuallensi abbati[3] in illo itinere adeo factus est familiaris ut illis solis presentibus ipse quoque presens adesset, ubi per orationem eorum fertur sanitas collata cuidam egroto. Insignia etiam amoris, baculum scilicet, tam presulis quam abbatis accepit ab utroque, in quibus quedam facte sunt uirtutes, et orarium cum manipulo ei dedit abbas in monimentum sui.

15. *Ordinatio canonicorum*

Reuersus denique ad sua pater Gilebertus, quoniam suo proposito defraudatus est quo per humilitatis intentionem pastoralis cure pondera refugiens congregatarum ecclesiarum magisterium gubernationi monachorum Cistercie subdere decreuerat, nec impetrauerat. Hac itaque diuina ordinatione, ut credi fas est, commonitus, hac necessitate compulsus, uocauit in partem sollicitudinis, et omnium quos adunauerat regimini prefecit, uiros litteratos et ecclesiasticis ordinibus insignitos: uiros ut possent, litteratos

---

[a] *Od inserts new material here (see p. 345)*

[1] Cf. M. Maccarrone, *Vicarius Christi* (Rome, 1952); John of Salisbury, *Letters*, ii. 228–9n.
[2] Pope Eugenius III finally pronounced the deposition of William FitzHerbert, archbishop of York (the future St William of York) early in 1147, and confirmed the election of Henry Murdac, the Cistercian, abbot of Fountains, later in the year—the pope himself consecrated Henry on 7 Dec. (D. Knowles, *The Historian and Character and Other Essays*, Cambridge, 1963, p. 90).

which had summoned him to this enterprise; but, worried that if he maintained an obstinate resistance he would deprive himself of the other good qualities in which he excelled, he devoutly embraced obedience to God and to His vicar the pope,[1] hoping for a greater reward because he derived no pleasure from this action. He put aside his own particular interest in order to win the salvation of many. After long experience in the practice of contemplation, he now agreed to devote himself to performing pious deeds, so that he might gather fruit from both types of life. Justly could he be made steward of what he had previously possessed since, in granting these possessions to the poor and becoming poor himself, he exercised power as a servant over things entrusted to him rather than as a lord over his own property. Because of this and similar signs of holiness and the consistent evidence of many men, it is said that Pope Eugenius lamented not having known Gilbert before; he would have liked, he said, to have elevated him to the archbishopric of York, the see of which was vacant at that time, if news of his merits had reached him sooner.[2]

Gilbert also became so intimate with St Malachy, archbishop of Ireland, and St Bernard, abbot of Clairvaux,[3] during his visit that in the presence of those men alone he too was present when it is recorded that through their prayers health was restored to a sick man. Moreover, he received tokens of the affection of bishop and abbot alike, in the shape of a staff from each, the instruments of certain miracles; and the abbot gave him a stole and a maniple as keepsakes.

15. *The ordering of canons*

Eventually Father Gilbert returned home, since he was frustrated in his plan; he had determined, prompted by humility and the desire to avoid the responsibility of pastoral care, to transfer the government of all his churches to the control of Cistercian monks, and this he had not achieved. And so he was instructed by what we should properly consider a divine destiny and forced by this crisis to summon men to share pastoral care who were educated and distinguished by ecclesiastical orders; these he set to govern all those he had gathered together. He chose men for their ability, scholars

[3] See pp. xli, xlvi. St Malachy of Armagh died at Clairvaux in 1148; on Bernard's *Life* of him, and his reconstruction of the Irish Church, see J. A. Watt, *The Church and the Two Nations in Medieval Ireland* (Cambridge, 1970), pp. 19–28.

f. 52ᵛ ut nossent regere ceteros, ordinatos ut | ecclesie iure ualerent
preesse; uiros qui tuerentur mulieres, litteratos qui tam uiris
quam mulieribus uiam panderent salutis, clericos qui omnibus
pastorale officium exiberent. Hoc autem nutu Dei et consilio
fecit uirorum sanctorum et sapientum, quoniam, sicuti patrum
decreta diffiniunt, necesse est ut monasteria puellarum presidio
et administratione monachorum uel clericorum regantur,[1] eo
quod salubre sit Christo dicatis uirginibus si patres eis spirituales
eligantur, quorum non solum gubernaculis tueri sed etiam doc-
trinis possint edificari.

16. *Separatio coniunctorum*

Verum quoniam sacri inhibent canones ne monachi uel clerici
habitent cum mulieribus, sed remoti ab earum familiaritate, nec
usque ad uestibulum habeant accedendi familiare permissum,[2]
eandem secutus est domnus Gilebertus sententiam, quo nemo
umquam forcius zelatus est castitatem, et habitacula clericorum
procul sisti statuit a domibus monialium, tanquam in uno uico
uel in una ciuitate diuersas mansiones religiosorum, ita quod
canonici, longius ab illis remoti, nullum ad eas haberent acces-
f. 53 sum nisi pro administrando aliquo diuino | sacramento sub
multorum testimonio. Basilica tantum, qua diuina celebrantur,
communis est omnibus, sed non nisi tantum in missarum sollem-
niis, semel scilicet uel bis in die, pariete undique intercluso, non
uisis maribus nec auditis mulieribus.[3] Nam est suum canonicis
oratorium in quo diuina complent offitia. Quociens autem ad eas
ingredi urgentior causa compulerit, nemini licet, nec omnium
presbitero, uisitandi gratia intrare nisi sub plurium comitantium
testimonio. Sed et tunc audiri possunt que locuntur, uideri autem
a quoquam masculo detecta facie omnino non possunt. Si quid
uero a foris intro uel deintus foras oportet significari, quatuor
specialiter ad hoc deputantur, duo senes, scilicet probati,
extrinsecus et due sorores mature interius, per quos tantum se
audientes et non mutuo uidentes quicquid necesse est nuntiatur.

---

[1] Cf. Gratian, *Decretum*, C. 18 *q.* 2 *c.* 24 (with clerks added to monks).
[2] Cf. ibid. C. 18 *q.* 2 *cc.* 21–3 (with clerks added to monks).
[3] Cf. p. xxvi; Rose Graham, *S. Gilbert*, pp. 213–15, for Watton; and W. H. St John
Hope in *Archaeological Journal*, lviii (1901), 1–34 (with plan at end).

for their skill in ruling others, clerks in order to exercise authority over the church in accordance with law; men to look after women, scholars to open the way of salvation to both men and women, and clerks to supply the pastoral office to all. This he did observing God's will and the counsel of holy and prudent men, for as is laid down in the decrees of the fathers it is essential that communities of maidens be controlled through the support and administration of monks and clerks.[1] For it is beneficial for virgins who have given themselves to Christ if spiritual fathers are chosen for them so that they may not only be protected under their direction but also be fortified by their teaching.

16. *The setting apart of those joined together*

The sacred canons of the Church declare that monks and clerks must not live in the company of women, but apart from all contact with them; nor should they commonly receive permission to approach even as far as their threshold.[2] For this reason, Master Gilbert, than whom no one ever laboured more strenuously in the cause of chastity, observed this ruling. He ordered dwellings for the clerks to be established far away from the houses of nuns, as if there were in one village or one city diverse households of religious, so that the canons lived a long way distant from the women and had no access to them except for administering some divine sacrament when there were many witnesses present. Only the church where divine service is celebrated is common to all, but then only for the solemn rite of the mass, once or twice a day, and there is a wall which blocks it throughout so that the men cannot be seen or the women heard.[3] For the canons have an oratory of their own in which they perform the divine offices. But whenever a very pressing reason forces them to enter the nuns' quarters, no one, not even the priest who attends them all, is allowed to go in to visit them unless observed by several companions. Yet even then the nuns who are speaking can be heard, but in no circumstances can they be seen with uncovered faces by any man. If any message from outside needs to be given inside, or any from inside without, four persons are appointed especially to do this: from outside two older men, of known integrity, and from within two of the older sisters. Everything necessary is passed on by these four, who may only hear and not see one another.

17. De regulis omnium

His ita dispositis, quoniam omnes tam mares quam feminas in unitatem societatis et uinculum pacis uocauerat, ut per unum in uno omnes perduceret ad unum, multitudinis fecit cor unum et animam unam in Deo,[1] singulis pro sexu, etate et gradu certum uite modum f. 53ᵛ presignansᵃ et metam 'ultra quam citraque nequit procedere | rectum'.[2] Vt autem superiori niteretur auctoritate, ne arrogans aut presumptuosus iudicaretur, si abiectis alienis sua impudenter ingereret, cum tamen magisterium haberet Spiritus Sancti, ceterum ut subditi preostensam sibi uiam sollicicius seruarent, duplicem monastice uite imposuit suis disciplinam, monialibus regulam beati Benedicti, clericis uero regulam sancti Augustini tenendam proponens, omnibus autem Christi et sanctorum exempla et euangelicam apostolicamque doctrinam annuntians,[3] quatinus, dum in subditis tam monachilem quam clericalem iustitiam haberet, ipse in se a nulla monasterii perfectione discreparet.

18. De scriptis

Et quia pro locis et temporibus personisque ex causis incidentibus uariantur et mutari oportet iura constitutionum, ea que minus in illis regulis inuenit ad sic datam normam sufficientia a multarum ecclesiarum et monasteriorum statutis et consuetudinibus, quasi flores quosdam pulcherrimos, excerpsit,[4] collegit et preelegit que magis necessaria et competentiora sic infirmatis hominibus iudicauit. In quibus eruendis et explanandis tanta in eo uiguit sollicitudo ut non solum magna et maxime necessaria, f. 54 uerum etiam minima | quedam et abiecta, quasi uerus angelus super scalam Iacob ascendens et descendens,[5] non omisit, ne ipse inperfecte doctrine uel subditi ignorantie legis rei arguerentur. Hec omnia, ut pro lege haberentur et magis uitaretur transgressio, quoniam 'lex est constitutio scripta',[6] hec, inquam, omnia ad

---

ᵃ presignans LcOd; uel prefigens s.l. Lc¹

---

[1] Cf. Eph. 4: 3; Acts 4: 32 (quoted in many religious rules, e.g. 'Regula tertia S. Augustini' ad init.).

[2] A hexameter (cf. Horace, Sat. 1. 1. 107).   [3] For the rules, see pp. xlviii–l.

[4] A topos also used in Scripta Leonis, etc., ed. R. B. Brooke (OMT, 1970), pp. 88–9, by St Francis's companions.

[5] Cf. Gen. 28: 12 (a topos for the religious life: see pp. 242–3, 250–1).

17. *The rules observed by them all*

When all these arrangements had been made and he had called them all, both men and women, into the unity of fellowship and the bond of peace, that through and in the One he might lead them all to the One, then he made from the multitude one heart and one soul in God;[1] before each individual, varying according to sex, age, and rank, he set a certain way of life and a goal 'which right living cannot fall short of or exceed'.[2] In order, however, to rely upon a higher authority, so that he might not be judged arrogant or presumptuous if he was shameless in rejecting other men's ways and imposing his own, even though he was under the control of the Holy Spirit, and to ensure that those under him kept carefully to the way which had been shown them, he imposed upon his followers a double discipline of religious life. Before the nuns he set for observation the rule of St Benedict, before the clerks the rule of St Augustine, and to all he preached the examples of Christ and his saints and the teaching of the gospels and the apostles.[3] Thus while he upheld the righteousness of monks and of clerks for those under his authority, in himself he strayed not at all from the monastic standard of perfection.

18. *The* Scripta

The regulations which govern institutions differ and need changing as reasons arise, in accordance with place, time, and persons. Therefore when he did not find enough in those rules for the monastic life he had established in this way, he picked what he needed like so many beautiful flowers[4] from the statutes and customs of many churches and monasteries, collecting and choosing those which he considered more vital and more relevant to human beings in all their weakness. He took such care in searching them out and in clarifying them that he included not only the great and most important regulations but also some small and trivial ones, like a true angel ascending and descending Jacob's ladder,[5] so that he himself might not be charged with imperfect doctrine or his subjects with ignorance of the law. To ensure that all these might be kept as law and that offences might more easily be avoided, because 'law is a decree which is written down',[6] all these things,

---

[6] Isidore, *Etymologiae*, V. iii. 2 (ed. W. M. Lindsay, Oxford 1911), quoted e.g. in Gratian, *Decretum*, D. 1 c. 3. *Scripta* below may be a play on *Scriptura*.

memoriam in posterum litteris mandauit et appropriato uocabulo scripta uocauit, ut nomine sicut et sensu quantum reuerentie et obeditionis eis debetur indicaret. Horum omnium tenorem et omnem de omnibus factam institutionem scripto innotuit pape Eugenio, ut si quid fuerat emendandum corrigeret, quicquid uero rectum et rationabile ratum faceret, quatinus omnis uox calumnie auferretur*a* et securitas ea seruantibus condonaretur, si summi pontificis fuerint communita consensu. Qui diligenter singula perlegens et nichil reprehensibile inueniens, perpetua commendauit ea firmitate, et misso priuilegio suo quicquid sanccitum fuerat a patre Gileberto uel foret sanctiendum, de his que ad cultum religionis pertinent, decreuit eterna*b* debere subsistere stabilitate. Hoc idem a successoribus Adriano et Alexandro ceterisque Romanis pontificibus robustius confirmatum est cum illustrium cardinalium subscriptione.[1]

19. *Commendatio ordinis*

f. 54ᵛ His rationibus fretus, his auctoritatibus suffultus, pater Gilebertus filios Dei a .iͦͬͥiͬ uentis collegit et in unam fabricam domus Dei in quatuor parietibus compegit, quadris lapidibus super humile fundamentum compositis, ipso summo angulari lapide Christo Ihesu.[2] Hic est discus Petri .iͦͬͥiͬ lineis de celo summissus, omnigenis animalibus plenus, que mactauit a uiciis seculi et in corpus ecclesie transiecit hic Petri uicarius et imitator.[3] Hic est currus Dei decem milibus multiplex iustis, humilibus et quietis, quos se uehentes*c* in [se]*d* locum interminalem*e* prouehit Dominus: milia habet diuersarum conditionum, sexuum, etatum et linguarum, spe futura et caritate gratuita letantium, quia in eis est Dominus in Synai sancto, id est in mandato suo impleto et implendo.[4] Hec est quadriga Aminadab, id est spontanei populi, uoluntariorum scilicet pauperum Christi, que duo habet latera, unum uidelicet uirorum, alterum mulierum; rotas iͦͬͥiͬ, duas masculorum, clericorum et

---

a auferretur *Lc*²*Od;* auferetur *Lc*
c quod se uehementem *Lc*
b eterna *LcOd;* uel firma *s.l. Lc*¹
d *Deleted by Winterbottom*
e interminabilem *Od*

---

[1] See pp. xxii, 154–5.
[2] Cf. Matt. 24: 31; Eph. 2: 20.
[3] Cf. Acts 10: 11; ('macta' in Ital. for 'occide' in Vulgate; for 'transicio' as 'pass' by eating, cf. Bede, *Expos. in Actus, Corpus Christianorum*, 121, p. 51). For the Pope as *Vicarius Petri*, a commoner phrase in the 11th c., Maccarrone, above p. 44, n. 1; John of Salisbury, *Letters*, ii. 472–3. The meaning of 'mactauit' is very unclear.

I repeat, he committed to writing as a lasting memorial; and he called them by the appropriate word *Scripta*, to show by their name and its meaning what profound reverence and obedience are due to them. He notified Pope Eugenius in a letter of the contents of all these precepts and of the entire code formed from them all, so that if anything needed alteration he could correct it, while confirming all that was right and sensible; thus if they were strengthened by the pope's approval every accusing voice might be silenced and security conferred upon those who kept these laws. The pope read through each article carefully and, finding nothing to criticize, he approved them to stand for ever; and having sent his privilege he decreed that of the laws relating to religious observance, whatever had been authorized by Father Gilbert, or would later be so, should endure and last for ever. This document was confirmed in stronger terms by his successors Adrian and Alexander and by other Roman popes, with the signatures of eminent cardinals.[1]

19. *A commendation of the Order*

For these reasons and because he was supported by these authorities, Father Gilbert brought the sons of God together from the four winds, and confined them between four walls within the single structure of God's house, placing four stones upon a humble foundation, Jesus Christ himself being the chief cornerstone.[2] This is Peter's vessel let down from heaven on four ropes, full of every type of animal, which this man, Peter's vicar and imitator, killed ⟨to remove them⟩ from worldly evil and passed into the body of the church.[3] This is God's chariot containing many tens of thousands of righteous, humble, and innocent people, whom the Lord drives, carrying him, to a limitless place; it holds thousands who differ in their circumstances, in sex, age, and tongue; but yet they rejoice at the hope which is to come and at the love so freely given, because the Lord is amongst them on holy Sinai, that is, in the commandment he has fulfilled and will fulfil.[4] This is the chariot of Aminadab, in other words of a willing people who of their own accord have become poor for Christ. It has two sides, one of men, the other of women; and four wheels, two of men, clerks and

---

[4] Cf. Ps. 67: 18 (68: 17); Augustine, *PL* xxxvi. 828–9 = *CC* xxxix. 887–8.

laicorum, et duas feminarum, litteratarum et litteras nescientium; iumenta duo quadrigam trahentia, clericalem et monachicam disciplinam. Clericatui beatus presidet Augustinus, monachatum precurrit sanctus Benedictus.[1] Quadrigam ducit per aspera et plana, alta et profunda, pater Gilebertus. Via per quam incedunt | f. 55 angusta est semita, brauium autem uita eterna.[2]

Videntem hunc currum talibus ministris et ministeriis procurrentem, exclamare libet etiam maliuolum quemque et inuidum cum Balaam: 'Quam pulchra tabernacula tua, Iacob, et tentoria tua, Israel', et qui fausta optat cum Iacob et Helya: 'Castra Dei sunt hec'.[3] Quid enim uidebis in Sunamite hac nuper conuersa nisi choros castrorum: castra propter hostium repulsionem, choros propter Dei glorificationem; castra propter acerrimum congressum, choros propter felicem de triumpho exultationem?[4] Quid enim maiorem uel tantam faciat hosti inuidiam, quid tantum uel talem[a] adquirit de hoste tropheum, quam ut[b] discordantium tot differentiis hominum una sit concordia morum? Ibi habitat lupus, quondam in seculo raptor, cum agno miti quouis et mansueto, et pardus peccatorum maculis uarius cum hedo accubat, qui se despicit et peccatorem fatetur.[5] Ibi uitulus corde contritus et leo olim seuerus et ouis innocentia simplex simul morantur, et[c] puer paruulus, Christus uidelicet siue sanctus iste humilis, minat eos per ardua discipline ad gaudia uite.[6] Ibi rinoceros docet ouem mansuetudinem et iuuencus f. 55ᵛ indomitus sponte subicit iugo ceruicem.[7] | Ibi damula canem et alauda uenatur accipitrem, et testudo aquilam comitatur ad astra.[8] Ibi uulpis nescit astutias et coruus contemnit cadauer oblatum.[9] Ibi iuuenes et uirgines, senes cum iunioribus laudant[d] nomen Domini, quia omnis etas, omnis conditio et uterque sexus exaltant ibi non suum, sed nomen Domini solius.[10] Quinni[e] Spiritus eius congregat dispersos, qui quamlibet diuerse morigeratos[f] inhabitare facit unius moris in domo, adeo caritas tollit inuidiam et iocunditas socialis facit habitare fratres in unum.[11] Quid tam unum quam

---

[a] The author should have written tale (Winterbottom)   [b] Perhaps supply e (Winterbottom)   [c] quia Od   [d] laudent Lc   [e] Perhaps for Quin (Winterbottom)
[f] diuerse morigeratos Lc corr., Od; morigeratos diuerse Lc

---

[1] See pp. 336–7 and above pp. l, lxxvii; and for the echoes in this sentence cf. S. of S. 6: 11–12.   [2] Cf. Matt. 7: 14; Phil. 3: 14.
[3] Num. 24: 5; Gen. 32: 2.   [4] Cf. S. of S. 7: 1 (6: 13).
[5] Cf. Isa. 11: 6.   [6] Ibid.   [7] Cf. Jer. 31: 18.
[8] Cf. H. Walther, *Lateinische Sprichwörter* (Göttingen, 1969), vi. 190, s.v. *testudo*.
[9] We have not identified specific sources for the rhapsody.

laymen, and two of women, educated and unlettered; the two beasts drawing the chariot are the clerical and monastic disciplines. St Augustine directs the clerks and St Benedict guides the monks,[1] while Father Gilbert drives the chariot high and low over places rough and smooth. The way along which they go is a narrow path, but the prize they seek is everlasting life.[2]

As he sees this chariot rolling onwards equipped with such officers and offices, even the hostile and envious person is pleased to cry out with Balaam, 'How beautiful are thy tabernacles, O Jacob, and thy tents, O Israel', while the man who desires their success cries with Jacob and Elijah, 'These are the camps of God'.[3] For what shall ye see in this Shunammite maiden, recently admitted to the religious life, but the companies of an army: an army to repel the enemy, companies to glorify God; an army for fierce combat, companies to exult joyfully in victory?[4] What could do greater harm, or even as great, to the enemy, what wrests a similar trophy or one as important from him, than that from so many differing and conflicting sorts of people there should emerge one agreed way of life? In that place the wolf, who in the world was once a robber, dwells with any mild and gentle lamb, and the leopard, multicoloured with the spots of sins, lies down with the kid, who despises himself and confesses himself a sinner.[5] There the calf, contrite of heart, the lion which was formerly so fierce, and the sheep, simple in its innocence, dwell together, and a little child, who is Christ or this humble saint, leads them through the rough path of discipline to the joys of everlasting life.[6] There the rhinoceros teaches the sheep gentleness, and the untamed bullock bows his neck willingly to the yoke.[7] There the young deer hunts the dog and the lark the hawk, and the tortoise accompanies the eagle to the stars.[8] There the fox knows no cunning and the crow spurns the carcass offered to him.[9] There young men and maidens, old and young, praise the Lord's name, because in that place all ages, all human conditions, and both sexes exalt not their own name but the Lord's name alone.[10] Yea also His Spirit brings together scattered individuals and causes them, however they differ in their character, to dwell in a house sharing one way of life: so true is it that charity overcomes envy and a delight in their fellowship makes them live in unity as brothers.[11] What is so much at one as

[10] Cf. Ps. 148: 12–13; 113(2) (115): 1.
[11] Cf. Ps. 67: 7 (68: 6); 132 (133): 1.

unumquemque magis rem communem curare quam propriam,
omnis ab uno et ex uno uite sumere necessaria, omnia sub
pondere, numero et mensura pro singulorum gradibus sine
murmure distribui? Quid tam unum quam omnes ecclesias,
ubique terrarum distantes, in uictu et uestitu personarum ceterisque uite contingentibus a se non distare? Quelibet persona
tocius ordinis quamlibet domorum eque habet sibi debitam, nec
aliquid in aliqua uendicare licet alicui, nisi quod a prelato
omnium cuiusque fuerit indultum potestati. Ita uni capiti omnia
compaginantur et subiacent menbra ut eius magisterio singula
singulis compatiantur et congratulentur, et siue in uita siue in |

f. 56   morte unumquodque extat alterum alterius, omnia autem insimul
Domini.[1]

Mirabilis hec unitas tam personarum quam ecclesiarum et
inaudita rerum omnium communio que sic unum omnia et omnia
unum efficit in tot cordium et tantorum monasteriorum diuersi-
tatibus. Preter illam enim quam caritas texit cordium unitatem,
quecunque instituta uirorum apta sunt uite mulierum uel que a
mulieribus ad uiros transferri possunt, salua honestate et regu-
larum quas professi sunt tenore, propter pacem et concordiam
iussit altrinsecus obseruari. Vnde patet quante fuerit uir iste
scientie et discrecionis, qui sic cuique sua distribuit ut omnibus
idem adaptaret.[2] Sed et proinde quante fuerit constat sanctitatis,
quia nisi esset hic homo a Deo, non posset facere quicquam; nec
potuit aliter docere quam uixit, cum doctrina eius opus operata
sit in hiis quos docuit. Doctrina enim illius suam expressit sanctitatem et sanctitas adquisiuit doctrine effectum. Cui enim, nisi
superne pietati et magnis meritorum titulis, est ascribendum quod
uir humilis, de plebe electus, infra paucos annos tanta opera tam
strenue consummauit? Nam preter pauperum et infirmorum,
languidorum et leprosorum, uiduarum et orphanorum xenodochia

f. 56ᵛ   que stabi|liuit et gubernauit, tresdecim ecclesias conuentuales
cum pertinenciis, quatuor scilicet canonicorum seorsum com-
manentium et nouem monialium cum suis rectoribus et fratribus
degentium, in uita sua non sine magno labore et industria constituit, in quibus, ut estimamus, duorum milium et ducentorum

---

[1] Cf. Rom. 14: 8, 12: 5.
[2] The precise meaning is not clear.

that each and every person has more regard for common property than for his own, that all take the necessities of life from and out of one alone, and that all things are divided out by weight, number, and quantity according to individual rank without dissension? What is so much at one as that, although they lie scattered all over the earth, each and every church makes no distinction from the others in the food and clothing of its members and in other practices? Each person in the entire Order has an equal share in each of its houses as his due, and no one is allowed to claim anything in any one of them unless he who is set over all grants it to the power of each. In this way all members are united and made subject to one head so that under his rule they suffer together and rejoice together, and in life and in death alike everything belongs to another, though all belongs together to the Lord.[1]

How marvellous is the unity achieved both by individuals and by churches, and how exceptional the sharing of all possessions which in this way makes one all and all one, in spite of the differences between so many souls and such great religious houses! Charity knits our hearts together; but, apart from that unity, to promote peace and harmony Gilbert gave orders that those customs observed by men but appropriate to the religious life of women and those which can be transferred from women to men should be kept by both sides, saving their integrity and the substance of the rules which they professed. It is clear, then, how very experienced and judicious this man was, for he gave each what was appropriate in such a way as to adapt a single way of life to all.[2] Furthermore it is plain what great holiness he possessed, because had this man not come from God he would not have been able to do anything; nor could he teach other than he lived, since his teaching worked so effectually in those who heard it. His teaching was an expression of his holiness, and his holiness made his teaching effective. For to what save to God's fatherly care and to the great claims of his merits can we attribute the fact that a humble man, chosen from amongst ordinary people, accomplished such important achievements so energetically within a few years? Thus he established and controlled hospitals for the poor and infirm, for the sick and for lepers, and for widows and orphans; moreover, during his lifetime with great labour and effort he founded thirteen conventual churches with appurtenances, of which four were for canons living apart and nine for nuns in association with men to guide them and with lay brethren. In these houses we estimate that at his death he left communities containing 2,200

uirorum et religiosarum mulierum collegia in obitu suo reliquit, preter innumeros antea defunctos: unde liquido constat quod fuit Dominus cum eo, per quem erat uir in cunctis prospere agens.[1] Liquet etiam hunc Dei docibilem eo per magisterium unius magistri Christi et unctionem Spiritus Sancti fuisse edoctum, quod tot Deo famulantibus utriusque sexus hominibus uite formam et uiuendi exempla prestiterit, que ab homine non didicit: nullus enim ordinis illius inuentor, sed nec ordo ipse ante illum fuit inuentus.

20. Ratio contra detrahentes

Quocirca obstruitur os cuilibet ingrato et inuido, qui cum uitam non possit, eius doctrinam reprehendere conatur, cum ex uita laudabili non possit doctrina uituperabilis oriri. Sane nec bonis moribus uita nec fidei catholice obuiat eius doctrina, cum fides per f. 57 dilectionem tanta in eo operata sit bo|na:[2] unde et nec aliqua ab eo constituta consuetudo est retractanda. Sed nec uniuersali ecclesie officit, immo plurimum proficit hec nouelle religionis adinuentio, cum non omnis nouitas, set tantum profana, debeat uitari, et doctrine religionis, ut ait beatus Augustinus, congruentes sint uerborum nouitates.[3] Porro nec legibus humanis nec diuinis abrogat hec recens constitutio, nec sacros canones offendit sed statuit, quandoquidem a principibus seculi ueneratur, a pontificibus prouinciarum acceptatur, a Romanis presulibus in perpetuum corroboratur, per totum orbem quo eius fama pertingit maxima laude celebratur, et, quod his est amplius, signis et miraculis Deo placita comprobatur. Que cum ita sint, ut facta clamant et orbis perhibet testimonium, qualiter se gesserit in pastorali officio pater Gilebertus, ad Dei laudem et illius gloriam et auditorum utilitatem, deinceps declarabimus.

21. Qualiter se habuit in prelatione

Postquam beatus Gilebertus, iterum parturiens filios in euangelio, bonum illud et iocundum, quod est 'habitare fratres in unum',

---

[1] See p. xxxii.
[2] Cf. Gal. 5: 6.
[3] Augustine, *Tractatus in Ioannis Euangelium* 97, *PL* xxxv. 1879 (we owe this reference to the kindness of Père G. Folliet).

men and professed women, quite apart from countless others who had died beforehand. Thus it is an agreed and obvious truth that the Lord was with him, and by His aid he was a man who prospered in all his undertakings.[1] It is also clear that this disciple of God was instructed through the rule of Christ, his one master, and through the outpourings of the Holy Spirit, since he displayed to so many of God's servants of both sexes a way of life and pattern of living which he had learnt from no man. There was no founder of that Order, but neither was the Order found in existence before him.

20. *An argument against detractors*

Any thankless and envious person who tries to censure Gilbert's teaching because he is unable to find fault with his life therefore has his mouth stopped, because faulty doctrine cannot arise out of an exemplary life. Clearly Gilbert's life does not conflict with right conduct nor his teaching with the catholic faith, since faith through love worked such good and mighty deeds in him,[2] and therefore no custom which he established should be revised. This devising of a new type of religious life does not damage the Universal Church; on the contrary it is greatly to its advantage, as not every new thing, but rather worldly novelty, should be avoided and, according to St Augustine, new forms of words are proper to the teaching of the religious life.[3] Now this recent Order does not detract from either human or divine laws, and it strengthens the holy canons of the church rather than transgressing them; for it is venerated by princes of this world, accepted by provincial bishops, confirmed in perpetuity by Roman popes, celebrated with great glory throughout the entire world wherever its fame extends and, still more important, is proved by signs and wonders to be pleasing to God. Since this is the situation, as his achievements proclaim and the world bears evidence, we shall reveal next how Father Gilbert conducted himself in his pastoral office, to God's praise, to Gilbert's glory, and to the benefit of those who hear our words.

21. *How he conducted himself in authority*

St Gilbert again bore sons in the gospel, and after he had accomplished with God's help that 'good and pleasant thing', which is 'for brothers to live together in unity', he became in honour,

f. 57ᵛ | opitulante Deo peregerat, factus est barba ueri sacerdotis Aaron
decore, fortitudine et alacritate uirtutum, et tanquam hora indi-
uisibilis tunice Christi, que est ecclesia, per os suum extremo hoc
tempore introduxit Christum in domum suam per fraternam
quam ipse sarciuit concordiam.¹ Et quia suscepit unguentum
gratie spiritualis, quod descendit a capite Christi,² omni floruit
uirtutum experientia, ut dignus esset ceteris preponi in exemplum uiuendi. Nam ut arbor bona fructus bonos faceret³ et a
radice firma solida pullularent germina, studuit omni custodia
seruare cor suum, ne unquam illud cogitatio inmunda macularet
nec delectatio praua ad consensum peccati pertraheret. Eandem
nempe quam ab utero matris contraxerat illibatam custodiens
carnis integritatem, muliebris spurcicie incitamenta, aliquotiens
acriter a muliere pulsatus,⁴ contempsit, ut esset mundus qui
ferret uasa Domini et manus impoluta que alienas sordes habuit
detergere. Et ut boni pastoris impleret officium,⁵ preter ea que
sunt uirtutum opera, utpote pietas et humilitas, misericordia et
ueritas, que pure mentis exibent efficatiam, extitit in corporali

f. 58 exercitatione laborator | strenuissimus. Nam pro adquirendis uel
tuendis subditorum necessariis, regum et pontificum palatia et
procerum curias, ultra citraque mare, frequentius adibat, ubi
multa incommoda pro commissa sibi ecclesia multociens sus-
tinuit, ita ut inuisibilis hostis instinctu, qui eius actus semper
nisus est impedire, a uisibilibus inimicis non modo uerborum sed
etiam uerberum aliquociens contumelias subiret.

Omnes ecclesias equaliter dilexit, et ideo circa omnium nego-
tia sollicitus fuit: omnium uero grauiores cause et singulorum
maiores culpe semper reseruabantur eius examini, unde et plus
omnibus laborauit. Cum autem, intermisso itineris labore, ad
aliquod monasterium uisitandi gratia deuenisset, panem ociosus
non comedit,⁶ sed preter maiorum negotiorum consilia et auxilia
manibus suis aliquid quod conferret laborauit. Scripsit quandoque libros, et multa alia opera in suppellectilibus uariis et
edificiis construendis ipse confecit. Inter hec agendum cum hominibus quidem erat silentium, cum Deo uero clamor cordis

---

¹ Cf. 1 Cor. 4: 15 ('in Christo Iesu per euangelium ego uos genui'—hence Gilbert
'iterum parturiens . . .'); Ps. 132 (133): 1–2; John 19: 23–4.
² Cf. Ps. 132 (133): 2.   ³ Cf. Matt. 7: 17.
⁴ Or 'deeply disturbed'.   ⁵ Cf. John 10: 11, 14.
⁶ Cf. Prov. 31: 27.

courage, and his eagerness to do good the beard of Aaron the true priest; and like the hem of Christ's indivisible robe, the Church, through his own teaching at this late hour he brought Christ into his own house, by means of the brotherly fellowship which he himself repaired.[1] And because he received the ointment of spiritual grace which descends from the head of Christ,[2] he triumphed in every trial of virtue, so that he deserved to be put above all other men as an example of how to live. That the good tree might bring forth sound fruit[3] and healthy shoots spring from a well-established root, he took every precaution to protect his heart, so that no filthy thought should ever stain it nor evil pleasure tempt it to consent to sin. He preserved unimpaired that purity of flesh which he derived from his mother's womb, and on several occasions when vigorously wooed[4] by a woman he spurned the inducements of the filth attached to her, that he might be clean to bear the vessels of the Lord and that the hand might be untainted that had to wipe away the filth of others. Moreover, apart from those deeds springing from virtues like piety and humility, pity and truth, which demonstrate the strength of a pure heart, to fulfil the office of a good shepherd[5] he showed himself a most energetic worker in the demands he placed upon his body. In order to obtain or safeguard what was vital to those under his charge, he would very often attend the palaces of kings and bishops as well as princely households, both on this side of the Channel and beyond. In these places he experienced many hardships on behalf of the church entrusted to his care; for through the goading of the invisible enemy, who tried always to obstruct his activities, he suffered on several occasions from visible adversaries insults inflicted not only by words but also by whips.

He loved all his churches equally and was therefore concerned about the affairs of all; the more serious issues of all the churches and graver offences of individuals were always kept for his attention, so that he worked harder than anyone else. When he broke an arduous journey and came to visit a religious house, he did not eat the bread of idleness;[6] for apart from the advice and assistance in more important business, Gilbert laboured with his own hands to have something to offer them. Sometimes he copied books, and he personally carried out many other tasks, constructing various household articles as well as buildings. Before men silence had to be observed during these activities, but before God the cry of his

inmensus, et motus labiorum in psalmodia et oratione continuus. Hinc factum est ut cum loqui necesse esset, ex habundantia cordis f. 58ᵛ et concordia operis | loquebatur, quia sicut inspiratus est edidit, et ut docuit sic fecit. Verba eius nichil aliud quam sermonem sapientie et scientie sonuerunt: sapientie quidem in docendis uel discendis supernis et celestibus, scientie in disponendis et dispensandis temporalibus; sapientie in exortatione uirtutum et abdicatione uiciorum, scientie in correptione peruersorum et laude bonorum. Hec omnia adeo caute, adeo discrete gerebat, ut, siue taceret siue loqueretur, et sermo eius utilitatem et silentium haberet discretionem. Nam secundum sapientiam a Deo sibi concessam contra singula uitia congruam opposuit correptionis mensuram.

Monialem quandam inpacientis igne libidinis per maligni hostis machinamenta succensam aspera castigatione sanauit, et fratrem quendam, ire stimulis adeo agitatum ut a monasterio uellet recedere, leui ictu baculi sui in maximam mansuetudinem statim conuertit.[1] Hoc enim semper tenuit in castigando moderamen, ut et culpas ad plenum purgaret et caritatem, tam sui in illos quos arguit f. 59 quam illorum in se, illesam conserua|ret.[a] Viderunt qui affuerunt in sui sanguinis proximos atrocius eum deseuire cum peccarent, ita ut rebelles quosdam et peruersos, nisi omnimodam exhiberent cum summa humilitate satisfactionem, a sua uellet precidere societate. Pretulit autem illis extraneos quoslibet bene agentes, quos recto ordine sanctior copula caritatis ei fecerat propinquiores, et quos tenebatur diligere ex paterna conditione dupla amplexatus est propter iustitiam affectione. Vidimus quod precibus et premiis multimodis diuitum et magnatum denegabat, hoc simplici fratrum uel unius alicuius quem uita commendauerat annuere petitioni. Erat enim homo hylaris et urbane eloquentie, nec habens quicquam in eloquio reprehensibilitatis admixtum,[b] unde et miro affectu tam a suis quam ab alienis diligebatur.

22. *De asperitate uite eius*

Exteriori quoque scemate conformis, immo forma factus gregis, ens in illis quasi unus ex illis,[2] omnia que minoribus imperauit in se

---

[a] conseruaret *LcOd;* uel ob(seruaret) *s.l. Lc*[1]   [b] hylaris . . . admixtum *Lc;* iocundissimus seruata tamen in hiis uerborum grauitate et quantum etiam ad seculi pertinet honestatem facetissimus in factis *Od*

---

[1] See above, pp. liv–lv.   [2] Cf. Ecclus 32: 1.

heart knew no bounds, and the movement of his lips as he repeated psalms and prayers was continuous. So it happened that when speech was necessary, he spoke from an overflowing heart consistent with his deeds, because as he received inspiration so he imparted it, and whatever he taught he himself carried out. His words were a pure expression of wisdom and knowledge: wisdom in teaching or learning the things of heaven above, knowledge in ordering and managing temporal matters; wisdom in the encouragement of virtue and the rejection of vice, knowledge in the reproof of wrongdoers and in praise of the righteous. All this he did so carefully and with such discernment that, whether speaking or silent, his speech was beneficial and his silence well judged. For according to the wisdom God had granted him, he applied the appropriate degree of correction to each individual fault.

With a sharp reproof he cured a nun, inflamed with an unbridled lust by the devices of the wicked Enemy; and one of the brothers who was so roused by anger as to wish to leave his monastery, he changed in a trice into the gentlest of men with a light tap of his staff.[1] This was the criterion which he always followed in his punishments: to secure full expiation of faults which had been committed and to preserve intact both his love for those he censured and the love which they bore him. Those who attended upon him saw that he turned more fiercely upon those to whom he was related by blood, when they sinned, so that he was ready to cut off some of them who were rebels and wrongdoers from his company unless they showed complete penitence and deep humility. To them he preferred outsiders of virtuous behaviour; quite properly the holier bond of charity had brought such persons closer to him, and bound as he was to love them as a father, he embraced them for their righteousness with twice as much affection. We observed that what he refused to the various prayers and bribes of rich men and magnates, he conceded to the simple request of the brethren or anyone recommended by his style of life. He was a cheerful man possessed of a refined eloquence, and because no fault could be found in what he said, he was loved with remarkable strength of feeling both by his own followers and by strangers.

22. *The austerity of his life*

Conforming in outward appearance, or rather being the pattern for his community, and present among them like one drawn from their[2]

prius quantum decuit excepit: non uestis nitidior, non cibus
f. 59ᵛ accuratior, non sequester in illoᵃ tempore dormi|endi locus, nec
mensa, nisi propter hospites, et hoc rarissime et quasi necessario,
diuersa. Equitatura simplex et comitatus honestus, non in multitudine equorum et famulorum, sed uno de laicis conuersis,
duobus uero de clericis honestioribus semper actus eius intuenti-
bus. Viam equitando non fabulosis sermonibus sed psalmodiis et
orationibus seminauit, semper aliqua deferens que occurrentibus
pauperibus erogaret. Hospitium satis frugi et habundans, et
expense nec pares prodigis nec heedem auaris. Cum commede-
bat, non quod sibi sumeret, sed potius quod ceteris tribueret,
uoluit apponi. Hylaris conuiua quosᵇ escis non poterat uultu
saciabat. Interim aliis largus satis, sibi parcus apparuit. Conques-
tus est multotiens surgens a mensa quod deliquisset in crapula,
cum mirarentur sodales tam paruo cibario uitam posse transigi
humanam. Si quid enim sapide suauitatis sensisset in dapibus
quod gustatum appetitum prouocaret, uel quasi sanum et bene
paratum laudaretur a circumsedentibus, uolentibus sic persua-
dere ut comederet, mox ipsi laudatori uel alicui alii transmissum |
f. 60 a se amouit, ne uideretur offendere si uel modicam haberet inde
uoluptatem.

A carnibus et carnium nutrimentis omni tempore nisi in maximo
langore abstinens, ab esu etiam piscium per totum Quadragesime
et dominici tempus Aduentus temperauit, olera et legumina et
huiusmodi uilia frequentius et libentius sumens. Piscium et huiusmodi, queᶜ ne nimia debilitate deficeret aliquantulum laucius
nescienti et nolenti parabantur, primam partem Deo, reliquam
fere totam commensalibus communicauit.ᵈ Erat omni cena pre
oculis mense suppositum uas quoddam, quod discum Domini
Ihesu appellauit, in quo non modo ciborum reliquie sed et primitie
et partes precipue ad opus pauperum imponebantur. Vidimus cum
ad mensam accederet uel sederet lacrimas eum fudisse inter
epulas, quod pro humana conditione urgeretur satisfacere coti-
diane necessitati. Vasis ligneis et testeis et coclearibus tantum cor-
neis utens, omnem exclusit mundi uanitatem et metallorum

ᵃ in illo *Lc;* ullo in *Od*   ᵇ quos *Winterbottom;* quod *Lc;* commensales *Od,*
which gives a different wording for this story   ᶜ que *(or* qui*) Winterbottom;* quo *LcOd*
ᵈ commensalibus communicauit *Lc;* uel sociis uel diuisit *s.l. Lc¹;* sociis diuisit *Od*

midst, he first applied to himself, as far as was right and proper, all that he enjoined upon lesser men: he was not more elegantly dressed, he was no more fastidious in his food, he had at that time no separate place for sleeping and no separate table except to entertain his guests, and then only very rarely and if necessary. He rode simply with upright companions, not in a crowd of horses and servants but with one lay brother and two of the more virtuous clerks always witnessing what he did. As they rode along he interspersed the journey, not with story-telling but with psalms and prayers; he always carried something to give to the poor they met along the way. His household was very frugal yet generous, and his expenses those neither of a prodigal nor a miser. When he ate he liked to be served not his own portion for himself to eat, but what he might give to others. He was a cheerful companion; those he could not satisfy with food he satisfied with his countenance. Generous enough to others, he showed himself sparing to himself. Often as he rose from the table he complained that he had offended through gluttony, when his fellows marvelled that life could be sustained by so little food. If in the course of a meal he discovered a pleasant and tasty dish which roused his appetite on tasting it, or if one was praised as wholesome and well prepared by those who sat round him, trying in this way to persuade him to eat, he immediately moved it away from himself over to the person who had recommended it, or to someone else, in case he appeared to do wrong by deriving even moderate pleasure from it.

He abstained at all times from meat and from any food made with meat except when afflicted by serious illness, and he also avoided eating fish throughout the whole of Lent and Advent, though he would very often eat freely of vegetables, pulses, and similar cheap things. Fish and food of this kind would be a little more luxuriously prepared without his knowing and against his wishes, to prevent him from fainting through excessive weakness; but of this he allocated the first portion to God and almost all that remained to his companions. At every meal a vessel which he called 'Lord Jesus' dish' was set down in full view on the table, and not just the leftovers but both firstfruits and special portions would be placed in it to relieve the poor. We saw how when he came to table or sat down there, his tears would fall among the dishes of food because the human condition compelled him to satisfy his daily needs. He used vessels made of wood and earthenware, and spoons made only of horn, and thus he banished all worldly vanity and the tempting extravagance of

illecebrosam superfluitatem. Post refectionem magis mentis ex uerbo diuino quam uentris ex corporali cibario, quod modicum temporis labori surripere | potuit lectioni et orationi sacreque meditationi indulsit. Toto anni circulo equalibus utens indumentis, nec plura in yeme nec pauciora*a* estate quesiuit. Vna tantum tunica contentus usum pellicee penitus refutauit. Mirari posses et misereri si uideres senilis corporis membra uix ossibus coherentia,[1] concussis humeris et collisis dentibus, subtracto tam naturali quam accidentali calore, multotiens contracta. Inter linum et cilicium mediam lanam propter subditorum conformitatem et popularis aure fugam potius utendam censuit. 'Cum nocturna quies ad stratum menbra uocaret',[2] dictis prius quibusdam psalmis familiaribus pro se suisque, pro regibus et pontificibus, pro fidelibus uiuis et defunctis, post completam septimam horam super lectum tota nocte non iacuit sed sedit, non depositis diurnis uestimentis nec adiecto capiti plumari sustentaculo, sed, quia a tergo non erat quod occiput sulleuaret, sopor irruens pendulum caput nonnunquam in anteriora depressit, ut sic somnum*b* fugaret et orationi pernoctans uacaret. Lectisternio laneo mediante | sic super stramenta residebat, nichil cuiquam usque mane locuturus.

Post nocturnas laudes, recitatis sanctorum passionibus et absolutis defunctis, tam pro se quam pro cuncto sibi grege commisso, humilem et prolixam edidit confessionem, petiitque a fratribus et suam dedit, tam absentibus quam presentibus, culparum omnium absolutionem, conferens postea benedictionem, quasi more beati Iob, singulis diebus offerens holocaustum pro singulis*c* filiorum.[3] Diei autem nichil passus est preterire ociosum, sed orationi, lectioni, contemplationi iusteque actioni uicissim incumbens, temporum uices temperanter distribuit. Singulis uicissitudinibus, non singulatim sed simul, se totum impendit, nec tamen aliquid debite cure succedentis operis derogauit. Nec propriam salutem propter aliorum sollicitudinem omisit, nec diuina propter humana pretermisit, nec internorum curam propter externorum occupationem diminuit. Cunctis compassione proximus, pre cunctis contemplatione suspensus. Flebat multociens

a ins. in Od *b* sompnum Od; somnium Lc *c* pro singulis Brooke (cf. Job 1: 5); per singulos LcOd

[1] Cf. Virgil, Eclog. i. 103.
[2] A hexameter, unidentified.
[3] Cf. Job 1: 5.

precious metals. After he had refreshed his spirit with the divine word rather than his belly with bodily food, the little time he could snatch from his work he gave to reading, prayer, and holy meditation. He wore the same clothes throughout the whole year, seeking neither more in winter nor less in summer. He was content with only one tunic and refused adamantly to wear a pelisse. You would have been struck by wonder and pity to see how the bones scarcely held the limbs[1] of his aged body together and how, when deprived of their natural as well as any additional warmth, on many occasions his shoulders shook, his teeth chattered, and his limbs shrank away. He considered that he should wear a layer of wool in between his garments of linen and his hair shirt to conform with his subjects and also avoid popular favour. 'When the peace of evening summoned his limbs to bed',[2] he first of all recited some familiar psalms for himself and his followers, for kings and bishops, and for the faithful, living and dead; and when the seventh hour had passed he spent the whole night, not lying, but sitting upon his bed. He did not take off his daytime clothes. Also he did not place a feather pillow under his head, and because there was nothing to raise the back of his head from behind, the onset of sleep sometimes made his nodding head fall forwards; by this means he avoided sleeping and was free to spend the night in prayer. Thus he would sit, with a woollen sheet between him and a straw mattress, speaking to no one until morning.

After lauds, when he had recited the martyrdoms of the saints and the collect for the dead, he made a humble and lengthy confession, both on his own behalf and that of the whole flock entrusted to his charge; from the brothers he asked for absolution of all offences and himself absolved those who were absent as well as those who were present; afterwards he bestowed his blessing in the manner of Job, offering a daily sacrifice on behalf of each one of his sons.[3] He permitted no part of the day to drift idly by, but divided the passing hours evenly, alternately engaged in prayer, spiritual reading, contemplation, and good deeds. He gave his whole attention to every single thing that happened, viewing it in context rather than in isolation, and he shunned no part of his proper responsibility for what followed. In looking after others he did not forget his own salvation, nor neglect the divine for the human; and his concern over things within did not lessen through preoccupation with those outside. He was very close to all men in sympathy but far above them all in contemplative prayer. He would often

in ymnis et canticis, suaue sonantis ecclesie uocibus uehementer illectus, uerborum tamen sentenciis magis delectatus. Nam ne |

f. 61ᵛ quis forinsecus euentus uel internus cogitationis occursus mentem suam a sapore et intelligentia diuini uerbi auerteret, cum illud protulit uel audiuit, composuit sibi signa quedam in digitis, et singulis articulis singula uerba uel orationes deputans, tali artificio infixit animo tenacius dictorum memoriam.[1]

Defecate mentis hoc docuit deuotio, que soli sponso speculando suasit uacare,[2] et ipsum in membris eius amplectens omnia effudit uiscera caritatis. Sicut enim ex deuotione pre amore Dei gaudendo plorabat, ita ex compassione proximi lacrimando miseris condolebat. Vidimusᵃ cum quis grauius usque ad separationem deliquisset, cum rediret ad ueniam, durus primitus et pene inexorabilis obstitit, ut contritionem penitentis probaret et culpam ad plenum exquoqueret timoremque ceteris incuteret; sed cum ueram et plenam intellexit emendationem, lacrimas fudit coram cunctis, et pro oue uel dragma perdita sed inuenta conuocans fratres et amicos, ipse uberius gaudebat et omnes congaudere fecit.[3] Sic se affligendo afflictisque compaciendo cum cruce Ihesum sequebatur:[4] sic se bene regens ceterorum fuit rectissi-

f. 62 mus rector, et que | sunt boni pastoris per omnia agens,[5] summi regis meruit membris honorabilioribus annumerari. Sic Deum diligens dilectus est a Deo et hominibus adeo ut illi, quibus quasi necessario preerat utpote primus pater et omnium fundator, susceptor et institutor, ardenti desiderio perpetuum sibi, si fore posset, prelatum illum adoptarunt. Vnde dux constitutus, licet ipsum non constituissent ducem, sed ipse omnes suo ducatu instituerat, cum per omnia esset in illis quasi unus ex illis,[6] exterius quoque habitus signaculum non refugit suscipere ut omnimodam gregis haberet conformitatem. Vsque ad id enim temporis habitu canonico quem tradiderat non erat usus, nec speciale uotum fecerat alicui regule, sed grisiis quas dicunt uestibus utens fucatos fugit pannorum colores.[7] Quam profitendi dilationem, ut

---

ᵃ *ins.* etiam quod *Od, providing a construction*

[1] A technique described e.g. in Quintilian, 11. 2. 17 f. On monastic sign language see esp. W. Jarecki, *Signa Loquendi* (Baden-Baden, 1981), a reference we owe to Professor Giles Constable.
[2] Perhaps echoing Tobias 6: 18 (Vulg.).   [3] Cf. Luke 15: 6, 9.
[4] Cf. Matt. 16: 24.   [5] Cf. John 10: 11, 14.   [6] Cf. Ecclus. 32: 1.
[7] Like the Cistercians, who in early days made their habits of undyed wool. For Gilbert's late entry, in a formal sense, into his own Order, see pp. 68–71.

weep during hymns and spiritual songs; he was beguiled by the voices which rang so sweetly through the church, but he took greater pleasure in the sense of the words. To ensure that no external happening or inner train of thought distracted his attention from the savour and meaning of the divine word, as he expounded it or listened to it, he invented for himself signs upon his fingers, and, attributing to each joint individual words or prayers, by this device he impressed the memory of what was recited more firmly upon his mind.[1]

His piety taught him this, the piety of a mind discharged of every taint, which persuaded him to concentrate on looking at the Bridegroom alone,[2] and, embracing Him in all his limbs, poured out all the bowels of charity. Just as he wept out of devotion, rejoicing in God's love, so he grieved with the unfortunate, weeping out of compassion for his neighbour. We observed that when someone offended so gravely that he set himself apart and then returned to seek pardon, Gilbert at first opposed him, appearing almost relentlessly severe in his determination to test the penitent's contrition, to purge his fault completely, and to inspire fear in everyone else; but when he understood that the penitent's change of heart was total and sincere, he wept before them all and, summoning his brethren and friends on behalf of the sheep or the coin which had been lost but was found, he would rejoice deeply and cause them all to rejoice with him.[3] Thus by abasing himself and sharing in the sufferings of the afflicted, he followed after Jesus with his cross.[4] Since he governed himself so well he was the most proper governor for the others, and by acting the part of a good shepherd in every circumstance,[5] he deserved to be included among those members of the high king more deserving of reverence. As he loved God, so he was loved by God and men; with the result that those whom he was almost bound to command, being their earliest father, and founder, guardian, and teacher of all, wished ardently to choose him as their prelate for ever, if this should be possible. In this way he became their leader, not because they appointed him to the office but because he had brought them all up under his leadership; and because in every respect he took his place amongst them as if drawn from their number,[6] he also agreed to accept the outward sign of the habit, in order to conform in every detail with his community. Until that time he had not worn the canon's habit which he had bestowed upon others, nor made a special vow to any rule; but dressed in what are termed 'grey' garments he avoided clothes with dyed colours.[7] In our opinion

credimus, ideo subintulit quoadusque nouella sua plantatio caperet incrementum et solidamentum; timuit tamen[a] ne arrogantie notaretur si ipse suis adinuentionibus, licet a Deo essent, sollemne uotum deferret. Sed precauentes discipuli perniciosum esse si alterius habitus homini profiterentur, ne forte post obitum illius extraneus aliquis posset loco eius, ui uel potestate principum, ut solet, substitui, | si ille, cui prima facta est professio, de suo numero non esset, pecierunt et probabilibus rationibus persuaserunt ut habitum illius ordinis, quem preesse ceteris statuerat, ipse susciperet, quatinus uiam quam premonstrauerat ingrediens, suo exemplo alacriores duceret et securiores. Quorum precibus et monitis permotus, maxime quia diuino consilio uiderat opus suum et inchoari et eatenus perduci, cum non tantum sua sed et Romana accessisset auctoritas, deuote assensit facere quod postulauerunt.

f. 62ᵛ

23. *Quod suscepit habitum canonici*

Erat quidam ex primoribus canonicis, nomine Rogerus, origine Sempinghamensis, prepositus ecclesie Maltone, uir prudens et probate per omnia religionis, quem fere omnium monasteriorum congregationes successorem[b] beati Gileberti desiderabant habere.[1] Hunc etiam ipse pre nota probitate talem esse arbitrans, sicut et erat, qui merito uices eius, si sic contingeret, agere posset, ex filio patrem et ex discipulo magistrum sibi prefecit, et obedientiam illi, professionem uero loco et ordini de Sempingham rite deuouit, et sic de manu eius habitum canonicum apud Buling|tonam suscepit. Huic postmodum tantum detulit quoad uixit insigne humilitatis[c] honorem, ut, cum ipse omnibus, ille uero sibi preesset, nichil fere de agendis suorum sine eius consilio et assensu disponeret, nichil quod ille ageret irritum[d] haberet. Credidit namque eius fidelitati et presumpsit de illius prudentia, unde fidelem seruum et prudentem primo super se, deinde super familiam suam, constituere proposuit.

f. 63

ᵃ enim *Od*   ᵇ successorum *Lc*   ᶜ insigne humilitatis] *these words have no construction. Holford-Strevens suggests* insignis, 'honour consisting in conspicuous humility'   ᵈ irritum *Lc³Od; om. Lc*

¹ Roger became prior of Malton between 1169 and 1174, and Master of the Order by 1178 (see p. lix, correcting *Heads*, pp. 203-4).

he deliberately delayed making his profession until his new foundation gained in size and strength, because he was afraid that he would be accused of arrogance if he took a solemn vow to rules which, even though they were inspired by God, were of his own devising. But his disciples were afraid it was dangerous for them to profess obedience to a man clothed in a different habit; perhaps after his death some outsider might be intruded into his position by force or through princely influence—a common event—if the man to whom their first profession was made did not belong to their number. They therefore begged him and urged him with cogent arguments to put on the habit of the Order which he had determined to be superior to all others, that, as he set out along the path which he already indicated, he might lead them all the more swiftly and safely by means of his own example. He was greatly affected by their prayers and advice, particularly since, following God's counsel, he had seen his work not just begun but brought to the point where it acquired not only his own authority but also that of Rome; and so he piously agreed to do what they asked.

23. *How he received the habit of a canon*

Amongst the original canons was one called Roger, who came from Sempringham and became head of the house at Malton. He was a discreet man who had thoroughly proved his religious vocation, and the communities of almost all the religious houses wished to have him as St Gilbert's successor.[1] Because of Roger's known integrity the saint too considered him, with ample justification, as the sort of person who could well take his place if the occasion arose. So from the position of son he appointed him father, from disciple his own master, and with ritual solemnity vowed obedience to him, making his profession to the place and Order of Sempringham; thus he received a canon's habit from Roger's hand at Bullington. Thereafter as long as he lived he displayed such great reverence and such obvious humility(?) towards Roger that (for although he commanded all, he was himself under Roger's command) he would take scarcely any decisions about what should be done for those in his care without Roger's advice and approval, and he would cancel nothing that Roger did. He trusted to his loyalty and assumed his good judgement, so that he planned to give his loyal and prudent servant authority first over himself and then over his community.

Consummatis igitur et corroboratis omnibus que ad tantam Dei edificationem uidebantur necessaria, cum quatuor pretaxatos parietes in quadratis lapidibus uideret hostis antiquus contra se erigi,[1] et tam solido bitumine caritatis compingi et ne quando soluerentur tam strenuo seruatore muniri, sed et magis dolens alterum eius supparem et coadiutorem ad perpetuum illius domus firmamentum prouideri, cum itaque perspiceret omnia inpedimenta sua que contra hanc domum ab initio obiecerat cassari, quia f. 63ᵛ principia eius destituere[a] non poterat, iam erectam et | perfectam fabricam deicere uel saltem in aliquo ledere machinatus est. Veruntamen hec eius peruersa cogitatio qui semper uult nocere in aliquo, Dei fuit recta dispositio, qui nouit bene uti malis, et quod ille parauerat ad perniciem, hoc Dei clementia uertit ad utilitatem. Erat enim ecclesia iam facta et oculis eius bene placita, et ideo decreuit eam ecclesiastico more excercere, quam frequens est et familiare fluctibus tundi et flatibus aduersitatum iactari, sed tandem illesam portum subire salutis. Voluitque Dominus, sicut antea multis eam probauerat, dum construeretur, assultibus, et semper inexpugnabilem inuenerat, unde et debitam meruit accipere perfectionem; uoluit, inquam, Dominus iam consummatam[b] examinare, ut firmaret si immobilem uideret, quatinus sicut per primam constantiam suam adquisierat staturam, ita per iugem perseuerantiam eternam sortiretur stabilitatem.

24. De constantia eius

Efferbuit illo in tempore, diebus scilicet regis Anglorum Henrici secundi, notissima illa persecutio que in beatum Thomam Cantuariensem archiepiscopum pro diuinis legibus et libertate uniuersalis | f. 64 ecclesie stantem grassabatur.[2] Huius gloriose uictorie noluit diuina prouidentia beatum Gilebertum eiusque ecclesiam esse exsortem; sed ut inter filias uniuersalis ecclesie digna esset computari, fecit

---

[a] destruere *Od, probably rightly*   [b] consummatam *Winterbottom;* consummatum *LcOd*

---

[1] See above, c. 19.
[2] See Foreville, *L'Église et la royauté,* pp. 122–326, esp. pp. 165–6, 209–10. In his flight from Northampton in Oct. 1164, Thomas had a Gilbertine canon as guide, and seems to have stayed at Sempringham, Haverholme, and Chicksands on his way to Kent and the Channel (*MB* ii. 399–400, iii. 323–4, iv. 54–5). The accusations against the Order were evidently made early in 1165 (Foreville, p. 210).

Accordingly everything which seemed vital to so great an edifice of God was completed and established. Then the ancient Enemy saw that these four walls had been raised against him out of square-cut blocks of stone;[1] and, moreover, that they were joined so firmly with the cement of love and defended by so energetic a guardian that they could never be demolished; but what grieved him even more was that another man, almost equal to the first, was being found to assist him in establishing the house on a permanent footing. Thus he saw with dismay how all the obstacles which from the start he had placed in the way of this house were being brought to naught; and because he had been unable to destroy its beginnings, he plotted how he might tear down the structure, now that it was completely built, or at least damage it in some respect. But this sinister intention on the part of one who is constantly wishing to do harm somewhere was in fact the providence of God: for He knows how to employ evil in a good cause, and now in His mercy turned to advantage what the Devil had intended in the way of destruction. And because the house was now finished and well pleasing in His sight, He decided to deal hardly with it as He tends to deal with churches, for it frequently and commonly happens that such a church is buffeted by waves and tossed by the winds of adversity, but eventually reaches the harbour of salvation unharmed. The Lord willed it thus: just as earlier, while the house was being built, He had tested it with many assaults and always found it impregnable, so that later it deserved to reach its proper completion, so, I repeat, the Lord wished to examine it now that it was complete, in order to give it firmness if it appeared unshakeable; that in the same way that it had acquired stature through its early firmness of purpose, it might by reason of unfailing perseverance succeed in enduring unto all eternity.

24. His constancy

At that time, in the days that is of King Henry II of England, the celebrated persecution arose and raged against St Thomas, archbishop of Canterbury, as he took his stand on God's laws and the liberty of the universal church.[2] Divine providence did not wish St Gilbert and his community to be excluded from this glorious victory, but, in order that his church should deserve to be reckoned among the daughters of the universal church, made her

eandem simul cum matre legitime certare et beate triumphare. Igitur cum in excidium ecclesie et beati Thome tota fere Anglia coniurasset, nec inueniret ubi requiesceret pes eius,[1] obstantibus iunctis et insidiantibus ut eum comprehenderent et regis traderent uoluntati, susceptus est pacifice in monasteriis et mansionibus patris Gileberti, et acceptis ex fratribus eius comitibus et ministris, itinera eius et latibula satis circumspecte sunt directa. Sed in-grauescente malitia cum idem beatus antistes ad regem Francorum Lodowicum exul ab Anglia confugisset, notatus est domnus Gile-bertus et sui quod post relegationem illius multam ei trans mare pecuniam misissent et quibus indiguerat contra regis preceptum ministrassent. Quod licet falsum esset, quia tamen ita creditum est a fidelibus regis et ministris, coacti sunt tam ipse quam omnes omnium cenobiorum suorum prepositi et procuratores iudicibus f. 64ᵛ regis coram assistere, ut si rem ita se habere | conuinceretur, omnes pariter subirent exilium. Miserentibus ergo iudicibus, quia eius sanctitas nota erat omnibus, oblatum est ei ut prestito sacramento fidem faceret falsum esse quod suggestum est, et ita cum suis indem-nis ad propria remearet.

Quod uir sanctissimus et sapientissimus quamuis integra fide et consona ueritate facere potuisset, quia id tamen in iniuriam ecclesie redundaret, renuit, dicens malle se subire exilium quam tale prestare iuramentum.[2] Considerauit enim quod quamuis rei ueritas aliter se haberet quam putabant, et uerum iurare non noceat iuranti si compellitur, licet a malo sit exigentis pocius quam prestantis, contra fidei tamen et pietatis iustitiam agere uideretur si iuraret, et prauum posteris presentibusque relinqueret exem-plum, quasi impium esset et sacrilegum pastori et ecclesie sub tali casu succurrere, cum magis prophanum sit in hoc articulo eccle-siam pro uiribus non defendere. Simili modo sub Machabeis senex Eleazarus nec propter timorem mortis carnem suillam comedere, f. 65 nec propter amorem uite | et ueterem uirorum amicitiam uoluit simulare se comedisse, ne triste iuuenibus senex daret exemplum quod pro metu mortis patrias leges uiolasset.[3] Ita et senex noster

---

[1] Cf. Gen. 8: 9.

[2] In the Gilbertine Constitutions, as in most monastic constitutions, the swearing of an oath in a law court was forbidden (cf. *Monasticon*, vi, iii, lxix* (xlii*)).

[3] Cf. 2 Macc. 6: 18–31.

struggle in this lawful cause alongside her mother church and happily to triumph. Thus when almost the whole of England had conspired to destroy the church and St Thomas, when he could find nowhere his foot might rest,[1] when united by their hostility men lay in wait to capture him and deliver him up to the king's will, he found a peaceful refuge in the monasteries and houses of Father Gilbert, and plans for his journey and his hiding places were most carefully drawn up, companions and servants being received by Thomas from among Gilbert's brethren. But the crisis deepened and the blessed archbishop fled as an exile from England to King Louis of France; then it was alleged that, after the sentence of banishment imposed upon the archbishop, Gilbert and his followers had sent him large sums of money across the Channel and had provided what he lacked against the king's command. Although this was a lie, it was believed by the king's vassals and servants, and both Gilbert and all the heads of all his monastic houses together with their representatives were compelled to appear before the king's justices, so that if the accusation was substantiated all alike might suffer exile. However, the justices relented because Gilbert's holiness was well known to them all, and it was put to him that he should swear a solemn oath that the allegation was untrue and so return home safe and sound along with his followers.

This the wisest and holiest of men could have done with entire good faith, adhering strictly to the truth, but because it meant injuring the church he refused, saying that he preferred to undergo exile rather than take such an oath.[2] The real situation was quite other than what they thought and to take a true oath does not harm the person who does so if he acts under compulsion, since the action arises from the wickedness of the man demanding the oath rather than the one taking it. Nevertheless he considered that if he swore an oath he would appear to be acting against the just requirements of faith and piety; moreover, to the living and those coming after him he would leave a bad example, as it would be an impious sacrilege to help a pastor and his church in such a way, although in such a crisis it is more wicked not to defend the church to the utmost of one's strength. In similar fashion, in the time of the Maccabees old Eleazar would neither eat pork because he was afraid of death, nor, out of his love of life and long-standing personal friendship, pretend that he had eaten it, lest an old man should give a bad example to the young in violating the laws of his people through fear of death.[3] Thus while it lay within his power, our aged Master

nec indefensam ecclesiam dum potuit relinquere, nec se quasi reliquisse uoluit fingere, ne apud homines factus eneruis ceteros eneruaret, et apud Deum tanquam pro facto incurreret offensam. Itaque suspensa diu sententia, cum nec ipse se hoc modo purgare adquiesceret et iudices illum condemnare timerent, apud urbem Lundoniarum cum suis moratus est prestolando quid ei mandaretur a tribunalibus, paratus semper ad omnia pro ueritatis constantia. In qua expectatione cum nimis timore desolarentur omnes sui, utpote iam iamque et genus et patriam relicturi, ita ut quidam eorum sane se iurasse posse arbitrantes, et impium esse ducentes loca sue professionis pro tali causa deserere, iuramentum illud prestare essent parati, ille ita terrenum oblitus est timorem quod in curia cum suis cunctis merentibus residens ludicra quedam fusilia deferente puero emisset, ad nullam aliam utilitatem uel usum nisi ut iocum faceret sociis, et quantum
f. 65ᵛ causam tristitie | eorum paruipenderet ostendit.

In hospitio quoque suo maiori iocundabatur in illa mora leticia, et inter diuina sollemnia mirationem fecit omni populo super dulcissono spiritalis chori illius concentu. Omne enim gaudium estimabat, cum in tribulationes uarias incidisset. Die igitur ultimo cum ab auditione mala cuncti timerent ut sine dilatione et obstaculo intentatum preciperentur subire exilium, aduenerunt de transmarinis regii ad iudices nuncii, qui eis ex parte regis mandauerunt ut questionem magistri Gileberti et suorum differrent quousque rex ipse plenius cognouisset de causa. Ilico dimissus est in pace, et cum suis omnibus ad sua redire permissus. Tunc cum ab omni exactione et coactione solutus esset nec opus haberet quicquam inficiari uel confiteri, dixit manifeste iudicibus, sed nec tactis uel inspectis sacris, nec sub conditione litis, uerbis tamen quibus bene crederent, quod obiecte falsitatis penitus esset inmunis. Vnde mirati sunt uniuersi constantiam uiri, quod nec in tanta minarum asperitate et sui suorumque periculo id agere uellet coactus, quod tamen tam tute
f. 66 agere posset, | quod post egit spontaneus.

would neither leave the church defenceless nor cause it to look as if he had done so, lest, by becoming feeble in the sight of men, he should make others feeble, and in the sight of God commit an offence as great as a positive action. And so judgement was suspended for a long while, as he would not agree to clear himself in this way and the justices were afraid to convict him; and he remained with his followers in the city of London to await whatever command should be sent him by those in authority, always prepared for every eventuality in his steadfast defence of the truth. While they waited all his followers were seized by a heavy foreboding that they were on the point of leaving both family and country. Some of them, therefore, thinking that they could really have sworn and judging it wicked to desert the places of their profession in such a cause, were ready to take that oath. But the Master so far forgot earthly anxiety that, as he was sitting in the court along with all his sorrowful followers, he bought some spinning-tops from a boy with no other use or purpose but to make sport for his companions, thus showing how unimportant he thought the cause of their sadness.

In his lodging he rejoiced with great delight during the delay, and during divine service he caused the entire congregation to marvel at the sweet harmony of that spiritual brotherhood. He reckoned everything joyful though he had fallen into manifold tribulations. Then on the last day, when they were all frightened by an evil rumour that they would be ordered without delay or hindrance into their threatened exile, royal messengers from across the sea arrived before the justices and commanded them in the king's name to postpone the dispute concerning Master Gilbert and his followers until the king himself had taken fuller cognizance of the case. Thereupon he was peacefully dismissed and allowed to return home with all his companions. At that moment, when he was free from every pressure and compulsion and had no need to deny or admit anything, he said openly to the justices (not touching or observing holy objects and without legal constraint, but in words which they might readily believe) that he was entirely innocent of the false charge made against him. Then everyone was amazed at the man's iron resolve, because not even when there were so many grave threats and such danger both to himself and his followers would he perform an action under coercion which he could nevertheless have performed quite safely, and which he later performed of his own accord.

25. *Vexatio falsorum fratrum*

Videns igitur hostis inquietus se in premisso temtandi genere defecisse et uirum cum suo populo gloriosiorem reddidisse, acriori seuit inuidia, et si quo modo alio aliaue causa uel aliis instrumentis opus diuinum subuertere posset exquisiuit. Quia enim predicta iuuare non poterant, ad alterius modi se contulit negocii sui expedimenta. In predicta enim temptatione, causam habuit illum criminandi pietatis defensionem, modum potentiam magis quam iustitiam, instrumenta extera et affectata, que omnia, que[a] magis prodesse poterant quam obesse illi contra quem parabantur, sine magna difficultate poterant adnichilari. In hac autem temptatione se conuertit ad contrarium, et causam temptandi adinuenit religionis inpugnationem, modum quo hoc prosequeretur iustitiam, instrumenta ex propria domo illius sibi assumpsit. Dixit enim per os mendatium quorumdam ipsum esse sacri ordinis et ecclesiasticarum institutionum subuersorem, que causa facile posset mouere contra eum uni|uersos, et ut cautius hoc probaret iuris ordinem et iustitie processum seruauit in lite, et quo ueracius credi faceret quod intendit, de suis domesticis actores constituit et testes. Quis non contra eum in hac causa se erigeret? Quis sancte religionis subuersionem pateretur inultam? Quis non iustam causam crederet illum habere, qui in sua causa tam iuste uellet procedere? Inpetrauerat enim per suos satellites, laicos scilicet conuersos, a principibus tam secularibus quam ecclesiasticis, quos aduersus eum commouerat, monita et precepta multiformia ad iudices satis constantes, quorum examini secundum tenorem legum et canonum commisit sue cause cognitionem.[1] Quis autem non crederet dictis proximorum et sibi indiuisibiliter coherentium, zelum Dei, quantum uideri poterat, et formam pietatis habentium?

Hec erant que temptationem grauius urgebant, quia rationem maior comitatur uirtus quam uiolentiam. Accedit ad pondus grauaminis quod homines pacis sue in quibus sperauit, qui edebant panes suos et quos maxime dilexerat, ampliauerunt aduersus

f. 66ᵛ

---

[a] *Perhaps* quia *or* quod *(Winterbottom)*

---

[1] For all this see pp. lv–lxi.

25. *Trouble from false brethren*

Then the unresting Enemy saw that he had failed with this kind of temptation and had made the man of God and his following all the more glorious; so a fiercer hatred raged within him, and he investigated whether he could overthrow God's work by other means, another pretext, or other instruments. Because his previous devices had proved unable to help him, he turned to a different means of fulfilling his purpose. For in the temptation already described he had used Gilbert's fidelity to his religious profession as the pretext to incriminate him; power rather than justice had been his means, and his instruments were external and contrived; and because all these factors could more easily work to the advantage rather than the detriment of the man against whom they were devised, they could be eliminated without any great difficulty. But for this new temptation he took an opposite course; he found a pretext for his attempt in an attack upon the religious life, and the means to bring this about in justice, while the instruments he took from St Gilbert's own house. Speaking through the mouths of some lying men, he asserted that Gilbert himself was a subverter of the sacred order and of ecclesiastical institutions—an issue which might easily influence everyone against him. To prove this accusation all the more cunningly he preserved the form of law and process of justice in the dispute, and to make his assertions more easily credible he appointed accusers and witnesses from amongst the Master's own household servants. Who could not rise against the Master in such a cause as this? Who could allow such damage to the religious life to go unavenged? Who would believe that a person wishing to act so properly in his own case did not have a just cause? For through his underlings, the lay brethren, the Enemy had obtained many different warnings and instructions from both secular and ecclesiastical dignitaries whom he had influenced against St Gilbert, warnings to the perfectly sound judges to whose jurisdiction, following the letter of secular and church law, Gilbert committed the trial of his case.[1] And who would not believe what was said by his intimates and those inseparably associated with him, men who were, as far as could be seen, zealous for God and outwardly pious?

It was these considerations which gave the crisis such serious impact, since reason is stronger than violence. To add to the weight of the offence, the men who shared his peace and partook of his bread, whom he trusted and had loved most dearly, enlarged their

eum supplantationem, unde magis doluit.[1] Rursum preter senectu-
f. 67 tis | incommoda debilitate corporis uexabatur, cum tamen procul et
in ultimis finibus Anglie in causarum uentilationibus cogeretur
multociens in propria persona apparere. Itemque, quod super
omnia grauat, serui dominum, despicabiles conspicuum, ignoti
nobilem impetere presumpserunt, et quorum patres (ut ait Scriptura) non dignabatur ponere cum canibus gregis sui, nunc in eorum
canticum uersus est et factus est eis in prouerbium.[2] Quippe forma
erat hec prime persecutionis primitiue ecclesie, in quam surrexer-
unt quidam de synagoga libertinorum, id est manu missorum,[3] qui
primo fidei Christi restiterunt. Que omnia qui plenius cupit cogno-
scere, ex beati uiri dictis plenius addiscet in scripto illo quod de fun-
datione monasteriorum reliquerat, ubi sic ait:[4]

Huius discidii et discordie exstiterunt caput duo fratres laici, quibus
commiseram pre ceteris curam omnium domorum nostrarum. Eis uero
associati sunt alii duo, quorum unum fere mendicantem suscepi uictum
queritantem arte textrina, et alterum Oggerum fabrum nomine, quem
puerum suscepi, non fabrum arte,[a] cum tribus fratribus suis, arte im-
peritis, et patrem eius pauperrimum et fere decrepitum, et matrem eius
f. 67ᵛ uetulam cum duabus filiabus suis | mendicantibus et diutina infirmitate
languentibus. Oggerum uero et alium de fratribus suis arte fabrili a
nostris permisi instrui, et alios duos arte carpentaria. Hii uero predicti,
associatis sibi aliis fratribus, insurrexerunt aduersum me et canonicos
nostros—Deus scit—mentientes, et diffamauerunt nos per multas
regiones. Ipsum etiam domnum papam Alexandrum, magne sanctitatis
uirum, et curiam Romanam aduersum nos concitauerunt. Ipse uero
domnus papa, credulus uerbis predicti Oggeri, nimis seuerum mandatum
et sententiam crudelem aduersum nos dedit.

Et post pauca:[b]

Veritatem, teste Deo, dicam et non mentiar: hec fuit causa insanie Oggeri
et Gerardi, qui aggregauerunt sibi proprietates furto, sequentes proprias
uoluntates, a professione et religione sua deuii, proprios habentes pale-
fridos cursitabant huc et illuc, minus parcentes castitati et honestati in
subsannationem et derisum facti sunt clero et populo.[c] Quod cum
audirem et eos ab errore ad uiam ueritatis reuocare uellem, ab infamia

---

ª arte *om. Lc*   ᵇ et post pauca *om. Od, which adds at the end of the previous extract*
quod postea reuocauit   ᶜ *This sentence is ill written, and it is difficult to know how it
should be articulated*

---

[1] Cf. Ps. 40: 10 (41: 9).   [2] Job 30: 1, 9.   [3] Cf. Acts 6: 9.
[4] On Gilbert's *scriptum* see pp. 30–1.

crookedness against him, which caused him to grieve even more deeply.[1] Moreover, apart from the troubles of old age he suffered from bodily exhaustion; yet he had often to appear in person to attend judicial hearings at great distances and on the furthest confines of England. And most offensive of all, servants presumed to attack their master, contemptible men to assail a person of distinction, and obscure men one of noble birth; and he became the song and byword of those whose fathers (in the Bible's words) he disdained to set with the dogs of his flock.[2] This indeed was what happened during the early church's first persecution, when some of the synagogue of the libertines, that is of freedmen,[3] who at the beginning opposed the faith of Christ, rebelled against her. Whoever wishes to learn more about all this can gain fuller information from the saint's own words, for in the account he left of the foundation of the religious houses he says:[4]

At the head of this discord and strife were two lay brethren to whom I had entrusted the care of all our houses, preferring them before all others. Two other men were associated with them, one of whom I received when he was scarcely more than a beggar endeavouring to make a living from his skill at weaving. The second Ogger, a smith by name but not by craft, I took in when he was a boy, along with his three brothers, who were unskilled in any craft, his destitute, almost moribund father, his aged mother, and his two sisters, who were living in beggary and were weak from a long illness. I allowed Ogger and one of his brothers to be taught the blacksmith's trade by our people, and the other two the carpenter's. These men, having united other brethren to them, rebelled against myself and our canons, lying, God knows, and slandering us in many parts of the country. They also stirred up against us no less a person than Pope Alexander, a man of great sanctity, as well as the Roman curia. For the pope, trusting Ogger's words, issued an unduly severe mandate and a cruel judgement against us.

A little further on:

As God is my witness, I will speak the truth and not lie. This was the pretext for the madness which seized Ogger and Gerard, for they accumulated possessions for themselves by theft, and followed their own desires, turning away from their profession and the religious life; they chased hither and thither on their own mounts with very little respect for continence and honest living, until they became objects of mockery and derision to clergy and people. When I heard of this I wished to call them back from error to the way of truth, from shame

ad bonam famam, ab incontinentia ad castitatem, contempta correptione nostra et nostrorum, diffamauerunt me et canonicos nostros, et facti f. 68 sumus in admiratione et | fabula per diuersa locorum spacia.

Hiis uerbis suam deplorat uir pacientissimus molestiam, quam nisi naturali sentiret affectu non ex hoc mereretur.[a] Sed quia omnia constanti tolerancia superauit, magis eorum plangit perditionem, ut asseuerauit, quia magis doluit, quam suum laborem. Nam cum peruersi illi scismatici, furtim asportantes possessiones domorum, auribus summi pontificis multa falsa instillassent et litteras sue uoluntatis efficaces tacita uoluntate inpetrassent, omnem exhibuit apostolicis mandatis licet sibi perniciosis obedientiam, et nunciis quamuis aduersariis suis reuerentiam. Igitur in illarum causarum conflictibus sepe in ius uocatus, et coram pontificibus et prelatis pulsatus, cum multa in eum intenderentur, ille immobilis animi constantiam seruans, nec timore penarum nec suasu iudicum a recto proposito deuiare consensit, ita ut prius secandum guttur assereret quam primam eorum professionem et ordinis institutionem immutaret, que multorum priuilegiis apostolicorum fuerat sanccita et per longum tempus eatenus seruata. Cumque in probationibus eorum que obiecerant omnino deficerent, nec ui uel arte obtinere possent quod optabant, contulerunt se f. 68ᵛ | ad preces, ueniam postulantes et suppliciter duntaxat deprecantes quatinus pauca de proposito rigore temperaret.[1] Quos omnes in filios sicut uir mansuetus in osculo pacis benigne suscipiens, in temperandis nimis asperis et emendandis ordinis institutis auctoritate domini pape et uirorum religiosorum consilio promisit prono animo se in omnibus pariturum. Solus tamen Oggerus, uiri sancti ut ita dicam malleus, in sua perstitit malitia, nec fratrum suorum precibus nec iudicum uel assessorum commonitionibus motus redire uoluit ad ordinis unitatem, nisi sepedictus magister ad arbitrium eius nouas in ordine conderet institutiones. Quod quia noluit (non enim expediuit), ille in sua pertinatia abscessit, et fere usque ad diem obitus tam sui quam beati Gileberti illum inpugnare non destitit. Parum tamen uel nichil profecit:

---

[a] mireretur *Lc before correction. The word is corrupt. Perhaps* pateretur *(Winterbottom)*

---

[1] A promise not fulfilled until St Hugh's intervention, between 1186 and 1189 (see pp. 116–19, 344).

to good repute and from incontinence to chastity. But, spurning my reproaches and those of my followers, they slandered my canons and myself, so that in different localities we provoked shocked surprise and gave rise to gossip.

With these words the most patient of men laments the distress caused to himself, which he would not have suffered from this matter, were it not for his natural feelings. But because by steadfast endurance he overcame everything, he bewails the plight of these men more than the vexation to himself for, he said, it grieved him more deeply. Those obstinate schismatics had secretly removed possessions belonging to the houses; they had filled the pope's ears with many falsehoods; and by keeping their intentions concealed they obtained letters securing what they desired. Yet Gilbert displayed total obedience towards the pope's mandates even though they were damaging to him, and showed reverence to his messengers although they were opposed to him. In the disputes arising from this case he was often summoned to a court of law and arraigned before bishops and prelates. But even when many charges were preferred against him, he maintained the steadfastness of unwavering courage; and so far was he from agreeing to depart from his correct position, either through fear of the punishment or the judges' persuasion, that he declared his throat should be cut before he would alter the first profession of these men and the first institution of the Order, authorized by the privileges of many popes and hitherto preserved over a long period of time. When they failed entirely to prove their accusations and were unable to get what they wanted by force or cunning, they resorted to entreaty, begging for pardon and humbly requesting him only to moderate a little the strictness of their regime.[1] Being a merciful man he graciously received them all as sons with the kiss of peace, and he promised gladly that, with the pope's authority and the advice of the religious, he would obey in all respects in tempering and reforming over-harsh regulations of the Order. Ogger alone, whom I may call the hammer of the saint, persisted in his wickedness; influenced neither by his brothers' prayers nor by the warnings of judges and assessors, he would only return to the united body of the Order if the Master established new regulations for it which accorded with his own wishes. Because the Master refused (for it was not expedient), Ogger, still obstinate, departed and, almost to the day both of his own death and that of St Gilbert, he lost no opportunity to attack the saint. But it did him

nam semper iuxta nominis sui interpretationem interclusus recessit.[1]

Cuius peruersitas quantum Deo displiceret non sine euidenti inditio preteriuit: nam quia in posteritate carnali qua caruit puniri ut plerique non potuit, in sua radice damnata reprobus ostensus est. Pater siquidem eius carnalis,[a] uiciis filii non reni- f. 69 tens sed forte consentiens et | condelectans, quotiens sacramentum dominici corporis percepisset,[b] dictu mirum et terribile aspectu, dedignatus Dominus indigni hospicii habitaculum quandoque per os, quandoque per nares aut aures illud eiecit, ostendens manifeste non esse participem communionis ecclesiastice, quam quantum in ipso erat disciderat, qui sacramenta unitatis ecclesie retinere non poterat. Qui et ipse morte inprouisa defunctus est. Complicum etiam suorum, qui principales illius scismatis extiterant conditores uel factores, uix aliquis decenti obitu diem clausit extremum. Reuelata tandem sua et complicum eius nequitia, cum in hoc camino sanctus satis esset probatus,[2] et pacem reddere ecclesie decreuisset pietas superna, pene omnes episcopi Anglie ceterique prelati, qui uel ex propinquitate et confrequentia uel ex fame preconio eum nouerant, scripta sua cum sigillis et nuntiis, omnem rei ueritatem continentia, ad domnum papam Alexandrum direxerunt, quibus Deo dignam magistri Gileberti personam eiusque opera mirifica et laudabilem subditorum gregem satis magnifice commendauerunt, et illorum rebellium insolentiam dilucide et ueraciter innotuerunt, supplicantes | f. 69ᵛ unanimiter ut memoratum uirum in suo proposito quod a Deo erat stabiliret et inuiolabiliter roboraret, necnon et scismaticorum insidias eluderet.[c] Ipse quoque illustris rex Henricus secundus suum scriptum idem testificans idemque obtestans cum regiis nunciis transmisit, in fine firmissime contestans quod si rusticorum illorum et qui erant, ut ait, ascripticii glebe machinationibus ordo ille mutaretur, dominia et possessiones que ob religiosam ibidem conuersantium deuotionem cum suis proceribus contulerat omnino retraheret.[3] Quod si prefatum ordinem et primam institutionem debito rigore faceret papa obseruari,

---

[a] carnaliis *Lc*   [b] percepiscet *Lc*   [c] elideret *Od (cf. below, p. 146 n.d.)*

---

[1] See below, Appendix 2 (note by Cecily Clark).
[2] Cf. Ecclus. 2: 5; and cf. Wisd. 3: 6; Prov. 17: 3.
[3] See the king's letter, pp. 142–5.

little or no good, for always according to the interpretation of his name he was prevented and forced to retreat.[1]

How deeply this man's wrongdoing offended God did not pass unmarked by a clearly visible sign; for because he could not, like most men, be punished in the descendants of his body, since he had none, his guilt was demonstrated by the condemnation which fell upon his stock. Since his father in the flesh did not repudiate his son's vices but perchance agreed to them and shared in their pleasure, whenever he received the sacrament of Our Lord's body an event occurred which is amazing to relate and was horrifying to see. Our Lord, disdaining to dwell in an unworthy lodging, cast the sacrament out, sometimes through the mouth, sometimes through the nostrils or the ears; thus he clearly showed that the man who was unable to retain the sacrament of the Church's unity was no member of the ecclesiastical community which he had torn apart as far as he could. He died, moreover, an untimely death; and scarcely any of Ogger's accomplices who had originally provoked or brought about the division came at the end of his days to die honourably. But when at last the wickedness of this man and his associates had come to light, when the saint had been tried in this furnace[2] and heavenly providence had determined to restore peace to the church, then almost all the English bishops and other prelates who knew him, either because they lived nearby and had met him or because they were acquainted with his reputation, sent by messenger sealed letters containing all the facts of the matter to Pope Alexander. In these they commended the person of Master Gilbert and in glowing terms deemed him acceptable to God, his deeds marvellous and the community of his subjects worthy of high praise; and clearly and truthfully they described the insolence of the rebels. With one accord they begged the Pope to establish this man in his purpose, which derived from God, making it strong and unassailable; and in addition they asked him to frustrate the deceitful works of the schismatics. The illustrious King Henry II himself also sent with royal messengers his own letter giving the same evidence and making the same requests. At the end of it he stated categorically that if the Order was altered through the machinations of these peasants and (as he put it) former serfs, he would take back in entirety the estates and possessions which, along with his magnates, he had granted to the house because of the devotion to the religious life shown by its inmates.[3] But if the pope would ensure that this Order and the original form of its constitution were observed with proper strictness,

ipse quantum ad secularem iustitiam pertinet eum pro posse suo
manuteneret et in maximo honore et reuerentia sicut consueuerat
haberet.

Indulgentie[a] domini pape

Quibus beatus papa commonitus testimoniis precibusque com-
motus apostolicam scripto remisit auctoritatem, indulgens beato
Gileberto et successoribus eius ut nulli liceat religionem eorum et
iura uel rationabiles institutiones, sine maioris et sanioris partis
consilio et consensu, corrigere uel mutare, uel aliquid superaddere
f. 70 quod predicte religioni eorum et sa|lubribus institutionibus uide-
atur obuiare.[1] Sed quecunque in ordine illo de cetero emerserint
corrigenda, ille uel successor eius ea cum consilio priorum eiusdem
ordinis secundum statuta sua corrigere et emendare ⟨possint et⟩[b]
secundum quod magis uiderint expedire reforment. Alias etiam
plurimas inmunitates et dignitates ad perpetuum firmamentum
domnus[c] papa Alexander sancto patri Gileberto successoribusque
eius et sancto conuentui de Sempingham dedit et concessit, que et a
successoribus suis Romanis pontificibus plenius et robustius con-
firmate sunt, quatinus in posterum tollatur omnis malignandi occasio suoque robore gaudeat hic ordo et illesus consistat.[2]

26. Item alia temptatio

In hac igitur pugna gloriosus uictor pater Gilebertus semper se ipso
robustior apparuit, et quanto acrius[d] impetebatur ab hoste, tanto
forcius uiriliusque restitit et felicius uicit. Nam instar beati Iob, tot
hactenus extra accidentibus periculis nichil detrimenti passus, eo
grauiori quo propinquiori et diuturniori fuerat certamine interro-
gandus, ut tanquam aurum quod per ignem tercio probatur et quasi
f. 70ᵛ argentum purgatum | septuplum Christi diademati infigeretur.[3]
Deuictis enim bellis multis tam extraneis quam ciuilibus, sibi ipsi
ipsemet obicitur superandus, ut nullo genere uictorie priuaretur.
Nam preter naturalem corporis imbecillitatem, quam tum[e] morborum molestia, tum senectus importuna, tum labor cicius
senectam importans inflixerat, corporalis uisus incurrit caliginem.

---

[a] indulgentiam Lc; indulgentia Lh corr.   [b] Supplied by Winterbottom (cf. the original letter, below, p. 156)   [c] Perhaps domus (Winterbottom)   [d] arctius Lc
[e] quam tum Brooke; quantum LcOd

[1] See pp. 156–9.   [2] See pp. lviii–lx, lxvi.
[3] Cf. Ecclus. 2: 5; Prov. 17: 3 (and Wisd. 3: 6); Ps. 11 (12): 7; 65: 10 (66: 9).

then as far as secular justice was concerned he would maintain it to the height of his powers, and regard it with the greatest honour and reverence, as he had always done.

The pope's privileges

The pope was impressed by their evidence and moved by their prayers, so that he sent back written papal confirmation; this granted to St Gilbert and his successors that no one might correct or change their form of religious life, customs, or reasonable institutions, without the advice and consent of the greater and wiser part of the Order; neither was anything to be added which might appear to stand in the way of their religious rule and its sound organization.[1] But if problems arose in the Order needing correction in future, he or his successor, with the advice of the priors of the Order, could correct and amend it according to their statutes, and reform it as they thought best. Pope Alexander also granted and conferred upon holy Father Gilbert, his successors, and the holy community of Sempringham many other immunities and privileges to strengthen it for ever; these were confirmed in fuller and stronger terms by the Roman popes who succeeded him, to remove all possibility of injury and to ensure that the Order flourished vigorously, standing firm and free from harm.[2]

26. Another trial

In this battle Father Gilbert appeared as a glorious conqueror, all the time increasing in strength; the more fiercely he was attacked by the Enemy, the more bravely and energetically he fought back and the more splendidly he triumphed. Up to this point he had suffered no harm from so many external dangers, but like Job he was to be tested by a trial which was all the more severe for being a more intimate and long-drawn-out struggle; that, just as gold is tried three times by fire and silver purified seven times, he might be set into the crown of Christ.[3] Since he had victoriously concluded many wars, foreign as well as civil, his own person was presented to him as something to overcome in order that he should not be deprived of any sort of victory. Apart from the natural weakness of his body which troublesome illnesses, grievous old age, and the toil which hastens on old age had inflicted on him, he went blind.

Quam temptationem utrum nature deficienti an casui siue inimico persequenti attribuam, ignoro. Talis etenim fortassis erat complexio corporis[a] naturalis que uisus aciem, maxime in tanta etate, diutius non poterat conseruare. Sed si casu uel uiolentia hoc contigit illi nescimus; cum crebris lacrimarum inundationibus, dum mitteret semina sua, eosdem oculos nouimus eum debilitasse, et multas uentorum, puluerum et uigiliarum aliorumque incommodorum pertulisse iniurias. Si autem spiritualis hec fuerit percussio incertum est; quocumque tamen modo uel Dei iudicio hoc ei euenerit,[b] non inde erubescimus cum idem Ysaac et Iacob multisque aliis acciderit sanctis, sed ex hoc amplius gratulamur quia non hoc iram et indignationem sed Dei scimus fuisse clementiam.

27. *Qualis erat in senio*

f. 71 Accreuit enim illi uirtus ex defectione, et pro lumine corporis amisso maiore et meliore meruit gratia spiritus illustrari. Nam uigorem animi licet decrepitus, licet egrotus, licet uisu priuatus, in nullo relaxauit, immo quantum zelum et feruorem habuit cure pastoralis in minore etate, tantum quoad uixit indefesse seruauit. Quam uigil sensus, discreta ratio, docile ingenium, herens memoria ei fuerit, mirati sunt quotquot uiderunt. Auditus penetrabilis, lingua diserta, manus intremula, pes solidus suum officium alteri Caleph non[c] denegabant.[1] O quantus feruor diuine dilectionis, quantum studium fraterni amoris in illa mente resedit, cum eius cordi et ori Christus numquam defuit, eius lingue et manibus semper inerat quod proximis profuit. Iugis oratio, iuge suspirium et lacrimarum crebra inundatio quid mens senserit interius non potuerunt celare. Et quia speculator constitutus a Domino domus Israel supra speculam suam per se stare prout oportuit non potuit, oculos, manus et pedes, id est ministros qui horum gererent officium loco suo, preparauit.[2] Sollicitudinem omnium cenobiorum pretaxato domino Rogero
f. 71v priori Maltone commisit, | ut consilio suo maiora tractaret, sub eo uero singulis gradibus marium et feminarum unum uel duos,

[a] corporalis *Lc; perhaps read* corporalis nature *(Winterbottom), cf. p. 118* [b] euenerat *Od* [c] non *Lc*[1] *Od; om. Lc*

[1] Presumably Caleb son of Jephunneh, Num. 13–14; Josh. 14.

[2] Cf. John of Salisbury's celebrated analogy of the body and the kingdom in the *Policraticus*, ultimately based on 1 Cor. 12: 12ff.

I do not know whether to attribute this trial to man's deficient nature or to an accident or to the persecution of the devil. Perhaps his body was naturally so made that he could not preserve his keenness of vision any longer, especially at such a great age. But we do not know for certain whether this happened to him by accident or through some act of violence: we do know that he weakened those eyes of his with frequent floods of tears while he was preaching, and that he suffered much harm from winds, dust, vigils, and other discomforts. It is also uncertain whether this was a spiritual affliction, but by whatever means or judgement of God this occurred to him, we do not blush for it, since the same thing happened to Isaac, Jacob, and many other holy men; on the contrary we give thanks all the more fervently because we know that this was proof not of God's anger and indignation, but of his mercy.

27. *What he was like in old age*

For he derived new strength from his weakness and, in return for having lost light from his body, he received the illumination he merited from the greater and more important blessing of the spirit. Although he was infirm, sick, and blind he lost none of his mental energy; on the contrary, as long as he lived he preserved undiminished the zeal and enthusiasm which he devoted to his pastoral office at a younger age. All those who saw him wondered that he possessed in so generous a measure an unflagging intellect, a discerning judgement, and a receptive spirit linked to an excellent memory. His acute hearing, eloquent tongue, steady hand, and firm foot did not refuse their functions to this second Caleb.[1] How deeply his passion for divine love and his concern for brotherly affection were impressed upon his mind! For Christ was never absent from his heart and lips, and his tongue and his hands were always occupied by what was of profit to those around him. His continual prayer, repeated sighs, and frequent bursts of tears could not hide what his mind perceived within him. And because, as the watchman of the house of Israel appointed by God, he was unable through his own powers to stand on watch as he should, he appointed eyes, hands, and feet—in other words, servants to carry out their functions in his place.[2] To Roger, prior of Malton, he entrusted the care of all the religious houses, in such a way that this man handled the more important business following his advice; under him for each rank of men and women there were one or two

quos circatores uel summos scrutatores appellant, qui omnium domorum statum diligenter inspicerent et[a] ut oporteret corrigerent, grauiora autem semper ad ipsum referrent.[1] Ipse uero caput omnium, utpote sensu et sanctitate preminens omnibus, omnium ad se causas detulit et manuscriptas omnium professiones quoad uixit suscepit. Quocirca ut nichil de partibus officii sui omitteret, quia equo non poterat, gestatorio se fecit semper per singulas domos circumferri.

In itinere, hospitio, mensa et lecto et ceteris omnibus locis regularibus et horis, eandem quam prius, immo rigidiorem, tenuit discipline censuram. Nam rebus secularibus pro carentia uisus exemptus et absens, totus in celestibus habitauit, et post iustos sancte actionis labores, dulcis contemplationis meruit deliciis indesinenter confoueri. Toto spatio diurno preter corporalium indigentiarum supplementa, aut lectioni aurem inclinauit, aut mentem manusque et os precibus accommodauit, aut spiritali fratrum confabulationi indulsit. Nichil autem inter loquendum ei |
f. 72 placuit uel pacienter audire potuit, nisi quod de Deo et uera uita sonuisset. Pauca tamen et breuia, licet essent sancta et utilia, edidit uerba, memorans illud Psalmiste: 'Obmutui et humiliatus sum et silui a bonis.'[2] Nam mox mentem ad celeste desiderium et uotum in preces conuertit, dicens hec et huiusmodi: 'Vsque quo, Domine, obliuisceris me in finem' et cetera, et 'Heu me, quia incolatus meus prolongatus est.'[3] Cumque quiescentem dormitare putaremus, manus sub pallio cum oculis ad celum erectas uidimus, et diuina uerba secum inmurmurantem porrectis auribus deprehendimus. In mediis autem sermonibus, cum se forte uel circumsedentes excessisse in uerbis arbitraretur, mox confessionem ecclesiasticam magna cum deuotione protulit, se petens humiliter absolui et suam subdens absolutionem. Nocte nichilominus pristinas seruauit in orationibus uigiliarum excubias, latenter ut potuit se deponens de grabato, ut ante lectum quas posset faceret genuflexiones. Cumque a comitibus sic iacens repertus fuisset, quasi culpauit eos quod stratum eius uespera male parauissent. Solum enim Dominum et sanctos eius, cum quibus nocte confabulatus est, huius rei desiderauit habere conscios et testes. |

---

[a] et *Lc*[1] *Od; om. Lc*

---

[1] See pp. 68–71.
[2] Ps. 38: 3 (39: 2).
[3] Ps. 12 (13): 1; 119 (120): 5.

persons called inspectors or chief scrutineers, who were to examine carefully the condition of all the houses and correct them as necessary, but were always to refer the more serious matters to him.[1] For as the head over them all, surpassing all in understanding and in holiness, he referred the cases of them all to himself and, as long as he lived, he received the written professions of all. So, in order not to neglect any aspect of his responsibility, as he could not ride, he always had himself carried round to each house upon a litter.

While travelling or staying in lodgings, at table and in bed, and at all the other regular times and places, he maintained the same standard of discipline as hitherto, or rather one even stricter. Released and removed by his loss of sight from attending to secular preoccupations, he dwelt entirely among the things of heaven; and after carrying out the good deeds of pious activity, he earned the reward of being strengthened ceaselessly by the delights of sweet meditation. All day, besides satisfying his bodily needs, he listened to a reading, busied his mind, hands, and mouth with prayer, or engaged in spiritual discussion with the brethren. While they were talking he enjoyed no theme and could not listen patiently unless it concerned God and the life of truth. The words he uttered were few and to the point although holy and edifying, for he remembered the Psalmist's saying: 'I was silent and chastened, and I spoke not even of good things.'[2] Then his mind would turn to heavenly longing and his will to prayer, as he spoke these words and others like them: 'Lord, wilt thou forget me unto the end?' and so on, and 'Woe is me, for I dwell here too long.'[3] And when we thought that he was quietly asleep we noticed that his hands underneath his blanket, as well as his eyes, were raised heavenwards, and by listening intently we caught him whispering holy prayers to himself. Also in the middle of discussion, when he considered that perhaps he or those sitting around him had said too much, he immediately and with great piety offered the church's rite of confession, humbly asking that he might himself be absolved, and bestowing his own absolution. At night he kept all his former vigils, spending them in prayer and getting out of bed as secretly as possible in order to make the genuflexions he could manage before his bed. When he was discovered by his companions in such a position, he made a show of blaming them for having prepared his bed badly in the evening. For he wished that only God and his saints, with whom he spoke at night, should be witnesses of this practice.

f. 72ᵛ   28. *De abstinentia eius*

Quid de ciborum loquar parsimonia, cum etiam in maximo morbi languore, qui senium solet comitari, nec fratrum precibus coactus in suo adquieuit comedere dormitorio? Numquam enim quantum in ipso erat a fratrum mensa uoluit separari, licet cubiculum eius a publico refectorio procul distaret, et gradus plurimi difficultatem facerent ascendendi in cenaculum.¹ Rogatas enim a fratribus ut sue parceret aliquantulum infirmitati, respondit substomachando, dicens: 'Non erit Gilebertus exemplum successoribus suis comedendi delicias in camera', et sic utroque latere manibus fratrum portatus, magno cum labore accessit ad mensam: ubi corpusculum magis inedia affecit quam refecit, numquam uasis dominici et fratrum memoriam pretermittens.² Surgens a mensa et reportatus ad cubiculum, quod reliquum erat diei in similes usus expendit.

29. *De magnificentia eius*

Hic est beati patris Gileberti uite excursus, uiuendi modus; hec uirtutum experimenta et morum insignia, quibus et potentissimorum principum factis magnificis supergressus est magnitu-
f. 73 dinem, | et sanctissimorum hominum non solum imitatus est sed etiam imitandum in se exhibuit exemplum. Quis enim summatumᵃ seculi, regum dico uel pontificum, tantam tantorum operum potuit in nostris temporibus summam adequare, cum ille pauper ut dicitur clericus primo totum patrimonium suum, omnia scilicet que habuit,³ largitus, ex diminutione incrementum et ex paupertate tantas congregauit diuitias. Sed quod magis arbitror mirandum, homo secularis et in curia ministrans monastice discipline normam ab homine non didicit, quam tamen tenuit, nec solum ipse seruauit sed multis custodiendam contradidit. Vnde pre sanctitate Deo amabilis et ex magnificentia hominibus factus est admirabilis, ex utroque autem omnibus uenerabilis. Reges et principes illum honorabant, pontifices et prelati deuote suscipiebant, propinqui

---

ᵃ summatum *LcOd;* optimatum *Lc*²

¹ Nothing survives above ground of the buildings at Sempringham, but this passage seems to make clear that the refectory was on the first floor, up a flight of stairs from the cloister (as at Watton: see p. 46, n. 3). For air photographs and the excavations of 1938–9, see D. Knowles and J. K. S. St Joseph, *Monastic Sites from the Air* (Cambridge, 1952), pp. 242–5; R. Graham and H. Braun in *JBAA*, 3rd ser. v (1940), 73–101.
² i.e., to see that the poor and the brethren were fed: see pp. 62–3.
³ Cf. Luke 18: 22.

28. *His abstinence*

What should I say about the spareness of his diet? Even when he was extremely weak from the sickness which usually accompanies old age, he would not agree to eat in his own sleeping-chamber despite the brethren's importunity. He wished, as far as in him lay, never to be parted from the brethren's table, although his bed-chamber was situated a long way from the common refectory[1] and a large number of steps made it difficult to climb up to it. When he was asked by the brethren to make some allowance for his infirmity he answered them with spirit, declaring: 'Gilbert will not provide his successors with the example of eating delicacies in his own room'; and so he came to the table, supported on both sides by the brethren's hands and with great effort. While there, rather than refreshing his frail body he made it fast, although he never forgot our Lord's plate or the brethren's.[2] When he arose from table and was carried back to his bedchamber he spent what was left of the day in similar practices.

29. *His greatness*

This is an account of blessed Father Gilbert's life and this his mode of living; these are the proofs of his fine qualities and the indications of his character, which enabled him to surpass in achievements the greatness of the most powerful princes; more-over, not only did he follow the example of the holiest men but he himself supplied an example for imitation. For who among the supreme men of our age, I mean kings or pontiffs, could in our time equal so high a total of mighty deeds? Though a poor clerk, as is said, he first of all gave away his whole inheritance, in other words all that he had,[3] but from this reduction gathered increase and from poverty great wealth. But even more remarkable in my opinion, as a secular serving at court he maintained a standard of monastic discipline which he had not learnt from any man, and not only did he himself observe it, but he handed it over so that many should keep it. Thus he became beloved of God for his sanctity, admired by men for his distinction and, for both reasons, venerated by all. Kings and princes honoured him, pontiffs and church dignitaries received him devoutly, those who were intimate

et extranei ualde diligebant, omnis plebs ut sanctum Dei colebat. Vidimus episcopos genibus eius prouolutos benedictionem suam petere, et de extraneis regionibus, in quibus fama sanctitatis eius personuerat, quosdam episcopos aduentantes aliquid de uestimentis eius postulare, quod in terris suis locis celebribus suspen-

f. 73ᵛ derent pro reliquiis. De eo | quoque quidam presules in suis scriptis et sermonibus popularibus illud propheticum interpretati sunt: 'Erubesce, Sydon, ait mare',[1] se Sydonem, illum uero mare appellantes, eo quod homo secularis et nullius ecclesiastice dignitatis summos ecclesie pastores non modo equiparare uerum etiam superare in promotione ecclesie uideretur.

Rex etiam inclitus Henricus secundus tantum ei detulit munus honoris ut illum ad curiam pro negotiis ecclesie uenientem non sit passus ad se uenire, sed ipse magis ad illum in hospitio suo audiendum cum proceribus suis ire non erubuit, et benedictioni eius se humiliter summittere et monita salutis ab eo audire non recusauit. Regina quoque Alienor filios suos reges futuros ab eo gaudebat benedici.[2] Statum enim regni sui et rerum successum uiueᵃ illius presentie et precum eius obtentui deputabant. Vnde cum postea nuntium obitus illius idem rex Henricus audiret, cum impugnaretur a filiis,[3] grauiter ingemiscens ait: 'Vere cognoui illum migrasse a seculo: nam ideo inuenerunt me mala ista quia non superest ipse.' Loquebatur ex magnitudine doloris et amoris, quoniam si rationem uis doloris admitteret scire poterat quod effi-

f. 74 catius in celestibus | quam in terra pro eo intercederet. Quod ut ei ab assidentibus proceribus suggestum est, tandem consolationem recepit.

30. *De miraculis in uita sua factis*

Taliter nouit Dominus glorificare sanctos suos apud homines, qui quos iustificat hos et magnificat, et qui lucernam accendit et in abscondito non ponit sed super candelabrum, ut qui ingrediantur lumen uideant.[4] Quales quoque aput se illos habeat, etiam in conspectu hominum manifestat, qui future in eis dignitatis gratiam

---

ᵃ uiue *Holford-Strevens*: uite *LcOd*

[1] Cf. Isa. 23: 4.
[2] i.e. Richard I and John, who was the king when the *Vita* was written.
[3] St Gilbert died on 4 Feb. 1189; Henry II was in Maine or Touraine. Richard was in revolt against his father, Henry II, in alliance with Philip II of France, and John joined them in the summer, shortly before Henry himself died at Chinon on 6 July

with him as well as strangers loved him dearly, and the whole people revered him as a holy man of God. We witnessed bishops seeking his blessing at his knees; and we saw some bishops, coming from foreign parts where the fame of his holiness had penetrated, beg items of his clothing to hang as relics in the famous shrines belonging to their lands. Again some prelates applied to him in their writings and public sermons the prophecy 'Blush, Sidon, says the sea',[1] terming themselves Sidon and Father Gilbert the sea because a secular without ecclesiastical office was seen not only to match the highest ministers of the church but even to surpass them in promoting the church's interest.

The renowned King Henry II also honoured him so highly that he would not allow Father Gilbert, when he came to court on church business, to wait upon him; rather he was not ashamed to go himself with his magnates to hear him in his lodgings, and he made no objection either to humbly accepting the saint's blessing or to hearing the lessons of salvation from his lips. Queen Eleanor also rejoiced that her sons and future kings were blessed by him.[2] They attributed the kingdom's well-being and their success in worldly affairs to the influence of his presence and the protection of his prayers. For this reason, when King Henry later heard the report of his death, while he was under attack from his sons,[3] he groaned loudly and said: 'Truly I realize now that he has departed this life, for these misfortunes have befallen me just because he no longer lives.' He was speaking from the depths of grief and love, for if the force of his sorrow had permitted thought he might have realized that Gilbert would intercede more effectively for him in heaven than upon earth. When the magnates who were in attendance suggested this to him, he eventually took comfort.

30. *Miracles performed during his lifetime*

In such a fashion does the Lord know how to make his saints glorious in men's eyes: those whom he justifies, he also exalts, and, lighting a candle, he places it not in a secret place but upon a candlestick so that those who enter may see the light.[4] The esteem in which he holds such men, he also makes visible to men's sight; he causes the grace of their future dignity to be

(R. W. Eyton, *Court, Household and Itinerary of King Henry II* (London and Dorchester, 1878), pp. 292–7; W. L. Warren, *Henry II* (London, 1973), pp. 620–6).

[4] Cf. Matt. 5: 16 (cf. pp. 214–15 etc.).

preire facit miraculis, quatinus quam teneant homines uiam agnoscant, et de spei ueritate securi fiant, ut ad uitam perueniant. Simili pietate et circa hunc sanctum suum usa est bonitas diuina, gratiam primitus infundendo qua meritis eniteret, et misericordiam postmodum augendo, qua eadem merita uirtutibus illustrarent.[a] Hec sunt igitur que per beatum patrem nostrum Gilebertum adhuc in carne positum operatus est Deus mundo miracula.

Licet enim non sint hec tempora signorum, iuxta illud: 'Signa nostra non uidimus, iam non est prophetia',[1] et ipse magis moribus studuerit quam miraculis, in attestationem tamen piorum[b] operum et confirmationem sermonum, preter multarum que fecit lucra f. 74ᵛ animarum que preiudicant miraculis, | quedam per eum diuinitus facta sunt signa quibus et sanctitas uite eius et sinceritas doctrine commendatur. Sic enim reuelatum est cuidam uiro nobili et fideli totam scilicet terram per eum letificandam. Adam de Amundauilla hic erat, miles opulentus et fide dignus.[2] Vidit hic per somnium, quasi in medio populorum multorum in quadam planitie consistentium, descendere pontificem quendam pontificalibus ornatum. Quem cum interrogasset quis esset, 'Nonne' inquit 'me nosti qui iam in meo seruitio bis fuisti?' Fatenti se nescire, respondit presul: 'Ego sum Thomas Cantuariensis archiepiscopus, quem sanctum Thomam appellant.' Gauisus ille et admiratus 'Gratias' inquit 'Deo qui tanta pro te, domine, operari dignatus est. Nam numquam fuit nec erit aliquis, ut putamus, in terra nostra de quo tanta oriatur leticia.' Ad quem ille: 'Erit, inquam.' Querenti nomen eius, sanctus uno uerbo respondit 'Gilebertus'. Quem non alium nisi hunc nostrum presumimus[c] esse Gilebertum. Quod enim nondum talis fuerit certi sumus; quod autem nec futurus est per hec colligimus: nam preter ea que futura speramus gaudia, que de quo maior poterit esse letitia quam de uiro qui tot hominibus et animarum et cor-f. 75 porum prouidit stipendia? Que maior leticia in terra nostra | quam quod eam tantorum operum magnificentia et tanta signorum honorat frequentia? Que maior letitia quam quod non solum suam regionem uerum totum orbem Romanum sua illustrat gloria? Que

---

[a] *Perhaps* illustrarentur *or* illustraret *(Winterbottom)*   [b] uel piorum *s.l. Lc*²; priorum *LcOd*   [c] presummimus *Lc*

[1] Ps. 73 (74): 9 (reading 'propheta').
[2] See p. lxxiv; C. T. Clay, 'The Family of Amundeville', *Lincs Archit. and Archaeol. Soc. Reports and Papers*, iii. 2 (1948), 109–36, at p. 131. Adam was a younger brother of Walter de Amundeville, the head of a family whose main holdings were in Lincolnshire. They probably came from Mondeville, now a suburb of Caen.

foreshadowed in miracles, so that men may recognize the path they should take and be confirmed in the true expectation of reaching everlasting life. With similar piety God's goodness found expression in the case of this his saint, first in pouring down grace so that he might shine with merit, and afterwards by increasing his compassion so that his merit might gain lustre from human virtues. These, then, are the miracles which God worked for the world through our blessed Father Gilbert, while he was still alive.

This is not an age of miracles, according to the saying 'We have not seen our miracles, now there is no prophecy';[1] and Gilbert himself paid more attention to honest conduct than to miraculous events. However, to bear out his good works and to confirm what he preached (apart from the wealth of souls he won for God, which are preferable to miracles), certain signs were accomplished by God's power working through him which prove the holiness of his life and the sincerity of his teaching. A revelation that he would bring joy to the whole land was granted to a faithful believer of noble birth. This was Adam de Amundeville, a wealthy and trustworthy knight.[2] In a dream he saw an archbishop, distinguished by the robes appropriate to his rank, descend into the middle of a great crowd of people who were standing together in an open place. When Adam asked him who he was, he said: 'Do you, who were twice in my service, really not recognize me?' As Adam confessed ignorance, the prelate replied: 'I am Thomas, archbishop of Canterbury, whom they call St Thomas.' Filled with wonder and joy Adam exclaimed: 'Thanks be to God who has seen fit to perform such mighty works on your behalf, my Lord. For we reckon that there never was anyone in our land, and never will be, to give rise to such rejoicing.' St Thomas replied, 'I say that there will be.' When asked his name the saint answered with the one word 'Gilbert'. We presume that this meant no other than our own Gilbert. For we are certain that there has not yet been a man like him, and we conclude as follows that there will not be one in the future either. For apart from the joys which we look for in the future, who can cause greater happiness than a man who has supplied so many with provision for both body and soul? What greater source of rejoicing exists within our land than that the distinction of great deeds and the remarkable frequency of miracles brings honour upon it; and again, than that his glory illumines not only his own region but the whole of the Roman world? What

maior letitia quam que hominibus simul et angelis collata est?
Videmus eam iam et tenemus et pre gaudio que nouimus silere non
possumus, sicut nec debemus.

31. De febribus

Domnus Albinus,[1] uir fidelissimus, et qui omnes eius a multo
tempore nouit actus, utpote diutius et usque ad diem transitus eius
perseuerans cum eo comes et capellanus familiarissimus, refert ea
que refero. Pater Gilebertus febrium molestia aliquotiens anxia
pulsabatur. Cui condolens Albinus, cum more uulgari moneret
eum torporem excutere et sese mouere, ut motu corporis febres
amoueret, interrogauit senex si ille numquam per experientiam
didicisset quanta esset febrium anxietudo. Respondit ille nunquam se febres pertulisse. A quo, cum quesisset senex an febres
illas uice sua uellet suscipere, ut ipse liberaretur, annuit Albinus.
Nec mora, mane sequenti, hora scilicet qua solebat pater Gilebertus uexari, corripitur febre Albinus et, patre liberato, diutino
ardore torquetur, ut disceret non in hominis arte uel potestate, sed
f. 75ᵛ in Dei | tantum uoluntate positam esse morborum continentiam.

32. Item de eisdem

Alio tempore, cum prefatus Albinus, post internam quandam
egritudinem qua laborauerat, febribus apud Sempingham arri-
peretur, nec solitum per monasteria circuitum cum patre Gileberto agere posset, expectauit idem pater aput cenobium Insulam
nomine,[2] perhendinans donec sanitati redditus iter consuetum
cum illo aggredi ualeret. Cumque inibi aliquamdiu commorans
moras illius fastidiret, misit ad eum pater mandans et in ui obedientie[a] prohibens ne ulterius febres susciperet, sed ad illum quamtocius festinaret, morbo quoque illi per eundem nuntium in uirtute
obedientie interdicens ne ad illum amplius accederet. Accepto
obedientie uerbo, caput ex more humiliter inclinat[b] Albinus
precepto. Crastino, subsequente die scilicet, et hora accessionis,

---

[a] obidientie Lc   [b] inclinauit Od

[1] See pp. 8–9, 108–9, and 280–1, where this story is repeated.
[2] Probably Newstead-on-Ancholme (as below, pp. 120–1), or perhaps Haverholme
(cf. Heads, p. 202 and nn. 4–5).

greater joy is there than that which is bestowed upon men at the same time as upon angels? We are firm witnesses of it, and because of our joy we are unable, and indeed ought not, to keep silence about what we know.

31. *Attacks of fever*

Dom Albinus[1] is an entirely trustworthy man who, because he remained with Father Gilbert for a very long time, right up to his death, as his companion and the most intimate of his chaplains, knows all that he had done over many years. He tells this story which I now relate. Father Gilbert used to be afflicted sometimes with troublesome and distressing fevers. Albinus would pity him and urge him, as people often do, to pull himself together and get moving, so as to drive away his feverish attacks by the activity of his body. The old man asked him if he had never learned through experience the great distress caused by fever. Albinus replied that he had never suffered from fever, and he gave his consent when the venerable Gilbert enquired of him whether he would endure these attacks of fever for him, so that he himself might secure relief. Immediately, the following morning at the exact time when Father Gilbert used to be troubled, Albinus was taken with a fever and, while our father enjoyed relief, he was long tormented by a burning heat so that he should learn that the control of disease resides not in human skill or ability but in God's will alone.

32. *Another case of the same*

On another occasion this Albinus was gripped by fever at Sempringham after some internal complaint from which he suffered; and he was unable to go on his rounds of the monasteries with Father Gilbert as usual. Our father waited for him at the monastery called *Insula*,[2] staying until Albinus recovered his health and could make the customary journey with him. After our father had been there for some while he grew tired of Albinus' delay and sent him instructions ordering him by virtue of his obedience not to give hospitality to the fever any longer but to hurry to join him as quickly as possible; by the same messenger he also commanded the disease, by virtue of its obedience, not to approach him again. Albinus received the word of obedience and, as was his custom, bowed humbly to this order. On the morrow, that is the following day, at the hour it usually came,

ecce solita signa et nota sinthomata accedentium febrium presentit
Albinus, et plena fide quasi ad intelligibilem personam sic ad morbum clamat, dicens: 'Quid est quod me inuadis? Nonne prohibuit
tibi magister ne ad me amplius accederes? Et ego in nomine
Domini et eiusdem magistri obedientia tibi impero ne me diucius
f. 76   uexare presumas.' Quo dicto, | signum crucis sibi inprimens, mox
suaui somno carpitur, nec ab illo die usque*^{a}* ad obitum suum
febrium ualitudine lacessitus est.

33. *De dolore pedum sedato*

Quidam ecclesie Sixlensis[1] canonicus uehementem pedum passus
est dolorem. Is, de magistri uirtute confidens, aquam petiit a
ministro qua pedes domni Gileberti ex more uespera cum iret
cubitum lauabantur. Accepit aquam, pedes perfudit, et mox omnis
dolor conquieuit.

34. *De podagra*^{b}* curata*

Alter quidam, quondam in seculo miles, tunc ecclesie de Oseneia
canonicus, regulariter professus et officio celerarius,[2c] podagrico
dolore diutius cruciabatur. Videns is mirabilia que per patrem
Gilebertum patrauerat Deus in tot ecclesiarum et tante religionis
edificatione, credidit, ut uere erat, celestem tanto uiro inesse uirtutem, et tota mentis confidentia conuertens se ad subsidium
sancti, petiit*^{d}* a domesticis eius saltem ueteres pedules sibi dari
quos magister aliquando pedibus suis habuerat calciatos. Dati
sunt ei pedules, calciauit, et protinus dolor omnis aufugit. Inter-
iecto postea aliquanto tempore, dolor qui pedes reliquerat manus
arripuit, et secundum sui tenorem durius contorquet. At ille ad |
f. 76ᵛ   expertum auxilium confugit, manus in pedules iniecit, et protinus
omnimodam tam manuum quam pedum sanitatem recepit. Hec
idem Radulfus domno Rogero, nunc ordinis de Sempingham
prelato,[3] paulo postquam id ei acciderat retulit, dicens se non
audere mirifica Dei circa se acta infructuoso silentio tegere.

   ^{a} usque *LcOd;* uel et deinceps *s.l. Lc*^{1} ^{b} *ins.* et ciragra *Lc index* ^{c} *ins.*
nomine Radulphus *Od, probably rightly (see n. 2 and* idem Radulfus *at the end of the section)*
   ^{d} petit *Lc*

   [1] In Lincolnshire: see pp. xxxi, xxxiii.
   [2] Ralph Bidun: see pp. 202–3.   [3] See p. lxv.

lo!—Albinus sensed the usual signs and well-known symptoms of the approaching fever, and he cried out confidently, addressing the illness as if it was a rational person: 'How is it that you are attacking me? Did not the master forbid you to approach me again? I too command you in the Lord's name and in obedience to this same master that you dare to trouble me no longer.' Having said this, he crossed himself and soon fell into a sound slumber, and from that day he was not afflicted by a feverish attack right up to the time he died.

33. *Painful feet relieved*

A canon of Sixhills[1] suffered from a terrible pain in his feet. Trusting in the master's powers, he asked a servant for the water used to wash Gilbert's feet, following his usual custom, in the evening when he retired to bed. He obtained the water and poured it over his feet, and soon all his pain abated.

34. *A case of gout cured*

There was another man who in secular life had formerly been a knight and who then took vows as a regular canon of the church at Osney and became cellarer;[2] he suffered for a very long time from painful attacks of gout. When this man saw the wonders which God had worked by means of Father Gilbert—the foundation of so many churches and the encouragement given to the religious life— he believed correctly that the heavenly spirit resided in this great man. Fully assured in his own mind he turned to the saint for help, and asked the members of his household to give him at least the old slippers which the master had worn sometimes on his feet. The slippers were given him, he put them on, and immediately all his pain vanished. After some time had elapsed the pain which had deserted his feet attacked his hands and, following its usual course, tormented them more severely. But the canon sought refuge in the proven remedy; he thrust his hands into the shoes and immediately, just like his feet, his hands were entirely cured. Shortly after this experience, this same Ralph described it to Roger, now head of the Order of Sempringham,[3] asserting that he did not dare to conceal by an unprofitable silence the wonderful things which God had done for him.

35. *De febre*

Missus est cyfus magistri, quia fractus erat, ad reparandum ad quendam de Beuerlaco artis argentarie peritum. Is quia tunc febribus laborauit gauisus est ad presentiam uasculi, cum cognosceret quod magister ex eo potare soleret, sumensque ex poculo potum, suam pariter hausit exinde salutem.

36. *De fistula*

Fistule morbo exesum habuit pedem unus de numero laicorum fratrum domus de Chikesande.[1] Die dominice Cene, dum abluendis fratrum pedibus diligens et deuotus minister procumberet pater Gilebertus, ex industria positus est eo loco frater ille infirmus quo sacrarum manuum contactum posset percipere. Venit ergo ad egrotum, et utraque manu pedem illum cepit constringere, constrictoque ex ulcerum concauitatibus sanguinem elicere f. 77 et effluentem saniem aqua sacri ministerii | eluere. Quid multa? Cum sordibus pedum et sanguine uulnerum omnem ulcerati artus detersit infirmitatem.

37. *De constipatione*

Iuete preposite ad extrema uite perducte mortis inhibuit accessum in uirtute obedientie, eo quod necessaria ordini eius adhuc uita uideretur. Qua uisitata, uix dorsum conuertit abscedens cum confortata concito natura per sudorem expulit humorum[a] noxietatem et uentris resoluit qua mori timuerat constrictionem.

38. *De morti proximo*

Moribundus successor suus, nunc noster prelatus, et a medicis in desperatione relictus, ad eius imperium mortis euasit periculum.

---

[a] homorum *Lc*

[1] See p. xxxii.

35. *A fever*

A goblet belonging to the master broke and was therefore sent for repair to a craftsman of Beverley skilled as a silversmith. This man, because he was suffering from fever at the time, rejoiced at the vessel's appearance when he learnt that the master used to drink from it, and on taking a draught from the goblet he derived an instantaneous cure from the same source.

36. *An ulcer*

One of the number of lay brethren belonging to the house of Chicksands[1] had an ulcerated foot. On Maundy Thursday, while Father Gilbert took the part of a loving and devout servant and knelt to wash the feet of the brethren, the sick brother was purposely brought to the place so that he might be touched by his holy hand. Father Gilbert came to the sick man and began to grasp that foot with both hands; when he squeezed it he caused blood to flow from the bases of the ulcer and he washed away the discharge of pus with the water he used for this holy office. What then? Along with the dirt from the feet and the blood from the wound he removed every trace of sickness from the ulcerated limb.

37. *A case of constipation*

When Prioress Yvette had been brought to the end of her life, he prevented the approach of death through the power of obedience, because her life still seemed so necessary to his Order. Father Gilbert visited her, and scarcely had he turned his back upon her to depart when nature, immediately reassured, discharged the poison of the humours in a sweat, and relaxed the tightness of her bowels from which she had feared she would die.

38. *A man close to death*

Father Gilbert's successor, now our head, was about to die and the doctors had given up all hope of him. Yet at Gilbert's command he escaped the peril of death.

39. *De uirtute uerborum eius*

Sanctimonialis quedam domus de Sempingham, lumen ferens noctu per coquinam partem candele peruste alteri arsure compegit, ut ambe simul illuminarentur. Sed cum pars compacta pene esset consumpta, cecidit in aream ubi multum straminis parati incendio colligebatur. Negligens illa et ignem per se credens extinguendum, preteriuit, hostium clausit. At flamma, pabulum inueniens, primo paleas prope iacentes, demum totam domum simul et contiguas officinas cum contentis deuastauit, unde magna iactura ecclesie | contigit.[a] Adueniens illuc pater Gilebertus, uolens expiare delictum, rogauit, monuit et precepit ut culpam confiteretur si qua se ream super hoc cognosceret. Negauere omnes. Hoc sepius actum est; cumque nulla peteret ueniam, imprecatus est ut talis animaduersio obstinate illi que hoc perpetrauit et abscondit ante mortem infligatur, qua coacta reatum confiteatur. Nec caruit effectu imprecatio. Nam tantum sustinuit postea miserabilis illa corporis cruciatum quod non solum factum illud sed et inobedientie crimen et confessionis dilationem et paterne sentente iustissimam ultionem coram omnibus confessa, pastoris[1] peteret absolutionem et sororum orationem.

f. 77ᵛ

40. *Aliud miraculum*

Altera quedam monialis eiusdem domus, procacitatis lingue et inquiete suspitionis uitio laborans, omnes sorores suas anxie molestabat; super quo delicto cum nullam patris admitteret correptionem, orauit ille ut Christus filius Dei eam castigaret. Hec itaque post transitum ipsius sub feretrum cui corpus exanime incubuit se dedit in lamentum et orationem, nec inde auelli poterat quamdiu funus ibi iacebat, continue petens ut illam tolleret secum a seculo, ne forte recederet ab ordine in quem eam susceperat, si diutius in hac uita permaneret. Postera die | sepulture eius, resoluta est illa paralisi, et accipiens communionem migrauit a seculo. In quo facto et corporalem sustinuit, iuxta

f. 78

---

[a] contigit *Lh;* contingit *Lc (def. Od)*

[1] Either St Gilbert himself or her superior.

39. *The force of the master's words*

A nun belonging to the house of Sempringham was carrying a light through the kitchen quarters at night-time when she pressed the piece of candle which had burnt low against another to light it, so that both should burn together. But because the piece she pressed was almost burnt out, it fell into the space where there lay ready a great quantity of straw which had been gathered for the fire. Thinking the fire would go out of its own accord, the nun went on her way without troubling and shut the door. But the flame, finding fuel, burnt first of all the straw lying nearby, and finally the whole house along with its adjacent workshops and their contents. This event caused great loss to the church. When Father Gilbert arrived upon the scene, wishing to purge the guilt he asked, urged, and ordered anyone who knew herself responsible for it to confess her fault. They all denied it. This occurred time after time; and because no nun sought absolution he swore an oath that, before she died, such a punishment would be inflicted upon the obstinate person who had committed this deed and concealed it as would make her confess her guilt. Nor was his curse without effect. For afterwards this unhappy woman endured such great bodily pain that in the presence of them all she admitted not only her action but also the sin of disobedience, her delay in confession, and the very just punishment meted out by the father; and so she asked her pastor[1] for absolution and her sisters for their prayers.

40. *Another miracle*

Another nun belonging to the same house suffered from the vice of a shameless tongue and a restless, suspicious nature, and annoyed all her sisters with her troubles; because she would not accept any reproach from the father on the subject of this fault, he prayed that Christ the Son of God might punish her. Accordingly, after the father died this woman gave herself up to lamentation and to prayer under the bier upon which his lifeless body lay, and as long as the corpse lay there she could not be removed from that place. Ceaselessly she begged him to take her with him from the world, in case she might leave the Order into which he had received her if she remained alive any longer. The day after his burial she was struck by paralysis, and after taking communion she departed this life. In this way she suffered the bodily punishment she deserved in accordance

sententiam patris, quam promeruit penam, et celerem obtinuit, quem optauit ne amplius peccaret, uiuendi finem.

41. *Aliud*

Nam[a] quidam canonicus super delicto suo correptus, instigante penitentie aduersario, obduratus ad disciplinam, in immoderatam effrenatus est iram. Statutis ordinis et rigori capituli rebellis, non admisit correctionem, uoti sui immemor et reuerentie patris simul et assidentis conuentus oblitus, nec corporali pena nec etiam compedum ligatione que minabatur potuit coherceri. Egresso tandem a capitulo magistro occurrit ille plenus iracundia et rixa, uultu minaci et toruo aspectu, ab ordine minatus abscessum. Tunc uir prudentissimus et spiritu mansuetudinis plenus baculi sui superiori parte uesanum illum leuiter percussit in frontem. Mira res: qui modo nudi corporis flagella non erubuit nec uinculorum constrictionem timuit, leui illo ictu ita est perterritus[b] quod in se reuersus, quid egerit quidue dixerit admiratus, factus est deinceps mansuetissimus.

42. *Predicta ab eo rerum mutatio*

f. 78ᵛ　Cogitans mecum quandoque de uenerabilis patris nostri factis | et dictis mirificis, recolo me quiddam ab eius ore audisse cui simile est illud quod beatus Gregorius in Libro Dialogorum ponit pro miraculo.[1] Refert enim idem sanctus quod Redemptus, Ferentine ecclesie episcopus, a beato martire Zotico, iuxta cuius sepulchrum nocte iacuerat, talem tercio audierit uocem: 'Finis uenit uniuerse carni'; quod licet uniuersaliter dictum sit, non tamen mox omnis caro iuxta hanc comminationem consumpta est, quamuis hoc de mundi sed longe post futuro fine intelligi possit, sed pronostica fuit uox illa, ut interpretatur idem doctor, uastationis illius quam exercuerant Longobardi in finibus Romanorum. Simili modo, tempore quo ad restaurationem captiuitatis Ierosolimitane crucem sumpserunt fere omnes principes et nobiles occidentalium regionum, audiens pater Gilebertus regem Anglorum Henricum secundum

---

　　　[a] nam *om. Od*　　　[b] perteritus *Lc*

[1] Gregory, *Dial.* iii. 38 (ed. de Vogüé, ii. 428–31). For the 'I' of this passage, see p. lxxiv.

with the father's judgement; and she also secured the swift end to her life which she desired, in order that she might sin no more.

41. *Another*

Now a certain canon was rebuked for a fault and at the instigation of the enemy of penitence he resisted discipline and fell victim to a fit of uncontrollable rage. Rebelling against the statutes of the Order and the chapter's strictness, he refused correction, disregarded his vow, and forgot the reverence which he owed both to the father and the assembled community, so that he could not be restrained either by bodily punishment or even by the threat of being bound with fetters. At length, whilst still extremely angry and quarrelsome, with a menacing expression on his face and a wild look about him, he encountered the master, who had left the chapter, and threatened that he would leave the Order. Then the wisest of men, filled with the spirit of gentleness, struck this rash fellow lightly on the forehead with the upper part of his staff. A strange thing happened. He who even now had not blushed to feel the whip on his bare body and who had no fear of imprisoning chains, was so terrified by that light tap that he came to his senses, wondered at what he had done and what he had said, and subsequently became the gentlest of men.

42. *The master predicts a change*

When I sometimes run over in my mind the remarkable deeds and sayings of our venerable father, I remember hearing him say something which resembles an episode cited by St Gregory as a miracle in his *Dialogues*.[1] For this saint tells how after Redemptus, bishop of Ferentino, had lain at night next to the tomb of the blessed martyr Zoticus [Euthicius], he heard him utter this phrase three times: 'The end of all flesh approaches.' Although this was said of all men, nevertheless all flesh was not destroyed soon after in accordance with this direful prophecy; it might indeed be thought of as implying the end of the world at some time far in the future, but the teacher Gregory interprets this utterance as prophesying the destruction which the Lombards wrought within the Roman boundaries. A similar thing happened at the time when almost all the princes and noblemen of the west took the cross to recover Jerusalem from its captivity. Father Gilbert, hearing that Henry II, king of England,

cruce insignitum, ingemiscens hec ipsa Latino eloquio protulit
uerba: 'Placuit Deo finem rebus ponere.'[1] Quod quam ueraciter de
rebus se sicut ut tunc[a] habentibus dictum sit, sic probauit euentus.
Nam non longe post obiit, sed non in itinere illo, idem rex Henricus; imperator quoque Romanorum Fredericus uersus Ierusalem[b]
obiit in Persida.[2] Baldewinus similiter, Cantuariensis archiepis-
f. 79   copus,[3] | necnon et innumeri alii diuersarum linguarum et regio-
num, tam de potentibus seculi quam de prelatis ecclesiarum, in
expeditione illa defuncti sunt, statusque omnium tam orientalium
quam occidentalium ecclesiarum et regnorum ita ab illo tempore
mutati sunt quod rerum seriem in pristinam formam unquam
posse reuerti omnino desperemus. Quin pocius, per illam que tunc
inchoata est ecclesie tribulationem, finem omnium rerum esse
ualde propinquum certioribus quam huc usque indiciis colliga-
mus, quamuis non omnibus generaliter rebus sed rebus indefinite
pronuntiauit finem esse ponendum. Quod tamen si dixisset, uel ex
dictis quisquam conicere uellet, attendi tamen posset exceptio in
parte, sicut est illud in Genesi: 'Finis uniuerse carnis uenit coram
me'; quod sic intelligi debet quod omnium mortalium finis aduen-
erit, preter eos qui saluandi erant in archa,[4] et illud in Euangelio:
'Non inueni tantam fidem in Israel', exceptis his scilicet qui cum
Domino erant.[5]

43. Alia eius reuelatio

Alio quoque prenoscendi genere reuelauit ei Deus futura. Tempore
bellice infestationis inter Stephanum regem Anglorum et Henricum
ducem Normannie,[6] cum generalis depopulatio occuparet uniuer-
f. 79[v] sam terram Anglie, agris iacentibus incultis | et uillis desertis, meniis
dirutis et urbibus desolatis, predas et rapinas, incendia et cedes sibi
inuicem incolis agitantibus, grauis meror obsedit cor uiri Dei,

---

[a] sicut ut tunc] corrupt. Perhaps tunc sicut et nunc (Winterbottom)   [b] A verb like
pergens (Winterbottom) seems to have dropped out

---

[1] Henry II took the cross on 21 Jan. 1188—after other abortive talk of a crusade; but
he died before the vow could be fulfilled (Councils and Synods, ii. 2, ed. D. Whitelock,
M. Brett, and C. N. L. Brooke (Oxford, 1981), p. 1024, and refs.).
[2] Henry II died at Chinon on 6 July 1189; Frederick I in Cilicia, 10 June 1190.
[3] Archbishop Baldwin died in the Holy Land on 19 or 20 Nov. 1190 (Fasti, ii. 5).
[4] Cf. Gen. 6: 13.   [5] Matt. 8: 10.
[6] Henry became duke in 1150 and only resumed his campaigns against Stephen in
England in 1153–4; but it is clear from the context that the author was thinking of the

had been signed with the cross, groaned and in an expressive Latin phrase delivered himself of these words: 'It has pleased God to end all things.'[1] How truly this was said about the circumstances which then prevailed, the course of events was to prove. For not long afterwards King Henry died, although not on the Crusade. Frederick, the Emperor of the Romans, also died on the way to Jerusalem in Persia.[2] Similarly Baldwin, archbishop of Canterbury,[3] and countless other men of different tongues and diverse lands, holding high office in both the church and the world, also died upon that enterprise; moreover from that time the condition of all the churches and kingdoms in both east and west has been so greatly changed that we entirely despair of ever being able to see the state of affairs restored to its previous case. On the contrary, because of the tribulation which then began for the church, we may understand from signs which are clearer than ever before that the end of all things is at hand, even though the master declared that there must be an end not to everything in general, but to certain things which he did not specify. However, if he had made the previous [i.e. the general] statement, or if anyone wished to interpret his words in this way, a partial omission could be allowed such as occurs in Genesis: 'The end of all flesh is come before me'; this must be understood in this way: that the end came for all mortal beings apart from those who were to be saved in the ark.[4] There is also the Gospel verse 'I have not found so great a faith in Israel', apart, that is, from these men who were with Our Lord.[5]

43. *Another revelation*

God also revealed the future to this man by another type of prescience. During the troubled wars between Stephen, king of England, and Henry, duke of Normandy,[6] when widespread destruction gripped the whole of England, when fields lay untilled, villages were deserted, walls torn down, cities abandoned, and the inhabitants of this country gave themselves up to plundering, pillaging, burning, and slaughtering one another, the heart of this godly man

whole period of civil war, perhaps from Stephen's accession in 1135, in any case from the Empress Matilda's landing in 1139, to the peace of 1153 or the death of Stephen in 1154. (For Henry as duke of Normandy see Z. N. and C. N. L. Brooke in *EHR* lxi (1946), 81–9; W. L. Warren, *Henry II* (London, 1973), pp. 38–53.)

et pro publica deuastatione regionis sue et pro priuata nouelle religionis quam inchoauerat inminenti desolatione. Qua super afflictione uehementer afflicto et pro pace continue oranti, talis data est diuinitus consolatio. Ostensus est ei in somnis tomus*a* in quo erat scriptus numerus annorum illorum illius hostilitatis. Legens ille scripturam, mente consternatus est, eo quod crediderit omnes annos illos esse adhuc durature persecutionis, quod si esset ad nichilum omnia deuenirent. Tunc ammonuit iudex totalem illum numerum totius guerre presentis esse significatiuum, nec omnes annos illos in posterum elapsuros, sed quosdam iam preteritos, quosdam autem adhuc futuros, et quot essent hii uel illi certa significatione monstrauit. Nam finito termino quo predixit, pariter finiuit grassatio. Quo presagio certificatus homo Dei et consolationem accepit et pluribus effecit.

44. *Item alia*

Post aliquantos annos ex quo corporea luce priuatus est pater Gilebertus,[1] iter faciens per monasterium puellarum cui nomen est
f. 80 Aluestonha, ad petitionem sororum | ingressus, uerbum fecit edificationis in conuentu. Cuius suauissima uerba et celestem saporem quem gustauerat redolentia, tanquam 'sagitte potentis acute'[2] corda multarum audientium conpungentia, ex cordibus deuotionem et ex oculis lacrimas eduxerunt. Finito sermone recedens, cum per uiam uersus Chikesandam pergeret, interrogauit Albinum canonicum et capellanum suum si uidisset que uiderat ipse.[3] Quesiuit Albinus quid uidit. 'Vidi' inquid 'plures ex sororibus illis ad auditum sermonum Dei multas et grossas lacrimas effundere.' Idem protestatus est monialibus de Chikesanda, cum eo uenisset, arguens illas quod non essent tam deuote ut ille que uidebantur minus religiose. Vnde colligimus quod tunc et forte sepius, ut sepe putauimus, apertos habuerit oculos carnis, cum ex defectu etatis et multo lacrimarum profluuio usum corporei uisus multo ante perdiderit. Vtrum tamen hoc in spiritu uiderit ignoramus.

---

a tomus in somnis *Lc, but marked for transposition*

[1] For Gilbert's blindness, see pp. 84–7, 118–19. Elstow was an abbey of Benedictine nuns in Bedfordshire (KH, pp. 253, 258; *Heads*, p. 211).
[2] Ps. 119: 4 (120: 3).
[3] Chicksands was a Gilbertine house, also in Beds (see p. xxxii); for Albinus, see pp. 8–9, 96–7, 280–1.

was beset by a deep sorrow both on public grounds for the devasta-
tion of his country and on private grounds for the disintegration
which threatened the new religious order he had founded. He suffered severely under this affliction, but as he prayed constantly for
peace heaven bestowed this comfort upon him. He was shown in a
dream a book inscribed with the number of years the war was to
last. As he read what was written, his mind fell into turmoil,
because he assumed that all the years signified related to the future
duration of the troubles, and if this were true everything would be
brought to destruction. At that point a doomsman(?) counselled
him that the number comprised the entire length of the present
war and not all the years which were to follow afterwards, for some
had already passed and some were still to come; and with a careful
reckoning he demonstrated how both these separate totals were
made up. And so when the term of years he had foretold was completed, the disturbances also came to an end. Assured by this
knowledge of the future, the man of God both received comfort
and imparted it to many others.

44. *Yet another revelation*

Several years after Father Gilbert lost the sight of his eyes,[1] he was
travelling by the nunnery called Elstow; at the request of its sisters,
he entered and delivered an edifying sermon in the convent. His
eloquence, savouring of the heavenly banquet of which he had
tasted, pierced the hearts of many who heard him like the 'sharp
arrows of the mighty',[2] calling forth devotion from their hearts and
tears from their eyes. His sermon over, he departed, but as he
journeyed along the road to Chicksands he asked the canon
Albinus, his own chaplain, if he had seen what he himself had witnessed.[3] Albinus asked what this was. 'I saw', he said, 'many of
those sisters weep many great tears as they listened to God's word.'
He asserted this too to the nuns of Chicksands when he arrived
there, rebuking them because they were not as devout as those who
appeared less strict in their religious observance. Thus we infer
that on this occasion and perhaps more frequently, as indeed we
often suspected, he kept his fleshly eyes open even though he had
lost the normal use of his eyes long before through the weakness of
old age and the outpouring of many tears. But whether he saw this
with the eyes of the spirit, we know not.

45. *De uento precibus eius conuerso*

Sicut per primi hominis inobedientiam amisit homo et sui et suorum dominationem, ita per secundi hominis humiliationem qui eum perfecte fuerit secutus recuperat omnium propter se factorum f. 80ᵛ subiectionem.[1] Veritas est enim que dicit: | 'Si quis habuerit fidem sicut granum synapis, dicet huic monti, tollere et mittere in mare, et fiet ei'; et iterum: 'Amen dico uobis, si quid orantes pecieritis credetis quia accipietis, et fiet uobis.'[2] Habemus huius promissi exhibitionem in beato Gileberto, qui, quia debitam soluit suo creatori, qui imperat uentis et mari,[3] obedientie integritatem, et ipse uirtutum eius imitator factus est, etiam operum mirificus patrator. Ad nutum enim eius elementa muta famulabantur, cum uenti et mare obedierunt ei,[3] et ad uoluntatem ipsius uim uirtutis sue oblitus est ignis.

Transiturus namque aliquando pastor sollicitus Humbrie fluuium, uisitandi gratia opposite regionis monasteria, resistente uento austro, ceterisque aeris motibus mare turbantibus, prohibitus est transmeare. Cumque apud grangiam Heselscoch nomine[4] celi serenitatem et transfretandi exspectaret facultatem, fastiditus moram, sed magis credo ecclesiarum quas peciit gerens sollicitudinem, quesiuit a suis qua parte celi aura suo itineri daretur commodior, quis uentus sue nauigationi commodaretur secundior. f. 81 Responsum est ei boream satis si flaret fore prosperum. At | ille asseruit credere se uulturnum ceteris destinato cursui esse gratiorem.

Tunc confidens in Domino propter quem ierat, sed suis uiribus nichil attribuens et elationis simul et proprie laudis, ut semper solebat, caueriᵃ declinans, suasit ab omnibus dominicam dici orationem. Post finita orationis uerba, iussit equos sterni, frenos immitti, socios iter aggredi. Appropinquantibus illis ripe fluminis, cessat paulisper tempestas. Hortantur se mutuo naute aquas inuadere, quoniam de tanti uiri transferendi confidebant uirtute; parato nauigio irruit idem qui prius petebatur uentus, scanditur nauis,

---

ᵃ *The word is corrupt (perhaps* causam *Brooke)*

[1] Cf. Rom. 5: 19. For this miracle, see pp. 202–3.
[2] Matt. 17: 20 and Luke 17: 6; Mark 11: 23–4.
[3] Cf. Luke 8: 25; etc.
[4] A grange belonging to Watton priory, in the East Riding of Yorkshire, north of the Humber near Market Weighton (*VCH Yorks, East Riding*, iv. 155–7, 159).

45. *A wind diverted by his prayers*

Just as men lost dominion over themselves and their world through the disobedience of the first man, so, through the humbling of the second Man who fulfilled him in every way, they have regained control over all those things created for them.[1] For very Truth says: 'Whoever has faith like unto a grain of mustard seed shall say to this mountain "arise and depart into the sea" and it shall obey him'; also 'Amen I say unto you, if you desire anything as you pray, believe that you will receive it and it shall be done for you.'[2] We see the fulfilment of this promise in the case of St Gilbert: because he observed the obligation of total obedience to his Creator, who rules over wind and sea,[3] he himself came both to imitate His powers and to perform wonderful deeds. At his nod the voiceless elements would do his bidding, for wind and wave obeyed him[3] and in accordance with his will fire forgot the force of its own nature.

For example, once when our pastor was anxious to cross the River Humber to visit the monasteries on the other side, he was prevented from crossing by an adverse southerly wind and by other gusts which whipped up the water. And while he waited at the grange of Hessleskew[4] for the sky to clear and for an opportunity to cross, he grew weary of the delay, but, more important in my opinion, he felt anxious for the houses which he intended to visit; and so he asked his companions from what direction a breeze more favourable to his journey would arise and which wind would promote his voyage more successfully. They answered him that if a north wind blew it would bring about a happy enough outcome. He, on the other hand, said that he thought an easterly would be better for the crossing he intended.

Then, trusting to the Lord who had prompted his journey, but ascribing no importance to his own powers and refusing as was his practice any occasion of pride or vainglory, he urged them all to recite the Lord's prayer. When this prayer came to an end he ordered the horses to be saddled and harnessed and instructed his companions to set out. As they approached the banks of the river the storm abated for a while. The sailors urged one another to put out, because they trusted in the power belonging to the great man who had to be taken across; the ship was made ready; the wind he had prayed for played upon it; they embarked, the

implentur uela, et directo cursu ad optatum concito portum trans-
ponuntur. Quodque magis mirandum, ut referunt qui affuerant, eo
transuecto, rediit ad priores plagas pristina tempestas, ut manifeste patesceret non ad aliud quam ob gratiam ipsius faciem celi
fuisse mutatam. Huic rei interfuit eius successor, nunc prelatus
noster, domnus Rogerus, qui eo quo refero modo et ipse rem ges-
tam referre consueuit.

46. De incendio fugato

Contigit incendium in urbe Lundoniarum, ubi, cum flamma uehementer crescens hospicio magistri Gileberti immineret, et iam
f. 81ᵛ propinquiora loca inuasisset, | admonitus est a suis a domo illa
secedere et tantum periculum deuitare.[1] Renuit ille, et iussit omnia
que inibi erant remanere immota, precepitque se duci ad fenes-
tram ex qua prospici posset ignis. In qua cum paululum resedisset
orans et psallens, accessit propius ignis, sed ceteris fugientibus ille
remansit inmotus. Mox alteram partem domus depascens, flamma,
quasi abhorrens eius presentiam, illam partem ubi resedit transu-
olauit et uiciniora loca circumquaque arripuit, sicque omnia alia
edifitia hospitii[a] intacta reliquit, quod paterfamilias domus Dei
gratie et hospitis sui meritis ascribens, nulli nisi Deo et illi gratias
egit[b] de rerum suarum saluatione.

47. De partu miraculose dato

Vir quidam de Stanfordia cum uxore sua diu uixerat absque liberis.
Diuertit forte ad domum eorum pater Gilebertus hospitandi
gratia. Hospita cauta, de sanctitate suscepti hospitis confisa,
locum ei parat[c] in proprio grabato, ut meritis eius tanquam altera
Sunamitis suscipere filium mereretur per Helyseum.[2] Quod
factum est ut credidit mulier. Nam dormiendi[d] ueniens domum
maritus eius mox genuit ex ea filium et uocauerunt eum nomine
f. 82 huius patris Gileberti. Audiens autem uir | Domini rem gestam,

---

ᵃ hospitii *Winterbottom;* hospitis *Lc;* eius hospitis *Od*   ᵇ egit *Od (perhaps after
correction);* agit *Lc*   ᶜ parauit *Od*   ᵈ dormiendi *om. Od; otherwise perhaps* dormiendi ⟨causa⟩ *(Sharpe, Winterbottom)*

[1] The Order owned property in the parish of St Sepulchre in London by the end of
the 12th c. (*Cartulary of St Bartholomew's*, ed. N. Kerling (London, 1973), no. 137). For
fires in London in the 12th c. see C. Brooke and G. Keir, *London 800–1216* (London,
1975), pp. 116, 212n.   [2] Cf. 4 Kgs. (2 Kgs.) 4.

sails filled, and they were swiftly carried over on a direct course to the harbour they sought. What was more remarkable, according to those who were present, after this man had crossed the earlier storm returned to its former quarter; thus it was clearly demonstrated that the face of heaven had been transformed solely because of Gilbert's grace. His successor, Dom Roger, who is now our head, was present when this happened, and he used to describe the event exactly as I am doing.

46. A fire put to flight

It happened that a fire broke out in the city of London, and when the flames, spreading fast, threatened the inn where Master Gilbert was staying, and already had a hold upon properties close by, he was urged by his companions to leave the house and avoid such terrible danger.[1] He refused, ordered them not to move anything in the place, and asked to be taken to a window from which the fire could be observed. When he had sat there for a little reciting prayers and psalms, the fire came closer; but although everyone else fled he remained motionless. Then the flames which were burning another part of the house leapt over the place where he was sitting as if shunning his presence, and attacked the neighbouring places round about. Thus the fire left all the other buildings of the inn untouched, an event which the head of this household attributed to the grace of God and the merits of his guest, so that he offered up thanks to God and Master Gilbert alone for the preservation of his property.

47. The birth of a child, accomplished by a miracle

A man from Stamford had lived a long time with his wife without having children. It happened that Father Gilbert stopped at their house to spend the night. The discreet lady of the household put her trust in the holiness of the guest she had received, and prepared a place for him on her own couch so that through his merits she might be found worthy to bear a son, as the Shunammite did through Elisha.[2] It turned out just as she believed. For when her husband came home to sleep he before long fathered a son upon her, and they named him after Father Gilbert. When Our Lord's servant heard what had happened,

ut erat iocundus et liberalis, tanquam proprio filio uaccam misit ad nutriendum.

48. *De eodem*

Nobilem nouimus mulierem que quociens concepit totiens abortiuit. Data est ei ab altera potente matrona zona qua sanctus subtus ad carnem fuerat succinctus. Hanc et ipsa tali modo continue usa concepit et peperit filium, et post ipsum alterum, qui adhuc supersunt diuiciisque et honoribus pollent. Si diligenter attendas, lector, non minorem, ut arbitror, aduertere poteris uirtutem quam mortuorum suscitationem. Quid est enim aliud mortem imminentem arcere quam a morte liberare? Quid est facilius reformare quod erat in predictis quam quod non erat statuere? Proinde quamuis non legeris eum alicui non enti suum esse restituisse, quoniam non ad tanta sed nec ad minima aliqua uoluit accingi signa facienda, scire per hec poteris illum quosdam in suo esse conseruasse, quibusdam autem ut penitus essent suam essentiam per Dei gratiam contulisse. Suscitauit tamen mortuos multos, non carne quidem sed spiritu, sicut quosdam, ut predictum est, curauit in anima, cum multi per ipsum curati essent in corpore. Vt autem ait beatus papa Gregorius: 'Maius est
f. 82ᵛ miraculum predicationis uerbo atque orationis solatio pecca|torem conuertere quam carnem mortuam suscitare.'[1] Hoc uero genere miraculi pre omnibus nostri temporis claruit hic sanctus Domini precipuus.[a]

Sunt quidem multa et alia eius opera et uerba omni admiratione digna, que quod facta sunt non ignoramus, sed quia modum factorum non nouimus, silentio preterimus. Vidimus certe dum adhuc iuueret pre nota eius sanctitate et expertis uirtutibus multos aliquid de uestimentis, calciamentis et cingulis eius, seu de rebus quas contigerat uel quibus usus fuerat, loco reliquiarum petere, et quosdam audiuimus uiros religiosos et ueraces constanter asserere se ueraciter scire multas per eius reliquias factas fuisse uirtutes.

ᵃ claruit . . . precipuus *Lc;* studuit . . . precipue clarescere *Od*

---

[1] Gregory, *Dial.* iii. 17 (ed. de Vogüé, ii. 340–1).

being a cheerful and generous person he sent the boy a cow to supply him with food, acting just as if the boy had been his own son.

48. *The same*

We know of a noblewoman who miscarried every time she conceived. Another great lady gave her the girdle which had been tied about the saint under his clothing, next to his skin. Wearing this constantly in exactly the same way, she conceived and bore a son and another after him, who are still living and flourish in riches and honours. If, reader, you pay careful attention you may, in my opinion, observe a power at work which is not inferior to that of raising the dead. For what is the difference between warding off imminent death and freeing from death? Is it easier to transform the situation which prevailed in these cases than to create what did not exist? I grant that you will not read that he restored life to anyone without it, since he did not wish to gird himself to perform great or even small miracles. Yet from these examples you may recognize that the Master preserved the life of some men and moreover by God's grace imparted to some the reality of existence in order to realize the fullness of their human nature. He did indeed rouse many who were dead, but dead in spirit, not in the flesh; similarly, as I have already described, he cured the minds of some, although many received bodily cures from him. But as blessed Pope Gregory says: 'To convert the sinner by preaching the word and with the consolation of prayer is a greater miracle than to raise flesh which is dead.'[1] This eminent saint of Our Lord won renown before all others of our age for this type of miracle.

There are many others of his deeds and sayings which deserve all our admiration. We are not unaware that they happened, but because we do not know how they came about we pass over them in silence. However, while he was still alive, we did see that, because of his well-known holiness and his well-tried powers, many men asked for a piece of his clothing, shoes, and belts or for things which he had touched or used, to serve as relics. And we heard religious and truthful men say firmly that in all honesty they knew of many powerful works performed by means of his relics.

49. De pane[a] incorrupto

Extat adhuc panis splendidus et incorruptus quem nobili mulieri, uxori Symonis de Bellocampo,[1] deuote petenti benedictionis gratia ante annos quatuordecim tradiderat, ex quo multi sumentes sanitatem morborum sunt consecuti. Ipse tamen non modo signorum gloriam non quesiuit, sed tota intentione fugit, ita ut cum multociens a deuotis aliquibus sanis uel egris peteretur benedictionem, uix dare consensit, tali se munere uel tanto honore reputans indignum, uel |
f. 83 suam potius ab hominibus abscondens dignitatem.

50. De pace cum laicis facta

Hiis aliisque pluribus sanctitatis testimoniis sanctam et Deo placitam fuisse beati Gileberti uitam, etiam dum adhuc in carne[b] uiueret, comprobauit diuinus respectus. Hii sunt quos utcumque prediximus, nam ut debuimus dicere non potuimus, ipsius mores, hec opera, hec in mundo gloria. Mores proponuntur in imitationem, opera in admirationem, gloria in congratulationem. Iam quid inde expectandum quidue sperandum attendas. Finis omnium indifferenter mors est.[2] Sed mors tamen differens est. Nam 'mors peccatorum pessima', 'preciosa autem in conspectu Domini mors sanctorum eius'.[3] Proinde, cum iudicat Dominus fines terre et remunerat finalia, ultima queque istius fecit laudabilia, ut esset cuius fines poneret pacem sempiternam.[4] Igitur ut omnis consummationis uideret finem, pacem etiam temporalem composuit suis, ut dicere posset discedens: 'Pacem relinquo uobis, pacem meam do uobis.'[5] Ante pauca enim decessus sui tempora, prouidens perpetue in posterum collecti gregis firmitati, quia nouit quod 'non minor est uirtus quam querere parta tueri',[6] discidium illud quod a laicis conuersis quondam fuerat exortum propter occa-
f. 83[v] sio|nem cibi, coram bone memorie Hugone Lincolniensi episcopo,[7]

---

[a] ins. diu Lc index   [b] carne Winterbottom; carnem LcOd

[1] On Simon (fl. c. 1164/5–c. 1206/7) see The Cartulary of Newnham Priory, ed. J. Godber, i (Beds Hist. Rec. Soc., xliii, 1963), pp. x, xi, 11–12; etc. He was half-brother of William de Mandeville, earl of Essex, a member of the Bedfordshire branch of the family rather than that of Elmley (The Beauchamp Cartulary 1100–1268, ed. E. Mason, Pipe Roll Soc., NS 43 (1980 for 1971–3), p. xxii).   [2] Cf. Rom. 6: 21.
[3] Ps. 33: 22 (34: 21); 115 (116): 15.   [4] Cf. Wisd. 6: 2; Ps. 147: 14 (and pp. 132–3).
[5] John 14: 27.   [6] Ovid, Ars am. 2. 13.
[7] St Hugh, bishop of Lincoln 1186–1200, canonized 1220 (Fasti, iii. 3; Magna Vita

49. *Uncorrupted bread*

There still remains fresh and incorrupt some bread which the Master gave in blessing fourteen years ago to a noblewoman, the wife of Simon de Beauchamp,[1] when she was his devout suppliant. Many people who have tasted it have been healed of their ills. However, the Master himself not only did not seek fame from these miracles, but he made every effort to escape from it. Thus when on many occasions his blessing was sought by devout persons in good or bad health, he only bestowed it reluctantly, either considering himself unworthy of such a gift or so great an honour, or, more likely, preferring to conceal his merits from human view.

50. *Peace made with the lay brethren*

By these and many other proofs of sanctity, Providence established even while he was still living in the flesh that St Gilbert's life was holy and pleasing to God. This is his conduct, about which we have spoken as best we could, though we have not been able to speak as we ought, these his deeds, and this his glory in the world. His conduct is put before you to be copied, his deeds to be admired, his glory to prompt rejoicing. Consider what grounds they give for optimism and for hope. Death is the end of all men without distinction.[2] Nevertheless death itself varies. For 'the death of sinners is a most evil one', 'but precious in the sight of the Lord is the death of his saints'.[3] Accordingly since the Lord is judge over the ends of the earth and gives the final reward, He made every circumstance surrounding Gilbert's end praiseworthy so that he might be one of those whose ends He made everlasting peace.[4] Therefore to see the end of every issue, he also arranged peace in temporal affairs for his followers, that he might say as he departed: 'Peace I leave with you, my peace I give unto you.'[5] Concerned that the stability of his whole flock should continue ever afterwards, he knew that 'to protect one's possessions is as great a virtue as to acquire them'.[6] And so, a short while before his death, in the presence of Hugh, bishop of Lincoln, of happy memory,[7]

S. Hugonis, ed. D. L. Douie and H. Farmer (2 vols., NMT, 1961–2; OMT 1985); D. H. Farmer, 'The Canonization of St Hugh of Lincoln', *Lincs. Archit. and Archaeol. Soc. Reports and Papers*, vi. 2 (1956), 86–117).

cum communis capituli assensu, pacificauit, quem modum et mensuram in uictu et uestitu et ceteris moribus[a] tenerent satis rationabili moderamine decernens. Quam constitutionem sibi gratam et ratam debere esse iudicantes omnes laici amplexati sunt, nichil addendum uel minuendum fore statuentes, ubi tamen secundum priorem constantie sue rigorem illud excepit, quod si quid contra primam eorum professionem constitueretur, hoc non ad eum spectare asseruit, nec se uoluit laudari auctorem.

51. *De infirmitate*[b] *qua obiit*

Perfectis igitur tam sue perfectionis meritis quam suarum congregationum necessariis instrumentis, cum disponeret Dominus labores illius eterna requie munerare, appropinquante tempore uocationis sue, cepit plus solito lascessere,[c] pronuntiauitque se in hac uita diutius non posse subsistere, quia tocius nature corporalis amminiculis destituebatur. Morbo nempe et senio confectus hinc compellitur migrare, et morbus quidem ex proprietate inhesit nature: nam solet semper senium comitari. Sed senectus ex dono durauit gratie, quoniam mirabile fuit hominem tot penis attritum f. 84 hiis diebus cum tanto corporis uigore posse peruenire ad cen|tennium, cum ipse centenariam excesserit etatem, membris omnibus sui corporis preter uisum oculorum incolumis.[1] Sed uoluit Dominus multis eum excercere laboribus et complere labores illius, quatinus merces eius multa esset in celis.[2] Non est ergo de quo queratur natura, non est in quo derogetur gratie, quoniam utrique satisfacere paratus est ipse: nature quidem ut desinat uiuere, gratie uero ut si expedierit uitam uelit protelare. Mox igitur insinuauit per litteras omnibus ecclesiis sui resolutionem imminere, orans ut orationibus suis exitum eius munirent, et relinquens post se benedictionem. Omnes qui post[d] eius decessum futuri essent ordinis amatores et unitatis congregationum defensores absoluit ab omnibus contra regulam et instituta presumptis excessibus. Machinantibus autem discidium et discordiam contestatus est suam non posse prodesse absolutionem, cum in conspectu Dei nisi penituerint constet eos penitus esse reprobatos.

---

[a] moribus *Winterbottom;* motibus *LcOd*   [b] *ins.* eius *Lc index*   [c] lascessere *Lc¹Od;* lacessere *Lc*   [d] post *Lc¹Od; om. Lc*

[1] See pp. xxiv–xxv.
[2] Cf. Luke 6: 23.

and with the agreement of the whole chapter, he settled the dispute over their food which the lay brethren had earlier raised, judging with quite reasonable moderation the style and quantity they should observe in their rations, clothing, and other customs. All the lay brethren considered that this rule should be welcomed and approved, and they agreed upon it, deciding that nothing should be added to it or taken away from it. But at that point, following the earlier strictness which he consistently upheld, he made a condition, arguing that if anything was determined which contravened their first profession he would have nothing to do with it and he did not wish to be held up as its author.

51. *The illness from which he died*

So he accomplished both the meritorious actions leading to his own perfection, and the purposes necessary for his communities. Then the Lord prepared to reward his labours with everlasting rest. As the time of his summons approached he began to grow weary more than usual, and he declared that he could no longer endure this life since the supports of his whole bodily nature had deserted him. One worn out by illness and old age is bound to leave this world. Illness attached itself to Gilbert in the proper course of nature: for it always accompanies old age. But his old age lasted so long because of the gift of grace. It was remarkable that a man exhausted by so many hardships could in these days reach a hundred years with so vigorous a body; yet this man lived beyond the age of a hundred, preserving every part of his body save his eyesight.[1] But the Lord wished to test him with many trials and to crown his labours so that his reward might be great in heaven.[2] There is, then, no reason for nature to complain and no cause to disparage grace. This man was prepared to satisfy both; nature by ceasing to live, but grace by wishing to prolong life if the occasion arose. Accordingly he informed all his religious communities by letter that his death was imminent, begging them to aid his departure with their prayers and leaving behind him his blessing. He absolved all those who after his death should love the Order and defend the unity of its houses from every offence committed against its rule and its laws. But he asserted that his absolution could be of no benefit to those plotting dissension and discord; for while they remain impenitent it is clear that they stand entirely condemned in the sight of God.

Instante itaque tempore quo sancta illa anima carnis erat relictura hospitium, nocte qua natus est Dominus, apud monasterium quod est[a] insula de Kadeneia,[1] extreme unctionis dominicique corporis munitus est sacramentis, et sic horam exitus qua decuit et oportuit expectauit deuotione. Sed cum necdum carnis uinculis solueretur, accepto tempore oportuno quam citius potuerunt comites | et capellani eius illum inde remouerunt, et timentes ne forte a potentibus seculi per quos erat transiturus raperetur aut ui retineretur in suis ecclesiis aut monasteriis sepeliendus, diuertentes a recto itinere, quam occulte, quam uelociter potuerunt, ad Sempingham detulerunt, ut ibi sepulturam acciperet ubi caput constituerat monasteriorum. In quo spacio sibi diuinitus indulto, accedentes ad eum omnium ecclesiarum eius[b] prelati[c] et plures alii eius discipuli benedictione eius et colloquiis sunt firmati, et de pace et de unitate ordinisque rigore post dies suos seruando sollicicius admoniti et instructi. Vltimo autem die uite ipsius temporalis, cum omnes abscessissent a domo qua iacebat agens in extremis, solus ante grabatum ipsius resedit qui ei successit in offitio.[2]

f. 84[v]

Cumque diu antea siluisset utpote in extremo alitu constitutus, nec quisquam aliquid ei fuisset locutus, neminem uidens, neminem audiens, in spiritu tamen ut intelligimus assidentis intelligens presentiam, morose, distincte et aperte hunc uersiculum psalmi inmurmurauit, dicens: 'Dispersit, dedit pauperibus',[3] et repetiuit quasi exponens: 'Dispersit multis, dedit non uendidit, pauperibus non diuitibus', et subnectens 'Tibi' inquit 'amodo | incumbit', quedam alia que non nouimus subiungens. Quorum sententiam uerborum absque sanioris interpretationis preiudicio eidem ipsi maxime arbitror conuenire, qui sua omnia multis quos ad Dei seruitium adunauerat dispersit, et respectu caritatis dedit, non pro terrena aliqua recompensatione uendidit, pauperibus, scilicet qui eum recipiant in eterna tabernacula, non diuitibus, quibus dare superfluum est et non meritorium cum et ipsi difficile intrant in regnum celorum.[4] Vnde pro hiis in fine mercedem recepturus exultat, et ei quem sibi successurum predicit[d] similitudinem agendi indicit. Sic gloriatur Paulus in his

f. 85

---

[a] Perhaps add in (Winterbottom)   [b] eius Lc²; om. Lc; suarum Od, perhaps rightly
[c] prelati LcOd; uel prepositi s.l. Lc²   [d] preuidit Od

[1] Christmas 1188 (see below); at Newstead-on-Ancholme (above, pp. xxv, 96–7; Heads, p. 203 n. 4).
[2] Roger: pp. xxiii, lxvn., 68–9, etc.   [3] Ps. 111 (112): 9.   [4] Cf. Luke 16: 9; Matt. 19: 23.

Just before his sanctified spirit was about to leave its home in the flesh, on the night when Our Lord was born, he was strengthened by the sacraments of extreme unction and eucharist at the monastery belonging to the isle of Cadney;[1] and so with fitting and proper devoutness he awaited the hour of his passing. But when he was still not released from the chains of the flesh, his companions and chaplains seized their opportunity and took him away from that place as quickly as they could. And fearing that the secular powers whose land he had to cross might capture him or hold him by force, so as to bury him in their own churches or monasteries, they left the direct route and carried him as secretly and as fast as they were able to Sempringham, that he might receive burial in the place which he had appointed the head of his religious houses. In the space of time God allowed him, there came to him the heads of all his houses and many other disciples. Strengthened by his blessing and by their conversation with him, they were most carefully advised and instructed how to preserve the Order's peace, unity, and strict discipline after his days were over. On the last day of his earthly life when all had left the house where he lay at death's door, there remained by his bed only the man who succeeded him in office.[2]

Earlier the master had been silent a long while as if he had reached his last breath, and no one had said anything to him since he saw and heard no one. Nevertheless he was conscious in his spirit, we understand, that someone was present and close by for he whispered to him slowly, distinctly, and clearly this verse from the Psalm, saying: 'He has distributed and given to the poor';[3] and, as if expounding the theme, he repeated: 'He distributed to many, he gave and did not sell, to men who were poor, not rich', adding: 'Upon you the responsibility rests, from now on' and some other words which we do not know. Without excluding a more valid interpretation I believe that the sense of these words fits the Master himself best of all. For he distributed all his possessions to the many whom he had united in the service of God; he gave out of charity, not selling for any earthly recompense; and he gave to poor men, who might receive him into everlasting dwelling-places, not to rich men, because it is unnecessary and without merit to give to those who with difficulty enter the kingdom of heaven.[4] Thus at the end, when he was about to receive the reward for these things, he rejoiced and prescribed a similar course of action to the man he said would succeed him. Thus does Paul glory in these things,

unde magis confidit cum tempus resolutionis sue instat, dicens:
'Bonum certamen certaui, cursum consummaui, fidem seruaui; de
reliquo reposita est mihi corona iustitie, quam reddet mihi Dominus in illa die iustus iudex.'[1] Et Dauid Scottorum rex sanctus, cum
mors esset ei in ianuis, septies hunc uersum psalmi ubi spem suam
posuerat repetiuit, dicens: 'Feci iuditium et iustitiam, non tradas
me calumniantibus me.'[2]

52. *De obitu eius*[a]

Postera die que preteriri non poterat illuxit sabbatum, tempus
scilicet quo requiesceret[b] a laboribus suis.[3] 'Nox precessit, dies
f. 85ᵛ   autem appropinquauit', quia dicere potuit: | 'Non me tenebre com-
prehendent nec conculcabunt me.'[4] Hora erat matutinarum lau-
dum et hora exitus matutini; nec deerant que[c] Deum laudabant
astra matutina, dicat quod sequitur.[5][d] Vix aliquid dicere poterant
qui interfuerant: singultus enim et lacrime adherere fecerunt
linguas suas faucibus suis; lacrimosa enim illa dies[6] que tulit nobis
patrem et pastorem nostrum, germanum et amicum. Nec qualem
patrem habent uel amittunt ceteri in monasteriis subditi, sed qui
omnes nos quotquot fuimus, quotquot fueramus genuit in uerbo
euangelii et fouit ut nutricius, quemadmodum gallina congregat
pullos suos sub alas.[7] Ceterum quid faciemus te facto de medio,
domine? Ad quem ibimus? Quem sequemur? Timemus enim te
percusso dispergi sicut oues errantes absque pastore.[8] Nam non
oportet flere super te, sed super nosmet ipsos[e] et super posteros
nostros. Sed non est quod queramur[f] de tempore nec quod dole-
amus de casu, quia extunc cepit consolatio nostra et tibi prouenit
gloria sempiterna. Non est ergo quod pro te, non est quod pro
nobis lugeamus, sed pocius tibi congaudeamus, et omnes nobis.
Hoc enim secutum est: sabbato ergo illo, pridie scilicet nonas Februarii, anno ab incarnationis dominice[g] M̊.C̊.LX̊X̊X̊.IX̊., cum nox
f. 86   immutaretur | in diem, dum celebrarentur laudes a conuentu,

---

[a] ipsius *Lc index, Od*   [b] *ins.* deus *Lc, but marked for deletion*   [c] que *Winterbottom (cf. Job 38: 7); qui LcOd*   [d] dicat quod sequitur *om. Od; the words are corrupt
(perhaps ut indicat quod sequitur Winterbottom)*   [e] ipsos *Lh;* ipso *Lc (def. Od)*
[f] queramur *Winterbottom;* queramus *Lc (def. Od)*   [g] incarnacione domini *Od*

---

[1] 2 Tim. 4: 7–8.   [2] Ps. 118 (119): 121.
[3] Cf. Job 14: 5; Gen. 2: 2–3.
[4] Rom. 13: 12; cf. John 1: 5; Ps. 138 (139): 11–12.
[5] Cf. Ps. 64: 9 (65: 8); Job 38: 7. In medieval usage what is now usually called lauds

which gave him greater confidence when the time of his death was at hand, saying: 'I have fought a good fight, I have finished the course, I have kept faith; for the rest a crown of righteousness is assigned to me which the Lord, the righteous judge, will give me upon that day.'[1] And David the holy king of the Scots, when death was upon him, repeated seven times this verse from the Psalm, in which he placed his trust, saying: 'I have performed judgement and justice: do not deliver me to those who work my downfall.'[2]

52. *His death*

Next day was the one whose bounds he could not pass; it dawned, the Sabbath, a time therefore when he might rest from his labours.[3] 'The night was far advanced and the day was at hand', because he could say: 'The darkness shall not encompass me, neither shall it cover me.'[4] It was the hour of lauds and the hour of the morning outgoing, and there was no lack of morning stars to praise God[5]— as is shown by what follows(?). Those who were present could scarcely say anything; their sobbing and their tears caused their tongues to stick in their throats, for it was that sad day[6] which took from us our father and pastor, our brother and friend. He was not such a father as others under monastic authority possess and lose; but a man who begot us all, however many we were or had been, in the word of the gospel and cared for us like a guardian, in the same way that a hen gathers her chicks under her wings.[7] What then shall we do, lord, now that you have been taken from our midst? To whom shall we go? Whom shall we follow? We are afraid that now you are struck down we shall be scattered, like sheep wandering without a shepherd.[8] We should weep, not for you, but for ourselves and those who come after us. But it is not fitting to complain of the occasion or to lament what happened, because that moment saw our comfort begin and everlasting glory descend upon you. Therefore it is not fitting to grieve for you or for ourselves; rather let us rejoice with you, and let all rejoice with us. For this is what followed: on that Saturday which was 4 February 1189, as night was giving place to day and while the community was celebrating lauds,

(following matins) was often called matins—but commonly matins and lauds were virtually a single office and usage in such cases is not entirely clear.

[6] Perhaps echoing a common source with the Requiem hymn, the *Dies Irae* —'Lacrimosa dies illa ...'.

[7] Cf. 1 Cor. 4: 15; Matt. 23: 37.   [8] Cf. 2 Chron. 18: 16.

a tenebris huius seculi et laboribus mundi ad ueram lucem
requiemque eternam migrauit, plus quam centennis senex et plenus
dierum, habitaturus in domo Domini et Deum in secula lauda-
turus,[1] ubi in ordine suo, ut dignus erat, sicut cuidam postea reuela-
tum est,[2] credimus eum inter agmina uirginum beatam sedem
percepisse a Domino. Non enim defuerant manifeste uisiones et
reuelationes, personis fide dignis facte, quibus certissime colligatur
ipsum sanctorum consortio coniunctum esse in celis.

53. *Visio cuiusdam preposite*

Nam nocte eadem qua migrauit a seculo pater Gilebertus, uisio
talis apparuit uni ex non suis sed ex alterius ordinis monialibus,
Agneti nomine, preposite de Apeltona, quod est monasterium
uirginum in prouincia Eboraci.[3] Vidit illa quasi in loco ameni-
simo ecclesiam magnam, et ab occidente ipsius domum spa-
tiosam, in qua parabantur exequie uelut alicuius magnatis,
feretrum scilicet pannis sericis ornatissimum, cum crucibus et
candelabris et ceteris ministeriis solemnibus. Admirata tantum
apparatum quantum non uiderat uspiam circa defunctum, quesiuit a quodam e turba, que ibi erat copiosa, quisnam esset de-
f. 86ᵛ functus cui tanta obsequia | deferebantur. Tunc responsum est
magistrum Gilebertum de Sempingham migrasse de mundo, et
eum cum tanta ueneratione debere sepeliri. Nec mora, erexit se
in loculo qui intus iacebat, et sumpta in manu uirga pastorali,
inchoauit uoce altiori et dulciori quam*ᵃ* unquam illa audierat hunc
uersum sequentie ita modulando: 'Pure mentis gaudia ostendamus
eya in uocis melodia.'[4] Omnes etiam qui aderant elatis in celum
uocibus concinebant cum eo, et cantantes processerunt uersus
basilicam. Videns illa uiuentem qui dicebatur mortuus, indignata
respondit ei qui rem sibi indicauerat: 'Putas me non nosse
magistrum Gilebertum? Noui eum optime et iam non est mortuus
iste quem dicis ipsum esse.' Ad quam ille: 'An ignoras quid contigit beato Iohanni euangeliste? Sicut enim ille matrem Domini
accepit in sua,[5] ita iste eam imitantes sumpsit in custodiam.'

ᵃ quam *Winterbottom;* quod *LcOd*

---

[1] Cf. 1 Chron. 23: 1; and above, pp. xxv, 118–19.   [2] See below, c. 54 (pp. 128–9).
[3] Nun Appleton (Yorks.), included among the houses of Cistercian nuns in KH,
pp. 272, 275; it was founded *c.* 1150.   [4] Unidentified.
[5] Cf. John 19: 26–7. Nun Appleton was dedicated to St Mary and St John the Evangelist.

he left the darkness of this age and worldly labours for the true light and everlasting rest; more than a hundred years old and full of days, he went to dwell in the house of the Lord and to praise God for ever.[1] There he has occupied the station which befitted him, according to the revelation granted to one person:[2] we believe that he has received from the Lord a blessed seat among the ranks of the chaste. For there has been no lack of unambiguous visions and revelations vouchsafed to reliable witnesses, to permit the certain inference that this man has been made a member of the company of saints in heaven.

53. *A prioress's vision*

On the same night that Father Gilbert died, the following vision appeared to a woman who belonged not to his own community but to nuns of another Order; she was called Agnes and was prioress of Appleton, a house of nuns in the province of York.[3] This woman saw a great church in what seemed a most pleasant place, and to the west of it an airy house where arrangements were being made as if for the funeral of some great man; the bier was lavishly decorated with silk hangings, crosses, candlesticks, and the other customary ornaments. She marvelled at preparations more imposing than she had seen anywhere surround a dead man, and she enquired of someone in the crowd thronging that place who it was that had died in whose honour such magnificent rites were being observed. The reply was that Master Gilbert of Sempringham had died and had to be buried with such great reverence. On the instant the man lying within rose upright in his coffin and, taking his pastoral staff in his hand, began this verse of the hymn, singing in a voice higher and sweeter than any she had ever heard: 'O joy!—let us express the delights of a pure mind in the melody of song.'[4] All those who were present lifted their voices to heaven, joined in with him and sang as they processed towards the church. When the prioress saw the man was alive despite the report of his death, she indignantly answered the person who had explained the situation to her: 'Do you think that I do not know Master Gilbert? I know him extremely well, and the man you say this person is, is not yet dead.' To which the reply was: 'Do you not know what happened to St John the Evangelist? Just as he received our Lord's mother in his home,[5] so this man took into his charge those women who followed her example.'

Tunc illa 'Noui' ait 'quia dominus meus est et aduocatus huius loci, et uitam ipsius fere totam memoriter teneo.' Mox ille 'Sicut' inquit 'actum est ei, ita fiet et isti.' Procedentibus igitur cunctis, interrogauit illa quonam erant processuri, et responsum est omnes mundi processiones illi processioni obuiaturas. Ingredien-

f. 87 tibus autem illis in ecclesiam | et ante magnam crucem consistentibus, ecce ex omnibus mundi partibus innumeri populi confluentes, precedentibus choris et altissone*a* concinentibus, plures confecere quarum quasdam nouerat processiones. Videns illa tantas turbarum multitudines, timens ne ab eis comprimeretur, exiuit, et statim excusso somno tantam sensit in naribus odoris suauitatem quod tota die et multo tempore sequenti retinens fragrantiam*b* miro modo reficiebatur. Tunc pulsatum est ad matutinas, et ueniens in basilicam innuit circumstantibus sororibus magistrum Gilebertum de Sempingham certissime obisse, ut cognouerat in somnis. Acceptoque post modicum mortis ipsius nuntio, collegit ipsam fuisse transitus eius noctem et horam qua hec uisa ei paruerunt.

54. *Alia uisio*

Similia etsi non eadem uidit mulier ingenua et optimis moribus instituta, uxor uiri boni Radulfi de Hauuilla.[1] Videbatur sibi uidere et audire in somnis multitudinem angelorum, cum inmensis laudibus et concentibus dulcissonis ascendentem in celum, post quam ascenderunt alie due turme spirituum beatorum oppositis uultibus ferentes intra se tres pueros in lintheamine. Medius a cingulo sursum apparebat | caluus capite, puer tamen facie, duo circa resi-

f. 87ᵛ dentes ab humeris sursum eminebant, multum eo inferiores. Querenti qui essent, responsum est medium illorum esse magistrum Gilebertum de Sempingham qui mortuus mundo iturus erat ad Deum. Putanti et percunctanti si alii duo essent ordinis illius canonici, dictum est non eos esse canonicos, bonos tamen et sanctos ad Dominum suum transferendos. Hec uidit mulier fidelis ipsa*c* nocte obitus eius, et experrecta retulit uisionem marito,

---

a altissone *Winterbottom (cf. p. 190);* altissonis *LcOd*   *b* fragantiam *Lc*
c ipsa *Lc;* uel illa *s.l. Lc*¹; illa *Od*

---

[1] See above, p. lxxiii n. 1.

The prioress then said: 'I know that he is my lord and a patron of this house, and my knowledge of him covers almost the whole of his life.' He replied: 'As it has happened to this man, so shall it be for Master Gilbert.' Since everyone was now moving in procession the prioress asked where they were going and was told that processions from the whole world were to meet this one. They entered the church and stopped before a great cross; and lo, as numberless peoples from every part of the world massed together, preceded by choirs and those who joined them in lofty song, many processions were formed, some of them composed of people she knew. When she saw such a dense mass of crowds, she was afraid she would be crushed by them, and so she went outside; and immediately, waking from her dream, she caught in her nostrils a smell so sweet that she did not lose its fragrance for the whole day and a long time afterwards, and was refreshed in a marvellous fashion. At that moment the bell rang for lauds, and on entering the church she told the sisters who stood around her there that Master Gilbert of Sempringham had most assuredly died, as she had learnt in her dream. And when shortly afterwards news of his death was received, she discovered that it had taken place on the same night and at the same hour that this vision appeared to her.

54. *Another vision*

Similar but not the same things were seen by a woman of noble birth imbued with the highest principles, the wife of that good man Ralph de Hauvilla.[1] In a dream it seemed to her that she saw and heard a host of angels going up into heaven, voicing endless praise and singing sweetly; and after them two other hosts of the blessed spirits ascended, facing one another and bearing between them three boys dressed in linen garments. The one in the middle appeared from his girdle up, and was bald-headed though he had the face of a boy; the two on either side of him were visible from their shoulders upwards and were far below him. When she asked who these people were, the reply came that the middle one was Master Gilbert of Sempringham who, having died to the world, was going to God. She enquired whether she was right in thinking that the other two were canons of his Order, and was told that they were not canons but good and holy men on the point of departure to their Lord. This devout woman saw these things on the very night of Master Gilbert's death; when she awoke she described her vision to her husband and,

annotansque diem inuenit ipsam esse qua sanctus migrauit e seculo.

Quo autem portaretur uel ubi reponeretur, reuelatum est postea cuidam ex suis canonico. Nam non[a] multo tempore post decessum sancti elapso, uidit in somnis quidam canonicus ordinis de Sempingham unum ex fratribus suis nuper antea defunctum. Quem cum de pluribus interrogasset et ille suis interrogationibus satisfecisset, de statu etiam magistri, ubi esset uel quid ageret aut pateretur, sciscitatus est. Ad quem ille 'Non est' inquit 'nobiscum, altior enim locus tenet eum. Nam ex quo migrauit e seculo, statim inter choros uirginum collocatus est.' Non abhorret a uero ista uisio, quoniam si, ut credimus, redditur unicuique secundum opera eius, et teste | ueritate amici de mammona iniquitatis facti factores recipiunt in eterna tabernacula,[1] iuste uirginibus est adunatus, qui et uirgo corpore et mente, carnis scilicet et fidei integritate, sanctus permansit in euum, et omnia sua uirginibus largiens pro multarum seruanda uirginitate tota uita sua laborauit. Vnde sicut qui recipit iustum in nomine iusti mercedem iusti accipit,[2] ita qui recipit non unam sed quamplures uirgines in nomine uirginum, mercedem uirginum merito accepit. Sed et prelatus multarum ecclesiarum hominum precipue continentiam uouentium, digne fructum centesimum percepit,[3] qui debetur uirginibus et martyribus et prelatis.

55. *De sepultura eius*

Hec circa sanctam animam illam gesta fuisse credimus officia celestia, circa corpus uero exanime rite per quatriduum celebrate sunt exequie, donec mandati omnes ordinis priores et preposite ad tanti patris funus conuenissent, qui eo die, cum reliquis omnibus eiusdem professionis secum annumeratis, plus quam duo milia ducenti inuenti sunt. Quarta die, hoc est feria .iii.,[4] astantibus quibusdam abbatibus et tam de suis quam de aliis cenobiis et ecclesiis prepositis, multisque utriusque sexus religiosis[b] personis, necnon et nobilibus et diuitibus | seculi cum innumero populo, qui audito transitu

---

[a] non multo ... martiribus et prelatis] *these words are repeated by Lc at ff. 106ᵛ–107ʳ*
[b] religionis *Lc*

---

[1] Cf. Luke 16: 9.   [2] Cf. Matt. 10: 41.
[3] Cf. Matt. 13: 23.   [4] 7 Feb. 1189 (see c. 52).

f. 88

f. 88ᵛ

making a note of the day, she found it to be the same as that on which the saint departed this life.

Where the saint was carried and where set down was also revealed later to one of his own canons. For not long after the saint's death a canon belonging to the Order of Sempringham saw in a dream one of his brethren who had died shortly before. When the canon had asked him about various matters and his brother had answered his enquiries, he wanted to know also about what had happened to the Master, where he was, what he was doing and experiencing. The brother said to him: 'He is not with us; he occupies a higher position. For as soon as he left the world he immediately took his place amongst the choirs of virgins.' Such a vision is not inconsistent with the truth, since we believe that each man is rewarded according to his deeds and Bible truth assures us that those who have become friends of the mammon of unrighteousness receive others of their kind into the everlasting dwelling-places.[1] Hence it was right for him to join the virgins, because chaste both in body and mind, that is with the wholeness of his flesh and his faith intact, he preserved his holiness unto eternity; and in distributing all his possessions to virgins, he laboured the whole of his life to protect the virginity of many women. Therefore as the man who receives a righteous man in the name of a righteous man receives the righteous man's reward,[2] so he who receives not one but many virgins in the name of virgins deserved to receive the virgins' reward. Again, as the head of many communities of men dedicated especially to continence, he rightly received the fruit of one hundredfold[3] which is owed to virgins, martyrs, and religious superiors.

55. *His burial*

We believe that these were the services performed for his holy soul in heaven; for his lifeless body funeral rites were celebrated according to the custom over four days, until all the priors and prioresses of the Order duly arrived for the burial of their noble father. That day, if we add in all the other members of this same Order, they totalled more than 2,200. On the fourth day, this being a Tuesday,[4] there were present abbots, priors belonging both to his own and other monastic houses and communities, and many religious of both sexes; also layfolk both noble and wealthy, together with countless people who, having heard of the saint's death, had

sancti undique confluxerant, completis missarum sollemniis, uenerabile illud corpus prius aqua perlotum, que multis egrotis postea data in potum profuit ad salutem, sacris et sacerdotalibus uestimentis inuolutum in loco sepulchri inter maiora altaria, scilicet beate Marie et beati Andree apostoli cenobii de Sempingham, quasi in spelunca duplici, ubi ex utraque parte parietis interclusi, hinc a uiris, illinc a mulieribus, possit cum ueneratione adorari, honorifice collocatur.[1] Nec tamen lapis fouee superponitur donec omnes qui affuerant, tanquam ultimum uale dicentes, sanctum et dilectum corpus qua quisque poterat parte contingere amplexati certatim oscula infigerent. Nec erat alicui, etiam pueris et puellulis, horror in extincti cadaueris deosculatione, quia fides tangendi prebuit ausum et deuotio indidit amoris indicium. O quantus luctus omnium, quanta precipue lamenta clericorum et uirginum chori, cum primum et precipuum amitterent pastorem, nec similem post eum se habiturum sperarent. Sed qui in electo famulo suo opera sua omnia operatus est Deus, per quem erat uir in cunctis prospere agens, nec operarium | mercede nec opera debita defraudauit consummatione.[2] Quod e uicino sequentia signa manifeste declararunt.

f. 89

56. *Substitutio primi successoris eius*

Maximum enim et mirandum contigit ipso die humationis eius miraculum, quod scilicet tradito sepulture corpusculo mox contra spem omnium, consensu et petitione omnium, absque omni obstaculo et contradictione omnium, ab utroque sexu et omnibus personis pater et pastor qui nunc preest eligitur, et in caput quod menbra regat, disponat et contineat sullimatur.[3] A nonnullis enim et fere ab omnibus comprouincialibus quasi certum presumebatur quod ex quo tam strenuum decideret caput, illico contingeret a domo de Sempingham menbrorum suorum discessio.[4] Vnde stupentibus cunctis, et quid egissent mirando, secum conferentibus non erat aliud respondere nisi quod qui semper paci studuerat dum iuueret, pacem quoque perpetuam mox ut in

---

[1] See p. xxvi.

[2] Cf. 1 Chron. 17: 19; Gen. 39:2; Luke 10: 7 (and 1 Tim. 5: 18).

[3] This was evidently written while Roger was still Master, i.e. before 1204.

[4] Evidently a reminiscence of the revolt of the lay brethren in the diocese of Lincoln and the province of Canterbury; those of the see and province of York did not join in; see pp. 150–3. But 'comprouincialibus' may have a less specific sense.

come flooding in from every side. When solemn masses had been sung the holy body was first of all cleansed with water, which later when given as a drink to many sick persons restored them to health; then, wrapped in holy and priestly vestments, it was laid with honour in its place of burial. This was between the high altars of St Mary and St Andrew the Apostle belonging to the conventual house of Sempringham, in a sort of double hollow where he could be venerated and adored on both sides of the intervening wall, on this side by the men and on the other by the women.[1] But the stone to cover the grave was not put in position until everyone present, in the manner of those who say their last farewell, could vie to embrace his dear and holy body to impress a kiss upon whatever part each person could reach. No horror at kissing the lifeless body affected anyone, even the boys or the little girls, because faith gave them the courage to touch it and piety prompted them to demonstrate their love. How great was the grief which they all felt, how great in particular the lamentations expressed by the gathering of clerks and virgins, for they were losing their first and greatest pastor and did not expect to have another such after him. But God, who worked all His purposes in His chosen servant, and through whom Gilbert was prosperous in all matters, neither denied the worker his reward nor robbed his deeds of the conclusion they deserved,[2] a fact clearly demonstrated by the miracles that happened soon afterwards.

56. *The appointment of his first successor*

A very great and wonderful miracle occurred on the very day of his burial; immediately his emaciated body had been placed in its tomb, contrary to everyone's expectations, the father and pastor who now exercises authority was, with the agreement and advice of all and without any hindrance or gainsaying, unanimously elected by both men and women and raised to be the head, to rule, govern, and control the limbs.[3] For it was regarded almost as a certainty by some, and by nearly everyone belonging to the province, that the moment so vigorous a head was lost a secession of his limbs from the house of Sempringham would take place.[4] So they were all amazed and, marvelling at what they had done, they could after discussion find no other explanation but that one who had always devoted himself to the cause of peace during his lifetime successfully petitioned for perpetual peace amongst his followers as soon

conspectu Dei uenerat suis impetrauit. Secuta sunt et alia innumera cum his que subiecta sunt et*a* miraculorum insignia, quibus non modo humanorum corporum uerum et cordium curantur dispendia, dum per eorum exhibitionem et operum eius emuli confunduntur, et de gloria dubii absoluuntur, et factorum expressioni f. 89ʳ dero|gantibus ora clauduntur. Ipse nobis meritorum suorum interuentu et precum obtentu uitia compescat, inimicicias*b* depellat, uirtutem subministret, profectum et augmentum uere religionis sue et uniuersali ecclesie conferat, et fines nostros pacem eternam disponat,[1] prestante Domino nostro Ihesu Christo cui cum Patre et Spiritu sancto honor et gloria in secula seculorum. Amen.

EXPLICIT VITA SANCTI GILEBERTI CONFESSORIS.*c*

---

a *Apparently to be deleted (Winterbottom)*   *b* inimicicias *Lc;* uel aduersitates *s.l.* *Lc*¹; aduersitates *Od*   *c* *There is no colophon in Od*

[1] Cf. Ps. 147: 14 (and pp. 116–17).

as he entered the presence of God. Countless other miraculous signs followed, along with these which are added below. Not only human bodies but also human hearts are cured by them of their failures. At the same time the demonstration of such miracles puts to shame those who envy his works, frees from their doubts those who doubt his glory, and stops the mouths of those who would belittle the telling of his deeds. May St Gilbert, by means of his prayers, his own merits interceding for us, check our faults, drive away enmities, supply virtue, cause his own and the universal Church to flourish and increase in true religion, and bestow eternal peace throughout our land,[1] through our Lord Jesus Christ, to whom with the Father and the Holy Spirit be honour and glory, world without end. Amen.

THE END OF THE LIFE OF ST GILBERT THE CONFESSOR

INCIPIVNT EPISTOLE EPISCOPORVM[a]

[1]

1166

Sanctissimo domino et patri Alexandro, Dei gratia summo pontifici, W(illelmus) sue sanctitatis seruus, Norwincensis episcopus,
salutem et deuotam obedientiam.[1]

Mandatum uestre sanctitatis uenerabili[b] domino et fratri nostro,
deuoto filio uestro, Wintoniensi episcopo et nostre paruitati communiter destinatum debita ueneratione suscepimus. Et quia dominus Wintonie graui languore prepeditus adesse non potuit, nos,
quamuis debiles et languidi, pro modulo nostre[c] possibilitatis in eo
processimus, ascitis nobiscum uiris religiosis quos ad ⟨rei⟩[d] com-
misse nobis examen esse cognouimus idoneos. Assistentibus
itaque in presentia nostra magistro Gileberto de Sempingham et
tam canonicis quam conuersis sui ordinis, conquesti sunt conuersi
quod magister G(ilebertus) compulit eos nouam facere professionem abbatie de Sabaneia[2] et iuramenta prestare contra primam
f. 90 professionem | quam dudum fecerant uenerabili domui de Sem-
pingham secundum formam ordinis Cistercie; et eos qui iurare
nollent excommunicasset. Magister uero G(ilebertus) contra dif-
fitebatur quod neque secundum formam ordinis Cistercie professionem unquam ei fecerant, nec illi professioni quam primo apud
Senpingham, postea apud Sabaneiam coacti fecerant professionem contrariam, sed nec aliquam. Verumptamen constanter
astruebat quod neminem eorum coegit ad aliquod sacramentum
prestandum. Quosdam tamen, qui de conseruando ordine suo
iuramentum spontanei[e] prestiterant, iampridem coram domino

---

[a] Hic incipiunt littere contra laicos fratres ad papam *Od*
Letter 1 *Text based on LcOd (neither MS gives a heading)*   [b] *ins.* et *Lc (but marked for
deletion)*   [c] *ins.* paruitatis et *Od*   [d] *Supplied by Winterbottom*   [e] *sponta-
neum Od*

---

[1] For all these letters, see pp. lxxxiv–xc. William de Turba, bishop and formerly prior
of Norwich (bishop 1146/7–1174, *Fasti*, ii. 56); and Henry of Blois, bishop of

LETTERS CONCERNING THE LAY
BRETHREN'S REVOLT

HERE BEGIN THE BISHOPS' LETTERS

[1. *Letter from the bishop of Norwich to the pope on behalf of St Gilbert*]

To his most holy lord and father Alexander, pope by God's grace, W(illiam), his holiness's servant, bishop of Norwich,[1] sends greetings and devout obedience.

We have received with proper reverence your holiness's mandate, sent jointly to our venerable lord and brother, your devout son, the bishop of Winchester, and to our poor self. And because the bishop of Winchester was hampered by a serious illness and could not be present, although we ourselves are weak and ill, we have acted in this matter to the small extent of our powers, joining to ourselves religious whom we knew to be suitable to investigate the matter entrusted to us. Thus Master Gilbert of Sempringham and both canons and lay brethren of his Order came forward in our presence. The lay brethren complained that Master Gilbert forced them to make a new profession to the abbey of Savigny[2] and to swear oaths which were contrary to their first profession, made earlier to the venerable house of Sempringham, following the example of the Cistercian Order; moreover, he had excommunicated those who refused to take such an oath. Master Gilbert on the other hand denied either that these men had ever made him a profession following the custom of the Cistercian Order, or that under compulsion they later made at Savigny any profession contrary to their first profession at Sempringham—or any at all. Indeed he firmly asserted that he had not compelled any of them to take any oath. But some who of their own free will had sworn to preserve his Order he had long ago absolved from their oath in the

Winchester (1129–71, *Fasti*, ii. 85). They were among the few English bishops who had been religious: see esp. D. Knowles, *Episcopal Colleagues of Archbishop Thomas Becket* (Cambridge, 1951), pp. 31–3, 34 ff.; L. Voss, *Heinrich von Blois* (Berlin, 1932).

[2] Identified by David Knowles (*EHR* l (1935), 470 and n. 1) as Savigny, probably correctly, although this part of the story has never been explained.

Lincolniensi episcopo[1] a iuramento absoluerat. Conuersi uero ad hec, sepius interrogati utrum intentata probare possent, in probationibus defecerunt.

Preterea magister G(ilebertus), commonitus a nobis ut fratrem Oggerum[2a] et alios in domibus suis secundum formam mandati uestri reciperet, benigne concessit quod omnes qui cum debita humilitate uellent redire paterna susciperet affectione, et caritatis communionem quam ratio ordinis exigit, salua ordinis professione eorum, eis exhiberet; tamenetsi plerique eorum impetratis litteris dimissoriis et absolutoriis exierant, de quibus fratres W. et Dionisius coram nobis palam protestabantur se nulla ratione uelle reuerti, sed ad alium ordinem migrare. Sed nec Oggerus |

f. 90ᵛ nec alii qui aderant (sic dicebant) reuerti uoluerunt[b] donec in alterum statum ordo reduceretur, quem exprimebant hoc modo, ut scilicet de quatuor ordinibus quos in domibus suis esse asserebant, canonicorum uidelicet, monialium, fratrum et sororum, unus omnibus preponeretur[c] et ab omnibus communiter et pariter obseruaretur. Inquisiuimus etiam si quis ex fratribus captus esset uel incarceratus, et nullum audiuimus captum nisi unum qui, iam per spatium anni ab ordine fugitiuus, pridie quam ad hanc causam agendam uenimus in habitu seculari et accinctus gladio deprehensus fuit a ministris domini regis et tentus.

Illud quoque studiose satis et sollicite inquisiuimus, utrum magister G(ilebertus) litteras uestre celsitudinis, capitulo ordinis sui directas, falsas iudicasset uel latorem earum excommunicasset; quod ipse penitus negabat, affirmans quod nec ipsas inspexerat, nec ei unquam porrecte fuerant, et hoc ipsum Oggerus diffiteri non potuit sed publice confitebatur. Asserebat quoque quod neminem excommunicasset indiscrete, et quod quando peruersores ordinis sui, fures etiam et latrones, generali excommunicatione illaqueasset, excepit nominatim ob reuerentiam litterarum uestre sullimitatis[d] Oggerum qui eas attulit, et Oggerus id confitebatur. Quod autem sanctitati uestre suggestum audiui-

f. 91 mus, canonicos cum | monialibus in una ecclesia commorari,

---

ᵃ Oggerum *Od;* Rogerum *Lc. There are similar variants elsewhere in this letter*   ᵇ uoluerunt *Winterbottom;* noluerunt *LcOd*   ᶜ preponetur *Lc*   ᵈ uestre sullimitatis *Knowles;* uestrarum sullimitatis *Lc;* uestrarum *(om.* sullimitatis*) Od, perhaps rightly*

---

[1] Presumably Robert de Chesney, bishop 1148–66 who died *c.* 25 Dec., probably on the 27th (*Fasti*, iii. 2); but his predecessor Alexander (1123–48) had been much involved

presence of the bishop of Lincoln.[1] On this point, when the lay brethren were asked repeatedly whether they could substantiate their charges, they failed to supply proof.

Next we advised Master Gilbert to receive brother Ogger[2] and the others in his houses, following the terms of your mandate. He graciously agreed that he would welcome with fatherly affection all who wished to return in proper humility, and would demonstrate to them the loving fellowship which the Order's procedure requires, saving their profession to the Order. However, many of these men had left, having obtained letters of dismissal and absolution; among these Brothers W. and Denis asserted openly in our presence that they wished on no account to return, but to transfer to another order. Neither Ogger nor others who were there wished, they said, to return to their houses until the Order was remodelled. This was what they proposed: from the four classes which they said existed in their houses—namely canons, nuns, lay brethren, and lay sisters—one ought to be given charge over all and should be jointly and equally obeyed by all. We also asked whether any of the brethren had been captured or imprisoned. We heard that none had been seized apart from one man who had been a fugitive from the Order for a year, and who, the day before we came to hear this case, was arrested by the king's servants, wearing secular clothing and carrying a sword, and committed to prison.

Further, we made a very diligent and careful inquiry as to whether Master Gilbert had judged to be forged a letter sent by your highness to the chapter of the Order, and whether he had excommunicated the bearer of it. This charge he utterly repudiated, saying that he had not seen this letter, nor had it ever been delivered to him; and Ogger could not deny this but publicly admitted that it was so. Master Gilbert also asserted that he had not rashly excommunicated anyone, and that when he had embraced in a general excommunication those who overturned his Order, together with thieves and robbers, he excepted by name, out of reverence for your highness's letter, Ogger who brought it; and Ogger admitted as much. We have also heard of the charge made to your holiness that canons live alongside nuns in one church

---

in the formation of the Order: see pp. xxx–xxxi. On Robert, see Knowles, *Episcopal Colleagues*, pp. 15–16; *GFL*, p. 535.

[2] In spite of the confusion of the MSS, it is clear that his name was Oggerus, Ogger: see pp. 78–83, 338–40.

et inde plurima scandala suboriri, in uehementem nos ducit admirationem, cum et oratoria habeant canonici et claustra per
singulas domos suas diuersa et separata penitus a monialibus, ubi
meditantur et orant, donec statuta diei hora, facto grege, ad signum
quod dant eis moniales, ad celebranda eis missarum sollemnia
conueniunt, iterumque post expleta missarum officia, grege facto,
ad propria reuertuntur. Veruntamen secundum formam mandati
uestri precepimus eis ut uel duo uel tres deinceps ad agenda missarum sollemnia preficiantur, alii uero canonici separatim in
diuersis ecclesiis permaneant; et magister quidem ad id pronum se
exhibuit et pacientem, quamuis ordini perniciosum sit, quousque
uestrum susceperit inde responsum; et ad omnem suspicionem
remouendam et scandalum, fratribus conuersis, qui in nocturnis
horis ecclesiam monialium ingredi consueuerunt et earum matutinas audire, iniunximus ut ad oratorium ubi canonici separatim
diuina celebrant interim frequentarent, et ab eis horas suas
audiant, ut nec illis, sicut nec canonicis, ad ecclesiam monialium
pateat accessus. Sed neque pretereundum ducimus quod de sanc-
f. 91ᵛ timonialibus et sororibus magistro precepimus | uestra auctoritate
ne deinceps ad officia immittantur qui[a] delinquendi materiam
preparant, et idipsum benigne concessit, et quecumque ei ad ordinis emendationem, uel uestra auctoritate uel religiosorum uirorum
qui nobiscum aderant discreta prouisione, dicebantur prono
animo et satis deuote suscepit. Nunc igitur, uenerande pater,
placeat sanctitati uestre memoratum uirum in proposito suo, quod
a Deo est, paterna pietate stabilire, et eam moderationem his ad
que nos minus sufficimus adhibere, ut et[b] ordinis religio floreat et
Deo placita consistat. Conseruet omnipotens Deus miseratione
sua incolumitatem uestram, piissime pater.

[2] *Epistola Norwicensis episcopi ad dominum papam*[1]

1169–76

Sanctissimo patri et domino[c] summo pontifici A(lexandro) sue
sanctitatis seruus W(illelmus) Norwincensis episcopus,[d] salutem
et cum[e] deuotione obedientiam.

---

[a] que *Od, probably rightly*   [b] et *om. Od, more elegantly*
Letter 2 *LcOd; 17th cent. transcripts in Paris, Bibl. Nat. Lat. 14615, ff.   358–9 = Par, and
J. Picard's edition of William of Newburgh, Paris, 1610, pp. 697–9 = Pic (select readings only of
Par and Pic)*   [c] et domino *om. Pic,* domino *om. Par*   [d] *om. ParPic*   [e] *ins.*
summa *ParPic*

and that many scandals arise from this situation. This causes us great surprise, because in every one of their houses the canons possess oratories and enclosures which are entirely different and separate from the nuns'; here they meditate and pray until at a fixed hour of the day, when the community has assembled, at a sign given them by the nuns they come together to celebrate mass for them. When mass is over they return once again in procession to their own quarters. However, following your instructions, we gave them orders that either two or three canons are to be appointed in future to perform the service of mass, while the other canons stay separate in their different churches; and the Master showed himself patient and agreeable to this measure, although it is harmful to the Order, until he receives your answer on the matter. And in order to remove all suspicion and scandal we have ordered that the lay brethren, who used to enter the nuns' church during the night office and attend their matins, should for the time being visit the church where the canons hold their separate services, and that they should follow the canons' offices. Thus access to the nuns' church is to be available neither to the lay brethren nor to the canons. We do not think that we should pass over the fact that on the subject of nuns and lay sisters we instructed the Master on your authority that in future those who cause occasion for misbehaviour should not be admitted to services. This the Master graciously allowed, and every proposal to improve the Order made to him either on your authority or reflecting the considered judgement of the religious present with us, he embraced willingly and with great piety. Now therefore, venerable father, may it please your holiness out of paternal affection to strengthen this man in his purpose, which derives from God, and to bring your authority to bear on the matters where we are not sufficient; that the religious observance of the Order may both flourish and continue acceptable to God. May Almighty God of his mercy keep you safe and well, most holy father.

[2] *Letter from the bishop of Norwich to the Pope*[1]

To his most holy father and lord Pope A(lexander), W(illiam), bishop of Norwich, his holiness's servant, sends greetings and obedience with devotion.

---

[1] This letter is also in the letter-book of Saint-Victor (see textual note; cf. also A. Luchaire, *Étude sur quelques manuscrits de Rome et de Paris* (Paris, 1899), p. 133).

Statuta paternitatis uestre ex pietatis et rationis fonte manare[a] nulli dubium est; et ea sola spiritui[b] uestro placent[c] que Spiritus Sanctus suggerit et ueritatis dulcedine condiuntur. Inde est quod uestre maiestati audeo scribere, cum sim puluis et cinis,[1] et testimonium perhibere ueritati, quam uisu et rerum argumentis expertus sum. Gilebertus de Sempingham, tum ex uicinitate, tum ex celebritate sanctitatis qua preminet, mihi incognitus esse non

f. 92 potest. Anima eius | sedes est sapientie[d] et mens eius haurit de Spiritu Sancto quod aliorum auribus excellenter infundit. In ⟨lucrandis et⟩[e] conseruandis Deo animabus tam studiosus et efficax est ut ex comparatione eius tedeat me ignauie mee, et mihi et consimilibus meis[f] propheta improperet,[g] dicens 'Erubesce Sydon, ait mare.'[2] In sanctimonialibus, quarum multitudinem et numerum[h] Deo adquisiuit, feruet religionis amor et castitatis diligentissima custodia, et ⟨se ab hominum uisu et⟩[i] colloquiis gloriantur esse exemptas, ut merito eis conueniat quod scriptum est: 'Dilectus meus mihi et ego illi, qui pascitur inter lilia.'[3] De canonicis, quorum innocentie audio apud clementiam uestram esse derogatum, testor Deum in[j] animam meam quod nec uerbum infamie memini me audisse, cum ex propinquitate loci et confrequentia uenientium ad nos ignorare non possem. Accessus ad sanctimoniales sic eis penitus inhibitus est ut nec priori quidem eorum uidendi uel loquendi cum aliqua licentia pateat; et in perceptione eucharistie et dans et accipiens inuicem ignorat.[k] Habent siquidem domos suas, claustrum et oratorium in quibus dormiunt, meditantur et orant. A conuersis suis tantum exigit[l] ut uitam quam professi sunt inuiolabiliter conseruent; quod et ipsi me presente se deuotissime facturos promiserunt. Quod enim predecessorum

f. 92ᵛ uestrorum[m] et uestra | auctoritate firmatum est, et quod illi post longam experientiam profitentes deuouerunt, ipse inmutare non presumit, ne leuitatis et presumptionis arguatur. Lis tamen, quam aduersus eum suscitauerunt plus tepidi quam feruentes caritate, utinam dirimeretur talium iudicio et testimonio, qui haberent zelum Dei secundum scientiam, qui ex inspectione apostolicorum

---

[a] manare *LcOd;* procedere *ParPic*   [b] sola spiritui *Lc corr., Od ParPic;* spiritui sola *Lc*   [c] placent *Od;* et placent *Lc;* complacent *ParPic*   [d] sapientiae est *ParPic*   [e] *Supplied from ParPic*   [f] meis *LcOd Par;* mei *Pic*   [g] improperet *Lc¹Od Pic;* improperat *Lc;* improbet *Par(?)*   [h] et numerum] innumeram *ParPic*   [i] *Supplied from ParPic*   [j] in *LcOd Par;* et *Pic*   [k] ignorantur *ParPic*   [l] exigit *LcOd Pic;* exigunt *Par*   [m] uestrorum *Od;* nostrorum *Lc ParPic*

[1] Cf. Gen. 18: 27.

No one doubts that laws flow from you, father, as from a fount of piety and reason; and those things alone delight your spirit which are prompted by the Holy Spirit and given savour by the sweetness of truth. This is why, although I am dust and ashes,[1] I dare write to your majesty and bear witness to the truth which I have learned with my own eyes and by experience of the case. Gilbert of Sempringham cannot be unknown to me both because we live in neighbouring regions and because he is famous for exceptional holiness. His soul is the seat of wisdom, and his mind takes from the Holy Spirit the draughts which he pours into the ears of other men in a wonderful fashion. He is so industrious and successful in winning and keeping souls for God that in comparison with him I am ashamed of my idleness, and the prophet reproaches me and those like me when he says 'Blush, Sidon, says the sea.'[2] He brought to God a great host of nuns, amongst whom there burns a love of the religious life and a most scrupulous regard for chastity; they delight in being free from the sight and converse of man, so that the writing may be properly applied to them: 'My beloved is mine and I am his, who feeds among the lilies.'[3] About the canons, whose purity I hear has been slandered before your clemency, as God is my witness I declare I do not recall hearing even a single word of evil rumours, and these I could not have missed because the place is close by and many people come to visit us. Access to the nuns is so entirely forbidden to the canons that not even their prior is allowed to see or speak with one, and when they receive the eucharist, both the person who gives and the person who receives are ignorant of each other. They possess their own dwellings, their own enclosure and church in which they sleep, meditate, and pray. The only obligation the Master lays upon his lay brethren is to keep inviolable the life which they have professed; and this they have promised in my presence most faithfully to do. For what was established on your and your predecessors' authority, what those men vowed when they made their profession after a long trial of it, Master Gilbert does not presume to alter, in case he is charged with unconsidered rashness. If only the case mounted against him by those who are lukewarm in their love, rather than red-hot, might be settled by the judgement and evidence of such men as possessed zeal for God according to knowledge, recognized the truth by inspecting papal

[2] Cf. Matt. 16: 27; Isa. 23: 4.   [3] S. of S. 2: 16; 6: 2.

priuilegiorum et rerum ipsarum euidenti cognitione ueritatem agnoscerent, et regularis obseruantie nec inexperti essent nec ignari, et quos non tederet suscepte religionis et manu missa ad aratrum non respicerent retro.[1] Vir uero confectus senio, et uirtutum plenior quam dierum, non est deterrendus[a] ne a proposito[b] ad multorum ruinam deficiat, sed hortandus et demulcendus, ut perseueret ad conseruandam salutem quam Deus per eum operatus est in medio terre nostre. Rarescunt cotidie grana in Domini area,[c] sed palee multiplicantur.[2] Deus sanctitatem uestram ecclesie sue conseruet incolumem. Amen.

[3] *Epistola regis Henrici ad dominum papam[d] pro sancto Gileberto[3]*
1166—7

Dilectissimo domino et patri spiritali A(lexandro), Dei gratia summo pontifici, H(enricus) eadem gratia rex Anglie, et cetera, salutem ⟨et⟩[e] cum summa deuotione debitum obsequium.

Vestre diligenter supplicamus paternitati quatinus pro Dei amore et nostro interuentu au|res benignas adhibeatis uniuersis scriptis episcoporum et aliorum uirorum religiosorum quibus magnifice commendant personam et sanctitatem uenerabilis uiri Dei, magistri G(ileberti) de Sempingham, et singularem fructum utriusque sexus quem fecit in domo Domini, et iuxta eorum testimonium et deprecationem petitionem illius executioni[f] mandare dignemini, precipientes rebellibus ipsius ordinis conuersis et omnibus aliis[g] professionis domorum[h] de Sempingham, ut inuiolabiliter obseruent professionem et uotum suum, sicut priuilegio uestro et predecessorum uestrorum sanccitum est et eximie confirmatum; et si obedire contempserint, placeat sanctitati uestre precipere episcopis in quorum diocesi prefatus uir Dei habet domos suas ut eos auctoritate uestra coherceant obedire per omnia uoto et professioni sue, secundum tenorem priuilegii uestri et predecessorum uestrorum. Vestre etiam discretioni in ueritate que Deus est notificamus quod rebelles illi grauiter perturbauerunt totum ordinem et grauem iacturam fecerunt domibus ordinis, furtim asportando possessiones earum, et in factis eorum nichil est

---

[a] deterrendus *Pic (and Par?);* deterendus *LcOd*   [b] ne a proposito *Lc ParPic;* a proposito ne *Od*   [c] in area Domini *ParPic*

Letter 3 *LcOd*   [d] papam *erased in Lc*   [e] *Supplied by Winterbottom*
[f] execucioni *Od;* executionem *Lc*   [g] aliis *om. Lc*   [h] *ins.* ordinis *Od*

f. 93

privileges and, clearly understanding the matter itself, were neither unused to nor ignorant of observance of a rule, did not tire of the religious life they had undertaken, and did not look back when their hand was put to the plough.[1] But a man worn out by old age, yet fuller of virtues than days, should not be deterred, lest in failing in his purpose he cause the downfall of many; rather he should be encouraged and reassured so that he may continue to uphold the salvation which God has worked in the midst of our land by his means. Daily the seed upon the Lord's threshing-floor diminishes, while the chaff multiplies.[2] May God preserve your holiness safe and well for His Church. Amen.

[3] *Letter from King Henry to the pope on behalf of St Gilbert*[3]

To his dear lord and spiritual father A(lexander), by God's grace pope, H(enry), by the same grace king of England, etc., sends greetings and due service with deep devotion.

We earnestly beg you, father, considering God's love and our intercession, to turn your gracious attention to all those letters from bishops and other religious men, which commend in generous measure the person and holiness of the venerable man of God, Master Gilbert of Sempringham, and the remarkable fruit drawn from both sexes which he has brought forth in the house of the Lord. Also, following the evidence and entreaty of these people, may you be pleased to order the carrying-out of his petition, ordering the rebellious lay brethren of the Order and all others professing membership of the Sempringham houses to observe without deviation their profession and vow, as was decreed and particularly confirmed by your privilege and those of your predecessors; and if they refuse to obey, may it please your holiness to instruct the bishops in whose dioceses this man of God has his religious houses that on your authority they are to compel these men to obey their vow and profession in every detail, following the terms of your and your predecessors' privilege. Relying upon the truth which is God, we also lay before your discreet judgement the fact that those rebels have seriously disturbed the entire Order and have caused severe damage to the Order's houses by secretly carrying away their possessions. There is nothing but violence in their deeds, because they would before now have thrown out of the Order's houses, or caused

[1] Cf. Romans 10: 12; Luke 9: 62.   [2] Cf. Matt. 3: 12; etc.   [3] See pp. lviii, lxxxvi.

nisi furor, quia magistrum ordinis et plures canonicorum suorum,
per quos integritas religionis ibi uiget, uel iam eiecissent a domibus ordinis uel neci tradidissent, nisi timuissent nos et alios funda-
f. 93ᵛ tores domorum, qui | nullatenus sustineremus ipsos laicos
dominari in elemosina nostra, nec moniales alienari a custodia
magistri G(ileberti) de Sempingham et canonicorum suorum, quorum prouisione et doctrina usque in presentiarum satis mirabiliter
floruit ipsarum uita et tocius ordinis status. Nec uolumus uos
latere quod ipsi peruersi nobis dedissent .CCC. marcas argenti, si
sustinuissemus eos dominari ad libitum et canonicos eliminari a
domibus, quibus uoto et professione tenentur; sed non ausi sumus,
tam pro metu Dei quam pro reuerentia uestri priuilegii et prede-
cessorum uestrorum, quibus ordinis corruptores anathematis
uinculo innodantur, eis in tanta et tam maligna fauere stultitia,
quia nobis constat, si in hoc assensum preberemus, quod totius
ordinis excidium hinc proueniret. Quod ne ullo modo contingat,
sanctitas uestra malignantibus medullitus resistat.ᵃ

[4] *Epistola Wintoniensis episcopi ad eundem pro eodem*
1166—7

Alexandro, Dei gratia summo pontifici, H(enricus) Wintoniensis
ecclesie humilis minister, salutem et deuotam obedientiam.[1]
   Pro dilecto fratre G(ileberto) de Sempingham, uiro probate religionis et honestatis, celsitudini uestre preces pie porrigimus,
optantes attestatione paruitatis nostre negocii ipsius iusticiam erga
sullimitatem uestram commendabiliorem esse. Siquidem locum
f. 94 religiose | habitationis sue et canonicorum suorum et sanctimonia-
lium, quas ministerioᵇ doctrine et institutionis sue regulariter Deo
seruire certum est, non inspeximus; sedᶜ lucernam sanctitatis eius
et odorem deuotionis eius, qui longe lateque diffunditur, fame pre-
conio creberrime persensimus. Hic est enim qui, ab ineunte etate
Christo militare disponens, usui pauperum patrimonium suum
deputans, multorum animas in utroque sexu Christi iugo assue-
fecit, et precipuus uirginitatis et sacre continentie cultor ouile
dominicum per distinctas et separatas mansiones sacrarum ouium

---

ᵃ quod . . . resistat *Lc;* proinde . . . reportent. ualeat *Od (from the end of Henry II's second*
letter (no. 12) to the pope: see p. 162; cf. p. lxxxvi)
   Letter 4 *LcOd*   ᵇ ministerio *Knowles;* misterio *LcOd*   ᶜ non inspeximus
sed *Lc;* inspeximus et *Od*

to be killed, the master of the Order and many of his canons who are responsible for the strength and integrity of religious observance there, if they had not been afraid of us and of the other founders of houses. For on no account would we permit these lay brethren to rule in houses founded on our charity, or the nuns to be separated from the guardianship of Master Gilbert of Sempringham and his canons, because it is through their care and teaching that their life and the state of the entire Order has flourished up till now in a most remarkable way. We also do not wish to hide from you that these same wrongdoers would have given us 300 silver marks if we had allowed them to rule as they wanted and the canons to be cast out of the houses to which they are attached by vow and profession. But we were not so rash as to support them in so great and so wicked a folly, both out of fear of God, and in reverence for your and your predecessors' privilege, according to which those who undermine the Order are bound by the chain of anathema. We are sure that if we were to agree to this, it would result in the downfall of the entire Order. To prevent this from happening at all costs, we pray that your holiness will strive against the wicked with all your energy.

[4] *Letter from the bishop of Winchester to the same on behalf of the same*

To Alexander, pope by God's grace, H(enry) the humble servant of the church of Winchester sends greetings and devout obedience.[1]

We offer your highness sincere prayers for our dear brother G(ilbert) of Sempringham, a man of proven faith and integrity, hoping that by our humble witness the rightness of this man's case may recommend itself more powerfully to your highness. We have not, indeed, seen the site of the religious dwelling which belongs to this man, his canons, and also to nuns, women who assuredly serve God under their rule by means of the Master's teaching and instruction. But we have very often been made aware by popular report of the lamp of his holiness and the sweet savour of his piety, which spreads far and wide. For this is the man who, on becoming an adult, determined to enter Christ's service and made over his inheritance to the use of the poor. He accustomed the souls of many of both sexes to the yoke of Christ, and, as an especial exponent of virginity and holy continence, brought fruit to the Lord's sheepfold in the shape of a great number of blessed sheep distributed throughout distinct and separate dwellings. The

[1] See pp. 134–5 n.

numerositate fecundauit. Virgines inclusas seorsum, canonicosque eis diuina ministrantes separatim agere, aditumque ad illas non patere, nisi per extreme necessitatis urgentiam, et tunc cum utriusque sexus testimonio, totum Anglorum regnum approbat et admiratur. Inde est quod quamplures de regno nostro nobiles, odore religionis eorum illecti, et beneficiis eorum propositum caritatiue iuuerunt*a* et pro conuersione[1]*b* gregem suum adauxerunt. Verum perniciosus hostis innocentie, qui caput eorum insidiis nequiuit deicere, calcaneo saltem per conuersorum suorum insolentiam, qui ad aratrum diuine culture manum per professionem miserunt[2] et iam post fere .xl. annos conuersionis sue retro abire

f. 94ᵛ moliuntur, insidias | tendit.*c* Vestrum est igitur insidias illas eludere,*d* et conuersorum adquiescere professioni sancte religionis recusantium insolentiam edomare, ut quod ob senii et debilitatis impeditionem proprius pastor dominici gregis, pro quo scribimus, minus potest, sanctitatis uestre sollicitudo*e* suppleat.

[5] *Epistola Norwicensis episcopi ad sanctum Gilebertum*[3]

1166

W(illielmus), Dei gratia Norwincensis episcopus, alteri sibi, Gileberto de Sempingham, salutem et se.*f*

Mira est prerogatiua caritatis, que unit quos replet et corporum uarietate discretos uelut in unam animarum conflat substantiam. Vocasti me, frater karissime, ad ortum deliciarum tuarum. Venientem me*g* magnifice suscepisti et benignitate qua precellis me et meos constituisti ciues ciuitatis tue Ierusalem, quam studio tuo elegit Deus in hereditatem sibi, de qua dicit: 'Hec requies mea in seculum seculi, hic ha(bitabo), quoniam elegi eam.'[4] Hac incomparabili connexione unisti me tibi, immo, quia qui suscipit beneficium inferior est conferente, paruitatem meam sic tuis subiugasti imperiis dominationis*h* ut tuus non esse non possim, etiam si hoc esse desiero. Ergo quicquid tibi

---

a iuuerant *Lc*   *b* conuersacione *Od*   *c* tendunt *Lc*   *d* elidere *Od (cf. above, p. 82 n. c)*   *e* celsitudo *Od*

Letter 5 *LcOd; 17th-c. transcript in Paris, B.N. Lat. 14615, ff. 359–60 = Par (select readings)*
f *Possibly for* seipsum *(Brooke)*   *g* me *om. Par (but repeats* me *after* ciuitatis*)*
h tuis . . . dominationis *LcOd;* tuae dominationis subiugasti imperiis *Par*

---

[1] The meaning of 'pro conuersione' is far from clear; possibly 'per conuersionem' should be read.

[2] Cf. Gen. 3: 15; Luke 9: 62.

whole kingdom of England approves and admires the fact that the virgins are enclosed on their own, while the canons who administer the sacraments to them live apart, and that access to the nuns is not allowed except under the pressure of extreme need and then only when witnessed by both sexes. This is why many nobles of our kingdom, carried away by the sweet fragrance of their religious life, have charitably assisted their purpose with gifts and have increased his flock with the means for their conversion.[1] However, the dangerous enemy of innocence, who was unable by his stratagems to cast down their head, is laying plots at least against their heel, using the insolence of his own lay brethren, men who put their hand to the plough[2] of divine service by their oath of profession and now, after nearly forty years of living a life of religion, are endeavouring to turn back and depart. We therefore look to you to foil these plots, and to subdue the insolence of the lay brethren who are refusing to acquiesce in the profession of the holy religious life. Thus what the proper shepherd of the Lord's flock, on whose behalf we write, is unable to do, hindered as he is by old age and infirmity, your holiness's loving care may perform.

[5] *Letter from the bishop of Norwich to St Gilbert*[3]

William by God's grace bishop of Norwich sends greetings, together with himself, to Gilbert of Sempringham, his other self.

How wonderful is the privilege of love, which unites those it enters and fuses as into one substance compact of souls those separated from one another by dwelling in different bodies. You summoned me, dear brother, to the garden of your delights. You welcomed me generously when I came and, with the graciousness in which you excel, you appointed myself and my followers citizens of your city of Jerusalem. Because of your zeal God chose your city as His own inheritance, and says of it: 'This is my rest for ever, here will I dwell, for I have chosen it.'[4] With this incomparable bond you have joined me to you, or rather, since he who receives a gift is less than he who bestows it, you have subjected my humble self so completely to the authority of your will that, even if I cease to be your subject, I could not help but belong to you. For this reason let

---

[3] See p. 134 n. This letter is also in the letter book of Saint-Victor: see textual note; also Luchaire, loc. cit. (p. 139 n. 1).

[4] Ps. 32 (33): 12; 131 (132): 14.

scripsero uero amori imputa, qui coegit me ut scriberem. Venient ad te littere domini pape, quas meo consilio diuina ueneratione suscipies, et earum delatores nulla uerborum asperitate, nulla uultus truculentia, exacerbes,|memor illius uulgaris prouerbii: 'Qui diligit me, et canem meum honorat.'[1] Hoc enim pre ceteris debemus Deo et domino pape, ut nuntiis eorum diuinam exhibeamus reuerentiam.[a] Quicquid tibi a domino papa mandatum fuerit, a Domino prolatum estima, et sic ei obedi ut Deo, iuxta illud: 'Qui uos audit me audit, et qui uos spernit me spernit.'[2] Prophetauit Cayphas et[b] filius Cis inter prophetas fuit, sed uterque ex officio.[3] Quanto magis dominus papa, organum Spiritus Sancti et Christi uicarius et successor Petri,[4] cuius sapientiam precellentem orbis predicat, cuius sanctitatem nec liuor capit[c] et miracula manifesta protestantur. Quod si in litteris illis tue uoluntati aliquid contrarium inueneris, pacienter sustine, nec cum illis uelis communicare consilium qui oderunt pacem,[5] qui, ut tibi placeant, fallacibus animum tuum demulcent blandiciis; sed sapientum[d] utere consilio qui uelint et sciant animarum prouidere saluti, qui in scola religionis eruditi ex eo quod iudicati sunt de aliis iudicare didicerunt. Argumentosa res apis ex multis floribus mel conficit et, ut aiunt,[6] non sine salis aut salsuginis admixtione. Esto et tu apis Dei, et ex multorum sapientum sentenciis unam confice Deo placitam[e] et tibi salutarem, quam condiat sapientia diuina,[f] que est Christus, que[g] et dicit: 'Ego in consiliis habito, et thronus|meus in columna nubis';[7] ac si diceret: 'Habito in consiliis sapientum, quibus[h] Spiritus Sanctus spiritalem fortitudinem subministrat.' Valete.[i]

f. 95 (marginal)

f. 95ᵛ (marginal)

[6] *Epistola R(oberti) Lincolniensi[j] episcopi*[8] *ad eundem pro eodem*
1166

Sanctissimo patri et domino A(lexandro), Dei gratia summo pontifici, minimus suorum R(obertus), eadem gratia Lincolniensi[j]

    [a] *ins.* et mandatis omnimodam obedientiam *Par*   [b] *ins.* Saul *Par*   [c] capit *LcOd;* carpit *Par*   [d] sapientum *Par;* sapienter *LcOd*   [e] placitam *Par;* placidam *LcOd (Od adds* responsionem*)*   [f] Dei *Par*   [g] qui *Od*   [h] *ins.* tota domus nostra que est gloria uestra in Christo Iesu *Par*   [i] Valete *LcOd;* Valeat sanctitas uestra nostri memor *Par*
    Letter 6 *Lc*   [j] R. Eboracensis ... R. eadem gratia Eboracensis *Lc, wrongly; see p. lxxxviii*

---

[1] *The Oxford Dictionary of English Proverbs*, 3rd edn., rev. F. P. Wilson (Oxford, 1970), p. 492, cites as an early source St Bernard, *Sermo in Fest. S. Michaelis:* 'qui me amat, amat et canem meum'.   [2] Luke 10: 16.

whatever I write to you be attributed to the true affection which compels me to write. Letters will be coming to you from the pope. It is my advice that you receive them with godly respect, and do not provoke those who bear them by any roughness of speech or fierce looks, remembering the common saying 'Love me, love my dog.'[1] For we owe this above all to God and to the pope, to show godly reverence towards their messengers. Whatever instructions there are for you from the pope, consider them as issuing from the Lord and obey him as you would God, in accordance with the saying 'Whoever hears you, hears me and whoever despises you, despises me.'[2] Caiaphas prophesied and the son of Kish was among the prophets, but both acted thus on account of their office.[3] How much more is the pope [to be respected], the instrument of the Holy Spirit, Christ's vicar and the successor to Peter,[4] for the whole world declares his wisdom superior, while no envy touches his holiness, and evident miracles attest it. But if you find anything in those letters which opposes your will, bear it patiently and do not take counsel with those men who hate peace,[5] who to please you soothe your spirit with deceitful flattery. But take advice from wise men who possess the will and knowledge to obtain the salvation of souls: men experienced in the school of the religious life, who have learned to judge others by being judged themselves. That assiduous creature the bee makes honey from many flowers and, they say,[6] not without an addition of salt or salty fluid. Do you too become therefore God's bee, and from the opinions of many wise men form one which is pleasing to God and beneficial to yourself, spiced by the divine wisdom which is Christ and which says: 'I dwell in wise counsels and my throne is among the cloudy pillars';[7] as if he should say, 'I dwell in the counsels of the wise, by whose means the Holy Spirit supplies spiritual courage.' Farewell.

[6] *Letter from R⟨(obert), bishop (of Lincoln) to Pope Alexander⟩*[8]

To his most holy father and lord A(lexander), by God's grace pope, the least of his servants R(obert), by the same grace bishop of

---

[3] Cf. John 11: 51; 1 Kgs. 10: 11 (of Saul). The argument of the passage seems to be: if even Caiaphas and Saul could be prophets (even though only on the strength of the offices they held, as high priest, and anointed king), how much more can the pope speak with authority as the mouthpiece of the Holy Spirit, as Vicar of Christ and successor of Peter.

[4] See pp. 44–5, 210–11.   [5] Cf. Ps. 119: 7 (120: 6).

[6] We have not found the source of this.   [7] Ecclus. 24: 7.

[8] Robert de Chesney, bishop of Lincoln 1148–66; see p. xxxi n.

ecclesie episcopus, salutem et debitam in omnibus et per omnia obedientiam.

Audiuimus et dolemus quod quedam sinistra significata sunt sanctitati uestre de domibus illis que subiecte sunt regimini magistri G(ileberti) de Sempingham, uidelicet quod canonici et fratres et moniales simul habitent; sed longe aliter se res habet. Seorsum enim habitant, seorsum comedunt, et ita ab inuicem sunt segregati quod nulli canonico uel fratri pateat aditus ad moniales. De domibus autem illis quas in diocesi nostra habet, certissime audemus asserere quod honestissime et religiosissime reguntur. Vir siquidem prefatus suaue olentis opinionis est, et domibus suis prouidere omnimodis intendit. Si uero longe separarentur^a canonici et fratres a monialibus, sicut ad suggestionem quorundam uos precepisse accepimus, non possent stare domus ille. Aduocati namque, qui canonicis et monialibus illis possessiones suas pietatis intuitu concesserunt, nullatenus sustinerent, sed facillima f. 96 sumpta occasione libenter eis subtraherent quicquid | benigne prius ipsis inpenderant. Valete.

[7]   *Item eiusdem ad eundem pro eodem* [sic]

1166–7

Domino pape A(lexandro), Rogerus Eboracensis archiepiscopus^b et H(ugo) Dunelmensis episcopus.^{1c}

Iuxta formam quam in scripto paruitati nostre dedit sullimitas uestra, in causa processimus que inter magistrum G(ilebertum) de Sempingham et fratres eius uertebatur, et quidem quod ad prouinciam nostram de facili expediuimus. Vnica quippe domus est in Eboracensi diocesi in qua canonici et conuersi cum monialibus,^{2} infra eadem septa, que quidem ampla sunt, sed seorsum, ut fama publica est, honeste habitant; in qua nec iusiurandum nec aliud quippiam contra primam professionem^d predictus magister ab ipsis exegerat, nullum eorum carcerali deputauit custodie, neminem eorum excommunicauerat, sed omnes in ea uocatione manserant in qua ab eo uocati fuerant. Precepimus

---

^{a} separentur *Lc before correction*
Letter 7 *LcOd* ^{b} archiepiscopus *Od;* episcopus *Lc* ^{c} ins. salutem *Od*
^{d} professionem *om. Lc*

---

^{1} Roger of Pont l'Évêque, archbishop of York (1154–81) and Hugh du Puiset, bishop of Durham (1153–95): Knowles, *Episcopal Colleagues*, pp. 8, 12–14, etc.; *Letters of John of*

Lincoln, sends greetings and the obedience owed in all matters and in every respect.

We have heard with grief that some evil allegations have been made to your holiness concerning those houses subject to the rule of Master Gilbert of Sempringham; namely that canons, lay brethren, and nuns all dwell together. The situation is quite different. They live apart, they eat apart, and they are kept so completely separate from one another that entry to the nuns is not permitted to any canon or lay brother. Moreover, of those houses which he has in our diocese, we dare state most confidently that they are ruled with complete integrity and the strictest regard for the religious life. The man himself has a glowing reputation and aims in every possible way to care for his houses. If the canons and brethren were really put a great distance away from the nuns, which we have heard you have been prompted by some men to command, those houses could not survive. For their patrons, who, moved by piety, granted their possessions to these canons and nuns, would on no account permit it; rather, seizing so apt an opportunity, they would promptly take away from these people whatever they had kindly given them previously. Farewell.

[7] ⟨*Letter from Roger archbishop of York and Hugh bishop of Durham to Pope Alexander*⟩ [1]

To Pope A(lexander), Roger archbishop of York and H(ugh) bishop of Durham, [greetings].

We have proceeded in the dispute which arose between Master Gilbert of Sempringham and his lay brethren according to the instructions which your highness gave in writing to our humble selves; and indeed we have easily settled what concerns our province. For there is only one house in the diocese of York where canons and lay brethren dwell alongside nuns within the same enclosures,[2] which are particularly spacious; but, as is public knowledge, they live apart with propriety. In this house Master Gilbert has not demanded from its inhabitants either an oath or anything else contrary to their first profession; he has sent none of them to prison; he has excommunicated no one; on the contrary, all have remained in that calling to which he had summoned them. So,

Salisbury, ii, nos. 306–7 and p. 747 n. 15; G. V. Scammell, *Hugh du Puiset* (Cambridge, 1956); *Fasti*, ii. 13, 30; Foreville, *L'Église et la royauté*, index s.vv. Hugues, Roger.

[2] At this date Watton was the only *double* Gilbertine house in the see of York.

itaque ei ut canonicos a monialibus, iuxta formam mandati uestri, separaret. Quod libens concessit. De litteris quoque uestris, quas uniuerso ordini illi direxistis, quas ipse de falso notasse dicebatur, nichilominus solliciti fuimus, et diligenter quesiuimus cur eas falsitatis arguisset, cum nec in scriptura nec in dictamine nec in bulla aliqua falsa nota appareret. Ipse uero constanter negauit quod nec eas receperat nec uiderat. Et quoniam fratres ad hoc f. 96ᵛ conuincendum non satis instructi uenerant, ad | uoluntatem eorum dies prorogata est. Veniente autem die, ego Rogerus archiepiscopus, immo seruus uester, quoniam dominus Dunelmensis ex necessaria causa absens fuit, accitis abbatibus et prioribus et aliis uiris prudentibus maturi consilii, deuotum mandato uestro obsequium exhibui; et quoniam eadem die fratres predicti in eorum probatione que proposuerant omnino defecerunt, hii qui in diocesi nostra morantur, circa quos sicut dictum est nichil contra primam professionem et ordinis institutionem innouatum fuerat, absque ulla murmuratione iam dictum magistrum in patrem et ipse eos in filios benigne suscepit, supplices dumtaxat preces porrigentes quatinus pauca temperaret, quibus sopitis non solum extra sed intus pacem perfectissimam affuturam esse firmiter asserebant; in quibus temperandis nec mandato uestro nec consilioᵃ magistrum credimus defuturum. Reliquos quoque qui extra nos positi sunt, in osculo, sicut uir mansuetus est, non minus benigne recepit, preter solum Oggerum, qui cornua peccatorum assumens[1] nec ad fratrum suorum lacrimas motus nec ad commonitionem abbatum et priorum qui nobis assistebant uel nostram redire uoluit, nisi sepedictus magister ad arbitrium eius nouas in ordine suo conderet institutiones.

f. 97   Superest igitur, domine, | quatinus uirum innocentem et per quem Deus multa et magna et usque ad tempus eius inaudita operatus est in medio nostri,ᵇ mansuetudo consoletur apostolica, ut qui iam in diebus suis processit, nature debitum in breui redditurus, pacifice e carcereᶜ mortis huius egredi possit; nec paciamini ipsum ab his conculcari, qui non que religionis sunt querentes sed sua, imitari pro uoto suo querunt magistros prurientes auribus.[2]

ᵃ ins. nostro Od   ᵇ ins. mirabilia Od (but cf. p. 162 n. b)   ᶜ One expects corpore (Winterbottom), cf. Rom. 7: 24

---

[1] See pp. 78–83; and cf. Ps. 74: 11 (75: 10).
[2] Cf. Ps. 73: 12 (74: 13); Rom. 7: 24 ('de corpore mortis huius'); 2 Tim. 4: 3.

following the instructions in your mandate, we have ordered him to separate the canons from the nuns. This he has willingly granted. Moreover, we have been no less painstaking about the letter which you sent to the whole of that Order and which it is said the master aspersed as being forged; and we have enquired carefully why he accused it of being false when no sign of any inauthenticity appeared in its writing, its phraseology, or its seal. However, he consistently denied either receiving or seeing it. And because the lay brethren had come insufficiently prepared to prove this point, there was an adjournment at their request. When the day arrived I Roger, archbishop or rather your servant, the bishop of Durham being absent for an urgent reason, gathered abbots, priors, and other prudent men of mature wisdom and demonstrated my reverent obedience towards your mandate. That same day the lay brethren entirely failed to prove those allegations. As a result these men who dwell in our diocese, in connection with whom, as has been said, there had been no innovation contrary to their first profession and to the Order's rule, embraced Master Gilbert as their father without a murmur, and he embraced them graciously as sons. They merely offered humble prayers that he would moderate a few things; when these had been settled, they stoutly asserted that absolute peace would reign not merely outside but also within. In making these adjustments we are certain that the master will not fail to obey your authority or your advice. Because he is a mild man he also received with a kiss and no less kindness those other men based outside our diocese, excepting Ogger alone; taking upon himself the horns of the wicked,[1] this man was influenced neither by the tears of his fellow lay brethren nor by the warning given by the abbots and priors who were our assessors, and by ourselves. He refused to return unless the Master made new rules in his Order following his own judgement.

It remains then, lord, for your apostolic grace to comfort an innocent man through whom God has worked in our midst many great deeds, unheard-of until his lifetime; that he who is already advanced in years and will shortly pay nature's debt may peacefully depart from the prison of this death; nor must you allow him to be trampled underfoot by these men who, seeking not what concerns the religious life but their own advantage, try in accordance with their whims to ape teachers who tickle their ears![2]

[8] *Epistola prioris de Bridlingtona ad dominum papam*^a *pro
sancto Gileberto*

1169–76

Domino pape^a prior de Bridlingt(ona).[1]

Credi non licet ex iuris et equi moderamine non procedere
quicquid sancta paternitas uestra filiis suis obseruandum precepit. Verum ut id quod a pie memorie sanctissimis patribus
Eugenio et Adriano institutum est et uestre sanctitatis auctoritate
munitum funditus euertatur, quis crediderit uestram prudentiam
precepisse?[2] Neque enim consueuit grauitas Romani pontificis
familiaribus litteris priuilegiorum decreta conuellere. Et quidem
notissimum est quod transmissis a magistro G(ileberto) ad
memoratum predecessorem uestrum papam^a Eugenium utrique
sexui competentibus uite monasterialis institutis, habito cum
uiris religiosis tractatu, idem summus pontifex ea in perpetuum
sanxerit obseruanda, nec ex his que patris G(ileberti) studio pro-
bata fuerant quicquam censuerit immu|tandum. Papa quoque
Adrianus, eiusdem patris inherens uestigiis, suo eadem priuilegio
roborauit; sed et sancta sinceritas uestra ab eorum sententia non
discrepauit, sed decreta priorum patrum sacri priuilegii pagina
subsecuta est.

Vnde et usque ad hec tempora, in uiris pariter et feminis, sub
memorati patris diligentia, religiosa conuersatio magnifice floruit.
Nec ut uestre sanctitati falso persuasum est unquam ex canonicorum contubernio sinistri rumoris^b apud nos saltem percrebuit,
quin pocius ne laicorum fratrum insolentia sinceritas religionis tur-
baretur, prouide procurata est a uiro in huius modi studiis experien-
tissimo litteratorum fratrum, non quidem in eisdem ecclesiis, sed
seorsum, extra ambitum feminarum, et intra clausuram laicorum
satis remota habitatio; quos uidelicet in eo numero congregandos
oportunum censuit qui et sollicitudinibus monasteriorum et obser-
uationibus regularibus fratrumque laicorum regimini inseruire sufficeret. Inque multis id probatum causis, quantum uidelicet ad ipsorum monasteriorum disciplinam, quantum ad sanctitatis integritatem conseruandam, profuerit canonicorum prouisio.

f. 97^v

Letter 8 *LcOd*   ^a *Erased in Lc (the first* papam *is in a part omitted by Od)*
^b *Deficient (add e.g.* quicquam *Winterbottom)*

[1] The prior of Bridlington in 1166 was Gregory, who succeeded Robert the Scribe
before 1159 and was prior until after 1181 (*Heads*, p. 154).

[8] *Letter from the prior of Bridlington to the pope on St Gilbert's behalf*

To the pope, the prior of Bridlington.[1]

It is impossible to imagine that you, holy father, have instructed your sons to observe anything which does not stem from a regard for law and justice. But who would believe that in your wisdom you have ordered the complete overthrow of what was established by the holy fathers Eugenius and Adrian, of blessed memory, and strengthened by your holiness's authority?[2] For the dignity of the Roman pontiff used not to destroy by means of a personal letter what was decreed in solemn privileges. Moreover, it is very well known that rules of the monastic life pertaining to both sexes were sent by Master Gilbert to your predecessor, Pope Eugenius; and that, after discussions with men of the religious life, this same pontiff ordained that they should be obeyed thereafter in perpetuity; he also laid down that none of these measures, which had passed the test of Father Gilbert's zeal, should be altered. Pope Adrian, also, following in this holy father's footsteps, strengthened the same decrees with a privilege of his own. Again, in your integrity you did not differ from the judgements of these men, but supported the decrees of earlier fathers with a document conveying a solemn privilege.

And so up to the present moment the religious way of life has flourished magnificently among men and women alike under their father's care. Contrary to the false allegations made to your highness, no evil report stemming from the community of canons has ever gained currency, at least with us. Quite the reverse; to ensure that the purity of religious observance was not disturbed by unruliness on the part of the lay brethren, the master, who was most experienced in taking precautions of this kind, wisely arranged that the dwelling of the educated brethren should be situated some distance away, and not within the nuns' churches at all, but separate and outside the area occupied by women, within the lay brethren's enclosure. He judged it useful to gather such men together in a number sufficient to supervise the business affairs and regular observance of the religious houses, as well as rule over the lay brethren. Many factors combined to prove how beneficial was this regulation concerning the canons, in preserving the discipline of those houses and the purity of their holiness.

[2] See pp. xxii, lxi, 50–1.

Vnde supplicamus sancte paternitati uestre, quatinus insolentiam fratrum laicorum, quos in elationis tumorem erexit spiritus huius mundi, Spiritum Dei extinguere non paciamini, ne quod, Deo operante, per sanctos patres cum summa grauitate inchoatum f. 98 est, et in plurima sanctitate | probatum, uestris, quod absit, diebus, per homines animales, per homines seipsos amantes, per homines carni et sanguini deditos, nimia leuitate subruatur, fiatque ex hostis antiqui molimine ut, preualentibus apud aures discretionis uestre falsorum fratrum suggestionibus, quod in fundo patrimonii sui memoratus pater G(ileberti) Dei Spiritu animatus iuuenis instituit, iam decrepitus deserere compellatur. Valeat uestra paternitas sancta in Domino et Virgine benedicta.[a]

[9] *Epistola Alexandri pape ad sanctum G(ilebertum) et ad ordinem*[1b]
20 September 1169

Alexander episcopus, seruus seruorum Dei, dilecto filio G(ileberto), magistro ordinis de Sempingham, salutem et apostolicam benedictionem.

Quoniam in commissis tibi domibus dissensiones audiuimus et scandala quedam suborta fuisse, eorum correctionem quibusdam personis alterius religionis semel et iterum nos iam pridem meminimus commisisse. Verum ne quis occasione illa predicti ordinis correctionem[c] sibi in posterum uendicare presumat, deuotioni tue et per te successoribus tuis apostolica auctoritate concedimus ut, si in ordine uestro aliqua de cetero emerserint corrigenda, tu uel successor tuus[d] ea cum consilio priorum eiusdem ordinis secundum statuta uestra corrigere et emendare possitis, et secundum quod magis expedire uideritis[e] reformare. Adicimus insuper ut, si quis subditorum uestrorum statutis uestris contraire presumpserit aut ea contempserit obseruare, eum ecclesiastica sententia percellatis, secundum institutiones prescripti ordinis, quam utique sententiam rationabiliter latam tam a diocesano episcopo quam ab aliis f. 98ᵛ firmam et inconcussam usque ad dignam satisfactionem | precipimus obseruari. Decernimus ergo ut nulli omnino hominum liceat hanc paginam nostre concessionis infringere uel ei aliquatenus

---

[a] *The sentence is lacking in Lc (which has the gloss:* Idem concedunt Lucius Clemens Celestinus et Honorius*)*
   Letter 9 *LcOd Cartulary of Malton (BL, Cotton Claud. D. xi; PUE, i, no. 103) (selected readings)* [b] ad ... ordinem *Lc;* sub plumbo ad sanctum G. et capitulum sui ordinis *Od; no heading in the Cartulary* [c] quibusdam ... correctionem *Lc²Cartulary (but* illius regionis ... prescripti*); nullus LcOd* [d] *Lc² adds the gloss:* Honorius dicit 'tu et successores tui' [e] noueritis *Cartulary*

Therefore we beg you, holy father, not to allow the insolence of the lay brethren, whom the spirit of this world has filled with swelling pride, to vanquish the spirit of God; lest what the holy fathers began, acting with God's help and in high seriousness, and what was established amid the greatest piety, should in your day (which God forbid) be too lightly overthrown by men of lower nature, men who love only themselves, men dedicated only to flesh and blood. Let it not come about through the efforts of our ancient enemy that the allegations made by false brethren sound authoritative in the ears of your wise self; and that what Father Gilbert, as a young man inspired by God's spirit, founded upon his inherited estates, he is forced to abandon now that he is old. May you fare well, holy father, in the Lord and the Blessed Virgin.

[9] *Letter from Pope Alexander to St Gilbert and his Order*[1]

Alexander, bishop, servant of the servants of God, to his dear son Gilbert, master of the Order of Sempringham, greetings and papal blessing.

Because we heard that disputes and scandals had arisen among the houses entrusted to your care, we recall that more than once, some time ago, we entrusted their correction to various persons belonging to another Order. But in case anyone, on that pretext, should later dare to take upon himself the Order's amendment, we make this grant to your devout self and, through you, to your successors by virtue of our papal authority: if any further troubles arise within your Order which need correction, you or your successor may make such alterations and improvements with the advice of the Order's priors in accordance with your statutes, and make those changes which you consider expedient. Furthermore we also lay it down that if any one of those under your authority presumes to contravene your statutes, or refuses to obey them, you are to lay the Church's judgement heavily upon him, following the Order's regulations; and we order that both the diocesan bishop and other men are to regard this sentence, in so far as it is sensibly applied, as firm and unshakeable until a suitable penance has been performed. Accordingly we determine that, without exception, no person is permitted to infringe these terms of our grant, or to contravene

[1] Also in *PUE* i, no. 103, from the Cartulary of Malton.

contraire. Si quis autem hoc attemptare presumpserit, indigna-
tionem omnipotentis Dei et beatorum apostolorum eius Petri et
Pauli se nouerit incursurum.
⟨Datum Beneuenti .xii. kalendas Octobris.⟩[a]

[10] *Item eiusdem ad episcopos*

1169

Alexander episcopus, seruus seruorum Dei, uenerabilibus fratribus archiepiscopis, episcopis et dilectis filiis archidiaconis, in
quorum parrochiis domus et ecclesie ordinis de Sempingham sunt
constitute, salutem et apostolicam benedictionem.

Si tenemur omnibus ecclesiasticis uiris patrocinium apostolice
protectionis impendere, multo forcius et attentius illos protegere
cogimur et fouere qui sub regulari disciplina famulantur[b] ab
inquietatione secularium personarum debent omni tempore
manere quieti. Inde est quod dilectos filios nostros de Sempingham et eorum domos caritati uestre sollicite commendamus.
Monemus uniuersitatem uestram attencius et precipimus quatinus
eosdem canonicos et uniuersas domos prescripti ordinis manute-
nere curetis propensius et defendere, ne canonicos aut moniales
etiam seu conuersos eiusdem ordinis permittatis a quolibet contra
iuris ordinem fatigari, et si qui eos indebitis uexationibus inquie-
tare presumpserint[c] ipsos, nisi commoniti quamtocius resipuerint,
auctoritate apostolica freti, censura ecclesiastica compescatis;
f. 99 porro, si aliqui homines uestre iurisdictionis in aliquem | canoni-
cum uel professum prescripti ordinis uiolentas manus iniecerint,
aut ipsum de equitatura deposuerint uiolenter, ipsos cognita ueritate, contradictione et apellatione cessante, excommunicatos
publice nuncietis, et faciatis sicut excommunicatos arctius euitari,
donec passo iniuriam congrue satisfaciant, et cum litteris uestris
satisfacturi apostolico se conspectui representent.

[11] *Item eiusdem ad regem contra laicos rebelles*

1169

Alexander episcopus, seruus seruorum Dei, karissimo in Christo
filio H(enrico), illustri Anglorum regi, salutem et apostolicam
benedictionem.

---

[a] *Supplied from the Cartulary*
    Letter 10 *LcOd Hence also* PUE, *i, no. 185*   [b] famulantes *Holtzmann,* PUE, *i, no. 185,*
rightly, unless we add et *(Winterbottom)*   [c] presumpserint *Holtzmann;* presumpserit *LcOd*

them in any way. If, however, someone dares to attempt this, he should know that he will draw upon himself the wrath of Almighty God and his blessed apostles Peter and Paul.

Given at Benevento, 20 September.

[10] *Letter from the pope to the bishops*

Alexander, bishop, servant of the servants of God, to his venerable brothers the archbishops and bishops, and to his dear sons the archdeacons in whose jurisdictions the houses and churches belonging to the Order of Sempringham are founded, greeting and papal blessing.

If we are bound to extend to all churchmen the benefit of papal protection, a much stronger and livelier obligation rests upon us to look after and encourage those who live under the discipline of a rule and should remain at all times free from disturbance at the hands of secular persons. It is for this reason that we warmly commend our dear sons of Sempringham and their houses to your love. Also, we caution and order you all most especially to see that you readily support and defend these same canons and all the houses of this Order. You are not to allow the canons, nuns, or lay brethren of this Order to be troubled by anyone in an unlawful manner; and if people dare to disturb them with uncalled-for provocation, unless they come quickly to their senses after being cautioned, you are to discipline them by means of ecclesiastical censure, relying upon papal authority. Further, if any man within your jurisdiction lays violent hands upon any canon or professed religious of this Order, or if they pull him violently from his horse, as soon as the truth has been established and opposing arguments and appeals abandoned, you are publicly to announce the excommunication of such men; and you should ensure that, as excommunicates, they are rigidly shunned until they make proper satisfaction to the person who has suffered injury, and, bearing letters from you, appear before us to do penance.

[11] *Another letter from the pope to the king, against the rebellious lay brethren*

Alexander, bishop, servant of the servants of God, to his dear son in Christ H(enry), illustrious king of the English, greetings and papal blessing.

Letter 11 *LcOd* Hence also PUE, *i, no. 184*

Dilecti filii nostri prior et canonici ac moniales ordinis de Sempingham, non sine multa serenitatis regie commendatione, mon-
strauerunt quod ordinem ipsorum et cetera que ad eos pertinent,
diuini amoris intuitu, specialiter diligis, eisque tue defensionis pre-
sidium subministras; super quo tanto gaudemus amplius quanto ex
hoc excellentie tue maius speramus premium cumulandum.

Verum quia scriptum est: non qui ceperit, 'sed qui perseuerauerit
usque in finem, hic saluus erit',[1] celsitudinem regiam monemus,
hortamur attentius et in remissionem tibi iniungimus peccatorum[a]
quatinus bonum[b] principium meliori fine concludas, et predictos
canonicos et moniales, nostre commonitionis obtentu, et intuitu
salutis proprie, necnon et consideratione religionis sue, habeas
more solito commendatos, et contra potentiam omnium laicorum
f. 99ᵛ qui tue sunt | potestati subiecti facias manere securos.

Fratres autem laicos contumaces et ordini rebelles, qui per eccle-
siasticam sententiam corrigi noluerint, regia potestate, prout tibi
expedire uisum fuerit, ad aliorum timorem et ipsorum correctionem, sine sanguinis effusione, districte corripias, ita quod sub
regia tutela[c] prefati canonici et moniales debita pace letentur, et tu
perhenne premium a Domino et a nobis uberes[d] ualeas gratias
expectare.

[12] *Epistola regis ad papam pro sancto Gileberto*

1169—76

A(lexandro) domino pape, Henricus rex Anglie, et cetera.

Sanctitati uestre gratias quanta possumus deuotione referimus
pro magistro G(ileberto) de Sempingham et fratribus et conuentibus eiusdem ordinis quod eos sub protectione uestra suscepistis et
eundem ordinem autentico scripto confirmastis, quodque[e] eorum
quieti et paci paterna affectione prouidetis. Nouerit autem sanctitatis uestre discretio quod certissime credimus eos debite et
deuote in domibus suis Domino ministrare, et se in exterioribus ita
gerere[f] ut conuersatio illorum Deo et hominibus merito credatur
acceptabilis, unde circumstantium tam clericorum quam laicorum
gratiam non modicam meruisse noscuntur, et ob hoc solum in

---

[a] peccatorum *om. Lc*   [b] bonum *Brooke;* bonorum *LcOd*   [c] regia tutela
Holtzmann, no. 184; regie tutele *LcOd (to which perhaps add* presidio *or the like: Winterbot-*
tom)   [d] a Domino et a nobis uberes *Winterbottom;* uberes a nobis *Lc;* uberes a
domino et a nobis *Od*

Letter 12 *LcOd*   [e]quodque *Winterbottom;* quod quia *Lc;* et quod *Od*   [f] gerere *om. Lc, leaving a gap*

Our dear sons the prior, canons, and nuns of the Order of Sempringham have shown, with the aid of your royal highness's frequent recommendations, that, inspired by divine love, you bear a special affection for their Order and for everything which concerns them, and that you offer them the benefit of your protection. We rejoice all the more over this since it leads us to hope that a greater reward must thereby be stored up for your excellency.

But because it is written that not he who begins, 'but he who perseveres unto the end will be saved',[1] we advise your royal highness, earnestly beg you, and for the remission of your sins command you to bring this honourable start to a yet better end: that following our advice, for the sake of your own salvation and also bearing in mind their religious vocation, you hold these canons and nuns in your customary high regard, and ensure that they remain secure in the face of the power exercised by all the laymen subject to your authority.

And as for the lay brethren, obstinate rebels against the Order, who refuse correction by means of an ecclesiastical penalty, you should bring them to strict account, using your royal power in the way you think most fit, without shedding blood, to inspire fear in other men and to work the correction of the lay brethren themselves. Then under your royal protection the canons and nuns may rejoice in the peace they deserve, while you may expect from the Lord an everlasting reward and from ourselves abundant thanks.

[12] *Letter from the king to the pope on behalf of St Gilbert*

To Pope A(lexander), Henry king of England, etc.

As devoutly as we may, we thank your holiness on behalf of Master Gilbert of Sempringham and the brethren and houses of that same Order for taking them under your protection and confirming the Order with an authentic privilege, and for ensuring their peace and quiet with a father's affection. In your wisdom your holiness must know that we firmly believe that these men serve the Lord with propriety and devotion within their houses, and outside bear themselves in such a way that their behaviour is rightly thought acceptable to God and man. Therefore they are reckoned to have earned in no small degree the good opinion of the clergy and laity about them, and for this reason alone they have achieved

---

[1] Matt. 10: 22; 24: 13.

oculis nostris et nostrorum gratiam et fauorem non modicum promeruerunt. Innotescat autem uestre serenitati quod prenominatus magister ordinis, quamuis debilitatem corporis incurrerit,

f. 100 animi tamen constantiam et robur | nullatenus relaxauit, immo quanto feruore et zelo in fortiori etate ordinem prefatum regebat, tanto adhuc, ut credimus, id ipsum satagere non cessat, nec ad idem regimen in regno nostro idoneor posset[a] inueniri.[b] Et quoniam quidam ex fratribus dissolutius uiuere et ordinis primam institutionem infringere nituntur, mouet nos non modicum et eos qui in domos prefatas elemosinarum suarum largitiones contulerunt. Proinde obnixe rogamus quatinus ordinem prefatum faciatis inuiolabiliter obseruari, secundum quod a prefato magistro prestitutus est et confirmatus a uobis. Si enim, quod Deus auertat, contigerit illicitis[c] quorumdam conatibus et maxime rusticorum et conuersorum laicorum, et qui ante conuersionem suam ascriptitii glebe fuerunt, institutionem prefati ordinis inmutari ut, quod absit, dissolute uiuere incipiant, firmissime sciatis quod et nos et barones nostri possessiones et domania nostra, que eisdem domibus contulimus ob eorumdem religiosam conuersationem et sanctum propositum, eadem ordine mutato retrahemus. Que enim ob causas prefatas prenominatis domibus collata sunt, causis eisdem cessantibus licite poterunt, ut credimus, reuocari. Et si ordinem prefatum secundum primam institutionem a uobis et predecessoribus uestris approbatam et firmatam debito rigore feceritis

f. 100ᵛ obseruari, nos quod ad secularem | iustitiam nostram pertinet eum pro posse nostro manutenebimus, et personas illius in maximo honore et reuerentia, sicut habere consueuimus, exactiori si fieri poterit diligentia uenerabimur. Hec et que alia prefatis domibus expedire credidimus nunciis nostris magistro I(ordano), archidiacono Cicestrie, et magistro O., clerico,[1] secrecius intimauimus, ut uobis ea fideliter exponant et super his nobis consilium uestrum reportent.

[a] posset *Winterbottom;* posse *LcOd*   [b] *After this word, Od completes the letter as follows* [*see p. lxxxvi*]: quem ignis diuinus ita inflammauit ut magne multitudinis uirorum et mulierum animos in Dei amore succenderet, et ipsius plantacionis institutor primus fieret et inuentor. Per illum enim Deus multa et magna et usque ad eius tempora inaudita operatus est [Deus] *(deleted by Knowles, cf. p. 152)* in medio terre nostre. Et licet teneamur omnibus religiosis et ecclesiasticis uiris parmam regie protectionis impendere, multo forcius et attencius illos protegere cogimur et fouere *(Winterbottom, cf. p. 158:* fauere *Od)* quos in regno nostro Anglie et de gente nostra primo sancte religionis normam originaliter nouimus suscepisse ad Dei laudem et uniuersalis ecclesie gloriam et decorem. Valete.   [c] illicitis *Knowles;* licitis *LcOd (see p. 144 note a)*

considerable grace and favour in our eyes and those of our subjects. Your highness must also learn that although the master of the
Order has grown weak in body, yet he has not in any way relaxed
the firmness and vigour of his mind. On the contrary, the energy
and zeal with which he used to rule the Order at a more robust age,
we believe he still continues to employ as he busies himself with its
affairs; and no man more suitable for this responsibility could be
found within our kingdom. The fact that some of the brethren are
attempting to lead a less disciplined life and break the Order's first
requirement shocks us not a little, as well as those who have conferred gifts of alms upon these houses. So we earnestly beg you to
ensure that the Order is rigorously obeyed in the form in which it
was established by Master Gilbert and confirmed by yourself. God
forbid that the Order's organization should be altered by the illicit
attempts of certain persons, especially villeins and lay brethren
and those who before entering the religious life were tied to the
soil, to allow them to enter on a life without restraint. But if this
happens, you should know for certain that both we ourselves and
our barons will take back from an Order so changed our possessions and our estates, which we granted to these same houses
because of their religious life and holy purpose. For whatever has
been granted to these houses for the reasons already mentioned
may properly, we believe, be withdrawn when these same reasons
fail to operate. If you will see that the Order, in its original form as
approved and confirmed by you and your predecessors, is strictly
and properly obeyed, then as far as our secular justice is concerned
we shall support it to the height of our powers; and, just as we used
to regard its members with great honour and reverence, we shall
revere them with more considerate care if this is possible. We have
privately informed our messengers Master J(ordan), archdeacon of
Chichester and Master O., clerk,[1] of these things and others which
we believed advantageous to these houses, so that they may report
them accurately to you and bring back to us your advice on these
matters.

---

[1] For Master Jordan of Melbourne, archdeacon of Lewes in the diocese of Chichester (and so commonly called archdeacon of Chichester), see H. Mayr-Harting, *Acta of
the Bishops of Chichester, 1075–1207* (Canterbury and York Soc., 1974), pp. 211, 213; he
was archdeacon 1154/64–1173/4, and dean of Chichester, 1173/4 to 1176 or shortly after.
He had formerly been one of Becket's *eruditi*, and was one of the messengers who
fetched his pallium in 1162 (*MB* iii. 526; Ralph de Diceto, *Opera*, ed. W. Stubbs, RS,
i. 307).

[13] *Epistola sancti Gileberti ad canonicos Maltone*[a]

1176—8 or 1186—9

Gilebertus de Sempingham, misericordia Dei hoc quod est, immo quod fuit, dilectis filiis suis canonicis et fratribus de Maltona, salutem perpetuam in Domino cum Dei benedictione et sua.

Dum licuit, dum Deus facultatem secundum suam misericordiam mihi ministrauit, solebam quandoque sicut filios meos karissimos uos corporali presentia uisitare, et doctrina qua potui, qua noui, ad amorem diuinum inuitare et allicere. Vtinam efficatia meam sollicitudinem sequeretur! Sed modo uiribus corporis omnino destituor, ita ut me oporteat, carnis uelamina exeundo,[b] hinc migrare ex hac uita, mihi longo tempore amara et tediosa. Et quoniam amodo uos uoce uiua alloqui non potero, hac cedula attentius quantum possum admonere non desisto, quatinus pro Dei amore et salute animarum uestrarum diligentius quam f. 101   hucusque | diuino amori inuigiletis, uicia reprimendo, ueritatem et iustitiam exaltando, institutiones et traditiones ordinis uestri obseruando, et tanto uigilantius et districtius quanto expeditiores estis ab occupationibus quibus ceteri[c] in ordine occupantur, et oportunitatem habetis rigorem ordinis excercere, ita ut insolentia aliorum rigore uestro cohibeatur. Ad hoc enim uos specialiter congregaui, ut ordo noster protegatur et exaltetur rigore uestre religionis. Si autem meam sollicitudinem uobis in aliquo profuisse perpenditis, labori meo mercedem impendere non denegetis, attentius diuinam clementiam precibus deuotissimis implorando ne mecum intret in iuditio, sed pocius sua magna dulcedine dignetur peccata mea delere et requiem eternam mihi concedere. Vobis autem, quos superstites desero, pacem Dei et misericordiam dono et relinquo cum Dei benedictione et mea. Absoluo quoque, auctoritate mihi a Deo tradita, quantum ad me pertinet, omnes amodo ordinis nostri amatores et unitatis nostre congregationis defensores ab omnibus reatibus quos ignorantia uel infirmitate seu negligentia uel contemptu contra ordinis nostri institutiones commiserunt. Machinantes uero discidium et discordiam in nostra f. 101ᵛ   congregatione nouerint | sibi meam absolutionem non posse prodesse, cum in conspectu Dei, nisi penituerint et ad dignam satisfactionem peruenerint, constet eos esse reprobatos. Neminem

Letter 13 *Lc: Od gives a version of the letter as part of the Vita*   [a] Littera sancti G. directa omnibus suis per ordinem canonicis *Od*   [b] *Possibly for* exuendo *(Knowles)*
[c]ceteri *Lc;* laici fratres *Od*

[13] *Letter from St Gilbert to the canons of Malton*

Gilbert of Sempringham, by God's mercy whatever he is, or rather was, to his dear sons the canons and brethren of Malton, everlasting salvation in the Lord together with God's blessing and his own.

While it was allowed and while in His mercy God furnished me with the ability, I used occasionally to pay personal visits to you as to my dearest sons; and with such teaching as matched my knowledge and my powers, I would summon and draw you towards the love of God. Oh that success had crowned my efforts! But now I am entirely bereft of bodily strength, so that by passing beyond the veil of flesh I must depart from this life which has been bitter and wearisome to me for a long while. And because from now on I shall not be able to speak with you face to face, I do not hesitate in this written form to urge you as strongly as I can: for God's sake and for the salvation of your souls pay more careful attention to divine love than you have up till now, by repressing vice, exalting truth and justice, and keeping the rules and traditions of your Order. And you can do this the more carefully and strictly because you are free from the concerns which occupy others in the Order, and because you have the opportunity to exercise discipline within the Order in such a way that the unruliness of others may be prevented. For this is why I have particularly brought you together, that our Order may be protected and exalted through the strictness of your religious observance. If you think that my care has helped you in any way, do not refuse to grant me a reward for my labours: with devout prayers earnestly beg that God in His mercy will not enter into judgement upon me but of His great kindness may instead see fit to obliterate my sins and grant me everlasting rest. To you whom I leave behind, I give and bequeath the peace and mercy of God, together with God's blessing and my own. By the authority entrusted me by God, as far as I may, I also absolve all those who shall in future love our Order and defend the unity of our congregation, from all the offences which, through ignorance, weakness, negligence, or contempt, they committed against the rules of our Order. But those who scheme to bring about dissension and discord in our community must know that my absolution can be of no use to them, for, unless they are penitent and arrive at a suitable penance, it is clear that they remain guilty in the sight of God. However, I do

tamen ex uobis suspectum huius facinoris habeo, sed de omnibus uobis confido in Domino, quod diligentius acturi sitis amodo quam hucusque in omnibus agendis uestris que ad salutem anime pertinent, adiuti gratia saluatoris, ut de societate uestra gaudium meum coram Deo augeatur, quod ipse prestare dignetur, cuius regnum et imperium manet in secula seculorum. Amen.[a]

[a] Valete *Od*

not suspect any of you of this fault, but am confident in the Lord concerning you all, that from now on you will be more diligent than hitherto in performing all your duties which relate to the soul's salvation, helped as you are by our Saviour's grace; and thus my joy in your fellowship will be increased in God's presence. May He see fit to provide such joy, whose kingdom and power endure unto everlasting. Amen.

INCIPIT CANONIZATIO BEATI GILEBERTI[1]

Quantum apud se magnificauerit beatum Gilebertum gratia superni conditoris, qui uiuenti in omnibus cooperatus est, etiam defuncti gloriam confirmare dignatus est sequentibus signis.[a] Quorum ueritas manifesta qualiter in lucem uenerit ne quis presentium uel futurorum de ea possit ambigere, breuiter rei ordinem prout gesta est retexemus. Cum igitur uir Domini Gilebertus migrasset e seculo, ad declarandum Deo accepta fuisse ipsius merita ceperunt primo depositionis sue anno et deinceps ad tumbam eius crebro fieri uirtutum insignia. Sed fratres Sempinghamensis cenobii, ut religiosorum mos est secreta querere et mundi gloriam fugere, ea palam facere neglexerunt, ne f. 102 suas | uiderentur uelle 'philactereas dilatare', si ea que per suum institutorem patrata sunt diuulgarent.[2] Euolutis denique ab obitu ipsius plusquam .xi. annis, cum multa multis in locis per eum facta fuissent miracula, aduerterunt quidam ex fratribus per illam factorum occultationem Dei et sancti[b] eius necnon et ecclesie sancte honorem non reuelari, et sapientum freti consilio ad uirum sapientissimum, Hubertum Cantuariensem archiepiscopum, rem detulerunt. Qui tot et tantis auditis mirabilibus, abortis[c] pre gaudio lacrimis, gratias Deo exsoluit multiplices, qui talia illis temporibus pro uiro indigena operari dignatus est. Et licet de eius sanctitate quem bene nouerat et cuius honestas et opera tam late claruerant non dubitauerit, ad ingerendam tamen aliorum mentibus pleniorem certitudinem celebri decreuit inuestigatione audita perquirere, mittensque ad quosdam prouincie illius abbates mandauit per litteras suas ut diligentem[d] super hiis facerent inquisitionem, et inquisita suis scriptis ei notificarent, quatinus de hiis omnibus plenius instructus ad celebrandam illius sancti canonizationem apostolice sedis securius posset petere auctoritatem.[3]

---

[a] *The author loses his way in this sentence* LcOd [c] *Perhaps* obortis *(Winterbottom)* Lc[1]; diligenter *Od* [b]sancti *Winterbottom (cf. p. 190)*; sanctis [d] diligentem *Lc;* uel (diligen)ter

---

[1] For the texts that follow, see pp. xc–xcvi.
[2] Cf. Matt. 23: 5. [3] See pp. xcii–xcvi.

THE CANONIZATION

THE CANONIZATION OF ST GILBERT[1]

It is clear how much the grace of the heavenly Creator exalted St Gilbert; for just as He worked with him in his lifetime in all things, so also He has seen fit to confirm the man's glory, now he is dead, by the signs which have followed. So that no one, present or future, can have any doubts about the way the obvious truth of these miracles came to light, we shall briefly describe the course which events took. When Gilbert, the man of God, had departed from the world, to show that his merits were found acceptable to God, mighty works began frequently to be performed at his tomb in the first year after his burial and thereafter. But as it is the custom of those in religious orders to seek privacy and shun worldly glory, the brethren of the monastery of Sempringham omitted to make these things public knowledge; for they were afraid they would appear anxious to 'make broad their phylacteries' if they made known what had been done through their founder.[2] At last, more than eleven years after Gilbert's death, when many miracles had been performed through him in many different places, it occurred to some of the brethren that by hiding works in this way they were suppressing honour due to God, His saint, and His holy Church. So, taking the advice of wise brethren, they brought the matter to the attention of the wisest of men, Hubert archbishop of Canterbury. Having heard about so many great and marvellous deeds, this man repeatedly thanked God with tears of joy, that He had seen fit to perform such things in those days on behalf of a man belonging to our own country. Hubert himself had no doubts about Gilbert's holiness, because he had known him well, and his goodness and achievements had been so widely famous. But, to impress greater certainty upon other men's minds, he decided to sift the reports by means of an investigation publicly carried out; and, sending to some of the abbots belonging to that province, he ordered them by letter to make a careful enquiry into these events. They were to tell him in writing what they had discovered, so that, better informed on all this, he could with greater assurance seek papal authority to celebrate the canonization of that saint.[3]

Abbates autem que iussa fuerant exequentes, adiunctis secum
plurimis tam secularibus quam religiosis*a* ecclesiasticis personis
f. 102ᵛ pariter | accesserunt ad domum de Sempingham .ix. die Ianuarii
anni incarnationis Domini .Ṁ.ĊĊ. primi, quo die inclitus rex
Anglorum Iohannes cum suis proceribus domum illam uisitauit,[1]
et omnia que ibi inuenerant de miraculorum euentu sub districta
examinatione discusserunt, suisque scriptis tam illi quam domino
pape significauerunt.[2] Dominus autem Cantuariensis ea que
acceperat ad Romanam curiam nuntiauit, directisque epistolis
personam sancti et magnifica opera digna laude commendauit,
eiusque reuelationem prout iustum fuerat postulauit. Eius etiam
hortatu plures ex episcopis et sullimioribus abbatibus Anglie
plurimique priores et prelati ecclesiarum litteras commendatiuas
et idem petentes transmiserunt. Sed et illustris rex Anglorum
Iohannes cum quibusdam suis proceribus eadem nichilominus
prosecutus est. Proficiscentes igitur duo ex litteratis fratribus, cum
omnibus hiis testificationibus necnon et scripto seriem uite et
operum eius continente, Romanam curiam adierunt; in quibus
illud non sine miraculo contigit, quod in maximo estiui temporis
caumate quando pestis plurimos peremerat redierunt incolumes;
inter medios hostes qui eis insidias tetenderant quasi acroisia*b*
percussos ad instar Helysei transierunt illesi.[3]

f. 103   Redeuntes autem a curia | mandatum apostolicum ad memora-
tum archiepiscopum Cantuariensem, et ad episcopum Eliensem,
et de Burgo et de Wardonia abbates reportauerunt,[4] quo iniunctum est eis quatinus ad locum sepulture eius pariter accedentes
triduanum ieiunium toti collegio ipsius ordinis sollemniter
indicerent, ut uniuersi fratres orantes et rogantes ab eo qui est
uia ueritas et uita postularent et implorarent aperiri uiam
inueniendi super hoc ueritatem ad uitam; ac deinde non solum
per testimonia sed per testes, per famam quoque uulgatam et
scripturam auctenticam, de uirtute morum et de uirtute signorum,

---

a regularibus *Od (omitting* ecclesiasticis personis)   *b* acrisia *Od; properly*
aorasia *(see MLD s.v.)*

---

[1] See p. 215 n. 2.   [2] See pp. xcvii–xcviii.
[3] Cf. 4 Kgs. (2 Kgs.) 6: 18–22. Cf. the high mortality among the monks of Christ
Church, Canterbury, on embassy to Rome in 1188, reported in *Epistolae Cantuarienses*,
ed. W. Stubbs (RS, 1865), pp. 254–5, 269.
[4] Hubert Walter (see pp. xcvii–c, 2 n. 1); Master Eustace, bishop of Ely, 1197/8–1215;
Acharius or Akarius, abbot of Peterborough; Warin or Roger, abbot of Wardon, Cistercian house in Bedfordshire (*Fasti*, ii. 45; *Heads*, pp. 61, 146. *Heads* gives the sequence

The abbots carried out their instructions and together with many men, both religious and secular, holding positions within the church, they came to the house of Sempringham on 9 January 1201, the same day that John, the noble king of England, visited the house with his magnates.[1] They subjected everything they found out there about the occurrence of miracles to careful examination and reported it in writing both to the archbishop and the pope.[2] The archbishop of Canterbury sent on what he had received to the Roman curia, and in his own personal letter he commended the saint's character and his mighty works with due praise; and he petitioned for the disclosure about this man which justice demanded. Urged by him, many of the bishops and more senior abbots of England, together with very many priors and monastic heads, also sent letters of commendation making the same request; and John, the illustrious king of England, along with some of his barons did exactly the same. So two of the learned brethren set out with all these testimonials and also a document containing an account of the saint's life and works, and they went to the Roman curia. It happened only by a miracle that in the most intense summer heat, when pestilence had carried off so many, they returned safe and sound; they travelled unharmed, like Elisha, through the midst of enemies who had laid an ambush for them but were like men struck blind.[3]

On their return from the curia they carried a papal mandate back to the archbishop of Canterbury, the bishop of Ely, and the abbots of Peterborough and Wardon;[4] in this they were instructed to arrive together at Gilbert's place of burial and solemnly pronounce a three-day fast for the whole community of that Order. All the brethren, as they prayed and entreated Him who is the way, the truth, and the life, were to beg and beseech that a way might be revealed to discover the living truth in this matter; and then they were to seek confirmation of his virtuous character and mighty wonders, that is his deeds and miracles, relying not only upon statements of evidence but also upon witnesses, as well as popular report and authentic documents; and when they had faithfully written an account of all these things, authenticated by their seals,

Warin I, Roger (occurs 13 Oct. 1200), Warin II for Wardon, which perhaps makes Roger the most likely for this date; but as his existence depends on a single document, there must be some doubt about it. 'De Burgo' could possibly mean 'of Bury'—but Acharius is named on pp. 192–3).

operibus uidelicet et miraculis, certitudinem inquirerent, cunctaque fideliter conscribentes sub testimonio sigillorum suorum per
uiros ydoneos, qui etiam super*a* hiis fidem facerent in presentia
domni pape iurati, ad sedem apostolicam destinarent. Que omnia
iuxta formam mandati apostolici rite peracta sunt. Nam .v̂i. kalendas
Octobris sepedictus archiepiscopus cum Eliensi, Batoniensi et
Bangoriensi episcopis, abbates quoque de Burgo et de Brunna,[1]
quia ille de Warduna ad capitulum Cisterciense fuerat profectus,
priores etiam plurimi et quidam archidiaconi, necnon et canonici et
officiales Lincoln(iensis) ecclesie, famosique magistri multi cum
f. 103ᵛ multa*b* turbarum frequentia domum de Sempingham aduenientes, |
post celebratum triduanum ieiunium, inuocata primitus Spiritus
Sancti gratia, testes iuratos tam religiosos quam seculares, tam clericos quam laicos, tam uiros quam mulieres super uirtute signorum
que facta sunt prestito prius sacramento diligentissime examinauer-
unt. Quorum attestationes fideliter in scripturam redactas sub sigillis suis clausas domino pape transmiserunt, adicientes insuper de
uita et conuersatione eius et fama uulgata audita testimonia. Vbi
dum per quatriduum morarentur aperta est diuinitus ueritas quam
querebant per quoddam insigne miraculum ad sepulchrum sancti
tunc factum de curato iuuene quodam, iugem capitis rotationem et
uicariam mentis alienationem pre angustia morbi patiente. Qui non
multo post ad hoc testificandum Romam missus, sanus perrexit
sanusque repedauit. Nam missi sunt ilico Romam .v. canonici
sacerdotes et .vi. laici seculares, quorum quidam per merita sancti a
suis incommodis fuerant liberati, quidam illorum et aliorum interfuerant curationibus, ut quod antea fuerat per litteras domino pape
suggestum, modo per uiuam presentium uocem fieret indubitatum.

Pergunt igitur dicti nuntii alacres itinera sua de Dei et sancti
propter quem ierant confisi suffragiis, maxime cum leta quedam
somnia, et ante profectionem suam et in profectione uisa, et
f. 104 itineris | prosperitatem et negotiorum perfectionem sibi promisis-
sent; et non cum magna difficultate uenientes quo tetenderant,
licet Sathanas uel ad modicum iter eorum impedire conaretur, .ii.
kalendas Ianuarii uenerunt Romam, et .iiii. nonas eiusdem
Agnaniam ubi tunc forte dominus papa morabatur.[2] Tantam

---

a sub *Lc*   *b* magna *Od*

[1] The bishop of Bath was Savaric (1191/2–1205); for Bangor, see p. 221 n. 3; the abbot
of Bourne (Lincs, Augustinian–Arrouaisian) was possibly Henry (*Heads*, p. 153).
[2] Innocent III was at Anagni *c.* Oct. 1201–Feb. 1202.

they were to send it to the pope by suitable messengers, who after taking an oath in the pope's presence would also submit sworn evidence on these points. All this was properly carried out in accordance with the terms of the papal mandate. For on 26 September the archbishop, with the bishops of Ely, Bath, and Bangor, also the abbots of Peterborough and Bourne[1] (because the abbot of Wardon had set out for the Cistercian general chapter), many priors, some archdeacons, canons, and officials belonging to the church of Lincoln, and many famous masters came to the house of Sempringham, accompanied by a great throng of people. After they had observed a fast for three days, they began by invoking the grace of the Holy Spirit, and then, having first exacted an oath from them, they most carefully questioned the sworn witnesses— both religious and secular, clerks and laity, men and women— about the power of the miracles which were performed. The evidence given by these people they faithfully wrote down and sent to the pope as letters close under their own seals, adding the evidence they had heard concerning Gilbert's life and conduct and his popular reputation. During the four days they stayed there, the truth which they sought was revealed through divine intervention, in the shape of a remarkable miracle which occurred at that time at the saint's tomb. It involved the cure of a young man suffering from a constant dizziness in the head, associated with intervals of loss of reason caused by the distress of such an ailment. Not long afterwards this lad was sent to Rome to give evidence in this case; he arrived there healthy and returned healthy. Further, five canon-priests and six laymen were promptly dispatched to Rome: some of them had been relieved of their afflictions by the merits of the saint; some had been present at the cures of these and of other people. They went so that the statements made earlier to the pope by letter might now, through the live witness of those present before him, become certainties.

Thus the messengers proceeded eagerly upon their way, trusting in the support of God and the saint on whose behalf they went. They derived especial confidence from some happy dreams experienced both before their departure and on their journey, which promised them a successful journey and the completion of their business. They arrived at their destination without great difficulty, although Satan made some efforts to obstruct their journey. On 31 December they reached Rome, and on 2 January Anagni, where the pope happened to be staying at that time.[2] God bestowed such

autem dedit eis Deus gratiam in oculis summi pontificis et cardinalium quod decimo die aduentus sui impetratis gauderent postulationibus. Habito namque coram apostolico inter cardinales
super hiis deliberatiuo tractatu inspectisque testimoniis que attu-
lerant, et iuratis testibus qui uenerant et diligenter examinatis,
cum maxima in omnibus inueniretur concordia, et pro humana
ratione rem debere perfici potuisset iudicari, placuit tamen diuine
dispositioni suam enodare censuram, et ipsi domino pape diuinum
consilium et auxilium super hiis flagitanti quesite rei taliter
innotuit ueritatem. Nocte quadam infra .x. dies illos post aduentum eorum ad curiam iacuit plus solito dominus papa peruigil in
lecto et cepit secum cogitare de sancti G(ileberti) quam^a petebatur
canonizatione, rogauitque Deum ut ei aliquo indicio reuelare dig-
naretur quid esset inde acturus, et si id foret agendum suum lar-
giretur auxilium. Intercepit ilico somnus cogitationem et in somnis
f. 104^v talis | uisio apparuit. Vidit pre oculis turrim ingentem et eminen-
tem, in quam uolens ingredi manibus constipantium ex more
introductus est. Inuenitque in ea lectum stratum et ornatum
pulcherrimum,^b et circa lectum cortinam sericam et preciosam
appensam sanctorum iconiis insignitam. Admiratus decorem et
splendorem cortine quia talem circa lectum suum cum esset serica
non haberet, nitebatur ad se eam trahere, et cepit quasi suere ut
illam super suum grabatum adaptaret. Interim diuertens in aliam
cameram que prope uidebatur, et reuersus quesiuit secum attentius quidnam esset acturus de negotio canonicorum de Sempingham, et de canonizatione sancti illius quam petebant. Vox
ergo de sursum lapsa est dicens ad eum: 'Michael archangelus erit
adiutor tuus in illo negotio.' Expergefactus summus pontifex de
tanta et tam manifesta reuelatione exhilaratus intellexit apud diuinum arbitrium illud perfectum esse negotium, et a se apud
homines esse perficiendum; statimque specialem orationem de eo
composuit, quam et secretam et postcommunionem quas postea
edidit decreuit in commemorationem ipsius esse dicendas. Oratio
autem hec est: 'Plenam in nobis' etc.; secr(eta): 'Accepta sit tibi'
f. 105 etc.'; postcommunio: 'Quod a te, Domine' etc.^{1c} | Porro uir

---

^a *Perhaps* que *(Winterbottom)*   ^b *Perhaps* pulcherrime *(Winterbottom)*
^c *The prayers are given in full in Od (printed* Gilbertine Rite, *ii. 26—7)*

¹ For the full text, see n. *c*. Application to the pope for collects became common
from this time on: see Cheney, *Innocent III and England* (Stuttgart, 1976), p. 56 and
n. 14.

grace upon them in the eyes of the pope and the cardinals that on the tenth day after their arrival they could rejoice at obtaining what they sought. For a careful discussion of these matters took place among the cardinals in the pope's presence; the evidence which the messengers had brought was inspected and the witnesses who had come were put under oath and carefully examined. Then total unanimity was discerned in every aspect and, as far as human reason could judge, the affair deserved successful completion. Nevertheless it pleased God in His providence to make known His own judgement; and in this manner He revealed the truth of the matter in question to the lord pope in person, who was praying for divine counsel and help in this affair. One night during those ten days after the messengers' arrival at the Curia, the pope lay in bed more wakeful than usual; he began to turn over in his mind the canonization petitioned for St Gilbert, and he asked that God might show him in some way what he should do about it and grant him the aid he needed if this were to be accomplished. Immediately sleep interrupted his thoughts and as he slept the following dream came to him. He saw before his eyes a huge and lofty tower; as he wanted to enter it he was led in, according to the custom, by the hands of the people crowding around. In the tower he found a bed most beautifully covered and adorned, and around the bed hung a precious silk curtain decorated with images of the saints. He admired the curtain's elegance and splendour because he did not have one like it around his own bed, since it was made of silk. He tried to pull it towards himself and began, in his dream, to sew in order to alter the curtain to hang above his bed. Then he turned aside into another room which appeared to be nearby, and coming back he carefully considered what he was going to do about the business of the canons of Sempringham, and the canonization of the holy man which they petitioned for. At that moment a voice came down from above saying to him, 'The Archangel Michael will be your helper in that matter.' Waking from his sleep the pope was full of joy at so great and clear a revelation. He perceived that the business had been completed before the divine judgement-seat and must be brought to an end in the sight of men by himself. And immediately he composed a special prayer about Gilbert which, with the secret and post-communion prayers he wrote later, he decreed should be said in commemoration of him. This is the prayer: *Plenam in nobis*, etc.; the secret: *Accepta sit tibi*, etc.; the post-communion: *Quod a te, Domine*, etc.[1] Then, being a

cautissimus omni certitudine fieri uolens suffultus interpretationem somnii quesiuit a uiro quodam sanctissimo et eruditissimo, abbate Reinero,[1] qui solitariam in montibus agens uitam
pre nota sanctitate et scientia tam pape quam toti ecclesie Romane
habebatur uenerandus. Hunc ergo ascitum iussit dominus apos-
tolicus de somnio cogitare et significationem illius enodare. Cui
ille spiritu Ioseph siue Danielis repletus: 'Non est' inquit 'diu
super hoc cogitandum, quoniam somnium et interpretatio eius
manifesta sunt. Turris enim alta et eminens quam uidisti papalis
est excellentia, in quam ut uolebas ab aliis es delatus, quoniam non
tu eam aripuisti, sed alii te ad illam elegerunt. Lectus ornatus con-
scientia est munda, in qua uelut in lecto pausandum est[a] iuxta illud
psalmiste: "Lectum meum lacrimis meis rigabo."[2] Cortina circa
lectum ymagines habens sanctorum commemoratio est sanctorum
que ornat conscientiam, dum corde et opere eorum retinetur
memoria. Suere cepisti in ea dum de hoc sancto de quo agitur
tractasti, qui et meo iudicio inter sanctos deinceps est commemor-
andus. Quod petisti uigilans dormiens postulasti, et annuit Deus
uoto tuo, dum Michael archangelus promittitur tibi adiutor, nec
f. 105ᵛ inmerito: Michael enim | prepositus est paradisi, et princeps con-
stitutus a Deo super omnes animas suscipiendas. Qui et hanc
sanctam animam inter sanctorum animas suscepit, et in illa
superna curia spirituum beatorum cui presidet Michael decretum
est, et istum nomine sancti et honore debere amodo censeri. Insue
ergo illum ut dignus est cortine illi: id est, sanctorum commemora-
tioni adiunge.'

Placuit pontifici sententia abbatis: nec mora, conuocata omni
curia Romana, que tunc erat ibi bene generalis, presente archiepiscopo Remensi, qui magnum sanctitati beati G(ileberti), quem

---

[a] est om. Lc

---

[1] Reiner or Rainier of Ponza (died 1207×1209) was a Cistercian monk and associate
of Joachim of Fiore who later became intimate with Innocent III. In 1198 he was legate
in León, Castile, and Portugal and in Dec. that year was appointed legate in Languedoc.
In 1199 he returned to the Curia and seems to have become Innocent's confessor; he
appears to have made Fossanova his base but continued to visit the Curia. In June 1201
he was one of a commission to investigate the First and Second Orders of Humiliati,
and in Nov.–Dec. he witnessed two bulls at Anagni and advised on the canonization
process of St Gilbert. Caesarius of Heisterbach recounts another dream legend concerning him involving Innocent's narrow escape from Hell. He retired to the island of
Ponza off Terracina, where he lived as a hermit till his death. On him see H. Grund-
mann, 'Zur Biographie Joachims von Fiore und Rainers von Ponza', *Deutsches Archiv*,

very cautious person and wanting the assurance of complete certainty, he asked for an interpretation of his dream from a most holy
and learned man, Abbot Reiner.[1] Leading a solitary life among the
hills, he was held in great reverence not only by the pope but also
by the whole church of Rome, because of his remarkable sanctity
and knowledge. So when this man had answered his summons the
pope ordered him to consider his dream and unravel its meaning.
Filled with the spirit of Joseph or of Daniel, the abbot said to him,
'There is no need to spend long in consideration of this, because
the dream and its interpretation are obvious. The tall and lofty
tower which you saw is the excellence of the papal office; you were
borne into it by others as you wished because you yourself did not
seize it, but other men chose you for it. The ornate bed is a spotless
conscience, in which one must rest as in a bed, following the
Psalmist's saying "I shall moisten my bed with my tears."[2] The
curtain around the bed with its pictures of saints is the commemoration of saints which adorns conscience as long as the
recollection of these men is kept in one's heart and work. You
began to stitch at this curtain while you were considering the holy
man in question; and it is my judgement too that he ought now to
be commemorated among the saints. What you sought while you
were awake, you asked for as you slept, and God has granted your
request, since the Archangel Michael is promised you as a helper;
and with justification, for Michael is the lord of paradise and the
prince appointed by God to receive all souls. He has received this
holy soul too among the souls of the holy, and it has been decreed,
in that heavenly court of blessed spirits over which Michael
presides, that Gilbert too should from now on be accorded a saint's
title and dignity. Therefore, since he is worthy, sew this man upon
the curtain: in other words, add him to the number of commemorated saints.'

The pope assented to the abbot's judgement, and without
delay he summoned the entire Roman Curia, which was then in
full public session in that place. Amongst those present was the
archbishop of Reims, a man who bore ample witness to the
holiness of blessed Gilbert, whom he had known while himself

xvi (1960), 437–546; B. Griesser, 'Rainer von Fossanova und sein Brief an Abt Arnald von
Cîteaux (1203)', *Cistercienser Chronik*, lx (1953), 152–5; C. Thouzellier, *Catharisme et
valdéisme* (Louvain and Paris, 1969), pp. 139–58; Caesarius of Heisterbach, *Dialogus
miraculorum*, vii. 6. (We owe the substance of this note to the kind help of Brenda Bolton.)

  [2] Ps. 6: 7 (6).

nouerat dum iuuenis esset in Anglia, tulit testimonium,[1] coram omni clero et populo circumsedentibus omnibus, solis nunciis illis stantibus, papa ipse grandem et prolixum texuit sermonem super meritis et miraculis sancti G(ileberti), et testimoniis acceptis testibusque admissis multisque propositis rationibus et allegatis que necessarie erant quampluribus causis, canonizauit eum de communi assensu tocius ecclesie memoriamque eius inter sanctos celebrandam esse decreuit. Facta est autem hec canonizatio beati G(ileberti), exigentibus propriis meritis, atestantibus miraculis multis, suadentibus reuelationibus plurimis sanctorum cathalogo f. 106 ascripti, anno ab incarnatione Domini .M̊. C̊C. i̊i. tercio idus | Ianuarii, .v̊i. uidelicet etate seculi, .v̊i. die apparitionis Domini, et feria .v̊i. hora .v̊i. diei, anno .v̊i. decem nouenalis cicli, .v̊i. littera alfabeti dominicali,[2] apud Anagniam a domino Innocentio papa .ii̊i., per generalem curiam Romanam, regnante in Anglia Iohanne, Henrici regis secundi filio, pontificante sedem Cantuarie Huberto, imperante ubique Domino Ihesu Christo, cui est honor et gloria in secula seculorum. Amen.

f. 106ᵛ INCIPIVNT VISIONES ET REVELATIONES DE SANCTO GILEBERTO CONFESSORE

Quod uenerabilis pater G(ilebertus) sanctorum consortio sit aggregatus in celis et inter sanctos merito sit uenerandus in terris, multe uisiones et reuelationes personis fide et gratia dignis diuinitus declararunt, quatinus precedentia merita et subsecuta miracula et celestia monita sibi inuicem attestentur ad sanctitatem ipsius sufficienter comprobandam. Post descripta igitur uite et morum eius insignia signorumque subiuncta experimenta, superest ut que apparuerunt ueratia cum suis significationibus referantur somnia. . . .ᵃ

f. 107 Tempore illo quo secundum mandatum apostolicum inquirenda erant que per eum facta sunt miracula, sollicitus erat successor suus

---

ᵃ *Lc (ff. 106ᵛ–107ʳ) here repeats the first vision of Gilbert's heavenly reward from ff. 87ᵛ–88ʳ (see above, p. 128 n. a)*

[1] William aux Blanchesmains, brother of Henry count of Champagne and so nephew of King Stephen and Henry of Blois, was also brother-in-law of Louis VII of France, bishop of Chartres 1165–76, also archbishop of Sens 1168–1176/7, archbishop of Rheims 1176/7–1202, and in his later years also a cardinal (for dates and refs., *Letters of John of Salisbury*, ii. 567–9 n.). With this reference to his early life cf. ibid. no. 307, pp. 746–7.

a young man in England.[1] Before all the clergy and people, who all sat round him, the messengers alone standing, the pope himself preached a great and lengthy sermon upon the merits and miracles of holy Gilbert. The evidence was received, the witnesses admitted, many causes were adduced and a host of compelling reasons put forward; and so he canonized him with the common assent of the whole church and decreed that his memorial should be celebrated among the saints. St Gilbert was added to the catalogue of the saints through the strength of his own merits and the witness of many miracles supported by frequent revelations; and his canonization was accomplished in the year of Our Lord's incarnation 1202, on 11 January, during the sixth age of the world, on the sixth day of Epiphany, on the sixth day of the week, at the sixth hour of the day, in the sixth year of the nineteen-year cycle, the sixth letter of the Dominical alphabet,[2] at Anagni by Pope Innocent III acting through the full Roman Curia, while John, son of King Henry II, was ruling in England, Hubert presiding over the see of Canterbury, and Our Lord Jesus Christ reigning everywhere, to whom is honour and glory world without end. Amen.

HERE BEGIN VISIONS AND REVELATIONS ABOUT ST GILBERT THE CONFESSOR

Many visions and revelations have been granted to people reckoned worthy of belief and of grace. Such signs, sent from God, have made plain that our venerable father Gilbert has been gathered to the fellowship of saints in heaven and should properly be revered among the saints on earth; for the merits which came first, the subsequent miracles, and the lessons supplied by heaven support each other's witness in adequate proof of this man's sanctity. So now that we have described the remarkable features of his life and character, followed by the experience of miracles, it remains to recount the truthful dreams which occurred, together with their meanings. . . .

At the time when, in accordance with the papal mandate, the miracles worked by St Gilbert were to be investigated, his successor took great pains to track down people who had been

---

[2] 'The sixth of the nineteen-year cycle' was the Golden Number; the Dominical Letter for 1202 was F, the 6th (for the meaning of these terms, see C. R. Cheney, *Handbook of Dates*, London, 1945, pp. 8–9).

in personis curatis et eorum testibus perquirendis, quoniam, licet plura haberet certa et manifesta, multa tamen per diuersa loca patrata sunt que seu per incuriam seu per quorumdam simplicitatem non fuerunt precognita. Huic ergo per uisum apparuit sanctus dicens: 'Vt quid tantum sollicitaris super multis miraculis querendis? Non sit tibi cure, non est enim necesse.' Quibus uerbis intellexit uir prudens non tantum debere fidem facere sanctitatis miracula, quantum uite honestas et merita testificata. |

f. 107ᵛ Vnde et spem concepit quod ex facili per Dei gratiam eius canonizatio foret impetranda. Nec fefellit eum spes. Cum enim recitarentur in curia Romana quedam pauca tamen signa, dixerunt quidam ex cardinalibus sola ea que audierant debere sufficere, alii uero dicebant ea superhabundare. Quamobrem cito et facile est canonizatio illa celebrata.

Prouisa sed non preparata legatione ad sedem apostolicam pro canonizatione beati G(ileberti) celebranda, in preparandis itineri suo necessariis aliquam moram innectebant nuntii profecturi. Erant autem multi ex fratribus suis et sororibus pro eis solliciti et compacientes quia tam magnum laborem fuerant aggressuri, nec sciebatur qualem exitum erant sortituri. Cogitabant super hiis maxime, quarum est plerumque deuotio feruentior, et pro eis orabant instantius moniales, presertim una ex illis de Hauerholm, que maiori circa eos pietate mouebatur. Huic dormienti uisio huiuscemodi apparuit. Vidit in uisu beatum G(ilebertum) quasi in ecclesia consistentem et cum eo magnam quandam personam ante altare residentem, puerum pulcherrimum in genibus

f. 108 tenentem: ad quam | pater: 'Quare' inquit 'tam diu tardant canonici uestri ire Romam?' Respondit: 'Domine, non sunt adhuc penitus parati, et quidam ex ipsis iuuenes sunt et trepidant illuc ire.' Tunc ille: 'Ne timeant', ait, 'quia puer iste quem tu uides bene ducet eos et reducet.' Qua uisione excitata illa et ea recitata, ad celerandum iter dictos canonicos plurimum excitauit. Credimus nempe puerum illum beate Virginis fuisse filium, qui eis dux extitit in uia et comes: quod ex consequentibus patuit. A multo enim tempore non est auditum quod tot homines ex nostris regionibus simul Romam proficiscentes tam prospere iuissent tamque prospere remeassent. Non enim uel uno die pre infirmitate aliqua que alicui eorum accidisset a suo itinere sunt retardati, nec permissus est aliquis eis nocere inimicus, licet inter

cured and their witnesses; for although there were many clear and obvious cases, many miracles were performed in different places which were not recognized as such because of the carelessness or the simplicity of some men. The saint appeared to him in a vision, saying: 'Why do you take such trouble over seeking out large numbers of miracles? Do not worry, for it is not necessary.' From these words the wise man understood that he should put his trust not so much in the saint's miracles as in his virtuous life and well-attested merits. For this reason he began to hope that by God's grace Gilbert's canonization would be obtained without difficulty. Nor did this hope deceive him. For when just a few miracles were described in the Roman Curia, some of the cardinals said that what they had heard should alone suffice, while others said that they were more than enough. In this way the canonization was celebrated swiftly and easily.

When an embassy to visit the pope and obtain blessed Gilbert's canonization had been planned but not organized, the messengers who were to go incurred some delay in preparing what they needed for their journey. Moreover, many of their brethren and sisters were anxious about them and felt pity for them because they were about to embark on such a great enterprise and it was not known what sort of outcome they would secure. The nuns, who commonly possess a more lively devotion, thought very seriously and prayed very earnestly for the messengers, especially one of those belonging to Haverholme who was moved by great piety on their account. While she slept this sight appeared to her. In a vision she saw blessed Gilbert, as though standing in a church, and with him a large figure seated before the altar, holding a most lovely boy upon its knees. Father Gilbert said to her, 'Why do your canons delay so long in going to Rome?' She replied, 'Lord, they are still not entirely ready, and some of them are young men and are frightened to go there.' Then he replied, 'They must not be afraid, because the boy you see will lead them well and bring them back.' Waking from this dream, she described it and roused the canons most strongly to hasten upon their journey. We believe that that boy was the son of the Blessed Virgin, who acted as their guide and companion upon the journey, as was clear from what followed. For over a very long time it was unheard of for so many men setting out together for Rome from our land to travel so successfully and return so successfully. They were not held up even for one day by any illness occurring to any of them; nor was any enemy allowed to harm them, even though at one time

medios predones quandoque transierint, qui et ante et post se transeuntes alios uiatores spoliauerunt. Verum omnes cum quibus agebant gratos sibi habuerunt et fauentes, super hiis que petebant gaudentes et id quod optabant uotis omnibus affectantes. Domnum etiam apostolicum et omnes sacri palacii proceres faciles sibi inuenerunt et beneuolos: unde et peractis melius et cicius quam petere auderent negociis sani et iocundi ad

f. 108ᵛ | sua quamtocius sunt reuersi. Angelus enim Domini bonus comitatus est cum eis, qui bene disposuit iter et actus suos, sicut ex quadam uisione que eis aparuit in uia collegerunt.[1]

Cum enim iter suum conficerent uersus Romam, erant nimis solliciti et in multis dubii, utpote tam longinqui itineris et tantorum periculorum inexperti, et de tanto negotio consummando incerti. Quibus pater piissimus talem adhibuit consolationem: apparuit in somnis cuidam ex ipsis, Rad(ulfo) de Insula nomine,[2] tanta perfusus iocunditate quantam mirabatur qui hec uidit posse alicuius hominis animo inesse. Erat autem ibi presens, ut uidebatur, quidam ex sociis suis, nomine Gamelus, qui in prima profectione propter hoc negotium arrepta fuerat secundus,[3] et multam de eo gesserat sollicitudinem. Hunc pater conueniens quasi increpauit eum quia tantam in redeundo moram fecisset. Cuius uerba reueritus uisus est uultum deicere, sed pater blande et hilariter consolatus est eum, dicens: 'Noli, fili, mestus esse nec nimium angustieris, quia factum est factum est factum est negotium.' Quibus auditis, supra quam credi potest factus est ille

f. 109 iocundatus. Et uere sic erat. Recitata enim mane | uisione tam ille quam omnes alii satis sunt letificati, et sperantes in eo qui facit que facta sunt et futura habet pro preteritis,[4] ad exequendum ceptum opus quod peragendum plene presumpserant uehementer sunt animati.

Non solum sanctis consertum in celo beatum G(ilebertum) et sancti ueneratione dignum declarandum in mundo reuelauit Deus quibusdam ex domesticis eius, et ut huic operi insisterent ammonuit et animauit, sed extraneis, et non leuibus personis, uerum eis in quorum censura summa rei constitit, idem propalauit. Preter id namque quod de executione huius rei ipsi

---

[1] See p. lxxv.
[2] See pp. lxxiii–lxxv.
[3] See p. xcviii.
[4] Cf. Wisd. 8: 8.

they travelled through the midst of robbers who, both before and after them, stripped other men upon that journey. Indeed everyone with whom they dealt regarded them agreeably and with favour, rejoicing in their aims and supporting with all their prayers what they were hoping to obtain. They also found the pope and all the officers of his holy palace helpful and well disposed towards them. And so, having completed their business to better effect and more speedily than they dared to ask, they returned home as soon as possible, cheerful and in good health. For the Lord's good angel went with them, who managed their travelling and their activities well: a fact they learned from a vision which appeared to them on the way.[1]

For while they were travelling towards Rome, they were extremely anxious and afflicted by many doubts, because they had no experience of such a long journey and such great perils; also they were uncertain whether they would complete so important a piece of business. The most holy father supplied them with this comfort: he appeared in a dream to one of them, called Ralph de Insula,[2] radiating such cheerfulness that Ralph, who saw this, wondered that so much could dwell in any man's spirit. It seemed to him that one of his companions, Gamel by name, was also present there; he had been the second man in the first party to set out on this business[3] and had taken much trouble over it. On meeting him the holy father appeared to reproach him for causing such a long delay in returning to Rome. Gamel listened to his words with reverence and looked crestfallen, but Father Gilbert comforted him kindly and cheerfully, saying, 'Do not be sad, my son, or distress yourself too much, because the work is accomplished—it is accomplished—it is accomplished.' Hearing this, Gamel was filled with more joy than can be imagined. And so it really was. For in the morning when Ralph had described the vision, both he and all the others were greatly cheered; and trusting in Him who accomplishes what has been done and considers the future as the past,[4] they were strongly encouraged to continue the work which they had begun, and had ventured to accomplish.

God has revealed that blessed Gilbert is united to the saints in heaven and must be declared worthy of veneration as a saint upon earth, not only to members of Gilbert's own household, urging and encouraging them to pursue such a course, but also to outsiders, not persons of trivial importance, but those with whom final judgement of the case rested. For quite apart from what heaven revealed

summo pontifici diuinitus innotuit, cuidam domini pape conso-
brino, Iohanni Hodeline nomine,[1] summe prudentie uiro, de
beatitudine eius talis facta est manifestatio: uidebatur sibi uidere
in somnis regiam quandam sullimem et spaciosam alteramque
prope domum quasi thalamum siue capellam, in qua uidit, ut
uidere poterat, Dei maiestatem. Aspexit et ecce uir quidam
longeuus innuit ei ut accederet. Illo autem pre foribus stante,
senex ille in interiorem domum ubi maiestas residebat ingressus
est. Stetit ille admirans luminis magnitudinem, et recolens secum
f. 109ᵛ illam Dei esse maiestatem, cogitabat quod ad eam | usque si posset
pertingere uellet. Talia cogitanti respondit maiestas: 'Non potes
modo huc intrare; sed magister G(ilebertus) de Sempingham te
introducet.' Excitatus ille a somno mane facto quesiuit diligenter a
canonicis cuius forme fuerat homo magister G(ilebertus) dum
uiueret, an scilicet senex, lati uultus, caluus et canutus, capite
uersus pectus pendulo. Cui cum respondissent eum talem in hac
uita fuisse, iurauit se illum nocte preterita manifeste uidisse, quia
uirum eiusdem speciei conspexerat in somnis, et referens uisionem adiecit quod si unquam ad Deum peruenturus est adiuuanti-
bus ut sperat ipsius meritis eo perueniet.[a]

De translatione sancti Gileberti confessoris

Revelata igitur beati Gileberti gloria et canonizatione eius in princi-
pali sede ut predictum est sollemniter celebrata, summus pontifex
sua direxit scripta ad archiepiscopos Anglie et ad capitulum ordinis
de Sempingham, omnia in eis retexens que a principio prime
inquisitionis signorum et sanctitatis eius facta sunt, quamque
mature et discrete eatenus processum esset ostendens, demandans
in fine quatinus quod ipse sollemniter et caute statuerat, illi
humiliter et deuote conseruarent, facientes festiuitatem ipsius per
f. 110 suas prouincias sollemniter | celebrari.[2] Archiepiscopo autem
Cantuariensi dedit in mandatis ut cum a fratribus illius ordinis
fuisset requisitus, quia in sua prouintia tumulatus est sanctus, corpus confessoris eiusdem cum honore debito ac reuerentia eleuaret.

---

[a] esset . . . ut sperauit . . . perueniret Od

---

[1] Probably John Odonis (son of Odo or (H)odelino), occ. 1204 (*PL* ccxv. 387–8—a
reference we owe to Professor Cheney).   [2] See pp. 254–9.

to the pope himself about the completion of this matter, a clear
sign of Gilbert's blessedness was granted to a relative of the pope's
called John Hodeline,[1] a man of profound judgement. It seemed to
him that as he slept he saw a lofty and spacious palace, and another
building nearby rather like a chamber or chapel where he saw, as
far as he was able, the majesty of God. He looked and, behold, an
elderly man beckoned him to approach. As he stood upon the
threshold, the old man went further inside the dwelling where
God's majesty was present. He stood, wondering at the strength of
the light, and when he remembered that the splendour belonged to
God, he felt that he wished to reach it as far as possible. While he
was considering this, God's majesty spoke to him: 'You cannot
enter here now; but Master Gilbert of Sempringham shall bring
you in.' When it was morning and he awoke from sleep, he asked
the canons carefully about the appearance of Master Gilbert
during his lifetime: that is, whether he had been an elderly man
with a broad face, bald apart from a few white hairs, with his head
bent towards his chest. When they replied that during his life
Master Gilbert had been just like this, he swore that he had seen
him clearly the previous night, because he had seen a man with
exactly the same appearance in a dream. And as he described the
vision he added that if he ever was to come to God he hoped he
would approach him with the help of this man's merits.

The Translation of St Gilbert the Confessor

When blessed Gilbert's glory had been revealed and his canonization, as already described, celebrated with great solemnity in the
principal see, the pope sent letters to the archbishops of England
and the chapter of the Sempringham Order. He related in these
everything which had been done from the beginning of the first
enquiry into Gilbert's miracles and holiness; he showed in what a
timely and well-judged manner affairs had progressed to their
present state; finally he asked them to observe humbly and
devoutly what he himself had decreed with all solemnity and
care, making sure that Gilbert's festival was celebrated with
solemn dignity throughout their provinces.[2] He also instructed the
archbishop of Canterbury, since the saint was buried in his province, to raise the confessor's body with appropriate honour and
reverence when asked by the brethren belonging to that Order.

Quod mandatum tanquam de celo missum tam predictus archiepiscopus quam fratres ordinis predicti implere cupientes, prepar-
atis que necessaria erant eleuando corpori quamtocius institerunt.
Licet enim, sicut in antiquis et quondam ignotis sanctis, quosᵃ ipsa
uetustas, uel hominum incuria seu inscicia, diu occultauerat, nulla
uisio premonuerit hanc facere translationem, sufficere sibi tamenᵇ
credebant ad hoc opus aggrediendum, primo per Deum postea per
homines, ita manifeste factam eius reuelationem, presertim cum
mandatum super hoc apostolicum suscepissent, cui tanquam
diuino precepto obedire censuerunt. Et quoniam a summo ponti-
fice adhuc superstite et ipsi uiuentes ad hoc incitabantur, timentes
moram fore periculo, que iussi fuerant absque tarditate executi
sunt.

Anno igitur Domini .M̊.C̊C̊.I̊I̊. memorati fratres in uigilia sancte
Crucis iam dictum archiepiscopum per magistrum suum et
maiores ordinis conuenerunt, instantes ut die dominica proxima
f. 110ᵛ   post festum sancti Dionisii translationem | beati G(ileberti) confes-
soris perageret.[1] Quod deuotus annuit et libens, et pro sollemnitate quam tanti processus negocii desiderabat, hoc omnibus
coepiscopis suis per Angliam constitutis denuntiare curauit,
mandans et exhortans ut omnes qui possent una cum ipso ad diem
predictum interessent, et per dioceses suas id publicari facerent,
quatinus diem tante sollemnitatis notum haberent qui uellent eiusdem sancti limina uisitare. Die igitur prefixo, hoc est .I̊I̊I̊. idus
Octobris, negocium istud executioni demandatum est. Nec defuit
gloria supernarum reuelationum, cum attestationibus diuinis
manifestata. Tempore enim illo dum de hiis tractaretur, apparuit
cuidam consorori sue dormienti altera quedam illius ordinis
monialis eodem anno defuncta: que inter cetera que cum ea habuit
colloquia, hoc etiam asseruit quod in celestibus facta est generalis
citatio sanctis, ut die statuto quem prediximus ad translationem
beati Gileberti conuenirent. Adiecit etiam quod omnes ordinis
illius defuncti, qui in purgatoriis sue saluationis tempus expecta-
bant, ab hora citationis illius eis facte usque ad diem illius celebri-
tatis nullam penam sustinerent. Nec enim debet esse ambiguum

ᵃ quos *Winterbottom;* quod *Lc (def. Od)*   ᵇ tamen *Lc*[1]; non *Lc (erased); def. Od*

[1] The vigil of the Invention of the Cross, 2 May 1202; the Sunday after St Denis or
Dionysius, 13 Oct. 1202 (see pp. 258–9).

Both the archbishop and the brethren of the Order were as eager to obey this instruction as if it had been sent from heaven, and they devoted themselves entirely to the preparations necessary for raising the body. Just as in the case of ancient and previously unknown saints, shrouded in antiquity owing to men's negligence or ignorance, so no vision advised them in advance to carry out this translation. Nevertheless they believed that the revelation about him made so clearly, first through God and afterwards through men, was sufficient for them to embark upon this work, especially since they had received a papal mandate for it, which they judged they should obey as a command from heaven. And because they were urged to this measure by a pope who was yet living, as they were themselves, fearing that delay would be dangerous they performed what they had been bidden with all promptness.

Thus in the year of Our Lord 1202, upon the vigil of the Holy Cross, the brethren, represented by their master and senior members of the Order, met the archbishop, and urged him to carry out the translation of St Gilbert the Confessor on the Sunday following the feast of St Dionysius.[1] The archbishop devoutly and willingly agreed, and out of regard for the solemnity which the performance of such an important ceremony required, he took care to announce it to all his fellow bishops holding office throughout England. He commanded and exhorted all those who could to be present with him on that day and to have the occasion made known throughout their dioceses, so that whoever wished to visit the saint's dwelling might know the day of so solemn an event. The ceremony was appointed to be carried out on the day already arranged, that is 13 October. Nor was there lacking the glory of divine revelations, made manifest with heavenly witnesses. For during the time these matters were being discussed, a nun belonging to the Order, who had died that very year, appeared to one of her fellow sisters as she slept. In the course of the rest of the conversation which she had with her, the nun declared that in heaven the saints had been given a general summons to meet together for St Gilbert's translation on the appointed day already mentioned. She added that all the members of the Order who had died and were in purgatory awaiting the time of their salvation would endure no punishment from the hour this summons was issued to the day the service was celebrated. There should be no doubt that the

f. 111 | beatos spiritus ibi tunc fuisse presentes, sicut manifesta quedam signa declararunt. Nocte enim huius eleuationis, que dominica habebatur, cum sepedictus archipresul ceterique episcopi et ministri mausoleum quo sacra pignora condebantur aperuissent, et ea honorifice eleuassent, ut sic lota suis locis collocata absque mora possent in crastino in sacrata capsa decenter componi, dum hoc ministerium ageretur cum ymnis et canticis spiritualibus, uiderunt quidam religiosi, et cum eis seculares plurimi, globum igneum immensum, quasi candelas multas ut dicebant simul accensas, seu uelut stellam magnam uibrantem, semel et secundo et tercio de celo descendere et rursum ascendere supra tectum basilice contra sepulchrum. Tercio autem impetu facto quasi penetrare culmen ecclesie et intro cadere uidebatur. Quod uidentes aliqui inuitabant alios exire ad uidendum, ut dixerunt, luminare Christi supra ecclesiam. Similia uiderunt quidam excubantes in orationibus ante sepulchrum sancti quadam nocte ante translationem, lumen scilicet immensum per uitrinam prope tumulum tercio intrare, et tercia inmissione in fossam ubi sanctus iacuerat descendere; mira etiam odoris fragrantia impleuit nares

f. 111ᵛ omnium qui aderant, cum remo|uerent artifices aliquantulum mausoleum a spelunca ubi prius steterat, ut pararetur locus feretro ibidem componendo. Nec solum ista sed et alia apparuerunt diuine illustrationis testimonia. Amoto enim lapide a monumento inuentus est rubicundus puluis carnis liquefacte, qualis esse dicitur uirginum defunctorum.

De casula[1]

Casula quoque serica, in qua corpus humatum erat inuolutum, incorrupta reperta est. Extractis igitur sacris reliquiis et ablutis, uenerabilis antistes cum lecto paululum pausasset, arripuit eum grauis infirmitas, et ita uehementer afflixit quod sacrum officium quod inceperat,ᵃ propter quod tot reuerendas personas et tantam plebem conuocauerat, explere desperaret. Super quo magis quam de suo incommodo contristatus, cum nil proficeret adhibitis humanis amminiculis que profutura credidit ad salutem, preces supplices

---

ᵃ ins. et Od

[1] This heading (omitted by Od) only refers to the first sentence of what follows.

blessed spirits were present at that place and time, as certain clear signs made obvious. For on the night of the raising, which was a Sunday, the archbishop together with the other bishops and celebrants opened the grave where the holy relics were buried and reverently lifted them out so that, after being washed and put back together in their places, they could be decently put together, without delay, in a sanctified casket on the following day. While they were performing this service with hymns and spiritual songs, a few religious and with them many secular people saw a huge fiery globe, resembling they said many candles all lit at once or perhaps a great twinkling star. Once, twice, and a third time it descended from the heavens and rose again over the church roof opposite the place of burial. The third time it moved it appeared to penetrate the church roof and fall inside. Some who saw this asked others to go outside and look at what they called Christ's lantern shining over the church. Those who spent a night preceding the translation in prayer before the saint's tomb saw much the same thing; an immense light which entered three times through the window near the tomb and which on its third entry went down into the grave where the saint had lain. Also, a wonderfully sweet smell filled the nostrils of all who were present, when the workmen removed the tomb a little distance from the pit where it had previously stood, in order that the site might be prepared for the shrine to be raised there. Apart from this, other examples also appeared to reveal God's glory. For when the stone was removed from the tomb there was discovered a rosy dust of dissolved flesh, of the sort said to belong to those who die chaste.

The chasuble [1]

Again, the silk chasuble in which the body was wrapped when buried was discovered to be without corruption. When the sacred relics had been taken out of it and washed, the venerable archbishop rested a little while upon his bed. Then a serious illness attacked him and affected him so badly that he despaired of completing the holy office he had begun and for which he had called together so many clergy and such a crowd of people. This, rather than his own discomfort, depressed him, and there was no improvement after he had applied the human remedies which he believed would benefit his health. Then he poured out prayers

fundit ad Deum et ad sanctum Gilebertum, quatinus uirtus ei donaretur per merita sancti exequendi quod inceperat eorum[a] obsequium. Vix preces compleuit et tota illa incommoditas concito euanuit, maiusque robur ei accreuit quam habuerat ante tempus doloris. Tunc statim pulsatum est ad nocturnale officium,

f. 112 et ille gratias agens et·acturus cum suis | clericis presentauit se officiis canonicorum in conuentu, que pro honore et amore sancti de quo agebatur cum magna deuotione sollemniter celebrauit. Mane facto conuocatis maioribus ecclesie sanus et hilaris quod sibi acciderat exposuit, laudans Dei et sancti eius uirtutem, quam in se ipso tam manifeste probauerat affuisse. Hora igitur competenti diei sacris insistens obsequiis, benedicta aqua episcopali et dedicata theca reliquiarum, impositaque humeris quorundam principum et maiorum Anglie qui affuerant, sollemnis processio ordinatur, precedente clero et subsequentibus ante pontifices cum innumero populo nobilibus multis tam sacras reliquias quam earum sacratam capsam deferentibus. Vbi quidam egroti propius accedentes et sancta illa contingentes a suis periculis, ut pro certo cognouimus, eadem hora saluati sunt. Facto itaque ab archipresule publico sermone de sanctitate et signis beati Gileberti, et de tocius huius processu negocii, missa de ipso sancto altisone celebratur, circa cuius finem, sumpta scilicet eucharistia, ante cantatam communionem, uenerande reliquie in bysso munda infra pannum sericum preciosum, que domnus archiepiscopus ad hoc dederat, inuolute in uase dedicato reconduntur.

f. 112ᵛ Vbi | carta seriem uite et miraculorum eius necnon et canonizationis et huius translationis summatim continens, signis pontificum et abbatum sibi assistentium munita, simul cum lamina plumbea ad perpetuam memoriam eadem prestruente, reposita est. Clausa autem techa et supra marmoreum parietem in loco ubi prius sanctus iacuerat erecta, missaque completa et omnibus rite peractis ad sua singuli cum gaudio sunt reuersi.

---

[a] eorum om. Od, perhaps rightly; otherwise, the word is corrupt

to God and to St Gilbert, asking that through the saint's merits
he might be given strength to carry out the service which he had
begun on their behalf. Scarcely had he finished his prayers when
the entire illness swiftly disappeared, and he enjoyed greater
vigour than he had possessed before the time of his affliction.
Just at that moment the bell rang for the night office; giving
thanks and ready to give more, he took his place with his clerks
for the canons' offices amid the community; these he celebrated
solemnly and with great devotion out of honour and love for the
saint, for whom the celebration was being performed. When it
was morning and the senior members of the church had been
called together, he explained, cheerful and healthy as he now
was, what had happened to him, and he praised the power of
God and of His saint, which he had so clearly proved to exist in
his own case. Then at a suitable hour of the day he continued
with the holy ceremonies, blessing the bishop's water and dedi-
cating the reliquary. When this chest had been laid upon the
shoulders of some of the princes and the most important men of
England who were present, a solemn procession was drawn up;
the clergy went first, and before the bishops, along with a countless host of people, many nobles followed bearing both the holy
relics and their consecrated chest. At this point some sick people
came closer, and as they touched those holy objects they were
delivered from their illnesses, we know for certain, that very same
hour. The archbishop preached a public sermon about St Gilbert's holiness and miracles and about the course of the whole
business. Then in lofty tones the saint's proper mass was celebrated; towards its end, that is when the eucharist had been
received, before the singing of the communion, the revered relics
were wrapped in spotless linen within a precious silk cloth, both
given by the archbishop for this purpose. Then they were placed
within the consecrated vessel. A document was also placed inside
containing a concise account of St Gilbert's life and miracles,
and of his canonization and this translation; it was authenticated
by the seals of the bishops and the abbots present with them,
along with a strip of lead to provide a perpetual memorial for the
events. The chest was then closed and placed upon a marble wall
in the place where the saint had previously lain; and when the
mass was finished and all rites had been observed everyone
returned rejoicing to their own homes.

Lamine autem plumbee scriptura hec est

Hic iacet sanctus Gilebertus, primus pater et institutor ordinis de
Sempingham, translatus in hunc loculum a domno Huberto Cantuariensi archiepiscopo per mandatum Innocentii pape tercii, .ɪɪɪ.
idus Octobris anno ab incarnatione Domini .ṁ.ċċ.ɪ̇ɪ.[a]

Rescriptum carte in feretro posite hoc est

In hac capsa continentur reliquie beati Gilberti presbiteri et confessoris, primi patris et institutoris ordinis de Sempingham, cuius
uitam licet multa preclaram reddiderint et commendabilem, hoc
tamen precipue eum insigniuit, quod spontaneam eligens paupertatem, omnia temporalia sibi a Deo prestita fratrum et sororum, quos
sub regulari disciplina prudenter instituit et sollicite custodiuit,
f. 113   necessitatibus | deputauit. Cui processu temporis tantam Deus
adauxit gratiam et uirtutem quod .ɪ̊ɪ̊ɪ̊ɪ. canonicas regulares et .ɪx.
monasteria sanctimonialium construxit.[1b] In quibus eo tempore
quo migrauit ad Dominum, preter innumeros antea defunctos,
circiter septingentos uiros religiosos, mille et quingentas sorores
iugiter Deo famulantes reliquit. Obiit autem in senectute plusquam
centenaria anno incarnationis Domini .ṁ.ċ.ʟx̊xx.ɪx̊. pridie nonas
Februarii, tempore incliti regis Anglorum Henrici secundi. Exigen-
tibus uero propriis meritis, attestantibus miraculis multis, et
suadentibus reuelationibus diuinis, canonizatus cathologo sanctorum est asscriptus a domino papa Innocentio tercio per generalem
curiam Romanam aput Anagniam coram clero et populo anno
Verbi incarnati .ṁ.ċċ.ɪ̇ɪ. tercio idus Ianuarii, anno regni illustris
regis Iohannis .ɪɪɪ., presidente sedi Cantuarie uenerabili archiepiscopo Huberto: qui de mandato memorati summi pontificis
Innocentii tercii, cum collegis suis Heliensi episcopo Eustachio, et
abbate de Burgo Achario, diligentem super miraculis per eum
diuinitus patratis fecerat inquisitionem, et ipsi eorum attestationes
f. 113ᵛ   fideliter in scripturam redactas, | sub sigillis suis clausas, ad sedem
apostolicam transmiserunt.[2] Vnde cercioratus dominus papa de
sanctitate eius et signis, ipsum sanctis Domini decreuit annumer-
andum anno pontificatus sui .ɪɪɪɪ. Et eodem anno per mandatum

---

     [a] *So Lc after correction by the rubricator from* primo; secundo *Od*   [b] construit *Lc*

     [1] See pp. xxx–xxxii, 54–5.   [2] See pp. 240–5.

This is the writing upon the strip of lead

Here lies St Gilbert, first father and founder of the Order of Sempringham, translated to this shrine by Hubert, archbishop of Canterbury by the mandate of Pope Innocent III on 13 October in the year of Our Lord's Incarnation 1202.

This is a copy of the document placed in the shrine

In this casket are contained the relics of St Gilbert, priest and confessor, first father and founder of the Order of Sempringham. Although many things made his life remarkable and worthy of commendation, this was his special distinction: choosing poverty of his own accord, he made over all the temporal possessions granted him by God to meet the needs of those brethren and sisters whom he wisely placed under the discipline of a rule and carefully protected. In the course of time God so increased his grace and virtue that he built four houses for regular canons and nine for nuns.[1] In these houses, at the time he departed to Our Lord, he left, besides the countless numbers who had died beforehand, about 700 male religious and 1,500 sisters constant in their service of God. He died at the advanced age of more than one hundred years, in AD 1189, on 4 February, during the time of the noble king of England Henry II. By the force of his own merits, the witness of many miracles, and the persuasion supplied by divine revelations, he was canonized and added to the list of saints by Pope Innocent III, acting through a general assembly of the Roman Curia at Anagni, before clergy and people in the year of the Incarnate Word 1202 on 11 January, in the third year of the illustrious king John, while the venerable archbishop Hubert was presiding over the see of Canterbury. The archbishop, acting on the mandate of Pope Innocent III, had made a careful enquiry into the divinely inspired miracles performed through Gilbert, along with his colleagues Eustace bishop of Ely and Acharius abbot of Peterborough; and they sent evidence about the miracles, faithfully copied into written form and closed under their seals, to the apostolic see.[2] Thus the pope was assured of his sanctity and his miracles, so that in the fourth year of his pontificate he decreed that Gilbert should be added to the number of saints. And the same year, in accordance

prefati pape a predicto archiepiscopo Huberto translatus est in hunc loculum .iii. idus Octobris, assistentibus uiris sibi uenerabilibus Norwicensi, Herefordensi et Landauensi episcopis,[1] et abbatibus aliisque ecclesiarum prelatis plurimis, cum maioribus et nobilioribus Anglie, magno ibi presente cetu cleri et populi. Ad cuius rei perpetuandam memoriam iam dictus archiepiscopus et coepiscopi sui et abbates sua signa huic scripto appenderunt, et in hoc loculo reposuerunt.

De diebus indulgentiarum H(uberti) archiepiscopi et suffraganeorum eius

Quicumque autem hunc locum sanctum pro honore Dei et sancti Gileberti uisitauerint uel ei aliquid de bonis suis contulerint, relaxantur eis de iniuncta sibi penitentia a sepedicto archiepiscopo .xL. dies in perpetuum, et a suffraganeis suis auctoritate ipsius .c.lx. dies, sicut eorum auctentica testantur. Insuper conceditur eis tam uiuis quam mortuis participium orationum et omnium beneficiorum que fiunt in omnibus ecclesiis tocius ordinis | de Sempingham et ecclesie Cantuariensis, similiter in perpetuum.

f. 114

De uisione R(oberti) prioris de Wathona[2]

In uisione nocturna uidit Robertus prior Wattone quasi paratas exequias pro funerando sancti corpore ipsumque corpus super feretrum in ecclesiam deferri, ut celebraretur missa pro eo. Cumque ex more introitus misse pro defunctis inciperetur a sacerdote, erigens se sanctus resedit in loculo, inchoans missam unius confessoris modulando hanc antiphonam: 'Statuit ei dominus' et cetera.[3] Aduertens[a] ille missam in eius commemoratione tanquam de uno confessore celebrandam, cogitauit secum quales in nocturnalibus eius officiis lectiones deberent recitari. Cuius cogitationi sic sanctus respondit: 'Vnius confessoris.' Nec caruit effectu huius somnium,[b] quoniam, cum in noua eius canonizatione apud curiam Romanam missa de eo esset celebranda, quesitum est a cardinalibus et clericis ibi consistentibus quale officium misse inciperetur; placuitque omnibus ut hec antiphona 'Statuit ei dominus'

---

[a] aduertens *Winterbottom, cf. p. 276;* aue- *LcOd*   [b] somnium *Mynors;* som(p)num *LcOd*

---

[1] John de Grey, bishop of Norwich (1200–14, *Fasti,* ii. 56); Giles de Braose, bishop of Hereford (1200–15); Henry of Abergavenny, bishop of Llandaff (1193–1218).

with the pope's command, he was translated to this shrine by Archbishop Hubert on 13 October; assisting him were the venerable bishops of Norwich, Hereford, and Llandaff,[1] many abbots and other heads of religious houses, together with the more important and noble men of England; and a large gathering of clergy and people was present in that place. To make a perpetual memorial of this event the archbishop, his fellow bishops, and the abbots have added their seals to this document and have placed it in this shrine.

Concerning the days of indulgence of Archbishop H(ubert) and his suffragans

Whoever visits this holy place for the honour of God and of St Gilbert, or who grants him any of his possessions, secures in perpetuity from the archbishop forty days' remission from the penance imposed upon him; and from his suffragans, on his authority, he secures remission of one hundred and sixty days, as their own letters testify. In addition he is granted in perpetuity, while living and after death, a share in the prayers and all benefits which exist in all the churches of the whole Order of Sempringham and in the church of Canterbury.

The vision of R(obert), prior of Watton[2]

In a vision which came to him at night, Robert, prior of Watton saw funeral ceremonies as if prepared for the burial of a saint's body, and he saw the body itself borne into the church upon a bier so that mass might be celebrated for him. When the priest according to custom began the introit of the mass for the dead, the saint, lifting himself up, sat in his coffin and started the mass for one confessor by intoning the antiphon *Statuit ei dominus*.[3] Robert noticed that mass in his memory should be celebrated as if for one confessor, and he thought over what lessons should be recited in the night offices for him. The saint answered his query, saying 'Those for one confessor.' This man's dream was not without result, because when in the course of Gilbert's recent canonization at the Roman Curia mass had to be celebrated for him, the cardinals and clergy present there were asked how the office of the mass was to begin. They all agreed that the antiphon *Statuit ei Dominus* should be

---

[2] Robert occurs as prior of Watton in 1200 and 1202, and had been succeeded by 1205 (*Heads*, p. 205). [3] Cf. *Gilbertine Rite*, ii. 57.

imponeretur, asserentibus cunctis eam sue excellentie uix sufficere, licet esset unius confessoris pontificis propria. Nec inmerito, f. 114ᵛ satis nempe competit ei quod sonat in uerbis: | 'Statutum est enim ei a Domino testamentum pacis',[1] qui per se tot et tam diuersis uocatis in uinculum pacis hominibus, pacem quoque firmissimam post suam mortem iure testatoris reliquit. Princeps etiam factus est a Deo tanquam 'fidelis seruus et prudens quem constituit dominus super familiam suam, et inuentus uigilans constitutus est super omnia bona domini sui', unde et debetur ei regalis sacerdocii dignitas in eternum.[2]

---

[1] Ecclus. 45: 30.
[2] Matt. 24: 45, 47; Ecclus. 45: 30.

used, declaring that it hardly matched his distinction, although correctly it belonged to one confessor bishop. And with good reason, for the words 'The Lord appointed a covenant of peace for him',[1] are entirely appropriate for a man who through his own efforts called so many different persons into the bond of peace and also left behind him as a legacy after his death the most unshakeable peace. He was also made a ruler by God like 'the faithful and wise servant whom the lord appointed steward over his household and who, being found watchful, was given authority over all his lord's possessions', and so for this reason the royal dignity of the priesthood is owed to this man too for all eternity.[2]

EXEMPLARIA EPISTOLARVM DE CANONIZATIONE
SANCTI GILEBERTI

Exemplaria epistolarum a diuersis personis ad diuersas editarum quibus beati G(ileberti) sanctitas et magnificentia operum eius merito commendata est et probata, in unam seriem congessimus, ut ex hiis liqueat quam ordinate, quam ueraciter et discrete gloria eius et ueneratio in sancta ecclesia decreta est celebranda.

[1] *Epistola Philippi notarii ad prelatos Anglie*[1]

Dominis et amicis in Christo karissimis omnibus ecclesiarum prelatis per Angliam constitutis, Philippus domini pape nuncius et notarius, eternam in Domino salutem.

Eos quos apud se habet superna diuinitas in celis honoros, congruum est ut humana infirmitas ducat in terris commendabiles: f. 115 quatinus dum eorum dignis uenerationibus | insistimus, piis intercessionibus fulciamur. Hinc est quod cum pie recordationis magister G(ilebertus) de Sempingham in presenti uita sanctissime conuersatus fuerit, et post mortem multis, ut accepimus, illustratur[a] miraculis, fraternitatem uestram rogamus attencius et exhortamur in Domino ut, de tantis beneficiis gratias agentes, ipsius glorie pariter congratulemini eiusque uestigiis inherentes sanctorum consortio digni inueniamini. Cumque aliqui ex uobis a fratribus ordinis ipsius ad indagationem miraculorum faciendam fuerint inuitati, monemus et ex parte domini pape iniungimus ut cum omni deuotione et promta uoluntate eorum inquisitioni intendatis, quatinus ad diuinum honorem rerum ueritas perspecta tam domino pape quam sacrosancte Romane ecclesie possit per uos euidentius declarari.

Letter 1 *Lc*   [a] uel coruscat *s.l. Lc*[1]

---

[1] On Master Philip, papal subdeacon, notary, and messenger, see C. R. Cheney in *EHR* lxiii (1948), 342–50; Cheney, *Innocent III and England*, pp. 243–6; *Councils and Synods*, i, ii, 1074. He came to England in Apr. 1200 to raise money for the Crusade; this letter was written before the first inquiry (9 Jan. 1201), probably late 1200.

LETTERS CONCERNING THE CANONIZATION

COPIES OF THE LETTERS CONCERNING THE CANONIZATION OF ST GILBERT

We have collected together into one sequence copies of the letters from various persons, addressed to a variety of recipients. By these letters the sanctity of blessed Gilbert, and the greatness of his works, are rightfully commended and proved. Our purpose is to make plain by what orderly procedure, how truly and wisely, it was decreed that his glory and reverence should be celebrated in Holy Church.

[1] *Letter of Philip, notary, to the prelates of England*[1]

To the lords and dearest friends in Christ all the prelates appointed to churches throughout England, Philip, nuncio and notary of the lord pope, sends everlasting salvation in Our Lord.

It is only fitting that human frailty should consider praiseworthy upon earth those whom the Deity above honours in His presence in heaven; thus while we strive to venerate them appropriately we may be supported by their pious intercessions. Since therefore Master Gilbert of Sempringham of holy memory lived a most saintly life here on earth and, we have heard, is being made famous after his death by many miracles, we most particularly ask you our brethren and urge you in the Lord's name, that, acknowledging such great benefits with gratitude and rejoicing in this man's glory, you may by following in his footsteps be found worthy to share in the fellowship of the saints. And because some of you have been asked by brethren of the Order to carry out an investigation into this man's miracles, we caution and instruct you on behalf of our lord pope to make your enquiry into them reverently and promptly, so that to God's honour you can openly demonstrate the clear truth of these matters both to the lord pope and to the sacred church of Rome.

[2] *Epistola H(uberti) Cantuariensis archiepiscopi de*
inquisitione miraculorum facienda

Hubertus Dei gratia Cantuariensis archiepiscopus, tocius Anglie primas, dilectis filiis de Swinesheued, de Brunna,[a] de Croxtuna abbatibus,[1] salutem, gratiam et benedictionem.

Audiuimus et letati sumus quod ad tumbam uiri uenerabilis magistri G(ileberti) de Semp(ingham) frequentius fiunt miracula f. 115ᵛ et in testimonium sanctitatis uite ipsius multa ibidem | preclara diuinitus patrantur. Que si ita sunt ut fama refert, ad laudem Dei et fidei nostre firmamentum ea fieri non est dubitandum. Vnde, quia ad officii nostri sollicitudinem spectare dinoscitur opera Dei reuelare que in prouintia nostra in diebus nostris tam gloriose sunt facta, discretioni uestre, de qua plene confidimus, significamus quatinus ad locum sepulchri eiusdem sancti uiri pariter accedentes diligenter et sollicite, tam per eos qui curati dicuntur[b] quam per eorum testes fideles, de generibus morborum et diuturnitate et curationum ueritate et de opinione eorundem inquiratis, et cum miraculorum serie tam nobis quam domino pape inquisitam inde rescribatis ueritatem.

[3] *Epistola abbatum ad archiepiscopum de inquisitione facta*

Reuerendo domino et patri H(uberto), Dei gratia Cantuariensi archiepiscopo et tocius Anglie primati, de Swinesheued, de Brunna,[c] de Croxtuna, abbates[1] salutem, et tam deuotam quam debitam reuerentiam.

Ad mandatum uestrum per litteras uestras ad nos directum accedentes ad domum de Sempingham, inuenimus plures tam uiros quam mulieres, tam religiosos quam seculares, per merita uenerabilis uiri magistri G(ileberti) de Sempingham a uariis langoribus ut asserebant curatos. De quibus omnibus ut sanctita-f. 116 tem uestram sicut iussistis | certificaremus, tam eos qui curati sunt quam eorum testes fideles de ueritate morborum et curationum necnon et opinione eorum prestito prius sacramento, diligenter

Letter 2 *LcOd*   [a] *ins. et Od*   [b] dicuntur *LcOd;* uel sunt *s.l. Lc*[1]
Letter 3 *LcOd*   [c] *ins. et Od*

---

[1] William, abbot of Swineshead (Lincs., Cistercian), who occurs in 1202 and after 1209 and was later abbot of Furness; the abbot of Bourne (Lincs., Augustinian), probably Henry (see p. 172, n. 1); Adam, abbot of Croxton Kerrial (Leics., Premonstratensian),

[2] *Letter from H(ubert) archbishop of Canterbury concerning the enquiry to be made into the miracles*

Hubert, by God's grace archbishop of Canterbury and primate of all England, to his beloved sons the abbots of Swineshead, Bourne, and Croxton,[1] greeting, grace and blessing.

We have heard with great joy that miracles are taking place very often at the tomb of the holy man Master G(ilbert) of Sempringham and that by divine inspiration many wonderful things are performed there in evidence of that man's holy life. If these things are what report suggests, they must undoubtedly be happening so that God may be praised and our faith strengthened. It is well known that it is the responsibility of our office to bring to light those works of God which have been so wonderfully accomplished in our province during our lifetime. Therefore we instruct you, in whose discernment we have full trust, that you should travel together to the place of this holy man's burial and investigate most carefully, on the evidence both of those who are said to be cured and also of reliable witnesses, the different types and length of illness, and the truth of their cure, and general opinion about them; you should send an account both to us and the lord pope of the facts you have discovered, together with a list of miracles.

[3] *Letter from the abbots to the archbishop concerning their enquiry*

To their reverend lord and father H(ubert), by God's grace archbishop of Canterbury and primate of all England, the abbots of Swineshead, Bourne, and Croxton[1] send greetings and all devoted and proper reverence.

According to your mandate sent to us in your letter we came to the house of Sempringham, and found many people, men as well as women, religious as well as seculars, who said that they had been cured of various illnesses through the merits of the venerable Master G(ilbert) of Sempringham. So that we might inform your holiness about all these matters as you commanded, we questioned carefully upon oath both those who have been cured and reliable witnesses of these events as to the truth of their illnesses and of

who occurs in 1202 and 1221. See *Heads*, pp. 144, 153, 194. This letter is calendared in *EEA* iii, no. 607.

examinauimus, et horum omnium seriem, sicut subscripta est et sigillis nostris munita, inquisiuimus, eamque paternitati uestre presenti scripto comprehensam transmisimus.ᵃ

Domnus prior R(ogerus) ordinis de Sempingham, in animam suam iuratus, dixit se uidisse ad preces magistri G(ileberti) dum adhuc uiueret uentum ualidum et tempestuosum subito mutatum, cum transiturus esset Humbriam, et ea parte celi qua uoluit flasse secundum, post transitum quoque ipsius pristinam redisse tempestatem.¹ Idem dixit quod, cum graui morbo relinqueretur a medicis desperatus, ad eius imperium, ut credit, euasit mortis periculum. Idem adhuc dixit quod accepit a Radulfo Bidun canonico de Osenei,² multis coram positis, quod idem R(adulfus) per quosdam predicti magistri pedules qui ei dati sunt, a diuturno pedum necnon et manuum dolore intolerabili liberatus est. Hec eadem testantur plures alii uiri religiosi.

Secuntur quedam aliorum miraculorum atestationes que ab archiepiscopo Cantuariensi et collegisᵇ eius cum celebriori examine discussa sunt, unde ea f. 116ᵛ *hic ponere non est necesse. Post descripta autem tunc ibi | inuenta miracula, hoc subiniunxeruntᶜ memorati inquisitores in fine litterarum:*

Hec de multis in presentia nostra a fidelibus uiris et honestis personis iuratis et examinatis excipientes, et multa alia proposita et proponenda pre sui numerositate intermittentes, tam excellentie sanctitatis uestre quam coepiscoporum uestrorum notitie ceterorumque uirorum ecclesiasticorum audientie, per mandatum uestrum incitati, dignum duximus significare, sigillis nostris apensis, credentes ea sufficere debere ad manifestationem gratie et glorie memorato magistro G(ileberto) diuinitus collate, cum et ipsi uiderimus uitam eius ualde comendabilem, et in lucrandis Deo animabus et sancte religionis institutione, amplificatione et gubernatione admirabilem.

Vos igitur de cetero prouidebitis, Domino prosperante, quod preclara Domini lucerna amodo sub modio diu non lateat, sed super candelabrum posita tanto lucidius effulgeat quanto radiantibus signis clarius choruscat.³ Nam nos que a tot et tantis tam

---

ᵃ transmittimus *Od*　　ᵇ *Corrected from* collegiis *in Lc (def. Od)*　　ᶜ subiunxerunt *Od*

¹ See pp. 110–13.
² See pp. 98–9.
³ Cf. Matt. 5: 15; Luke 11: 33.

their cures and also their reputation. We have drawn up a report containing the whole sequence of them, as follows below, authenticated with our seals; and this we have sent to you, our father, included in the present document.

Lord R(oger), prior of the order of Sempringham, swore by his soul and declared that he himself had seen, while Master G(ilbert) was still living, a strong and stormy wind, when he was about to cross the Humber, veer at his prayers and blow from the direction he wished; then after Gilbert had crossed over the earlier storm returned.[1] The same man said that when the doctors gave him up as a hopeless case of a serious disease he believes he escaped the danger of death because of Gilbert's influence. He said, moreover, that he heard from Ralph Bidun, canon of Osney,[2] before many witnesses that he, R(alph), had obtained relief from daily and unendurable pain in both feet and hands by means of some slippers belonging to the Master which were given to him. Many other religious testify to these same facts.

There follow sworn statements about other miracles which were examined by the archbishop of Canterbury and his colleagues at the formal enquiry, so that it is not necessary to put them down here. Having described the miracles which they discovered on that occasion, the above-mentioned investigators added this at the end of their letter:

We have selected these cases from the many examples submitted upon oath by reliable and truthful people examined in our presence, and we have put on one side many others which were, and are yet to be, adduced, because there are just too many of them. Spurred on by your mandate, we considered it important to make these events known to your holiness as well as to bring them to the notice of your fellow bishops and to the ears of other churchmen. We have attached our seals to this in the belief that it must sufficiently reveal the grace and fame given to the same Master G(ilbert) by divine favour, and because we ourselves have seen that this man's life was worthy of high praise and remarkable for the souls which he won for God and for the foundation, development, and organization of a holy religious rule.

Moreover, as the Lord prospers your undertakings you will surely take care that His famous candle is not long hidden from henceforth under a bushel, but is put on a candlestick so that it shines the more brightly as it gleams more brilliantly with shining miracles.[3] We do not dare to keep silent in future about what we

uiris quam mulieribus prestito sacramento accepimus, de cetero tacere non audemus. Vigeat et ualeat sanctitas uestra in Domino.

Testimonia aliorum

Ego Arcadus, abbas de Barling, huic inquisitioni apud Sem-
f. 117 pingham | facte interfui et sigillum meum appendi.

Ego Walterus, prior de Chikesand, huic inquisitioni interfui et sigillum meum appendi.

Ego, R(ogerus), prior de Kime, huic inquisitioni similiter interfui.[1]

Nos uero omnes, scilicet de Brunna, de Croxtuna,[a] de Barlinga abbates, de Kima, de Swinesheued, de Chikesand,[a] de Cateleia priores,[2] in animas nostras iurati, dicimus nos apud Sempingham, .ix. die Ianuarii, uidisse et audisse suprascriptos uiros iuratos protestari coram nobis magnalia Dei per uenerabilis uiri Gileberti merita prouenisse, sicut suprascripta sunt.

[4] *Epistola abbatum ad papam de miraculis*

Reuerentissimo domino et patri Innocentio, Dei gratia summo pontifici, de Suinesheued, de Brunna, de Croxtuna, de Barling abbates, de Kima, de Chikesand, de Cateleia priores, salutem et deuotum in omnibus famulatum.

Cum nemo possit ambigere sanctitatem uestram glorie Dei et sancte ecclesie, cui Deo auctore presidetis, profectui et magnificentie congratulari, cuius gloriam et honorem omni studio queritis, diligitis et amplificatis, dignum duximus serenitati uestre insinuare quantum Deus in finibus nostris hac etate suam extulerit
f. 117ᵛ ecclesiam, quantam operatus sit | salutem in medio terre nostre per uirum uenerabilem et Deo dignum magistrum G(ilebertum) de Sempingham, ut cum mirabilia opera Domini ad apostolicam peruenerint[b] noticiam, perhennem de cetero sorciantur memoriam, et sancte Romane ecclesie approbata auctoritate indubitatam obtineant fidei firmitatem.

Ex mandato itaque uenerabilis patris nostri Huberti Cantuariensis archiepiscopi hec plenius nosse desiderantis accedentes ad

---

ᵃ *ins.* et *Od*
Letter 4 *LcOd*   ᵇ peruenerunt *Lc*

---

[1] Roger occurs as prior of Kyme (Lincs., Augustinian) in the late 12th c. and 1202 (*Heads*, p. 169).

have heard from so many men and women of high standing speaking upon oath. May your holiness prosper and be strong in the Lord.

The evidence of the others

I, Achardus, abbot of Barlings, was present at this enquiry carried out at Sempringham and have attached my seal.

I, Walter, prior of Chicksands, was present at this enquiry and have attached my seal.

I, R(oger), prior of Kyme, was also present at this enquiry.[1]

Thus we all, that is the abbots of Bourne, Croxton, and Barlings and the priors of Kyme, Swineshead, Chicksands, and Catley,[2] having sworn on our souls, declare that on 9 January at Sempringham we all saw and heard these men declare on oath in our presence that God's miracles as they are described above took place through the merits of the venerable Gilbert.

[4] Letter from the abbots to the pope concerning miracles

To our most revered lord and father Innocent, by God's grace supreme pontiff, the abbots of Swineshead, Bourne, Croxton, and Barlings and priors of Kyme, Chicksands, and Catley send greetings and their devoted service in all matters.

No one can doubt that your holiness rejoices in the splendid increase in the glory of God and of His holy Church, over which you preside on His authority; with utter zeal you seek, love, and enlarge the church's honour and glory. We have thought it proper to make known to your serenity how greatly God has exalted His Church in our country in our days, and how great a salvation He has brought to the midst of our land by means of the venerable and godly Master G(ilbert) of Sempringham. Then, when the Lord's wondrous deeds receive the pope's attention, they may in future obtain an everlasting memorial and, sanctioned by the authority of the holy church of Rome, secure the indisputable status of faith.

According to the mandate of our venerable father Hubert, archbishop of Canterbury, who wished to find out more about these events, we came to the house of Sempringham, and found there

---

[2] Presumably, as below, it was the *abbot* of Swineshead, not the prior, who was the witness. For the abbots and priors see p. 200 and p. 204 n. 1; Achardus or Akarius was abbot of Barlings (Lincs., Premonstratensian), Walter of Chicksands (Beds., Gilbertine), and possibly 'B.' of Catley (*Heads*, pp. 192, 201–2).

domum de Sempingham, inuenimus ibi plures tam uiros quam
mulieres *et cetera ut supra*[a]. . . .

In fine sic: hec de multis excipientes quoniam omnia, pre sui
numerositate et immensitate, presentibus litteris comprehendi
nequeunt, uestram omni supplicatione et deuotione monemus et
exoramus in Domino sanctitatem, ut fratrum ordinis illius quem[b]
uir ille Deo plenus instituit et fundauit, scriptis et nuntiis omnia
fideliter et diligenter exprimentibus fidem adhibeatis, eorumque
petitionibus assistatis, que ad laudem Dei omnipotentis et sancte
uniuersalis ecclesie decus et utilitatem, necnon et laudabilis ordinis illius qui nouella patris plantatio est, in quo infinite anime
salue facte sunt per ipsum, indissolubile firmamentum spectare
dinoscuntur. Vt enim nostrum iudicium suggeramus, cum uiro
f. 118 prenominato[c] et semper | nominando nichil defuerit de meritis
sanctitatis, liquidum est quod sanctorum meritorum debitis
premiis non sit defraudatus. Vnde, cum tam manifestis indiciis
eius sanctitudo et beatitudo declaretur, rectum arbitramur ut per
gratiam uestram merita eius celebrentur et suffragia petantur in
terris, cui per gratiam Dei tanta premia credimus collata in celis.

[5] *Epistola magistri R(ogeri) et capituli ordinis de Sempingham*
ad dominum papam

Reuerentissimo domino et patri Innocentio, Dei gratia summo
pontifici, Rogerus, humilis minister, tam deuotus quam debitus
sue sanctitatis seruus, totumque capitulum ordinis de Sempingham, salutem et omnem reuerentiam, uitamque longeuam et
felicitatem eternam.

Gloriam Dei et ecclesie decus, pater karissime, sicut prohibere
uel imminuere sanctitas uestra nouit esse sacrilegum, sic ea non
querere uel aumentare nolle torporis et negligentie filiorum
scimus estimare[d] delictum. Si enim uoce psalmiste tociens monemur afferre Domino gloriam et honorem, afferre gloriam nomini
eius, si censura legali[e] edicto diuino honorare patrem et matrem
iubemur,[1] que culpa est oblatam Deo gloriam subtrahere, quanti
reatus paratum[f] a Deo parentum honorem non suscipere! Cum ergo

---

[a] *Lc mg. refers back to p. 200*   [b] quem *Winterbottom;* quam *LcOd*   [c] prenomi-
nato *Lc*[1]*Od;* nominato *Lc*
Letter 5 *LcOd*   [d] *Perhaps* estimari *(Winterbottom)*   [e] *Perhaps insert* et
(Winterbottom)   [f] *Perhaps* imperatum *(Winterbottom)*

[1] Ps. 28 (29): 2; Exod. 20: 12.

many persons, both men and women *and so on, as written above*
[*pp. 200—2*].

At the end: Out of so many we have concentrated on these cases
because as a whole they are too numerous and long to be included
in our present letter. With humble devotion we ask your holiness
and urge you in the Lord's name to give credence to the letters and
envoys most carefully describing all these matters, sent by brethren of the Order which that godly man both instituted and
founded; and to grant their petitions, which we know redound to
the praise of Almighty God, the honour and advantage of Holy
Church Universal, and also the unshakeable strengthening of this
praiseworthy order, which is our Father's new foundation and in
which countless souls have been saved by him. We should add that
in our judgement this man, whose name we have given before and
must constantly repeat, lacked none of the attributes of holiness,
and so has obviously not been deprived of the rewards attendant
upon his holy merits. Since there are so many clear indications of
his holiness and blessedness, we consider it only just that the
merits of a man who we believe has received such great rewards in
heaven through God's favour should be celebrated and his intercession sought upon earth through yours.

[5] *Letter from Master R(oger) and the chapter of the Order of Sempringham to the pope*

To our most revered lord and father Innocent, by God's grace
pope, Roger the humble servant and both devoted and proper slave
of his holiness, and the whole chapter of the Order of Sempringham send greetings and all reverence, wishing him a long life
and everlasting joy.

Dearest father, just as your holiness knows that it is sacrilege to
obstruct or diminish God's glory and the Church's honour, so we
know that not wishing to search them out and increase them
counts as the sin of laziness and negligence in his children. For if
we are told so frequently by the psalmist 'to give unto the Lord
glory and honour, give unto the Lord the glory due unto His
name',[1] if we are commanded by the judgement of the law and
divine decree to honour our father and mother, what a sin it is to
detract from the glory offered to God, what an offence not to pay
the honour enjoined by God as due to our parents! Therefore,

f. 118ᵛ preceptis diuinis astringimur 'annuntiare inter | gentes gloriam eius, in omnibus populis mirabilia eius',[1] contemptus crimen ueremur si que a Deo manifestataᵃ sunt nobis, uestre excellentie et aliis pandere negligamus. Glorificauit se ipsum Deus pater, honorificauit matrem nostram, ecclesiam suam, pre oculis nostris per quemdam filium suum patrem nostrum G(ilebertum) de Sempingham, cuius opera mirifica, quia Deum omnium opificem ex quo sunt commendant,ᵇ uos quoque hominum patrem credimus letificatura, iuxta illud: 'filius sapiens letificat patrem';[2] uenerabilem quoque matrem nostram sanctam Romanam ecclesiam, cui Deo auctore presidetis, non minus reddent iocundam: hec enim pia mater nostra, sicut de filiorum cui semper studet gaudet multiplicatione, ita de eorum magnificentia gloriatur.

Hinc est quod non priuatam gloriam nostram, Deus scit, queritantes, sed Dei et sanctorum gratie aggratulantes, ea que de memorato patre nostro nouimus, que ad laudem Dei sunt, diuino timore et amore ducti, ex consilio magnorum et auctenticorum uirorum uestre duximus proponere sanctitati ut, cum ad apostolicam et sancte Romane ecclesie peruenerint notitiam, laus Dei et exultatio ecclesie non modicum inde sumat incrementum. Verum ne prolixi-

f. 119 tas orationis et dicendi | facultas epistolarem modum excedant si in presenti pagina textus uite ipsius et signorum tam in uita quam post mortem factorum comprehendantur, ea in aliis scriptis, sigillis et testimoniis tam nostris quam aliorum Anglicane ecclesie prelatorum munitis, plenius explicamus, quorum ueritati in uerboᶜ Domini et in animam nostram iurati attestamur. Preter illa namque que per eum operatus est Deus miracula, que sunt manifeste sanctitatis inditia, talem nouimus eius a puero conuersationem, ita preter modernam humane uite consuetudinem scimus eum uixisse, quod tota ipsius uita magnum mundo aparuit miraculum. Sed et manifesti labores ipsius, non solum in construendis monasteriis, sed etiam in fundandis et sustentandis pauperum et infirmorum mansionibus, non sine magne admirationis uirtute clarescunt. Sane, si signa queruntur curationum, multa sunt que uidimus, plura que audiuimus, et innumera que negglectui tradita ignoramus. Que autem scimus hec testamur, et que nouimus ecce coram Deo et

---

ᵃ manifestata *Foreville;* manifesta *LcOd*   ᵇ uel mirificant *s.l. Lc*¹; mirificant *Od*
ᶜ *Perhaps* uerbum *(Winterbottom)*

---

[1] Ps. 104 (105): 1–2.
[2] Prov. 15: 20.

since God's commandments oblige us 'to proclaim his glory among the nations and his wondrous works among all people',[1] we fear to incur the accusation of contempt if we fail to display to your excellency and to other men those works made manifest to ourselves by God. Before our very eyes God our father has brought glory upon Himself and has honoured our mother, His Church, by means of one of His sons, our father, Gilbert of Sempringham. His wonderful works, because they exalt God, maker of all, from whom they come, will, we believe, also bring joy to you as the father of men, according to the saying 'a wise son maketh a glad father';[2] moreover, these achievements will make our venerable mother the holy Roman church, over which by God's authority you preside, equally joyful; for as our holy mother always looks to and rejoices in the increase of her sons, so she in turn takes pride in their greatness.

God knows, we do not seek glory for ourselves, but we give thanks to the grace of God and His saints. And so, swayed by the fear and love of God and advised by great men of authority, we have decided to lay before your holiness what we have learnt about our same father which tends to God's praise; that when it reaches the attention of the pope and the holy Roman church, God's praise and the rejoicing of His Church may receive from it no small increase. But if we included in our present account the details of his career and the miracles performed both in his lifetime and since his death, our lengthy phrases and fluent speech would overrun a letter's bounds. Thus we describe these matters more fully in other letters and in evidence authenticated by our seals and those of other prelates of the English church. That these are true we confirm with a solemn oath upon the Lord's word and on our soul. For as well as those miracles—clear signs of holiness—which God performed by his means, such was the way of life we know he led from childhood on, so differently (as we know) did he live from the modern custom, that this man's entire life appeared to the world like a great miracle. What is more, his well-known achievements, not only building monasteries but also founding and maintaining houses for the poor and infirm, is famous and a source of great inspiration. If examples of his cures are sought, there are many that we have seen, even more that we have heard about, and countless numbers about which through neglect we know nothing. But what we know we testify to, and behold, we declare before God and

uobis, uniuersorum patre et pastore, quia non mentimur.[a] Ad
tumbam eius ceci uident, claudi ambulant, muti loquntur, parali-
tici restaurantur, febricitantes frigescunt, ydropici detumescunt,
surdi audiunt, demoniaci liberantur,[1] et alia morborum genera |
f. 119ᵛ curantur, que alibi expressa hic non memorantur.

Cum ergo tam sancte uixerit, tot et tantis sanctitatis indiciis
claruerit, quis non auderet sanctum illum estimare, quis non sanctum Dei gaudeat proclamare? Sed quoniam nonnisi per apostolice
sedis conniuentiam fas est alicuius nomen sanctum predicare,
uestrum qui estis lux mundi, sal terre, uicarius Petri immo Christi
flagitamus consilium,[2] petimus assensum, obsecramus in Domino
misericordiam, ut ad laudem et profectum fidei tam preclara
Domini lucerna erigatur super candelabrum, ut qui ingrediuntur
lumen uideant, tam preciosa margarita a lutea gleba sub qua
obruitur effodiatur ut possint inde negotiari[3] qui sponsi presto-
lantur aduentum, et memoratum uirum de loco quo iacet humatus
erectum in eminentiori condiri et canonizatum sanctorum cathalogo conscribi iubere dignemini, quatinus in diebus uestris, sicut
in aliorum retro Romanorum pontificum temporibus, ecclesia Dei
qui tantam uobis optulit occasionem sullimetur, honorificetur,
debitam gratiam et gloriam consequatur. Nos autem memoriam
uestri et dominorum cardinalium faciemus semper in orationibus
nostris, nomenque uestrum martirologio nostro insertum die
depositionis uestre quotannis in perpetuum celebrabimus, pro
f. 120 spiritus uestri[b] commendatione | per omnia facientes sicut pro
prelato ordinis nostri defuncto.

Ad hec sanctitati uestre uice nostra insinuanda dilectos fratres
nostros presentium baiulos cum hac testificationis nostre pagina
ceterisque scriptis et negociis nostris expediendis, ad sedem apostolicam destinamus, uiros quantum experti sumus fide dignos et
probate religionis, quos petimus per clementiam Dei et beatis-
simorum apostolorum Petri et Pauli uestra pia paternitas habeat
commendatos, eorumque iustis postulationibus, que ad religionis
profectum fiunt, grato assensu annuere dignetur.

---

[a] *Something is wrong with this sentence; we give what is clearly the general sense*   [b] nostri
L*c*

---

[1] Cf. Matt. 11: 5.
[2] Cf. Matt. 5: 13–14; St Bernard, *De consideratione*, iv. 7. 23 (*Opera*, iv. 466); pp. 148–9.
[3] Cf. Luke 11: 33; Matt. 13: 46.

before you, the father and shepherd of us all, that what we say is true. At this man's tomb the blind see, the lame walk, the dumb speak, the paralysed are restored, the fevered grow cool, the dropsical lose their swelling, the deaf hear, those possessed with devils are set free,[1] and other kinds of illness are cured which, because they are described elsewhere, are not recorded here.

Since he lived such a virtuous life and was distinguished by so many great signs of holiness, who then would dare not reckon him holy, who would not rejoice to proclaim him God's saint? But because it is only lawful to call someone holy with the approval of the Holy See, we beg your advice, you who are 'the light of the world, the salt of the earth', the vicar of Peter or rather of Christ;[2] we ask your approval, we beg for your mercy in the Lord that, for the glory and advantage of our faith, the Lord's candle which shines so brightly may be lifted 'on a candlestick, that they which come in may see the light': that a pearl of such great price[3] may be plucked from the muddy field where it lies buried so that those who await the coming of the bridegroom may traffic with it: that you may give orders for this man to be taken from where he lies buried and interred in a more eminent place, and that when he has been canonized you may deign to order him to be entered in the lists of saints. Thus has God offered you so great an opportunity that in your days, just as in those of other previous Roman popes, His Church may be exalted and honoured, securing the grace and glory which rightly belong to it. For our part we shall always remember you and the lords cardinals in our prayers. When we have placed your name in our martyrology, we shall celebrate it on the day of your death every year in perpetuity, and perform all rites for the commendation of your soul as for a deceased prelate of our Order.

To recommend our findings to your holiness on our behalf, we are sending to the Holy See our dearly beloved brethren who carry our letter together with this account of our evidence and other documents and business to be dealt with. These men so far as we have experience of them are trustworthy and of proved religious life, and we ask through the mercy of God and the most blessed Apostles Peter and Paul that you, holy father, may accept their credentials, and may favour with your gracious approval their just requests, which are made for the advancement of the religious life.

[6] *Littere testimoniales H(uberti) archiepiscopi Cantuariensis ad
dominum papam Innocentium*[1]

Sanctissimo patri ac domino I(nnocentio), Dei gratia summo pontifici, H(ubertus), diuina permissione Cantuariensis ecclesie
minister humilis, totius Anglie primas, salutem et debitam patri ac
domino in omnibus reuerentiam.

Dum periculose presumat taciturnitas humana supprimere
quod dignatur deitas reuelare, dignum credo ut reuelatam
hominibus Dei gloriam ad salutem credentium ecclesia faciat
manifestam. Sane quanti meriti fuerit uir uenerabilis magister
G(ilebertus), primus ordinis de Sempingham institutor et fundator, quantumque per eum fuerit religio propagata, ad uestram,
pater, credo notitiam uel saltem audientiam peruenisse. Scio
f. 120ᵛ   utique ut hiis que | de eo uidi et notaui dum uiueret perhibeam tes-
timonium ueritatis, quod sancte conuersationis fuit, quod cultum
religionis summo opere propagare studuit, adeo ut incredibilem
multitudinem religiosarum feminarum et fratrum ordinis quem
instituit reliquerit moriens, cum ante eum nullus ordinis illius,
immo nec etiam ordo ipse fuisset inuentus. Scio quoque quod et
adhuc floret et mirabiliter propagatur ab eo inchoata et instituta
religio, adeo quod meritis ipsius et miraculo hoc censeant omnes
adscribendum.

Nec in hoc solum eiusdem sancti uiri merita propalat Deus, sed
et in multis et magnis miraculis que per eum, ut pro certo didici,
dignatus est operari. Attamen cum rumor miraculorum eius ad me
primo peruenisset, nolui statim fidem fame adhibere, sed religiosis
et discretis uiris de partibus illis scripsi, scilicet de Brunna, de
Swinesheued, de Croxtuna, de Barlinga abbatibus, et de Kyma et
de Chikessand et de Cateleia prioribus, ut ipsi ad locum sepulchri
eiusdem sancti uiri pariter accedentes diligenter et sollicite, tam
per eos qui curati dicebantur quam per eorum testes fideles, de
morborum et curationum ueritate, et de opinione eorumdem
inquirerent, et cum miraculorum serie tam uobis, pater, quam
f. 121   mihi inquisitam inde rescriberent ueritatem. | Ipsi autem, man-
datum meum fideliter executi, in eadem forma mihi super hoc
rescripserunt in qua ab eisdem uestre scribitur sanctitati.

Letter 6 *LcOd*

---

[1] Also in *EEA* iii, no. 608.

[6] *Testimonial letter from H(ubert) archbishop of Canterbury to*
Pope Innocent[1]

To his most holy father and lord I(nnocent), by God's grace pope, H(ubert), by divine permission the humble servant of the church of Canterbury, primate of all England, sends greetings and that reverence in all matters due to a father and lord.

Since only at their peril do men venture silently to conceal what God is pleased to disclose, I consider it right that the Church should proclaim God's glory, which has been revealed to men for the salvation of believers. Now I am sure, father, that news has come to your attention, or at least to your hearing, of the great virtues of the holy man Master Gilbert, who first began and founded the Order of Sempringham, and of how greatly the religious life has spread through him. I know assuredly that I must testify truthfully to what I observed about him and observed while he was alive: his conduct was saintly, and he devoted enormous energy to spreading the practice of religion, with the result that when he died he left an amazing number of religious women and brethren in the Order which he began. Before him there had been no one belonging to that Order, or rather the Order itself had not even been established. I know also that the religious rule he founded and organized is still flourishing and spreading so wonderfully that everyone considers it a miracle and attributes it to his merits.

God displays the virtues of this holy man not by this alone, but also by the many great miracles which He has seen fit to perform, to my certain knowledge, by his means. However, when the rumour of his miracles first reached me, I was unwilling to trust common talk straight away, but wrote to religious and discerning men of those parts, namely to the abbots of Bourne, Swineshead, Croxton, and Barlings and the priors of Kyme, Chicksands, and Catley. I instructed them to meet together at the place of this holy man's burial and thoroughly and carefully to inquire into the truth of the illnesses and the cures, and opinion concerning them, both from those who were said to be healed and also from reliable witnesses; I asked them to reply both to you, father, and to me with the facts they had discovered, together with a list of the miracles. These men have faithfully carried out my mandate; they have written to me about this affair in a document identical with that which they have drawn up for your Holiness.

Cum igitur, pater sancte, ad uos pertineat prouidere ne 'lucerna hec ulterius sub modio abscondatur sed super candelabrum posita luceat omnibus in domo Domini exsistentibus',[1] uestre supplico sanctitati quatinus, tot et tantorum religiosorum qui uobis scribunt fideli testimonio comprobato, secundum quod eundem sanctum uirum meruisse et Deo placere noueritis, in negotio illo ad honorem Dei procedatis. Commendo[a] autem paternitati uestre presentium latores, G(amelum) et W., fideles et discretos canonicos ordinis de Sempingham, obnixe supplicans quatinus intuitu Dei et nostri eos habere uelit uestra paternitas commendatos. Valeat paternitas uestra in Domino.

[7] *Littere regis testimoniales ad papam*[2]

Reuerendo domino et patri in Christo I(nnocentio), Dei gratia summo pontifici, I(ohannes) eadem gratia rex Anglie, dominus Hibernie, dux Normannie et Aquitanie, comes Andegavie, salutem et debitam ac deuotam in omnibus reuerentiam.

Ea que uobis dominus Cantuariensis scribit super sanctitate magistri G(ileberti) de Sempingham uera esse credimus, et fama eadem de eo predicat in regno nostro.[b] Teste me ipso | apud Eboracum .ĩi. die Martis.[c]

f. 121ᵛ

[8] *Epistola archiepiscopi ad episcopos et abbates exhortans eos ad scribendum*

Hubertus Dei gratia Cantuariensis archiepiscopus, tocius Anglie primas, uenerabilibus in Christo fratribus W(illelmo) Lundoniensi, E(ustachio) Eliensi,[d] G(alfrido) Couentrensi, eadem gratia episcopis, et uenerabilibus uiris I(ohanni) Sancti Albani, W(altero) de Waltham et M(artino) de Certerseia, abbatibus,[3] salutem in auctore salutis.

---

[a] commendo *Lh corr.;* commendendo *Lc (and Lh) (cf. p. 234 n. b);* commendando *Od*
Letter 7 *LcOd*   [b] *Od adds:* Supplicamus igitur paternitati uestre quatinus nuncios fratrum eiusdem ordinis de Semp(yngham) in hiis que secundum Deum a uobis postulauerint cum ad uos peruenerint si placet exaudire et promouere uelitis. Valete.
[c] *Od adds:* Similia quoque et ceteri magnates scripserunt domino pape testimonia quorum tenorem huic opusculo longum esset interserere.
Letter 8 *LcOd*   [d] Eliensi *Brooke;* Eliensis *Lc (def. Od)*

Holy father, it is your duty to see that 'this candle is no longer hidden under a bushel but is placed upon a candlestick to give its light to all that are in the house'.[1] Therefore, when you have tested the evidence submitted to you in good faith by so many distinguished religious, I beg your holiness to act in the affair so as to promote God's honour according to your knowledge of this holy man's deserts and God's will. I also commend to you, father, the bearers of these letters G(amel) and W., who are faithful and prudent canons belonging to the Order of Sempringham, and I earnestly request that for God's sake and our own you may receive them, father, in accordance with our recommendation.

Farewell, father, in the Lord.

[7] *Testimonial letter from the king to the pope*[2]

To his reverend lord and father in Christ I(nnocent), by God's grace pope, J(ohn), by the same grace king of England, lord of Ireland, duke of Normandy and Aquitaine, count of Anjou, sends greetings and proper and devout reverence in all things.

We believe that what the archbishop of Canterbury writes to you concerning the holiness of Master Gilbert of Sempringham is true, and it is confirmed by popular opinion about him in our kingdom. Witness myself at York, the second day of March.

[8] *Letter from the archbishop to bishops and abbots urging them to write*

Hubert, by God's grace archbishop of Canterbury, primate of all England, to his venerable brothers in Christ W(illiam) of London, E(ustace) of Ely, G(eoffrey) of Coventry, by the same grace bishops, and to the venerable J(ohn) of St Albans, W(alter) of Waltham, and M(artin) of Chertsey, abbots,[3] greetings in the author of our salvation.

---

[1] Luke 11: 33; Matt. 5: 15; etc.

[2] John's presence at York in early Mar. 1201 is attested by several charters: cf. T. D. Hardy, *Rotuli Literarum Patentium*, i, Introduction, *Itinerary of King John* (Record Commission, 1835).

[3] William of Sainte-Mère-Eglise, bishop of London 1198/9–1224 (*Fasti*, i. 2); Eustace, bishop of Ely (see p. 170 n. 4); Geoffrey Muschamp, bishop of Coventry 1198–1208; John de Cella, abbot of St Albans 1195–1214; Master Walter of Ghent, abbot of Waltham, 1184–1201 (died 2 May); Master Martin, abbot of Chertsey 1197–1206 (*Heads*, pp. 39, 67, 188). This letter is calendared in *EEA* iii, no. 609.

Pro meritis sancti uiri magistri G(ileberti) de Sempingham,
quem Deus dignatus est miraculis illustrare apud homines extol-
lendis, domino pape scripsimus in hac forma: Sanctissimo patri et
domino I(nnocentio), Dei gratia summo pontifici, H(ubertus) permissione diuina *et cetera*,[a] salutem *et cetera*. Cum periculose presumat taciturnitas humana supprimere *et cetera ut supra*. . . .

Vestram igitur uniuersitatem exoramus quatinus, considerata
hac litterarum nostrarum continentia inspectisque religiosorum
uirorum scriptis patentibus que uobis super hoc presentium
latores ostendent, in ea forma quam uideritis competere, secundum datam uobis a Deo super hoc intelligentiam, litteras uestras
uelitis formare et domino pape per ituros ad eum eosdem nuntios
destinare.

[9] *Epistola W(illelmi) Lundoniensis episcopi*

Reuerentissimo domino et patri[b] I(nnocentio), Dei gratia summo
pontifici, W(illelmus), diuina permissione Londoniensis ecclesie
minister, salutem et tam deuotum quam debitum in omnibus obe-
f. 122 dientie | famulatum.

Quoniam ea que Dominus pro dilatanda sui nominis gloria
modernis temporibus manifestare dignatus est non sunt digna
latere sub modio, sed super candelabrum ponenda,[1] ut lucem
ceteris ad augmentum fidei simul et salutis amministrent, licet per
se clara satis et gloriosa consistant, oportunum tamen est ut a
sacrosancta Romana ecclesia, de qua cetere per orbem terrarum
late diffuse fundamentum habent religionis et honestatis, auctoritatem uenerationis accipiant, ut sic a cunctis deuocius et licentius
honorentur. Sane quante fuerit uir sanctitatis et innocentie magister G(ilebertus) de Sempingham primus ordinis illius institutor et
rector, quantumque tempore suo religionem ordinis quam instituit
prouexerit et ampliauerit, ad notitiam sedis Romane iampridem
peruenisse credendum est. Verumptamen quanta miraculorum
insignia, sicut a cunctis penes nos publice predicatur, per illius
sancti uiri merita post transitum ipsius frequenter ille qui in
sanctis suis semper est mirabilis operatus sit, nec sic euidenter nisi

---

[a] *Lc mg. refers back to p. 212*
Letter 9 *LcOd*   [b] domino et patri *Lc;* patri et domino *Lc corr., Od*

---

[1] Cf. Matt. 5: 15; Luke 11: 33; etc.

Since God has deigned to make him famous for miracles which deserve celebration amongst men, we have written to the lord pope urging the merits of the holy Master Gilbert of Sempringham in this form: To his most holy father and lord I(nnocent), by God's grace pope, Hubert by divine permission *etc.* greetings *etc.* Since only at their peril do men venture silently to conceal *etc. as above*....

When you have thought over the contents of our letter and examined the unsealed letters from the religious about this affair, which the bearers of this document will show you, we beg you all, according to such understanding of this matter as God may have given you, to draw up your own letters, couched in terms you think appropriate, and to send them to the pope by those same messengers who are about to visit him.

[9] *Letter of W(illiam), bishop of London*

To the most revered lord and father I(nnocent), by God's grace pope, W(illiam), by divine permission the servant of the church of London, sends greetings and the devout and proper service of obedience in all matters.

It is wrong that those things which in recent times the Lord has seen fit to reveal for the greater knowledge of His glorious name should be hidden under a bushel; rather they should be placed upon a candlestick,[1] serving to give light to other men to the strengthening both of their faith and of their hope of salvation. Although such manifestations are sufficiently obvious and wonderful in their own right, nevertheless it is appropriate that they be deemed worthy of reverence by the holy Roman church, from whom the other churches spread throughout the world derive the foundation of religion and of their good life. Then all men will accord them greater devotion and authority. Now doubtless it long ago came to the attention of the Roman See that Master Gilbert of Sempringham, the first founder and Master of that Order, was a very holy and upright man; also that during his lifetime he greatly advanced and increased the religious observance of the Order which he founded. However, it is not so easily appreciated, except from the truthful evidence of eminent and religious men, how great are the miraculous signs (that is what everyone here openly proclaims them) which He who through His saints always inspires wonder has often performed through the merits of this holy man

per magnorum et religiosorum uirorum ueridicum testimonium[a]
eidem constare posse dinoscitur. Vestrum igitur erit, pater reuer-
ende, auditis et pro certo cognitis tot et tantorum uirorum super
f. 122[v] hac re multiplicatis testimoniis, prouidere quali | et quanto sit
honore dignus in terris, qui ob suorum magnitudinem meritorum
habundanter apud Deum honorari creditur in celis.

[10] *Epistola G(alfridi) Couentrensis episcopi*

Reuerendo domino et patri sanctissimo I(nnocentio), Dei gratia
sacrosancte Romane ecclesie summo pontifici, G(odefredus),
diuina permissione Couentrensis ecclesie humilis minister, salutem et tam deuotam quam debitam reuerentiam.

Inter cetera sullimitatis uestre insignia, que immensa Christi
bonitas nobis dignata est exibere, etiam illud sanctitatis[b] uestre
titulis non immerito credimus ascribendum, uidelicet quod per
merita magistri G(ileberti) de Sempingham, a cuius institutione
ordo ille de Sempingham originem sumpsit et fundamentum,
crebro et frequenter, ut dicitur, miracula uestris temporibus Deus
operatur. Sicut enim ex certa relatione multorum uirorum fide
dignorum recepimus, et maxime illorum qui ex parte uenerabilis
patris nostri domini Cantuariensis ad inquirendam huius rei ueritatem ad sepulchrum predicti boni uiri missi fuerant, quanta sint
apud Deum ipsius merita signorum et uirtutum declarat frequentia. Supplicamus itaque uestre sanctitati deuotissime, quatinus
uestra deliberet prouidentia quid super hoc ad honorem Dei et
sancte ecclesie fuerit statuendum.

[11] *Epistola I(ohannis) Norwicensis episcopi*[1]

f. 123 Reuerendo domino et patri sanctissimo I(nnocentio), Dei gratia
sacrosancte Romane ecclesie summo pontifici, I(ohannes), diuina
permissione Norwicensis ecclesie humilis minister, salutem et tam
deuotam quam debitam obedientiam et reuerentiam.

Inter cetera sullimitatis uestre insignia que immensa Christi
bonitas nobis dignata est exhibere, etiam illud sanctitatis uestre
titulis non immerito credimus ascribendum, uidelicet quod per

---

[a] ueridicum testimonium *Brooke;* ueridico testimonio *LcOd (rightly if we delete* per*)*
Letter 10 *Lc (Od gives much of the same material, but regards it as the letter of the bishop of Nor-*
wich = *Letter 11)*   [b] sanctitatis *Mynors;* sanctitati *Lc (also Od: see previous n.)*

after his death. Thus, reverend father, when you have heard and verified the substantial evidence on this subject submitted by so many worthy men, it will fall to you to decide what earthly distinction befits a man who, we believe, because of his great merits receives lavish honour before God in heaven.

[10] *Letter of G(eoffrey) bishop of Coventry*

To his revered lord and most holy father I(nnocent), by God's grace pope of the holy Roman church, G(eoffrey), by divine permission humble servant of the church of Coventry, sends greetings and both devout and proper reverence.

Among the other signs of your majesty which Christ in His great goodness has seen fit to show us, one which we consider should rightly be added to your holiness's renown is this: that through the merits of Master Gilbert of Sempringham who began the Order of Sempringham, giving it both origin and foundation, in your lifetime God is working miracles time and time again, as it is said. According to what we have heard from the faithful account of many trustworthy men, and especially from those who were sent to this good man's tomb to inquire into the facts of the matter on behalf of our venerable father the archbishop of Canterbury, the frequent occurrence of signs and miracles makes clear that his merits find great favour with God. Thus most devoutly we beg your holiness to consider in your wisdom what decision should be taken about this to further the honour of God and His holy Church.

[11] *Letter of J(ohn) bishop of Norwich* [1]

To his revered lord and most holy father I(nnocent), by God's grace pope of the holy Roman church, J(ohn), by divine permission humble servant of the church of Norwich, sends greetings, and obedience and reverence both devout and proper.

Among the other signs of your majesty which Christ in His great goodness has seen fit to show us, one which we consider should rightly be added to your holiness's renown is this: that through the

Letter 11 *Lc (for Od see on Letter 10)*

---

[1] John de Grey, bishop of Norwich 1200–14 (*Fasti*, ii. 56).

merita magistri G(ileberti) de Sempingham, a cuius institutione ordo ille de Sempingham originem sumpsit et fundamentum, late in partibus nostris ad honorem sancte ecclesie sancte religionis propagatio*a* crescit et aumentatur. Hinc est quod sanctitati uestre duximus supplicandum quatinus nuntios fratrum predicti ordinis de Sempingham in hiis que secundum Deum a uobis postulauerint cum ad uos uenerint, si placet, exaudire et promouere uelitis.

[12] *Epistola G(ileberti) Roffensis episcopi*[1]

Reuerentissimo domino et patri in Christo karissimo I(nnocentio), Dei gratia sacrosancte Romane ecclesie summo pontifici, G(ilebertus) diuina miseratione Roffensis ecclesie minister, salutem et tam deuotum quam debitum omnimode subiectionis et obedientie famulatum.

Scio, pater, scio quod in hiis que Dei sunt[2] delectetur anima uestra, presertim ut in diebus uestris cultus ecclesie sancte crescat f. 123ᵛ et deuotio fidelium augeatur; ea|propter, domine, sanctitatem uestram desidero non latere quod in partibus nostris fuit uir quidam nomine Gilebertus, uite quidem sancte, opinionis illese, conuersationis honeste, plurimarum domorum religiosarum fundator egregius que temporibus illius inchoate, de die in diem per gratiam Dei in melius proficiunt et in diuinis obsequiis augmentantur. Nunc autem ipsius merita que gesserat in uita non sinunt defuncti memoriam occultari; fiunt etenim ad tumbam eius, ut publice predicatur, de diuino nutu admiranda miracula, prout de litteris super hoc ad uos missis plenius poteritis edoceri. Vnde et ad cumulum ueritatis credite paruitatis mee suffragium ad celsitudinem uestram duxi*b* litteratorie transmittendum, ut de tam sancto uerbo et tam manifesto quod sanctitas uestra faciendum decreuerit ordinare dignemini.

Sub eadem forma scripsit abbas de Waltham.

[13] *Littere Bangorensis episcopi*[3]

Reuerendo domino et patri I(nnocentio), Dei gratia summo pontifici, R(obertus), eiusdem permissione Bangorensis episcopus, salutem et debitam cum omni deuotione subiectionem.

a propagatio *Foreville;* propago *Lc (def. Od)*
Letter 12 *Lc*   *b* duxi *Winterbottom;* duxit *Lc*
Letter 13 *LcOd*

merits of Master Gilbert of Sempringham who began the Order of
Sempringham, giving it both origin and foundation, there has been
a great flowering of holy and religious life, which is growing in
strength throughout our country to the honour of Holy Church.
For this reason we have decided to ask that your holiness may
graciously listen to messengers from the brethren of this Order of
Sempringham when they come to you, and that you may assist
them in those godly requests which they will make of you.

[12] Letter of G(ilbert) bishop of Rochester[1]

To his most revered lord and dearest father in Christ I(nnocent), by
God's grace pope of the holy Roman church, G(ilbert), by divine
mercy servant of the church of Rochester, sends greetings and the
devout and proper service of all submission and obedience.

I am fully aware, father, that your soul delights in the things that
are God's[2] and you are especially concerned that in your lifetime
the worship offered by Holy Church should increase and the devotion of the faithful be strengthened. Therefore, my Lord, I desire
your holiness to know that there lived in our country a man called
Gilbert, who was holy in his manner of living, unblemished in
reputation and virtuous in behaviour; he was the distinguished
founder of many religious houses, which were begun in his lifetime
and are daily by God's grace making great progress and increasing
in the service of God. Moreover, the good deeds which he performed while alive do not permit his memory to fade now that he is
dead, for according to popular report amazing miracles inspired by
God are taking place at his tomb. You will be able to learn more
from the letters which have been sent to you about this. On this
ground, to add to the body of believed truth, I have thought it right to
send your highness my petition in this letter, humbly requesting
that on the basis of such holy and indisputable evidence you may
give orders for whatever your holiness decides should be done.

The abbot of Waltham has written in the same terms.

[13] Letter of the bishop of Bangor[3]

To the reverend lord and father I(nnocent), by God's grace pope,
R(obert), by his same permission bishop of Bangor, sends greetings and proper submission with all devotion.

---

[1] Gilbert de Glanville, bishop of Rochester (*Fasti*, ii. 76).   [2] Cf. Matt. 22: 21.
[3] Robert of Shrewsbury, bishop of Bangor 1197–?1212–13.

Vt felicis memorie magistri G(ileberti), quondam prioris de Sempingham, merita ad honorem eius qui in sanctis suis gloriosus est, ad exemplum quoque aliorum in lucem prodeant, et ut ipse |

f. 124 condignam meritis in ecclesia Dei uenerationem*a* obtineat, excellentie uestre cum aliorum testimonio notificare dignum censui, sicut publica fama predicat et per diuersas Anglie partes notorium habetur, quod ad memoriam ipsius crebro fiunt miracula. Et non solum a populo post ostensa miracula sanctus iudicatur, uerum et dum superstes esset, adeo sancte conuersationis extitit, domibusque religiosis fundandis aliisque piis operibus excercendis tam studiose et efficaciter preter humanas fere uires insudauit, quod adhuc uiuens sanctus Domini habebatur. Intellecta itaque, pater uenerande, huius rei ueritate multorum testimonio, prouidere uelit sanctitas uestra quatinus is*b* quem Deus miraculorum celebritate honorabilem facit inter homines ab hominibus ea qua decet reuerentia honoretur, ut et Domini magnificentia collaudetur in sanctis suis et ipsis in ecclesia Dei honor debitus exhibeatur.*c*

[14] *Littere E(ustachii) Eliensis episcopi*

Sanctissimo patri ac domino dilectissimo I(nnocentio), Dei gratia summo pontifici, E(ustachius), diuina miseratione Eliensis ecclesie minister humilis, salutem et omnimode deuotionis obsequium.

Cum spiritus ubi uult spiret et occulta sint Dei iuditia, confidendum est de misericordia eius qui nunquam deest sperantibus

f. 124ᵛ in se,[1] quod illi sint ab eo retributionem multiplicem | recepturi quorum uita et conuersatio perseuerauerit usque in finem apud Deum et homines commendabilis, et honestati religionis extiterit ecclesiastice fructuosa. Vnde quia pro Gileberto de Sempingham, qui dies suos in honestate et in augmentando religionem domus Domini, ut publice creditur, consummauit dignatus est Dominus*d* post mortem in miraculis operari, sicut audiuimus et per litteras religiosorum et discretorum uirorum qui melius et plenius quam nos ueritatem inde nouerunt sanctitati uestre nuntiatur, uestre paternitatis prouidentie deuotissime supplicamus quatinus quod

---

a ueneratione *Lc*   *b* hiis *Lc*   *c* exibiatur *Lc*

Letter 14 *LcOd*   *d* dignatus est Dominus *Od (the order probably intended by the corrector of Lc);* Dominus dignatus est *Lc*

---

[1] Cf. John 3: 8; Prov. 30: 5.

In order that the merits of Master Gilbert of happy memory, formerly prior of Sempringham, may be brought to light to honour Him who is glorified through His saints and supply an example for others, and in order that this man may be venerated in God's Church in a way appropriate to his merits, I have judged it meet to inform your excellency, along with the evidence of others, of a matter well known throughout the different regions of England: that frequent miracles are taking place at the tomb of this man. And he is not only considered holy by the people after miracles have been witnessed; even while he was still with us he was so outstandingly holy in his way of life and he laboured so earnestly and strenuously, almost beyond the limits of human strength, founding religious houses and performing other pious works, that whilst still alive he was accounted a saint of the Lord. Thus, venerable father, when you have learned the truth of this matter from the evidence supplied by many men, may your holiness take steps so that he whom God is making worthy of honour amongst men by the fame of his miracles may be accorded all fitting reverence by them; so may the splendour of the Lord be exalted through His saints and due honour be shown them in the Church of God.

[14] *Letter of E(ustace) bishop of Ely*

To his most holy father and dearest lord I(nnocent), by God's grace pope, E(ustace), by divine mercy the humble servant of the church of Ely, sends greetings and the service of all devotion.

Since 'the wind bloweth where it listeth' and God's judgements are hidden from us, relying on the mercy of Him Who never fails those who put their trust in Him,[1] we must be confident that those will receive from Him a manifold reward who continue until death in life and behaviour acceptable to God and to men, bearing fruit in the good reputation of the religious life within the Church. According to popular belief Gilbert of Sempringham passed his days in all righteousness, increasing the religious life of the Lord's house. We have heard, and a report is being sent to your holiness in letters from religious and discriminating men who are better and more fully acquainted with the facts of the matter than we, that since his death the Lord has deigned to work miracles on his behalf. For this reason we most respectfully ask, father, that in your wisdom you may take that action over this affair which seems to

uestra discretio uiderit expedire super hoc ad honorem ecclesie et
gloriam Dei dignemini prouidere. Conseruet Dominus uos ecclesie sue sancte per tempora longa.*

[15] *Epistola I(ohannis) abbatis Sancti Albani*

Reuerentissimo patri et domino I(nnocentio), Dei gratia sacrosancte Romane ecclesie summo pontifici, I(ohannes), permissione
diuina minister humilis ecclesie sancti Albani, salutem et deuotum
tocius reuerentie et obedientie famulatum.

Cum immensa bonitas creatoris nulla tempora gratie sue largitate
uacua esse permittat, sed in salutem credentium ecclesiam suam
nunc ornare miraculis, nunc uelit misericorditer erudire flagellis,
f. 125 iam et uestris dignatur*b* temporibus eam copiosa gratie | plenitudine
preclara sanctorum merita declarando diuiniter illustrare. Iam enim
in ecclesia Anglicana per cuiusdam uiri sanctissimi Gileberti
nomine merita, qui primus ordinis de Sempingham institutor fuit et
rector, miraculorum uirtus et gloria reflorescit. Qui quidem uir
quante innocentie quanteque fuit sanctitatis, ad tumbam eius, ut
publice predicatur, gloriosissima sanitatum signa locuntur, prout
poterit excellentia uestra per litteras super hoc uobis destinatas*c*
patenter agnoscere. Ego igitur mirabilibus Dei credulus, et uirorum
uenerabilium et magnorum qui similiter uobis scribunt exempla
secutus, super hac re testimonium coram uobis litteris credidi per-
hibendum, ut prudentia uestra deliberet qualiter eum honorent
homines qui tanta gloria diuinitus honoratur.

Idem mandauerunt de Selebi et de Wardona abbates.[1]

[16] *Epistola abbatis et conuentus de Kirkestal*[2]

Reuerentissimo domino suo et patri in Christo dilectissimo
I(nnocentio), Dei gratia summo pontifici, deuoti filii sui abbas et
conuentus Sancte Marie de Kirkestal, salutem et tam deuotam
quam debitam subiectionem et reuerentiam.

Ne preclara Domini lucerna uitio taciturnitatis sub modio
obscuritatis diucius lateat,[3] paternitatis uestre pietati ea que de

---

  a *Od adds:* Sub tali et simili forma scripserunt alii episcopi.
  Letter 15 *LcOd*   *b* dignatur *Winterbottom;* dignata *LcOd*   *c* destinatas
uobis *Lc before correction*
  Letter 16 *Lc*

  [1] Richard abbot of Selby 1195–1214 (*Heads*, pp. 69–70); for Wardon see pp. 170–1.

your discerning mind most likely to enhance the church's honour and the glory of God. May the Lord preserve you over many years for His holy Church.

[15] *Letter of J(ohn) abbot of St Albans*

To his most revered father and lord I(nnocent), by God's grace pope of the holy Roman church, J(ohn), by divine permission the humble servant of the church of St Albans, sends greetings and the devout service of all reverence and obedience.

Our Creator in His great goodness does not allow any age to be bereft of His generous grace; for the salvation of believers it is His pleasure at one time to adorn His Church with miracles and at another to teach it by the merciful use of His scourge. But now in your lifetime He has seen fit to lighten it in divine fashion with the full abundance of His grace, by asserting the outstanding merits of His saints. For at this present time miracles are flowering once more in the English church in all their strength and beauty, through the merits of a most holy man, named Gilbert, who first founded and ruled the Order of Sempringham. The most wonderful demonstrations of healing at his tomb, which have received public acclaim, testify how guiltless and holy this man's life was; this your excellency may easily ascertain from letters which have been sent to you about the matter. Trusting, therefore, in God's wonders and following the example of the worthy and great men who are writing to you in a similar vein, I judged that I must offer you testimony in a letter. Then in your wisdom you may decide how best men should honour this man so gloriously singled out by God.

The abbots of Selby and Wardon have written in the same terms.[1]

[16] *Letter of the abbot and monks of Kirkstall*[2]

To their most revered lord and dearest father in Christ I(nnocent), by God's grace pope, his devoted sons the abbot and community of St Mary of Kirkstall send greetings, and submission and reverence both devout and proper.

Lest the Lord's bright candle be longer concealed under the bushel of obscurity by our sinful reticence,[3] we have decided to put down for you in this letter what we have heard concerning that

---

[2] Turgisius was abbot of Kirkstall (Yorks., Cistercian) 1192/3–1201/2 (*Heads*, p. 136).
[3] Cf. Matt. 5: 15; etc.

f. 125ᵛ uere uenerabili uiro magistro Gileberto, fun|datore et institutore ordinis de Sempingham audiuimus, presenti scripto significare decreuimus. Nouerit siquidem sancta paternitas uestra, sicut a uiris admodum religiosis et ueredicis accepimus, eum tam in uita quam in morte multis et innumerabilibus claruisse miraculis, ut in claudorum, cecorum et aliarum infirmitatum curatione. Magnam autem religionis propagationem quam, Deo auctore, late per Angliam instituit, quam ex magna parte inspeximus, laudabili ualde religione et uite honestate pollere noueritis indubitanter. Et quoniam singula eiusdem patris et ordinis nec uerbo nec scripto sufficimus explanare, excellentie uestre ea qua possimus deuocione supplicamus quatinus hiis que uenerabiles fratres ordinis de Sempingham uobis de uita predicti et felicis memorie G(ileberti) sub testimonio uirorum proposuerint auctenticorum fidem habeatis et eadem incunctanter facere dignemini, quia de Dei misericordia plurimum confidentes certi sumus quod in cathalogo sanctorum Dei miseratione et eius efficientibus meritis dignus est canonizari.

Simili modo scripserunt prior et conuentus de Giseburna et magister Columbus,ᵃ domini pape subdiaconus.[1]

[17] *Littere abbatum de Kyrchestede et de Reuesbi*[2]

f. 126 Innocentio, Dei gratia summo pontifici, Th.ᵇ de Kirkestede | et H(ugo) de Reuesbi dicti abbates ordinis Cisterciensis, salutem et tam debitam quam deuotam cum omni subiectione reuerentiam.

Quamuis signa que per magistrum G(ilebertum) de Sempingham post ipsius decessum operatus est Dominus, ut multi protestantur, non uiderimus, ex multa tamen confidentia sanctitatis eiusdem prospectaᶜ dum uiueret, et post mortem circumquaque signis radiantibus lucidius approbata, sed et immensa religionis propagatione per illius, ut credimus, merita cotidie reflorente, confidenter audemus tanti uiri uirtutibus testimonium ueritatis

---

ᵃ Columber *Lc before correction*

Letter 17 *Lc*   ᵇ *Reading of Lc uncertain (*h *Lh)*   ᶜ *Perhaps* perspecta *(Winterbottom), cf. p. 230*

[1] Roald occurs as prior of Guisborough (Yorks., Augustinian) 1199–1202 (*Heads*, p. 164). Master Columbus occurs as papal subdeacon and proctor for the archbishop of York in cases of 1201 and 1198×1204 (Cheney and Cheney, *Innocent III*, nos. 304, 588; cf. Cheney, *Innocent III and England*, pp. 149 n., 200 n.). He probably made several journeys from Rome to England and was there during the first inquiry into Gilbert's life and miracles in 1201.

truly venerable man Master Gilbert, who founded and instituted
the Order of Sempringham. For, holy father, you will know what
we have learnt from men of impeccable faith and truthfulness: that
this man was famous both in his lifetime and in his death for many,
nay countless miracles involving the healing of the lame, the blind,
and other infirmities. You will also surely know that the great
development in religious observance which, with God's help, he
promoted throughout England and which to a large extent we have
witnessed, draws its strength from his exemplary and upright religious life. And because we are unable either in speech or in writing
to describe every detail concerning our father and his Order, we
beg your excellency with all possible sincerity to trust what the
venerable brothers of the Order of Sempringham tell you about the
life of this Gilbert, of happy memory, on the evidence of reliable
men, and to do this without delay. For, relying above all upon the
mercy of God, we are sure that through God's pity and his own
effective merits he is worthy to be canonized and placed in the list
of saints.

The prior and community of Guisborough and Master Columbus,[1] *the
pope's subdeacon, have written in similar fashion.*

[17] *Letter of the abbots of Kirkstead and Revesby*[2]

To Innocent, pope by God's grace, (Thomas) abbot of Kirkstead
and H(ugh) abbot of Revesby, of the Cistercian Order, send greetings and reverence both devout and proper together with complete
submission.

We ourselves have not witnessed the miracles which many
affirm the Lord has performed by means of Master Gilbert of Sempringham since his death. Nevertheless we derive great assurance
from the holiness which was evident while he lived and which
since his death has been more clearly established by the radiance
of his miracles visible on every hand. Because, moreover, religious
observance has spread enormously and in our opinion is flourishing daily through his merits, we are emboldened confidently to
offer evidence concerning the truth of this great man's virtues and

---

[2] The abbot of Kirkstead (Lincs., Cistercian) could have been Richard (occurs from
before 1185 to 1199), but was much more probably Thomas (occurs 1202–6: *Heads*,
p. 136); the reading of Lc is far from clear; the abbot of Revesby was Hugh (occurs 1172
to after 1203: *Heads*, p. 140).

perhibere, nostrumque super eo iuditium uestre paternitati suggerere, dignum uidelicet fore maiori de cetero inter homines gloria
quem sanctis associatum fides nostra presumit.

Sub eadem forma scripserunt de Bardeneia et de Swinesheued abbates et
prior et conuentus de Bridlintuna.[1]

[18] *Littere decani et capituli Lincolniensis ecclesie*

Sanctissimo patri et domino I(nnocentio), Dei gratia summo pontifici, humiles filii sui R(ogerus) decanus et capitulum Lincolnie,[2]
salutem et tam deuotum quam debitum subiectionis et obedientie
famulatum.

Scimus, pater sanctissime, quod sanctitatis uestre constantie
congaudet uniuersalis ecclesia, que tanti pastoris illustrata exemplo secundum Deum proficit de die in diem; et quia in deuotione
f. 126ᵛ fidelium et religionis augmento | delectatur anima uestra, ea que
Deus temporibus uestris ad honorem ecclesie sue operari dignatus
est, discretioni uestre dignum duximus notificare. Vidimus utique
et nouimus uirum uite uenerabilis magistrum G(ilebertum), ordinis de Sempingham primum fundatorem et institutorem, quantum
ad humanum iuditium magne religionis, presbiterum bonum,
pudicum, mansuetum et pium. Plura etiamᵃ construxit monasteria,
quedam canonicorum, plura uero feminarum religiosissimarum,
que de die in diem proficiunt et incrementum suscipiunt. Audiuimus etiam post pretaxati uiri decessum eius meritis Dominum
plura operatum esse miracula. Vestre itaque discretionis erit,
secundum potestatem uobis desuper datam, super hoc prout ratio
dictauerit et Spiritus Sanctus intimauerit ordinare, ne (quod absit)
tanta lucerna sub modio abscondatur, sed super candelabrum
posita luceat omnibus qui in domo sunt.[3] Supplicamus igitur sanctitati uestre ut in cathalago sanctorum eum annumerare et sicut
credimus dignum canonizare dignemini gratiose.ᵇ

Letter 18 *LcOd*   ᵃ enim *Od*   ᵇ ne quod . . . gratiose *om. Lc*

---

[1] The abbot of Bardney was either Robert, occurs 1192, or Ralph de Rand, occurs
before 1206, deposed 1213/14; Elias, the prior of Bridlington occurs 1200–10 (*Heads*,
pp. 27, 154); for Swineshead, see p. 200 n. 1.

[2] Master Roger of Rolleston was dean of Lincoln *c.* 1195–1223 (*Fasti*, iii. 10).

[3] Cf. Matt. 5: 15; etc.

to submit to you, father, our testimony of him: which is that a man who in our belief has joined the saints will in future deserve greater glory amongst men.

The abbots of Bardney and Swineshead and the prior and community of Bridlington have written in the same terms.[1]

[18] *Letter of the dean and chapter of the church of Lincoln*

To our most holy father and lord I(nnocent), by God's grace pope, his humble sons R(oger), dean, and the chapter of Lincoln,[2] send greetings and the service both devout and proper of submission and obedience.

We know full well, most holy father, that the Universal Church, adorned by the example of so great a pastor, rejoices in your holiness's steadfast character and prospers daily in God's eyes. And because your soul delights in the devotion shown by the faithful and in the increase of religious observance, we think it right to inform your discerning mind of those works which God has deigned to perform to the honour of His Church during your lifetime. From the evidence of our own eyes we know that Master Gilbert, that man of venerable life who first founded and organized the Order of Sempringham, was a mighty example of the religious life, as far as mere men may judge, and a good priest, modest, gentle, and pious. In addition he built many monasteries, some for canons but many for the most dedicated women religious; these are flourishing daily and increasing in number. We have also heard that, since the death of this same man, through his merits the Lord has performed many miracles. Thus it will be a matter for your judgement, according to the power bestowed upon you from on high, to act in this affair prompted by reason and guided by the Holy Spirit; to ensure that such a great candle is not hidden under a bushel (God forbid!), but rather is placed upon a candlestick to give light to all who are in the house.[3] We ask therefore that your holiness may be pleased to add this man to the list of saints and to canonize him, as we think he deserves.

[19] *Littere A(cardi) abbatis de Barlinga*[1]

Reuerendo domino et patri I(nnocentio), Dei gratia summo pontifici, A(cardus) de Barlinga ⟨abbas⟩[a] et eiusdem loci conuentus,
salutem et debitam cum omni subiectione reuerentiam.

Auditis signis que per magistrum G(ilebertum) de Sempingham,
et in uita et post eius obitum, operatus est Dominus, necnon et[b]
multa eiusdem sanctitate perspecta dum uiueret, et immensa religionis propagatione per illius ut credimus merita cotidie reflorente, confidenter audemus tanti uiri uirtutibus testimonium
f. 127 perhibere | ueritatis, nostrumque super eo iuditium paternitati
uestre suggerere, dignum uidelicet fore maiori de cetero in terris
gloria et honore, quem in celis sanctis associatum indubitanter
presumimus, ne (quod absit) tanta lucerna sub modio abscondatur, sed pocius auctoritate[c] uestra super candelabrum posita
luceat omnibus qui in domo sunt,[2] et si excellentie uestre uisum
fuerit, tam in letaniis quam in priuatis orationibus locum habeat.

[20] *Littere W(alteri) prioris et conuentus de Kyrkeham*[3]

Sanctissimo domino et patri I(nnocentio), Dei gratia summo pontifici, Walterus humilis prior et conuentus canonicorum de Kirke-
ham, salutem et omnimodam reuerentiam et obedientiam.

Significamus sanctitati uestre quod magister G(ilebertus) sancte
recordationis, dignissimus institutor ordinis de Sempingham et
multarum domorum religionis deuotus fundator, sapientia, religione et preclaris uirtutibus in uita sua late claruit, et post obitum
suum multis miraculis prefulsit; cuius sanctitati tanto cercius testimonium perhibemus quanto uerius, cum uirum uirtutis et sapientie et gratia Dei plenum uidimus et cognouimus, et de miraculis
que post obitum eius Deus propter eum operatus est certo relatu
satis audiuimus. Supplicamus itaque sanctitati uestre ut in catho-
f. 127ᵛ logo | sanctorum eum annumerare et, sicut credimus dignum,
canonizare dignemini.

Letter 19 *Lc*   *ᵃ Supplied by Brooke*   *ᵇ Perhaps* ex *(Winterbottom), cf. p. 226*
ᶜ auctoritate *Lh;* auctore *Lc*
Letter 20 *Lc*

---

[1] For Acardus or Akarius see p. 205 n. 2.
[2] Cf. Matt. 5: 15; etc.
[3] This is puzzling, since Andrew seems, on other evidence, to have succeeded Walter

[19] *Letter of A(cardus) abbot of Barlings*[1]

To our revered lord and father I(nnocent), by God's grace pope, A(cardus) of Barlings and the community of this place send greetings and proper reverence with all submission.

We have heard of the miracles which Our Lord has performed by means of Master Gilbert of Sempringham, both during his lifetime and after his death. Because of his great holiness, which was evident while he lived, and the great spread of religious observance which in our opinion is flourishing daily through his merits, we are emboldened confidently to offer evidence concerning the truth of this great man's virtues and to submit to you, father, our testimony of him: which is that a man who we consider has most assuredly joined the saints in heaven will in future deserve greater glory and honour on earth. God forbid that this great candle should be hidden under a bushel; rather, on your authority, may it be placed upon a candlestick to give light to all who are in the house.[2] And, if your excellency sees fit, may he secure mention both in the litany and in our private devotions.

[20] *Letter of Prior W(alter) and the community of Kirkham*[3]

To our most holy lord and father I(nnocent), by God's grace pope, Walter the humble prior and the community of canons of Kirkham send greetings and all reverence and obedience.

We inform your holiness that Master Gilbert of holy memory, who was the most worthy originator of the Order of Sempringham and the devout founder of many religious houses, was famous far and wide during his lifetime for wisdom, religious life, and outstanding virtue, and since his death has shone out through many miracles. We offer testimony concerning his holiness all the more confidently because of its truth: we have seen and learnt to our complete satisfaction that he was a virtuous and wise man overflowing with God's grace; and from reliable sources we have heard sufficient information concerning the miracles which God has performed on his account after his death. Thus we ask that your holiness may add him to the list of saints and canonize him as we believe he deserves.

as prior of Kirkham by 1200 (*Heads*, p. 168); it is just possible that Walter was writing as ex-prior.

[21] *Littere R(ogeri) prioris et conuentus de Kyma*[1]

Reuerentissimo et karissimo domino I(nnocentio), Dei gratia summo pontifici, R(ogerus) prior humilisque conuentus canonicorum de Kima, salutem cum debita reuerentia.

Licet prophetam obmutuisse et a bonis quandoque siluisse nouerimus,[2] impietatis tamen esset negotium si pietatis opera que Dominus per merita uenerabilis uiri G(ileberti) de Sempingham sub oculis nostris operatus est sub silentio deperirent. Excellentie igitur uestre pro certo significamus prefatum uirum uenerabilem G(ilebertum) tam ex propriis redditibus et substantiis que ei de iure cesserant quam etiam nobilium procerum largitione plura construxisse monasteria, in quibus multa floret religio, multusque Deo militantium hactenus accreuit et cotidie accrescit numerus cum propriis meritis, tamen etiam prefati uiri pollens uirtutibus, multas enim uirtutes necdum carne solutus operatus est; qualiter uero uixerit, qualem diuino conspectui se uiuus exibuerit, miraculorum gloria post ipsius decessum e uestigio declarauit. Que ut succincta breuitate perstringantur, que ipsi uidimus, que etiam a uiris probatissimis accepimus, hec testamur, quia ad eius tumbam f. 128 ceci uident, claudi | ambulant, ydropici curantur, paralitici redintegrantur, multa morborum genera eliminantur, multi per ipsius merita tam in terra quam in mari optate quietis portui restituuntur.[3] Et quia nemo accendit lucernam et ponit eam sub modio, sed super candelabrum,[4] prefatum uirum uenerabilem dignum gloria arbitramur in terris, quem Dominus radiantibus signis, ut omnes credimus, coronauit in celis.

[22] *Littere G(alfridi) comitis Essexie*[5]

Reuerentissimo patri in Christo et domino I(nnocentio), Dei gratia summo pontifici, G(alfridus) filius Petri comes Essexie, salutem et debitum obedientie famulatum.

Ad aures uestras credo peruenisse quante sanctitatis et religionis magister G(ilebertus), qui fundator fuit ordinis de Sempingham et rector extiterit. Crebra namque miracula, ut pro certo

Letter 21 *Lc*   Letter 22 *Lc*

---

[1] See p. 204 n. 1.   [2] Cf. Ps. 38: 3 (39: 2).
[3] Cf. Matt. 11: 5.   [4] Cf. Matt. 5: 15; etc.
[5] Geoffrey FitzPeter, earl of Essex 1199–1213, chief justiciar 1198–1213.

[21] *Letter of Prior R(oger) and the community of Kyme*[1]

To our most revered and dearest lord I(nnocent), by God's grace pope, R(oger), prior, and the humble community of canons of Kyme send greetings together with proper reverence.

Although we know that the prophet held his tongue and sometimes kept silence even from good words,[2] nevertheless it would be scandalous if the pious works which the Lord has performed before our very eyes through the merits of the venerable Gilbert of Sempringham were to perish through our silence. And so we give your excellency our firm assurances that this holy man Gilbert built many monasteries, devoting to this purpose both his own rents and his legally inherited wealth, and also generous contributions from noble men. There is in these houses a great flowering of religious life, and the number of God's warriors has increased greatly up to this present moment and is still growing day by day in proportion to their merits. And yet their strength lies also in Gilbert's virtues, for he performed many pious works before being released from this earthly life. Exactly how well he lived and how he bore himself in the sight of God has been established by the glory of those miracles which followed immediately upon his death. To be brief, we testify to what we ourselves have seen and to what we have heard from men of the highest standing: namely that at his tomb the blind see, the lame walk, the dropsical are healed, the paralysed become whole, many types of illness are banished; also through his merits many men both on land and sea reach the haven of peace they so much desire.[3] And because no one lights a candle and puts it under a bushel but upon a candlestick,[4] we consider that this holy man whom we all believe the Lord has crowned with brilliant miracles in heaven is worthy of glory here on earth.

[22] *Letter of G(eoffrey), earl of Essex*[5]

To his most revered father in Christ and lord I(nnocent), by God's grace pope, G(eoffrey) FitzPeter, earl of Essex, sends greetings and the due service of obedience.

I am sure news has reached you of the great piety and faith shown by Master Gilbert, who founded and ruled the Order of Sempringham. Indeed, according to my certain knowledge and to

didici et fama publica predicat, ad ipsius tumbam ostensa sanctitatem eius et quanta sint eius merita testantur: prout poteritis per litteras uirorum uenerabilium super hoc uobis destinatas[a] patenter
agnoscere. Vnde paternitati uestre presentium latores G(amelum)
et W., canonicos predicti ordinis, commendo,[b] deuote supplicans
quatinus intuitu Dei eos benigne audiatis, et eorum negotium ad
honorem Dei et sancte ecclesie promoueatis.

[23] *Rescriptum domini pape ad archiepiscopum Cantuariensem et alios*
de iterum facienda inquisitione

f. 128ᵛ Innocentius episcopus, seruus seruorum Dei, uenerabilibus fratribus H(uberto) Cantuariensi archiepiscopo, et E(ustachio) Eliensi[c]
episcopo, et dilectis filiis de Burgo et de Wardona abbatibus, salutem et apostolicam benedictionem.[1]

Licet apostolica sedes pastoralem in omnibus seruare debeat
grauitatem, in hiis tamen que diuini iudicii sunt pocius quam
humani, tanto cum maiori debet maturitate procedere quanto etsi
iuditia Dei semper sunt iusta, eorum tamen cause amplius sunt
occulte. Sane multum sumus meritis inequales apostolo, qui
sapientie et scientie Dei altitudinem admiratus, 'quam incompre-
hensibilia sunt' inquit 'iuditia, et inuestigabiles uie eius. Quis enim
cognouit sensum Domini aut quis consiliarius eius fuit?'[2] Vnde cum
dilecti filii R(ogerus) prior et conuentus de Sempingham a nobis
humiliter postulassent ut sancte recordationis G(ilebertum), qui
quondam eorum fuit ordinis institutor, et quem piis operibus
floruisse fatentur in uita, certisque tam ante quam post mortem
miraculis claruisse, sanctorum ascriberemus cathalogo ueneran-
dum, noluimus protinus petitioni eorum annuere, sed et[d] de uita et
miraculis eius proposuimus prius plenius indagare, licet tam karissimi in Christo filii nostri I(ohannis), regis Anglorum illustris, quam
f. 129 uenerabilium fratrum nostrorum Cantuariensis | archiepiscopi et
quorundam suffraganeorum ipsius, multorum quoque abbatum et
priorum et magnatum prouintie super hiis nobis litteras testimoniales direxissent. Significauit quidem nobis archiepiscopus memora-
tus quod cum olim fama miraculorum que Dominus ad sepulchrum

---

[a] destinatas uobis *Lc before correction*   [b] commendo *Winterbottom;* commendendo *Lc (cf. p. 214 n. a)*
Letter 23 *LcOd*   [c] Eliensi *Foreville;* Eliñ *Lc*   [d] et *om. Od*

---

[1] Calendared in Cheney and Cheney, no. 345A.   [2] Rom. 11: 33–4.

the claims of popular report, the frequent miracles displayed at his tomb are witness of his holiness and the richness of his merits. This you may clearly ascertain from letters about the matter which have been sent to you by men who deserve respect. Therefore I commend to you, father, the bearers of this letter G(amel) and W., who are canons of this Order, and I respectfully ask that in God's name you listen favourably to them and advance their business to the honour of God and Holy Church.

[23] *Reply from the pope to the archbishop of Canterbury and others ordering another inquiry*

Innocent, bishop, servant of the servants of God, to his venerable brothers H(ubert), archbishop of Canterbury, and E(ustace), bishop of Ely, and his beloved sons the abbots of Peterborough and Wardon, greetings and apostolic blessing.[1]

Although the Holy See must maintain its pastoral dignity in all matters, nevertheless in those involving divine rather than human judgement it must proceed with all the greater deliberation, since although God's judgements are always just, the reasons for them are better concealed. We are very far from sharing the merits of the apostle who wondered at 'the depth of God's wisdom and knowledge. How unsearchable', he said, 'are His judgements, and His ways past finding out! For who hath known the mind of the Lord? or who hath been his counsellor?'[2] It was for this reason that we did not wish to grant their petition immediately, when our dear sons Prior R(oger) and the community of Sempringham humbly asked us to enrol Gilbert of holy memory in the catalogue of saints that he might be held in veneration; this Gilbert was originally the founder of their Order and, according to their account, excelled in pious works during his lifetime and won fame by the well-established miracles he performed both before and after his death. Instead we proposed first to carry out a thorough investigation into this man's life and miracles, even though they had sent us testimonial letters on these points from both our dear son in Christ J(ohn), renowned king of the English, and from our venerable brothers the archbishop of Canterbury and some of his suffragans, and also from many abbots, priors and nobles of the province. The same archbishop told us that when news first reached him of the miracles which Our Lord works repeatedly at that holy man's tomb,

illius sancti uiri frequentius operatur peruenisset ad eum, quibusdam abbatibus et prioribus constitutis in partibus illis scripsit, ut
ad sepulchrum eius sancti uiri pariter accedentes tam per eos qui
dicebantur fuisse curati quam per testes ydoneos inquirerent de
omnibus diligentius ueritatem, et quod inuenirent tam nobis quam
ipsi per suas litteras intimarent. Qui tam ab hiis qui curati fuerant
quam ab aliis iuramento recepto, multa nobis de miraculis eius per
litteras suas expresserunt. Nos autem in tanto iuditio diligentiam
curantes omnimodam adhibere discretioni uestre, de qua plene
confidimus, per apostolica scripta precipiendo mandamus quatinus auctoritate nostra suffulti ad locum pariter accedentes triduanum ieiunium toti collegio ipsius ordinis sollemniter indicatis, ut
uniuersi fratres[a] orantes et rogantes ab eo qui est 'uia, ueritas et
uita'[1] postulent et implorent aperiri uiam inueniendi super hoc
f. 129[v] ueritatem ad uitam, ac deinde non solum | per testimonia sed per
testes, per famam quoque uulgatam et scripturam auctenticam, de
uirtute morum et uirtute signorum, operibus uidelicet et miraculis,
certitudinem inquiratis, cunctaque fideliter scribentes sub testimonio sigillorum uestrorum per uiros ydoneos, qui etiam super
hiis nobis fidem faciant in presentia nostra iurati, ad sedem apostolicam destinetis, ut per inquisitionem uestram sufficienter
instructi ad diuini nominis gloriam et catholice fidei firmamentum
securius in ipso negotio procedere ualeamus.

[24] *Littere archiepiscopi et aliorum ad ordinem de die inquisitioni
statuto*[2]

Hubertus Dei gratia Cantuariensis archiepiscopus, tocius Anglie
primas, E(ustachius) eadem gratia Eliensis episcopus, et abbas de
Burgo dilectis sibi in Christo fratri R(ogero) magistro ordinis de
Sempingham et toti eiusdem ordinis capitulo, salutem in Domino.
  Mandatum domini pape suscepimus ut ad domum de Sempingham pariter accedentes triduanum ieiunium auctoritate suffulti
apostolica toti uestri ordinis collegio sollemniter indicamus, quatinus uniuersi fratres et sorores orantes et rogantes ab eo qui est
'uia, ueritas et uita'[1] postulent et implorent aperiri uiam inueniendi

---

[a] *ins.* et sorores *Od, no doubt rightly*
Letter 24 *LcOd*

---

[1] Cf. John 14: 6.   [2] Calendared in *EEA*, iii, no. 610.

he wrote to certain abbots and priors who hold office in the area instructing them to go together to the holy man's tomb and to find out the truth of all these matters most carefully, both from those who were said to have been cured and from suitable witnesses; they were to relate what they discovered in letters sent both to us and to him. After sworn evidence had been taken both from the people who had been cured and from others, these men gave us in their letters a full description of Gilbert's miracles. Because we are anxious to take every care over a decision of such importance, we are sending you, whose discretion we trust completely, apostolic letters with our instructions: on the strength of our authority, you are to go together to the place and solemnly to declare a three-day fast for the whole community of this Order: that while all the brethren pray and entreat Him who is 'the way, the truth, and the life',[1] they shall beg and beseech that the way to discover the living truth in this matter may be revealed. Next you must seek confirmation of his virtuous character and powerful wonders, in other words his deeds and miracles, relying not merely upon statements of evidence but also upon witnesses, popular report, and authentic documents. When you have faithfully written an account of all this and attested it by your seals, you are to send it to the Holy See by suitable messengers, who, after they have taken an oath in our presence, will also submit sworn evidence to us on these points. Then, sufficiently informed by your inquiry, we may be able to proceed more confidently in this affair to the glory of God's name and to the strengthening of the Catholic faith.

[24] *Letter from the archbishop and others to the Order concerning the day appointed for the inquiry*[2]

Hubert, by God's grace archbishop of Canterbury, primate of all England, E(ustace), by God's grace bishop of Ely, and the abbot of Peterborough to their beloved brother in Christ R(oger), master of the Order of Sempringham, and the whole chapter of the same Order, greetings in the Lord.

We have received a mandate from the pope to the effect that we are to go together to the house of Sempringham, and on the strength of his apostolic authority solemnly to declare a three-day fast for the whole community of your Order; that while all the brothers and sisters pray and entreat Him who is 'the way, the truth, and the life',[1] they shall beg and beseech that the way

super meritis sancte recordationis magistri G(ileberti), institutoris
f. 130 uestri ordinis, ueritatem | ac deinde non solum per testimonia sed
per testes, per famam quoque uulgatam et scripturam auctenticam,
de uirtute morum et uirtute signorum, operibus uidelicet et miraculis, certitudinem inquiramus, cunctaque fideliter conscribentes
sub testimonio sigillorum nostrorum per uiros ydoneos, qui fidem
etiam super hiis domino pape faciant in presentia eius iurati, ad
sedem apostolicam destinemus, ut per inquisitionem nostram sufficienter instructus, ad diuini nominis gloriam et catholice fidei
firmamentum securius in ipso negotio ab eo possit procedi. Cum
igitur prouiderimus quod ad domum uestram de Sempingham
proxima quarta feria ante festum sancti Michaelis propter hoc,
Domino fauente, pariter accedemus, uobis auctoritate apostolica
per duos antecedentes dies, scilicet secundam et tertiam feriam,[1]
necnon per ipsam quartam feriam, ut sic triduum compleatur,
ieiunium indicimus, ut sic ieiunantes postuletis uiam aperiri super
predicti uiri sancti meritis et miraculis ueritatem inueniendi.
Mandamus quoque uobis eadem auctoritate et iniungimus quatinus contra eundem terminum uobis de omnibus que necessaria
fuerint ad inquisitionem ueritatis, scilicet tam de testibus quam
aliis, prouidere curetis, ut cum illic uenerimus expedite[a] in negotio
procedere ualeamus.

f. 130ᵛ   [25] *Littere R(ogeri) prioris et capituli ordinis de| Sempingham ad*
dominum papam commendatiue pro nunciis

Sanctissimo patri et domino I(nnocentio), Dei gratia summo pontifici, R(ogerus) dictus prior ordinis de Sempingham eiusdemque
ordinis capitulum, salutem et tam deuotum quam debitum obedientie famulatum.

Ad pedes sanctitatis uestre duos ex canonicis nostris pro urgen-
tissimis negociis nuper destinauimus. Vnde excellentie sanctitatis
uestre nec tales nec quantas debemus sed quas sufficimus gratiarum
referimus actiones quod ipsos tam benigne suscepistis tamque
paterne super negociis nostris pro temporis congruentia exaudis-
tis. Nunc autem pedibus sanctitatis uestre corde et animo prouo-
luti omni intentione supplicamus quatinus quinque canonicos

ᵃ expedite *Winterbottom;* expedire *Lc;* expediti *(-i after correction) Od*
Letter 25 *LcOd*

[1] 24–5 Sept. 1201.

may be revealed to discover the truth concerning the merits of Master Gilbert of holy memory, the founder of your Order; and further we are to seek certain confirmation of his virtuous character and powerful wonders, in other words his deeds and miracles, relying not merely upon statements of evidence but also upon witnesses, popular report, and authentic documents; and when we have faithfully written an account of all this and attested it by our seals we are to send it to the Holy See by suitable messengers, who after they have taken an oath in his presence will also submit sworn evidence to the pope on these points. Then, sufficiently informed by our inquiry, he can proceed more confidently in this affair to the glory of God's name and to the strengthening of the Catholic faith. Therefore, since we have arranged to meet for this purpose at your house of Sempringham, God willing, on the Wednesday before the feast of St Michael [26 September] next, acting on papal authority we ask you to fast on the two preceding days (Monday and Tuesday)[1] and also on that Wednesday so that the three days may be made up in this manner; then as you fast you are to pray for a way to be revealed which will uncover the truth about the merits and miracles of this holy man. We also command and instruct you, on the same authority, to take care to have available by this date all that is necessary for an investigation into the facts, both the witnesses themselves and other evidence, so that when we arrive we may proceed to business straight away.

[25] *Letter from Prior R(oger) and the chapter of the Order of Sempringham to the pope commending their envoys*

To our most holy father and lord I(nnocent), by God's grace pope, R(oger), called prior of the Order of Sempringham, and the chapter of the same Order send greetings and the respectful and due service of obedience.

Not long ago we sent two of our canons with matters of the greatest importance to the feet of your holiness; in this connection we return our grateful thanks (in quality and quantity matching our capabilities rather than our obligations) to your excellent holiness for receiving them so kindly and listening to them on our business with such fatherly concern as the time allowed. But now, as we lie prostrate in heart and soul at the feet of your holiness, we earnestly beg you to accept the credentials of our five canons who bear this

nostros presentium baiulos pro negociis nostris ad sedem apostolicam destinatos commendatos habere, tueri atque fouere, et pre
omnibus exaudire dignemini. Vt sanctitas uestra ex testimonio
paruitatis nostre circa statum ipsorum cercior efficiatur, ipsis tamquam uiris sub monastica disciplina penes nos conuersantibus testimonium perhibemus, quod zelum Dei habent, et in agendis et in
disponendis negociis sibi commissis fideliter et discrete tamquam
Dei timorem habentes se habuerint.

[26] *Rescriptum H(uberti) archiepiscopi et ceterorum ad dominum
papam super inquisitione facta*[1] |

f. 131   Sanctissimo patri et domino I(nnocentio), Dei gratia summo pontifici, H(ubertus), permissione diuina Cantuariensis ecclesie
minister humilis, tocius Anglie primas, et E(ustachius), eadem
gratia Eliensis ecclesie minister, et A(charius) abbas de Burgo,[2]
salutem et obedientie integritatem.

Mandatum sanctitatis uestre nobis et abbati de Warduna directum suscepimus, quo nobis fuit iniunctum ut ad Sempingham
pariter accedentes triduanum ieiunium toti collegio ipsius ordinis
solemniter indiceremus, ut uniuersi fratres et sorores orantes et
rogantes ab eo qui est 'uia, ueritas et uita'[3] postulent et implorent
aperiri uiam inueniendi ueritatem super sanctitate magistri
G(ileberti) de Sempingham, ac deinde non solum per testimonia
sed per testes, per famam quoque uulgatam et scripturam auctenticam, de uirtute morum et de uirtute signorum, operibus uidelicet
et miraculis, certitudinem inquireremus, cunctaque fideliter conscribentes sub testimonio sigillorum nostrorum per uiros idoneos,
qui fidem etiam super hiis uobis faciant in presentia uestra iurati,
ad sedem apostolicam destinaremus. Quod si non omnes hiis
interesse possemus, tres nostrum nichilominus ea exequerentur.
Cum autem predictus abbas de Wardona ad generale capitulum
Cisterciense[a] secundum ordinis morem fuisset profectus et ideo
predictis exequendis interesse non posset, nos mandatum uestrum |
f. 131ᵛ   prompta uolentes exequi deuotione, apud Sempingham sub ea qua
potuit fieri celeritate in propriis personis conuenimus, et triduano
ieiunio secundum formam mandati uestri toti collegio ordinis

Letter 26 *LcOd*   [a] Cistercensis *Lc(?)*

---

[1] Calendared in *EEA*, iii, no. 611.   [2] See p. 170 n. 4.   [3] See p. 236 n. 1.

letter and have been sent to the Holy See on our business; may you protect and encourage them and, above all else, grant them a favourable hearing. In order that our humble witness may inform your holiness about their position, we testify concerning them that they behave in our midst as befits men under monastic discipline, and that they are full of godly zeal, and in performing and transacting the business committed to their charge they have borne themselves honourably and with discretion like God-fearing men.

[26] *Reply from Archbishop H(ubert) and the others to the pope concerning the inquiry which has taken place*[1]

To the most holy father and lord I(nnocent), by God's grace pope, H(ubert), by divine permission humble servant of the church of Canterbury, primate of all England, and E(ustace), by the same grace servant of the church of Ely, and A(charius), abbot of Peterborough,[2] send greetings and complete obedience.

We have received your holiness's mandate sent to us and to the abbot of Wardon, in which we were instructed to go together to Sempringham and solemnly to declare a three-day fast for the whole community of this Order; that while all the brethren and sisters prayed and entreated Him who is 'the way, the truth, and the life',[3] they should beg and beseech that the way might be revealed to discover the truth concerning the holiness of Master Gilbert of Sempringham; and further, we were to seek certain confirmation of his virtuous character and powerful wonders, in other words his deeds and miracles, relying not merely upon statements of evidence but also upon witnesses, popular report, and authentic documents; and when we had faithfully written an account of all this and attested it by our seals we were to send it to the Holy See by suitable messengers, who after they had taken an oath in your presence would also submit sworn evidence to you on these points. If we could not all be present, then at least three of us were to carry out these instructions. But although the abbot of Wardon had set out for the general chapter, according to the custom of the Cistercian Order, and thus could not help fulfil these instructions, as we wished to execute your mandate promptly and reverently we came in person to Sempringham as quickly as possible. When by a solemn pronouncement we had declared and observed the three-day fast for the whole community of the Order

ipsius solemniter indicto et expleto, testes iuratos tam religiosos quam seculares, tam clericos quam laicos, tam uiros quam mulieres, super uirtute signorum que per merita ipsius magistri G(ileberti) facta dicuntur diligenter examinauimus. Quorum attestationes fideliter in scripturam redactas, sub sigillis nostris clausas, uestre paternitati transmittimus.

Licet autem honestas ipsius et conuersatio religiosa nobis publice uiderentur innotuisse, uiros tamen religiosos, qui ei multis temporibus familiarius asistere consueuerant, et quos eius secreta conuersatio latere non potuit, diligenter requisiuimus: qui omnes concorditer et constanter testificati sunt quod uita eius sancta fuit et immaculata. Erat enim in abstinentia admirandus, in castitate preclarus, in orationibus peruigil et deuotus, circa curam gregis sui prouida discretione sollicitus, horis quibus uacare potuit contemplationi deditus. Sicque in terris positus actionis et contemplationis uices alternabat, ut in scala Iacob angelos nunc ascendentes f. 132 nunc descendentes imita|retur;[1] cui, quando cum fratribus aut sororibus familiaris fuit collatio, iuxta quod de Samuele legitur, non cecidit de uerbis eius in terram, sed secundum apostoli doctrinam sermo ociosus ex ore eius raro procedebat,[2] sed qui bonus erat ad edificationem fidei ut daret gratiam audientibus. Licet autem multa uitam eius preclaram reddiderint et commendabilem, hoc tamen precipue eum insigniuit, quod spontaneam eligens paupertatem omnia temporalia sibi a Deo collata sanctimonialium quas in unum congregauit et sub regulari disciplina prudenter constituit et uigilanter custodiuit sustentationi deputauit. Cui processu temporis Deus tantam gratiam adauxit quod quatuor canonicas regulares et nouem monasteria sanctimonialium construxit:[3] in quibus eo tempore quo migrauit ad Dominum multos uiros religiosos, mille et quingentas sorores quas adunauerat, Deo iugiter famulantes, preter innumeros antea defunctos, relinquebat. De fama autem uulgata iuxta mandati uestri formam diligenter inquirentes, inuenimus quod sanctitatem uite ipsius et uirtutes signorum fama uicinie plenius attestatur. Inquisitionis igitur a nobis facte seriem et tocius negocii processum uestre paternitati f. 132ᵛ per presentium latores, | qui fidem etiam, ut dicunt, super hiis

---

[1] Cf. Gen. 28: 12, cited in a similar context by Gregory the Great, *Registrum*, i. 24; St Bernard, *Epistola* 91 (*Opera*, vii, ed. J. Leclercq and H. Rochais (Rome, 1974), p. 240); cf. pp. 48–9, 250–1.

[2] Cf. 1 Kgs. (1 Sam.) 3: 19; Eph. 4: 29.

[3] See pp. xxx–xxxii, 54–5, etc.

in accordance with the terms of your mandate, we carefully examined the sworn witnesses—religious as well as secular, clerks as well as layfolk, men as well as women—concerning the power of those miracles which are said to have been performed through the merits of this Master Gilbert. We are sending to you, father, their sworn evidence which has been faithfully copied down and enclosed under our seals.

Although this man's integrity and devout conduct appeared to us to be well known to everyone, nevertheless we questioned carefully the religious who were often more intimately associated with him and from whom his private conduct could not be concealed; all these men have testified unanimously and consistently that his was a holy and chaste life. For his abstinence was wonderful and his chastity exemplary; he was watchful and devout at prayer, scrupulous in looking after his flock carefully and prudently, and, at times which he could set aside, much given to contemplation; thus, while on earth, he filled alternately the active and the contemplative roles, so that he followed the example of the angels upon Jacob's ladder ascending and descending in turn.[1] When he was at ease talking with the brethren or sisters, as we read of Samuel, he 'let none of his words fall to the ground'; following, rather, the apostle's teaching, he rarely spoke anything superfluous but that which, in bestowing grace upon those who heard him, served to strengthen their faith.[2] But although there were many characteristics which rendered his life remarkable and praiseworthy, this especially marked him out: that in choosing poverty of his own free will, he put aside all the worldly possessions which God had granted him to support the nuns, whom he gathered into a single community, placed wisely under the discipline of a rule and carefully protected. With the passage of time God lavished such grace upon him that he built four houses for regular canons and nine for nuns.[3] At the time of his death he left behind him in these establishments in the constant service of God many men in religious orders and 1,500 sisters whom he had brought together, apart from countless others who were already dead. Moreover as we carefully investigated popular report, according to the terms of your mandate, we discovered that opinion in the area fully supports the holiness of this man's life and the power of his miracles. Thus we are sending you, father, an account of the inquiry we have carried out together with a record of all that was done; those who bear this

uobis facere iurati in presentia uestra parati sunt, destinamus, ut quod ad gloriam diuini nominis et honorem sancte ecclesie uobis celitus fuerit inspiratum super negotio pretaxato*a* sanctitas uestra decernat. Vitam et incolumitatem uestram sibi et ecclesie sue conseruet omnipotens in tempora longiora.

[27] *Rescriptum domini pape ad H(ubertum) Cantuariensem archiepiscopum de canonizatione facta*[1]

Innocentius episcopus, seruus seruorum Dei, uenerabili fratri archiepiscopo Cantuariensi, salutem et apostolicam benedictionem.

Cum secundum euangelicam ueritatem nemo accendat lucernam et ponat illam sub modio sed super candelabrum, ut omnes qui in domo sunt uideant,[2] pium pariter et iustum est*b* ut quos Deus merito sanctitatis coronat et honorat in celis, nos uenerationis officio laudemus et glorificemus in terris, cum ipse pocius laudetur et glorificetur in illis 'qui est laudabilis et gloriosus in sanctis'.[3] Pietas enim promissionem habet uite que nunc est et future, dicente Domino per prophetam: 'Dabo uos cunctis populis in laudem, gloriam et honorem', et per se pollicente: 'Fulgebunt iusti sicut sol in regno patris eorum.'[4] Nam ut sue uirtutis potentiam mirabiliter manifestet et nostre salutis causam misericorditer f. 133 operetur, | fideles suos quos semper coronat in celo frequenter etiam honorat in mundo, ad eorum memorias signa faciens et prodigia, per que prauitas confundatur heretica et fides catholica confirmetur. Nos ergo, frater archiepiscope, quantas possumus etsi non quantas debemus omnipotenti Deo gratiarum referimus actiones, quod in diebus nostris ad confirmationem catholice fidei et confusionem heretice prauitatis euidenter innouat signa et mirabilia potenter inmutat,*c* faciens eos coruscare miraculis qui fidem catholicam tam corde quam ore necnon et opere tenuerunt. Inter quos beate memorie magister Gilebertus, fundator et institutor ordinis de Sempingham, qui degens olim in mundo magnis meritis

---

a pretexato *Lc*

Letter 27 *LcOd*   *b* est *om. Lc*   *c* *An odd word to use here*

[1] Also in *Selected Letters of Pope Innocent III concerning England*, ed. C. R. Cheney and W. H. Semple (NMT, 1953), pp. 26–32; calendared in Cheney and Cheney, no. 374; Potthast, no. 1612.

[2] Cf. Matt. 5: 15; etc.

[3] Cf. Dan. 3: 52.

letter are also prepared, they say, to give you firm assurances concerning these matters when they have taken an oath in your presence. Then your holiness may judge in this affair according to the inspiration heaven visits upon you, to the glory of God's name and the honour of His holy Church.

May the Almighty long preserve your life, keeping you safe for Himself and for His Church.

[27] *Reply from the pope to H(ubert), archbishop of Canterbury, about the canonization*[1]

Innocent, bishop, servant of the servants of God, to his venerable brother the archbishop of Canterbury, greetings and apostolic blessing.

According to the gospel truth 'no one lights a candle and places it under a bushel, but upon a candlestick, so that all who are in the house may see'.[2] Therefore it is a pious practice and a just that we upon earth should praise and glorify by the service of veneration those whom God because of their holiness crowns and honours in heaven, since He 'who is worthy of praise and glorious in His saints',[3] is the more effectively praised and glorified in them. For piety holds the promise of life which is now and to come, as our Lord said through the prophet 'I will place you before all people for praise, glory and honour' and as He Himself promised 'the righteous shall shine like the sun in the kingdom of their Father'.[4] In order, then, wonderfully to display the power of His strength and mercifully to work our salvation, He also honours frequently in the world His faithful sons whom He always crowns in heaven, performing miracles and amazing deeds at their tombs by which evil heresy may be routed and the Catholic faith strengthened. Therefore, brother archbishop, we offer grateful thanks to Almighty God, as much as we may although not as much as we ought, that in our day, to strengthen the Catholic faith and confound the evil of heresy, He is clearly renewing His signs and working powerful wonders, so that those who have adhered to the Catholic faith in thought, word, and deed are made radiant by miracles. Among these Master Gilbert of blessed memory, the founder and establisher of the Order of Sempringham, who was famous when he lived formerly in the world for his great virtues,

[4] Cf. Zeph. 3: 20; Matt. 13: 43.

prepollebat, nunc uiuens in celo magnis[a] coruscat miraculis, ut eius sanctitas ueris et certis inditiis comprobetur. Licet enim ad hoc ut aliquis sanctus sit apud Deum in ecclesia triumphante sola sufficiat finalis perseuerantia, teste ueritate que dicit quoniam 'qui perseuerauerit usque in finem, hic saluus erit', et iterum: 'Esto fidelis usque ad mortem, et dabo tibi coronam uite',[1] ad hoc tamen ut ipse sanctus apud homines habeatur in ecclesia militante duo sunt necessaria, uirtus morum et uirtus signorum, merita uidelicet

f. 133[v] | et miracula, ut hec et illa sibi inuicem contestentur. Non enim aut merita sine miraculis aut miracula sine meritis plene sufficiunt ad perhibendum inter homines testimonium sanctitati, cum interdum angelus Sathane transfiguret se in angelum lucis, et quidam opera sua faciant ut ab hominibus uideantur.[2] Sed et magi Pharaonis olim signa fecerunt, et antichristus tandem prodigia operabitur, ut si fieri posset in errorem etiam inducantur electi.[3] Vnde quandoque testimonium operum est fallax et deceptorium, ut in ypocritis, et miraculorum quoque testimonium interdum fallit et decipit, ut in magis. Verum cum et merita sana precedunt et clara succedunt miracula, certum prebent inditium sanctitatis, ut nos ad ipsius uenerationem inducant quem Deus et meritis precedentibus et miraculis subsequentibus exibet uenerandum; que duo ex uerbis euangeliste plenius colliguntur, qui de apostolis loquens aiebat: 'Illi profecti predicauerunt ubique Domino cooperante et sermonem confirmante sequentibus signis.'[4]

Licet ergo iamdudum dilecti filii prior et conuentus de Sempingham postulassent a nobis ut sancte recordationis magistrum

f. 134 Gilebertum, qui quondam fuit eorum ordinis | institutor, et quem piis asserunt ante mortem operibus floruisse certisque post mortem coruscare miraculis, sanctorum ascriberemus cathalago uenerandum, noluimus petitioni eorum protinus acquiescere, sed de operibus et signis et miraculis eius indagare uoluimus plenius ueritatem, preter id quod karissimus in Christo filius noster, Iohannes, rex Anglorum illustris, cum magnatibus suis, et tu cum tuis suffraganeis, necnon et memorati prior et conuentus de Sempingham cum multis abbatibus et prioribus de uirtute morum

---

[a] uel multis s.l. Lc[1]; multis Od

[1] Cf. Matt. 10: 22; Rev. 2: 10.
[2] Cf. 2 Cor. 11: 14; Matt. 23: 5.
[3] Cf. Exod. 7: 11–12; oddly echoes Deut. 6: 22, but there referring to God's works.
[4] Cf. Mark 16: 20.

is radiant with great miracles now that he lives in heaven, so that
his sanctity receives true and incontestable proof. For a man to be
deemed a saint before God in the Church Triumphant this alone
suffices: that he persevere to the end, according to the word of
Truth, which states 'that whoever endures to the end shall be
saved'; also 'Be faithful unto death and I will give thee a crown of
life.'[1] However for this same man to be deemed a saint before men
in the Church Militant two things are necessary: a virtuous life and
mighty signs, in other words merits and miracles, so that these two
things bear witness one to the other. Neither merits without
miracles nor miracles without merits are properly enough to prove
sanctity among men, since occasionally an angel of Satan transforms himself into an angel of light, and there are some who
perform their deeds in order that they may be seen of men;[2] even
Pharaoh's magicians once performed signs, and in the end Anti-
christ will work great wonders, so that if it were possible even the
elect may be led into error.[3] Thus sometimes the evidence
provided by deeds is false and misleading, as we see in the case of
hypocrites, and the evidence of miracles also sometimes deceives
and misleads, as in the case of the magicians. But when sound
merits come first and conspicuous miracles follow, they offer
indisputable proof of sanctity, and thus they persuade us to revere
the man whom God, by reason of both his antecedent merits and
succeeding miracles, presents as worthy of our veneration; the two
forms of proof are entirely deduced from the words of the evangelist, who said, speaking of the apostles: 'They went forth, and
preached everywhere, the Lord working with them and confirming
the word with signs following.'[4]

  Therefore, although some while ago our dear sons the prior and
community of Sempringham begged us to enter Master Gilbert of
holy memory in the catalogue of saints for veneration (he was
formerly the founder of their Order and according to their account
excelled in pious works before his death and afterwards has
become famous for undoubted miracles), we were reluctant to
agree immediately to their request; instead we wished to make our
own full investigation into the facts surrounding his deeds, signs,
and miracles, quite apart from what our dearest son in Christ John,
renowned king of the English, together with his nobles and you,
your suffragans and the same prior and community of Sempringham and many abbots and priors had faithfully related to us

et uirtute signorum ipsius nobis fideliter intimastis. Quocirca, uolentes in tanto iuditio diligentiam omnimodam adhibere, tibi et uenerabili fratri nostro episcopo Eliensi, ac dilectis filiis de Burgo et de Warduna abbatibus per scripta nostra dedimus in mandatis ut auctoritate nostra suffulti ad locum pariter accedentes toti ipsius ordinis collegio ieiunium indiceretis sollemniter triduanum, ut fratres et sorores postularent et implorarent ab eo qui est 'uia, ueritas et uita' super hoc aperiri uiam inueniendi ueritatem ad uitam,[1] ac deinde non solum per testimonia, sed per testes, per famam quoque uulgatam et scripturam auctenticam, de uirtute morum et de uirtute signorum, operibus uidelicet et miraculis, f. 134ᵛ inquireretis certitudinem diligenter, | cunctaque fideliter conscribentes sub testimonio sigillorum uestrorum per uiros idoneos, qui fidem etiam nobis super hiis facerent in presentia nostra iurati, ad sedem apostolicam transmittere curaretis, ut per inquisitionem uestram diligenter instructi ad diuini nominis gloriam et catholice fidei firmamentum securius in ipso negotio procedere ualeremus. Quod si non omnes hiis possetis exequendis adesse, tres ea nichilominus adimplerent.

Qui mandatum nostrum fideliter exequentes, cum quartus propter necessariam causam interesse non posset, tres ex uobis, uidelicet tu, frater archiepiscope, et memorati episcopus et abbas de Burgo, ad locum pariter accedentes et peragentes uniuersa secundum mandati nostri tenorem, testes iuratos, tam religiosos quam seculares, tam clericos quam laicos, tam uiros quam mulieres, super uirtute signorum que per merita ipsius magistri G(ileberti) dicebantur ostensa, examinare diligentius procurastis, quorum atestationes fideliter conscribentes sub uestris nobis sigillis transmisistis inclusas, que licet euidentia fuissent et certa, quia tamen tam multa fuerunt et uaria ut non oportuerit ea presentibus litteris annotare;[a] f. 135 super honestate uero conuersationis ipsius que | per se publice innotescit, uiros religiosos qui ei multis temporibus familiarius assistere consueuerant et quos eius secreta conuersatio non latebat diligenter requirere studuistis: qui omnes concorditer testificati sunt et constanter quod eius uita inmaculata perseuerauit et sancta. Erat enim

---

[a] *The writer loses control of this sentence*

[1] Cf. John 14: 6.

concerning this man's virtuous life and mighty signs. For this reason, as we wished to take every care over a case of such importance, we sent to you and to our venerable brother, the bishop of Ely, and to our dear sons the abbots of Peterborough and Wardon, a mandate in our letter: on the strength of our authority, you were to come together to the place and solemnly to impose a three-day fast upon the whole community of this same Order, so that the brethren and sisters might beg and implore Him who is 'the way, the truth, and the life'[1] to reveal the way to discover the living truth in this affair; you were then to investigate carefully the facts concerning his virtuous life and mighty signs, in other words his deeds and miracles, relying not only upon statements of evidence but also upon witnesses, popular report, and authentic documents; and when you had faithfully recorded all these things under the witness of your seals, you were to see that it was sent to the Holy See by suitable messengers, who, after they had taken an oath in our presence, were also to make depositions to us about these matters. Thus, sufficiently informed by your inquiry, we should be able to take action more confidently in this business, to the glory of God's name and the strengthening of the Catholic faith. But if you could not all be present to perform these instructions, at least three of you should carry them out.

Since for a compelling reason the fourth person could not take part, three of you faithfully executed our mandate, that is you our brother archbishop and the same bishop and abbot of Peterborough; when you came together to the place and had done everything in accordance with the contents of our mandate, you took care meticulously to examine the sworn witnesses—religious as well as secular, clerks as well as laymen, men as well as women—concerning the power of those miracles which were said to have been revealed through the merits of this same Master Gilbert. After you had copied down their sworn depositions carefully you sent them to us closed under your seals; although these constituted reliable evidence, there were so many of them and they were so varied that it would not be right to record them in this letter. About this man's integrity of conduct, which is public knowledge in its own right, you took care to question closely the religious who used to be intimate with him on many occasions as members of his household and from whom his private conduct was not concealed; all these men have testified unanimously and consistently that his life remained chaste and holy to the end. For

admirandus in abstinentia, preclarus in castitate, in oratione deuotus et in uigiliis assuetus, circa curam gregis sui prouida discre-
tione sollicitus, et horis quibus poterat libenter contemplationi
uacabat, ut in terris positus actionis et contemplationis uices mirabiliter alternaret, tanquam in scala Iacob nunc ascendentes nunc
descendentes angelos sequeretur; cui quando cum fratribus et
sororibus fuit familiaris collatio, iuxta quod de Samuele legitur
non cecidit de uerbis eius in terram, sed secundum doctrinam
apostoli ociosus sermo de ore eius rarius procedebat, sed qui ad
edificationem fidei bonus erat ut daret gratiam audientibus.[1]
Quamuis autem multa uitam eius preclaram reddiderint, hoc
tamen eum precipue insigniuit, quod, spontaneam eligens paupertatem, omnia temporalia sibi a Deo prestita fratrum et sororum
quos sub regulari disciplina prudenter instituit et sollicite cus-
f. 135ᵛ todiuit necessitatibus | deputauit; cui processu temporis tantam
Deus adauxit gratiam et uirtutem quod nouem construxit sanctimonialium monasteria et quatuor canonicas regulares, in quibus,
eo tempore quo migrauit ad Dominum, preter quamplures uiros
religiosos, mille et quingente sorores uiuebant Deo iugiter famulantes.[2] Ad maiorem uero cautelam quinque de fratribus ordinis
memorati ad nostram presentiam accedentes examinari fecimus
sub iuratoria cautione, qui de piis eius operibus et claris miraculis
multa nobis concorditer retulerunt.

Nos ergo de meritis et miraculis eius multis et magnis non
solum testimoniis sed et testibus cerciores effecti, cum iuxta
testimonium angeli ad Tobiam 'sacramentum regis abscondere
bonum sit, opera uero Dei reuelare et confiteri sit honorificum', ut
secundum prophetam 'laudetur Deus in sanctis suis', ipsum beatum
Gilebertum cathalogo sanctorum ascripsimus eiusque memoriam
inter sanctos decreuimus celebrandam.[3] Quapropter fraternitatem
tuam monemus et exhortamur in Domino, per apostolica tibi scripta
mandantes, quatinus quod nos sollemniter et caute statuimus, tu
humiliter et deuote conserues, faciens festiuitatem ipsius per tuam
prouintiam sollemniter celebrari, ut meritis eius et precibus apud
f. 136 misericordissimum iudicem mi|sericordiam consequaris, et cum a
fratribus ordinis de Sempingham fueris requisitus corpus confessoris eiusdem cum honore ac reuerentia debita eleuareᵃ procures.

ᵃ releuare *Lc*

[1] Cf. Gen. 28: 12 and above p. 242 n. 1; 1 Kgs. (1 Sam.) 3: 19; 1 Tim. 5: 13; Eph. 4: 29.
[2] See pp. xxxii–xxxiii.   [3] Tobias 12: 7; Ps. 150: 1.

his abstinence was wonderful, his chastity exemplary; he was devout at prayer and assiduous in vigils; he was scrupulous in looking after his flock carefully and prudently, and whenever it was possible he devoted himself wholeheartedly to contemplation. Thus while on earth he filled alternately the active and contemplative roles in a wonderful manner, as if he followed the angels upon Jacob's ladder ascending and descending in turn. When he was at ease talking with the brethren and sisters, as we read of Samuel, he 'let none of his words fall to the ground'; following, rather, the apostle's teaching, he rarely spoke anything superfluous but that which, in bestowing grace upon those who heard him, served to strengthen their faith.[1] But although there were many characteristics which rendered his life exceptional, this especially marked him out: that, in choosing poverty of his own free will, he put aside all the worldly possessions which God had granted him to meet the necessities of the brethren and sisters, whom he wisely placed under the discipline of a rule and carefully protected. With the passage of time God lavished upon him such grace and virtue that he built nine houses for nuns and four for regular canons. By the time he died, apart from a large number of male religious, 1,500 sisters were living in these houses, constant in the service of God.[2] Then as a further precaution we had questioned under oath five of the brethren of this same Order who came before us; in complete agreement they told us much about his pious deeds and conspicuous miracles.

Thus acting on the information about this man's many great merits and miracles, based on both written and oral evidence—and since, according to the angel's advice to Tobias, 'to conceal a king's trust is good, but to reveal and confess the works of God is honourable', in order that, in the prophet's words, 'God may be praised in his saints'—we have added blessed Gilbert to the catalogue of saints and decreed that he shall be commemorated amongst the saints.[3] Therefore we advise you, brother, and urge you in the Lord's name, by the apostolic letter we are sending you, humbly and devoutly to observe our solemn and careful decision, causing this man's festival to be celebrated solemnly throughout your province, so that by his merits and through his intercession you may obtain mercy before our most merciful judge. And when you are so asked by the brethren of the Order of Sempringham, you are to make arrangements to translate this same confessor's body with appropriate respect and reverence.

Collectas autem in commemorationem eius dicendas edidimus, quas in hac pagina duximus subscribendas:[1]

Plenam in nobis, eterne saluator, tue uirtutis operare medelam, ut qui preclara beati Gileberti confessoris tui merita ueneramur, ipsius adiuti suffragiis a cunctis animarum nostrarum langoribus liberemur. Qui uiuis *et cetera.*

Accepta tibi sit, Domine, quesumus hec oblatio salutaris, ut sicut beato Gileberto confessori tuo proficit ad honorem, ita nobis famulis tuis proficiat ad salutem, per Dominum. . . .

Quod a te, Domine, descendit ad nos, ad te, quesumus, a nobis ascendat,[2] ut intercedente beato Gileberto confessore tuo purificet quos redemit Ihesus Christus, filius tuus, Dominus noster, qui tecum. . . .

Data Anagnie, .iĩi. kalendas Februarii, pontificatus nostri anno .IIII.

Sub hoc tenore litterarum scripsit dominus papa Galfrido Eboracensi archiepiscopo, eadem que supra retexens, et idem de sollemnitate celebranda et collectis dicendis precipiens, nisi quod de eleuatione funeris sacri, quia ad
f. 136ᵛ *eum non pertinuit, nullum dedit | ei mandatum.*

Ad totum etiam ordinis huius collegium simile scriptum transmisit, filo serico ad perpetuam memoriam appense bulle apostolice insertum.[3]

[28] *Littere archiepiscopi Cantuariensis ad ordinem de Sempingham exortatorie ad gratiarum actiones*[4]

Hubertus Dei gratia Cantuariensis archiepiscopus, tocius Anglie primas, dilectis in Christo filiis R(ogero), magistro ordinis de Sempingham, et capitulo, salutem, gratiam et benedictionem.

Benedictus Dominus de cuius munere uenit quod ei a fidelibus suis laudabiliter et digne seruiatur, qui sibi seruire dilectos et electos suos simul hortatur et docet, gratis infundens gratiam seruiendi. Seruitus eius totis appetenda uisceribus, totis uiribus amplectenda, regnum decoris acceptura pro munere, diadema

Letter 28 *LcOd*

---

[1] These are reproduced as collect, secret, and postcommunion in the *Missale Gilbertinum*, ed. R. M. Woolley, *Gilbertine Rite*, ii. 26–7 (*in* Accepta . . . *reading* quesumus Domine *and in* Quod a te . . . *omitting* a nobis); cf. i. 123, 126 (from Od). The Missal is 13th-c.

[2] Cf. Cheney and Semple (p. 244 n. 1), p. 32 n. 33.

[3] i.e. a solemn 'littere cum serico' 'ad perpetuam rei memoriam' with the bulla or papal seal of lead attached by silk threads (cf. Cheney and Cheney, p. xiv). These two

We have also issued collects to be recited in his commemoration and we have thought it right to add these to this document:[1]

Eternal Saviour, may thy full healing power work in us, so that we who revere the great merits of the blessed Gilbert Thy confessor may be assisted by his prayers and relieved of all the ills of our souls. Who liveth *etc.*

Grant, we beseech Thee, O Lord, that this redeeming sacrifice may be acceptable to Thee, so that as it serves to honour blessed Gilbert Thy confessor so it may bring us,[2] Thy servants, to salvation, through Our Lord. . . .

We beseech Thee, O Lord, may that which descends to us from Thee rise again to Thee from us, so that by the intercession of blessed Gilbert Thy confessor it may purify those redeemed by Jesus Christ, Thy son Our Lord, who with Thee. . . .

Given at Anagni, 30 January, in the fourth year of our pontificate [1202].

The pope wrote a letter to the same effect to Geoffrey archbishop of York, relating the above and giving the same instructions about the rites to be celebrated and the collects to be recited, except that he sent him no mandate about translating the sacred body because this was not his concern.

He also sent to the whole community of this Order a similar letter with the papal seal attached by silk thread, that it might serve as a perpetual record.[3]

[28] *Letter from the archbishop of Canterbury to the Order of Sempringham urging them to give thanks*[4]

Hubert, by God's grace archbishop of Canterbury, primate of all England, to his beloved sons in Christ R(oger), master of the Order of Sempringham, and the chapter, greetings, grace, and blessing.

Blessed be the Lord, whose own gift ensures that He is laudably and worthily served by His faithful believers; who encourages His dear and chosen followers even as He teaches them to serve him, freely pouring upon them the grace of obedience. His service is to be sought with all our hearts, and embraced with all our strength. It will receive the kingdom of glory as its reward and a crown of

lost letters are noted in Cheney and Cheney, nos. 374A and 375, the second also in Potthast, no. 1611.
  [4] Calendared in *EEA*, iii, no. 612.

speciei de manu Domini pro mercede, sicut ipse Dominus notum facit, qui sanctos suos tota die mirificat, pro temporalibus eterna retribuens, et faciens eos in conspectu hominum miraculis choruscare, nomina eorum in eternum uiuere, corpora etiam non solum in pace sed honorifice sepeliri.[1] Hec uobis sub breuitate perstrinximus penes quos in presentiarum ueritas specialiter eorum elucescit. Beatus quidem G(ilebertus), primus ordinis |

f. 137 uestri institutor, quia uixit innocenter, laudabiliter inter homines conuersatus, digne usque in finem in Dei seruitio perseuerans, in signum et argumentum retributionis quam in celis obtinuit gloriam similiter assecutus est et in terris. Dominus enim papa, de uita ipsius magistri meritis et moribus et conuersatione instructus, necnon et de miraculorum uirtutibus quibus eum Dominus illustrauit, sicut ex tenore mandati apostolici liquet omnibus, ipsum magistrum de consilio fratrum sicut sañctum Domini sanctorum cathalogo sollemniter ascribi censuit, sollemnitatem eius celebrari constituit; quod quia in gloriam ipsius uehementer accrescit, misericorditer indulsit et corpus cum honore processu temporis eleuari. Super hoc multipliciter exultauit spiritus noster, quod nostris in diebus acciderit quod nostre sollicitudinis interuentu conuersationis et miraculorum inquisita et inuenta sit ueritas, et Romane sedi super omnibus fides sit facta. Hoc est etiam quod nobis exultationem et iocunditatem inducit, scilicet quod per eum in eiusdem professionis regulam congregati efficatius ad firmiorem eius obseruantiam inuitantur, et ipsius obtentu de cetero penes omnes amplioris reuerentie conscribuntur.[a] Gratuletur

f. 137ᵛ igitur uestra uniuersitas hiis que | uobis a Domino prius et sede Romana[b] posterius indulta sunt, et gratiarum actiones deuotas et uberes pro tantis beneficiis compensate, supplicantes atencius ut inchoata feliciter ipse finiendo perficiat qui se principium et finem omnium nominauit.[2] Nos autem secundum mandatum domini pape cum fratribus et coepiscopis sollemnitatem denuntiauimus sollemniter celebrandam, et cum requisiti fuerimus, preparatis que necessaria fuerint eleuando corpori humiliter insistemus.

---

[a] *A strangely worded clause*   [b] Romona *Lc*

[1] Cf. Wisd. 5: 17; Ps. 4: 4 (3).   [2] Cf. Rev. 22: 13.

honour from the hands of the Lord as its payment. This Our Lord Himself makes known. The whole day He exalts His saints, repaying the temporal with the eternal and causing them to shine with miracles in the sight of men, ensuring that their names live for ever and also that their bodies are buried not only peacefully but with honour.[1] These points we have mentioned briefly to you in whose presence their truth is now especially clear. Blessed G(ilbert), the first founder of your Order, because he lived a guiltless life, winning praise by his conduct amongst men and persevering honourably in God's service to the end, has, as a sign and proof of the reward he has secured in heaven, in like fashion won glory also upon earth. For the pope has been informed about the life of Master Gilbert, his merits, his character and conduct, and the power of the miracles for which Our Lord has rendered him famous. As is clear to all from the contents of the papal mandate, he has decided on the advice of his brethren that this Master should be solemnly added to the catalogue of saints as a saint of the Lord, and has appointed that his festival be observed. Because this redounds greatly to Gilbert's glory, he has also mercifully granted that in the course of time his body may be translated with honour. Our spirit has rejoiced abundantly for this reason: that in our day it has come about, through our careful mediation, that the facts concerning his way of life and his miracles have been examined and established, and that firm assurances have been given to the Roman see on all these points. This also promotes our joy and happiness, that those who were gathered by this man under the rule of this monastic profession are strongly encouraged towards a more rigorous observance of it; and further, because of this man they are accorded greater respect before all. Therefore your whole community must offer thanks for these advantages, granted you in the first place by our Lord and secondly by the Holy See; and you should return sincere and generous expressions of gratitude for such great benefits, asking all the more urgently that, what has been begun in prosperity, He who called Himself the beginning and end of all things may complete at the last.[7] In accordance with the pope's mandate we, together with our brethren and fellow bishops, have proclaimed that his festival is to be celebrated with all solemnity and, when we have been asked and all necessary preparations have been made, we will humbly undertake the translation of his body.

[29] *Item epistola eiusdem ad suffraganeos suos de sollemnitate sancti Gileberti celebranda*[1]

Hubertus Dei gratia Cantuariensis archiepiscopus, tocius Anglie primas, dilectis in Christo fratribus episcopis per prouintiam Cantuariensem, salutem, gratiam et benedictionem.

Dominus papa, sicut ex litteris ipsius manifeste perpenditur, de conuersatione, meritis et moribus beati G(ileberti), magistri ordinis de Sempingham, et miraculis a Deo per eum factis per testes et testimonia sufficienter instructus, de consilio fratrum cardinalium ipsum magistrum cathalogo sanctorum decreuit ascribi, sollemnitatem eius constituit, et mandauit per Cantuariensem prouintiam sollemniter celebrari. Insuper et corpus eius cum requisiti fuerimus precepit ad honorem Dei et gloriam eleuari. |

f. 138 Vestra igitur uniuersitas huic mandato cum deuotione congaudeat, et secundum formam in ipso mandato prescriptam predicti confessoris Domini depositionem annuam faciatis cum reuerentia et sollemniter obseruari, ut apud Deum et ab illo uestra debeat et possit deuotio commendari, necnon et ipsius sancti supplex intercessio uobis proficiat ad salutem. Valete.

[30] *Littere R(ogeri) decani et capituli Lincolniensis de eodem*[2]

Rogerus decanus et capitulum Lincolniensis ecclesie, uiris uenerabilibus et amicis in Christo karissimis uniuersis archidiaconis per episcopatum Lincolniensem constitutis eternam in Domino salutem.

Mandatum domini Cantuariensis in hec uerba suscepimus: H(ubertus) Dei gratia Cantuariensis archiepiscopus, tocius Anglie primas, dilectis in Christo fratribus episcopis, *et cetera ut supra*. Mandamus itaque discretioni uestre quatinus prescriptum mandatum domini Cantuariensis super hoc in archidiaconatibus uestris executioni reuerenter sicut decet demandetis, cui mandato nec resistere possumus sicut nec debemus, presertim cum domini pape auctoritate sit subnixum.[a]

Letter 29 *LcOd*
Letter 30 *LcOd*   [a] *Od adds:* Consimili modo scripserunt episcopi, adicientes ut secundum formam prescriptam beati confessoris G. sollemnitatem congruo honore facerent obseruari.

[1] Calendared in *EEA* iii, no. 613.   [2] See p. 228 n. 2.

[29] *Another letter from the same to his suffragans on celebrating the festival of St Gilbert*[1]

Hubert, by God's grace archbishop of Canterbury, primate of all England, to his dear brothers in Christ the bishops throughout the province of Canterbury, greetings, grace and blessing.

As emerges clearly from his letter, the Pope has received from witnesses and written evidence sufficient information about the way of life, the merits, and the character of blessed Gilbert, master of the Order of Sempringham, and about the miracles which God worked through him. On the advice of his brothers the cardinals he has decreed that Master Gilbert should be added to the catalogue of saints, and has established his festival and ordered its solemn celebration throughout the province of Canterbury. And further he has commanded that his body should be translated, for the honour and glory of God, when we are asked to perform it. Therefore you may all with respect rejoice together at this mandate, and in accordance with the terms set out within it you are to see that the death of Our Lord's confessor is observed reverently and solemnly every year. Then your devotion should, and indeed can, win his commendation before God, and also this saint's humble intercession may profit you unto salvation. Farewell.

[30] *Letter of Dean R(oger) and the chapter of Lincoln about the same*[2]

Roger, dean, and the chapter of the church of Lincoln to those venerable men, and dear friends in Christ, all the archdeacons holding office throughout the bishopric of Lincoln, everlasting salvation in Our Lord.

We have received a mandate from the archbishop of Canterbury in these terms: Hubert, by God's grace archbishop of Canterbury, primate of all England, to his dear brothers in Christ the bishops . . . *etc. as above* [*no. 29*]. Therefore we instruct you of your good judgement reverently and properly to put into execution in your archdeaconries this mandate on the subject sent by the archbishop of Canterbury. We neither may nor should oppose this mandate, particularly as it is supported by the pope's authority.

[31] *Littere I(ohannis) Norwicensis episcopi de eodem*[1]

I(ohannes), Dei gratia Norwicensis episcopus, uniuersis per
episcopatum suum constitutis ad quos littere iste peruenerint,
salutem, gratiam et benedictionem.

Mandatum domini Cantuariensis in hec uerba suscepimus:
H(ubertus) Dei gratia Cantuariensis archiepiscopus, tocius Anglie
f. 138ᵛ | primas, uenerabilibus in Christo fratribus uniuersis episcopis per
prouintiam Cantuariensem constitutis, salutem in Domino.
Dominus papa, sicut ex litteris eius manifeste perpendi potest, *et*
cetera.

Huius itaque auctoritate mandati uniuersitati uestre mandamus,
precipientes quatinus secundum formam prescriptam beati confessoris G(ileberti) solemnitatem honore condigno faciatis obseruari; collectas autem quas in commemoratione eius dicendas
summus pontifex edidit et litteris suis inseruit, huic mandato
nostro duximus inscribendas, et uobis denuntiamus in ipsius
memoria recolendas. *Collecta*: Plenam in nobis . . . [cf. p. 252].

[32] *Littere archiepiscopi ad episcopos ut convenirent*[2]

Sicut alias fraternitati uestre notum fecimus, dominus papa,
sufficienter instructus de sanctitate serui Dei G(ileberti),
quondam magistri ordinis de Sempingham, et miraculis quibus
dinoscitur choruscare, ipsum cathalogo sanctorum ascripsit, et
dedit nobis insuper in mandatis ut per prouintiam nostram facere-
mus festiuitatem eius sollemniter celebrari. Nunc autem noueritis
quod, cum in eodem mandato fuisset adiectum ut, cum a fratribus
f. 139 predicti ordinis requisiti essemus, corpus eiusdem confessoris
studeremusᵃ cum honore ac reuerentia debita eleuare, | ipsi fratres
in uigilia sancte Crucis nos super hoc per magistrum suum et
maiores ordinis conuenerunt, instantesᵇ ut die dominica proxima
post festum sancti Dionisii[3] mandatum apostolicum super eleuatione predicti corporis exequamur. Quia igitur tanti processus
negocii sollemnitatem desiderat, uobis hoc denuntiare curauimus,

Letter 31 *Lc*
Letter 32 *LcOd*   ᵃ studemus *Lc*   ᵇ instanter petentes *Od*

---

[1] See p. 219 n. 1.
[2] Calendared in *EEA* iii, no. 614. There were probably letters sent to individual
bishops, as Professor Cheney notes; cf. 'diocesim uestram' below.

[31] *Letter of J(ohn) bishop of Norwich about the same*[1]

J(ohn), by God's grace bishop of Norwich, to all those holding office throughout his bishopric to whom these letters come, greetings, grace, and blessing.

We have received a mandate from the archbishop of Canterbury in these terms: H(ubert), by God's grace archbishop of Canterbury, primate of all England, to his venerable brothers in Christ all the bishops holding office throughout the province of Canterbury, greetings in Our Lord. As may be clearly inferred from his letter, the pope *etc.* [*no. 29*].

Therefore on the authority of this mandate we issue instructions to you all that you cause the blessed confessor Gilbert's festival to be observed with fitting reverence following the terms set out above. We have also thought it right to enter in this our mandate the collects which the pope issued and included in his letter for use in his commemoration, and we urge you to record these in memory of this man. The collect: [Eternal Saviour, may Thy] full [healing power work] in us . . . [*p. 253*].

[32] *Letter from the archbishop to the bishops asking them to assemble*[2]

As we made known to you, brothers, on another occasion, since the Pope has received sufficient information about the holiness of God's servant Gilbert, formerly master of the Order of Sempringham, and the glittering miracles for which he is well known, he has added his name to the catalogue of saints, and further in his mandates asked us to see that his festival is celebrated solemnly throughout our province. Since it was included in this same mandate that we should take care to translate the confessor's body with proper pomp and reverence when we had been so asked by the brethren of this Order, you should also know now that these brethren, represented by their master and senior members of the Order, met us for this purpose on the vigil of the Exaltation of the Holy Cross [13 September] and urged that we should carry out the papal mandate on the translation of the same body on the next Sunday following the feast of St Denis [13 October].[3] Since a ceremony of such importance requires solemn celebration, we have taken care to report this to you so that,

[3] The dates must be the vigil of the Exaltation of the Holy Cross, i.e. 13 Sept. 1202, and the Sunday after St Denis, 13 Oct. 1202.

ut si placet una nobiscum ad diem quem prediximus intersitis, et per diocesim uestram*a* id puplicari uelitis, ut diem eleuationis notum habeant qui uoluerint beati confessoris limina uisitare.

[33] *Littere archidiaconorum*[1] *ad plebes*[b] *de eodem*

Auctoritate domini Cantuariensis uobis mandamus quatinus die dominica proxima post festum sancti Dionisii ei occurratis,[2] ut eleuationi corporis beati confessoris G(ileberti), quondam magistri de Sempingham, una cum illo intersitis. Tantam namque sollemnitatem in absentia uestra, presertim in partibus uestris, celebrari inhonestum est et indecorum. Vos autem, auctoritate domini Cantuariensis et nostra citati, accedere non postponatis, ita quidem ut ille uobis retribuat qui omnium est retributor bonorum.

[34] *Epistola archiepiscopi de translatione facta et de indulgentia quadraginta dierum*[3]

Omnibus Christi fidelibus presentes litteras uisuris Hubertus Dei gratia Cantuariensis archiepiscopus, | tocius Anglie primas, eternam in Domino salutem.

f. 139ᵛ

Dominus papa Innocentius iii, audito quod beatus Gilebertus, quondam magister ordinis de Sempingham, sancta conuersatione, morum et operum uirtute preclarus, adhuc in carne positus et carne deposita per gratiam Dei uariis et pluribus miraculis choruscaret, ueritatis inquisitionem sollicite faciendam nobis et nobiscum aliis per apostolica scripta commisit. Qua facta in sollicitudine qua iniunxit et sollemnitate qua decuit, sedi apostolice in forma prefixa certitudinem retulimus inquisitam. Cuius relationis et uerbis statera exquisite ueritatis et prudentie ponderatis, et nuntiis insuper examinatis attentius ad cautelam, idem dominus ac summus pontifex noster, superna instructione suppliciter inuocata, longaque deliberatione usus, et tractatu protracto cum fratribus, diuino tandem instinctu, de illorum communi consilio et assensu, beatum confessorem Gilebertum

---

a dioceses uestras *Od*
Letter 33 *LcOd* *b* plebem *Od*
Letter 34 *LcOd*

---

[1] Of the vacant see of Lincoln. [2] See p. 259 n. 3.
[3] Calendared in *EEA* iii, no. 615.

if it please you, you may be present with us on the day specified above, and that you may cause this to be announced throughout your diocese, so that those who wish to visit the blessed confessor's shrine may be aware of the day of his translation.

[33] Letter from the archdeacons[1] to the people concerning the same

On the authority of the archbishop of Canterbury we command you to meet him on the next Sunday following the feast of St Denis [13 October],[2] so that you may be present with him at the translation of the body of the blessed confessor Gilbert, formerly master of Sempringham. For it is a shame and disgrace that such a solemn rite should be celebrated without you, especially in your own part of the country. Summoned as you are upon the authority of the archbishop of Canterbury and upon our own, you are to hasten your arrival so that He who is the rewarder of all good deeds may reward you.

[34] Letter of the archbishop about the translation and an indulgence of forty days[3]

To all Christ's faithful people who will see this letter, Hubert, by God's grace archbishop of Canterbury, primate of all England, everlasting salvation in Our Lord.

When Pope Innocent III heard that blessed Gilbert, formerly Master of the Order of Sempringham—a man well known for his holy way of life and the virtue of his character and deeds—was, during his lifetime and after his death, achieving fame through God's grace for a great variety of glittering miracles, he sent papal letters both to us and to other men ordering a careful inquiry into the facts. After this had been accomplished, with the care that he prescribed and with all proper ceremonial, we sent back to the Holy See the truth we had discovered in the form laid down. When the words of this report had been weighed in the scales of accurate truth and of wisdom, and when as a further precaution the messengers had been carefully interrogated, this same lord, our pope, humbly entreated guidance from on high and engaged in lengthy deliberations and protracted discussion with his brethren. At last, divinely inspired and with their common advice and agreement, he judged that the blessed confessor Gilbert should be

inter sanctos et electos Dei censuit numerandum, cathalogo sanctorum asscripsit, sollemnitatem eius celebrandam indixit, corpusque ipsius confessoris precepit a nobis ad gloriam diuini
nominis fideique catholice firmamentum et perpetuum eiusdem
sancti titulum eleuari.

f. 140 Nosque secundi huius man|dati susceptis apicibus, pro tenore
iniuncto depositionis eius diem sollemnem constituimus obseruandum.[a] Tractuque temporis cum essemus a magistro ordinis et
fratribus requisiti, captata et data oportunitate, usque ad Sempingham cum quibusdam coepiscopis nostris in spiritu humilitatis
descendimus ad terminum eleuandi corporis publice nuntiatum.
Vbi simul in reuerentia debita et ueneratione deuota, cum maioribus ordinis memorati, nonnullis etiam regni principibus, coram
cleri et populi multitudine copiosa, .iīi. idus Octobris mandatum
eleuationis predicte fideliter executi sumus, ad gloriam Dei et
sancte matris ecclesie sempiternam.

Quia igitur beati Gileberti confessoris conuersationem nouimus
in hac uita, quia fructus operum eius inestimabiles[b] cognouimus et
alias inauditos, quia gloriam eius in ministerio eleuationis uidimus
manifestam, de sanctitate ipsius edocti plenius, quasi qui non
possumus dubitare de misericordia Dei, qui gloriatur in sanctis
suis, et beati confessoris meritis presumentes, ex potestate nobis
indulta misericorditer indulgemus, ut quicumque digne penitens
et uere confessus usque ad Sempingham sancti huius limina causa
f. 140ᵛ orationis quandocumque uisitaturus accesserit, | de iniuncta penitentia .XL. dies sibi gaudeat relaxatos, necnon et orationum ac
beneficiorum Cantuariensis ecclesie participatione perpetua se
nouerit gauisurum. Facta est autem hec a nobis relaxatio anno
dominice incarnationis .M.CC. secundo, die quo corpus eiusdem
sancti a nobis est eleuatum, scilicet .III. idus Octobris, in perpetuum duratura.

EXPLICIVNT EPISTOLE

---

[a] et seruandum *Lc*   [b] inestimabiles *Winterbottom;* inestimabiliter *Lc (def. Od)*

numbered amongst the saints and elect of God; he entered him in the catalogue of saints and established a festival to be celebrated in his honour; and he gave orders that the body of this same confessor should be translated by us to glorify the divine name, to strengthen the Catholic faith, and for his perpetual glory.

When we received the text of this second mandate we accordingly fixed the festival to be observed as the memorial of his death. And when in the course of time we had been so asked by the master and brethren of the Order, we grasped the opportunity we were given and, inspired by humility, went down with some of our fellow bishops to Sempringham on the date publicly announced for the translation of the body. At that place on 13 October, imbued with both proper reverence and devout respect, we, together with the senior members of this Order and also many of the kingdom's leading men, faithfully carried out the order for this translation before a great host of clergy and people, to the eternal glory of God and Holy Mother Church.

We know, therefore, how blessed Gilbert the confessor bore himself in this life; we recognize as beyond price and unprecedented the fruits of his works; we have witnessed his glory made manifest in the office of translation; we are fully convinced of his sanctity, for we cannot doubt the mercy of God, who delights in His saints. For all these reasons, trusting in the merits of the blessed confessor, by the authority which is granted to us we in our mercy issue this indulgence: whoever comes at any time to Sempringham properly penitent and having made true confession, in order to visit this saint's shrine for prayer, may enjoy forty days' remission from the penance imposed; moreover of a certainty he will enjoy a perpetual share in the prayers and benefits of the church of Canterbury. This remission was granted by us in the year of our Lord's incarnation 1202, on the day when this saint's body was translated by us, namely 13 October, and is to endure for ever.

HERE END THE LETTERS

INCIPIT PROLOGVS DE INQVISITIONE MIRACVLORVM

Ne cui ueniret in dubium placita Deo fuisse eius opera, dignatus est Dominus ea post decessum ipsius plurimis illustrare miraculis, que a uiris uenerabilibus, Huberto Cantuariensi archiepiscopo et Eustachio Eliensi episcopo et Achario abbate de Burgo,[1] cum multis aliis uiris illustribus, per mandatum domini pape Innocentii tercii, triduo ante festum sancti Michaelis, anno Incarnationis Domini .Ṁ.ĊĊ. primo, apud Sempingham inquisita sunt et ad sedem apostolicam sub hac forma transmissa.

EXPLICIT PROLOGVS

INCIPIVNT MIRACVLA POST MORTEM EIVS FACTA

[1] *De clerico arido*

Symon,[a] presbiter et canonicus domus de Hauerholm, que est ordinis de Sempingham, iuratus dixit quod circiter .XĪĪ. annos elapsos, cum ipse adhuc in seculari | habitu esset, die lune proximo post octabas Pentecostes, cum uersus scolas pergeret, obdormiuit in uia. Et cum euigilasset, sensit dextrum pedem suum cum tibia et crure emarcuisse et aruisse, ita quod usum illorum trium penitus amiserat, et surgens, alio pede, baculo sustentante, ad uillam proximam perrexit;[b] inde Radulfus laicus eum in humeris suis usque ad Hauerholm deportauit, ubi ad initium Septembris mansit continue predicta detentus infirmitate. Tunc uero quadam nocte dormiens somniauit quod quidam uir dixit ei: 'Si uis sanus fieri, hoc eodem die uisita sepulcrum magistri Gileberti de Sempingham.' Qui statim surgens in biga se illuc deferri fecit, et predicti Radulfi et quorundam fratrum de Sempingham manibus ad sepulcrum predicti deportatus, statim obdormiuit; uisumque

f. 141

Miracle 1 *LcOd*   [a] *ins.* canonicus *Lc*   [b] *ins.* et *Od*

---

[1] See p. 170 n. 4. For the date see pp. 172–3.

THE MIRACLES:
FORMAL COLLECTION

PROLOGUE TO THE INQUIRY INTO THE MIRACLES

In case anyone should doubt that Gilbert's works were pleasing to God, the Lord has seen fit to make them illustrious after his death with many miracles. These have been investigated by the venerable Hubert, archbishop of Canterbury, Eustace, bishop of Ely, and Acharius, abbot of Peterborough,[1] together with many other notable men, in accordance with our Lord Pope Innocent III's mandate, on the third day before the feast of St Michael [26 September], 1201, at Sempringham; they have been sent to the Apostolic See in this form.

END OF THE PROLOGUE

HERE BEGIN THE MIRACLES WORKED AFTER
HIS DEATH

[1] *A withered clerk*

Simon, a priest and canon of the house of Haverholme, which belongs to the Order of Sempringham, said on oath that about twelve years before when he was still in secular dress, on the Monday following the octave of Pentecost, he fell asleep on the way to the school. When he woke up he discovered that his right foot together with his leg and shin had so withered and shrivelled that he had entirely lost the use of all three. He got up and, on his other foot, with the help of a stick, went on to the next village, where Ralph, a layman, carried him on his shoulders as far as Haverholme; there he stayed, confined by this ailment, right up to the beginning of September. Then one night as he lay asleep he dreamed that a man said to him: 'If you want to be well, this very day go and visit the tomb of Master Gilbert of Sempringham.' He got up straight away and had himself taken there in a cart; when the same Ralph and some of the brethren of Sempringham had carried him bodily to the tomb, he promptly fell asleep. It seemed

est ei quod idem uir, qui prius ei in somnis apparuerat, astaret coram illo dicens: 'Vt quid hic diutius iaces? Ecce sanus factus es.' Et surgens sensit se non solum sanatum in pede et tibia et crure, sed etiam pes, tibia et crus, que prius arida, attenuata et quasi mortua fuerant, alii pedi, tibie et cruri in omnibus similia inuenta f. 141ᵛ sunt, ita quod maior | digitus dextri pedis, qui excoriatusᵃ in aduentu suo, penitus sanus inuentus est. Huius rei testes sunt adiurati Radulfus auriga et .iii. canonici.

Radulfus auriga laicus iuratus testatur satis idem per omnia quod Symon presbiter superius dixit de infirmitate et curatione sua, excepto eo quod dicit quod non portauit eum in humeris suis usque ad Hauerholm die qua infirmitas eum primo arripuerat.

TESTIS Radulfus, canonicus de Sempingham et sacerdos, iuratus dixit quod, cum esset sacrista ecclesie de Sempingham, predictus Symon manibus eius et alterius fratris et predicti Radulfi sustentatus ad sepulcrum predictum fuit deductus. Et cum ibi statim obdormisset, sudore magno profusus plangere cepit quinquies, et euigilans per se surrexit, diu pede illo aspecto; et cum iterum ad nutum factum ei a predicto obdormisset, euigilans est ab eodem Radulfo quomodo ei staret interrogatus. Et respondens dixit quod sentiebat se ex toto sanum; et uideret eum sanum recedere.

TESTIS Willelmus, canonicus de Sempingham et sacerdos, iuratus dixit quod fuit socius eiusdem sacriste, et uidit quod predictus Symon descendit de biga et uno pede, baculo sustentante, cum predictis | f. 142 sacrista et Radulfo laico iuit usque ad sepulchrum predictum; et ibi eo dimisso recessit, et post modicum tempus a monasterio sanum recedere.¹ᵇ

TESTIS Henricus, canonicus ordinis de Sempingham, tunc prior de Hauerholm,² iuratus dixit quod uidit predictum Symonem tali infirmitate detentum ut predictus Symon dicit; et motus doloribusᶜ eius sepe pedem et tibiam manibus contrectauit, et uidit quod articuli pedis infirmati excoriati erant, eo quod dum ipse incederet eos nudos per terram traheret, et pedi illi calceum quoddam de corio apposuit, quod nobis ostendit. Curationi non interfuit, sed curatum eum uidit. Credit tamen quod per merita magistri Gileberti ad tumulum eius sanitatem recepit.

ᵃ *A verb like* fuerat *seems to have dropped out (Winterbottom)*   ᵇ *The grammar of this sentence has gone astray*   ᶜ doloribus *Winterbottom;* doloris *Lc (def. Od)*

¹ The text seems corrupt and the precise meaning is not clear.
² Occurs 1201, 1208 (*Heads*, p. 202).

to him that the same man who had appeared to him before in his dreams stood by him saying, 'Why do you lie here any longer? Look, you are healed.' Then as he got up he realized not only that his foot, leg, and shin felt better but also, where they had previously been shrivelled, thin, and more or less dead, they were now found to be in every respect the same as his other foot, leg, and shin; moreover, the great toe of his right foot, which had been bare of skin when he arrived, appeared entirely healthy. Ralph the driver and three canons are sworn witnesses to this fact.

Ralph the driver, a layman, gives on oath in all respects much the same evidence supplied above by Simon the priest on his sickness and cure, except that Ralph says that he did not carry him on his shoulders to Haverholme on the day when his illness first struck.

Ralph, a canon of Sempringham and a priest, said on oath that when he was sacrist of the church of Sempringham, the same Simon was taken to the tomb, supported by himself, by another brother, and by Ralph. When he had at once fallen fast asleep there, he came out in a great sweat and five times began to lament. He woke up, arose without help, having examined his bad foot for some time, and went back to sleep at Ralph's suggestion. When he woke again Ralph asked him how he felt. He replied that he felt completely better, and Ralph saw him go away a cured man.

William, a canon of Sempringham and a priest, said on oath that he was the sacrist's colleague, and he saw Simon get down from the cart and come to the tomb on one foot supported by a stick, along with the sacrist and Ralph, a layman. William dismissed him and went on his way; and after a short time he saw him leave the monastery healed.[1]

Henry, a canon of the Order of Sempringham, then prior of Haverholme,[2] said on oath that he saw the same Simon confined by the illness Simon describes; touched by his suffering, he often massaged his foot and shin and saw that the toes of his weak foot were raw. This was because while Simon walked he dragged them uncovered over the ground. He put a kind of leather shoe, which he showed us, on that foot. He was not present at his healing, but saw Simon after he had been cured. He believes, however, that it was through Master Gilbert's merits that at his tomb Simon was restored to health.

[2] *De muliere contracta*[1] *per septem annos*

Brictiua de Sempingham iurata dixit quod, cum per .VII.^tem annos contracta fuisset, ita quod nullo modo incedere posset, sed sicut infantem eam oportuit reptare super terram, manibus et pedibus, delata ante sepulchrum magistri Gileberti, cum ibi per .VII.^tem continuos dies in orationibus perseuerasset, uisum est ei dormienti ante tumbam illius quod, scisso lapide quo tegebatur, uir sanctus erigens se resedit, maxima claritate circumfusus;^a et uidebatur

f. 142^v eidem mulieri quod | hostie quas ipse tenebat in manu sua multiplicabantur, ita quod manibus suis uix illas potuit continere; et duas imposuit ori egrotantis illius, et recepta benedictione ab ipso, excitata a somno sensit crepitum in extensione neruorum, et ita plene reddita est sanitati, et cepit rectis gressibus ambulare. Adiecit etiam quod de fistula quam per multos annos grauiter est perpessa per merita eiusdem uiri, ut credit, est tunc similiter a Domino liberata.

TESTES   Huius miraculi testes sunt iurati sacerdotes eiusdem uille et tota uillata cum illis iurata.

[3] *De sacerdote paralitico per annum et amplius*

Robertus de Multona presbiter iuratus dixit quod cum .VI.^a feria in balneo lotus fuisset, et^b in die sabbati sequenti proximo, et^b in talem et tam grauem incidit egritudinem continuam per annum et amplius quod officio menbrorum destitutus quasi paralisin incurrisset, et^b nisi alieno auxilio de lecto moueri non potuit. Sed cum ad ecclesiam de Sempingham in uehiculo delatus fuisset, circa meridiem ante uesperas facta oratione sua ad Dominum cum deuotione, per merita eiusdem sancti uiri, ut credit, ita fuit ab infirmitate liberatus quod ecclesiam exiuit et postea usum suorum

f. 143   habuit | menbrorum ad plenum.

TESTIS   Huius rei testis est iuratus Gilebertus seruiens eiusdem, qui in infirmitate illum custodiuit per annum, et hec uidit que de illo dicta sunt, quia idem seruiens manibus suis eum pauit in infirmitate sua et necessaria ministrauit.

Miracle 2 *LcOd*   ^a *ins.* hostias tenens in manibus *Od*
Miracle 3 *LcOd*   ^b et *in each case seems superfluous*

---

[1] Perhaps 'hunched' or 'shrivelled': see p. civ.

[2] *A woman crippled[1] for seven years*

Brictiva of Sempringham said on oath that for seven years she had been crippled so that she was completely incapable of walking and had to crawl on the ground on her hands and knees like a small child. She was brought in front of Master Gilbert's sepulchre and she persisted in her prayers there for seven consecutive days. As she slept before his tomb she dreamed that the stone which lay over him broke and the holy man, surrounded by a brilliant light, rose up and seated himself. And it seemed to this woman that the hosts which he was holding increased in number so fast that his hands could scarcely contain them; two of these he placed in the mouth of this sick woman. When she had received his blessing and woke from her dream she felt a tingling throughout all her nerves and in this way she completely recovered her health and started to walk, taking steps upright. She added, moreover, that she believes that through Gilbert's merits the Lord at the same time gave her similar relief from a fistula which she had endured with pain for many years.

The priests of this village, and the whole village with them, are sworn witnesses to this miracle.

[3] *A priest paralysed for more than a year*

Robert of Moulton, a priest, said on oath that he had taken a bath on Friday and on the following Saturday became so seriously ill for more than a year that he was without the use of his limbs as if he suffered from paralysis, and he could not move from his bed without another's help. But he was transported to the church of Sempringham, and about midday, before vespers, when he had prayed fervently to the Lord, he was so completely freed from his disability through the merits, he believes, of this holy man, that he walked out of the church and afterwards possessed the full function of his limbs.

Gilbert, his servant, who looked after him for a year during his illness, is a sworn witness of this miracle. He saw all that has been said about Robert, because as his servant he fed him with his own hands when he was ill and did whatever was necessary for him.

[4] *De dissenteria et aliis morbis*

Alienor, mulier de Amewic, iurata dixit quod cum uariis morbis, scilicet dissenteria, gutta, uomitu et aliis secretis quos fateri erubuit, detineretur[a] in lecto suo a festo Omnium Sanctorum usque ad diem tercium ante Purificationem sancte Marie, audiuit et sciuit quod due uicine sue, una surda, altera ex parte paralitica, ad tumbam magistri G(ileberti) receperint sanitatem, et ex hoc fidutiam recuperande sanitatis concipiens fecit se mensurari et cum candela qua se mensurauerat in una careta portari ad tumbam magistri; ibique uigilauit ab hora nocturnorum usque ad terciam decantatam; sentiens se conualuisse hilariter comedit et bibit, nec reiecit cibum ut antea consueuerat; et credit se per merita iamdicti G(ileberti) sanitatem recepisse.

TESTIS   Huius rei ueritatem et seriem testatur domina Hawisa de Amewic iurata.

[5] *De brachio inflato*

f. 143ᵛ Adiecit etiam de se ipsa quod brachium habuit inflatum | et rubicundum ex fleobotomia plus quam per unum mensem, et uenit ad Hauerholm, unam scilicet de domibus ordinis magistri G(ileberti), ubi ex aqua qua lotum fuerat corpus eiusdem magistri G(ileberti) defuncti brachium perfusum eadem die pristinam recepit sanitatem.

Galfridus de Amewic iuratus dixit quod duxit supradictam Alienor in careta sua ad tumbam magistri G(ileberti) predictis infirmitatibus pregrauatam, et scit quod sanitatem ibi recuperauerit.

[6] *De genu curato*

Felicia, mulier de Amewic, iurata dixit quod per duos menses habuit genu adeo contractum quod nullatenus incedere potuit, et fecit se portari in careta ad tumbam magistri G(ileberti), et ibi per duas noctes cum candela accensa uigilauit, et uouit quod ibidem, si ei Deus sanitatem prestaret, habitum religionis susciperet si permitteretur a conuentu. Secunda uero nocte obdormiuit et uidebatur ei in somnis quod flos rubicundus de ore

Miracle 4 *Lc*   [a] detineretur *Winterbottom;* detinetur *Lc*
Miracle 5 *Lc*   Miracle 6 *LcOd*

[4] *Dysentery and other ills*

Eleanor, a woman from Anwick, said upon oath that from the feast of All Saints [1 November] to the third day before the Purification of St Mary [30 January] she was confined to bed with various complaints, such as dysentery, gout, vomiting, and other secret ones which she was too ashamed to describe. She found out that two women, neighbours of hers, one deaf and the other partially paralysed, had recovered their health at Master Gilbert's tomb. Gaining confidence from this that she too would recover, she had herself measured and, equipped with a candle of her own size, taken by cart to the Master's tomb. She kept vigil there from the hour of matins to terce. Then, feeling herself restored, she ate and drank joyfully, not vomiting her food as she had done formerly. She believes that she recovered her health through Gilbert's merits.

Dame Hawise of Anwick witnesses on oath to the detailed truth of this event.

[5] *A swollen arm*

She also added on her own account that for more than a month she had an arm which was swollen and inflamed from a blood-letting. She came to Haverholme (one of the houses belonging to Master Gilbert's Order) where her arm was sprinkled with the water in which Master Gilbert's body had been washed after his death. That very day she recovered her former good health.

Geoffrey of Anwick said on oath that he took Eleanor, when she was suffering from these ailments, to Master Gilbert's tomb in his cart, and he acknowledges that she was restored to health there.

[6] *A knee healed*

Felicia, a woman from Anwick, said on oath that for two months the muscles of her knee were so tense that she could not walk at all. She had herself taken by cart to Master Gilbert's tomb, kept vigil there for two nights with a burning candle, and vowed that if God granted her good health she would take the nun's habit there if allowed by the convent. Then on the second night she fell asleep and dreamed that a red flower fell upon her knee from the mouth

ymaginis beate Virginis, que ibi fuit, cecidit super genu suum. Et euigilans statim se per merita magistri G(ileberti) et per gratiam Dei et beate Virginis intellexit sanatam, et statim exiliens deosculata est pedem ymaginis predicte.

TESTIS De morbo uero et sanitate et modo et loco testimonium perhibet
f. 144 | supradicta Hawisa de Amewic. Similiter Radulfus filius Suain iuratus, qui duxerat eam ad tumbam magistri G(ileberti) in careta sua. Supradicta quoque Felicia dixit quod singulis annis uisitat sepulchrum magistri G(ileberti) cum oblatione sua in memoriam huius miraculi.

[7] *De brachio curato*

Matildis, uxor Thome militis de Wilgebi,[1] iurata dixit quod tanta infirmitas arripuit eam in brachio sinistro ante festum sancti Petri ad Vincula, durans usque ad Natiuitatem beate Marie, quod nullo modo potuit manum suam ad caput leuare, nec aliquid operis facere; alio etiam morbo diu tenebatur. Adiens autem tumbam magistri G(ileberti) ibique uigiliis et orationibus pernoctans, ab utroque morbo sanata est.

TESTIS De morbo uero et sanitate testimonium perhibet Gilebertus miles, pater eiusdem Matildis, qui cum ea predicto modo afflicta uenit ad Sempingham, ad sepulchrum scilicet magistri G(ileberti), et cum eadem ibidem sanata rediit.

[8] *De squinanci*

Alexander de Sempingham iuratus dixit quod anno preterito, circiter .xv. dies post festum sancti Michaelis, obsedit quidam tumor quasi squinancis guttur eius, et adeo grauauit eum per .viii. dies quod detentus est lecto, non comedens, et per duos ultimos dies
f. 144ᵛ nil | bibere potuit; et circa mediam horam ultime noctis amisit loquelam usque ad uesperas diei sequentis, ita quod credebatur ab omnibus moriturus; et circa horam uespertinam allata est zona magistri G(ileberti) et aqua benedicta ipsius G(ileberti) in ciffo; et collum eius circumcinctum est zona, et aqua benedicta in os eius infusa, et totus tumor colli sui lotus aqua; et statim sensit interius fieri quandam ructuram paruam in gutture ipsius Alexandri, et

of a statue of the Blessed Virgin which was in that place. As she awoke, she realized at once that she had been healed through Master Gilbert's merits and by the grace of God and the Blessed Virgin. She leapt up immediately and kissed the statue's foot.

The same Hawise of Anwick testifies to the illness and the method and place of its cure. So also, upon oath, did Ralph, son of Swein, who had taken her to Master Gilbert's tomb in his cart. The same Felicia also said that to commemorate this miracle she visits Master Gilbert's tomb every year with her offering.

[7] *An arm healed*

Matilda, the wife of Thomas knight of Willoughby,[1] said on oath that from before the feast of St Peter ad Vincula [1 August] right up to the Nativity of St Mary [8 September] such weakness affected her left arm that she was completely unable to lift her hand to her head or do any work. She was also gripped by another illness for a long time. But she came to Master Gilbert's tomb and, having spent the night in vigil and prayer, she was cured of both ailments.

Gilbert, knight and father to Matilda, offers evidence concerning her illness and its cure. He came with her to Master Gilbert's tomb at Sempringham when she suffered in the way described, and he returned with her after she had been healed at that place.

[8] *A quinsy*

Alexander of Sempringham said on oath that the year before, about a fortnight after the feast of St Michael, a quinsy-like swelling blocked his throat and troubled him so badly for eight days that he was confined to bed. He did not eat, and for the last two days could drink nothing. From about midnight on the last night until vespers on the following day he lost his power of speech, so that everyone believed that he was on the point of death. But about the time of vespers Master Gilbert's girdle was brought to him along with Gilbert's holy water in a goblet. The girdle was tied round his neck, the holy water was poured into his mouth, and the entire swelling upon his neck bathed in it. Immediately there was a sensation within Alexander's throat like a small spasm, and

---

[1] Willoughby, probably Scott Willoughby (Lincs.).

exiuit una sola gutta sanguinis de ore eius, et sensit alleuiationem, ita quod ante noctem locutus est et comedit, et paulatim residente tumore infra tercium diem plene curatus est.

TESTIS   Thomas de Lincolnia canonicus[1] iuratus dixit se uidisse tumorem in gutture ipsius Alexandri, et cum illum alloqueretur, nullum uerbum potuit ei loqui. Ad instantiam autem uxoris ipsius Alexandri, domum rediens misit ei zonam et aquam benedictam, per Petrum ianitorem et per patrem ipsius Alexandri; sed non uidit eum usque in tercium diem, quando sanus fuit.

TESTIS   Petrus ianitor iuratus dixit quod attulit aquam benedictam cum patre eiusdem Alexandri, et zonam magistri G(ileberti), quam quidam iuuenis ei dedit, qui cum dicto G(ileberto) solebat esse. De
f. 145 infusione aque dicit uidisse | se eam infundi, sed non est memor a quo; sed post tres dies uidit eum sanum.

TESTIS   Christiana uxor Alexandri iurata concordat in omnibus cum Alexandro. Adiecit etiam quod tumor non tantum erat in gutture sed in toto capite.

[9] *De lippa*

Christiana mulier de Sempingham iurata dixit quod primo oculus eius dexter cepit dolere et lippus fieri, deinde sinister, qui usque adeo uehementer intumuit quod eo per triduum uidere non potuit. Ipsa uero spe sanitatis recuperande accessit ad tumbam magistri G(ileberti) cum candela sua, et ibi perstitit in oratione dum prior missam celebraret. Deinde domum reuersa obdormiuit. Et cum euigilasset, non sensit dolorem capitis uel oculorum, et ante solis occasum, sedato oculi tumore, potuit uidere, et postea de die in diem melioratus est uisus oculorum, ita quod tandem plene conualuit.

TESTIS   Alexander maritus eiusdem Christiane, homo domus de Sempingham, iuratus dixit de lippitudine, dolore et tumore oculorum Christiane uxoris sue idem quod Christiana, preterquam quod non recolit uter oculus magis fuerit infirmatus. Dicit etiam quod ipsa cum candela sua iuit ad sepulchrum magistri G(ileberti), sed ipse cum illa ⟨non⟩[a] iuit nec eam ibi uidit; sed dicit quod postquam domum reuersa est et obdormisset, conualuit sicut testata est |
f. 145ᵛ ipsamet.

Miracle 9 *Lc*   [a] *Supplied by Brooke*

[1] Presumably a canon of Sempringham, though just possibly of Lincoln (cf. e.g. *Fasti*, iii. 146).

a single drop of blood issued from his mouth. He experienced such relief that before nightfall he spoke and took food, and gradually the swelling went down so that within three days he was completely cured.

Thomas of Lincoln, a canon,[1] said on oath that he had seen the swelling in Alexander's throat and, when he spoke to him, Alexander was unable to say a word to him. At the insistence of Alexander's wife, when he returned home he sent him the girdle and the holy water by means of Peter the door-keeper and Alexander's father. But he did not see him until the third day, when he was cured.

Peter the door-keeper said on oath that, together with Alexander's father, he brought the holy water and also Master Gilbert's girdle, which a young man who used to be Gilbert's companion gave him. Concerning the pouring in of the water he says that he saw it being administered, but he cannot remember by whom. But three days later he saw Alexander cured.

Christina, Alexander's wife, agrees on oath with Alexander about everything. But she added that the swelling affected not just his throat but his whole head.

[9] *A woman suffering from inflammation of the eye*

Christina, a woman from Sempringham, said on oath that first her right eye began to hurt and grow inflamed, and then her left eye, which swelled up so greatly that for three days she could not see out of it. Hoping to recover, she came to Master Gilbert's tomb with her candle, and remained there praying until the prior celebrated mass. Then she returned home and went to sleep. When she woke up she felt no pain in either her head or her eyes, and before sunset the swelling in her eye had gone down so that she was able to see. Thereafter her vision improved day by day, so that eventually she fully recovered.

Alexander, Christina's husband and a servant attached to the house of Sempringham, said on oath exactly the same about his wife's inflammation, pain, and swelling of the eyes as Christina herself, except that he does not remember which eye was worse. He also says that she went to Master Gilbert's tomb with her candle, but he himself did not go with her or see her there; but he adds that after she returned home and slept, she got better just as she herself has testified.

TESTIS   Willelmus clericus, frater predicti Alexandri, iuratus satis concordat cum Christiana, eo excepto quod dicit eam antequam a
tumba recederet melius uidere posse quam potuit quando illuc
uenit.

[10] *De morti proxima*

Alina monialis de Chikesand, que est domus ordinis de Sempingham, iurata dixit quod per .xxx. annos, bis autem in anno,
graues solita esset sentire angustias et pressuras circa cor et toto
latere sinistro; tandem ita grauata est egritudine illa quod crede-
batur incontinenti moritura, et uocatis magistro et aliis sacerdoti-
bus, ut ei tanquam moriture in sacramentis extreme necessitatis
subuenirent, de consilio magistri infusa est ori eius aqua qua ablutum fuit corpus magistri G(ileberti) defuncti, inposito super eam
pelliceo magistri G(ileberti); et ipsa quasi de extasi surgens cepit
conualescere, et ita plene successu temporis sanitati restituta est
quod nunquam postea afflictionem illam sensit.

TESTIS   Sara, monialis de Chikesand, iurata testatur satis concorditer
cum predicta Alina de infirmitate ipsius Aline et modo curationis
eius.

[11] *De paralitico curato*

Frater Robertus, textor ordinis de Sempingham, iuratus dixit
f. 146 quod cum in uigilia beati Mathie apostoli post uesperas | texuit,
sequenti nocte proxima euigilans a somno, sensit manum dexteram retortam, ita quod non posset eam extendere et brachium
suum a cubitu infra; et destitutus est ab officio manus et brachii
usque ad festum dominice Annuntiationis proxime sequentis.
Contritus et uere penitens, confessus peccata sua patri peni-
tenciali, qui audit confessiones et iniungit penitentias, accessit ad
tumulum magistri G(ileberti), fundatoris ordinis de Sempingham,
cum candela, pernoctaturus ibi in oratione. Et cum ibi dormisset
modicum, euigilans sensit brachium uiuificatum et manum faci-
lem flecti et reflecti, et extendit eam, ⟨et⟩ aduertit[a] quod plene

Miracle 10 *LcOd*
Miracle 11 *Lc*   [a] et aduertit *Winterbottom, cf. p. 194;* auertit *Lc*

William, a clerk and Alexander's brother, on oath pretty well agrees with Christina, except that he states that she could see better before she left the tomb than she could when she arrived there.

[10] *A woman close to death*

Alina, a nun from Chicksands, which is a house belonging to the Order of Sempringham, said on oath that twice a year for thirty years she used to feel a terrible tightness and weight about her heart and the whole of her left side. Eventually she suffered so badly from this condition that it was thought that she was on the point of death. The master and other priests were summoned to strengthen her with the last sacraments as she lay like one about to die. Following the Master's advice, they poured into her mouth the water in which Master Gilbert's dead body had been bathed, and Master Gilbert's leather cloak was placed over her. Rising as if from a trance, she began to get better, and in the course of time she was so completely restored to health that she has never since experienced her previous condition.

Sarah, a nun from Chicksands, gives sworn evidence about Alina's sickness and how it was cured which agrees tolerably with Alina's own.

[11] *A man cured of paralysis*

Brother Robert, a weaver belonging to the Order of Sempringham, said on oath that he worked at his weaving after vespers on the vigil of St Mathias the Apostle [23 February]. Waking from a dream during the night which then followed, he found his right hand so bent back that he was unable to stretch out either his hand or his arm below his elbow. He was deprived of the use of his hand and arm until the following feast of the Annunciation of Our Lady [25 March]. Being contrite and truly penitent, he confessed his sins to the father penitentiary who hears confessions and determines penances. Then he came with a candle to the tomb of Master Gilbert, founder of the Order of Sempringham, to spend the night there in prayer. When he had slept there a little, he woke and felt his arm restored to life and his hand able to bend easily backwards and forwards. As he stretched out his hand he realized

per gratiam Dei curatus est. Et sic recepto usu manus et brachii, incolumis ad consuetum ministerium reuersus est, credens certissime quod per merita prefati G(ileberti) esset sanatus.

TESTIS Eudo, tunc prior domus de Sempingham,[1] iuratus dixit quod uidit manum prefati fratris recuruam, et dedit ei licentiam uigilandi ante tumbam prefati G(ileberti); et in crastino uidit manum fratris illius rectam et sanatam, ut ei uidebatur per merita magistri G(ileberti).

TESTIS Iohannes, sacerdos eiusdem domus, iuratus dixit idem de mortificatione brachii et manus curuatione et de liberatione fratris | f. 146ᵛ prefati quod ipse frater; sed non astitit ei presens quando curatus fuit.

TESTIS Frater Gilebertus laicus, tunc seruiens in refectorio fratrum eiusdem domus, iuratus dixit idem de mortificatione brachii et de manus curuatione et de diuturnitate temporis et de curatione prefati fratris quod ipse frater; sed non fuit presens in liberatione eius.

TESTIS Frater Rogerus, laicus eiusdem domus, iuratus dixit idem per omnia quod ipse frater Gilebertus, adiciens quod aliquamdiu fuit cum dicto fratre ante tumulum prefati G(ileberti), sed non quando curatus fuit.

[12] *De dolore colli*

Cyprianus, prior Maltone de ordine de Sempingham,[2] iuratus dixit quod cum graui dolore uexaretur in collo et occipite, quod*ᵃ* pre nimietate doloris attactum*ᵇ* manus sue proprie in loco dolente abhorreret, et per .viii. dies ea passione laborasset, ita ut caput in alterutram partem torquere non posset, nisi corpore moto; ad consilium cuiusdam fratris sui, Fabiani nomine, nunc defuncti, cum caput suum inuoluisset ueste qua magister G(ilebertus) uti consueuerat, incontinenti plenam recepit sanitatem. Et surgens de f. 147 lecto in quo decubuerat, ea nocte interfuit matutinis, psallens | et canens cum fratribus sicut consueuerat.

Miracle 12 *Lc*   *ᵃ The construction has got out of hand*   *ᵇ* actactum *Lc*

---

[1] Eudo occurs as prior in 1195 and had resigned by 1199; he is here evidently ex-prior (see *Heads*, p. 204 and n. 7).

[2] Occurs from 1201 to after 1204 (*Heads*, p. 203); and was possibly the same as Cyprian prior of Sixhills in the late 1190s, for the name is rare (*Heads*, pp. 200, 205).

that through God's grace he was completely cured. Thus having recovered the use of his hand and arm, he returned whole to his usual post in the firm belief that he had been healed through Gilbert's merits.

Eudo, who was at that time prior of the house of Sempringham,[1] said on oath that he saw Robert's hand when it was bent back, and he gave him permission to spend the night before Gilbert's tomb. The next day he saw that this brother's hand was straight, and it seemed to him that it had been healed through Master Gilbert's merits.

John, priest of the same house, said on oath the same as Robert concerning the paralysed arm and the hand's distortion and also his relief from them; but he was not standing by him when he was cured.

Gilbert, a lay brother who was then serving in the brethren's refectory at Sempringham, gave the same sworn evidence as Robert concerning the paralysis of his arm, the distortion in his hand, the length of time they lasted, and Robert's cure, but he was not present when he secured relief.

Roger, a lay brother of the same house, repeated on oath all Brother Gilbert's evidence, adding that he was present with Robert at Gilbert's tomb for some while, but not when he was cured.

[12] *A pain in the neck*

Cyprian, prior of Malton,[2] which belongs to the Order of Sempringham, said on oath that he suffered from a terrible pain in his neck and at the back of his head, and the agony was too great for him to bear even the touch of his own hands in the place where it hurt. For eight days he endured this affliction, which meant that he could not turn his head to either side without moving his body. Then, following the advice of one of the brethren called Fabian, who is now dead, he wrapped his head in a garment which Master Gilbert used to wear, and immediately he made a complete recovery. Rising from the bed where he had been lying, he took part in matins that very same night, chanting and singing with the brethren just as he had always done.

TESTIS   Thomas, prior de Sempingham,[1] iuratus idem testatur; sed non
interfuit quando frater Fabianus inuoluit caput suum in ueste
predicta.

[13] *De febre*

Domnus Albinus, quondam capellanus magistri G(ileberti), iuratus dixit quod idem G(ilebertus) cum adhuc uiueret, graui febre
correptus, dixit sibi: 'Frater Albine, si uelles loco meo febrem
istam recipere in te, eam transferrem in te.' Qui respondit se libenter suscepturum eam ut ipse liberaretur et posset uacare negotiis
domus que instabant, communiter spectantibus ad statum ordinis.
Veniente die tercio, iam plene magistro G(ileberto) curato, ter-
ciana febris arripuit Albinum et inualuit in eum per tres septimanas. Adiecit idem Albinus quod cum post aliquot annos iterum
egrotaret quadam interna egritudine, antequam plene de ea con-
ualesceret, iterum eum febris arripuit. Et cum hoc nuntiatum
fuisset magistro G(ileberto) tunc absenti, misit qui preciperet febri
ex parte Dei et sua ut relinqueret eum. Postera die, approprin-
quante hora accessionis, cum iam inciperet caro horrescere, quasi
ex frigore in proximo tremorem habitum,[2a] idem Albinus, memor
uerbi quod magister mandauerat, imperauit febri ex parte Dei et
f. 147ᵛ ipsius magistri G(ileberti) ne eum arriperet. Et facto | signaculo
crucis, penitus liberatus[b] a febre, nec postea ab ipsa uexatus,
credens certissime quod per merita prefati Gileberti esset sanatus.

[14] *De moribunda*

Alicia, priorissa de Hauerholm,[3] iurata dixit quod ⟨cum⟩[c] per .xv.
dies dolore illato grauiter laborasset, ita quod de uita sua desperaret, statim postquam aquam benedictam gustauit qua corpus
magistri ablutum fuit plene conualuit, uix adhuc ab ore ipsius
amoto ciffo in quo aqua ei allata fuit.

TESTIS   Huius rei testis est domina Diuia monialis iurata, socia familiar-
issima eiusdem Alicie,[4] que conscia fuit tam infirmitatis quam
sanitatis ipsius ita mirabiliter recuperate.

Miracle 13 *Lc*   ᵃ *The clause is corrupt*   ᵇ *Probably add* est *(Winterbottom)*
Miracle 14 *Lc*   ᶜ *Supplied by Winterbottom*

---

[1] Thomas had succeeded Eudo (see above) by 1199 and was still prior in 1204 (*Heads*,
p. 204).   [2] The text is unintelligible: see n. *a*.

Thomas, prior of Sempringham,[1] gives the same sworn evidence, but he was not there when Brother Fabian wrapped his head in the garment described.

[13] *A fever*

Dom Albinus, who was once Master Gilbert's chaplain, said on oath that this same Gilbert, while he was still alive and in the grips of a high fever, said to him: 'Brother Albinus, if you wished to take this fever upon yourself in my place, I would transfer it to you.' Albinus replied that he would willingly accept it to relieve Gilbert and allow him to attend to the urgent business of the house, affecting the condition of all the brethren and of the Order. When the third day came, Master Gilbert was now completely better, but the tertian fever gripped Albinus and held sway for three weeks. Albinus added that some years later when he was again unwell with an internal complaint, before he fully recovered from it, the fever attacked him again. When this was reported to Master Gilbert, who was away at the time, he sent commanding the fever to leave him, in God's name and his own. The next day, when the time of the fever's onset had almost arrived, indeed when his skin was beginning to shiver as if from cold, in advance of the usual shaking fit,[2] Albinus remembered the message which the Master had sent and he ordered the fever not to attack him, in the name of God and of Master Gilbert. Having made the sign of the cross, he was completely relieved of the fever and was never troubled by it thereafter. He believes most firmly that he was cured through Gilbert's merits.

[14] *A woman on the point of death*

Alice, prioress of Haverholme,[3] said on oath that for a fortnight she had suffered so badly from a pain which attacked her that she gave up all hope of living. But she tasted the holy water in which the master's body had been washed and immediately afterwards, when the chalice in which the water had been brought to her had scarcely been taken from her lips, she recovered completely.

Dame Divia, a nun and Alice's closest companion,[4] is a sworn witness of this case. She knew about both Alice's illness and the good health which she recovered so miraculously.

[3] This is the only known reference to her (*Heads*, p. 202).
[4] For the *socie* see *Institutiones* in *Monasticon*, vi. 2, p. *lxxvii (xlvii*).

TESTIS   Huius rei testis iurata est domina Matildis, monialis, que certissime conscia fuit tam infirmitatis quam sanitatis eiusdem Alicie ita
recuperate, utpote que interfuit.

[15] *De leprosa curata*

Iuliana monialis de Sempingham, et ab ipso magistro G(ileberto)
recepta in ordine, iurata dixit quod cum a pueritia sua lepre
macula laborasset, et eodem morbo inualescente totum corpus
eius successu temporis lepra perfusum fuisset, in tantum ut capillis
capitis et superciliis dipilaretur, oculos etiam eleuatis palpebris
aperire*a* non posset, et in infirmaria tanquam leprosa iugiter per
.xii. annos moram fecisset, ministrante ei et eam custodiente
f. 148 so|rore eius moniale, Claricia nomine, uidit per somnium in lecto
suo quod domina quedam ad eam ueniret, et admoneret eam ut ad
sepulchrum magistri G(ileberti) iret, dicens quod ibi curaretur.
Quo cum isset et ibidem obdormisset, apparuit ei in somnis
domina quedam uenerabilis et reuerenda,[1] que in circuitu
sepulchri magistri G(ileberti) pallium purpureum quo induta
fuerat expandit; et ad predictam Iulianam ueniens dixit ei: 'Surge,
quia curata es.' Que cum non surgeret, sed ut ei uidebatur iterum
obdormiret, iterum ei apparuit eadem domina dicens: 'Surge, quia
curata es.' Et uidebatur eidem Iuliane quod curata esset, et audiret
conuentum decantantem 'Te Deum laudamus' pro eius curatione.
Cumque ibidem dormiens requiesceret, donec pulsaretur cam-
pana ad matutinas, euigilans inde recessit, et in recessu suo
humorem colericum in magna quantitate subito reiecit, et infra
triduum proximum plenam sanitatem recepit, ita ut infra septima-
nam per totum corpus tanquam squame deciderent, et restitueretur*b* eius caro sanitati, sicut caro pueri.

TESTIS   Huius rei testis est iurata Lecelina monacha de Sempingham,
adiciens quod lepra ita grauiter totum corpus predicte Iuliane
occupauerat quod se manibus suis nec cibare potuit nec potare,
f. 148ᵛ nec | manuum suarum usum aliquem habebat.

TESTIS   Huius rei testis est iurata Claricia monialis supra memorata, que
magistra fuit eiusdem Iuliane dum esset nouitia, et in infirmaria corpus eius nudum unguentis medicinalibus perungere consueuit: adiciens quod nunquam uidit marem uel*c* feminam tam uniuersaliter

Miracle 15 *LcOd*   *a* aperiri *Lc*   *b* restitueretur *Winterbottom;* restituer *Lc,*
leaving a gap; restituetur *Lc corr.;* restituitur *Od*   *c* uel *om. Lc*

Dame Matilda, a nun, is a sworn witness of this case. She most certainly knew both of Alice's illness and of how she thus recovered her health because she was present at the time.

[15] *A woman cured of leprosy*

Juliana, a nun of Sempringham who was received into the Order by Master Gilbert himself, said on oath that she had suffered from leprous sores since she was a girl. As time went on and her whole body was afflicted by this disease, the leprosy spread to such an extent that the hair from her head and her eyebrows fell out, nor could she open her eyes by lifting up the eyelids. And so for twelve years altogether she stayed as a leper in the infirmary, looked after and protected by a sister, a nun called Clarice. As she slept in her bed she dreamed that an unknown lady came to her and told her to go to Master Gilbert's tomb, saying that she would be cured there. When she had gone to that place and had fallen asleep, there appeared to her in a dream a holy and reverend lady[1] who spread the purple cloak, which she had been wearing, around Master Gilbert's sepulchre; then approaching Juliana, she said to her, 'Arise, for you are healed.' When she herself did not get up but seemed to fall asleep again, the same lady appeared to her once more saying, 'Arise, for you are healed.' Then Juliana felt that she had been cured and that she heard the convent chanting the *Te Deum Laudamus* for her recovery. She rested there asleep until the matin-bell was rung. Then she awoke and withdrew from that place and as she went she suddenly vomited a great amount of bile. Within the next three days she recovered entire good health, so that within the week scabs fell off all over her body and she was left with skin as healthy as a child's.

Lecelina, a nun of Sempringham, is a sworn witness of this matter. She adds that leprosy had so badly affected Juliana's whole body that she could not give herself food or drink and she was completely unable to use her hands.

Clarice, the nun mentioned above, is a sworn witness of this matter. She was Juliana's novice mistress, and she used to treat Juliana's naked body with medicinal ointments in the infirmary. She adds that she has never seen either a man or a woman so completely |

---

[1] Presumably the Blessed Virgin Mary: see pp. 230–1.

et tam grauiter maculatam; asserens etiam quod quia consueuit eam unguento contrectare, et ipsa uitabatur ab aliis monialibus, timentibus ne ex ea maculam contraherent.

TESTES   Hoc idem testantur in periculo animarum suarum priorissa et magna pars conuentus de Sempingham in presentia Cantuariensis archiepiscopi, et in presentia Eliensis episcopi et abbatis de Burgo et multorum aliorum.

[16] De osse adherente gutturi

Emcina, monialis de Hauerholm, eiusdem ordinis de Sempingham, iurata dixit quod eodem anno quo obiit magister G(ilebertus) circiter festum sancti Iohannis Baptiste, cum comederet in refectorio ad prandium seruientum, os piscis ex transuerso adhesit gutturi eius, et inde grauiter anxiata manum apposuit ut extraheret, nec profecit, licet digito suo tangeret; bibensque pluries ut alleuiaretur, nichil profecit, sed pre anxietate potum ipsum reiecit; f. 149 sed et moniales temptauerunt ut extraherent, | nec potuerunt. Deinde crescente dolore assidue a meridie usque ad uesperam ita passa est. Tunc moniales adduxerunt eam in monasterium ante altare ut orarent pro ea, et ei genibus flexe dederunt aquam in qua ablutum erat corpus magistri G(ileberti) defuncti, et statim ex quo[a] sensit se liberatam, nec sciuit quo os id deuenit, et ideo credit ei hoc contigisse gratia Dei et meritis magistri G(ileberti).

TESTIS   Matildis, neptis magistri G(ileberti), monialis de Hauerholm, iurata testatur se uidisse Emcinam quodam osse laborantem sicut ipsa dixit, et eodem modo ut ipsa dixit liberatam esse. Dicit etiam[b] uidisse os id in gutture, et temptasse idem extrahere, sed non potuit.

TESTIS   Mabilia de Bugdene,[1] monialis de Hauerholm, iurata idem dicit per omnia quod Matildis.

[17] De pede leso et sanato

Mabilia de Stodfalde, monialis de Chikesand eiusdem ordinis, iurata dixit quod circiter .viii. annos transactos, tercia die post festum apostolorum Petri et Pauli, ex precepto priorisse iuit in

---

Miracle 16 *Lc*   [a] *Corrupt: perhaps read* eo *(Winterbottom)*   [b] *Perhaps add* se, *as just before (Winterbottom)*
Miracle 17 *LcOd*

and seriously blemished. She also states that, because she used to massage her with ointment, she herself was avoided by the other nuns, who were afraid that they would catch the infection from her.

Upon peril of their souls, the prioress and a large part of the convent of Sempringham give the same evidence in the presence of the archbishop of Canterbury, the bishop of Ely, the abbot of Peterborough, and many others.

[16] *A bone stuck in the throat*

Emcina, a nun of Haverholme, which belongs to the Order of Sempringham, said on oath that the same year that Master Gilbert died, about the feast of St John the Baptist [24 June 1189], she was eating in the refectory at the servants' lunch time when a fishbone stuck across her throat. In great distress she put up a hand to take it out but, although she touched it with her finger, she was unable to do more. She swallowed fluid several times to make it better, but there was no improvement, and in her worry she even vomited what she had drunk. Then the nuns too tried to take the bone out, but they could not do it either. Thus from midday to evening vespers she suffered continuously from increasing pain. Then the nuns led her into the church and before the altar so that they might pray for her, and as she knelt they gave her some of the water in which Master Gilbert's dead body had been washed. Immediately after this she felt great relief but she did not know what became of the bone. She therefore believes that this happened to her by God's grace and the merits of Master Gilbert.

Matilda, Master Gilbert's niece and a nun of Haverholme, testifies on oath that she saw Emcina suffering from a bone as she described and that she was relieved in the way she mentioned. She also says that she saw the bone in her throat and tried to get it out but was unable to do so.

Mabel of *Bugdene*,[1] a nun of Haverholme, says on oath exactly the same as Matilda.

[17] *An injured foot healed*

Mabel of Stotfold, a nun of Chicksands of the same Order, described on oath how about eight years before, on the third day after the feast of St Peter and St Paul [1 July], she went into the

---

[1] Very likely Bowden (Leics.).

coquinam cum magna festinatione, et collapsa ad lignum quoddam coopertum stramine cecidit, et in casu grauiter lesa est, ita quod pes eius recessit a iunctura, ita quod surgere non potuit, neque inde recedere. Tunc uenerunt moniales ad eius clamorem, et f. 149ᵛ ipsam tule|runt ad domum infirmarum, et sciderunt sotularem de pede, quia extrahere non potuerunt pro nimia inflatione; et cum multe multas adhiberent curas, tam trahendo, tum inplastra ponendo, nichil profecerunt sed pocius dolorem suum augmentauerunt. Et creuit dolor de die in diem toto illo anno et sequenti usque ad aniuersarium magistri G(ileberti), scilicet proximum diem ante festum sancte Agathe; et adeo desperata est illa cum aliis de curatione pedis quod quidam medicus dixit aliam non superesse uiam quam ut pes abscideretur; et dixit pedem nigrum esse ad similitudinem ueli sui; et cum infirmitate aggrauante uellet priorissa eam oleo infirmorum ungi, petiit id differri. Petiit etiam ut mensuraretur cum quodam lichno ad magistrum G(ilebertum), et candela facta portata est simul cum candela sua in monasterium; et priorissa inuoluit pedem eius in manutergio¹ quod iacuit supra pectus magistri G(ileberti) laborantis in extremis; et ibi uigilauit tota nocte aniuersarii magistri G(ileberti) ante altare, et etiam in die aniuersarii magistri G(ileberti) usque ad illam horam qua comedit conuentus, et tunc obdormiuit et in somnis uidebatur sibi uidere homines albis indutos, ingredientes monasterium, ornantes f. 150 altare quasi ad celebrandum; et post illos | uidit magistrum G(ilebertum) sacerdotalibus indutum, et ut uidebatur ei planeta erat rubea, et uidebatur ei quod magister G(ilebertus) conuertit se ad illam, et dedit ei ter benedictionem, singulis uicibus faciens ei signum ut surgeret. Ad tercium signum expergefacta surrexit, et uolens tenere magistrum G(ilebertum) cecidit in faciem; et tunc ueniente priorissa cum conuentu de prandio in monasterium, uocauit priorissam et dixit ei uisionem suam et dixit se sanatam esse per magistrum G(ilebertum), ostenditque ei pedem suum sanum, et priorissa dante ei manum surrexit, abiitque per se in domum infirmarum, usque hodie sana.

TESTIS   Cristiana, priorissa de Chikesand,² iurata huius rei per omnia testis est, dicens se ligasse manutergio pedem et soluisse propriis

---

¹ For liturgical towels see A. Watkin in *Archdeaconry of Norwich: Inventory of Church Goods temp. Edward III* (Norfolk Record Soc. 1948), pp. lxx–lxxi.
² This is the only known reference (*Heads*, p. 202).

kitchen in a great hurry on an errand from the prioress. Tripping against some wood which was covered with straw, she slipped and injured herself in falling so badly that her foot dislocated at the joint and she could neither get up nor leave the spot. Then the nuns came in answer to her cries and carried her to the infirmary and, because her foot was too swollen for them to take her shoe off, they cut it away from her foot. Although many nuns tried all kinds of remedies, putting the foot both in traction and in plaster, they brought about no improvement, indeed they even increased Mabel's suffering. Thus her pain grew day by day for the whole of that year and the one that followed, up till the anniversary of Master Gilbert's death, the day before the feast of St Agatha [4 February]. Mabel, along with the others, had so completely lost hope of a cure for her foot that a doctor stated that there was no alternative to amputating her foot, which was, she said, as black as her veil. As her complaint got worse the prioress wanted her to be anointed with the oil reserved for the sick, but Mabel asked for it to be put off. Instead she requested that her measurements should be used for a candle intended for Master Gilbert, and when this had been made, she was taken along with the candle into the church. The prioress wrapped her foot in the liturgical towel[1] which had lain upon Master Gilbert's breast when he was about to die. Mabel kept vigil there before the altar during the whole night of the anniversary of Master Gilbert's death and during the day itself, until the hour when the convent took a meal. Then she fell asleep; and she dreamed that men wearing albs came into the church and decorated the altar as if to celebrate mass there; behind these men she saw Master Gilbert dressed in his priestly robes and, she thought, in a red chasuble. In her dream Master Gilbert turned towards her and blessed her three times, each time signing her to rise. At the third sign she woke and stood upon her feet and, as she tried to take hold of Master Gilbert, she fell flat upon her face. When the prioress and the convent came from their meal into the church, she called to the prioress, described her vision to her and asserted that she had been healed by Master Gilbert. She showed her her healed foot, and when the prioress gave her a hand she got up and went away without help to the infirmary. She has been healthy ever since.

Christina, prioress of Chicksands,[2] is a sworn witness of all the details of this case. She says that she bound the foot with the liturgical towel and untied it with her own hands, and she asserts

manibus, et dicit quod post solutionem uidit omnino pedem detumuisse, et unum pedem adeo sanum et pulchrum ut alium.

[18] *De tumore uentris militis*

Henricus Biset, uir nobilis,[1] iuratus dixit quod, cum diu egrotasset et tumeret ei uenter, et tumor ille durasset circiter per duos annos et dimidium, ita ut cum resideret, obstante eodem tumore, non posset uidere de femore suo nisi ad quantitatem digitorum duorum, et timeret mortem sibi imminere, non proficiente sibi industria medicorum, licet in illum*a* multa expendisset, tandem, fere omnino | desperans de sanitate, de consilio uxoris sue misit ipsam uxorem suam et filias suas ad Sempingham custodiendas. Vxor autem eius inde reuersa attulit secum lineam zonam qua sancte recordationis magister G(ilebertus) precingi consueuit, ut ei dicebatur, super nudam carnem suam, et ampullam*b* cum aqua qua lotum fuit corpus eius, sicut ei dicebatur; quam aquam cum ipse bibisset et zona precinctus esset, cepit tremere et fremere, sed tamen non alsit et cepit dormire; et in ipsa dormitione erupit sudor, ita quod uxor eius, que uigilauit, uidit, sicut dixit, grossas guttas crocei coloris et mali fetoris. Idem uero cum euigilasset, uidit se perfusum magno sudore, et inde magnum fetorem sensit, et respiciens uentrem suum uidit tumorem resedisse sub zona ad quantitatem dimidii pedis; et postea per dies singulos conualescebat, ita quod post modicum tempus recuperata plena sanitate accessit ad tumbam sancti, gratias agens Deo. Requisitus autem utrum aliquis interfuit ubi ipse aquam bibit et zona precinctus est et ubi ita statim post potum conualuit, dixit quod non est memor quod aliquis interfuit, nisi uxor que mortua est et quidam seruiens eius, Warinus nomine sicut credit, qui tempore huius inquisitionis absens*c* in Scocia.

f. 150ᵛ

[19] *De uento dato in mari*

f. 151 Anselmus capellanus iuratus dixit quod fuit in naui quadam in mari quod est inter Angliam et Normaniam simul cum domino suo

Miracle 18 *LcOd*   *a* *Corrupt, unless we should emend the verb to mean 'they (the doctors) had worked much on him' (Od's* expendissent *can hardly mean that); it is just possible that* illum = tumorem   *b* ampulla *Lc (perhaps after correction)*   *c* *A verb (probably* erat*) seems to have dropped out (Winterbottom)*
Miracle 19 *LcOd*

that when she had unbound it she saw that the swelling had completely disappeared and the one foot was as healthy and fit as the other.

[18] *A knight with a swollen belly*

Henry Biset, a man of noble birth,[1] said on oath that he had been ill for a long while and his belly was enlarged with a swelling which lasted for about two and a half years. When he sat down this swelling got in his way, so that he could only glimpse two fingers' length of his thigh. He was afraid that his death was imminent for, although he had spent much money on them(?), the doctors' efforts had profited him nothing. Finally, when he had almost given up all hope of recovery, on his wife's advice he sent her and his daughters to be looked after at Sempringham. When his wife came back from there she brought with her the linen girdle which, she was told, Master Gilbert of holy memory used to tie around him on his bare flesh: also a flask containing, she was told, water in which his body had been washed. When Henry drank this water and tied the girdle about him, he started to shiver and groan, but he felt no cold, and fell asleep. As he slept he came out in such a sweat that his wife, who stayed awake, saw, as she stated, huge drops of a yellow colour and evil smell. When Henry himself awoke he noticed that he was covered in a heavy sweat, and he was aware of the great stench. Looking at his belly he saw that the swelling had gone down below the girdle by about half a foot. Each day afterwards he got better, so that after a little while, having fully recovered his health, he came to the holy man's tomb to offer thanks to God. But when he was asked if anyone else was present when he swallowed the water and put on the girdle, and when he got better so quickly after his drink, he replied that he cannot remember that any one was there apart from his wife, who is dead, and a servant of his, he thinks called Warin, who is away in Scotland at the time of this inquiry.

[19] *A wind bestowed upon the sea*

Anselm, a chaplain, said on oath that he was on board ship in the sea between England and Normandy, in the company of his lord,

---

[1] Perhaps the brother-in-law of John de Lacy: see below, p. 304 n. 1; *Early Cheshire Charters*, ed. G. Barraclough (Rec. Soc. of Lancs. and Cheshire, 1957, p. 15). See also Clay (art. cit. above, p. 94 n. 2), p. 126.

Iohanne, constabulario Cestrie, et Willelmo de Aubeni et Radulfo
Fraseir et aliis pluribus nobilibus;[1] sedata tempestate quam
grauissimam pertulerant, nec habuerunt uentum qui sufficeret
adhuc, ut de die applicarent in Normaniam, timebant nocturna
pericula.[a] Iohannes autem constabularius precepit eidem Anselmo
capellano suo ut proferret scapularium magistri G(ileberti) quod
ipse habebat loco reliquiarum, ex dono successoris ipsius magistri.
Idem uero Anselmus induens se uestibus sacerdotalibus, manibus
lotis idem scapularium a cofra domini sui protulit, et eleuans idem,
audientibus omnibus qui simul cum eo in naui erant, orauit dicens:
'Deus omnipotens, si placita tibi sunt magistri G(ileberti) opera,
fac nos per ipsius merita feliciter peruenire ad portum salutis.'
Hiis dictis, statim aura grata impulit scapularium inter manus suas
et a scapulario ascendit in uelum, et ita factum est ut eodem die
prospere nauigantes ⟨ante⟩[b] alias naues que cum illis in mare
ingresse fuerant in Normanniam applicuerunt.

TESTIS   Willelmus, canonicus de Sempingham, satis concordat cum
f. 151ᵛ Anselmo capellano, dicens se tunc temporis fuisse in | naue illa in
habitu seculari, et uidisse eadem que Anselmus dixit; et adiecit
quod alie naues que egresse erant de portu cum illa non applicuerunt eodem die, sed nec etiam in crastino, antequam recessissent a
Barbeflech. Adiecit etiam se ante idem tempus parum apprecia-
tum fuisse institutionem ordinis de Sempingham, sed postea, ex
quo fixum habuit propositum sumendi habitum religionis, miraculum istud fuit magna occasio quare habitum ordinis illius suscepit.

[20] *De frenesi*

Hugo de Noketun laicus iuratus dixit quod Ailiua, uxor fratris sui
Henrici, cum aliquamdiu egrotasset, tandem in frenesim incidit
aut morbum frenesi similem, quia quasi furibunda aliena loquebatur, fremebat dentibus et conspuebat in facies hominum, et ita se
gerebat quod oportuit eam ligari fere per mensem. Postea idem
Hugo et Agnes, soror eius, una cum uiro ipsius, eam traxerunt
usque ad Sempingham, ligatam in quadam biga. Quo cum uenis-
sent, detulerunt eam usque ad sepulchrum magistri G(ileberti),

---

[a] *The construction of the sentence is unclear; perhaps add* et *before* timebant *(Winterbottom)*
[b] *Supplied by the corrector of Od*
Miracle 20 *LcOd*

John, constable of Chester, William d'Aubeni, Ralph Fraseir, and many other nobles.[1] They had experienced a very severe storm, but when it died down they did not have enough wind to allow them to land in Normandy by day, and they were frightened of the night's dangers. Then John the constable ordered his chaplain Anselm to bring out Master Gilbert's scapular, which he kept among his collection of relics, since it had been given him by the Master's successor. Then Anselm put on priestly vestments, washed his hands, and produced this scapular from his lord's chest. He lifted it up, and all those who were with him in the ship listened as he prayed, saying: 'Almighty God, if Master Gilbert's works are pleasing to Thee, bring us successfully, through his merits, to a safe harbour.' As soon as he had said this, a pleasant breeze played on the scapular between his hands and then rose from the scapular up to the sails. So it came about that on that same day outpacing the other ships which had set sail with them they had an easy voyage and landed in Normandy.

William, a canon of Sempringham, agrees sufficiently with Anselm the chaplain, saying that he was on board the ship at that time in secular dress and that he saw those things which Anselm has described. He added that the other ships which left harbour with theirs did not make landfall the same day or even the following day, before they had left Barfleur. He also added that before this time he had valued the foundation of the Order of Sempringham very little, but later, when he became firmly determined to adopt the habit of religion, this miracle was the great turning-point which led him to receive the habit of this Order.

[20] *A case of delirium*

Hugh of Nocton, a layman, said on oath that Ailiva, the wife of his brother Henry, when she had been ill for some while, eventually fell into a mad fit or some delirious illness because she talked at random like a madwoman, ground her teeth, and spat in people's faces; and she behaved in such a way that she had to be tied up for almost a month. Later this same Hugh and his sister Agnes, together with her husband, took Ailiva, still bound, in a cart as far as Sempringham. When they arrived they carried her right to Master Gilbert's tomb.

[1] See p. 304 n. 1.

et ibidem nocte sequenti conualuit et resedit, gratias agens Deo; et
post tres dies sana ad domum reuersa est.

TESTIS   Agnes, soror predicti Hugonis, iurata satis concordat per omnia
cum predicto Hugone. Ipsa enim dicit se interfuisse et uidisse
f. 152 predictam | Ailiuam ita infirmatam et curatam ad tumbam magistri
G(ileberti) sicut Hugo dicit.

TESTIS   Emma, filia predicte Agnetis, iurata dixit se uidisse predictam
Ailiuam infirmatam ut dictum est; et dicit eam allatam fuisse ad
tumbam magistri G(ileberti) et ibi curatam, sed ipsa nec interfuit
nec hoc uidit, sed post paucos dies, cum Ailiua ad propria
remeasset, curatam eam uidit.

TESTIS   Robertus de Fulebech, laicus iuuenis, iuratus idem dicit per
omnia quod Emma, filia Agnetis; tempore huius examinationis
facte, mortui erant predicti Henricus et Ailiua uxor sua.

[21] De furioso [a]

Willelmus de Hoctona, pauper laicus, iuratus dixit quod cum ipse
apud Wattonam, que est domus ordinis de Sempingham, fere per
duos menses egrotasset in infirmaria pauperum, tandem incidit in
mentis alienationem; seruientes uero infirmarie eius miserti
posuerunt eum in quodam loculo ueteri in quo magister G(ilebertus) aliquando circumferri consueuerat, ex quo pre senectute
equitare non poterat. Vbi cum per duos dies et duas noctes ligatus
iacuisset, die tercio conualuit et ad mentem sanam rediit, credens
se per merita magistri G(ileberti) curatum.

TESTIS   Frater Martinus, nunc canonicus de Wattona, tempore uero
curationis predicti Willelmi sacerdos ministrans in parrochiali
ecclesia de Wattona, de infirmitate et curatione Willelmi dicit |
f. 152ᵛ idem per omnia quod idem Willelmus.

TESTIS   Frater Normannus, tunc temporis custos predicte infirmarie,
iuratus idem dicit per omnia quod idem Martinus.

TESTIS   Stephanus diaconus iuratus dixit se uidisse predictum Willel-
mum infirmantem et in lectulo magistri G(ileberti) positum, et scit
quod ibi curatus est, sed nescit post quot dies.

Miracle 21 LcOd   ᵃ furiosa (sic) Lc; furioso curato Od

There, on the following night, she got better and became calm, giving thanks to God; and after three days she returned home cured.

Agnes, Hugh's sister, on oath agrees with Hugh about all these details. She asserts that she was present and saw Ailiva incapacitated in this fashion and cured at Master Gilbert's tomb, just as Hugh relates.

Emma, Agnes's daughter, said on oath that she saw Ailiva afflicted in the way described. She states that Ailiva was taken to Master Gilbert's tomb and was healed there, but she herself was neither present nor witnessed it. But after a few days, when Ailiva had returned home, Emma saw that she had been cured.

Robert of Fulbeck, a layman and a young man, says on oath exactly the same as Emma, Agnes's daughter. At the time when this inquiry was carried out, the same Henry and Ailiva his wife were dead.

[21] *A madman*

William of Houghton, a pauper and a layman, said on oath that he had been sick for nearly two months in the paupers' hospital at Watton, which is a house belonging to the Order of Sempringham. Finally he went mad. Those who ministered in the hospital took pity on him and placed him in a kind of ancient litter, in which Master Gilbert sometimes used to be carried about when, because of his increasing age, he was unable to ride on horseback. After he had lain tied up there for two days and nights, on the third day he got better and became again of sound mind, convinced that he had been cured through Master Gilbert's merits.

Brother Martin, who is now a canon at Watton but at the time of William's cure was a priest serving in the parish church of Watton, says exactly the same about all that relates to William's illness and his healing as William himself.

Brother Norman, who was then warden of this hospital, repeats upon oath all that the same Martin has said.

Stephen, a deacon, said on oath that he saw William when he was unwell and put in Master Gilbert's litter. He knows that he was cured there but is not sure after how many days.

[22] De frenetica

Robertus de Thorp laicus iuratus dixit quod Maximilla, uxor illius, incidit in mentis alienationem, qua laborauit a festo sancti Michaelis usque ad festum sancti Thome apostoli proximum[a] sequens, ita quod aliquotiens solebat eam ligare; tandem ad sepulchrum magistri G(ileberti) eam duxit, ubi cum per duos dies et duas noctes iacuisset, tercio die circa horam terciam curata uisa est.

TESTIS   Walterus, laicus seruiens et homo domus de Sempingham, iuratus de infirmitate eiusdemque infirmitatis diuturnitate[b] idem dicit per omnia quod Robertus de Torp. Dicit etiam eam allatam ad sepulchrum magistri G(ileberti), et cum ibi per duos dies et unam noctem iacuisset, nocte sequenti curata est. Requisitus quomodo id sciret, dixit Maximillam, die tercio ab interiori cancello egressam,[1] dixisse nocte precedenti se curatam fuisse.

[23] De tumente

Antelina de Trikingham uidua iurata dixit quod ipsa post puerperium grauissimum | tumorem uentris per annum et .xⁱ̊L. duas ebdomodas sustinuit. Cumque aliquot loca sanctorum spe recuperande sanitatis uisitasset, nec profecisset,[c] tandem ueniens ad tumbam magistri G(ileberti) mane in uigilia inuentionis sancte Crucis circa horam nonam ibidem curata est.

f. 153

TESTIS   Erneburga, mulier de Trikingham, iurata de infirmitate et infirmitatis diuturnitate idem dicit quod Antelina et de curatione, sed non interfuit curationi; sed uidit eam infirmam proficiscentem ad tumbam magistri G(ileberti), et eodem die ad propria sanam reuersam.

TESTIS   Matildis de Trikingham iurata idem dicit per omnia quod Erneburga.

TESTIS   Walterus, filius Roberti, et Radulfus Neucumen iurati dixerunt se uidisse Antelinam infirmantem tumore uentris per annum et .xⁱ̊L. duas septimanas, et audierunt eam profectam ad tumbam magistri G(ileberti) et ibi sanatam fuisse, et, cum illa ad domum suam redisset, uiderunt tumorem uentris resedisse.

Miracle 22 *Lc*   [a] *One expects* proxime *(Winterbottom), cf. p. 276*   [b] infirmitatis diuturnitate *Winterbottom, cf. below;* diuturnitatis infirmitate *Lc*
Miracle 23 *LcOd*   [c] proficisset *Lc*

[22] *A madwoman*

Robert of Thorpe, a layman, said on oath that his wife Maximilla
went mad. From the feast of St Michael [29 September] to the feast
of St Thomas the Apostle following [21 December] she was so
badly afflicted that he sometimes used to tie her up. Finally, he
took her to Master Gilbert's tomb. After she had lain there for two
days and nights, on the third day, about the third hour, she was
seen to be cured.

Walter, a layman and a serving-man belonging to the house of
Sempringham, repeats on oath exactly what Robert of Thorpe says
about her illness and its duration. He also asserts that she was
taken to Master Gilbert's tomb, and when she had lain there for
two days and one night she was cured on the following night.
When he was asked how he knew this, he said that on the third day
Maximilla had come out of the inner chancel[1] and had declared
that she had been cured the preceding night.

[23] *A swelling*

Antelina of Threckingham, a widow, said on oath that after childbirth she suffered a most painful swelling in her belly for a year and
forty-two weeks. Although she visited various shrines in the hope
of recovering her health, there was no improvement. Finally she
came to Master Gilbert's tomb on the morning of the vigil of the
Invention of the Holy Cross [2 May] and she was cured there
about the ninth hour.

Erneburga, a woman of Threckingham, repeats on oath what
Antelina says about her illness, its duration, and its cure. However,
she was not present at the cure itself. But she saw Antelina set out
for Master Gilbert's tomb when she was sick and return home the
same day healed.

Matilda of Threckingham says on oath exactly the same as
Erneburga.

Walter, son of Robert, and Ralph Neucumen said on oath that
they saw Antelina suffering from a swelling in her belly for a year
and forty-two weeks. They heard that she had gone to Master Gilbert's tomb and had been healed there, and when she returned to her
own home they saw that the swelling of her belly had gone down.

[1] For the church at Sempringham, see pp. xxi–xxii, xxvi.

Omnes hii qui testificantur morbum et curationem Anteline
manent in uilla de Trikingham.

[24] *De uerme eiecto*

Eluiua de Folkingham iurata dixit quod cum per annum infirmata
esset ita quod extremam olei sacri inunctionem a presbitero
acceperat, credens se morti proximam,[a] conualescens modicum,
f. 153ᵛ in biga delata est ad | Sempingham; ubi cum per tres dies ad
sepulchrum magistri G(ileberti) iacuisset, tercio die saniem multam euomuit et cum sanie uermem[b] longum; et ita per duos dies et
duas noctes ibi iacuit, uicissim saniem uomens. Postea domum
adducta est, et sic de die in diem plene conualuit.

TESTIS   Cecilia filia ipsius Eluiue iurata dixit se uidisse que mater sua
predixit se passam fuisse, et eodem modo curatam sicut mater eius
predixerat.

TESTIS   Maloth, puella eiusdem uille, iurata idem dicit quod predicta
Cecilia.

TESTIS   Vmfridus, prepositus de Folkingham, maritus predicte Eluiue,
iuratus dixit uxorem suam Eluiuam ita infirmatam fuisse sicut ipsa
Eluiua predixit, et quod ipse eam duxit ad tumbam magistri G(ileberti), ubi credit eam curatam esse; sed non interfuit curationi.

[25] *De gibbosa*

Helwisa de Pointuna mulier iurata dixit se per triennium ita in-
curuatam et contractam fuisse quod non potuit pedibus suis
incedere, sed alii deferebant eam; nec potuit per se sedere uel sur-
gere uel erigi. Tandem a parentibus suis delata est ad sepulchrum
magistri G(ileberti), ubi prima nocte decubans, induta scapulario
magistri G(ileberti), aliquantulum sensit alleuiationem. Nocte
f. 154 sequenti apparuit ei dormienti senex canus baculum gestans | in
manu, qui dixit ei: 'Vis sana fieri?' Et deinde mulieri respondenti
'uolo' benedictionem dextera dedit. Requisitus ab ea quis esset,
respondit se magistrum G(ilebertum) de Sempingham esse. At
ipsa euigilans statim erexit se, statimque sensit se ire posse; et continue postea per se ire potuit.

Miracle 24 *LcOd*   [a] *The passage is very different in Od, which adds details of the illness:*
interno uiscerum dolore continue anxiebatur *(sic)*; nec tamen tumentem habuit aluum,
sed corrosuras et perunctiones circa cor et latera incessanter paciebatur.   [b]uer-
men *Lc*

Miracle 25 *LcOd*

All those who witness to Antelina's illness and her cure live in the village of Threckingham.

[24] *A worm cast out*

Elviva of Folkingham said on oath that for a year she had been so sick that she had received the holy oil of extreme unction from the priest, believing she was close to death. But as she got a little better, she was taken in a cart to Sempringham. There, when she had lain for three days by Master Gilbert's tomb, on the third day she vomited a great quantity of pus and, together with the pus, a long worm. Thus she lay there for two more days and nights, vomiting pus from time to time. Afterwards she was taken home and so day by day fully recovered.

Cecily, Elviva's daughter, said on oath that she had seen what her mother has described herself as suffering, and she claims that her mother was cured just as she had said.

Maloth, a girl from the same village, says the same on oath as Cecily.

Humphrey, reeve of Folkingham and husband to the same Elviva, said on oath that his wife had been ill in the manner she had described; he himself took her to Master Gilbert's tomb, where he believes she was cured, although he was not present at the cure.

[25] *A hunchbacked woman*

A woman called Helwise of Pointon said on oath that for three years she was so bent over and crippled that she could not walk on her own feet, but others used to carry her; nor was she able to sit down by herself, get up, or rise to her feet. Finally she was taken by her parents to Master Gilbert's tomb. When she lay down there on the first night and put on Master Gilbert's scapular, she experienced some relief. In the night which followed as she slept there appeared to her a white-haired old man, carrying a staff in his hand. He said to her, 'Do you wish to become well?'. When the woman then replied, 'I do indeed', he blessed her with his right hand. She asked him who he was, and he answered that he was Master Gilbert of Sempringham. Then as she awoke she immediately got up of her own accord and felt straight away that she could walk; and always thereafter she was able to walk without help.

TESTIS   Radulfus Raisun, pater Helewise, iuratus dixit de infirmitate eiusdem filie sue idem quod ipsa Helewisa. Dicit etiam quod ipse in humeris suis eam tulit ad sepulchrum magistri G(ileberti), et dicit eam tercia nocte, ut putauit, postquam illuc uenerat, curatam esse; sed non interfuit eius curationi, quia ei non patuit ingressus in interius cancellum monialium.

TESTIS   Willelmus Barath de Pointona, laicus, iuratus dixit de infirmitate Helewise idem quod ipsa Helewisa. Vidit etiam eam ad tumbam magistri G(ileberti) a patre suo deferri, ubi secunda nocte qua ibi iacuit curata est. Requisitus quomodo id sciret, dicit se illis duabus noctibus in ecclesia de Sempingham in cancello exteriori uigilasse. Puella autem in cancello interiori ad tumbam magistri G(ileberti) iacuit. Ipsa autem post aliquos dies domum reuersa dixit eidem Willelmo se secunda nocte curatam fuisse.

TESTIS   Gilebertus, filius Gerardi de Pointuna, laicus, iuratus dixit se uidisse Helewisam infirmatam fuisse sicut superius dictum est, et scit eam delatam esse ad tumbam magistri G(ileberti), ubi credit f. 154ᵛ eam | curatam esse, quia postquam domum reuersa est uidit eam sanam esse.

[26] *De clerico ydropico*

Alanus de Merstona iuratus dixit quod tumorem habebat et dolorem in pectore et uentre, ita quod timebat ne ydropicus esset. Et cum iam per duos annos et eo amplius tali egritudine laborasset, decubuit in lecto egritudinis iacens fere .xv. diebus; et audito quod Dominus operaretur in miraculis ob merita beate recordationis magistri G(ileberti), uouit se sepulchrum eius uisitaturum. Et facto uoto sensit eatenus se alleuiatum quod ambulare potuit; et hoc factum est in estate, circa festum sancti Iohannis Baptiste; et in yeme sequenti circa festum sancti Martini implens uotum suum, cum se super tumbam ipsius cum magna deuotione effusis lacrimis extendisset, repente ipsius uiscera commota sunt. Surgens itaque sensit se ita melioratum ut antequam recederet ab ecclesia illa, uisum fuerit illi plenam conualescentiam recepisse, quia ab eo tempore nullam ex illa egritudine sensit molestiam aut grauamen; et certissime credit per merita ipsius sancti uiri se fuisse ab illa infirmitate penitus liberatum; et in memoriam recepte sanitatis

Ralph Raisun, Helwise's father, said on oath the same about his daughter's disability as Helwise herself. He also says that he himself carried her on his shoulders to Master Gilbert's tomb, and he claims that according to his reckoning she was cured on the third night after she had arrived. But he was not present when she was cured, because he was not given entry to the nuns' inner chancel.

William Barath of Pointon, a layman, repeated on oath what Helwise herself had said about her illness. He also saw her taken by her father to Master Gilbert's tomb, where she was cured on the second night that she lay there. Asked how he knew this, he says that he kept vigil for those two nights in the outer chancel in the church of Sempringham. But the girl lay by Master Gilbert's tomb in the inner chancel. Helwise came home after a few days and told William himself that she had been cured on the second night.

Gilbert, son of Gerard of Pointon, a layman, said on oath that he had seen Helwise when she was sick in the manner described above. He knows that she was taken to Master Gilbert's tomb, where he believes she was cured, because he saw that she was healed after she returned home.

[26] *A clerk with dropsy*

Alan of Marston said on oath that he used to have swelling and pain in his chest and belly, so that he was afraid that he suffered from dropsy. When he had endured this disease for more than two years, he took to his sickbed and lay there for nearly a fortnight. When he heard what miracles the Lord performed on account of the merits of Master Gilbert of blessed memory, he vowed that he would visit this man's tomb. As soon as he had made the vow he felt himself so much improved that he was able to walk. This happened in the summer, about the feast of St John the Baptist [24 June]; and in the following winter, about the feast of St Martin [11 November], he fulfilled his vow. When he had stretched himself upon Gilbert's tomb, weeping and with great reverence, suddenly his entrails were stirred within him. And, as he got up, he felt so much better that before he departed from that church, he felt he had made a full recovery, because from that time he has experienced no harm or trouble from that disease. He is fully convinced that he was entirely freed from that disease through the merits of this holy man; and in memory of the good health which he

unum argenteum[1] singulis annis ad tumbam ipsius sancti uiri deportat.

[27] *De lippiente*

f. 155 Ysouda de Picworda, soror predicti Alani, iurata | dixit quod fuit presens ubi predictus frater suus ad tumbam predicti sancti uiri sanitatem recepit, et certissime credit quod ⟨per⟩[a] merita illius. . . .[b] Adiecit etiam quod cum illa ualidam passionem per mensem habuisset in oculis, ita quod parum aut nichil uidere potuisset, presertim ab hora nona usque ad noctem, quadam alia interna egritudine laborauit, ita ut in lecto decumberet. Visum erat ei per somnium quod si ad illius sancti uiri tumbam accederet, ibi reciperet sanitatem. Ad quam cum uenisset cum candela qua corpus suum mensurauerat, et de aqua qua corpus eiusdem sancti uiri lotum fuit hausisset et suis oculis infudisset, continuo ab infirmitate eadem, per merita eiusdem sancti uiri, sicut credit, fuit penitus liberata.

Et huic curationi interfuit predictus Alanus, frater eius, et hoc TESTIS iuratus asseruit. Hec autem Ysouda ad tumbam illam singulis annis refert oblationem.

Aliud.

Adiecit predicta mulier se uidisse quamdam mulierem laborantem in partu per duos dies, cum hausisset aquam benedictam in qua lota erat tonsura barbe predicti sancti uiri, statim enixam esse et peperisse.

[28] *De oculo maculoso*[c]

Adiecit etiam de filio quod per infusionem aque in qua lotum fuit corpus predicti sancti uiri, cum prius oblatus[d] esset super tumbam eius, curatus est a macula oculi, que obduxerat fere medietatem f. 155ᵛ oculi usque ad | pupillam,[e] ita quod dubitaretur ne per ipsam lederetur pupilla; et singulis annis memoriale recepte sanitatis affert puer ille in loco illo oblationem suam.

Miracle 27 *Lc*   [a] *Supplied by the corrector of Lh*   [b] *Something has fallen out, e.g.* hoc factum sit *(Winterbottom), cf. p. 302*
    Miracle 28 *Lc*   [c] *No break in the text of Lc; the rubric is added in the margin*
[d] *Corrupt*   [e] *ins.* oculi *Lc before correction*

recovered, he takes one silver coin[1] every year to this holy man's tomb.

[27] *A woman with inflamed eyes*

Ysouda of Pickworth, sister of the same Alan, said on oath that she was present when her brother was restored to health at this holy man's tomb, and she believes most firmly that [it happened through] Gilbert's merits. She added that she herself suffered for a month such a great pain in her eyes that she could see little or nothing, especially from the ninth hour until night time. She also suffered from some other internal complaint so that she took to her bed. She dreamed that if she went to the tomb of that holy man, she would recover her health there. When she arrived, with a candle the size of her own measurements, she drank some of the water in which the body of this holy man had been washed and poured it upon her eyes. At once she was completely freed from her illness through the merits, she believes, of this same holy man.

Alan, her brother, was there when she was cured, and he corroborated this upon oath. This woman Ysouda takes an offering to the tomb every year.

Another [miracle]

The same woman added that she had seen a woman who laboured in childbirth for two days. When she drank the blessed water in which the trimmings of the holy man's beard were washed, she gave birth and bore a child immediately.

[28] *An eye afflicted with a spot*

She spoke too about her son, saying that by administering the water in which the same holy man's body had been washed, after an offering had been laid upon Gilbert's tomb(?), he was cured of a spot upon his eye. This spot had obscured almost half the eye as far as the pupil, so that it was suspected that the pupil would suffer damage from it. Every year, to commemorate the recovery of his health, the boy brings his offering to the place.

---

[1] Presumably a penny (understand *denarium*).

[29] *De surda*

Emma, mulier de Amewic, iurata dixit quod cum obsurduissent ei aures per .ix. fere ebdomadas, ita quod sonum campanarum audire non posset, et ueniens ad tumbam predicti G(ileberti), et cum per noctem in orationem[a] pernoctasset, mane facto campanam audiuit, et postea infusa aqua eiusdem sancti uiri in auribus eius, homines colloquentes, et, cum inde recederet, strepitum pedum itinerantium comprehendit auditu.

TESTIS   Fulco de Amewic coniugatus huius rei testis est iuratus.

[30] *De tumente tibia*

Laureta de Horbling', uidua, iurata dixit quod, cum per mensem et amplius graui passionis incursu in tibia a genu infra tumescente laborasset, ita quod dextro pedi ad gradiendum niti non posset, cum uix equitando, fulta undique seruientium suorum auxilio, ad ecclesiam de Sempingham accessisset, et caligam sancti uiri super tibiam in qua paciebatur induxisset, passio ipsa ipsam continuo reliquit, et ibi curata est incontinenti, ut pedes in domum propriam plus quam per unum miliare a loco distantem sit reuersa.

f. 156   Huius rei testis est iurata Siride, uxor Adam, | de eadem uilla, que interfuit et uidit predictam et certissime credit quod hoc factum sit per meritum eiusdem uiri.

Item, Godefridus, filius predicte Laurete, iuratus infirmitatis et curationis matris sue testis est; sed tamen non interfuit ubi fuit curata.

Miracle 29 *Lc*   ᵃ *Perhaps read* oratione *(Winterbottom)*
Miracle 30 *Lc*

[29] *A deaf woman*

Emma, a woman of Anwick, said on oath that for almost nine weeks her ears had become so affected by deafness that she could not hear the sound of bells. She came to the same Gilbert's tomb, and when she had spent all that night in prayer and morning had dawned, she heard a bell; and later, when the water of this holy man had been poured into her ears she heard men as they spoke with one another; then as she departed, she could hear the noise made by the feet of travellers.

Fulk of Anwick, her husband, is a sworn witness of this fact.

[30] *A swollen leg*

Laura of Horbling, a widow, said on oath that for more than a month she suffered an attack of great pain in her leg, which grew swollen beneath the knee. As a result she could not support herself on her right foot in order to walk. Scarcely able to ride, propped up on every side with her servants' help, she came to the church of Sempringham. She put the holy man's shoe upon the leg which was troubling her, and immediately the pain left her and she was completely healed there, so that she returned on foot to her own home, which was more than a mile away from that place.

Sirida, Adam's wife, from the same village, is a sworn witness of this fact. She was present and saw Laura and she believes most firmly that this was brought about by Master Gilbert's merits.

Also Godfrey, Laura's son, is a sworn witness of his mother's illness and her cure. However, he was not present when she was cured.

ITEM ALIA MIRACULA

Multa quidem et alia signa fecit Deus per merita memorati serui sui G(ileberti) que non sunt sub hac inuestigatione discussa, quia pleraque neglectui tradita, quedam autem per talia testimonia non sunt probata, alia uero post hanc discussionem sunt patrata, unde[a] sub hac forma non sunt comprehensa. Quia tamen ea fuisse facta non dubitamus, preterire illa silentio nolumus.

[1] *De morti proximo*

Vir preclarissimus Iohannes, constabularius Cestrie,[1] patris Gileberti multum uenerans sanctitatem, peciit donari sibi baculum illius pro benedictione. Quem ad se per domnum Rogerum, nunc patronum nostrum, delatum gratanter accipiens et reuerenter deosculans, iurauit astantibus multis diuitibus et nobilibus se plus quam .XL. marcas argenti baculum illum carum habere propter uiri sancti cuius erat confidentiam. Quodam autem tempore cum baculum illum manu forte teneret, delinquentem seruum, ira superatus et reuerentie illius oblitus, eo percussit, f. 156ᵛ quem | et in tres partes confregit. Quo super facto graui penitentia ductus, ampliorem exhibuit baculo, immo Deo et sancto cuius fuerat honorem, et unam parcium illarum apud capellam castelli sui de Duningtona, alteram apud hospitale eiusdem uille, pro reliquiis seruandam, terciam uero partem secum in summagiis suis semper portari fecit.[2] Contigit autem post decessum beati G(ileberti) quod prepositus prefati hospitalis de Duningtona, nomine Helyas,[3] uir humilis et deuotus, morbo paralisis percussus, ad

---

[a] *ins.* et *Lc*
Miracle 1 *LcOd*

[1] John de Lacy, constable of Chester, was a leading baron in the Midlands and North-west, who died at the siege of Acre in 1190: see above, pp. 290–1; *Gesta Henrici II*, ed. W. Stubbs, RS, ii. 148; *Early Cheshire Charters*, ed. G. Barraclough (Record Soc. of Lancs. and Cheshire, 1957), pp. 14–17, etc.; W. Farrer in *VCH Lancs.* i. 299–300; G. Ormerod, *The History of the County Palatine . . . of Chester*, ed. T. Helsby, i (London, 1882), pp. 694–5.

THE MIRACLES:
INFORMAL COLLECTION

MORE MIRACLES

God also worked many other signs through the merits of this His servant Gilbert; they have not been investigated in the course of this inquiry because a large number fell into neglect, some were not proved by such testimony as these, and others were performed after this investigation, and so were not included in this schedule. But because we are sure these things took place we are unwilling to pass over them in silence.

[1] *A man on the verge of death*

John constable of Chester,[1] a most eminent man, held the holiness of Father Gilbert in high repute and asked that his staff might be given him as a favour. When it was brought to him by Roger, who is now our head, he received it with gratitude, and as he kissed it reverently he swore in the presence of many wealthy noblemen that he valued the staff at more than forty silver marks because of his faith in the holy man to whom it had belonged. But on one occasion, when he happened to be holding the staff in his hand, he was overcome by anger at a servant's wrongdoing and, forgetting his reverence for Gilbert, he struck the man with it and broke it into three pieces. His deep sense of penitence over this led him to pay greater respect to the staff, or rather to God and to the saint who had owned it. He had one piece kept in the chapel of his castle at Donington and another in the hospital of the same town, as relics; but the third piece he always had carried with him in his baggage.[2] Now after the blessed Gilbert's death it so happened that the warden of this hospital at Donington, a humble and devout man called Elias,[3] was struck by a paralytic illness and

---

[2] For the hospital at Castle Don(n)ington (Leics.), see *VCH Leics.*, ii. 39–40; Knowles and Hadcock, p. 351.

[3] Cf. *VCH*, loc. cit.; J. Nichols, *The History and Antiquities of the County of Leicestershire*, iii. 2 (London, 1804), p. 780.

extrema deductus est, ita ut ex more cereus accensus daretur illi in manum pro ultimi spiritus efflatione. In quo agone cum sic iaceret fere exanimis, uenit illi in mentem domni Gileberti sanctitas et mirabilium operum eius magnitudo, simulque meminit quid pro eo ipse aliquotiens egerit. Nam tempore transitus sancti G(ile-berti), cum idem Helyas esset in Hibernia, audito obitus illius nuntio, sicut mos est genti illi quociens audierint famam mortis alicuius magnatis ieiunare, et ipse*ᵃ* patrie ritu eo die in pane et aqua ieiunauit. Cumque hoc mente concepisset et patrem Gileber-tum Deo dignum et carum crederet, tota animi uirtute, nam lingua non poterat, suffragium illius exposcit, quatinus beneficium ora-tionis et ieiunii, quod pro eo fecerat, anime illius pariter et corpori f. 157 | in illa hora rependeret. Nec mora, data est illi ilico potentia loquendi, et mox pignus sancti quod apud se habuerat, baculi scili-cet illius fragmen, precepit afferri. Allatum est ligni frustum et super partem illam corporis quam*ᵇ* doluit positum, cum ecce subito et inopinate, non paulatim et pedetentim uel per partes, sed in momento et in ictu oculi tota sanitas et integra tocius corporis simul redintegratur, ut iam non semiuiuus uel egrotus appareret, sed nec ullum sensit infirmitatis uestigium.

[2] *De febre*

Per eandem quoque baculi fracturam tale rursum accidit miracu-lum. Medicus quidam in castello de Duningtona[1] incommodum pertulit febris terciane, quem morbum pacienter plerumque ferunt phisici, eo quod asserant febrem terciam si fuerit uera et morbum esse et medicinam. Sed cum iste diutius illa ualitudine detineretur, nec aliquibus medicamentis illam a se expellere ualeret, quesiuit anxius si qua inuenire posset morbi illius anti-dota. Cum autem semel descenderet ad pretaxatum hospitale, cui memoratus preerat Helyas,[2] ob querenda*ᶜ* sue salutis remedia in herbarum et radicum que ibi habebantur efficacia, interrogauit eum domnus Helias si omnino a febribus uellet liberari. Respon-f. 157ᵛ dit phisicus ualde | desuper*ᵈ* diuturnitate febrium et molestia anxiari, et libenter uelle si quo modo posset curari. Tunc ait

ᵃ ipso *Lc*   *ᵇ Perhaps read* qua *or* que *(Winterbottom)*
Miracle 2 *LcOd*   *ᶜ* quirenda *Lc*   *ᵈ Possibly* super *(Winterbottom) or* se super

---

[1] Castle Donington (see p. 305 n. 2).   [2] See p. 304 n. 3.

came so close to death that according to the custom a lighted candle was placed in his hand whilst his spirit breathed its last. As he lay like this, in agony and almost lifeless, Gilbert's sanctity and the greatness of his wonderful deeds came to his mind, and at the same time he remembered something he had once done on the saint's account. For this same Elias was in Ireland when St Gilbert passed away and, on hearing the report of his death, because those people customarily fast whenever they hear news of any great man's death, he followed the tradition of the country and fasted that day on bread and water. Because this thought had occurred to him and because he believed that Father Gilbert was a worthy man precious to God, he implored his help with all the strength of his spirit since he could not speak, asking him to repay that very hour to his spirit and body alike the good offices which he had performed for him of prayer and fasting. Without delay, instantly the power of speech was granted him, whereupon he ordered that the saint's relic which he had in his keeping, that is the fragment of the staff, should be produced. The piece of wood was brought and placed on that part of his body which gave him pain, when behold suddenly and unexpectedly, not slowly, gradually, or partially but in a second, in the twinkling of an eye, full and complete health was at once restored to his whole body, so that now he appeared neither at death's door nor even sick, and felt no trace of illness.

[2] *A fever*

This type of miracle occurred again, also by the same fragment of the staff. A certain doctor in Castle Donington[1] suffered the misfortune of tertian fever, which is an illness doctors bear patiently for the most part because they hold that if it is true tertian fever it is both disease and cure. But when he was gripped by this sickness for a very long time and could not rid himself of it by any treatment, he made anxious inquiries to see if he could find any antidote for this illness. Now on one occasion as he was going down to the hospital mentioned above, supervised by this same Elias,[2] to search among the powerful herbs and roots that were kept there for a means of restoring his health, Elias asked him if he wished to be completely relieved of fevers. The doctor replied that he was extremely worried about the length and severity of the fever and wished fervently to be cured if he possibly could. Then Elias said

ille manifestam et probatam se nosse medicinam, qua si uteretur continuo per Dei auxilium curaretur. Lotum est ilico baculi fragmen, et aqua perfusionis a medico exhausta, protinusque omnis febrium flamma est extincta.

TESTIS   Huius utriusque miraculi testis est sepedictus domnus cui euenerant, uir boni testimonii Helyas. Testantur et qui adhuc uiuunt plurimi qui uiderunt.

[3] *Item de febre*

Eodem modo per eandem baculi partem curatus est a febribus quidam predicti constabularii[1] famulus, nomine Henricus.

[4] *De surda*

Paupercula mulier, Kenna nomine, de Pointuna, surditatis officio diu depressa, per insensibilitatem aurium ita facta est stupida quod stolida a nonnullis putaretur. Veniens ad sepulchrum confessoris cum aliquamdiu orasset, uermis uiuus ab aure eius egressus, uidentibus que aderant sororibus, peruium iter auditui quod obstruxerat patefecit; et post uermem non modicum aquosi humoris e uestigio subsecutum patulas aeris uias in cerebro et in aure reserauit, caputque a dolore et aurium foramina ab inerti dolore alleuiauit.

[5] *De febre ter fugata*

f. 158   Febribus decoctus Robertus de Sixle[2] supprior uicaria | frigoris et caloris mutatione continuam pertulit corporis inquietudinem. Vexatus diutius uirtutis patris reminiscitur, et petit ad se afferri quam habuit repositam zonam ipsius pelliceam, ut ea precinctus optatum pro se consequeretur leuamen. Allata est corrigia, et in mediis estibus intemperantis caloris carni eius admota: nec mora, motu cicius repressus excedentis impetus ignis naturali cessit humane complexionis temperamento.

Miracle 3 *LcOd*   Miracle 4 *LcOd*   Miracle 5 *LcOd*

---

[1] See p. 304 n. 1.
[2] See pp. xxxi, xxxii.

that he knew a straightforward and tested medicine by which he would at once be cured by God's help if he availed himself of it. The fragment of staff was washed immediately and, when the doctor had drunk the water which had been used for this purpose, at once all the heat of the fever vanished.

The warden to whom these things happened, Elias, a man of honest reputation, is a witness of both miracles. And of those still living, many people who saw them add their testimony.

[3] *Another case of fever*

A servant belonging to the constable,[1] called Henry, was cured of fever in the same fashion by means of this same piece of staff.

[4] *A deaf woman*

A poor woman of Pointon called Kenna, who had long been weighed down by deafness, became so confused from the lack of sensation in her ears that she was considered stupid by some people. When she came to the confessor's tomb and had prayed for some time, a live worm emerged from her ear, as the sisters who were present witnessed, and made open and unobstructed the passage to her hearing which it had blocked; and after the worm there immediately followed a large quantity of watery fluid which unsealed passages in her brain and ear, opening them to the air, thus relieving her head of its hurt and her ears of the dead weight of pain.

[5] *A fever banished three times*

Robert of Sixhills,[2] who filled the office of subprior, was wasted by fever, and endured constant bodily pain from the alternation of cold and heat. When he had suffered for a very long time, he brought the father's powers to mind, and requested that his leather girdle, which he had stored away, be brought to him, so that when he put it on he might secure for himself the relief that he desired. The belt was brought and applied to his body in the course of an attack of excessive heat; immediately the fire was very swiftly quenched by the action of a power emanating from the belt, and it gave way to the temperature which is normal to the human constitution.

Alio quoque tempore eodem peruasus incommodo, eodem est medicamine liberatus. Tercia uice, non iam uicissitudine terciane febris ut prius, sed continuati incendii acumine urebatur, nec erat locus quieti, ubi nullam*a* laboris interpolatio uel modice requiei speciem preferebat. Quid ageret, quo se uerteret ignorauit. Ad notum tandem confugit auxilium, et probatum cingulum, immo in cingulo expertam*b* sancti uirtutem, in sui ascissit adiutorium. Quid multa? Vix corpus zona complectitur, cum ad tactum illius subito sudor erumpit, ardor depascens tepescit, naturalis temperies, quies salusque optata succedit. Hoc iam tercio manifestauit se Deus mirabilem in sancto suo circa eundem hominem, mirantem simul et congaudentem de subitatione sperate salutis, et de tam celeri subuentione diuine miserationis.

f. 158ᵛ   [6] *Visio cuiusdam monialis*

Quod uenerabilis patris et pastoris nostri G(ileberti) de Sempingham supra gregem suum etiam post carnis resolutionem cura inuigilet, quorum gubernationi in carne positus tota mente insudabat, sicut ex multis antea collegimus indiciis, ita ex quodam quod nuper contigit facto, ut subiecta docent, comprobamus.

Monialis quedam de Catteleia,¹ que est domus ordinis de Sempingham, aduersus unam consororem suam in iram uersa, cum egrederetur uespere hostium infirmitorii, cuius curam agebat, non se capiens pre furore, nomen antiqui hostis inclamauit. Qua uoce temerarie emissa, sensit sibi subito uenire in uerticem nescio quid ponderosum, cuius mole depressa corruit in terram, mortue simillima. Nam tota die illa et duabus noctibus sequentibus sic iacebat attonita ut, sublato omnium menbrorum officio, uix aliquod uite superstitis relinqueret uestigium, nisi quod rubor quidam uitalis in summitate nasi uidebatur. Cum enim sulleuarent caput illius uel aliquod aliud menbrum assidentes, decidit retrorsum tanquam mole*c* mortis pregrauatum. Secunda igitur nocte insecuta, apparuerunt ei tres uiri uenerabiles ante grabatum ipsius f. 159 transeuntes, sed ad uisum illius unus ad caput, | alter ad pedes, tercius in medio consistentes. Quos uidens penitus ignorauit;

---

a Perhaps read nulla *(Winterbottom)*   *b* expertam *Winterbottom;* expertem *LcOd*
Miracle 6 *LcOd*   *c* mole *Mynors;* male *LcOd*

---

¹ See pp. xxxi, xxxiii.

Again on another occasion when racked by the same illness, he obtained relief from the same remedy. The third time he ran a high temperature, not as before through the return of tertian fever, but from the heat of a persistent inflammation; and there was no chance of peace when he could command no respite from suffering nor the least semblance of rest. He did not know what to do or where to turn. At length he resorted to the girdle, a known and tested remedy, or rather in the girdle he summoned to his aid the saint's well-tried power. What more need I say? Scarcely was the girdle placed round his body when a sudden sweat broke out at its touch, the consuming heat of his body cooled and a normal temperature followed, together with rest and the recovery he had desired. So in His saint God revealed His wondrous nature a third time in the case of this same man, who marvelled as he rejoiced at the sudden onrush of the healing he had longed for and such speedy assistance by divine mercy.

[6] *A nun's vision*

Even after his death our father and pastor Gilbert of Sempringham labours in the care of his flock, which he devoted all his attention to ruling during his earthly life. This we have deduced before from many cases, and it is confirmed for us by the evidence of a particular event which happened recently.

A certain nun of Catley,[1] which is a house of the Order of Sempringham, was overcome with anger towards one of her fellow sisters. One evening, as she went out through the door of the infirmary where she was in charge, being beside herself with rage she called out the Devil's name. As soon as the reckless cry left her lips she felt something heavy come suddenly on to her head, and, sinking beneath its weight, she fell to the ground like one dead. For the whole of that day and the two following nights she lay so stunned that, since she had lost the use of all her limbs, scarcely any trace of residual life remained apart from a certain healthy pinkness visible at the tip of her nose. But when in attending on her they lifted her head or some other limb, it fell back as if borne down by death's weight. Then on the second night which followed there appeared to her three venerable men passing in front of her bed; but when they saw her one stopped by her head, another at her feet, and the third in between. She did not recognize them at all

sed qui essent tali recognouit indicio. Cum enim miseram illam respexissent, ait unus illorum qui ad pedes illius astitit ad alterum:[1] 'O bone magister, miserere illius'; ad quem ille quasi turbida uoce: 'Nichil ad me' inquit 'de ea; non enim est de meis, quia se illi commisit quem nominauit, et me contempto spretisque meis institutis, sicut multe alie faciunt, sui ordinis refugit disciplinam.' Tunc intercessor ille alterius comitis sui implorat auxilium, dicens: 'O sancte Andrea, adiuua illam.' Sanctus autem Andreas intercedens pro ea adiecit se illuc ad hoc uenisse, ut eius misererentur. Nondum autem perpetrata[a] subuentione ipsius, ait beatus Andreas ad illum qui se primo conuenerat: 'O sancte Clemens, succurre illi, quia te specialiter hactenus dilexit.' Nata enim erat in uico cuius basilica in honore sancti Clementis fuerat constructa,[2] et ideo specialem illius frequentabat memoriam. Tunc sanctus Clemens hortatus est eam petere ueniam et dicere confessionem, adiciens debere eos festinare, eo quod oporteret eos interesse missarum sollemniis, que illo die de beata Maria in conuentu erant in proximo celebrande. Illa igitur, que tamdiu iacuerat immota, | cepit mouere brachia, et quasi ad petendam ueniam conata est manus de more coniungere, uolensque dicere confessionem, repetitis sepius primis sillabis, tandem hanc totam dictionem 'confiteor' emisit, et prosecuta ea que sequuntur, sicut dicere solebat coram preposita sua: 'Confiteor' inquit 'Deo et beate Marie et omnibus sanctis et tibi, soror.' Quam sanctus Clemens correxit, dicens: 'Dicere debes "tibi pater".' Dicta autem tota confessione, tercius ille, qui uocabatur magister, qui reuera sanctus Gilebertus erat, nam eo nomine dum uiueret censebatur, subdidit absolutionem et dedit benedictionem, et sic omnes recesserunt. Viderunt hec et audierunt plurime ex sororibus que affuerunt; testatur et ipsa, sui casus pretendens testimonium diutinam infirmitatem, non sine magno lacrimarum profluuio rei geste referens ueritatem. Euanescente igitur uisione, cepit paululum respirare;

f. 159ᵛ

[a] impetrata *Od*

---

[1] It is clear from what follows that the three saints who appeared to the sick nun were St Clement, St Gilbert, and St Andrew; that Clement spoke first to Gilbert, who rejected her, and then appealed to Andrew; and that Andrew responded by asking Clement himself to succour her. This at last produced the beginning of her confession, and Gilbert's absolution and blessing; and they all hurried off to St Mary's mass, leaving her cured. Clement was the patron saint of her native village, Mary of both Catley and Sempringham priories, Andrew of the original church at Sempringham.

by sight but she knew who they were by this sign: when they had considered the unhappy woman the man who stood at her feet [St Clement] said to another [St Gilbert]:[1] 'O good master, take pity on this woman.' The other answered him in somewhat indignant tones: 'She is nothing at all to do with me; she is not one of mine, because she has entrusted herself to the one she named, and having scorned me and spurned my rules, just as many other women do, she has deserted the discipline of her Order.' Then the man who was interceding for her [Clement] implored help from his other companion, saying: 'O St Andrew, come to her aid.' Then St Andrew took her part and added that he had come there for this very purpose, that they might take pity on her. But as they had not yet secured Gilbert's help for her, blessed Andrew said to the one who had first addressed him: 'O St Clement, do *you* succour her, because up until now she had a special affection for you.' For she was born in a village whose church had been built in honour of St Clement,[2] and therefore used to commemorate him especially. Then St Clement urged her to ask for forgiveness and to make her confession, adding that they must hurry because they had to be present at St Mary's mass, which was shortly to be celebrated in the convent on that same day. Then she who had lain motionless for so long began to move her arms and tried to put her hands together in the manner of one asking for forgiveness and wanting to make her confession. After she had repeated the first syllables many times, she at last uttered the whole word *Confiteor* and managed those which followed, just as she used to say to the prioress: 'I confess', she said, 'to God and St Mary and to all the saints and to you, sister.' Here St Clement corrected her saying: 'You should say *to you, father*.' When she had made her complete confession, the third person who was called master and was in fact St Gilbert, for he was known by the name 'Master' in his lifetime, bestowed absolution and gave the blessing, and so they all departed. Very many of the sisters who were present saw and heard these things, and the woman herself testifies in her own case, citing her long illness as evidence and repeating, in floods of tears, the details of what had happened. So when the vision had disappeared she began to breathe again very slightly; she described to her

[2] For churches dedicated to St Clement, see F. Arnold-Foster, *Studies in Church Dedications* (London, 1899), iii. 349. There were a number in the Danelaw, several in Lincolnshire.

quid pertulerit, quid audierit, assidentibus indicauit; per .xv. dies
lecto decubuit, pristinamque sui corporis ualitudinem se deinceps
posse ex integro recuperare adhuc diffidit.[a]

Monemur per hec non facile irasci, nec male dicere proximis.
Monemur occulti hostis, qui circuit querens quem deuoret,[1]
cauere insidias. Monemur uotorum nostrorum, ne damnemur cum
f. 160 | impiis, effici debere solliciti executores. Monemur sanctorum
uenerationibus et uenerandis memoriis, qui curam nostri gerunt in
omnibus, diligenter debere insistere: qui, si quando eorum in-
diguerimus auxilio, promtiores apparent adiutores, quorum deuo-
tiores fuerimus cultores.

[7] *De ceca*

De Neuwerch mulier, nomine Cecilia, cecitatis tenebris diu obuo-
luta, diuini luminis radiante gratia, ad mausoleum memorati patris
corporalem uisum est consecuta.

[8] *Aliud*

Predicto in loco puella a matre, sed ignota, illuc adducta, oculorum detersa caligine, pristine lucis gauisa est adoptione.

[9] *De paralitica*

Coloni cuiusdam de Sempingham, Roberti cognomento Horn
filia, nomine Alicia, paralisi resoluta priori sospitati inibi est
restituta.

[10] *De surdo*

Willelmus surdus de Breicebi audiuit in somnis doctorem egregium
Gilebertum monita salutis populo predicantem; audiuit, et memoriter tenuit. Excusso somno et obturatis auribus illis fantasticis,
aperte sunt aures corporales, et audiuit campanam ecclesie ad
matutinas pulsatam: excitansque a somno uxorem, dixit pulsatum
esse et debere ire ad ecclesiam. Stupefacta illa interrogauit quo

[a] posse . . . diffidit *Lc* (tegro *before correction);* a Domino percepit *Od, more cheerfully*
Miracle 7 *LcOd*   Miracle 8 *Lc*   Miracle 9 *Lc*   Miracle 10 *Lc* .

[1] Cf. 1 Pet. 5: 8.

attendants what she had experienced and what she had heard; she lay upon her bed for a fortnight, and still despairs of ever again being able to recover completely her former bodily health.

This account teaches us not to give way to anger easily and not to curse our neighbours; we are cautioned to beware the snares set by the secret enemy who goes about seeking whom he may devour.[1] We are told to be scrupulous in the performance of our vows, lest with the impious we incur damnation. We are advised to attend carefully to the veneration of the saints and to their holy shrines, for they are concerned for us in every circumstance; if we ever need their help, the more devout we have been in their worship the more swiftly they come to our aid.

[7] *A blind woman*

A woman of Newark called Cecily, who had long been shrouded in blindness, obtained bodily vision at our father's tomb by means of the grace shining from the light divine.

[8] *Another*

At the same place a girl who was brought there by her mother, whose name is unknown, had the darkness wiped from her eyes and rejoiced at receiving her former eyesight.

[9] *A paralysed woman*

Robert Horn, a peasant of Sempringham, had a daughter called Alice, who was affected by paralysis. In this place she was restored to her former good health.

[10] *A deaf man*

William, a deaf man from Braceby, in a dream heard the famous teacher Gilbert preaching the lessons of salvation to the people; he heard them and retained them in his memory. Roused from sleep and those imaginary ears sealed, his real ears unblocked and he heard the church bell ringing for matins. He woke his wife from sleep, and told her that it had been ringing and they must go to church. She was amazed and asked him how he knew it had been

f.160ᵛ modo | sciret si iam pulsatum esset. At ille ex ordine exponens uisionem de restituto auditu se suosque reddidit gaudentes. Et ueniens Sempingham adorandi et gratias agendi gratia, capellanum uici cum ceteris conuicaneis secum adduxit, qui suam testarentur egritudinem, et de reddita sanitate gratias Deo et sancto eius exoluerent.

[11] *De moribunda*

Filia Alexandri de Creissi militis[1] moribunda per coopertorium patris G(ileberti), quod super morientis proiectum est menbra, non modo uite sed perfecte meruit sanitati restaurari.

[12] *De cecutiente*

Soror Matildis de Sempingham, tumentibus genis et dolentibus oculis, utriusque luminis uerebatur dispendium; procumbens tumulo peruigil in orationibus, et uultus planiciem et oculorum recepit lumen.

[13] *De contracto*

Puer, minister molendini de Sempingham, dum dormiret, utreque ei ulne cum palmis incuruate sunt, nec poterat dirigere. Surgens a somno, clamans et eiulans, cucurrit ad basilicam in qua sanctus requiescit et ibi sanitatem recuperatus est.

[14] *De quodam ceco*

Albinus et Gamelus,[2] canonici sacerdotes, testantur cecum quendam de Leuesingham ad memoriam eiusdem illuminatum, quem a
f. 161 pueritia cecum fuisse | omnes uicini eius testati sunt.

[15] *De intoxicato liberato*[3]

Miraculum quod factum est eo tempore quo archiepiscopus Cantuarie et clerus et populus conuenerant ad indagationem factorum

Miracle 11 *LcOd*   Miracle 12 *Lc*   Miracle 13 *Lc*   Miracle 14 *LcOd*
Miracle 15 *LcOd*

---

[1] Cf. L. C. Lloyd, *The Origins of some Anglo-Norman Families*, ed. D. C. Douglas and C. T. Clay (Harleian Soc., 1951), p. 35; *Red Book of the Exchequer*, ed. H. Hall (RS, 1896), i. 341.

ringing. But when he described from the beginning his dream about his restored hearing, he caused her and his family to rejoice. As he came to Sempringham to offer worship and to give thanks, he brought with him the village chaplain together with other neighbours, that they might testify to his illness and render thanks to God and His saint for the restoration of his health.

[11] *A woman close to death*

The daughter of Alexander of Crecy, knight,[1] was close to death; by means of Father Gilbert's coverlet, which was thrown over his limbs as he lay dying, she earned recovery not only of life but of perfectly good health.

[12] *A woman going blind*

Sister Matilda of Sempringham feared the loss of her sight in both eyes because her cheeks were swollen and her eyes in pain; from prostrating herself in prayer by the tomb all night she recovered both an unswollen face and her eyesight.

[13] *A deformed boy*

While the boy who served at the mill of Sempringham slept, both his arms and his hands bent inwards and he was unable to straighten them. He arose from sleep crying and shouting, ran to the church where the saint lies, and was there restored to health.

[14] *A blind man*

Albinus and Gamel,[2] canons and priests, testify that a certain blind man from Leasingham, who (as all his neighbours bore witness) had been blind from childhood, received his sight at the tomb of the saint.

[15] *A poisoned man relieved*[3]

A miracle took place at the time when the archbishop of Canterbury, the clergy, and people had assembled to carry out the

[2] See above, pp. 96–9, 182–3, 214–15, 280–1.
[3] The rubric does not belong to c. 15 and a miracle may be missing here.

faciendam, per quod et ceterorum miraculorum certitudo amplius est roborata, sic contigit et hoc modo innotuit.

Epistola

Reuerendo domino et patri Huberto, Dei gratia Cantuar(iensi) archiepiscopo, R. decanus et R. persona de Chilewell', salutem et omnem in Domino reuerentiam.

Significauit nobis uir uenerabilis R(ogerus), prior ordinis de Sempingham, ut nos diuine caritatis intuitu cum omni diligentia ad Dei laudem et honorem inquireremus certam ueritatem super quodam miraculo quod Deus ostendere dignatus est ob merita pie recordationis magistri G(ileberti), fundatoris et inuentoris ordinis de Sempingham, in curatione Radulfi de Adeneburch. Nos itaque, precibus tanti uiri admoniti et desiderio diuine glorificationis astricti, accessimus ad Adeneburch, et ibi coram nobis tam ipsum Radulfum predictum qui dicebatur curari quam testes suos, maturos, legales et bone fame uiros, conuocari fecimus. Testimonium etiam quod ipsi de illo predicto Radulfo perhibuerunt, tam de eius infirmitate et infirmitatis diuturnitate quam de eius cura-
f. 161ᵛ tione mirifica, diligenter | scripto annuntiantes sub sigillo nostro, paternitatis uestre excellentie transmittimus. Cuius rei geste series hec est.

TESTIS Radulfus, filius Brien, de Bartona super Trente, iuratus dixit quod ipse grauissima infirmitate infirmabatur, ita quod pre angustia non potuit caput suum per aliquam horam in pace tenere, quamuis inniteretur parieti uel petre alicui, sed semper infirmitatis grauitate cogente mouebat et excussit illud inuitus ad similitudinem furibundi; et hoc durauit ei per annum integrum et dimidium, excepto quod ex quo accepit baculum ad sanctum Iacobum circa Purificationem beate Marie usque ad reditum eius de sancto Iacobo circa Pentecosten proximum post, non grauauit eum illa infirmitas, sed statim, circa festum sancti Petri ad Vincula proximum post, iterum arripuit eum pristina infirmitas ualde grauius quam solebat, et durauit illi continue usque ad festum sancte Marie proximum post,[1] ita grauiter ut aliquando insane mentis putaretur, quia totam memoriam perdidit quandoque per integrum diem et eo amplius. Et cumᵃ plura sanctorum loca adisset nec profecisset ad sanitatem,

---

ᵃ cum *om. Lc*

---

[1] i.e. from 1 Aug. (St Peter ad Vincula) to 15 Aug. (the feast of the Assumption).

investigation into these events, which also further confirmed the truth of the other miracles. This is what happened and how it became known.

Letter

To our reverend lord and father Hubert, by God's grace archbishop of Canterbury, R. dean and R. rector of Chilwell send greetings and all reverence in the Lord.

R(oger), a venerable man and prior of the Order of Sempringham, has indicated to us that, inspired by divine grace, we should inquire with every care, and to God's praise and honour, into the exact truth of a miracle—the cure of Ralph of Attenborough—which God has seen fit to make known on account of the merits of Master Gilbert of holy memory, the founder and deviser of the Order of Sempringham. Thus, admonished by the request of a man of such standing and bound by our desire to glorify God, we came to Attenborough and caused to be summoned before us there both this same Ralph, who was said to be cured, and his witnesses, grown men answerable to the law and of good reputation. In our careful report written under our seal, we are sending you, excellent father, the evidence which these men submitted about this same Ralph, relating to his illness and its duration as well as to its amazing cure. This is the sequence of events.

Ralph, son of Brian, from Barton on Trent, said on oath that he used to be incapacitated by a most serious affliction: it was too difficult for him to keep his head still for a single hour even though he leant it against a wall or some stone; but compelled by the force of his illness he would perforce move and shake it constantly, as madmen do; and this went on for a whole year and a half, except that this ailment did not trouble him from the time when he went on a pilgrimage to St James [at Compostela], about the feast of the Purification of St Mary [2 February], until his return from St James about the following Whit Sunday. But suddenly, about the feast of St Peter ad Vincula [1 August] next following, his former illness attacked him again and was much worse than it had been; it stayed with him without remission until the next feast of St Mary [the Assumption, 15 August],[1] and was so serious that he was sometimes thought feeble-minded, because on occasion he completely lost his memory for a whole day and even longer; and although he visited many shrines his health did not benefit. Then he was urged

admonitus a suis ut iret ad tumbam magistri G(ileberti) de Sempingham spe sanitatis recuperande, confidens in Deum et magis-
trum Gilebertum, iuit et uenit illuc uigilia sancti Michaelis; et |
f. 162 nocte sequenti in orationibus pernoctans, post horas matutinas
meritis predicti G(ileberti), ut credit, ad tumbam ipsius plene
curatus est.

TESTIS   Brien, pater ipsius Radulfi predicti, iuratus dixit idem per
omnia quod ipse Radulfus de infirmitate et infirmitatis diuturnitate et curatione, adiciens quod sepe maluit eum mortuum esse
quam uiuere, pre dolore et tristitia quam habuit ex eoᵃ quod uidit
filium suum sic cruciari.

TESTIS   Radulfus de Adeneburch, auunculus predicti Radulfi, iuratus
dixit idem per omnia de infirmitate et infirmitatis diuturnitate
quod ipse Brien, adiciens quod nunquam uidit aliquem tali et tam
graui modo infirmantem, quia quandoque per duos dies integros,
quandoque per tres continue iacuit impotens sui nichil intelligens;
et precepit matri sue uidue ut custodiret illum et non permitteret
quoquam ire solum, et ut clauderet ianuas suas et firmaret cotidie;
timebat enim ne se in aquis precipitaret; et quod ipse inuenit sibi
necessaria uictus omni tempore infirmitatis sue, et quod circa eum
ab infantia nutritus fuit; et sciuit eum iuisse ad Sempingham, et ibi
eum curatum esse, ut credit meritis magistri G(ileberti), ad tumbam ipsius G(ileberti), quia sanum eum inde redire uidit et
redeuntem suscepit.

f. 162ᵛ   Ricardus, frater | predicti Radulfi, iuratus dixit idem per omnia de
TESTIS infirmitate et infirmitatis diuturnitate et curatione quod ipse Radulfus, excepto quod non ministrauit ei necessaria in infirmitate.

Martinus de Chilewell' iuratus dixit se uidisse predictum
Radulfum adeo infirmum quod non putauit eum posse uiuere per
dimidium diem, et monuit eum ire ad Sempingham ad tumbam
magistri G(ileberti), et sciuit eum iuisse illuc, et ibi eum ad tumbam predicti G(ileberti) plene curatum esse credit meritis magistri
G(ileberti), quia perfecte sanum eum inde redire uidit.

Herewardus iuratus dixit idem per omnia quod ipse Martinus,
excepto quod non locutus est cum eo quando iuit ad Sempingham.

Frater Willelmus ordinis de Sempingham iuratus dixit quod
ipse adduxit predictum Radulfum, predicto modo miserabiliter
infirmantem, ad tumbam magistri G(ileberti) predicti, et ante tumbam procumbere fecit, et ibi eum sepius uisitauit, et in die

ᵃ ea Lc

by his friends to go to the tomb of Master Gilbert of Sempringham in the hope of recovering his health; putting his trust in God and Master Gilbert, he set out and arrived there on the vigil of St Michael [28 September]; after spending the following night in prayer he was completely cured at this man's tomb after matins through the merits, he believes, of this same Gilbert.

Brian, Ralph's father, said on oath the same throughout as Ralph about his illness, its duration, and its cure; adding that he had often wished Ralph dead rather than alive because of the pain and distress caused him by seeing his son so tormented.

Ralph of Attenborough, Ralph's uncle, said on oath the same throughout as Brian about the illness and its duration; he added that he had never seen anyone so seriously ill with such an affliction, for Ralph lay with no understanding and no control over himself sometimes two, sometimes three whole days at a time; he instructed his own widowed mother to look after him and not to let him go out anywhere alone, but to shut and secure her doors every day, because he was afraid that Ralph would drown himself. He said also that he himself provided the necessities of life Ralph needed throughout the period of his illness, and that he had supported him from childhood; and he knew that Ralph had gone to Sempringham and was cured there at Gilbert's tomb, in his opinion by the merits of Master Gilbert, because he saw Ralph return from there healed when he met him as he arrived back.

Richard, Ralph's brother, said on oath the same throughout as Ralph about the illness, its duration and cure, except that he did not provide him with necessaries in his illness.

Martin of Chilwell said on oath that he had seen Ralph so ill that he did not believe he could survive for half a day, and he urged him to go to Sempringham to Master Gilbert's tomb and knew that he had gone there; and he believes that Ralph was completely cured there at Gilbert's tomb through the merits of Master Gilbert because he saw him return from Sempringham entirely healed.

Hereward said on oath the same throughout as Martin, except that he did not speak with Ralph when he went to Sempringham.

Brother William, of the Order of Sempringham, said on oath that it was he who brought Ralph, when pitifully sick in the way described, to Master Gilbert's tomb and made him lie in front of the tomb; he visited him there many times, and the following day

sequenti perfecte sanum et curatum ad tumbam prefati G(ileberti) uidit, meritis ipsius magistri G(ileberti), ut credit, et sanum reduxit ad patriam suam.

Huius rei testis est tota uillata de Adeneburch iurata, et capellani cum omnibus parochianis de Adeneburch, de Chilewell', de Bramcote, in animas suas iurati.

[16] *De manu curua*

f. 163   Mane uigilans a ⟨somno⟩,[a] filia Guidonis de Trikingham sensit sibi manum dexteram aruisse, nec[b] quicquam operis soliti peragere poterat. Conquesta patri manum suam ut uulgus loquitur obdormisse, ad consilium ipsius in aquam frigidam illam inmersit, ut ad tactum aque stupor ille euanesceret. Vix aqua attigit artus, et statim omnes digiti diriguerunt, manusque in aduersam brachii partem reflexa dupplicati morbi duplicauit dolorem. Tunc luctus et suspiria patri[c] filieque congeminantur. In meliorem tamen confidens mulier medicinam, que quosdam egrotos ex uico illo reddiderat sanitati, concepit in animo se posse, sicut et ceteros, per merita beati G(ileberti) liberari. Pergensque cum patre ad mausoleum sancti, tota die crastina plorans et orans iacuit ante sepulchrum ieiuna usque ad uesperum. Die uero cedente, cum recederet illa, recessit pariter morbus ab illa, et uoto facto in memoriam morbi et curationis, manum ceream tercia die rediens obtulit ad tumbam, nobisque coram clero et populo psallentibus et Deum glorificantibus manum directam et articulos flexibiles ut prius erant ostendit.

[17] *De surda*

f. 163ᵛ   Filia puella, audiendi uirtute priuata, illuc | a matre deducta, cum sepius in orationibus suis nunc unam nunc alteram aurem ad lapidem sepulchri inclinaret, circa mediam noctem pulsatis nocturnalibus horis, ruptis in ambabus auriculis quasi quibusdam neruis,

---

Miracle 16 *Lc*   [a] somno *Lh; om. Lc, leaving a space*   [b] nec *Winterbottom;* ne *Lc*   [c] *Perhaps read* patris *(Winterbottom)*
Miracle 17 *Lc*

saw him completely healed and cured at Gilbert's tomb, through the merits, he believes, of this same Master Gilbert; and he took Ralph home in good health.

The entire township of Attenborough on oath is a witness to this fact together with the chaplains and all the parishioners of Attenborough, Chilwell, and Bramcote, who have taken a solemn oath.

[16] *A deformed hand*

One morning as she woke from sleep, the daughter of Guy of Threckingham felt that her right hand had lost all sensation, and she was unable to do any of her accustomed work; she complained to her father that her right hand had, in the common phrase, gone to sleep, and on his advice plunged it into icy cold water, hoping that the numbness would disappear on contact with the water. But scarcely had the water touched her limb when immediately all her fingers grew rigid and her hand bent back in the opposite direction to her arm, thus increasing twofold the pain of her double affliction. Then the lamentations and the sighs of father and daughter redoubled. However the woman believed in a better remedy which had restored to health various sick people from that village, and it occurred to her that just like the others she might secure relief through the merits of blessed Gilbert. Arriving at the saint's shrine with her father, she lay weeping and praying before his tomb the whole of the following day, fasting until the evening. Then at nightfall as she was leaving, the illness likewise left her. Since she had made a vow in memory of her illness and its cure, she came back on the third day and offered a hand made of wax at the tomb; and, in the presence of clergy and people who were singing psalms and glorifying God, she showed us her hand straight and her fingers as supple as they had been before.

[17] *A deaf woman*

A young girl who had lost the power of hearing was taken to that place by her mother. As she prayed she would frequently lay first one ear and then the other against the stone tomb. About the middle of the night, when the bell had rung for the night office, something resembling certain nerves burst in the inner chambers of both ears and pus flowed from her ear out through each opening

exfluenteque ex utroque foramine super uelamen lamine sanie, primas in laudibus Dei editas uoces[1] patulo auditu clare deprehendit.

[18] *De collo curuo*

Puer super unum humerum caput diu habens recline, directum ibi et erectum, deinceps potuit illud attollere in sullime.

[19] *De fistula*

Filia Radulfi Raisun de Pointuna, M.[a] nomine, cuius soror Helewisa, per triennium curua, meritis sancti G(ileberti) fuit erecta, sicut testificatum est coram domino Huberto Cantuariensi archiepiscopo,[2] circiter duos annos fistulam in utroque pede paciebatur, dolorem tantum et tumorem sustinens quod per totum idem biennium altero pede terram non poterat contingere. Circumduxerat eam pater suus per medicos et per loca sancta, recuperande sanitatis gratia. Sed cum nichil proficeret, ammonita in somnis ut emplastrum factum ex gramine super quod sanctus ambulauerat f. 164 ulceribus apponeret, delata est ad | sepulchrum sancti, ubi uigilans nocte apostolorum Petri et Pauli unius pedis recepit sanitatem. Nocte uero sequenti commemorationis beati Pauli, alterius nichilominus pedis consecuta est integritatem. Fossas uidimus in pedibus clausas et siccas, tumorem agnouimus pene omnino sedatum. Dolorem sensit illa mitigatum, saliens coram nobis et utroque pede firmiter innitens, lacrimantibus pre gaudio parentibus,[b] gratias Deo et sancto Gileberto referentibus, quod filiam suam, quam nunquam talem se uisuros sperauerant, tam sanam uiderent.

[20] *De febre acuta*

Ex eadem uilla de Pointuna febre acuta decubans puella ad extrema perducta est. Biduo iacens inmota iam iamque ultimum spiritum efflatura expectabatur. Tunc uidit in spiritu sese quasi mortuam

Miracle 18 *Lc*
Miracle 19 *LcOd*   [a] M. *Lc, leaving a space;* Matild' *Od*   [b] parentibus *om. Lc;*
perhaps add et *(Mynors)*
Miracle 20 *LcOd*

---

[1] i.e. the words of the night office, matins.   [2] See pp. 296–9.

on to the lobe of her ear; then the first words she clearly distinguished with unimpeded hearing were raised in praise of God.[1]

[18] *A boy with torticollis*

There was a boy whose head for a long while rested upon one
shoulder; in this place it was straightened and raised, and henceforward he was able to lift it upright.

[19] *An ulcer*

The daughter of Ralph Raisun from Pointon, called M., whose
sister Helwise had been bent over for three years and was made
straight through the merits of St Gilbert, according to the evidence
given before Hubert, archbishop of Canterbury,[2] suffered for
about two years from an ulcer on each foot. She endured such great
pain and swelling that for the whole of this period she could not
touch the ground with one foot or the other. Her father had taken
her round the doctors and holy shrines in the hope of recovering
her health. But when she was none the better she was advised in a
dream to put on her ulcers a plaster made from the grass upon
which the saint had walked. Carried to the saint's tomb where she
spent the night of the feast of the Apostles Peter and Paul
[29 June], she had one foot healed. Then on the following night,
the feast of St Paul [30 June], she obtained an equal cure for the
other foot. We saw the sinuses in her feet after they had closed up
and healed; we perceived that the swelling subsided almost
entirely. The woman felt the pain decrease and in our presence she
leapt in the air and put her weight firmly on both feet; her parents
wept for joy and gave thanks to God and St Gilbert because they
saw that their daughter, whom they had never thought to see like
this, was so entirely restored.

[20] *An ague*

A girl from the same village of Pointon, who lay sick with ague,
came close to death. She had lain for two days without moving and
it was expected that she would breathe her last at any moment.
Then in the spirit she saw herself like a dead woman upon a bier;

super feretrum positam^a in montem qui inter . . .¹ et uillam de^b
Sempingham medius eminet, ubi erat, ut putauit, conflictus pug-
nantium. Sic iacenti astitit ad caput uir quidam, dicens: 'Quare
non uadis ad Sempingham ad tumbam sancti G(ileberti)?' Surgens
illa, ut credidit, ire cepit. Et cum uenisset ad portam cenobii, stans
senex increpauit patrem suum qui ei commitabatur quod ingres-
f. 164ᵛ sum filie | sue antea non petisset. Ingressa denique manibus et
pedibus reptans peruenit ad mausoleum, super quod toto corpore
extensa ilico se sensit alleuiatam. Quibus uisis excuciens se et
loquens retulit parentibus uisionem, peciitque a matre ut eam ad
tumbam sancti Gileberti mensuraret. Quo facto ilico conualuit, set
dolor capitis, qui talem morbum solet comitari, tam uehementer
eam detinuit quod sensum timuit amittere pre nimia anxietate.
Circumplexa autem caput filo mensurationis sue,² in momento
liberata est.

[21] *De febribus*

Duo pueri de uilla de Walecote,³ annorum circiter .vĩı. coeui, a
media .x̊ʟ. usque ad festum sancte Margarete tali laborabant
incommodo quod singulis diebus intollerabilis frigoris, noctibus
autem inmensi ardoris tolerauere molestias. Quibus angustiis
continue attriti, fere ad extrema deducti sunt. Venerunt pariter ad
sepulchrum; celebratis nocte uigiliis ita mane senserunt se alleuia-
tos ut omnino se crederent curatos. Tunc accitus suprior domus
ut rem cognosceret, suasit ut sustinentes per .xv. aut amplius dies
probarent si conualuissent, et tunc reuertentes darent gloriam Deo
f. 165 et sancto eius. Quod et factum est. | Nam recedentes, post tres sep-
timanas reuersi dixerunt nunquam postea aliquod morbi illius
uestigium se pertulisse et laudauerunt Deum.

[22] *De ceco*

Eadem nocte infantulus anniculus ex Quadaueringe, uilla Hoilan-
die,⁴ a matre illuc allatus, cecitate oculorum per mensem percussus,

---

^a positum *Lc*   ^b et uillam de *Lc (a name having dropped out after* inter; *perhaps sup-*
ply uillam de Pointuna *or* eam uillam*);* uillam et *Od*
Miracle 21 *Lc*   Miracle 22 *Lc*

¹ The name is missing—possibly Pointon (Lincs.).
² Cf. p. civ.
³ Presumably one of the Walcots in Lincs.   ⁴ Quadring (Lincs.).

this was placed on the hill which rises in between ...[1] and the village of Sempringham, where it seemed to her a battle was taking place. As she lay there a man stood by her head saying: 'Why do you not go to Sempringham, to the tomb of St Gilbert?' She thought that she got up and set off. And when she arrived at the monastery gate an old man standing there rebuked her father, who was accompanying her, because he had not requested entry for his daughter before. When at last she went in, she approached the shrine crawling on hands and knees, and after stretching out her whole body upon it she experienced immediate relief. After this vision she shook herself and spoke up; and she described her vision to her parents and begged her mother to measure her at St Gilbert's tomb. When this had been done she got better straight away, but the headache which often accompanies this illness troubled her so badly that she was afraid she was losing her senses through excess of pain. But the moment that the thread with her measurement was put round her head,[2] she was cured.

[21] *Fevers*

Two boys from the village of Walcot,[3] twins of about eight years, were troubled from the middle of Lent to the feast of St Margaret [20 July] with this misfortune: they endured the irritation of intolerable cold every day but great heat during the night. Constantly weakened by these afflictions they came almost to death's door. Together they visited the shrine and, having spent the night in vigil, they felt so much better in the morning that they believed themselves entirely cured. Then the subprior of the house was sent for to be told about the matter; he advised that they should wait for a fortnight or longer to see if they had recovered and should then return to give glory to God and to His saint. And so it happened. For they went away and when they returned after three weeks they said that they had never afterwards suffered the slightest symptom of that illness, and they praised God.

[22] *A blind boy*

The same night a baby boy a year old from Quadring, a village in Holland,[4] was carried there by his mother; he had been blind for a month and was brought to Sempringham following the advice

et ex consilio capellani de Trikingham cum eo ueniret mendicans et
ei ostenderet puerum cecum ad Sempingham ductus; cum resideret
in gradibus ante tumbam, aduertit frater conuersus puerum frequenter attollere oculos ad lampadem prope ardentem, dixitque
matri infantem uidere. Quod oblatis quibusdam signis clarissime
perpenderunt. Tollensque mater puerum circumduxit per uillas,
ostendens eum hominibus uidentem quem antea uiderant cecum.

[23] *De contracto*

Puer quidam nomine Willelmus, ex uilla*a* Brunne oriundus, dum
esset in famulatu uiri cuiusdam apud Torneiam, aruerunt ei, diriguerunt, et emarcuerunt utraque crura cum tibiis et pedibus.
Ceruix quoque ita debilitata est quod non nisi manu supposita
potuit caput sustinere; decidit enim deficientibus neruis super
humeros siue supra pectus, nec poterat idem nisi apposita manu
f. 165ᵛ attollere, nec propriis pedibus | ambulare. Iacebat illa detentus ab
infirmitate per duos annos et dimidium, nunquam se erigens a
lecto nisi alienis manibus deportatus. Missus a uiro cui seruierat,
proiectus est a portante ante hostium patris sui. Post cuius obitum
anno transacto procurauit eum mater sua plus quam per anni
spacium. Instante beati Gileberti translatione,[1] pergens illa ad
Lincolniam orationis causa, detulit eum secum ad Sempingham,
ibique dimisit habende sospitatis gratia. Nocte translationis ego
ipse qui hec scripsi propriis manibus illum contrectaui,[2] artus suos
quasi arboris ramos rigidos uidi, et misertus eius remoui eum a uia
qua iacebat in basilicam,*b* ne conculcaretur a turba. Sed tunc nichil
melioratus reportatus est a matre reuertente ad locum unde
uenerat. Et quoniam uir suus, uictricus scilicet pueri, obiurgauit
eam quod bona sua dissipasset in portatione et reportatione
et sollerti custodia ut ait contracti sui, reliquit eum mater sua, et
in ueteri casa solum nocte reclusit, que*c* a superueniente nobili
uiro Symone de Kyma[3] cum suis occupabatur. Verum licet pater
suus et mater sua dereliquerunt*d* eum, Dominus tamen assumpsit

Miracle 23 *LcOd*   *a* *ins.* de *Od, doubtless rightly*   *b* basilicam *Winterbottom;*
basilica *LcOd*   *c* que *Brooke;* quia *LcOd*   *d* derelinquerunt *Lc*

---

[1] 13 Oct. 1202.   [2] Cf. 1 John 1: 1.
[3] See above, p. xxxi. The meaning of 'superueniens' is not certain, but it probably
means he was a regular visitor—an outsider, not a member of the community: see R. E.
Latham, *Revised Latin Word-list* (London, 1965), p. 468.

which the chaplain of Threckingham gave when she went to beg in that place and showed him the blind boy. As the child sat on the steps before the tomb, a lay brother noticed that he often lifted his eyes to the lamp which was burning nearby, and so he told his mother that the child could see, a fact they checked easily by certain signs that were given. Picking the boy up, his mother took him around the villages showing his powers of vision to the people who had seen him before when he was blind.

[23] *A cripple*

While a boy called William, a native of Bourne, was in the service of a man at Thorney, both his legs, his shins, and his feet shrivelled, stiffened, and withered away; moreover, his neck was so weakened that he could not keep his head up unless he put a hand underneath it. Because his muscles were not strong enough, his head fell on to his shoulders or upon his chest, and he could not lift it without a supporting hand; nor could he walk on his own feet. For two and a half years he lay a victim to this disease, never getting up from bed unless he was carried in other people's arms. The man whose servant he had been sent him away, and he was laid down in front of his father's door by the person who carried him. After the father's death when a year had passed, his mother looked after him for more than a twelvemonth. On the occasion of St Gilbert's translation,[1] this woman, who was travelling to Lincoln in order to offer prayers, carried him with her as far as Sempringham and left him there hoping for a cure. On the night of the translation I myself, who have written this account, handled his body with my own hands;[2] I saw that his limbs were rigid like the branches of a tree, and in my pity for him I took him away from the pathway where he was lying into the church, so that he would not be trampled underfoot by the crowd. But then, as he had not got any better, he was carried back by his mother, when she returned to the place he had come from. And because her husband, that is the boy's stepfather, scolded her for wasting his substance on carrying her cripple, as he called him, there and back and on watching over him constantly, his mother abandoned him and shut him up alone at night in an ancient dwelling which was occupied by a noble visitor, Simon of Kyme,[3] and his household. But although his father and his mother forsook him, yet the Lord took

f. 166 eum.[1] Nam nocte illa uidebatur ei | in somnis quod esset in turre Sempinghamensi, in domo in qua tegule parabantur, et cum cepisset comburi domus illa, et fugientibus omnibus ille inmotus remansisset, apparuit ei senex admonens ut surgeret uelociter et curreret uersus basilicam. Ad cuius imperium uisum est ei surgere et currere quamtocius in ecclesiam directo collo et facie ad celum erecta, et sese ante sepulchrum sancti prosternere. Quod uisum cum mane referret matri, uix impetrauit illa lacrimis a uiro ut in uehiculo trahi eum faceret ad locum prenominatum, sub ea tamen conditione ut nunquam postea pateretur eum ad se reuerti. Quo cum uenisset die tercio, cum celebrarentur misse in altari sancti Gileberti a monachis qui illuc uenerant ad orationem, cepit conualescere, pedes et crura extendere, et pedetemtim ambulare, cunctisque uidentibus et Deum laudantibus gradus ascendere.

Noluerunt tamen canonici domus tam celeriter 'Te Deum laudamus' pro eius curatione decantare aut signa pulsare, donec, ut mos est ibi de omnibus sanatis ueritatem inquirere, mandati parentes eius et uicini omnia ut facta sunt narrarent[a] et testarentur. In dies autem semper ualidior effectus, colli et capitis motibus pedumque et crurum liberis potitus est deinceps gressibus.

f. 166ᵛ   [24] *De ydropica*

Adolescentula quedam ex . . . ,[b] a Pascha usque circa festum sancti Iohannis Baptiste tanquam ydropica uentre et cruribus inflata, tribus diebus ibi peruigil in orationibus detumuit, cibum sumpsit et sana recessit.

[25] *De squinanci*

Clericus quidam Ricardus nomine, cognatus Roberti de Birtona decani, suam illuc[c] deferens oblationem, retulit gratias agens quod, cum quasi morbo squinnancis guttur ei et fauces inflarentur, ita ut mortis timeret periculum, uidebatur ei in somnis adesse apud Sempingham in maiori ecclesia. Cumque orasset ante feretrum sancti

---

ᵃ narrent *Lc*
Miracle 24 *Lc*   ᵇ *Lc leaves a gap of almost a line*
Miracle 25 *LcOd*   ᶜ illuc *Lc;* ad Sempyngham *Od*

[1] Cf. Ps. 26 (27): 10.

him up.[1] For that very night he dreamt that he was in a tower at Sempringham, in a house in which tiles were being made. The building started to burn and everyone fled to safety, but he remained motionless; then an aged man appeared to him, urging him to get up quickly and run to the monastery church. So commanded, he thought that he arose and ran to the church as fast as he could, with his neck upright and his face lifted to the sky, and that he prostrated himself before the saint's shrine. In the morning he described his dream to his mother; and she was just able, by means of her tears, to make her husband agree to have the boy conveyed thither, but only on the condition that she never allowed him to return to them afterwards. The third day after his arrival, while mass was being celebrated at the altar of St Gilbert by monks who had come to pray there, he began to get better, stretching out his legs and feet and walking a little at a time and going up steps, with everyone watching and praising God.

However, the canons of this house were unwilling to sing the *Te Deum* for his cure straight away or to ring the bells until they had discovered the facts, which is the customary procedure in that place with all who have been healed; his parents and neighbours were told to give information and evidence about it all as it had happened. Day by day, growing stronger all the time, the boy obtained control over the movements of his neck and head and afterwards was able freely to take steps with his legs and feet.

[24] *A young woman with dropsy*

A young woman from ... whose stomach and legs had been swollen as if from dropsy from Easter until about the feast of St John the Baptist [24 June], spent three days praying constantly in this place; the swelling went down, she took food and departed cured.

[25] *A man with a quinsy*

A clerk called Richard, cousin to Robert dean of Burton, came to the place to make an offering. He described, giving thanks, how, when his throat and gullet were so swollen by a quinsy-like attack that he feared the peril of death, he dreamt that he was in the main church at Sempringham. And when he had prayed before the

confessoris, uisum est ei inponere caput et collum infra capsam
qua sacre continentur reliquie, que ei per se aperiebatur. Extra-
hens caput nullum omnino sensit dolorem. Quo uiso euigilans
contrectauit genas et guttur suum et inuenit totum resedisse
tumorem. Audiens autem decanus motus eius, quia prope lectum
eius iacebat, interrogauit quomodo se haberet: at ille, exponens
somnium, indicauit se tam a dolore quam a tumore fuisse liberatum.

[26] De furiosa

Lauans caput die sabbati post horam nonam, mulier quedam ex
f. 167 uilla Lennensi | subito incidit[a] mentis alienationem. Nam prope
iacentem filorum copiam, ad uestes faciendas preparatam,
arrepta securi incidit in frusta,[b] loquebatur aliena, uolutabatur et
spumabat ut furiosa. Sic se habuit ebdomadibus .xi., modicum
aut nichil interim comedens uel bibens.

Ducta est igitur a duobus filiis suis uersus Croilandiam, ut ibi
per merita et flagellum sancti Guthlaci, quod ibi habetur et solet
talibus mederi, liberaretur: sed cum essent in itinere, nescio quo
casu diuertit ab eis, et in inaccessibilibus paludibus[c] aliquamdiu
delituit uagabunda.[1] Tunc dolor multiplicatus compulit filios per
loca et uicos marisco proximos, unum ad austrum, alterum ad
aquilonem, huc illucque cursitantes querere matrem. Non in-
uenientibus autem illis, iuniori reuertenti per uiam qua uenerat, ut
iterum quereret, et dormienti in uilla Quadaueringa nomine, astitit
senex uenerandus baculum gerens manu, et sic eum alloquitur:
'Dormis an uigilas?' Respondenti se minime posse dormire pre
tristitia et sollicitudine, subiungit: 'Tristis es quidem nimium pro
amissione matris tue, licet frater tuus senior sit te tristior.' Dicenti
f. 167ᵛ se tristem esse, ait: 'Noli contristari, | sed surgens uade uersus
Sempingham ad domum meam, et ibi sanabitur mater tua.' Fatenti
se nescire ubi inueniret matrem suam, respondit: 'Vade ad uillam
proximam isti, et dum perrexeris repperies eam in agro siliginis.'

Miracle 26 LcOd   [a] Perhaps add in (Winterbottom)   [b] frusta Lc corr., Od;
frustra Lc   [c] plaudibus Lc

[1] The itinerary runs from Lynn south-west towards Crowland, then north to
Quadring, and west to Bridgend Causeway, Horbling, and Sempringham.

holy confessor's shrine, it seemed to him that he put his head and neck into the casket where the holy relics were kept, which opened of its own accord for him. When he took his head out, he felt no pain whatsoever. Waking from this dream he felt his cheeks and throat and found that the whole swelling had gone down. Because he was lying close by his bed the dean heard him moving and asked him how he felt; then Richard described his dream and showed that he had been set free from both pain and swelling.

[26] *A madwoman*

As she was washing her head one Saturday after the ninth hour, a woman from the town of Lynn suddenly lost her wits. For, snatching up an axe, she cut to shreds a pile of yarn which lay nearby ready for making into cloth; she said strange things, rolled on the ground, and foamed at the mouth like a madwoman. She remained in this condition for eleven weeks, eating and drinking little or nothing meanwhile.

So her two sons led her towards Crowland, to secure relief there through the merits of St Guthlac and his scourge, which is kept in that place and often cures such cases; but while they were travelling, by some obscure chance she went a different way from them and for some time disappeared from sight as she wandered about in inaccessible marshes.[1] Their increased grief then forced her sons to search for their mother through the countryside and the villages which bordered the fenland, running hither and thither, one to the south and the other to the north. But when they could not find her, the younger, to make further inquiries, turned back along the road he had taken. As he slept in a village called Quadring, a venerable old man holding a staff appeared to him and addressed him with the words: 'Are you asleep or awake?' When he replied that he was quite unable to sleep for grief and worry, the old man went on: 'Indeed you are very distressed at losing your mother, although your elder brother is even more distressed than you.' When the son declared his despair he said: 'Do not give way to sorrow, but rise and go towards Sempringham to my house and there your mother will be healed.' The son said that he did not know where to find his mother. He replied: 'Go to the village which is next to this one, and as you go along you will find her in a field of rye.'

Surrexit et abiit, et circumspiciens uidit agrum siliginis statim, et querens diligenter inuenit eam in quodam iugere, laceratis uestibus et corpore contrito iacentem. Quam cum uideret et ei panem porrigeret, quia antea eam sciuit diu non commedisse, apprehendens illa panem more canis momordit, et expuit, et lapidem quem in eum iecit corrodere cepit. Venientes ergo aurige quidam itinerantes eam ante se flagellis suis egerunt, quousque pontem Aslaci transissent, quorum uia exacta, alii homines superuenientes usque in uillam Horblingia nomine simul eam cum filio currere compulerunt.[1] Inde sumpto auxilio usque ad Sempingham pre se fugauit. Viderunt se procurrentem[a] habitatores uillarum, obstupuerunt impetuose prorumpentem custodes sepulchri, audierunt delirantem;[b] aduene et domestici aduerterunt, quotquot aduenerant, in gestis eius et tocius corporis inflatione ualidam et f. 168 diutinam | ipsius passionem.

Nocte sequenti, dominica scilicet proxima post aduincula sancti Petri, post terribiles clamores et horrificos strepitus, post multam uolutationem, et capitis ac menbrorum ad pauimentum frequentem tunsionem, tandem siluit, quieuit et dormiuit. Post somnum uero surgens, quo sanctus ei apparuerat et sanitatem promiserat, resedit et signum crucis sibi impressit, admirans ubi esset uel quomodo illuc uenisset, tota nocte Deum et sanctos eius adorans et gratias agens. Mane facto petita confessione et accepta sacra communione, ad presentiam filii et agnitionem sui largiter flens, cibum sumpsit et confortata est: et sic post diem tercium gaudens et sui compos inde recessit, defectionem uirium et plagas ante ei impositas plangens tunc primo et sentiens.

EXPLICIT LIBER VITE BEATI GILEBERTI[c]

---

[a] procurrentem *Winterbottom (or* pre- *Sharpe);* procurrentes *LcOd. The text and sense of this sentence are far from clear.*   [b] delicantem *Lc*   [c] *So the colophon of Lc (whose margin displays the same words, with* uite *omitted). Od has no colophon.*

[1] Bridgend Causeway is 3 km from Horbling . The opening of the next sentence but one may be corrupt.

He got up and set out, and as he looked about him he saw the field of rye straight away; and after a careful search he found his mother lying in a section of it, her clothes in tatters and her body emaciated. When he saw her, he offered her bread because he knew that she had not eaten for a long while; snatching it up she attacked it as a dog might do, spat it out and began to gnaw a stone which she threw at him. Then came some travellers in a cart who by using their whips drove her before them until they had crossed Bridgend Causeway; when they had completed their journey other men overtook them and forced her to run alongside her son right into the village called Horbling.[1] Having received help in that place, he made her hurry before him to Sempringham. The inhabitants of the villages saw her running. The custodians of the shrine were amazed at her bursting in, and listened to her ravings. Both strangers and inmates(?)—all who had come—noticed the extent and duration of her suffering, judging from the way she behaved and the swelling of her whole body.

The following night, which was the Sunday after St Peter's Chains [1 August], after emitting terrible shouts and horrifying noises, after much rolling on the ground and frequent beating of her head and limbs upon the floor, she at last became silent and calm and went to sleep. Awakening after a dream in which the saint had appeared to her and promised her recovery, she sat up and made the sign of the cross upon herself, wondering where she was and how she had got there. All that night she offered worship and thanks to God and His saints. When morning came she sought confession and received holy communion; then, weeping copiously to find her son present and to recognize him, she took food and was comforted. And so after the third day she departed, rejoicing and in full control of her faculties, but also lamenting and comprehending for the first time both her breakdown and the afflictions which had before assailed her.

HERE ENDS THE BOOK OF ST GILBERT

APPENDIX 1

The enigmatic figure of Aminadab in S. of S. 6: 11 has exercised the wisdom of exegetes old and new: the *New Jerusalem Bible* comments that it is the most difficult verse to interpret in the whole of the Song of Songs, and the text in the *Centenary Bible* is unintelligible. Thanks to Dom Jacques Dubois, OSB, of the Abbaye de la Source, Paris, I am able to throw some light on the medieval interpretations of the passage.

S. of S. 6: 11: 'nesciui: anima mea conturbauit me propter quadrigas Aminadab reuertere reuertere Sulamitis' (*Biblia sacra juxta uulgatam uersionem* . . . , ed. R. Weber (2nd edn., Stuttgart, 1975), p. 1000).

This is an obscure passage which the Glossa Ordinaria tried to elucidate according to the anagogical mode, following the advice of Ambrose and Paschasius Radbert (*PL* xiv. 487; cxx. 344A). The chariot of Aminadab is compared both with pious men, who work for the salvation of others, and with the Church, which preaches the Gospel to the four corners of the world (*Biblia Sacra cum Glossa Ordinaria* . . . , edition of Douai, 1617, cols. 1870–2). Aminadab was great-grandson of a patriarch of Judah, 'qui egressus est de Ægypto cum Naason filio suo', and also a figure of Christ himself, 'qui quasi currui presidens . . . et persona et nomine indicat saluatorem' (ibid., cols. 1871–2). Abbot Suger was inspired by such comments to have a window made in the abbey church of Saint-Denis in which God the Father, standing among the symbols of the four evangelists and holding the cross on which Christ hangs, appeared as the driver of a chariot—or altar or Ark of the Covenant— equipped with four wheels. The window carried the inscription 'Quadriga Aminadab' and these lines by Suger:

> Foederis ex arca Christi cruce sistitur ara;
> Foedere maiori uult ibi uita mori.[1]

It is not impossible that the biographer of St Gilbert had been on pilgrimage to Saint-Denis, perhaps while staying in Paris where many Englishmen studied or taught in the late twelfth and early thirteenth centuries. However that may be, he shows us Gilbert, represented as

[1] Suger, *Œuvres*, ed. A. Lecoy de la Marche, Paris, 1867, p. 205; E. Panofsky, *Abbot Suger on the Abbey Church of Saint-Denis*, Princeton, 1946, pp. 74–5, 198–9; L. Grodecki, *Le Vitrail roman*, Fribourg and Paris, 1977, no. 82; id., *Les Vitraux de Saint-Denis*, i (Paris, 1976), p. 100 and pls. v, 126–31; cf. H. de Lubac, *Exégèse mediévale*, ii. 2 (Paris, 1964), pp. 36–9.

Aminadab, leading the four-wheeled chariot in the way of salvation and so preserving the unity of the Order of Sempringham. If two oxen replace the four horses, it is no less true that 'eodem spiritu ad bellum unum currum trahunt' (*Glossa Ordinaria*, col. 1871A).

APPENDIX 2

OGGERUS

I am greatly obliged to Cecily Clark for her comments in connection with the following sentence in the *Life*, on the meaning of the name Ogger.

R.F.

> Solus tamen *Oggerus* . . . Ille in sua pertinatia abscessit, et fere usque ad diem obitus tam sui quam beati Gileberti illum inpugnare non destitit. Parum tamen uel nichil profecit; nam semper *iuxta nominis sui interpretationem* interclusus recessit (c. 25).

When found in a late twelfth-century English document the name-form *Ogger(us)* is of uncertain derivation. The period was one of rapidly shifting fashions, with 'Continental' (mainly French) names being widely adopted by the native English but pre-Conquest ones (ones, that is, of Old English or of Anglo-Scandinavian origin) still partly surviving, especially among the peasantry. *Ogger*, a fairly uncommon form, happens also to be one of the most ambiguous of those current at this time. Theoretically, it could be referred to any of several sources, partly interrelated: that is, to Continental Germanic *Audger / Odger / Otger* (cognate with Old English *Eadgar*) or, on the other hand, to either of two Scandinavian names, the corresponding but rare *Auðgeirr* or the *Oddgeirr* cognate with Old English *Ordgar*. As to 'meaning', none of these potential etymologies can be relevant to the context in question (*Aud- / Auð-* 'prosperity'; *Odd-* 'spear-point'; *-ger / -geirr* 'spear'). It is, in any event, wholly unlikely that a twelfth-century writer would have been able to work a true etymology out from information then available.

So presumably word-play is involved; and, if a pun could be confidently identified, it would have the further interest of throwing light on the language in which the hagiographer was thinking. The question thus arises of how the name might have been pronounced, a matter which the spelling by no means makes clear.

If representing a French derivative either from Continental Germanic or from Scandinavian, *Ogger* would probably have been pronounced with an assibilated medial [dʒ]. That such forms were current in medieval England is implied by Modern English surnames such as *Ogier* and *Odgers*. But, as to possible word-play based on such a pronunciation, searches through dictionaries of Old French as well as of Middle English have so far failed to bring to light any even remotely appropriate form.

If, however, *Ogger* here represented an English derivative from Scandi-

navian, then it would probably have been pronounced with a 'hard' *g*. Given that the bearer of it in question was a twelfth-century Lincolnshire peasant, this might seem a strong possibility. How widely current such a form was remains uncertain, because medieval spellings are ambiguous and among Modern English surnames *Odgers* (and similar forms) occurs far oftener than *Ogar*; but at least one early thirteenth-century occurrence in the Lincoln *Registrum Antiquissimum* implies a family with Anglo-Scandinavian traditions, that is, *Outy* [Anglo-Scandinavian *Auti*] *f. Ogeri*.

A pronunciation of this latter type proves to offer somewhat better opportunities for word-play. Admittedly, neither Latin nor French seems here to offer much scope for punning; but English offers a little. To a Middle English ear, what *Ogger* suggested must have been an agent-noun in *-er(e)*. Two possibilities seem to exist: neither, it is true, entirely conclusive.

(i) Of the terms in question, the nearer in pronunciation would have been Middle English *hoggere* 'herdsman', sometimes spelt (although mainly in documents later than the present one) *oggere* or *ogger*. Apt though this might seem for a gibe at a dissident lay brother, in the context it makes little sense; in order to contrive an interpretation, one would need to assume for herdsmen some sort of bad reputation unknown to the dictionaries.

(ii) There is a Middle English verb *uggen* used both transitively and intransitively so as to mean, respectively, 'to inspire loathing' or 'to feel loathing' [see *OED*, s.v. *Ug*, v.]. Derived from a Scandinavian verb *ugga* with a similar range of meaning, this appears mainly in the dialects of the old Danelaw, where indeed it survived until modern times [see J. Wright, *English Dialect Dictionary*, 6 vols. (London, 1898–1905), s.v. *UG*, v. and sb.]. From this verb *uggen* an agent-noun **uggere* might have been formed (that no such noun seems recorded is inconvenient but, given our imperfect records of Middle English vocabulary, constitutes no insuperable problem). As to the possible meaning of such a hypothetical noun, we may compare the adjectival forms *ugsome* and *ugging*, both of which mean 'loathsome'; if reflecting the verb's transitive sense, **uggere* would similarly mean 'one who inspires loathing'.

Such a noun **uggere*, although not identical in pronunciation with the Anglo-Scandinavian name *Ogger*, might conceivably (depending on the writer's standards in such matters) have been punned with it; and that seems to give reasonable sense. In so far as the man *Ogger* is represented as an instrument of the Devil, this passage from a devotional manual of *c.* 1230 may be relevant:

> ʒe schulen bihalde sum cheare toward te pine of Helle, þet ow uggi [transitive, used impersonally] wið ham & fleo þe swiðere ham-frommard

[Through divine enlightenment] you shall at some time behold the torments of Hell, in order that fear and loathing of them may fill you and that you may the more earnestly shun them: *Ancrene Wisse*, ed. J. R. R. Tolkien, Early English Text Society: Original Series 249 (Oxford, 1962), p. 50, the translation being my own.

Likewise, the impression given by the *Vita Gileberti* is that the man called Ogger was infernally inspired, was recognized as loathsome by most contemporaries, and was accordingly shunned.

CECILY CLARK

APPENDIX 3

This Appendix lists the discernible medieval marginalia, all of the late thirteenth or the fourteenth century, unless otherwise stated. It omits:

1. Corrections etc. by the original scribe (which are in the apparatus), and notes for rubrics, such as 'prologus in uitam sancti Gileberti' (f. 33).

2. The summaries added in a seventeenth-century hand, presumably by one of Cotton's Librarians, as in so many of their manuscripts.

f. 35	u[ita] Gr[egorii]
f. 38	Nota
f. 39	Nota (4) . . . Vita eius contine . . .
f. 39ᵛ	[illegible]
f. 40ᵛ	Nota
f. 41	docuit parochian . . . Lectio iiij; f. 41ᵛ magnanimus
f. 42	Lectio vta . . . de oracionibus eius
f. 43	Lectio—vj
f. 43ᵛ	de clericis . . . Lectio vij
f. 44ᵛ	Lectio viij
f. 45	archid. . . cons. . . oblac. . . contra. . .
f. 45ᵛ	Lectio ix [and an illegible note]
f. 46	Henricus primus [15th c.]
f. 48ᵛ	Nota hunc processum pro informacione nouiciorum
f. 50	de paupertate . . . Nota
f. 50ᵛ	Nota
f. 52	Nota de beato Bernardo . . . uiri sancti perit'
f. 53	[illegible]
f. 53ᵛ	meta recta
f. 54ᵛ	Religio
f. 55	contra mundos
f. 56	de doctrina eius
f. 56ᵛ	Nota de monaster. . . et . . .
f. 57ᵛ	pro uirtutibus Nota de eius continentia
f. 58ᵛ	de loquela eius . . . Nota sapiencie Nota de [? purgatione]
f. 59	pretulit extraneos . . . Dilectus ab omnibus [pro] affa[bilitate]
f. 59ᵛ	quando itinerauit
f. 60	abstinentia . . . de uase dicti(?) Domini
f. 61	confessio . . . de (?)accione: de contemplacione

f. 61ᵛ   misericordia . . . de eius misericordia
f. 62   . . . uestibus . . .
f. 64   beatus Thomas susceptus a suis(?)
f. 67   Nota discordia [15th–16th c.]
f. 69   De sacramento altaris
f. 69ᵛ   Nota (2)
f. 71   [. . .] relaxauit
f. 71ᵛ   rigid. . . de eius contemplatione
f. 72   Nota Dixit Vsque . . . confessio eius . . .
[Other notes, mainly illegible, on ff. 71ᵛ, 72ʳ, 73ʳ⁻ᵛ, 79ᵛ, 84ᵛ, 87ᵛ]
f. 112ᵛ   Translacio b. Gilberti fuit anno Christi mᵒ ccᵒ iiᵒ [15th–16th c.]
f. 113   Anno Domino mᵒ cᵒ lxx[x]ixᵒ obiit sanctissimus pater noster
                Gilbertus . . . Canonizatus fuerat b. G . . . tus anno Christi mᵒ
                ccᶜ iiᵒ 3ᵒ idus Ianuarii [both 15th–16th c.]
f. 117ᵛ   [by] etc ut supra: N supra [original hand]
f. 120   [by opening of letter] .W. [; and f. 121ᵛ has] .W. ut supra
f. 132   Nota pro monialibus

Thus the medieval marginalia almost entirely related to the *Vita*; of
special interest is its division into *Lectiones* for recitation. The N, W on
ff. 117ᵛ, 120 are symbols for cross-reference.

APPENDIX 4

THE CHRONOLOGY OF THE LAY BRETHREN'S REVOLT

See pp. lv–lxii, lxxxiv–xc.

Dates	Events	Documents	Lost documents
1164–5	First appeal of the lay brethren to Alexander III	1st letter of Thomas Becket to Gilbert (pp. 346–7)	Papal mandates to Becket and Gilbert
1166	Second appeal of lay brethren to the pope	2nd letter of Thomas Becket, as legate (after mid-May, pp. 347–8)	Papal mandates to the bishops of Norwich and Winchester, and the archbishop of York and the bishop of Durham
	Arbitration by the bishop of Lincoln	Letter of Robert, bishop of Lincoln, to the pope (no. 6)	Papal mandate to Gilbert
	Gilbert and the rebels before the judges-delegate in the dioc. of Lincoln	Letter of William, bishop of Norwich, to Gilbert (no. 5) Report of the hearing before William, bishop of Norwich, to Gilbert (no. 1, before the end of 1166)	
c. 1166–7	Gilbert and the rebels before the judges-delegate in the dioc. of York	Report of the hearing before Roger, archbishop of York, and Hugh, bishop of Durham (no. 7)	Petitions to the pope by bishops, abbots, and priors
		Petitions to the pope by Henry, bishop of Winchester (no. 4) and King Henry II (no. 3)	
c. 1167–8	Proceedings in the papal Curia		
1169		Privilege of Alexander III to Gilbert, 'prior' of Malton, etc., Benevento 30 July (*PUE*, i, no. 112)	Other privileges to the Order

1169 (*cont.*)		Papal letters to Henry II (no. 11) and to the archbishops, bishops, etc. (no. 10)	
		Papal letter to Gilbert, Benevento 20 Sept. (no. 9)	
1169–76	New hearing at the Curia; Gilbert again appears before judges-delegate	Letters of thanks and petition from Henry II to Alexander III (no. 12)	Papal mandates to new judges-delegate and to Gilbert
	Mission of Jordan, archdeacon of Lewes, and O. to Alexander III	Petition of William, bishop of Norwich, to the pope (no. 2)	New petitions from bishops, abbots, and priors to the pope
		Petition of the prior of Bridlington to the pope (no. 8)	The new judges delegate report to the pope
		Letter of Henry II to Gilbert (p. 348)	
1175–6	Legation of Cardinal Hugo Pierleone		
1176, *c.* Jan.– Feb.	The legate visits Sempringham		
1176–8	Gilbert resigns; Roger is made Master of the Order		
1178		Privileges of Alexander III for Malton, Alvingham, and Chicksands priories, Lateran 25 June (*PUE*, i, no. 154; Cheney, *Medieval Texts and Studies*, pp. 57–62)	Privileges for other houses of the Order
1176–8 or 1186–9		Letter of Gilbert to the canons of Malton (no. 14)	Similar letters to other priories
1186, 21 Sept.	Consecration of St Hugh as bishop of Lincoln		
1186–9	Arbitration by St Hugh, bishop of Lincoln		

APPENDIX 5

ADDITIONAL MATERIAL IN Od, f. 19^{r-v} (see p. 44 n. *a*)

Neque hoc silentio deputandum est, quod in hac peregrinacione mira Dei dispensacione fertur accidisse. Dum enim curiam Romanam, ut predictum*[a]* est, uir iste sanctus et sancte nouitatis inchoator adire disposuisset, tanta ac talis sollicitudo mentem illius preoccupauerat ut in eodem itineris procinctu curam uel custodiam Christi ancillarum, quas tanto studio Domino adunauerat, alicui hominum committere solummodo non reminiscens,*[b]* uerum claues de clausura et introitu ad easdem secum similiter detulisse perhibetur. Vnde cum maris ceraunea[1] pertransisset et hoc idem comperisset, eas patri orphanorum fusis lacrimis recommendans non minus sanas et incolumes ad propria rediens reperit quam progrediendo*[c]* reliquit, procuratis interim more consueto et ad|ministratis per eundem prout ei*[d]* uidebatur uite necessariis. Nam ut humiliter postea fatebantur, eius presencia medio tempore nusquam caruerunt.
f. 19^v

---

[a] predictum *Winterbottom;* predictus *Od*   *[b]* *This should be a finite verb*
[c] *ins.* dein *Od, but marked for deletion*   *[d]* ei *(i.e. the* pater orphanorum, *Christ) Winterbottom;* eis *Od*

[1] i.e. 'stormy waves'. The ultimate source of this usage is Lucan 5. 457, where John of Genoa, *Catholicon,* s.v., wrongly understood the word to mean 'exaltationes undarum in tempestate'. We are indebted to Mr R. Sharpe for this information.

APPENDIX 6

[1–2] *Two letters of Thomas archbishop of Canterbury to Gilbert
Master of the Order of Sempringham*

I am indebted to Dr Anne Duggan for sending me, in advance of the
publication of her *Correspondence of Thomas Becket* (OMT, forthcoming),
the critical text of these letters, formerly printed in *MB*, v, nos. 149, 148,
pp. 259–62; Foreville 1943, pp. 90–2.

[1] A letter issued in 1165, from France, at the time when Ogger and the
delegation of rebellious brethren appealed in person to the pope, then
exiled, as was Becket himself.

> Thomas Dei gratia Cantuariensis ecclesie minister humilis dilectis
> filiis Gileberto, canonicis, fratribus et sororibus, et omnibus ordinis
> de Semplingeham salutem et patris benedictionem.
>
> Quantum te, frater Gileberte, in persona tua omnesque ordinis de
> Semplingeham hactenus dilex⟨er⟩imus et adhuc diligamus, nouit
> Deus, nosti et tu, Gileberte, nouit etiam ordinis uniuersitas. Nos
> enim teste conscientia ordinem et ordinis uniuersitatem specialius
> pre omnibus aliis ordinibus semper dileximus, fouimus, et manu-
> tenuimus. Et iccirco quanto magis uos diligimus, tanto magis per-
> turbamur et dolemus cum talia a uobis et ordine uestro oborta fuisse
> audimus, que non solum oculos hominum offendunt, sed etiam
> ipsum Deum. Non enim credebamus, cum uos ita specialiter pre
> ceteris dilexerimus, uos aliquid magni in ordine uestro facere
> debuisse, nisi de consilio et conscientia nostra. Peruenerunt autem
> ad aures domini pape, peruenerunt et ad nos, quedam maxima
> scandala, que et ab ordine, et a domibus ordinis uestri, oborta sunt,
> que etiam per maximam orbis partem ignominiose sunt diuulgata.
> Itaque ad hec scandala corrigenda, et omnino per Dei misericordiam
> ab ordinis uniuersitate exstirpanda, noscat uniuersitas uestra domi-
> num papam nos constituisse, et ut ea corrigamus, et ordinem et
> domos ordinis in melius ordinemus, in mandatis nobis dedisse. Et
> iccirco, frater Gileberte, mandando precipimus, et in uirtute
> obedientie, in periculo possessionum, necnon et sub sententia

anathematis, firmiter iniungimus quatinus litteras domini pape et
nostras condigna reuerentia suscipias, et eas coram ordinis tui uni-
uersitate legi facias. Nichilominus tibi sub anathemate precipimus
quatinus infra terminum a domino papa litteris suis tibi constitutum,
quecunque tibi mandauerit, omni occasione et excusatione remota,
diligentissime labores perficere. Quod nisi feceris, nos iuxta mandatum a domino papa susceptum, uolente Domino, manus operi
apponemus, et, sicut litteris suis nobis mandauit, omnia Deo co-
operante studebimus adimplere diligenter et perficere. Verumtamen
si⟨c⟩ de consilio tibi mandando precipimus, ut te in Purificatione
beate Marie nostro conspectui represents, responsurus et satisfac-
turus domino pape et nobis de inobedientia, et aliis que tibi de
ratione poterunt obici; nisi omnia iuxta tenorem litterarum domini
pape, et infra terminum tibi ab eo constitutum, opere compleueris.

[2] A letter issued after the legatine powers had been granted to Becket
(papal bull of 24 April 1166: see p. lxxxix n. 1). Gilbert having failed to
appear before the archbishop.

Thomas Dei gratia Cantuariensis archiepiscopus et apostolice
sedis legatus Gileberto de Semplingham, salutem et in spiritu mansuetudinis congregare dispersos Israel.

Nos uobis alia uice scripsisse meminimus, ut fratres uestros, qui
occasione iuramenti seruande professionis (quod nulla sicut audiuimus religionis alicuius institutio exigere consueuit) dispersi sunt,
reuocaretis, remisso tanti scandali iuramento, et eos ea moderatione
de cetero tractaretis, que culpas cohibere et purgare sufficiat, et
patrem et pastorem deceat animarum. Hoc ipsum precipit et dominus papa, cuius non obedire mandatis maximi sceleris instar est, et
idolatrie crimini comparetur.[1] Sed sicut fratrum uestrorum indicat
querimonia sepius iterata, nostrum contempsistis aut dissimulastis
mandatum, nec de ecclesia curastis adhuc tantum scandalum
amouere. Scitis tamen quod Dominus, cuius essentia ueritas est et
uerba uita, ei ue denuntiat imminere, per quem scandalum uenit.[2]
Inde est quod fraternitati uestre, quam sicut Deus nouit sincera in
Christo diligimus caritate, iterata preceptione mandamus, in uirtute
obedientie iubentes quatinus fratres uestros reuocare et congregare
studeatis, et unitatem pacis reformare in domo Domini, ne nos ex
mandato apostolico aliquid in uos durius statuere compellamur.
Rogamus etiam, monemus, consulimus, et Christi uice in qua
preminemus auctoritate precipimus, ut sic zeli quem habetis in
Domino rigorem temperetis, quo laboris uestri fructus ualeat

---

[1] Cf. 1 Kgs. (3 Kgs.) 15: 23.   [2] Cf. John 14: 6; Matt. 18: 7, etc.

permanere, et ne post dies uestros tanti laboris opera pereat et impensa. Nam ut nostis, 'qui nimis emungit elicit sanguinem',[1] et immoderatio nouerca salutis est. Precamur etiam ut presentium latoribus, si deliquerunt in aliquo, misericordiam impendatis, et peregrinationem nostram sanctorum qui uobiscum sunt orationibus commendetis.

[3–4] Additional letters from Od

[3] Mandate from King Henry II to St Gilbert, to maintain the Order's constitution as confirmed by the privilege of Pope Alexander III and by the king's own charter (Od, f. 101ᵛ; Knowles, 'The Revolt of the Lay Brothers', p. 479, no. IV; Foreville, 1943, pp. 107–8; see pp. lxxxix, 344.

Littera regis Henrici secundi exhortatoria ad sanctum G(illebertum).

Henricus Dei gracia rex Anglie et cetera magistro Gilleberto de Sempyngham salutem.

Mando tibi sicut me diligis quod sicut bene incepisti studeas perseuerare, et custodias cum omni diligencia et sollicitudine institucionem ordinis domorum tuarum et firmiter obserues et teneas, desicut auctoritate priuilegiorum sedis apostolice et domini pape Alexandri priuilegio et propria carta mea tibi et successoribus tuis et ecclesiis ordinis tui confirmata est, et summopere caueas ne inde aliqua cuiuslibet personeᵃ suggestione auertaris. Test(ibus) etc.

[4] Letter of the papal legate, Cardinal Hugo Pierleoni, to Pope Alexander III, supporting petitions from St Gilbert and his canons and the houses of Gilbertine nuns: c.January–February 1176, when the legate crossed the diocese of Lincoln to attend the Council of Northampton (see pp. lxi–lxii, lxxxix, 344; Councils and Synods, i. 2, pp. 996–8; Od, ff. 104ᵛ–105ᵛ; Knowles, 'The Revolt of the Lay Brothers', p. 483, no. IX; Foreville, 1943, pp. 108–9).

Littere domini Hugonis cardinalis et legati pro sancto G(illeberto) m(agistro). Sanctissimo patri et speciali domino ac benefactori suo |
f. 105 Alexandro, sancte Romane ecclesie summo pontifici, Hugo uestre sanctitatis seruus et alumpnus, quod est et esse potest.

Ea que uidi, pater sanctissime, et oculata quasi fide cognoui maiestati uestre secura possum consciencia significare. Sane cum per Lincolniensem episcopatum transirem, contigit me ad domum

ᵃ persone corr. from persona Od

[1] Prov. 30: 33.

religiosarum monialium de Sempyngham,[a] quarum quidem conuersacio, ut pura uobis loquar consciencia, magis potest et uerius dici esse in celis quam inter homines. Et harum ancillarum Dei capud est et magister homo plenus dierum, simplex et timens Deum, Gillebertus de Sempyngham nomine. Nec ceterarum monialium habitum exteriorem habent, immo ita sunt abiecti habitus et arte religionis ut mundum uideantur penitus reliquisse, et, sicut pro certo audiui, ita sunt in abscondito faciei sue et ab habitacione hominum omnino secluse ne homines possint quomodolibet perturbare uel in quamcumque malam suspicionem inducere.[1] Ita eciam domus illa ad quam accessi et alie multe que de ipsa emanauerunt quasi in modico temporis spacio disposite sunt, sicut audiui, et adaucte ut circiter mille quingentas[b] esse dicantur, et cum eis [sic] intus concordia et tranquillitas uigeat et exterius bone opinionis fragrantia publicetur atque circumquaque redoleat. Set tante concor|die, honestatis et   f. 105ᵛ religionis antiquus inuidus hostis unum de fratribus conuersis, Oggerum nomine, non clericum, in arcum prauum conuertens ad hec machinacionibus suis induxit,[2] ut, licet a predicto magistro G(illeberto) paterne sit commonitus et sepe correptus, nondum tamen uult ad cor suum redire, immo aliquot de fratribus ad sue temeritatis foueam sicut dicitur inclinauit, statuta ordinis a sancte[c] recordacionis Eugenio papa et a paternitate uestra approbata et confirmata conans infringere et immutare. Vnde m(agister) G(illebertus) de communi fratrum et conuentus consilio in eum iuxta tenorem iam dicti domini Eugenii et uestrorum priuilegiorum excommunicacionis sentenciam promulgauit. Supplico igitur sancte discrecioni uestre ut eiusdem magistri G(illeberti) et fratrum suorum ac sororum sanctimonialium prescriptarum domorum peticiones quantum cum Deo et honestate poteritis benigne et paterne, si placet, admittat uestra clemencia. Valeat uestra p(aternitas).

---

[a] *As Knowles saw, an infinitive has dropped out, perhaps* uenire *or* accedere *(see below)*
[b] *sic Od*   [c] sancte *Knowles;* sancto *Od*

[1] Cf. Ps. 30: 21 (31: 22).   [2] Cf. Ps. 77: 57 (78: 58).

APPENDIX 7

18	De scriptis	
19	Commendatio ordinis	
20	Ratio contra detrahentes	Contra detractores
21	Qualiter se habuit in prelatione	
22	De asperitate uite eius	De asperitate eius uite
23	Quod suscepit habitum canonici	Quod suscepit habitum religionis [*with additional rubric before* 'Consummatis': Consummacio operis.]
24	De constantia eius	Noluit iurare
25	Vexatio falsorum fratrum	Vexacio falsorum fratrum
	Indulgentiam [*for* indulgentie] domini pape	Indulgentie domini pape
26	Item alia temptatio	Alia sancti G. temptacio
27	Qualis erat in senio	
28	De abstinentia eius	
29	De magnificentia eius	
30	De miraculis in uita sua factis	De miraculis sancti Gilleberti in uita sua factis
31	De febribus	De febribus curatis
32	Item de eisdem	Virtus obediencie eius
33	De dolore pedum sedato	De dolore pedum miraculose sedato
34	De podagra curata	
35	De febre	De febricitante curato
36	De fistula	De fistule morbo
37	De constipatione ⎤	De morti proximis et constipacione resoluta
38	De morti proximo ⎦	
39	De uirtute uerborum eius	[*The miracle is omitted.*]
40	Aliud miraculum	Correctio miraculosa
41	Aliud	Correptio cuiusdam rebelli (*sic*) canonici
42	Predicta ab eo rerum mutatio	[*The miracle is omitted.*]
43	Alia eius reuelatio	Reuelacio quedam facta sancto Gilleberto
44	Item alia	[*No rubric.*]
45	De uento precibus eius conuerso	De uento precibus eius sedato et ad uotum ipsius conuerso
46	De incendio fugato	De incendio fugato in suburbio Londoniarum
47	De partu miraculose dato	

48	De eodem	Qualiter mulier abortiens parturiuit
		Reuelacio facta sancto G. in sua cecitate (Lc c. 44)
49	De pane incorrupto	
50	De pace cum laicis facta	De pace cum laicis fratribus facta
		Littera sancti G. directa omnibus suis per ordinem canonicis
		[*See pp. 164—7.*]
51	De infirmitate qua obiit	De infirmitate qua pater Gillebertus obiit
		[*Additional rubrics not in Lc:*]
		Quod capellani eius detulerunt eum ad Sempyngham
		De uerbis eius in decessu ad successorem
52	De obitu eius	De obitu ipsius
53	Visio cuiusdam preposite	
54	Alia uisio	
55	De sepultura eius	De sepultura sancti G.
56	Substitutio primi successoris eius	Substitucio primi successoris sancti G.
	Explicit uita sancti Gileberti confessoris	[*No colophon.*]
[f. 89ᵛ]	Incipiunt epistole episcoporum	[*At f. 97ᵛ: see p. 134 n. a*]
	Incipit canonizatio beati Gileberti	Hic incipit canonizacio beati patris Gilleberti
	[*No rubric.*]	Visio domini pape
	[*See pp. 174–9.*]	[*No rubric for Oratio.*]
	Incipiunt uisiones et reuelationes de sancto Gileberto confessore [p. 178.]	Hic annotantur Reuelaciones de sancto Gilleberto
	[*See pp. 178—81; no rubrics in Lc.*]	Hic incipit translacio sancti Gilleberti. Visio successorum.
		De prouisione nunciorum ad curiam Romanam et quandam uisionem.
		Visio apparuit nunciis profecturis

	Visio apparuit Iohanni Hodoline consobrino domini pape
[*See below.*]	Visio domini Roberti prioris de Wattona
De translatione sancti Gileberti confessoris	Hic incipit qualiter translacio sancti Gilleberti confessoris fuerat sollemniter celebrata [*Om.* Licet enim ... executi sunt]
[*No rubrics in Lc.*]	De die translacionis assignato Visio cuiusdam monialis tempore translacionis Visio ignifera seu stelligera super ecclesiam
De casula	De infirmitate archiepiscopi
Lamine autem plumbee scriptura hec est	[*Omitting* autem *and reading* scriptua]
Rescriptum carte in feretro posite hoc est	
De diebus indulgentiarum H(uberti) archiepiscopi et suffraganeorum eius	[*No rubric.*]
De uisione R(oberti) prioris de Wathona	[*See above.*]

The Miracles: the formal collection (M1, pp. 264–303)[1]

Lc	Od
Incipit prologus de inquisitione miraculorum	Hic incipiunt miracula post mortem sancti G. facta
Ne cui ueniret in dubium ...	Ne cui ueniret in dubium ...
1. De clerico arido	2. De quodam clerico arido sanato
2. De muliere contracta per septem annos	1. De muliere de Sempyngham per septem annos contracta ...
3. De sacerdote paralitico per annum et amplius	3. De paralitico curato
4. De dissenteria et aliis morbis	[*Omitted.*]
5. De brachio inflato	[*Omitted.*]
6. De genu curato	4. De genu mulieris curato
7. De brachio curato	[*Omitted.*]
8. De squinanci	[*Omitted.*]
9. De lippa	[*Omitted.*]

[1] On Od's treatment of the miracles, see p. lxix.

10. De morti proxima	5. De morti proxima liberata
11. De paralitico curato	[Omitted.]
12. De dolore colli	[Omitted.]
13. De febre	[Omitted.]
14. De moribunda	[Omitted.]
15. De leprosa curata	25. De leprosa miraculose curata [Witnesses noted.]
16. De osse adherente gutturi	[Omitted.]
17. De pede leso et sanato	26. De pede leso et sanato
18. De tumore uentris militis	6. De tumore uentris sedato
19. De uento dato in mari	7. De uento in mari dato [Witness noted.]
20. De frenesi	20. De frenetica
21. De furiosa [sic for furioso]	8. De furioso curato
22. De frenetica	[Omitted.]
23. De tumente	22. De tumente curata
24. De uerme eiecto	23. De tortura uentris et uerme eiecto
25. De gibbosa	27. De gibbosa curata
26. De clerico ydropico	[Omitted.]
27. De lippiente	[Omitted.]
28. De oculo maculoso	[Omitted.]
29. De surda	[Omitted.]
30. De tumente tibia	[Omitted.]

The Informal Collection (M2, pp. 304–35)

Lc	Od
Item alia miracula Multa quidem . . .	
1. De morti proximo	9. De sanitate per baculum reddita
2. De febre	10. Aliud miraculum per eundem baculi fracturam
3. Item de febre	11. De eodem
4. De surda	19. De surda
5. De febre ter fugata	28. De febre a canonico ter fugata
6. Visio cuiusdam monialis	24. Visio cuiusdam monialis
7. De ceca	16. De ceca
8. Aliud	[Omitted.]
9. De paralitica	[Omitted.]
10. De surdo	[Omitted.]

11. De moribunda | 15. De moribunda curata
12. De cecutiente | [*Omitted.*]
13. De contracto | [*Omitted.*]
14. De quodam ceco | 14. De quodam ceco illuminato
  | [*Witnesses noted.*]
15. De intoxicato liberato [*sic*] Epistola | 13. De quodam paralitico curato
16. De manu curua | [*Omitted.*]
17. De surda | [*Omitted.*]
18. De collo curuo | [*Omitted.*]
19. De fistula | 12. De fistula curata
20. De febre acuta | 17. De febrium curacione
21. De febribus | [*Omitted.*]
22. De ceco | [*Omitted.*]
23. De contracto | 18. De quodam contracto
24. De ydropica | [*Omitted.*]
25. De squinanci | 29. De quodam a squinanci liberato
26. De furiosa | 21. De quadam furiosa
  | Multa quidem . . .

APPENDIX 8

CAPGRAVE'S USE OF *THE BOOK OF ST GILBERT*

(a) *Concordance of the Miracles*[1]

Capgrave	Lc: Life
c. 24	c. 31. De febribus c. 32. Item de eisdem
c. 25	c. 33. De dolore pedum sedato c. 34. De podagra curata
c. 36	c. 35. De febre c. 36. De fistula c. 37. De constipatione
c. 27	c. 43. Alia eius reuelatio c. 48. De eodem [De partu miraculose dato]
c. 28	c. 47. De partu miraculose dato c. 46. De incendio fugato
c. 29	c. 45. De uento precibus eius conuerso

Lc: Miracula, Formal Collection (M1)

c. 39	1. De clerico arido
c. 40	2. De muliere contracta
c. 41	7. De brachio curato 25. De gibbosa
c. 42	26. De clerico ydropico 3. De sacerdote paralitico per annum et amplius
c. 43	17. De pede leso et sanato
c. 44	14. De moribunda . . . 16. De osse adherente gutturi
c. 45	12. De dolore colli
c. 46	30. De tumente tibia
c. 48	10. De morti proxima 4. De dissenteria
c. 49	6. De genu curato 9. De lippa
c. 50	11. De paralitico curato

[1] The concordances are based on the text of the Miracles, not on the rubrics, which are sometimes inaccurate.

c. 51   { 20. De frenesi
          { 21. De furioso

c. 52   { 27. De lippiente
          { 28. De oculo maculoso
          { 18. De tumore uentris militis

c. 53   24. De uerme eiecto
c. 54   15. De leprosa curata
c. 55   19. De uento dato in mari

Miracula, Informal Collection (M2): these have no parallels in Capgrave.

(b) *Major borrowing from the* Life *both in St Gilbert's* Lectiones
and Capgrave's Life of St Gilbert *(first part)*

Lectiones	Life	Capgrave (first part)
I	c. 1, 2	c. 1
	c. 3, 4	c. 2
II	c. 5, 7–8	c. 3
III	{ c. 9, 10, 11	c. 4
	12, 17, 19	
IV	c. 21–2	c. 5–7
V	c. (24), 28	
VI	c. 24, (25), 29	
	c. 27, 29	c. 8
	c. 30, 51	c. 9
VII		
Evangelium		
VIII	c. 51	c. 10
	c. 52	c. 11
IX	c. 53	
	c. 55	c. 12
	Canonizatio }	c. 13
	Translatio	

APPENDIX 9

NOTE ON DR FREDEMAN'S SUPPOSED MANUSCRIPT

In the *Bulletin of the John Rylands Library*, lv (1972), 115–45, Dr J. C. Fredeman argued that Capgrave used a lost manuscript representing a branch of the Gilbertine tradition independent of, and different from, all our manuscripts. Capgrave in fact asserts in his prologue that he set out to translate the Life from the Latin exactly as he found it in the text provided by the Master of the Gilbertine Order, save that he added other material provided by the canons or which came to mind when he was writing.[1] This statement should give any reader pause before one accepts too readily Dr Fredeman's statement: 'Capgrave was working from a manuscript source that diverged in several striking ways from the extant *Vitae*.... There is no way of knowing how this particular difference came about, and it is not of great significance except in so far as it provides additional circumstantial proof that Capgrave's source represents a now lost branch of the transmission of the Life of St Gilbert.'[2] This seems to lay too little stress on the oral tradition invoked in his prologue, more or less embellished by the passage of two and a half centuries in which a certain amount of legendary matter could have grown up in the Order.

In a passing note almost hidden away Dr Fredeman observes: 'Obviously the evidence is always tenuous in discussing manuscripts no longer extant but which are presumed to have once existed',[3] an admission which might have induced the author to caution. The first point to be established is precisely how much detail is peculiar to Capgrave's translation, and for this two studies are needed: a thorough analysis of Lc, such as we have provided in this edition; a sifting-out from the contemporary evidence for Gilbert and that contained in Lc (that is of the twelfth and very early thirteenth centuries) of what I would readily call 'Capgrave's deposit'. Then and then only can one determine with any security whether we have evidence of a tradition separate from that of *The Book of St Gilbert*. Where we meet inconsistent interpretations, dislocations, comments inspired by more recent events, it may only be a question of intermediary strata between the thirteenth and mid-fifteenth centuries, whether due to oral tradition or the translator's embellishment.

This is not the place for a detailed critique of the accuracy of Capgrave's translation, but some examples will help us to a sound approach

---

[1] Capgrave, p. 62: see p. 359 n. 4 below.   [2] Fredeman, pp. 114, 128.
[3] Fredeman, pp. 116–17n.

to his manner of work. In the *Life*, c. 14, the meeting at Clairvaux of Bernard, Malachy, and Gilbert is described. Capgrave recaptures its themes, *non sine grano salis*, but brings the three future saints together on a common homeward journey: 'Thus came our father home in fellowship long time with St Malachy, the archbishop of Ireland, and St Bernard, abbot of Clairvaux, to which two men he was so familiar in that voyage that in their presence, through his devout prayers, a certain man was made whole of sickness which he had. He received eke tokens of love both of the bishop and the abbot, the staves of their crosses.'[1] Now St Bernard, great traveller that he was, never seems to have crossed the Channel and the journey of Malachy ended at Clairvaux itself, where he died soon after his arrival, on 3 November 1148.[2] According to the *Life* Gilbert was only the privileged observer of a miracle obtained by the prayers of Bernard and Malachy. Small details, perhaps: but the journey of the three saints and the first miracle of Gilbert are additions unknown to the *Life* and cannot survive sound criticism. Yet what a splendid picture a talented illuminator or painter of frescoes could have drawn from Capgrave's version! Though quite without historical support such a picture must have haunted the mind of nuns when they read and meditated the narrative intended for their use. They too were in view when he wrote '*our* Gilbert' and '*our* founder'.[3] It was a narrative intended solely for the Order's use, and particularly for nunneries. Dr Fredeman draws support for the word 'our', supposing it to come from a different *Life*, a standard text edited by a member of the Order. Must one invoke another tradition to explain what so clearly belongs to the *fioretti* of St Gilbert?[4] Such a narrative, we must recall, is never independent of the audience for which it is meant, in this case the Gilbertine nuns, justification enough for the words '*our* Gilbert, *our* founder'.[5]

From a slight episode like the anecdote of the three future saints, Bernard, Malachy, and Gilbert, we pass to a story elaborately developed: the canonization and translation of Gilbert, which fills the group of

[1] Capgrave, p. 91.—In the *Life* we read: 'in itinere illo', that is Gilbert's journey to and from Clairvaux with a stay at Clairvaux. Capgrave's interpretation introduces a new assertion manifestly false and not from a contemporary source: 'Thus came oure fader hom in felauschip long tyme with Seynt Malachie, archibischop of Yrland, and Seynt Bernard, abbot of Clarevalle.' The common understanding, as expressed in the modern marginal note, implies that Gilbert 'returned to England with St Malachy and St Bernard'. See above, p. xlviii.

[2] Above, p. xlviii.

[3] Fredeman, p. 118; see examples in Capgrave, pp. 65, 85, 89.

[4] 'Save some additions ... which men of that Order have told me, and eke other things that shall fall to my mind in the writing which be pertinent to the matter' (Capgrave, Prologue, p. 62, spelling modernized).

[5] See B. de Gaiffier, 'Hagiographie et Historiographie', *Recueil d'Hagiographie* (Brussels, 1977), c. IV, p. 165, about the 'Sitz im Leben'.

chapters LVI to LX in Capgrave's *Life of St Gilbert*.[1] Here we may perceive
the spirit in which he planned his work. He translated quite freely several
passages from the canonization dossier. There are several extracts from
the letters of Innocent III; ample passages from the bull of canonization,
an extract from the bull prescribing the second inquiry; then a further
extract from the bull of canonization, a literal translation of the document
deposited in the reliquary at the time of the translation, and finally yet
another piece of the bull of canonization, a free copy of the collect composed by the pope.[2] Capgrave presented this *mélange* as a sermon
pronounced by Innocent III at the canonization ceremony, which the
pope ordered to be copied in the relevant bulls. The canonization ritual,
which is precisely described in the *Book*,[3] does indeed imply a papal
homily; but the *cursus* of the papal chancery could not have been so
closely assimilated to the style of a sermon. It is possible to think that this
is an elaboration by Capgrave, drawing on the documents collected in the
Book as a bee gathers honey from flower to flower. It is impossible to
believe that a contemporary of the canonization could have proceeded in
this manner. An additional argument is that the division into five chapters
(LVI–LX) follows neither chronology nor any kind of logic: it answers
only to the need to break the text, not into *Lectiones*—which was not the
aim here—but into *loci* or sections capable of providing material for reading and meditation in the periods of leisure allowed by monastic use
between the recitation of the liturgical hours and the summons to
claustral duties.

We observe a similar treatment in the rearrangement of the stories of
miracles performed by Gilbert, both during his lifetime and after his
death: those which were elaborate and circumstantial furnished a chapter
each; others were grouped in twos or threes in a single chapter (see
pp. 356–7). In the first case we may detect a real care to expound the circumstances for the benefit of his audience. Some of Dr Fredeman's
points suggest a rather superficial knowledge of the manuscripts. Thus
she writes, apropos the miracles in Capgrave's version: 'neither the mode
of narration nor the specific miracles related accords with either the
Cotton or the Digby manuscript'.[4] It is true that in describing the
miracles Capgrave adopts a narrative style appropriate, as in the *Life*, to
edification, and so sets himself apart from the dry factual narrative appropriate to the report of the inquiry into the miracles, as it is in Lc. But in

---

[1] Fredeman acknowledges, but does not explain, the fact: 'the sermon itself is *in-explicably* broken into five chapters', p. 130.
[2] Above, pp. 192–5, 234–7, 244–53; Capgrave, cc. lvi–lx, pp. 136–41.
[3] Above, pp. 168–79. But not indeed, as Capgrave gives it, a homily incorporating the *carta* deposited in the shrine on the day of the translation!
[4] Fredeman, p. 134.

fact all the miracles recorded by Capgrave—during Gilbert's lifetime and after his death—occur in Lc, as is shown in the table on pp. 356–7, so long as one notes the content not the rubrics of the manuscript.

The posthumous miracles all, without exception, come from the official collection. The names of those cured have often been omitted and the sworn attestations of the witnesses have only been noted in exceptional cases. Capgrave did not undervalue the second collection, and quotes indeed its opening, placing it at the end of his recital: 'Multa quidem et alia signa ... : Many other tokens'—this was the note concerning the miracles not formally attested.[1] Before closing his final chapter on the life and the miracles and passing to the pope's 'sermon', he declares his aim anew, and justifies his narrative style: 'Therefore have we written them in such language as we could, to the praising and joy of our Lord God in whose name they were wrought, to the worship of Holy Church and profit of them that shall read or hear this life.'[2]

It is not impossible that in course of time, as the clear outlines of the contemporary view became blurred, miracle stories were copied and recopied, with names and other details omitted, and attached to the *Life*. This does not justify the hypothesis of another branch of the tradition, contemporary with but differing from that of the manuscripts, and takes no account of Capgrave's style of narrative, which sets beside more or less literal translations some freer adaptations making the *Life* of their father and founder accessible to the Gilbertine nuns. In truth, there is a deceptive phrase in Capgrave's own prologue: I 'translate out of Latyn rith [exactly]'.[3] A translator Capgrave could be at times; but none the less for that he was an adaptor, even a commentator.

The first part, cc. I to XIII of the English version, poses a different problem. As Dr Fredeman notes, it is very close to the nine lessons of the *seruicium S. Gileberti*: '... it seems likely that, rather than the first part being simply an abridgement of the longer *Life*, it is an elaboration of the *lectiones* coupled with material derived from the standard Latin *Life*.'[4] It has, in fact, a coherent structure, a concise style, and a different aim from the longer version; it also differs in arrangement, style, and tone: here are no digressions, no comments on particular points. Fredeman judiciously compares the short version by Capgrave with the lessons of the office for the feast of Gilbert and with the Latin *Life*, and notes some parallels. She concludes that this provides 'even more specific evidence that the author of Capgrave's source was using the service as his model', but that 'in addition, there are three more passages of the service, succinctly abbreviating

---

[1] Capgrave, c. LV, p. 135.
[2] Ibid.
[3] Capgrave, p. 62.
[4] Fredeman, p. 120.

details in the known Latin versions, which are carried over literally into Capgrave's work'.[1] From this she infers: 'it is possible to construct a revised manuscript tree leading from a common source to Capgrave's *Life*'. From this common source she would derive both Lc and Lh. 'Another non extant contemporary manuscript containing additional materials was the source of Digby 36. . . . Together, these manuscripts . . . may be behind the "standard life", but no single one is Capgrave's direct source. In addition, there existed *lectiones* associated with the *Servicium s. Gilleberti*. From these two sources a Latin manuscript was compiled, probably in the fourteenth century, by a brother of the Gilbertine Order. This manuscript was sent to Capgrave for translation.'[2] While adding to the manuscripts unknown Dr Fredeman strengthens her belief in the original hypothesis and overlooks the textual evidence—yet such evidence can be found in the *Book of St Gilbert* and provides, in my opinion, the key to the problem.

If we adhere to the texts, two conclusions may be drawn.

(1) The author of the *Life* (as represented in Lc, Lh, and Od) declares in his Prologue, the dedication to Hubert Walter, where he enumerates the component parts of the volume: 'Lectiones etiam ex hac legenda [i.e. the Life and the narratives attached to it] summatim excerptas et in sollemnitatibus eius legendas huic opusculo inserui.'[3] Thus the copy presented to the archbishop carried the lessons of the Office of St Gilbert, lessons drawn from the *Life*, and the author of the *Life* was also the author of the *Seruicium in festiuitatibus s. Gileberti*. For he mentions not only the lessons but the responses and the antiphons, saying he intends to draw them from the canonical Scriptures: 'Deo dante, in posterum excerpere proposui.'[4]

(2) Capgrave states that he wrote his Life of St Gilbert from a single manuscript. This manuscript must have contained both the *Life* and the *Seruicium*. This contradicts Dr Fredeman's assertion that the source of Capgrave had taken the *Seruicium* as its model: rather, the *Life* was the ultimate model both for the lessons and the short version in Capgrave. Table b in Appendix 8 shows the principal borrowings in one and the other from the *Life*. The conclusion seems clear: the manuscript lent to Capgrave by Nicholas Reysby must have been a copy of the archetype presented by the author, Ralph de Insula, to Hubert Walter—or at least a manuscript derived from the *Book*, as it survives in Lc. It seems probable indeed that the short version of Capgrave faithfully translated the original text of the lessons,[5] which corresponds with his first intention, to

---

[1] Fredeman, pp. 120–1.   [2] Fredeman, pp. 121–2.
[3] Above, p. 8.   [4] p. 10.
[5] As transcribed in Od, ff. 111ᵛ–114 (*Gilbertine Rite*, i. 117–20), the *lectiones* may be a later abridgement from the original text in the *Liber*. Anyway, there must have been

'translate out of Latyn rith', while his second aim, to make some additions, refers to the long version. It is therefore possible to simplify this hypothetical branch of the Gilbertine tradition, cutting back that part which postulates a tradition of lost manuscripts.

various attempts to introduce diversity into the *lectiones*, perhaps beyond liturgical purposes, as is shown in some medieval marginalia in Lc: *lectiones* not corresponding with the *lectiones* in the *Servicium* (see Appendix 3).

CONCORDANCE WITH PREVIOUS EDITIONS

In this concordance the page of the present edition is that on which the first word of the page in (I) Foreville (1943), and (II) *Monasticon*, editions of 1830 and 1846 (see p. xiv) will be found.

I

Foreville (1943)	This edn.	Foreville (1943)	This Edn.	Foreville (1943)	This edn.
1	2	37	254	73	334
2	2	38	256	74	96
3	6	39	258	75	96
4	8	40	260	76	98
5	178	41	260 (and 194)	77	102
6	180	42	264	78	104
7	182	43	264	79	108
8	194	44	268	80	110
9	198	45	270	81	112
10	200	46	272	82	116 (and 114)
11	200	47	274	(83–9, no text)	
12	202	48	276	90	346
13	204	49	278	91	346
14	206	50	282	92	347 (also 134)
15	208	51	284	93	134
16	212	52	286	94	136
17	214	53	288	95	144
18	216	54	290	96	148
19	218	55	292	97	150
20	220	56	296	98	152
21	222	57	298	99	148
22	228	58	300	100	140
23	224 (*sic*)	59	302	101	154
24	226	60	304	102	156
25	230	61	306	103	142
26	214	62	308	104	158
27	234	63	310	105	160
28	236	64	312	106	162
29	238	65	316	107	156
30	240	66	318	108	348
31	240	67	320	109	349
32	244	68	322	110	164
33	244	69	324		
34	246	70	326		
35	250	71	330		
36	252	72	332		

II

Monasticon, vi. 2		*Monasticon*, vi. 2	
1830	This edn.	1846	This edn.
*v	10	*v	10
*vi	14	*vi	16
*vii	18	*vii	26
*viii	24	*viii	34
*ix	28	*ix	42
*x	34	*x	52
*xi	38	*xi	60
*xii	44	*xii	68
*xiii	48	*xiii	76
*xiv	54	*xiv	84
*xv	58	*xv	92
*xvi	62	*xvi	124
*xvii	68	*xvii	168
*xviii	74	*xviii	176
*xix	78	*xix	190
*xx	84		
*xxi	88		
*xxii	92		
*xxiii	120		
*xxiv	124		
*xxv	130		
*xxvi	170		
*xxvii	176		
*xxviii	186		
*xxix	192		

INDEX OF QUOTATIONS AND ALLUSIONS

A. BIBLICAL ALLUSIONS

B. CITATIONS FROM CLASSICAL, PATRISTIC, AND MEDIEVAL SOURCES

GENERAL INDEX

Persons and places named in the text are indexed in the form given in the translation, usually their modern English equivalent. Most medieval personal names are indexed under Christian names; most after 1500 under surnames. Place-names in England are identified by their traditional English shire.